The Sound of Silence in European Administrative Law

"According to traditional theories, administrative law is the law relating to the control of government power, its main goal is to protect an individual right, and the courts decide which contrasts to impose on administrative action. While this face of administrative law is relatively well known, another is less known, that of administrative inaction. Administrative law, when viewed in this way, requires a focus on promoting rights. It also requires shaping the very form of judicial intervention in another manner. '*The Sound of Silence in European Administrative Law*' helps to fill the gap that exists in legal literature, by way of a wide-ranging comparative approach, focusing on both national and EU laws. This is an interesting and important book, for both public law scholars and practitioners."

—Giacinto della Cananea, *Professor of Administrative Law at Bocconi University, Italy*

"This new book on administrative silence, edited by Dacian Dragos, Polonca Kovač, and Hanna Tolsma, is a significant development in the literature in this area. It brings together a wide range of essays on European experiences with the problem of administrative silence, which can variously be caused by a simple error in public bodies, by administrative inertia, and sometimes even by a misuse of power. The essays develop normative and empirically-grounded points about how administrative silence is—and might be—addressed, including at the difficult interface between maladministration and illegality. The comparative dimensions to this book are as deep as they are wide, and the editors have achieved something remarkable in synthesizing the contributions and suggesting what is—and is not—possible in European law. I can think of no better or more comprehensive study of administrative silence in recent years."

—Gordon Anthony, *Professor of Public Law, School of Law at the Queen's University in Belfast, Ireland*

Dacian C. Dragos · Polonca Kovač ·
Hanna D. Tolsma
Editors

The Sound of Silence in European Administrative Law

palgrave
macmillan

Editors
Dacian C. Dragos
Center for Good Governance Studies
Babeş-Bolyai University
Cluj-Napoca, Romania

Polonca Kovač
Faculty of Public Administration
University of Ljubljana
Ljubljana, Slovenia

Hanna D. Tolsma
Faculty of Law
University of Groningen
Groningen, The Netherlands

ISBN 978-3-030-45226-1 ISBN 978-3-030-45227-8 (eBook)
https://doi.org/10.1007/978-3-030-45227-8

This Palgrave Macmillan imprint is published by the registered company Springer Nature Switzerland AG
The registered company address is: Gewerbestrasse 11, 6330 Cham, Switzerland

Preface

Making of "The Sound of Silence in European Administrative Law"

This book attempts for the first time to engage in a comparative assessment of the different models employed in order to tackle the administrative silence in administrative law. The comparative work will be the first on this theme to tackle both the legal aspects and some empirical evidences of how the legal institution works in practice.

Administrative silence occurs when administrative authority does not reply to an application in the legally prescribed time or does not take action when such action is legally prescribed. The legal fiction may be negative or positive. Negative fiction means that the law considers the silence as tacit rejection of the application and the interested parties have the possibility of a legal challenge in administrative or judicial venues. In the second instance, positive fiction, the presumption is that the silence means approval (the silent consent procedure or tacit agreement). The application is considered approved and the applicant can perform an activity. No legal system is exclusively working with just one of the legal assumptions. Both negative and positive assumptions are used, with different legal consequences.

Traditionally, administrative law and policy were concerned with ways of controlling and sanctioning administrative *action*, and less preoccupied with the administrative *inaction*. Nonetheless, administrative *silence* is as much relevant as the administrative *act*. It is an issue that lies at the intersection of legal and managerial aspects of governance and public administration. Moreover, it is a concept that is both reflecting and testing the principles of legal certainty, legality, and good administration and raises issues of rational organization and governance, as well as ethics in public administration.

The team of authors contributing to this book is based in most part on the network of researchers established under the umbrella of the Permanent Study Group X "Law and Public Administration" of the European Group of Public Administration.[1] The study group joins together at every annual EGPA conference in September to discuss and share research ideas related to the field of public law, but with a broader multidisciplinary perspective. Thus, the group is a permanent meeting place for scholars and practitioners from different fields: social scientists, jurists, and economists working in academia and public institutions, as well as civil servants working in national and supranational institutions. It tries to combine external and internal perspectives on law in a public administration context. Internal perspectives on law relate to juridical analysis and efforts to improve legal (sub)systems from the perspectives of rules and legal history, jurisprudence, and comments. The external perspectives can be of different kinds, as they confront (administrative) law with motives that often are external to law, like efficiency and timeliness of administration, the accountability of public agencies, transparency of government, and citizen's participation in decision-making.

This research proposal follows the EGPA's PSG X annual efforts to research and comparatively analyze topical issues from both a legal and empirical perspective. After research endeavors that finalized in published books—*ADR in European Administrative Law* (Springer, 2014) and *The Laws of Transparency in Action* (Palgrave, 2019)—we proposed for 2019 EGPA conferences the topic Administrative Silence in European law. The contributors are mainly from this study group, but also benefited from participation of other well-established scholars in the field of administrative law, most of them members of the ReNEUAL network (Research Network of European Administrative Law).[2]

[1] http://www.iias-iisa.org/egpa/e/study_groups/law/Pages/contact.aspx.

[2] http://www.reneual.eu/.

The book offers in-depth insights into the topic through national profiles provided by domestic scholars based on a common outline. The approach is mainly legal, but often enriched by an interdisciplinary perspective (such as public policy, management, and economics). Authors have gathered the most up-to-date case law and available empirical data to be able to assess the administrative silence as a complex dysfunction that needs to be dealt with systematically to enable good administration.

This book is structured as follows: Firstly, a comparative overview opens up basic principles, rules, and dilemmas that administrative silence is closely connected with. Further, an analysis of EU law is given, followed by country reports from Western and Southern (seven chapters) and Central and Eastern Europe (six chapters), respectively. Each chapter is organized in such a way to provide comparisons. Initially, the authors address the background legal tradition and system, and the general and sector-specific legal framework regarding administrative silence in a given country. The core research question is whether legal tools meant to deal with administrative silence (the positive or negative model) are effective and what is their effect in practice. Finally, an overall assessment of national regimes is performed in order to identify solutions for future policymaking and how to deal with the specific issues of administrative timeliness.

We hope the book will stir interest of students and academics from law, public administration, political sciences, and sociology, in Europe and elsewhere. Also, it will benefit practitioners from public administration in charge of applying or overseeing administrative procedure codes/laws, as the chapters will explain how comparable provisions from otherwise different jurisdictions are interpreted in practice. Legislators and initiators of legislation (members of parliament and of the government) could use the book in designing legal provisions and procedures that are effective in practice, taking into consideration comparative experiences.

Last but not least, lawyers should be interested in comparative examples of how administrative silence may be regulated, how provisions are interpreted, due to the fact that many national administrative procedures are similar in terms of how provisions are drafted. Cross-fertilization of legal principles and best practice may find a fertile ground here.

The editors wish to thank contributors to this book for their efforts to the European Group of Public Administration (Edoardo Ongaro and

Fabienne Maron) for enabling the research and the publication of its findings, and to Palgrave Macmillan (Jemima Warren) for considering our proposal in a timely and accommodating manner and for an excellent cooperation during production of the book.

Cluj-Napoca, Romania — Dacian C. Dragos
Ljubljana, Slovenia — Polonca Kovač
Groningen, The Netherlands — Hanna D. Tolsma

Contents

Notes on Contributors

Agnė Andrijauskaitė, LL.M is a Researcher at the German Research Institute for Public Administration (FOEV) and a Ph.D. student at the German University of Administrative Sciences Speyer, Germany, and Vilnius University, Lithuania. She holds a master's degree in law with specialization in European Union law from Vilnius University and the University of Hamburg (Europa-Kolleg Hamburg). Before joining the German Research Institute for Public Administration, she worked in the Supreme Administrative Court of Lithuania (2010–2016). Her main areas of research are Lithuanian and European administrative law.

Natassa Athanasiadou is Assistant Professor of EU law at the Faculty of Law of Maastricht University, The Netherlands. She obtained a doctorate with *summa cum laude* in 2016 from the University of Heidelberg. Her Ph.D. thesis on the legal instrument of "administrative contract" in EU law ("*Der Verwaltungsvertrag im EU-Recht*") was published in 2017 by *Mohr Siebeck Verlag*. Her research interests lie mainly in the area of European institutional and administrative law, comparative administrative law and fundamental rights, in particular procedural rights.

Mantas Bileišis is a Professor and Director of Public Security and Public Administration study programmes and acting vice-rector at the General Jonas Žemaitis Military Academy of Lithuania, Lithuania. He has a Ph.D. in social sciences in management with specialization in public administration. He also holds a master's degree in public administration from

Mykolas Romeris University. He is an expert in Lithuanian public administration. Before joining the General Jonas Žemaitis Military Academy of Lithuania, he was Head of the Public Administration Innovation Lab at Mykolas Romeris University. His main areas of research are public administration, public service, and multi-level public governance.

Ivo Carlens graduated from Ghent University in Diplomatic Sciences (1989), Development Cooperation (1990) and Maghrib Studies (1991). From 1994 till 1996, he was Researcher of Islamic Law and Aspects of Government in Africa for the Public Law Department at Ghent University, Belgium. While working as a civil servant in a local government administration, he graduated in Public Management at the Free University of Brussels (VUB). Since 2000, he was hired by the Administrative Law Department to cooperate as an expert in projects on behalf of the Flemish Authority. From 2007 on, he is teaching assistant of administrative law, and he mainly publishes about local government law issues.

Emilie Chevalier is Associate Professor in European and Public Law at the Faculty of Law at the University of Limoges, France. She obtained a Ph.D. from the University of Limoges in 2010, after an LL.M. in International, European and Comparative Law in Maastricht University (2004). Her Ph.D. analyzed the principle of good administration and European Union law (published with Bruylant-Larcier, 2014). She has taken part in international and European research projects, and published chapters and articles in French and in English, on European Administrative Law, on administrative procedure and the conditions of enforcement of European Law. She is part of the steering committee of the transnational administrative law network. Recently, she published *Institutions européennes* (with O. Dubos, Dalloz, 2019).

Vuk Cucić is Assistant Professor at the Faculty of Law, University of Belgrade, Serbia. He teaches administrative law, administrative procedural law, and comparative judicial control of administration. He is a member of the Serbian Association for Public Administration. His main research interests are administrative procedure and judicial control of administration.

Gonçalo De Andrade Fabião is a Guest Lecturer at the University of Lisbon, Portugal, Research Assistant at Lisbon Center for Research in Public Law (CIDP), and a Member of the Lisbon Legal Theory

Group (LxLTG). He is also a Legal Adviser to the Portuguese Government (2017–2019) and peer reviewer to e-Pública—Revista Eletrónica de Direito Público.

Tiago Fidalgo de Freitas is a Guest Lecturer at the University of Lisbon, School of Law, Portugal, LL.M., and Hauser Global Scholar with the New York University School of Law (2007), and Researcher at the European University Institute (2008–2012). He has European Academy of Public Law degree (2006). He is Associate Researcher and Executive Coordinator of the Lisbon Center for Research in Public Law, as well as Legal Adviser to JurisAPP (central legal services of the Portuguese Government). He has researched and published in the fields of public law, with a particular focus in international law, EU law, constitutional law and human rights.

Kars J. de Graaf is Associate Professor with a Chair in Public Law and Sustainability in the Department of Constitutional Law, Administrative Law, and Public Administration at the University of Groningen, The Netherlands. His research focuses on environmental law and adjudication in administrative law. He is a member of the Editorial Board of the Review of European Administrative Law (REALaw), chairman of the board of the Dutch association for Environmental Law (VMR), member of the board of the Dutch association for Administrative Law (VAR), and honorary judge at the District Court in the North of The Netherlands.

Dacian C. Dragos is Jean Monnet Professor of Administrative and European Law at the Babes-Bolyai University, Cluj-Napoca, co-director of the Center for Good Governance Studies, and co-chair of the "Law and Administration" Panel of the European Group of Public Administration since 2010. He acts also as a member of the scientific board of international journals: *European Procurement and Public-Private Partnerships Law*, *Transylvanian Review of Administrative Sciences*, and *International Journal of Court Administration*. His research publications include 2 edited books, over 40 chapters in international books, 8 books in Romanian as a single author, and over 50 papers in scientific journals.

Mariolina Eliantonio is Professor of European and Comparative Administrative Law at the Maastricht Center for European Law, The Netherlands. She carries out research on the enforcement of European law before national and European courts. She specifically investigates the concept and implications of the system of shared administration, especially from a judicial protection perspective, and she examines the role of courts in the new modes of governance (such as soft law and co-regulation) and the future of the system of judicial accountability in the European integration process.

Bettina Engewald is a Research Associate at the Institute for Regulatory Impact Assessment and Evaluation (InGFA) at the German Research Institute for Public Administration (FOEV), Germany. She studied law and her research focuses on retrospective assessment of laws, freedom of information and transparency laws, and planning regulation. On behalf of various public-sector clients, she studies and assesses the consequences of legislation projects and political measures in an interdisciplinary team.

Rafael Fernández Acevedo is Associate Professor of Administrative Law, at the Universidade de Vigo, Spain. He holds a degree in Law from the Universidad Complutense de Madrid and Ph.D. in Law (Summa Cum Laude) from the Universidade de Vigo. He has been Visiting Scholar at different Italian Universities, such as the Roma ("La Sapienza"), Bologna (Scuola di Specializzazione in Studi sull'Amministrazione Pubblica—SP.I.S.A), and Torino. He is author of more than 60 publications on administrative law. Its main lines of research are public procurement, the environment, the public domain, and transport. He has published several papers on administrative procedure and administrative silence. He has extensively published on public contracts, i.e., a monograph about "administrative concessions of the public domain," and the different papers regarding the strategic use of public procurement, award criteria, or compliance programs. He has participated in different national and international research projects. Finally, Professor Acevedo currently is also a consultant for public bodies and for private firms, advising clients mainly in the field of public domain and public procurement. One of the most important of these is the legal defense service provided by the Kingdom of Spain (Xunta de Galicia) before the Arbitration Court of Paris in relation to several mining concessions.

Vidmantė Giedraitytė is an Associate Professor, Head of the Department of Strategic Management at the General Jonas Žemaitis Military Academy of Lithuania, and Lecturer at Kaunas University of Technology, Lithuania. She has a Ph.D. in social sciences in management with specialization in public administration. She also holds a master's degree in law with specialization in law and governance from Mykolas Romeris

University. She is an expert in drafting legislation, providing consultations and conclusions on Lithuanian public administration issues. Her main areas of research are public-sector innovation and administrative law.

Nicole G. Hoogstra is Lecturer of Administrative Law and Researcher in the Department of Constitutional Law, Administrative Law, and Public Administration at the University of Groningen, The Netherlands. Her research focuses on general administrative law and on administrative silence in particular. She is member of the advisory committee for objections in the municipality Het Hogeland and of the municipality Oldambt.

Agata Jurkowska-Gomułka is a Head of Chair for Political Sciences and Administration at University of Information Technology and Management in Rzeszów, Poland. She obtained Ph.D. from Faculty of Law and Administration, University of Warsaw, in 2004, and habilitation from the Institute of Legal Studies, Polish Academy of Science in 2014. She is an associate member of Centre for Antitrust and Regulatory Studies, University of Warsaw. She is the Deputy Editor-in-Chief of Yearbook of Antitrust and Regulatory Studies. She is the author and co-author of many scientific papers on administrative law, economic law, European law, and public administration. She is a member of a Working Group for Social Responsibility of Public Administration at the Polish Ministry of Innovation and Development.

Polonca Kovač is a Full Professor of Administrative Law at Faculty of Public Administration at the University of Ljubljana, Slovenia. She is the author or co-author of numerous scientific articles and conference papers and the editor-in-chief of the "Central European Public Administration Review" and (co)editor of several edited books on public governance, reforms and Europeanisation in Eastern Europe, administrative (tax, inspection, etc.) procedures, transparency, regulatory impact assessment, etc. She is active in national and supranational committees and networks, such as the EGPA (co-chairing study group on law and public administration), NISPAcee (a member of the steering committee), European Law Institute, ReNEUAL, and EATLP and acts as an OECD/SIGMA and ReSPA expert.

Kamilla Kurczewska is a Researcher and Lecturer at the University of Information Technology and Management in Rzeszów, Poland. She is a graduate of the Faculty of Law and Administration (1997) and the Faculty of Philosophy (1997) of the Jagiellonian University, a Doctor of Juridical Sciences, and a Master of Arts in Philosophy.

Katarzyna Kurzępa-Dedo is an Assistant Professor of the Chair of Political Science and Administration at the University of Information Technology and Management, Rzeszów, Poland. She obtained Ph.D. from Faculty of Law and Administration, Jagiellonian University, in 2007. Her publications concern the public economic law, in particular administrative instruments for minimizing banking risk. She is a member of Association for Research on Sources and Functions of Law.

Albert T. Marseille is Professor of Public Administration in the Department of Constitutional Law, Administrative Law, and Public Administration at the University of Groningen, The Netherlands. His research focuses on procedures of dispute resolution in administrative law. He is chairman of the Editorial Board of The Netherlands Tijdschrift voor Bestuursrecht, co-chair of the Permanent Study Group Law and Public Administration of the European Group of Public Administration, honorary judge in the Central Appeals Tribunal of the Netherlands and member of the advisory committee for objections of the municipality of Delfzijl.

Anamarija Musa is an Associate Professor in the Department of Administrative Science, Faculty of Law, University of Zagreb, Croatia, where she has been employed since 2001. After obtaining her M.Sc. in European Politics and Governance, at the LSE, UK, in 2004, she earned her Ph.D. from Faculty of Law in Zagreb in 2009 on a thesis on the relationship between the Europeanisation of public administration and agencification. She (co)authored four books and published three co-edited volumes, and published more than 40 scientific and expert articles and chapters in edited volumes on topics such as transparency, public agencies, and Europeanisation. From October 2013 to October 2018, she served as the inaugural Information Commissioner of the Republic of Croatia, establishing the office and dealing with the access to information appeals and inspections and promoting the right of access to information.

Bogdana Neamtu is an Associate Professor, Ph.D., and Head of the Department of Public Administration and Management at Babes-Bolyai University, Cluj-Napoca, Romania. She obtained her Ph.D. in 2008, with a thesis in the field of urban studies (urban growth management). After obtaining her Ph.D., she continued to work on topics related to urban sustainability in the context of governance. She co-directs together with her colleague Dacian Dragos, the Center for Good Governance Studies, a small research unit dealing with topics pertaining to free access to documents and information, ADR in public law, public procurement, corruption studies, and other aspects pertaining to good governance. In the last years, she has been active at both national and international levels in the area of transparency and Ombudsman studies.

Jurgen Neuts graduated in Law in 2001 at the University of Antwerp. He was a lawyer at the bar of Antwerp from 2001 till 2007. Then, he became assistant senior officer at the Council of State (till 2009) and is now senior officer at the Council of State. From 2009 until now, he is Lecturer in the Public Management Department and Teaching Assistant in the EPIL Department at Ghent University, Belgium. Furthermore, he is volunteer at the Inter-University Centre for Education Law and contributor to the columns of jurisdiction issued by the Council of State of the Flemish journal *Tijdschrift voor Bestuurswetenschappen en Publiekrecht* (T.B.P.).

Mirko Pečarič is an Associate Professor of Administrative Law and Public Administration. From 2009 to 2011, he was the General Secretary of University of Ljubljana, and in 2011, he became an Assistant Professor of Administrative Law and Public Administration at the Faculty of Public Administration in Ljubljana where he teaches the courses of administrative law and public services. His main areas of research are the development of public administration and administrative law, public services, public participation in public matters, administrative structures, and good administration. In 2012–2018, he was the alternate member of the group of independent experts at the Council of Europe on the European Charter of Local Self-Government. In 2013–2014, he was the State Secretary of the Government of Republic of Slovenia at the Ministry of Education, Science and Sport, and responsible for the fields of higher education and science. He is also SIGMA expert and the author of six monographs and numerous scientific papers.

Bianca Radu is a Lecturer of Public Administration and has been employed at the Faculty of Political Administrative and Communication Sciences, Babeş-Bolyai University, Cluj-Napoca, Romania, since 2006. She specializes in public administration, community development, and urban planning. She conducts researches and publishes on public policy, transparency of public sector, regeneration of former industrial communities, and community resilience. She holds a Ph.D. in Sociology (2014) from Babes-Bolyai University, a M.A. in community development (2004) from Babes-Bolyai University, and another one in urban planning from Michigan State University (2007).

Miguel Assis Raimundo holds a Ph.D. in Administrative Law and is Assistant Professor, as well as a Senior Research Fellow, Lisbon Center for Research in Public Law (CIDP), Portugal. He is a member of the Coordinating Scientific Committee and Responsible for the area of Administrative Law research projects with CIDP, a member of the Working Group appointed by the Portuguese Government, in charge of drafting the transposition of the 2014 Public Procurement Directives (2015–2016), a member of the Editorial Board of the "Revista de Contratos Públicos" (Brazil) and *European Journal of Public Procurement Markets*. He acts as a peer reviewer to a number of legal journals [Lisbon Law Review, e-Pública, Católica Law Review, Revista de Direito Administrativo (Brazil) and Central European Public Administration Review] and is a member of ReNEUAL. He has researched and published extensively in fields of general administrative law, administrative justice, and public procurement law.

Tina Sever is an Assistant Professor at the Faculty of Public Administration, University of Ljubljana, Slovenia. In 2006, she obtained a B.Sc. degree at the Faculty of Law, UL, and in 2014, a Ph.D. at the European Faculty of Law. In 2007 and 2008, she was a trainee at the Administrative Unit of Ljubljana, European Commission (Directorate General for Translation in Luxembourg), and European Ombudsman. She passed a Bar Examination Traineeship at the Higher Court of Ljubljana in 2009. In October 2008, she became a teaching assistant at the UL, and in December 2016, she was appointed Assistant Professor. She publishes and researches in the field of public administration and administrative law.

Marko Šikić is Full Professor of Administrative Law in the Department of Administrative Law, Faculty of Law, University of Zagreb, Croatia, where he has been employed since 2000. He defended his master's thesis "Administrative Silence in Croatian Law" in 2006 and his doctoral dissertation "Legal Protection Against Non-solving Administrative Matter in Croatian and Comparative Law" in 2008. Since 2009, he has been the Head of the Chair of Administrative Law. He is (co)author of one book and more than thirty scientific papers in journals and edited volumes on the matters of administrative procedure and administrative dispute. He is a member of the Academy of Legal Sciences of Croatia.

João Tiago Silveira holds Ph.D. in Administrative Law and is Professor at the Lisbon Law School of the University of Lisbon, Portugal, where he teaches in the fields of administrative law, administrative litigation, legislative drafting, and constitutional law. He is a Deputy President of the Institute of Lisbon Law School for promotion of postgraduate courses and research on Public Law (Instituto de Ciências Jurídico-Políticas) and member of the board of the International Association of Legislation, and also acts in the private sector as partner in the law firm Morais Leitão, Galvão Teles, Soares da Silva & Associados, and arbitrator in the arbitration courts of the Economic and Social Council and Administrative Arbitration Centre. He has played an active role in public positions, namely as State Secretary of Justice, State Secretary of the Presidency of the Council of Ministers, and Director of the Legislative Policy and Planning Office of the Ministry of Justice. On these occasions, he conceived and executed policies on cutting red tape and simplification of registries and notaries, new technologies in courts, better regulation, simplification of legislative procedures, urban rehabilitation, and reform of administrative litigation. He has published extensively in the fields of administrative law and litigation, better regulation, legislative drafting, and constitutional law.

Anna Simonati, Ph.D. is a Full Professor of Administrative Law at the Faculty of Law of Trento University, Italy. At the supra-national level, she is a member of Permanent Study Groups in the International Institute of Administrative Sciences, in the European Group for Public Administration, and in the European Law Institute; she is also a Field Editor of the journal Central European Public Administration Review and a member in the Editorial Board of the journal Public Integrity. She has been accepted as an ECAS expert for the European Commission. She is the author of about 200 articles and papers and of three books; she is co-editor of various books.

Sara Sistero Ródenas is Lecturer and Researcher at Universitat Jaume I, Spain. She is within the Group for Public Law and Innovation (INNOVAP). She is participating in several projects linked to Transparency and Governance. Furthermore, her Ph.D. thesis is focused on the informative and cognitive dimensions of administrative procedures. Toward this end, she has benefited from a 2-year-long internship in the German University of Administrative Sciences (Speyer). Her research is partly funded by Spanish Education Ministry and by the Valencian Regional Government. As a teacher, she is leading NOVESMET, a group of innovative teaching. The involved activities include testing new methodologies on cooperative and dialogical learning. On this field, the main goal is to contribute to a better administrative culture, in line with the University Social Responsibility. Out of academic life, she has worked in the Environmental Department of the Valencian Regional Government and more recently in the Local Administration.

Dawid Sześciło is Assistant Professor and Head of the Public Administration Research Unit at the Faculty of Law and Administration, University of Warsaw, Poland. He authored or co-authored over 200 academic publications on public administration, public law, and human rights.

Hanna D. Tolsma is Assistant Professor in the Department of Constitutional Law, Administrative Law, and Public Administration at the University of Groningen, The Netherlands. She received her Ph.D. in 2008 on a thesis concerning legal aspects of the use of mediation by administrative authorities during the decision-making process. Her publication mainly relates to administrative law and environmental law. She is a member of the Editorial Board of AB Rechtspraak Bestuursrecht and honorary judge at the District Court in the North of The Netherlands.

Patricia Valcárcel Fernández is Associate Professor of Administrative Law (with the qualification for Full Professor), at the University of Vigo, Spain. She holds a Ph.D. in law (Summa Cum Laude and Extraordinary Doctorate Prize). She has been Visiting Scholar at different Universities, such as the Universitá degli Studi di Firenze (Italy), Universidade da Lusíada (Lisbon, Portugal), or the University of Nottingham (UK). Professor Valcárcel is author of nearly 100 publications on administrative law. She has extensively published on public contracts, i.e., a monography about "execution and financing of public works," different articles and chapters regarding public private partnership; the strategic use of public procurement; or innovation on public procurement. She is also editor of two books, the last one on "aggregated demand on public procurement" (Aranzadi Thomson Reuters, 2016). She has participated in different national and international research projects, and nowadays is responsible for a national research project, funded by the Spanish Ministry of Economy, Industry and Competitiveness (Spanish Government). Professor Valcárcel worked as a lawyer specialized in administrative law for Garrigues Abogados y Asesores Tributarios. Currently, she is also a consultant for public bodies and for private firms, advising clients in the field of administrative law.

Ludo M. Veny studied law at the Free University of Brussels (VUB), Belgium, where he graduated in 1986. He got his Ph.D. on March 22, 1994, with a thesis about education law. From October 1996 on, he was teaching administrative law, public law, and education law at Ghent University, Belgium. He was Director of the University Centre for Education Law at Ghent University. His research was mainly focused on the public and administrative law areas in general, and on public legal maintenance, local government law, and euthanasia in particular. From the foundation of the journal until December 2004, Ludo VENY was co-editor-in-chief of CDPK; he was also member of the editor's board of 4 other Flemish law journals. For more than 8 years (2006–2014), he was the chairman of the Department of Public Law, which shifted into the actual European, Public and International Law Department (EPIL). Professor Veny was also teaching constitutional law at the Free University of Brussels (VUB). He was Lecturer of legal subjects of the VLIR-UOS program and Master in Education and Research for Sustainable Development at the Anton de Kom University in Paramaribo (Suriname). Professor Veny died on July 17, 2018, in Paramaribo.

Bengt Verbeeck graduated in Law (2000) and Development Cooperation (2001) at Ghent University, Belgium. From 2001 till 2007 he was fulltime assistant of administrative law. In 2007 he became Ph.D. of Law with a thesis on education law. His main research areas are general administrative law and education law. He is volunteer at the Inter-University Centre for Education Law and as an external expert linked to the Support point Law and Education. He is currently working as the Head of the Legal advice Department at the University College Ghent.

Bosiljka Britvić Vetma is Associate Professor in the Department of Administrative Law, Faculty of Law, University of Split, Croatia. She earned her Ph.D. from Faculty of Law in Split in 2011 on a thesis on the full jurisdiction administrative dispute. She (co)authored several books and several dozens of scientific and expert papers in journals and conference proceedings. Together with Professor M. Gjidara she co-authored the Croatian-French Administrative Law Lexicon (2016, 2018). Since 2007, she has been the coordinator of the traditional annual conference Croatian-French Administrative Law Symposium in Split. Since 2008, she has been a general secretary of the Centre for European Documentation and Research Robert Schuman in Split, Croatia. She is a member of Academy of Legal Sciences of Croatia.

List of Figures

List of Tables

PART I

Introduction and Comparisons

CHAPTER 1

In Search of an Effective Model: A Comparative Outlook on Administrative Silence in Europe

Polonca Kovač, Hanna D. Tolsma, and Dacian C. Dragos

1.1 Introduction

Traditionally, administrative law and policy were concerned with ways of controlling and sanctioning administrative *action*, and less preoccupied with the administrative *inaction*—nonetheless, administrative *silence* as much relevant as the administrative *act*. It is an issue that lies at the intersection of legal and managerial aspects of governance and public

P. Kovač
Faculty of Public Administration, University of Ljubljana, Ljubljana, Slovenia
e-mail: polonca.kovac@fu.uni-lj.si

H. D. Tolsma
Faculty of Law, University of Groningen, Groningen, The Netherlands
e-mail: h.d.tolsma@rug.nl

D. C. Dragos (✉)
Center for Good Governance Studies, Babes-Bolyai University, Cluj-Napoca, Romania
e-mail: dragos@fspac.ro

D. C. Dragos et al. (eds.),
The Sound of Silence in European Administrative Law,
https://doi.org/10.1007/978-3-030-45227-8_1

administration. Moreover, it is a concept that is both reflecting and testing the principles of legal certainty, legality, and good administration and raises issues of rational organization and governance, as well as ethics in public administration.

Administrative silence occurs when administrative authority does not reply to an application in the legally prescribed time or does not take action when such action is legally prescribed. The legal fiction attached by the law to this situation may be negative (rejection) or positive (approval); over time, also various combinations thereof have been developed in individual legal regimes. Today, no legal system is exclusively working with just one of the legal assumptions.[1] Moreover, traditional national systems are lately redefined to offer more exceptions or mechanisms regulated beside a general rule, so that sometimes the number of exceptions overrides the basic principle.[2]

Public administration inactivity, or in other words the excessive length of administrative proceedings, is not a new phenomenon; however, it appears to be of limited interest for comparative law, and it occurred particularly as attempts to develop a European convergence in administrative procedural law in a pro-business paradigm.[3] In this context, there were initiatives at the EU level that attributed administrative silence as a positive legal fiction—namely Directive 2006/123/EC on services in the internal market (Service Directive).[4] It should be also noted that Article 41 on right to good administration of the EU Charter on Fundamental Rights generally requires that every person has a right to have his or her affairs dealt within a reasonable time.[5]

[1] More in Jansen (2008, 2016), de Graaf and Hoogstra (2013), and Kovač (2012). For the national reports, see chapters of this book for empirical data.

[2] See Jansen (2016). Similarly on other institutes such as access to information or administrative appeals and alternative dispute resolution mechanism (Dragos and Neamtu 2014; Dragos et al. 2019).

[3] See Hofmann et al. (2014), Auby (2014), Galetta et al. (2015), and Koprić et al. (2016).

[4] OJ L 376, 27 December 2006.

[5] More on the EU Charter and good administration in the CJEU jurisprudence in the EU chapter of this book. See the European Convention on Human Rights (ECHR), Article 6 on a fair trial, as well. On a national scale, usually such a guarantee is provided by a constitution and most often further on a statutory level (see the national reports in this book for more details). However, one should differ among (un)reasonable and (an infringement of) a prescribed timing, as addressed later on and in the national reports of

The tension between silence as *rejection* (negative) and silence as *approval* (positive) is to be found not only at the level of the EU procedural law, but also at the level of the national administrative law of the Member States. In this chapter, we critically synthesize the main aspects discussed in the following chapters that deal with this topic in national setting, trying to find a red line or identify common trends among the studied jurisdictions.

In comparative law, the administrative silence has been a field of constant changes as national legislators experiment the most efficient way to tackle the issue, and then search for refinement of their legal regimes based on legal traditions, comparative law, and EU law insights. The issue of administrative silence has been paid little attention in comparative law until now, so we hope that this chapter offers a sneak peek into the legal and practical problems raised by this legal institution and the interest of the reader to go into the more detailed analysis of the administrative silence provided by the national chapters was already sparked.

First, the concept of administrative silence is briefly discussed in this section. Subsequently, an outline is given of the national legal and administrative background as far as relevant for analyzing the administrative silence. The main trends regarding the regulation of timeliness and the length of time limits and calculation are described (Sect. 1.2). This is followed by an in-depth analysis of the response to administrative silence: the negative and the positive legal fiction (Sect. 1.3). The chapter ends with an overall assessment explaining the lessons to be learned on the basis of the comparative law study (Sect. 1.4).

1.2 The National Legal Systems as Background for the Treatment of Timeliness of the Administrative Procedure

1.2.1 The Context for Understanding Timeliness of Administrative Procedure

In most countries, administrative silence has been regulated since (deep in) the mid-twentieth century, and in some countries, the development of

this book. More in Venice Commission (2011). In this context, an inactivity (no response at all) and a procrastination (delayed or partial activity) are both seen as maladministration. For more on the differentiation thereof, see the Lithuanian chapter of this book.

administrative silence goes back further in time. France, Spain, Portugal, Italy, Netherlands, Slovenia, Serbia, and Croatia (among others) have quite extensive regulations on time limits, prolongation of time limits, and legal actions when time limits are exceeded. From a comparative perspective, it is interesting to note that the topic of administrative silence has received relatively little attention in Germany. Traditionally, in German administrative law and administrative science, the emphasis has been on tying and controlling the administration (arising from the rule of law) and not on fighting its inactivity. Originally, neither positive nor negative silence existed within the legal framework. The German Federal Administrative Procedure Act and the Code of Administrative Court Procedure were not influenced by French law or any other foreign legal system. Positive silence, implemented in 2009 in the Federal Administrative Procedure Act, is a product established by EU law. In addition, in Romania, one of the newest Member States of the EU, the regulation of administrative silence is scarce. An explanation for this is that during the communist regime (until 1989) it was practically impossible to challenge inaction of the public administration, as the state overlapped with the Communist Party. However, since the beginning of this century, the administrative silence has been evolving in the legal system from positive silence (influenced by EU law) shifting to silent rejection.

1.2.2 The Legal Framework of Administrative Timeliness

In most of the studied jurisdictions, the constitution does not provide *explicitly* for provisions related to timeliness of administrative decisions. General administrative deadlines are not provided in the constitution, nor specific provisions on legal protection against untimely decision-making by government. Most of the time, administrative timeliness is regulated in a general administrative law act or administrative procedure act, usually in combination with sector-specific laws.

In some countries, principles relating to administrative timeliness are laid down in the constitution. For example, the Spanish Constitution contains the principle of effectiveness, which is understood to include the obligation to resolve administrative procedures within a reasonable time. The Portuguese Constitution, in addition to codifying principles that can be associated with administrative timeliness (effective and non-bureaucratic administration), also contains a specific provision to ensure legal protection against administrative inaction. This constitutional guarantee is considered meaningful since in French-inspired administrative justice systems, forms of injunction in matters related to administrative acts were traditionally not in place, or were difficult to obtain, because of the understanding of the principle of the separation of powers. Some constitutions demand decision-making within a reasonable time (also) in administrative matters (Croatia, Slovenia). Although there is no explicit provision in the Portuguese Constitution for timely decision-making in administrative procedures, in case law a constitutional right to timely decision-making is derived from Article 6(1) of the European Convention on Human Rights and/or Article 41 of the Charter of Fundamental Rights of the European Union.

Administrative timeliness is regulated mainly through a general administrative procedure act in combination with sector-specific legislation. However, the interplay between the general act and special laws differs. In some countries, the general act provides a general provision on time limits, which only applies when the time limit is not specified in the specific legislation. The general provision functions as a "safety net" (Netherlands, Spain, and Portugal). In other countries, in principle, the general rule in the administrative procedure act applies, which can be deviated from in special legislation (France, Slovenia, Croatia, Serbian, and Poland). In Croatia, it has been a deliberate choice to move away from the principle of subsidiarity in order to ensure consistency in the implementation of general administrative law. Another approach is that there is specific time limit regulated by the general law, while specifying time limits in special laws (as in Germany, France, and Italy). Overlooking the whole, sector-specific regulation of issues of the administrative procedure seems to be widespread.

1.2.3 The Length of Administrative Deadlines

From a comparative perspective, it is noticeable that there is a dizzying variation in deadlines. Nevertheless, there are some red lines to be drawn. In general, complicated procedures can take longer time. Relatively simple cases, or cases in which an individual has a special interest, should be faster. In Poland, this distinction is translated into a general deadline of one month (simple cases) and two months (complex cases). This corresponds to the general deadline set in the Croatian Administrative Procedure Act, although the deadline is counted in days there ("without delay" with maximum of 30 days or 60 days conducting an investigatory procedure). The general deadline is slightly longer in, for example, the Netherlands (eight weeks), Portugal (90 business days), and Spain (three months).

The deadlines in special laws are sometimes shorter and sometimes longer than the ones established in the general administrative act. A short deadline can be set in days or even hours. For example, in France, the deadline to register an asylum seeker is 3 days and can be extended to ten. In Serbia, electoral law has time limits for decisions within hours. In more complex cases, for example in the field of environmental law, longer decision periods are usually used. In the Netherlands, if the extended preparatory procedure applies, it must be decided by the administrative body as soon as possible, but at the latest within 6 months of receipt of the application. It is possible to extend this period under certain conditions.

In most of the countries, prolongation of the deadline is allowed, although the possibilities to prolong a deadline may vary. For example, the Netherlands, Spain, and Portugal have extensive rules in the general administrative act on the extension of the time limit for taking a decision. A reason for suspending the decision period is, for example, when any interested party is required to correct defects or provide documents and other supporting evidence that may be necessary or when mandatory reports are requested from an administrative body.

In order to be able to determine exactly when there is administrative silence, it is very important that it is clear how the period is calculated. In almost all studied jurisdictions, there are specific rules for this. Again, we see variation between countries. Time limits may be calculated in months, weeks, days, and ours. In some countries, time limits are calculated in calendar days (France, Netherlands, and Croatia). There has been a notable change in this regard in Croatia. A deliberate choice has been made here to calculate in calendar days, instead of months. The ratio behind this shift is that counting in calendar days is fairer and contributes to procedural equality given the fact that months have an unequal number of days. Some countries, including Portugal, count in business days. The rational is that the deadline should be aligned with the working days of the employees and opening hours of public services. In most countries, the deadline starts when a party submits an application or in procedures ex officio, when the administrative authority performs the first official action. In general, the following also applies: counting deadlines is not limited by weekends or work-free days; however, when the last day is on a weekend or a public holiday, the deadline expires to the following weekday (Germany, Netherlands, Slovenia, Croatia, Serbia, and Poland).

The open concept of a "reasonable deadline" seems to have limited relevance in the administrative procedure of most countries (for instance, Portugal and France). In a legal system, such a concept only has added value in situations where there is no specific deadline set (see the development on this concept in Romanian law). For example, in the Netherlands, the requirement that a decision must be taken within a reasonable period applies only where the law does not provide for a time limit. In addition, the provision does prescribe a maximum deadline (see also Croatia).

1.2.4 Supervision of Administrative Timeliness

In most countries, the control of timeliness consists of legal actions by citizens in case of administrative inaction (appeal, judicial review, right to compensation). It is also common for a complaint to be submitted to the Ombudsman (Netherlands, Portugal, Croatia, Serbia, and Lithuania). In some countries, the general administrative law offers more options to control administrative timeliness. In Slovenia, for example, the administrative inspection can be informed in case of delay. The inspection can decide that an official person, or a head of the body, that violated prescribed time limits needs to go to additional training or propose a disciplinary procedure. The act requires that administrative authorities have a register of the number of applications, the number of solved administrative matters, and the time and means of conducting procedures. Disciplinary responsibility of the official also exists in Spain, Serbia, and Poland.

Although timeliness of administrative decision-making is high on the agenda in many countries, our study does not mention much government action. Interesting to mention here is regulation in Italy, aimed at speeding up and improving the efficiency of some administrative proceedings. Each year a group of administrative procedure whose particularly strong public interest needs quick conclusion (environment/public health) is selected for this so-called fast track method. Interesting to observe also is the implementation in Spain of a report from the Commission for Public Administration Reform. The Commission's proposal is to collect and disclose data (measurement of administrative unit workloads, calculate average processing times for procedures, assess productivity of each unit, and compare it with its counterparts).

1.3 Opposing Responses to Administrative Silence: The Negative and the Positive Legal Fictions

1.3.1 Intertwining the Basic Models: Negative, Positive, and Complementary Approaches

Administrative silence is generally understood to be a breach of the basic administrative law principle of good administration.[6] It is, therefore, common to legally regulate the consequences of such situations to mitigate dysfunction, and enable legal action and protection. Administrative silence is to be analyzed in relation to the principle of reasonableness.[7]

France was the first state to introduce administrative silence, doing so by a decree from 1865, which first adopted a negative model although with numerous exceptions; nevertheless, the legal fiction was reversed in 2013 to make room for a positive legal fiction.[8] Furthermore, Spain was one of the first countries to regulate administrative silence and its fictitious consequences in the APA, whereby a negative or a sustaining decision (*silencio positivo*) implies regarding procedure type.[9]

Pursuant to the important role of administrative silence and its legal treatment, this institution is commonly regulated by the (general) *Administrative Procedure Act* or *Code* or other legislation of the same level.[10] Additionally, sector-specific legislation determines different degrees of

[6] Cf. Galetta et al. (2015, p. 21): "*Timeliness, which pertains to the principles of fairness, means that decisions have to be taken within a reasonable time since slow administration is a bad administration and might be in violation of the concept of legal certainty.*"

[7] In the United Kingdom, for example, the term "administrative silence" is not used per se, which does not mean that such phenomenon does not occur (e.g., in environmental issues, see Anthony 2008, p. 39).

[8] See the chapter on France in this book.

[9] In principle, the fiction of negative decision applies, particularly in procedures conducted *ex officio*, including even the possibility of limitation of obligations under substantive law, while the fiction of a sustaining decision applies in procedures initiated upon the request of the party. In Spain, such cases have amounted to 122 out of 172 central proceedings (Jansen 2008, p. 12), which means that despite the general positive model there are in fact more cases with a negative outcome. In most countries under the Spanish influence (South America), a generally positive fiction prevails, with some corrections to the decision when such is inadmissible or excluded.

[10] Cf. Hofmann et al. (2014). See also the national chapters in this book. The majority of countries have APA as a general procedural law, some (like Spain or countries once

response timeliness as complementary solutions, whereby the principle of *lex specialis derogat legi generali* applies as long as these statutes comply with general principles and constitutional guarantees.

Most laws make reference to: (i) deadlines to issue an administrative decision, (ii) its legal effects, and (iii) legal remedies if the time limit is exceeded. In order to establish any legal consequences, especially a legal fiction (*praesumptio iuris et de iure*), certain conditions need to be fulfilled. These are at least the following: the case must concern a specific administrative matter, i.e., single-case administrative decision-making, the prescribed time limit for decision must be set specifically, and explicit legal protection is defined in case of administrative silence by a statutory law. If these and similar prerequisites are not met, there is no silence and consequentially legal effects do not occur. For instance, in Spain, these requirements are seen as a "double silence exception," since the Spanish APA requires various elements to be fulfilled in order to trigger the positive model.[11]

In both types of legal fictions, there is a presumption that either an express answer (negative) was given to the request addressed to the public authority, or an individual administrative act was issued. While the first model (negative) implies a balancing of interests and this is considered to be the exclusive competence of the public authority, in the second model (positive) there is merely a presumption that the opposing interests do not collide and hence the claim may be granted.[12]

Anthony[13] argues that understanding administrative silence based on a negative fiction is exaggerated and administration-centered. Alongside this opinion, it seems that lately the latter model (positive) is the predominant trend, although there are also objections by legal scholars against decision-making by default. The positive fiction is highly popular in EU candidate countries since candidates try to present themselves as progressive and compliant with the EU streamline, e.g., so Northern Macedonia or Albania.[14] However, the positive model raises specific issues, such as

part of Austrian-Hungarian Empire) cherish this tradition since nineteenth century or early twentieth century.

[11] See for details the Spanish chapter in this book.

[12] Jansen (2016, pp. 624, 639) and cf. Hofmann et al. (2014).

[13] Anthony (2008, p. 40).

[14] More in Koprić et al. (2016).

increased danger of corruption if other precautionary measures are not taken (e.g., control mechanisms and sanctions, a partnership awareness between the administration, and a citizen and realistic deadlines to be set in correlation with resources available).[15]

Table 1.1 presents previously dominant two-model comparison based on the national chapters, though it must be born in mind that "pure" codification has never existed in any country, but a mix of the two. Overall, the main model employed by the studied jurisdictions is negative, but exceptions enacted through sector-specific laws complement this model.

The legal tradition and culture need to be taken into account when judging the option for a model or another. In this sense, there are jurisdictions in Europe that cannot be easily categorized as positive or negative. Such an approach is particularly characteristic of Scandinavian and Anglo-Saxon legislation,[16] in which administrative inactivity is not supposed to burden parties and positive fiction is seen too extreme; this model is referred to as an *"informal dialogue"* between the administration and parties, potentially assisted by "third participants," most often ombudsmen, searching for win-win consensus resolution.[17]

In the jurisdictions from Western Europe, the consequences of administrative silence are not based only on the protection of the rights of parties and legality but also on the principle of transparency of the authoritative system and the need for procedural fairness. Informality is limited by law, yet it enables more flexibility as legally allowed in appellate and similar procedures. On a positive side, one can hereby establish a higher level of almost all stakeholders involved and fewer appeals and lawsuits in a consequence. On the other hand, the model implies goodwill on both sides and is effective only in the countries with a high level of service-minded administration. In these countries (or at the level of EU institutions), it is often that deadlines are not even set explicitly as a certain amount of time, but the law prescribes merely that authorities shall

[15] See Kovač (2012, p. 16).

[16] See Anthony (2008), Auby (2014), Hofmann et al. (2014), and Jansen (2016).

[17] Pursuing partnerships among the participants in the procedures, similarly to alternative dispute resolution mechanisms (cf. Dragos annd Neamtu 2014).

Table 1.1 Two main administrative silence models and their characteristics

	Negative model or deemed refusal	*Positive model or tacit/silent authorisation/approval/consent*
Social context	The model tries to insure that conflicting interests are balanced in the decisions. It relies on the pre-eminence of the public interest	The model tries to deal away with administrative red tape and to speed up administrative procedures. It relies on deregulation, legal certainty, it is business oriented
Legal context	The model is based on the fact that accountability lies with the public authority and that administrative competence is exclusive. It requires a merit review of the matter in order to insure that conditions to grant a right are fulfilled	The model relies on the principle that the burden of administrative inactivity must not be ascribed to the party, hence, any claim not refused in due time is deemed granted
Basic characteristics	Non-observance of the time limit by the administration leads to an application to be deemed to be rejected. The party can lodge an administrative appeal and/or court actio, leading to a devolution of competence	If there is a deadline breach in issuing an act, the application is deemed granted and rights claimed is acknowledged. However, some further procedural steps may be required in order to get the proof of that
Exceptions	When the system is mainly based on this model, the exceptions are usually those cases in which sector-specific laws regulate the positive model, mainly based on the Service Directive	For this model, the exceptions seem to be numerous, stipulated by general and sector-specific laws for sensitive cases where tacit approval is considered to be risky: international obligations, public finances, environment, heritage, social matters, urban planning
Advantages	There is no danger that public interest and third parties' rights may not be balanced during the decision making process. Also, there is a long tradition in some legal systems to employ this model	Stimulates authorities to comply with deadlines by "threat" that they will need to allow enforcement of private rights otherwise and then be held accountable

(continued)

Table 1.1 (continued)

	Negative model or deemed refusal	*Positive model or tacit/silent authorisation/approval/consent*
Disadvantages	Long procedures ("late decisions"). The principle of reasonableness is ineffective alone. The model legitimises inactivity and equalises situations of delays due to objective and subjective reasons; possible intentional delays in order to transfer accountability to decide to the courts	Potential recognition of rights disregarding the public interest. Risk of corruption. Problems with operational enforcement (e.g. no proofing document, not clear dates). False expectations of the beneficiaries. The alleged speeding up of procedures does not happen, as the administration quickly adapts to the model and requests new documents before the deadline expires. The assumption that deadlines cannot be observed for lack of resources is false premise for establishing a system of decision-making

decide *as soon as possible or without undue delay*. Still, it is then not fully clear what are the minimum formalities required to reach legal effects.[18]

Over time, there are some common—even though not unitary—trends discernible. The negative model has been the most common solution in European administrative law for long, based on the dominant role of the *Rechtsstaat* concept, in Central and Eastern Europe (e.g., in Romania, Serbia, Croatia) especially under Austrian influence.

A major turning point was in 2006 the adoption of the Service Directive. The Directive obliged EU Member States to adopt the positive silence model in their legal orders[19] when entrepreneurial licenses and

[18]As expressed in more depth by Jensen (2016), that, for instance in Italy, a special official or commissioner can be appointed by the court to replace the administrative authority that failed to take the decision required, which is a remarkable solution to solve the issue of separation of the judicial powers from the administrative power.

[19]Article 13, paragraph 4, reads: "*Failing a response within the time period set or extended in accordance with paragraph 3, authorisation shall be deemed to have been granted. Different arrangements may nevertheless be put in place, where justified by overriding reasons relating to the public interest, including a legitimate interest of third parties.*" Many countries have changed their laws only after several years, even after

grants are in question unless there is a specific need to regulate it differently, i.e., taking into account the concept of overriding reasons relating to the public interest. For some countries, this meant a major change in their traditional understanding of the phenomenon of administrative timeliness, while for some it presented merely a confirmation of a solution already in place for some time at least for sector-specific fields (Table 1.2).[20]

The EU administrative decision-making does not have a clear approach on this matter. Currently, there is no specific model of dealing with administrative silence and any conclusion can only be sector-limited. Member States are enjoying their national procedural autonomy as long as the EU substantive law does not apply directly or the principle of effectiveness and equivalence is not affected.[21]

The matter is complicated further by the fact that the CJEU does not want to set for a model or another, but leave as a principle the EU administration without immediate procedural sanctions. Thus, in Case C-123/03 P Commission v Greencore, it stated that "as a rule, mere silence on the part of an institution cannot be placed on the same footing as an implied refusal, except where that result is expressly provided for by a provision of Community law." We are wondering what is the consequence of silence of neither rejection nor approval are envisaged in the sector-specific laws? Is there a third way? We think not.

However, change may come at some point even at the EU level. A new proposal was envisaged but is yet to be adopted—the 2016 EU draft Regulation on open, efficient, and independent EU administration (2016/2610(RSP)) reads *inter alia* in Article 17: "*Administrative acts shall be adopted and administrative procedures shall be concluded within*

the transitional period provided by the Service Directive, for instance in Belgium and Slovenia only in 2010 (see more in the respective national chapters). Cf. Jansen (2016) or see de Graaf and Hoogstra (2013), where changes in domestic law pursuant to the Service Directive are discussed, and the Netherlands is seen as "enthusiastic," Germany "reluctant," and France as a "recent turnabout."

[20] See in details the respective chapters of this book.

[21] See in detail in the EU chapter of this book. For instance, as put forward by CJEU in the case C-123/03 P Commission v Greencore that "*as a rule, mere silence on the part of an institution cannot be placed on the same footing as an implied refusal, except where that result is expressly provided for by a provision of Community law.*" Cf. Galetta et al. (2015). For a background on a draft Regulation context and content, see Hofmann et al. (2014) and Harlow and Rawlings (2014, pp. 13–16).

Table 1.2 Some national examples of the prescribed deadlines and the silence model

	Deadlines in general & special law	*The main responses in a case of delay*
Spain	*Three months* provided by APA, and sector-specific laws cannot exceed six months; the deadlines are halved in urgent proceedings; all are valid also in *ex officio* proceedings	APA distinguishes between dispositive and official proceedings, in the latter negative model, and in the former a positive one, with some exceptions; imposed penalties and criminal liability for not complying with deadlines
The Netherlands	A decision must be given within the time limit prescribed by law or, in the absence of such *time limit in sector legislation*, within *a reasonable time but* in any event if not communicated otherwise within *eight weeks* of receiving the application	"From a negative interpretation to a procedural instrument" (cf. the national chapter) and a positive model, i.e. fictitious approval, unless exceptions provided by specific laws; also imposing periodic penalties when they exceed the time limit
Germany	To act within a *reasonable time* by APA, but the lawsuit may be lodged not prior to the expiry of *three months* unless a shorter period is required; deadlines are set by specific laws, e.g. *four weeks* by the Pressurised Air Decree or *60 days* or *seven months* by the Medicinal Products Act	Legal protection entails the action for the issuance of an administrative act, as the suit for inaction, whereby the party may skip the administrative appeal (which is not the case beyond silence); fictitious authorisations (*Genehmigungsfiktionen*) by laws based on the Service Directive and other special statutes
Croatia	*30 days* unless fact-establishing requires 60 days but only in the proceedings upon application; 60 days as well as in appellate proceedings; sector-specific law can determine only shorter deadlines as by APA	"From negative fiction to neutral position" (cf. the national chapter), with a devolution of competence upon a party's appeal/lawsuit; unless sector-specific law defines a positive model, if so a declaratory act is issued
Slovenia	*Two months*, also in *ex officio* and appellate proceedings; one month in summary proceedings; shorter or longer deadlines are (not often) set by sector-specific laws	Negative model, devolution of competence upon a party's appeal/lawsuit but also *ex officio* devolution if public interest is endangered

a reasonable time-limit and without undue delay. The time-limit for the adoption of an administrative act shall not exceed three months ... If the Union's administration does not acknowledge receipt of the application within three months, the application shall be deemed to be rejected."

It can be observed that the negative model, although preferred in the last 15 years, has been at times reorganized in terms of less rigid versions for the party in proceedings and toward stronger obligations for the administration. For instance, there are disciplinary or criminal liability and penalties imposed increasingly in various forms (e.g., see the national examples, in the chapters on the Netherlands, Belgium, Spain, Italy, Serbia, Romania, and Poland).

Some countries opted for a turnaround: from a negative to a positive legal fiction, and the most recent example is France. On the other hand, the positive model seems to allow for more and more statutory exceptions. At the same time, case law leads to strict interpretations, like for a positive approval in Italy or Belgium. The same goes for Romania, where silent approval was rendered almost impossible according to courts' judgments. Moreover, there are hybrid solutions as well, as in Germany, when in a case of silence a party goes to the court that requires from the administration that an act is issued. Some countries even set up an additional supervision, such as the administrative inspection (e.g., Slovenia, Croatia, and Serbia) which can adopt measures to ensure accountability in the events of violation of the APA if not repaired within the body itself. Based on fair trial requirements by the ECHR, there are other additional schemes of reconciliation, such damage compensations.

Overall, there is no one-size-fits-all recipe, and the approaches used by legislators combine the best elements of the two models and do the fine-tuning afterward. One of the issues discussed in the national chapters is whether, once the deadline expires, the competent body can still decide on the issue. In this case, a potential appeal or lawsuit would in some countries be rejected or proceeding ceased, e.g., in Serbia or in Italy and Romania, respectively. In others, even if the party withdraws an appeal already filed because of devolution and incompleteness of the case, the appellate body is nevertheless obliged to decide on the matter. In Poland, the delayed decision is taken as valid when a negative model is in place, also based on the case law; however, if a decision is issued after the expiration of the period when a silent approval occurs by a special law, the act is considered defective and unlawful, and the party may challenge it by an appeal. Within a positive model also in Italy, the delayed act could be disputed for annulment, while in Slovenia it would be illegal given the fact that competence has been transferred to the appellate body. The same applies in Belgium, where the Council of State ruled that the competent authority does not remain competent unlimitedly because it is bound to issue a decision within a reasonable deadline; furthermore, case law by the Council of State recognizes that delayed decisions can be harmful and lead to legitimate liability claims.

1.3.2 The Negative Model

The basic assumption of a negative model is a deemed refusal of party's application (and/or an appeal) when no individual administrative act is issued in a prescribed deadline. This model has been originally developed in central European law based on taking into account administrative procedures' *ratio*, which is primarily to protect public interest when endangered by parties' rights and their legal interest. Consequently, when in doubt, it is still better to assume that application has not been granted as opposed to positive model with the right claimed as deemed acknowledged, especially in certain fields where a public interest or third parties' rights are easily endangered, such as environment and public order.[22]

The legal nature of a negative decision can be (i) fictitious rejection, as in most Eastern European countries, or (ii) just an omission to act, as in Germany or Lithuania.

In the national chapters, the contributors were asked whether the administrative silence is restricted to procedures based on application or if functions also for ex officio decisions. In other words, when the law requires public authorities to act starting from one specific moment in time (when receiving a notification, for instance), is the general deadline applying? Further on, can the will of the administration be supplemented by a legal fiction?

From the national chapters, it emerges that the negative model applies in some cases also in *ex officio* proceedings, as in Spain, Slovenia, or Portugal (since 2015), in order to prevent the party to be uncertain of its legal position. In other countries, like Poland, this seems to be a controversial issue.

[22] See Harlow and Rawlings (2014, pp. 297–321), emphasizing trade-off in administrative matters.

Yet silence and the presumed negative decision in most legal systems are separated—the fiction of decision does not arise merely upon the expiry of the deadline for decision, as the party must first file an appeal or suit in an administrative dispute. The party has the right and not the obligation to seek a legal remedy although this only means that they assume the burden of action themselves. In some countries, it is required to firstly get a certificate that silence has occurred, whereby in Romania, for example, a party can choose administrative or judicial procedure to request to issue this document. In other countries, before access to court, the party is obliged to file an urging claim, as in Poland.

In some countries, it is allowed to file an appeal anytime until the issuing of the decision while in others within the preclusive deadline. This is the case in Serbia, with a limit of applying the appeal in one year after expiry of a deadline to issue an act, or in Portugal regarding the *ex officio* matters, also according to a Portuguese Supreme Court's judgment from 2018. The same goes for Lithuania, with two months after the expiry or one month from the publication of the challenged administrative act for appealing.

The negative fictitious act cannot achieve substantive effects per se; it is rather taken only as a procedural prerequisite to file an appeal or lawsuit.[23] The subject matter of an appeal on grounds of administrative silence is not to challenge the content of the decision, but the lack of a decision. By applying a legal remedy to administrative silence, the party claims that the authority has not decided yet and it should be forced by court to decide. Indirectly, the party indeed challenges the decision that does not recognize the legal interest they claimed, but essentially the party only files an appeal or an action to claim a right, not the violation thereof.

The administrative appeal may be filed directly with the superior instance authority, i.e., the appellate administrative body according to the general national appeal systems. Court proceedings are also an alternative or a subsequent possibility.[24]

[23] Given this, Croatian and Dutch rapporteurs describe their model as a neutral or a procedural one, respectively, as opposed to the (pure) negative one as applicable before the changes. In the Netherlands, such a stance has been pursued based on the highest court verdict from 1998, which was a different route taken than the legislator had envisaged according to the explanatory memorandum of the Dutch general administrative law (GALA).

[24] More in Dragos and Neamtu (2014), Auby (2014), and Koprić et al. (2016). Two major systems of administrative appeals are present—mandatory and optional. The first

The review bodies must within its supervisory powers ensure that action is taken. Thus, it frequently first examines the reasons for delay, and then it either imposes an additional time limit or takes upon itself to decide (e.g., in a case of endangered human lives or health, as in Slovenia).

In practice, the appellate body or the court commonly decides instead of a silent body, i.e., within not only a cassation function but also the court by merit judgment (e.g., in Slovenia or in Spain unless a discretionary act is in question). For instance, according to the Slovenian Administrative Dispute Act, the party may bring action in an administrative dispute even though there is no infringement of a single deadline but the procedure before the two administrative instances is still pending for more than three years.

We tried to gather in the national reports some empirical data on compliance with the deadlines prescribed by the law. It is difficult to draw any general conclusion since normally only average response data are provided which hide atypical cases, which may more or less frequent and may influence the perception of citizens toward timeliness of the administration.

Nonetheless, it seems that complementary measures enforced in the recent years—particularly under EU influence—have contributed to limit the phenomenon in many countries.

As to the usage of legal remedies, national rapporteurs (e.g., Belgium) reveal escalations of numbers of court proceedings at least in some sectors, such as environment. Other data are also interesting—in Serbia, approximately 20% of all lawsuits filed to administrative court were the result of administrative silence. In Croatia, this share is 5% despite 17% decrease of all administrative cases conducted in the same period, which is attributed to a higher awareness of parties to exercise their rights. In Germany, there are 2–15% of actions filed for failure to act in individual *Länder* (the highest in Berlin), with an increase of almost 19% in 2017—again in spite of the fact that the number of claims dropped by almost 4%. Lithuanian

one, adopted by the large majority of legal systems, e.g., in Germany (though not in the case of administrative silence), the Netherlands, CEE, and Balkan countries, precludes a lawsuit to a court in the absence of a prior administrative appeal. The second one (*recours administratif*), promoted by the French legal system and those inspired by it (e.g., Belgium), attaches certain effects to the exercise of the administrative appeal (prorogation of the statute of limitations for filing a lawsuit), without making it mandatory.

Ombudsman records in the last five years 2–5% of all complaints due to administrative silence but numbers have increased over time.

According to the EU Ombudsman, administrative inaction in the sense of total absence of a decision is not an issue when assessing the functioning of the EU administration, with only a small amount of cases.[25] Moreover, from the beginning of the functioning of the CJEU until the end of 2018, 263 cases were brought to court alleging a failure to act by an EU institution, body, office, or agency, and out of this total number, only 13 cases have been successful.

A further question was which administrative fields are mostly affected by administrative silence. The public authorities in their reporting have a manner of hiding the peculiarities in the average figures, and they do not offer any categorization. However, it is clear from other studies and from interviews conducted for the purpose of this study that one of such areas is access to information, where some countries record up to 70% of all complaints based on silence.[26] In other countries, like Germany and Slovenia, data available reveal silence as being a problem particularly in the field of granting social rights. In Romania, the problem is evident regarding building permits with 6–8 months to issue an act in practice, and taking in average 97 days in tax appeals in 2017. In the Netherlands, the most problematic sector seems to be the environment, as well as in Belgium with approximately 50% delayed decisions.

Given the long-standing tradition of the negative model, case law of the courts is rather rich. Frequently courts deal with the interpretation of duration of certain deadlines rather than the effects of the expiry of the deadline. That is particularly the case in countries with no defined deadline, e.g., Poland where the authority shall issue an act "promptly," "without a necessary delay." Further, according to German case law, the "suitable" timing runs a bit faster if the case is important for the party or the community and the public eye is watching.

As to the reasons for delays, in Germany and Poland, the case law from the last few years shows that work overload as well as absenteeism due

[25] See the EU chapter of this book. For example, there are cases of procrastination in the period 2013–2017 regarding a state aid complaint concerning four Spanish football clubs (with for years of a delay), access to documents connected with TTIP negotiations, delays in the authorization procedures for genetically modified food and feed, and chemicals.

[26] For FOIAs implementation, see Dragos et al. (2019), and the chapters in this book, such as Italian, Croatian, or Romanian.

to illnesses or vacation does not justify delays, so administrative silence occurs irrespective of the reason for exceeding the deadline and regardless of whether the deadline is statutory or set discretionary by an administrative body. If the law is not detailed enough, it is questionable whether the deadline to respond runs only when the application is complete as requested by the administrative body or from the time when the application was filed (e.g., in the Netherlands) regardless of subsequent requests for completion. Further on, sometimes dilemmas occur, in which procedural acts cause suspension of a proceeding and the suspension of the deadline to decide (e.g., preliminary rulings in Poland and Slovenia or when the administrative body requests new information from the party, in Romania).

Moreover, there is some case law also regarding the issue of lex generalis versus lex specialis when determining the deadlines. For example, Slovenian special law on children with special needs provides six months as opposed to the general deadline of two months, which the constitutional court found in 2010 not only against the equal protection of rights that require justified reason for different regulation in a certain field but also against the aim of the law—protection of children. In Romania, the special deadline for answering to requests for access to information (10 days) is usually disregarded and the more general deadline of 30 days from the petition law is considered.

1.3.3 The Positive Model

The positive model has been developed mainly to relieve parties when public administration is not conducting proceedings in due time. Its roots are found historically in Spanish and French laws, but nowadays it is a general issue in the EU and OECD.[27] According to this model, fictitious acts are legal ground for rights to be recognized and licenses to be granted if the administration fails to act in due time.[28]

[27] See Jansen (2016, p. 628) and Stelkens et al. (2012). See further on obligation to act as pursued by the EU Charter, Article 41, OECD, ECHR, and Council of Europe Recommendations CM/Rec(2007)7 on good administration, Rec(2004)6 on the improvement of domestic remedies, CM/Rec(2010)3 on effective remedies for excessive length of proceedings. More in Galetta et al. (2015) and Venice Commission (2011).

[28] In *ex officio* proceedings, a decision (also fictitious) that is unfavorable to the party may also be issued, which alters the legal relation (more in Kovač 2012, pp. 17ff). Positive decision is thus a broader term than sustaining decision. A positive decision is

However, the critics of this model argue that a positive model might compromise precisely those public interests for which the licensing requirement was introduced.[29] Therefore, there are many objections against the legal instrument of the fictitious positive decision (see Table 1.1). Despite this model being a general rule in some jurisdictions, all countries that adopt it provide also numerous exceptions, provided by sector-specific laws (as in Spain, Romania, France, Italy, etc.)—various protected categories, such as environment-related matters, public security matters, and even urban planning decisions. For instance, in Italy, the rule of fictitious positive decisions cannot be applied for the acts and proceedings concerning cultural heritage, environment, national defense, public security, immigration, public health, and all the cases in which European law requires a formal act. In France, the fictitious positive decision will not apply if it would be against public order, international law, the protection of liberties, or other constitutional rights if it involves a financial demand (except for social security).[30] In Belgium, an exception is adopted for the access to an administrative document and historical heritage. As an exception, the Portuguese law does not explicitly establish any legal matters where silent approvals are not accepted and even in traditional areas that are expression of state sovereignty, such as tax law, positive silence is permitted as a legal instrument.

Positive fictitious decisions have been a part of national systems for a long time, for instance in Spain or in the Netherlands, while some countries reversed to it recently, like France (2013) or some EU candidate countries. In addition, many national legislators pursue positive model as a general rule in the Administrative Procedure Act in special cases such as granting rights based on the consent of other body than a decision-maker (e.g., in Slovenia, Croatia, and Serbia).

A fictitious authorization or approval is regarded as any other individual act and can be legally challenged in the same way. If not disputed or enforced directly upon notification, with the fiction of positive decision,

either favorable for the party or unfavorable as it imposes obligations or restricts the rights and legal interests compared to the status prior to the initiation of the proceedings.

[29] See de Graaf and Hoogstra (2013, p. 9) and Kovač (2012, pp. 4–7). Moreover, almost all national rapporteurs in this book express some concerns or direct impediments in this regard.

[30] More in Jansen (2008, pp. 4, 13 and 2016, p. 644). See the respective national reports, for instance the Spanish "double silence exception."

a positive fictitious act acquires substantive finality (opposed to a negative one). Yet, especially with the positive fiction, the problem of finality and/or enforceability arises because of the non-materialized document and thus the problem of identifying the date on which the act entered into force. Hence, an additional proof should be provided, either from the authority upon request as in Germany or France, or certificated automatically (*ex lege*), like in the Netherlands.[31] In Spain, a certificate is also issued *ex officio* by the body with competences to decide within 15 days from the date of the expiry of the period allowed for resolving the procedure; additionally, the party may request it at any time based on the online registry. In Poland, in the event of silent authorization, the administrative body is bound by the decision issued in this mode from the day following the day on which the deadline for issuing expired, or the day on which the deadline for filing the objection expired. In Croatia, a declaratory act is issued upon a party's request. In Italy, there are many problems with the means of proof, so before starting the activity, the party must obtain an express decision by administration. In Romania, the document proving the silent approval must be obtained withers from the competent authority or from the court. In all systems, third parties aggrieved by the tacit approval have the right to appeal against the fictitious act from the date on which it has entered into force.

The case law on silent approval is not as many as in the case of negative silence, and those that have been initiated address mostly licensing proceedings under to the Service Directive and/or the scope of the exceptions. The Dutch Council of State noted in 2007/2008 paper that a tacit authorization is not based on an adequate balancing of interests, notably in environmental matters, where the interests of third parties and the public interest are always affected; accordingly, the law was amended. The Spanish Supreme Court, at its turn, dealt with some cases in the last two decades about when not to apply a positive fiction, like when requests that do not initiate the proceedings are in question. In Portugal, the same issue was in front of the courts in 2008 and 2012, and the courts stated that unlawfulness of the request does not prevent the occurrence of a silent decision, but it may cause the unlawfulness of that decision, in much the same way as would happen if an explicit act were issued. In

[31] See de Graaf and Hoogstra (2013, p. 32): "*To avoid discussion about whether or not a decision has been made within the time limit, the Dutch legislature opted to have the tacit authorisation come into effect three days after the expiry of the time limit.*"

Belgium, the Court of Cassation ruled in 2014 in a building permitting matter that administrative bodies have to decide in due time, but if they do not, the exceeding of a deadline might be the reason for a liability damage claim if some conditions are met, but is not sufficient to annul the decisions. An interesting ruling was made in Lithuania in 2017, in a case of a positive fiction by the special law to acquire a weapons license, where the Supreme Court ruled that the expiry of the deadline has no effect and considered a decision issued only few days after the deadline as valid since the applicant had a criminal record in connection with unlawful bearing of arms that precluded him from getting this license in the first place.

The case law confirms the overall approach that when regulated, positive silence model leaves room to many exceptions and that it may not be a principled rule for the conduct of administrative proceedings in other cases than repetitive ones with little importance or with no public interest stakes.

1.4 An Overall Assessment: The Importance of the Legal Design—Lessons Learned from Comparative Law

The comparative analysis of 14 reports for this book (EU law and 13 national reports) has revealed that administrative silence and responses to it are a recurrent European legal and administrative topic.

Regardless of the model applied, we want to emphasize the importance of setting specific deadlines instead of relying on the "reasonable time" concept. This is rather important in some legal traditions, more inclined to formalism or still in transition such as CEE countries. This is not only to make sure that decisions in the relations between authorities and individual parties are adopted within such time limits as promptly as possible, but also in order to foster the legal certainty and equality by providing exact time reference for the effects of administrative decisions.[32] One should have in mind that the deadlines for decision issued are seen in all countries as instructive ones, which are derived from the basic mission of the administrative body to conduct proceedings efficiently yet within

[32] In addition, certain cases require that decisions are adopted within such time that the matter as such does not become purposeless (Kovač 2012, p. 5).

the boundaries of law and with proportionate protection of public and individual legal interests. The rights and legal interests that the parties assert in administrative procedure are positive rights, particularly social and economic rights, in relation to which the parties have legally guaranteed expectations that the state will not only protect them but also create the possibilities for their actual implementation. In case deadlines are not defined in exact time limits, the promptness of decision-making has to be respected as a basic principle and if enacted by the law, legal effects and remedies are still applicable. Moreover, good administration requires response to any motion or complaint, in particular when well substantiated.[33]

Administrative silence should be considered to occur also if the deadline for decision is prolonged or if the decision is annulled at the appellate instance or in administrative dispute and no decision is taken by such additional deadline. Explicitly, the same goes for the discretionary act, even though the judicial review in these cases is often limited.

From comparing the different issues raised by the national chapters, the main conclusion is that there is no "one-size-fits-all" solution against the failure or the unwillingness of an administration to take a decision. Sometimes the cure—"lex silencio positivo"—may be deemed worse than the disease because there is no balancing of interests during decision-making.[34] The effect is not that decisions are taken within the deadline, but that procedural provisions are invoked to avoid the negative effects. So the envisaged positive effects are not realized.

The idea to replace the will of the administration by using a legal fiction may also raise issues of legitimacy and democracy. Consequently, the best available idea is still to foster the protection against administrative silence through legal instruments—judicial review, sanctions, Ombudsman intervention, in ways that insure a proper balance between legal certainty and effectiveness.

Despite these arguments against the positive silence mechanisms, a trend is discernible throughout Europe: the legal framework for the timeliness of administrative decision-making and for dealing with administrative silence has changed in the last decade. With it, the treatment of silence, which after decades of negative fiction, has moved to allowing

[33] More in Harlow and Rawlings (2014, pp. 156ff).

[34] See the Belgian and the Dutch chapters.

positive fiction for some specific procedures or even has been allowed to assume the primary role.

However, the underpinning motives of administrative delays and silence are tightly linked to the general problems of public administration in the jurisdictions studied: insufficient administrative capacity, lack of digitization and faulty record keeping, lack of interest from the central level of government for collecting data and analyzing systemic problems, lack of responsibility of civil servants, and lack of civic oversight. As a rule, administrative scholars scarcely discuss administrative silence, empirical data are not collected, while the discussion of timeliness considers procedures to be too long without empirical data (see, for instance, the German chapter). The review mechanisms alone are also ineffective in solving the timeliness problems, as courts are reluctant to police the administration too much (see, for instance, the case of Portugal).

In the national chapters, we tried to present also some empirical findings. It was hard to gather them, and they are not as relevant as we would have wished for. However, even the lack of data shows something: that record keeping must be improved and that governments should address the issue of timeliness not based on perceptions but on empirical data.

For a theme that is quite under-researched, we found a fair number of common issues and thus the legal tools envisaged purport to common conclusions.

For instance, public authorities do not keep a structured account of timeliness in solving administrative petitions that deadlines for answering petitions are in principle not exceeded but other tricks are used, such as requesting new documents, which can prolong the procedure indefinitely. Reporting on timeliness does not consider the completeness of the response given to the petitioner and they are not correlated with cases that end up in court. When assigned with litigation on administrative silence, the courts try to be effective and look at the underlying legal issue at hand (the rights or interests aggrieved) and treat administrative silence as a side-line issue. The system of negative silence is still predominant in most jurisdictions, even in those that declaratively adopted the positive silence as a principle. The positive silence, where generalized, has backfired, was criticized by scholars, and needed judicial intervention from courts in order to restrain its effects. On the other hand, there are also limited and specialized fields where positive silence works, for instance recognition of qualifications. In other instances, it works only as a sanctioning mechanism for the administration, and it pushes the authorities to respect the deadlines or at least to justify the extension of the deadline. Finally, apart from some declaratory political statements, there are no effective down-to-earth strategies aimed at reducing the processing time for citizen's requests or a coordinated analysis of this phenomenon.

As to the legal remedies, all jurisdictions use administrative appeal, a form of Ombudsman and the courts. Usually, the administrative appeal is a pretty effective method to make the administration pay attention to the deadlines, and it constitutes a good venue for pre-trial confrontation even in countries where it is not mandatory—such as France, where the administrative appeal helps the party to open the gates of judicial review. Another institution that takes care of delays is the Ombudsman, who can investigate both individual transgressions and systemic failures. The administrative and criminal law sanctions are not used in a consistent manner in order to be relevant; they work only as a scarecrow.

1.5 Conclusion

In order to ensure effective and responsive administration, in other words good administration, administrative silence must be properly addressed by both legal framework and organizational measures. Administrative silence can significantly influence administrative conduct in general, affecting not only individual rights and/or public interest in some cases, but generally the rule of law and trust into government. It has been a field of rather constant changes in pursuing the most efficient way to tackle the issue insofar, since various countries search for refinement of their legal regimes based on legal traditions, comparative insights, and EU measures.

So the solution is not to revert the legal fictions from negative to positive and expect a miracle, but to deal with delays in an integrated manner, using legal and managerial tools: negative fiction should be accompanied with accountability of civil servants that left the time to pass (as in the case of the Netherlands or Poland, where penalties are imposed), and finally, the courts should grant damages for not observing the deadlines, irrespective of how the case was decided on merits. The Ombudsman should be strengthened as an institution that deals with systemic breach of administrative timeliness.

In any case, we are convinced that administrative silence should be a theme that requires continuous attention from multidisciplinary scholars and from practitioners and that further insights into the workings of this institution are needed in order to draw firm conclusions on the effectiveness of tools envisaged to fight it.

References

Anthony, G. (2008). Administrative Silence and UK Public Law. *Ideas, 34–35*, 39–59. http://ideas.repec.org/a/pmu/cjurid/v34-35y2008p39-59.html.

Auby, J.-B. (Ed.). (2014). *Codification of Administrative Procedure*. Brussels: Bruylant.

de Graaf, K. J., & Hoogstra, N. G. (2013). Silence Is Golden? Tacit Authorizations in the Netherlands, Germany and France. *Review of European Administrative Law, 6*(2), 7–34.

Dragos, D. C., Kovač, P., & Marseille, A. T. (Eds.). (2019). *The Laws of Transparency in Action: A European Perspective*. London: Palgrave Macmillan.

Dragos, D. C., & Neamtu, B. (Eds.). (2014). *Alternative Dispute Resolution in European Administrative Law*. Berlin and Heidelberg: Springer.

Galetta, D.-U., Hofmann, H. C. H., Mir Puigpelat, O., & Ziller, J. (2015). *The General Principles of EU Administrative Procedural Law*. Brussels: European Parliament.

Harlow, C., & Rawlings, R. (2014). *Process and Procedure in EU Administration*. Oxford: Hart Publishing.

Hofmann, H. C. H., Schneider, J.-P., & Ziller, J. (Eds.). (2014). The *ReNEUAL Model Rules*. Oxford: Oxford University Press.

Jansen, O. (Ed.). (2008). *Comparative Inventory of Silencio Positivo. Institute of Constitutional and Administrative Law*. Utrecht: Utrecht School of Law.

Jansen, O. (2016). Silence of the Administration: General Comments and Dutch Law. In J.-B. Auby (Ed.), *Droit comparé de la procédure administrative/Comparative Law of Administrative Procedure* (pp. 623–646). Brussels: Bruylant.

Koprić, I., Kovač, P., Đulabić, V., & Džinić, J. (2016). *Legal Remedies in Administrative Procedures in Western Balkans*. Danilovgrad: ReSPA. http://www.respaweb.eu/11/library#respa-publications-2016-7.

Kovač, P. (2012). Fighting Administrative Silence in European and Slovene Law and Practice. In D. C. Dragos, F. Lafarge, & P. Willemsen (Eds.), *PSG Law & PA: Proceedings* (pp. 79–106). Bucharest: Economică.

Stelkens, U., Weiß, W., & Mirschberger, M. (2012). *The Implementation of the EU Services Directive: Transposition, Problems and Strategies*. The Hague, Netherlands: T.M.C. Asser Press.

Venice Commission. (2011). *Stocktaking on the Notions of Good Governance and Good Administration*, Study no. 470/2008.

PART II

The European Union

CHAPTER 2

Silence of the EU Authorities: The Legal Consequences of Inaction by the EU Administration

Natassa Athanasiadou and Mariolina Eliantonio

2.1 The Legal and Administrative Context of Regulating Silence in EU Law

2.1.1 The Distribution of Administrative Competences Between the EU and the Member States

The European Union (EU) is based on a system of so-called indirect administration; hence, most of EU legislation is implemented at national level, by national authorities and their own administrative decision-making procedures and structures. However, in some areas, a system of

N. Athanasiadou (✉) · M. Eliantonio
Faculty of Law, Maastricht Center for European Law, Maastricht University, Maastricht, The Netherlands
e-mail: natassa.athanasiadou@maastrichtuniversity.nl;
natassa.athanasiadou@maastrichtuniversity.be

M. Eliantonio
e-mail: m.eliantonio@maastrichtuniversity.nl

D. C. Dragos et al. (eds.),
The Sound of Silence in European Administrative Law,
https://doi.org/10.1007/978-3-030-45227-8_2

"direct administration" is in place, meaning that it is the EU institutions (mostly the European Commission and the relevant EU executive and decentralized agencies) that implement EU legislation.[1]

There are also increasingly more mechanisms of "composite" or "shared" administration, which comprise administrative decision-making processes, including actors from multiple jurisdictions (i.e., either the EU and national level, or horizontally multiple national levels).[2]

This contribution is only concerned with the instances of "direct administration" and the silence of EU institutions acting as administrative authorities (i.e., implementing EU legislation). Hence, it does not deal with the EU law requirements for national administration and the consequent Europeanization process brought onto national systems of administrative law.[3]

2.1.2 The Broader Cultural Context of Understanding Timeliness of Administrative Procedure by the EU Authorities

The legitimacy of the EU administration is based to a large extent also on its modus operandi. The Treaty on the Functioning of the EU (TFEU) proclaims the EU administration as an administration built on the principles of openness, transparency, and accessibility to EU citizens (see in particular art. 15 TFEU). From the early stages of the EU integration process, the Court of Justice of the European Union (CJEU) developed in its case-law the "reasonable period principle," which, in light of the fundamental requirements of legal certainty and good administration, prevents the institutions from indefinitely delaying the exercise of their powers and obliges them to act within a reasonable time.[4] The timeliness

[1] Further on these concepts, see Ziller (2014) and Craig (2018, p. 80).

[2] See, e.g., Hofmann (2009) and Eliantonio (2014).

[3] This matter will be indeed covered in each of the national chapters of this edited volume.

[4] Case 57/69 ACNA v Commission (ECLI:EU:C:1972:78), para 32; Case C-282/95 P Guérin automobiles v Commission (ECLI:EU:C:1997:159), para 36 and 37; and Joined Cases C-238/99 P, C-244/99 P, C-245/99 P, C-247/99 P, C-250/99 P to C-252/99 P and C-254/99 P Limburgse Vinyl Maatschappij and Others v Commission (ECLI:EU:C:2002:582), para 167–171.

of the administrative action became a component of the right to good administration, as enshrined in the EU Charter (art. 41 EU Charter).[5]

Already in the founding Treaty of the European Economic Community (EEC) of 1957, it was established that any physical or legal person could seize the Court of Justice in case an institution fails to address to that person any act other than a recommendation or an opinion (art. 175 of the EEC Treaty). This legal remedy, which is to be found in the current art. 265 TFEU, does not transform administrative silence into a negative or positive decision, but constitutes a means of control of the legality of inaction.

These provisions have created an administrative culture of fixed and relatively tight deadlines, in particular as regards access to the documents of the EU institutions or other procedures which involve applications. In general, the EU administration is characterized by its high responsiveness to queries by citizens. This is reinforced by the existence of platforms through which citizens may obtain information within fixed deadlines.[6]

2.1.3 The Main Principles of Administrative Law Regarding Timeliness of Administrative Procedures by the EU Authorities

The CJEU, drawing from the national constitutional traditions, used from the beginning of the EU integration the general principles of legal certainty and legitimate expectations in order to develop the obligation of the administration to act within reasonable time-limits which have to be foreseeable for the citizens.[7] This obligation exists even in the absence of a specific time-limit for a certain action and was defined by the court as the

[5] On the right to good administration in EU law, see Azoulai and Clément-Wilz (2014, p. 671), Chevalier (2014), Craig (2018, p. 348), and Galetta et al. (2015).

[6] For example, general questions on the EU may be sent via the "Europe Direct" platform and a reply is due within three working days (due to complexity a reply may take longer), available at https://europa.eu/european-union/contact/write-to-us_en; access to documents requests may be sent via a special platform and a reply is due within 15 working days, unless the deadline is extended because of the complexity of the request, available at https://ec.europa.eu/transparency/regdoc/index.cfm?fuseaction=fmb&language=en.

[7] Case 57/69 ACNA v Commission (ECLI:EU:C:1972:78), para 32; Case C-282/95 P Guérin automobiles v Commission (ECLI:EU:C:1997:159), para 36 and 37; and Joined Cases C-238/99 P, C-244/99 P, C-245/99 P, C-247/99 P, C-250/99 P to C-252/99 P and C-254/99 P Limburgse Vinyl Maatschappij and Others v Commission (ECLI:EU:C:2002:582), para 167–171.

principle of reasonable time.[8] This "reasonable time principle" became one of the elements of the principle of good administration, which was elevated to a fundamental right with the EU Charter.[9]

The right to good administration (art. 41 EU Charter) guarantees the right of every person to have their affairs handled impartially, fairly and *within a reasonable time* by the institutions, bodies, offices, and agencies of the Union (emphasis added). This article of the Charter aims to confer a justiciable right to individuals in the sense that it can be directly invoked before court.[10]

The elements of good administration have been rendered more concrete through codes of good administrative behavior, which had been existing even before the Charter became legally binding with the Lisbon Treaty. The European Ombudsman has compiled a code containing minimum standards of good administration relevant for all EU institutions when assuming administrative duties.[11] This code was first endorsed by the European Parliament through a resolution in 2001.[12] The European Commission follows its own code which is annexed to its rules of procedure[13] and which is in line with the one compiled by the European Ombudsman but adjusted to its own needs and specificities. Both codes crystallize the principle of reasonable time-limit and the need to inform the person who has addressed a request of the date on which they should expect a reply, as required by the principle of legal certainty (see Sect. 2.1).

[8] See Jansen (2016, p. 630).

[9] Case C-282/95 P Guérin Automobiles v Commission (ECLI:EU:C:1997:159), para 37; Case C-447/13 P Riccardo Nencini v Parliament (ECLI:EU:C:2014:2372), para 38.

[10] Case T-138/14 Randa Chart v European External Action Service (ECLI:EU:T:2015:981, para 113.

[11] Cf. European Ombudsman, European Code of Good Administrative Behaviour. On this, see Harlow and Rawlings (2014, p. 115 et seq).

[12] Cf. European Parliament Resolution on the European Ombudsman's Special Report to the European Parliament following the own-initiative inquiry into the existence and the public accessibility, in the different Community institutions and bodies, of a Code of Good Administrative Behaviour.

[13] Cf. European Commission, Rules of Procedure [C(2000) 3614], as last amended by Commission Decision of 9 November 2011 amending its Rules of Procedure [COM 2011/737/EU, Euratom].

2.2 The Legal Framework of Timeliness for EU Institutions

2.2.1 General Provisions on Timeliness

At the level of primary law, the EU Charter, as aforementioned, guarantees the right to good administration which encompasses the right of every person to have his affairs handled within a reasonable time by the institutions, bodies, offices, and agencies of the Union (art. 41 EU Charter). This fundamental right is safeguarded through the system of judicial protection before the CJEU. In case an institution or other body of the Union fails to act, including cases when it does not comply with a time-limit, the other institutions, Member States, or natural or legal persons may bring an action before the CJEU to have the infringement established under certain conditions (art. 265 TFEU). It derives from this provision that the EU Treaties do not deduce specific legal consequences from administrative silence in the sense of transforming it into a positive or negative decision, but they contain a specific legal remedy to challenge administrative inaction.[14]

At the level of secondary law, the EU does not dispose of a General Administrative Procedure Act which could have regulated in a horizontal way issues related to timeliness, and the legal consequences in case time-limits are not respected by the administration. However, there is legislation which contains horizontal rules on administrative procedures, but they cover a specific topic without being part of a general codex. In relation to the topic of time-limits, Regulation (EEC, Euratom) No 1182/71 determines the rules applicable to periods, dates, and time-limits.[15] An important horizontal rule in this respect is that any period mentioned in EU rules includes public holidays, Sundays and Saturdays, save where periods are expressed in working days.[16] In general, this horizontal piece of legislation regulates how time-limits are to be calculated,

[14] On the different choices of legal orders as to how to react to silence see Auby (2014, p. 22) and Jansen (2016, p. 623).

[15] Regulation (EEC, Euratom) No 1182/71 of the Council of 3 June 1971 determining the rules applicable to periods, dates, and time limits [1971] OJ L 124.

[16] Art. 3(3) Regulation (EEC, Euratom) No 1182/71.

but it does not mention the legal consequences in case of non-compliance with a deadline.[17]

Currently, there is an ongoing discussion on the codification of administrative procedural rules for the EU institutions, from both the academic and the policy-making side. The Research Network on EU Administrative Law (ReNEUAL) presented in 2014 model rules on EU administrative procedure, drafted by academics and aiming at inspiring the policymakers to this direction.[18] These model rules contain inter alia an article on time-limits in procedures leading to the adoption of individual administrative acts (rule III.9). Pursuant to this model article, there should be a default time-limit of three months unless otherwise provided by sector-specific rules (rule III.9(1)). The administration should have the possibility to extend the prescribed time-limit with adequate justification in cases of complex decisions, while informing the individual concerned about the expected time of the final decision (rule III.9(3)). The model rules do not provide for a consequence in case of violation of a time-limit, but mention the obligation of the sectoral rules to do so (rule III.9(4)).

This academic initiative triggered action from the European Parliament, which drafted a proposal for a Regulation for an open, efficient, and independent European Union administration and invited the Commission to consider it.[19] This draft Regulation includes a similar article on time-limits to the aforementioned model rule by ReNEUAL (see art. 17 of the draft Regulation). The added point concerning administrative inaction is that the administration, according to this draft Regulation, has an active obligation to inform the individual concerned about the legal consequences in case it violates the prescribed time frame (see art. 6(4)(f) and 7(3)(e) of the draft Regulation).

At the moment, no concrete steps have been taken by the Commission to propose legislation on this point. In particular, the Commission has expressed the opinion that relying only on sectoral law is not to be regarded as a problem, since this allows for flexibility to adapt to the

[17] See in detail von Danwitz (2008, p. 444).

[18] See Hofmann et al. (2014).

[19] European Parliament Resolution of 9 June 2016 for an Open, Efficient and Independent European Union Administration.

different policy areas.[20] As a consequence, administrative decision-making at the EU level is currently governed by general principles of EU administrative law, such as the principle of proportionality and legal certainty, the applicable sectoral laws, and the internal rules of procedure of the various institutions and EU agencies.[21]

These internal rules of procedure, as aforementioned, contain certain general guidelines on timely functioning, which reflect the European Code of Good Administrative Behaviour as drafted by the European Ombudsman. This code in its art. 14 provides that every letter or complaint to an institution shall receive an acknowledgment of receipt within a period of two weeks, except if a substantive reply can be sent within that period. No acknowledgment of receipt and no reply need to be sent in cases where letters or complaints are abusive because of their excessive number or because of their repetitive or pointless character. Art. 17 of this code crystallizes the so-called principle of a reasonable time-limit. According to this, every official shall ensure that a decision on a request or complaint to the institution is taken within a reasonable time-limit, without delay, and in any case no later than two months from the date of receipt. If a request or a complaint to the institution cannot, because of the complexity of the matters which it raises, be decided upon within the above-mentioned time-limit, the official shall inform the author as soon as possible. In such a case, a definitive decision should be communicated to the author in the shortest possible time.

The code which is annexed to the Rules of Procedure of the European Commission, in its Section 4 on "dealing with inquiries," restates these principles and adds that whenever the Commission services are not able to abide by a time-limit due to the complexity of the request or due to the need for interdepartmental consultation or translation, they should send a holding reply, indicating a date by which the addressee may expect the definitive reply. It is evident that the holding reply aims to restore legal certainty, which requires that the person who made a request should be able to foresee the time of the administration's reply.

These internal rules apply horizontally in every field of action, unless there are sectoral laws which provide otherwise. Sectoral rules normally

[20] See the position of the European Commission represented by the then Commission Vice-President Jyrki Katainen (2016) Protocol of the plenary debate, PV 8.6.2016-26; on this, see Athanasiadou (2017, p. 298).

[21] See Hofmann et al. (2011, p. 67) and Craig (2018, p. 263).

provide for specific time-limits, provide for any possibility of prolongation of deadlines, and often mention whether administrative inaction may be treated as a negative or positive administrative act. There are also instances, when secondary legislation does not determine a time-limit, e.g., the time-limit within which the Commission has to respond to complaints concerning State aid or anti-competitive behavior. However, also in these instances of absence of a time-limit in law, the Commission continues to be bound by the "reasonable time principle." For this reason, the Commission in internal codes of best practices sets indicative time-limits, i.e., in the codes on best practices for the conduct of State aid control procedures[22] and in proceedings concerning arts. 101 and 102 TFEU.[23]

2.2.2 Sector-Specific Legislation

In order to present the heterogeneous and wide-ranging sectoral laws in a comprehensive and systematic way, this contribution examines five representative pillars:

1. "*the EU administration as market regulator*": this pillar concerns rules in the field of market regulation, in particular notification procedures in competition and State aid law (where the main actor is the "Directorate-General Competition/DG COMP" within the European Commission);
2. "*the EU administration as risk regulator*": this pillar concerns rules on authorizations involving risk management (where the main actors are the Commission and several EU agencies, namely the European Chemicals Agency/ECHA, the European Medicines Agency/EMA, and the European Food Safety Authority/EFSA);
3. "*the EU administration as funding actor*": this pillar encompasses rules in the field of funding applications by private or public entities (where the main actors are various Directorates-General within the European Commission);

[22] European Commission, Code of Best Practice for the conduct of State aid control procedures.

[23] European Commission, Notice on best practices in proceedings concerning articles 101 and 102 TFEU.

4. "*the EU administration as transparent actor*": this pillar concerns rules on requests for access to documents by EU citizens (where the main actor is the institution to which the request is submitted); and
5. "*the EU administration as employer*": this pillar covers rules in the field of EU civil service law concerning employees of the EU institutions (where the main actor is the institution acting as the employer of the concerned civil servant).

For each of these four pillars, representative decision-making procedures are selected; for each of these procedures, the procedural steps are retraced and the average length of time-limits is examined. Furthermore, it is examined when a procedural step begins and what the rules about deadlines' expiry are. The legal character of the deadlines and the possibility of prolongation are also considered. Lastly, the consequences of deadlines' expiry beyond the general judicial remedies are investigated.

The EU Administration as Market Regulator

In the field of market regulation, two sets of rules have been considered, namely those concerning the authorization of mergers[24] and those concerning the authorization of State aid.[25] Both processes can be regarded as highly proceduralized, and they are composed of several steps, entailing the exchange of views and data between the Commission and the Member States. The aim of these exchanges is to acquire information on the relevant market in which the concerned enterprises operate, or the specifics of a certain national measure or scheme, in order for the Commission to be able to assess where a certain merger or aid is compatible with EU law.

Despite the high proceduralization in both areas, one notable difference is that while in the field of merger control, many steps have to be carried out by the European Commission "without delay" (such as the transmission of the applicant's submission concerning the effects of a

[24] Council Regulation (EC) No 139/2004 of 20 January 2004 on the control of concentrations between undertakings [2004] OJ L 24.

[25] Council Regulation (EC) No 659/1999 of 22 March 1999 laying down detailed rules for the application of Article 93 of the EC Treaty [1999] OJ L 83.

proposed merger to all Member States[26] or the transmission of the information to all Member States of one Member State's disagreement on transfer of proceedings concerning a proposed merger[27]), this is not the case in the field of State aid which contains exact deadlines.

What is furthermore peculiar in the field of merger control is that, where deadlines are provided in legislation, their expiry produces positive implicit decisions on the part of the European Commission. For example, the Commission has 25 working days starting from the receipt of the applicant's reasoned submission concerning effects of a proposed merger to refer the procedure to a specific Member State if a "distinct market" is deemed to exist. According to art. 4(4) of Regulation 139/2004, if this deadline expires "the Commission shall be deemed to have adopted a decision to refer the case in accordance with the applicant's submission."

Similarly, the Commission has 25 working days from receipt of the notification to examine a notified merger.[28] If a formal investigation is opened, the Commission is obliged to take a decision of the compatibility of the merger with the common market within 90 working days of the date on which the proceedings are initiated.[29] In both cases, if no decision is taken, the concentration shall be deemed to have been declared compatible with the common market.[30]

Interestingly, the same system of positive implicit decision is to be found in the rules concerning the authorization of State aid. While there are certain steps of the procedure which have to be completed within a "desirable" time-limit (such as the deadline to close a formal investigation),[31] whenever a fixed time-limit is provided, the consequence of its expiry is the creation of a positive implicit decision.

Hence, the Commission decision finding that the notified measure does not constitute aid, the decision finding that no doubts are raised as to the compatibility with the common market of a notified measure, and the decision finding that doubts are raised as to the compatibility with

[26] Art. 4(4) Regulation (EC) 139/2004.

[27] Art. 4(5) Regulation (EC) 139/2004.

[28] Arts. 6(1) and 10(1) Regulation (EC) 139/2004.

[29] Art. 8(1) and 10(3) Regulation(EC) 139/2004.

[30] Art. 10(6) Regulation (EC) 139/2004.

[31] In this case, the Commission has to "as far as possible endeavour to adopt a decision within a period of 18 months". Cf. Art. 7(6) Regulation (EC) 659/1999.

the common market of a notified measure have to be taken within two months from the day following the receipt of a complete notification.[32] In all of these cases, failure to comply with the deadline will cause the aid to be deemed to have been authorized by the Commission.[33] Whenever deadlines are not foreseen, according to the CJEU, the Commission should nevertheless act "diligently and take account of the interest of Member States of being informed of the position quickly in spheres where the necessity to intervene can be of an urgent nature by reason of the effect that these Member States expect from the proposed measures of encouragement."[34]

The EU Administration as Risk Regulator

Under this heading, a number of rules in the field of industry and market regulation have been considered, namely the procedure for marketing authorizations of medicines,[35] the procedure for marketing authorizations of GMOs,[36] and the procedure for marketing authorizations of plant protection products.[37]

The first two decision-making processes are characterized by similar procedural steps. As far as marketing authorizations for GMOs for cultivation are concerned, Regulation 1829/2003 foresees a procedure whereby, first, the opinion of the European Food Safety Authority (EFSA) needs to be obtained by the Commission. Thereafter, the Commission submits a draft authorization to the relevant comitology committee and, in case of a positive opinion on the draft authorization by the committee, the Commission issues a final decision in the form of an Implementing

[32] Arts. 4(2), 4(3), 4(4), and 4(5) Regulation (EC) 659/1999.

[33] Art. 4(6) Regulation (EC) 659/1999.

[34] Case 120/73 Gebrüder Lorenz GmbH v Federal Republic of Germany and Land Rheinland-Pfalz (ECLI:EU:C:1973:152).

[35] Regulation (EC) No 726/2004 of the European Parliament and of the Council of 31 March 2004 laying down Community procedures for the authorization and supervision of medicinal products for human and veterinary use and establishing a European Medicines Agency [2004] OJ L 136.

[36] Regulation No 1829/2003 of the European Parliament and of the Council of 22 September 2003 on genetically modified food and feed [2003] OJ L 268.

[37] Regulation (EC) No 1107/2009 of the European Parliament and of the Council of 21 October 2009 concerning the placing of plant protection products on the market and repealing Council Directives 79/117/EEC and 91/414/EEC [2009] OJ L 309.

Decision. The marketing authorization for medicines, when the so-called centralized procedure is activated, follows similar steps in that the application is first subject to an opinion by an agency (in this case the European Medicines Agency/EMA), with a subsequent step constituted by a comitology procedure and a final Commission Implementing Decision.

Despite the similarities in procedural steps, the regulation of deadlines in the two procedures is different. For example, while the opinion of the EMA must be received within 210 days after receipt of a valid application,[38] the EFSA shall only "endeavor" to provide an opinion within six months as from the receipt of a valid application.[39] Furthermore, according to the same provision, this time-limit may be extended (for a period of time which is not determined in legislation) whenever EFSA seeks supplementary information from the applicant.

Also, on the side of the Commission, which is in charge of issuing the final authorization, the deadlines in the process of marketing authorizations of medicines are shorter, since the Commission is obliged to submit the draft decision to be taken in respect of the application to be submitted to the comitology procedure within 15 days after receipt of the opinion of the EMA.[40] With regard instead to the regulation of GMOs, the same action must be undertaken by the Commission within three months after receipt of the opinion of the EFSA.[41]

The most striking difference is related to the deadline for finalizing the decision-making process. While the Commission has the obligation to take a final decision on the marketing authorization of a medicine within 15 days after the end of the comitology procedure,[42] there does not seem to be any deadline for the conclusion of the process with regard to the marketing authorization of GMOs.

A similar procedure to the one discussed above is that applicable to the marketing authorization of plant protection products. The relevant secondary rules also provide for some deadlines for the EFSA to circulate a draft assessment report prepared by the rapporteur Member State (at

[38] Art. 6(3) Regulation (EC) No 726/2004.

[39] Art. 6(1) Regulation No 1829/2003.

[40] Art. 10(1) Regulation (EC) No 726/2004.

[41] Art. 7(1) Regulation No 1829/2003.

[42] Art. 10(2) Regulation (EC) No 726/2004. See also Temple Lang & Raftery (2011).

the latest 30 days after its receipt)[43] and for the conclusion concerning the safety of product by the same authority (within 120 days of the end of the period provided for the submission of written comments by the Member States).[44] In the latter case, the rule provides for a possibility of extension until three months in certain circumstances.

Finally, as in the case of GMOs authorizations, while there is a deadline for the Commission to submit a draft Regulation to the comitology procedure (i.e., within six months of receiving the opinion from the EFSA),[45] there is no deadline foreseen for the final decision by the European Commission on the application. It is also to be noted that in none of these cases is there a specific regulation of the consequences of exceeding the time-limits set out above.

The EU Administration as Funding Actor

One of the major tasks of the EU administration consists in the distribution of various grants based on EU programs or actions adopted by the EU budgetary authorities (Parliament and Council). On the basis of such programs or actions, the Commission or its executive agencies adopt a "work program," which is subsequently implemented through the publication of calls for proposals (art. 110 Regulation (EU, Euratom) 2018/1046, "Financial Regulation").

The Financial Regulation requires that calls for proposals specify the planned date by which all applicants should have been informed of the outcome of the evaluation of their application and the indicative date for the signature of grant agreements or notification of grant decisions (art. 194 (1) (e)). Those dates shall be fixed on the basis of the following periods: (a) for informing all applicants of the outcome of the evaluation of their application, a maximum of six months from the final date for submission of complete proposals; (b) for signing grant agreements with applicants or notifying grant decisions to them, a maximum of three months from the date of informing applicants they have been successful (art. 194(2) Financial Regulation). Those periods may be adjusted in order to take into account any time needed to comply with specific procedures that may be required by the basic act and may be exceeded

[43] Art. 12(1) Regulation (EC) No 1107/2009.

[44] Art. 12(2) Regulation (EC) No 1107/2009.

[45] Art. 13 Regulation (EC) No 1107/2009.

in exceptional, duly justified cases, in particular for complex actions, where there is a large number of proposals or delays attributable to the applicants. The authorizing officer shall report in his or her annual activity report on the average time taken to inform applicants, sign grant agreements, or notify grant decisions (art. 194(2), sub-para 2 Financial Regulation). In the event of the aforementioned periods being exceeded, the authorizing officer shall give reasons and, where not duly justified in accordance with the third subparagraph, shall propose remedial action (art. 194(2), sub-para 3 Financial Regulation).

The EU Administration as a Transparent Actor

Openness is placed in the heart of the functioning of the EU institutions, because it guarantees that the administration enjoys greater legitimacy and is more accountable to the citizen in a democratic system (see recital 2 of Regulation (EC) No 1049/2001). One of the main elements of openness is the possibility of every EU citizen to have access to the documents of the EU institutions, which is guaranteed as a fundamental right.

In order to ensure that the right of access is fully respected, Regulation (EC) No 1049/2001 provides for a two-stage administrative procedure with precise deadlines. According to art. 7 of the Regulation, an application for access to a document shall be handled promptly. An acknowledgment of receipt shall be sent to the applicant. Within 15 working days from registration of the application, the institution shall either grant access to the document requested or state the reasons for the total or partial refusal. In the Commission Internal Rules of Procedure, it is provided that if an application is imprecise, the Commission shall invite the applicant to provide additional information making it possible to identify the documents requested; the deadline for reply shall run only from the time when the Commission has this information.[46]

The Regulation gives also the possibility, in exceptional cases, for example in the event of an application relating to a very large number of documents, to extend the time-limit by 15 working days, provided that the applicant is notified in advance and that detailed reasons are given (art. 7(3) Regulation (EC) 1049/2001). In the event of a total or partial

[46] Art. 2 of the Detailed Rules for the application of Regulation (EC) No 1049/2001 of the European Parliament and of the Council regarding public access to European Parliament, Council and Commission documents, annexed to the European Commission Rules of Procedure.

refusal, the applicant may, within 15 working days of receiving the institution's reply, make a confirmatory application asking the institution to reconsider its position (art. 7(2) Regulation (EC) 1049/2001).

The Regulation does not mention what happens in case of inaction of the administration following the first application. Nothing, however, prevents the applicants from making a confirmatory application also in the case that the administration does not respond to the first application within the prescribed time-limit.

For the administration's reply to the confirmatory application, the same time-limit and prolongation possibility apply. Failure by the institution to reply to a confirmatory application within the prescribed time-limit shall be considered as a negative reply and entitle the applicant to institute court proceedings against the institution and/or make a complaint to the Ombudsman (art. 8(3) Regulation (EC) 1049/2001). So, although for the first application the Regulation does not provide any legal consequences in case the administration violates the deadline, in the second stage of the confirmatory application the eventual silence of the administration is transformed into a negative decision.

The EU Administration as Employer

The rules which govern the relations between the EU institutions and agencies and their employees are the Staff Regulations and the Conditions of Employment of other servants. The Staff Regulations provide for general time-limits concerning requests and complaints of employees. According to art. 90(1), of these Regulations, any concerned person may submit to the competent authority a request that the latter take a decision relating to him. The authority has to notify the person concerned of its reasoned decision within four months from the date on which the request was made. If at the end of that period no reply to the request has been received, this shall be deemed to constitute an implied decision rejecting it, against which a complaint may be lodged.

Complaints may be submitted against an act affecting the person concerned adversely, or against an implied rejection of a request (art. 90(2) Staff Regulations). The complaint must be lodged within three months. The period shall start to run on the date of expiry of the period prescribed for reply where the complaint concerns an implied decision rejecting a request. The authority shall notify the person concerned of its reasoned decision within four months from the date on which the complaint was lodged. If at the end of that period no reply to the complaint has been received, this shall be deemed to constitute an implied decision rejecting it, against which an appeal may be lodged before the General Court (see art. 270 and 256, para 1, TFEU).

It can be concluded that in EU civil service law exist general provisions which transform administrative silence into an implied negative decision in all cases of requests and complaints by employees, unless otherwise provided by a *lex specialis*. The only *lex specialis* to be found in the Staff Regulations which provides for an exception to this general rule is art. 17a of the Staff Regulations. This article regulates the exercise of the right of freedom of expression by EU officials. More specifically, it requires that an official who intends to publish any matter dealing with the work of the Union shall inform their hierarchical superiors in advance. Where the hierarchical superiors are able to demonstrate that the matter is liable seriously to prejudice the legitimate interests of the Union, they shall inform the official of their decision in writing within 30 working days of receipt of the information. If no such decision is notified within the specified period, the hierarchical superiors shall be deemed to have had no objections.

It comes as no surprise that the only case of implied positive decision in the Staff Regulations concerns the fundamental right to freedom of expression (art. 11, para 1, EU Charter). The fact that staff members need to obtain prior authorization for any intended publication which concerns EU policies constitutes per se a significant limitation of their right to freedom of expression. The brief deadline of 30 days, which is one-fourth of the regular deadline of four months, alongside the creation of a fictitious positive decision in case of administrative inaction, aims to shape this limitation in a proportionate way.

2.3 The Responses to the Administrative Silence of the EU Authorities

2.3.1 No Prevailing Model of Administrative Silence at EU Level

From the analysis carried out above, it follows that the EU does not adhere to one specific model of administrative silence and any conclusion can only be sector-specific.[47]

As a general rule, unless it is expressly dictated by secondary law, no implied decision can be lawfully created. This has been confirmed by the

[47] On this, see also Sant'Anna (2016, p. 736).

Court of Justice of the European Union, which held that "as a rule, mere silence on the part of an institution cannot be placed on the same footing as an implied refusal, except where that result is expressly provided for by a provision of Community law."[48]

The two main sectors which contain general provisions on the creation of an implied negative decision in case of non-compliance of the administration by the prescribed time-limits are EU civil service law and the rules on access to documents. In these fields, the applicant requests from the administration to proceed to an action or to issue an act, i.e., to transmit a document, to make a payment, etc., and thus, an implied positive decision is here per definition not possible.

Among the examined fields, the main areas where general rules providing for fictitious decisions are absent are the areas of risk regulation and the distribution of funds. In these fields, the absence of fictitious positive decisions is easily comprehensible, since a delay from the side of the administration should not lead to fictitious decisions which, for instance, authorize substances unsafe for human health or lead to distribution of funds from the EU budget. What could have been indeed possible in these fields is the creation of implied negative decisions.

Lastly, EU secondary law provides for implied positive decisions in cases when the applicant seeks permission in order to proceed to a desired action which does not involve a risk for human health or the environment. The instances identified in the analysis above are to be found in the rules on merger control, authorization of State aid, and in EU civil service law when employees seek permission in order to make a publication.

2.3.2 The Legal Consequences of Non-compliance with a Time-Limit

As it was shown in the analysis of EU secondary law, sectoral rules often give to the administration the possibility to prolong the prescribed time-limit while providing for justification. This justification normally pertains

[48] Case C-123/03 P Commission v Greencore (ECLI:EU:C:2004:783), para 45. See also Case T-30/01 Diputación Foral de Álava v Commission (ECLI:EU:T:2009:314); Joined Cases T-189/95, T-39/96 and T-123/96SGA v Commission (ECLI:EU:T:1999:317), para 27 and 28; Joined Cases T-190/95 and T-45/96 Sodima v Commission (ECLI:EU:T:1999:318), para 31 and 32; Case C-27/04 Commission v Council (ECLI:EU:C:2004:436).

to the complexity of the case or the need to consult other departments, to make translations, to gather additional information, etc.

Even when the administration does not or cannot formally prolong the deadline, but nevertheless issues the given act after the time-limit has expired, this delay does not normally affect the validity of the act. For example, regarding the deadlines for the finalization of a disciplinary procedure in EU civil service law, the CJEU has ruled that the period prescribed by art. 7 of Annex IX to the Staff Regulations is not a mandatory time-limit. It constitutes a rule of sound administration the purpose of which is to avoid, in the interests both of the administration and of officials, undue delay in adopting the decision terminating the disciplinary proceedings. It follows that the disciplinary authorities are obliged to conduct disciplinary proceedings diligently and to ensure that each procedural step is taken within a reasonable period following the previous step. Failure to comply with that time-limit may render the institution concerned liable for any harm caused to those concerned but does not in itself affect the validity of a disciplinary measure imposed after it has expired. Infringement of the "reasonable time" principle can justify annulment of a decision taken at the end of an administrative procedure, only where the undue delay is likely to have an effect on the actual substance of the decision.[49]

However, there are also instances, when secondary law rules prevent the EU administration from acting after a specific deadline. For example, in the case of anti-dumping investigations concerning third countries, if the Commission has not completed an investigation within the prescribed time-limit, it cannot validly adopt a decision.[50]

2.4 Legal Remedies Against the Silence of the EU Authorities

2.4.1 *Administrative Remedies: The Internal Review Procedure*

Administrative remedies against the inaction of the EU authorities are mainly provided in the field of EU civil service law and in the rules on

[49] See Case C-39/00 P SGA v Commission (ECLI:EU:C:2000:685), para 44; Case T-390/10 P Füller-Tomlinson v Parliament (ECLI:EU:T:2012:652), para 116, and Joined Cases F-138/06 and F-37/08 Meister v OHIM (ECLI:EU:F:2009:48), para 76.

[50] See art. 11(5) Regulation (EU) No 2016/1036.

access to documents, as shown in the analysis of the sectoral law. The Staff Regulations (art. 90(2)) provide for the possibility to submit a complaint against the implied rejection of a request. Regulation (EC) 1049/2001 guarantees the right to submit a confirmatory application in case of a rejection (partially or in full) of a request of access to documents (art. 7(2) Regulation (EC) 1049/2001).

It is not expressly provided that such confirmatory request can be made also in case of inaction of the administration following the first request; however, this cannot be excluded.

2.4.2 The Action for Failure to Act Under Article 265 TFEU

The general remedy against silence of the EU authorities, when this is not transformed into an implied decision through secondary law, is the action for failure to act contained in art. 265 TFEU.[51] The subject matter of an action for failure to act is a determination as to whether an omission to issue a decision was unlawful. According to the case-law of the court, a failure to act, for the purposes of art. 265 TFEU, means a failure to take a decision or to define a position.[52] The action may be brought not only against a failure to adopt a final decision that is legally binding, but also against the failure to adopt a preparatory act, if it is a necessary preliminary act in a procedure leading to an act that has binding legal effects.[53] The case-law is consistent in that a failure to take a final or preparatory decision is unlawful only if the institution was under a duty to act, which can be derived from a provision of primary or secondary EU law.[54]

An action for failure to act will be admissible only if the institution concerned has first been called upon to act. The case-law has clarified that the claimant's request must be specific in that it must be clear what decision the institution should have taken.[55] There is no time-limit within

[51] On the action for failure to act see Lenaerts et al. (2014, p. 419), Hofmann et al. (2011, p. 848), Barents (2016, p. 305), and Cremer (2015).

[52] Case 8/71 Deutscher Komponistenverband v Commission (ECLI:EU:C:1971:82), para 2, and Case 196/12 Commission v Council (ECLI:EU:C:2013:753), para 22.

[53] Case 302/87 Parliament v Council (ECLI: EU:C:1988:461), para16.

[54] Case C-141/02 P Commission v T-Mobile Austria (ECLI:EU:C:2005:98); Case T-277/94 AITEC v Commission (ECLI:EU:T:1996:66).

[55] Case 25/85 Nuovo Campsider v Commission (ECLI:EU:C:1986:195), para 8.

which the request must be made. The Court of Justice has held, however, that the claimant may not delay the exercise of his rights indefinitely.[56] If, within two months of this request, the institution concerned has not defined its position, the action may be brought. Certainly, it can be considered that, by complying with the request, the institution will have defined its position. The Court of Justice has clarified that the same can be considered when the institution adopted a decision different from that which the claimant requested.[57]

If an action for failure to act is brought by a national or legal person, it will only be admissible if it concerns an EU institution's failure to adopt a binding act[58] which should have been addressed to them or whose lawfulness they are entitled to contest by bringing an action for annulment pursuant to art. 263 (4), TFEU.[59]

If the EU Courts declare an EU authority as having failed to act, the ruling has a mere declaratory nature. The courts cannot issue injunctions to the EU authorities.[60] In case the authority at stake defined a position even through a non-binding act, which cannot be challenged with an action for annulment, the action for failure to act will be declared inadmissible.[61] The action will also be declared inadmissible if there is a provision of EU secondary law creating an implied negative decision. In such a case, the person concerned will have to proceed with an action for annulment.

[56] Case 59/70 Netherlands v Commission (ECLI:EU:C:1971:77), para 19.

[57] Joined Cases 166 and 220/86 Irish Cement Ltd. v Commission (ECLI:EU:C:1988:549), para 17.

[58] art. 265 TFEU mentions 'any act other than a recommendation or an opinion'.

[59] See Case C-68/95 T. Port v Bundesanstalt für Landwirtschaft und Ernährung (ECLI:EU:C:1996:452), para 58 and 59 and Case T-773/16 Salehi v Commission (ECLI:EU:T:2017:739).

[60] Joined Cases C-199/94 P and C-200/94 P Pevasa and Inpesca v Commission (ECLI:EU:C:1995:360), para 24; Case C-137/16 P Petraitis v Commission (ECLI:EU:C:2016:904), para 31 and 32.

[61] Case T-407/09 Neubrandenburger Wohnungsgesellschaft v Commission (ECLI:EU:T:2012:1).

2.4.3 *The Action for Annulment Under Article 263 TFEU*

When EU secondary law transforms administrative silence into an implied decision, the person concerned may bring before the CJEU an action for annulment under art. 263 TFEU. In the course of the judicial proceedings, the administration may withdraw this implied decision and adopt an explicit one. In this case, the person concerned has to challenge the explicit decision, because the court acknowledges no interest anymore in challenging the implied one.[62] If the explicit decision is adopted by the administration after the person concerned has challenged the implied action, the applicant has to modify the form of order sought and challenge the explicit decision within two months from its adoption. If the applicant fails to do so, his claim against the implied decision will be declared inadmissible for reasons of lack of interest.[63] This approach is stricter than in other legal orders, where an explicit decision taken after the addressee has already challenged the implied decision is automatically co-challenged, as for example in Greece.[64]

2.4.4 *The Action for Union Liability Under Article 340 TFEU*

Pursuant to arts. 268 and 340(2) TFEU, an action for damages against the EU can be brought in order to have the Union held non-contractually liable for any damage caused by its institutions or its servants in the performance of their duties. It is possible to bring such action also if a prior action for annulment or for failure to act has not been brought.[65] The court has stated that the conditions under which the Union or a Member State may incur liability for damage caused to individuals have to be aligned, because the protection of the rights which individuals derive from Union law cannot vary depending on whether a national authority or a Union authority is responsible for the damage.[66] According to the case-law, Union law confers a right to reparation where three conditions

[62] Case C-127/13 P Strack v Commission (ECLI:EU:C:2014:2250), para 89.

[63] Case T-214/13 Rainer Typke v Commission (ECLI:EU:T:2015:448), para 25 et seq.

[64] Spiliotopoulos (2015, p. 102) and Gogos (2005).

[65] Case 5/71 Zuckerfabrik v Council (ECLI:EU:C:1971:116); Case 4/69 Alfons Lütticke GmbH v Commission (ECLI:EU:C:1971:40).

[66] Joined Cases C-46/93 and C-48/93 Brasserie du Pêcheur SA v Bundesrepublik Deutschland and The Queen v Secretary of State for Transport, ex parte Factortame

are met: the rule of law infringed must be intended to confer rights on individuals; the breach must be sufficiently serious; and there must be a direct causal link between the breach of the obligation resting on the State and the damage sustained by the injured parties.[67]

The decisive test for finding that a breach of Union law is sufficiently serious is whether the Member State or the Union institution concerned manifestly and gravely disregarded the limits on its discretion.[68] Where the Member State or the institution in question has only considerably reduced, or even no, discretion, the mere infringement of Union law may be sufficient to establish the existence of a sufficiently serious breach.[69] In case of administrative silence, a "sufficiently serious breach" would arise in cases in which there is a duty to act. According to the case-law, the institutions, bodies, offices, and agencies of the European Union enjoy no margin of discretion insofar as concern the observance of time-limits as required by the principle of sound administration. Consequently, a finding that the administration infringed that principle is sufficient in itself to establish the existence of a sufficiently serious breach within the sense of the criteria on Union liability.[70] Furthermore, in cases concerning omissions, the Court of Justice requires a rigorous examination as to whether the claimed damage can be attributable to the omission.[71]

(ECLI:EU:C:1996:79), para 42; Case C-352/98 P Bergaderm and Goupil v Commission (ECLI:EU:C:2000:361), para 41.

[67] Joined cases C-46/93 and C-48/93. Brasserie du Pêcheur SA v Bundesrepublik Deutschland and The Queen v Secretary of State for Transport, ex parte Factortame (ECLI:EU:C:1996:79), para 51.

[68] Joined cases C-46/93 and C-48/93. Brasserie du Pêcheur SA v Bundesrepublik Deutschland and The Queen v Secretary of State for Transport, ex parte Factortame (ECLI:EU:C:1996:79), para 55; Joined Cases C-178/94, C-179/94, C-188/94, C-189/94 and C-190/94 Dillenkofer and Others v Germany (ECLI:EU:C:1996:375), para 25; Case C-352/98 P Bergaderm and Goupil v Commission (ECLI:EU:C:2000:361), para 43.

[69] Case C-5/94 The Queen v Ministry of Agriculture, Fisheries and Food, ex parte Hedley Lomas (ECLI:EU:C:1996:205), para 28.

[70] Case T-138/14, Randa Chart v European External Action Service (ECLI:EU:T:2015:981), para 114.

[71] Case T-138/03 É. R., O. O., J. R., A. R., B. P. R. and Others v Council and Commission (ECLI:EU:T:2006:390); Case C-85/09 P Portela v Commission (ECLI:EU:C:2009:685).

2.4.5 *The Possibility to Submit a Complaint to the European Ombudsman*

The European Ombudsman is empowered to receive complaints from any citizen of the Union or any natural or legal person residing or having its registered office in a Member State concerning instances of maladministration in the activities of the Union institutions, bodies, offices, or agencies, with the exception of the Court of Justice of the European Union acting in its judicial role (art. 228 (1) (1), TFEU). Inquiries may be conducted also on the Ombudsman's own initiative. Where the Ombudsman establishes an instance of maladministration, the matter is referred to the institution, body, office, or agency concerned, which has a period of three months in which to inform him of its views. The Ombudsman then forwards a report to the European Parliament and the institution, body, office, or agency concerned. The person lodging the complaint is always informed of the outcome of such inquiries (art. 228 (1) (2), TFEU). The Ombudsman submits an annual report to the European Parliament on the outcome of his inquiries (art. 228 (1) (3), TFEU).

It derives from these provisions that the Ombudsman's decisions and recommendations are not legally binding for the institution concerned in the sense that they cannot be legally enforceable. However, the institutions tend to comply with the Ombudsman's recommendations. According to the Ombudsman's annual report of 2017, the EU institutions complied with the Ombudsman's proposals in 85% of instances.[72]

Examining the Ombudsman's annual reports from 2013 until 2017, it can be concluded that administrative inaction in the sense of total absence of a decision is not an issue when assessing the functioning of the EU administration. However, administrative delays constitute a recurrent issue in the work of the Ombudsman. In the annual report of 2013, it was mentioned that the European Commission took more than four years to take action following a complaint in relation to a State aid complaint concerning four Spanish football clubs.[73] In the annual report of 2014, the Ombudsman flagged the issue of delays in handling access to documents requests concerning the TTIP negotiations.[74] The

[72] See the European Ombudsman Annual Report for 2017, p. 44.

[73] European Ombudsman Annual Report for 2013, p. 26.

[74] European Ombudsman Annual Report for 2014, p. 9.

subsequent report of 2015 mentions the handling of complaints by the Ombudsman in relation to delays without mentioning a systemic problem or a specific case. The report of 2016 puts emphasis on the handling of 20 complaints concerning delays in the authorization procedures for genetically modified food and feed.[75] Finally, the last available annual report of 2017 mentions the carrying out by the Ombudsman of a strategic inquiry on delays in chemicals authorizations.[76] Chemical authorizations, such as other risk regulation procedures (see Sect. 2.2.2), often do not provide for legal deadlines for all different administrative steps.[77] For this reason, the Ombudsman stressed the importance of abiding by the "reasonable time principle" even in the absence of a specific deadline.[78]

None of the examined reports mentions total administrative inaction. The Ombudsman has so far dealt only with delays. Looking at the two latest reports, it can be concluded that administrative delays are observed mainly in risk regulation procedures, in the course of which many actors, including Member States, the Commission, and EU agencies, are involved. In general, the role of the Ombudsman toward ensuring that the EU administration is acting in a timely way can be assessed as crucial and complementary to judicial action, because it is not bound to the strict admissibility conditions which courts are. This means that the Ombudsman can act and make recommendations in cases where the principle of good administration is compromised, even if all the conditions required for a successful action before the CJEU are not met, for example the conditions for claiming damages.[79]

2.4.6 *Empirical Evidence*

Apart from the investigations carried out by the European Ombudsman, evidence on whether the EU administration indeed applies by the rules on

[75] European Ombudsman Annual Report for 2016, p. 8.

[76] European Ombudsman Annual Report for 2017, p. 35.

[77] For example, art. 51(7) Regulation (EC) No 1907/2006 concerning the Registration, Evaluation, Authorisation and Restriction of Chemicals (REACH).

[78] See European Ombudsman, Decision of 18.07.17, Case OI/2/2016/RH.

[79] See European Ombudsman, Decision of 18.07.17, Case OI/2/2016/RH, para 23, where it is recalled that "the Ombudsman looks at this issue from the perspective of good administration, and not simply from the perspective of enforceable legal rights."

timeliness can be extracted from the case-law of the CJEU. The main indicator is constituted by the cases brought before the court on the basis of art. 265 TFEU, which constitutes the main judicial means against administrative inaction. No official statistics on the proceedings brought on the basis of this article exist. For this reason, the authors of this contribution conducted a research using the search engine of the CJEU.[80] From the beginning of the functioning of the CJEU until the end of 2018, 263 cases were brought to court alleging a failure to act by an EU institution, body, office, or agency.[81] Out of this total number, only thirteen cases have been successful. When assessing these thirteen cases and after having subtracted those with peculiar facts,[82] two main categories of cases have a recurring significance. The first category concerns instances in which the Commission failed to investigate complaints concerning the functioning of the internal market, more specifically about anti-competitive behavior (art. 101 TFEU)[83] or unlawful State aid (art. 108 TFEU).[84] The second category consists of cases where the Commission did not act in a timely manner when exercising its role as risk regulator.[85] Given the very limited amount of cases over time, it can be concluded that administrative inaction is not a major issue in EU governance.

The vast majority of cases that were found to be manifestly inadmissible consist of instances where the Commission had no legal obligation to act. A recurring example are cases brought by individuals because the Commission did not start an infringement procedure against a Member

[80] http://curia.europa.eu/juris/recherche.jsf?language=en.

[81] Please note that appeals are not counted as separate cases.

[82] Joined Cases 42 and 49/59 S.N.U.P.A.T. v High Authority (ECLI:EU:C:1961:5); Case 13/83 Parliament v Council (ECLI:EU:C:1985:220); Joined Cases 167 and 212/85 Assider and Italy v Commission (ECLI:EU:C:1987:195); Joined Case T-79/96, T-260/97 and T-117/98 Camar and Tico v Commission and Council (ECLI:EU:T:2000:147); Case T-306/10 Yusef v Commission (ECLI:EU:T:2014:141).

[83] Case T-127/98 UPS Europe SA v Commission (ECLI:EU:T:1999:167); Case T-74/92 Ladbroke Racing Deutschland v Commission (ECLI:EU:T:1995:10).

[84] Case T-442/07 Ryanair v Commission (ECLI:EU:T:2011:547); Case T-95/96 Gestevisión Telecinco v Commission (ECLI:EU:T:1998:206); Case T-17/96 TF1 v Commission (ECLI:EU:T:1999:119). On this, see Laule (1999).

[85] Joined Cases C-596/15 P and C-597/15 P Bionorica v Commission (ECLI:EU:C:2017:886); Case T-521/14 Sweden v Commission (ECLI:EU:T:2015:976); Case T-164/10 Pioneer Hi-Bred International v Commission (ECLI:EU:T:2013:503); Case C-107/91 ENU v Commission (ECLI:EU:C:1993:56).

State following their complaint or did not respond to their complaint at all.[86] It is established case-law that the Commission enjoys a wide margin of appreciation when deciding whether to start an infringement procedure and therefore no failure to act may be established in this respect.[87]

However, an exception exists in two cases, in which the Commission, according to the case-law, is legally obliged to act following a complaint alleging violation of EU law rules, namely when such a complaint concerns the application of the rules on anti-competitive behavior[88] or State aid.[89] The Commission applies an indicative time-limit of four months to respond to a complaint concerning State aid[90] and four months in case the complaint concerns anti-competitive behavior.[91] In all other cases, if a complaint alleging violation of EU rules is left unanswered, the action for failure to act brought by a natural or legal person is deemed inadmissible on the ground that the Commission has no legal obligation to act.

[86] Case C-412/18 P King v Commission (ECLI:EU:C:2018:947); Case C-137/16 P Petraitis v Commission (ECLI:EU:C:2016:904); Case C-235/12 P H-Holding v Commission (ECLI:EU:C:2013:132); Case C-130/16 P Gaki v Commission (ECLI:EU:C:2016:731); Case C-570/12 P Concal v Commission (ECLI:EU:C:2013:440); Case C-569/12 P Micsunescu v Commission (ECLI:EU:C:2013:439); Case C-568/12 P Ioanovici v Commission (ECLI:EU:C:2013:438); Case C-567/12 P Barliba v Commission (ECLI:EU:C:2013:437); Case C-566/12 P Baleanu v Commission (ECLI:EU:C:2013:436); Case C-25/12 P Trevisanato v Commission (ECLI:EU:C:2012:409); Case C-474/11 P Smanor v Commission and Mediator (ECLI:EU:C:2012:121); Case C-411/11 P Altner v Commission (ECLI:EU:C:2011:852); Case C-52/11 P Fernando Marcelino Victoria Sánchez v Parliament and Commission (ECLI:EU:C:2011:693); Case C-26/10 P Hansen v Commission (ECLI:EU:C:2010:260).

[87] Ibid. See also Lenaerts et al. (2014, p. 423).

[88] Case T-127/98 UPS Europe SA v Commission (ECLI:EU:T:1999:167); Case T-74/92 Ladbroke Racing Deutschland v Commission (ECLI:EU:T:1995:10).

[89] Case T-442/07 Ryanair v Commission (ECLI:EU:T:2011:547); Case T-95/96 Gestevisión Telecinco v Commission (ECLI:EU:T:1998:206); Case T-17/96 TF1 v Commission (ECLI:EU:T:1999:119).

[90] Cf. European Commission (2004), para 61.

[91] Cf. European Commission, Code of Best Practice for the conduct of State aid control procedures, para 71.

In any event, despite the absence of a legal obligation for the Commission to initiate an *infringement* procedure following a complaint, the principle of good administration requires that such complaints, in particular if they are well substantiated, should not be left unanswered.[92]

2.5 Overall Assessment of the Rules and Practices Around Administrative Silence

Timeliness of administrative action is highly valued at the level of the EU administration and constitutes an element of the fundamental right to good administration as enshrined in the EU Charter. The average duration of time-limits depends on the complexity of each procedure, ranging from only three days for a general query on the EU to an undetermined maximum amount of time in the complex procedures of risk regulation. In general, it can be concluded that simple procedures such as queries on information or requests for access to documents are timely and citizen-friendly. In EU civil service law, the handling of requests and complaints by employees of the Union also follows stringent time-limits. In EU competition and State aid law, reasonable time-limits are provided for each procedural step. Mainly, only when the EU acts as risk regulator, procedures can be lengthy, and their total duration is not always foreseeable from the outset.

The respective sectoral rules which set the time-limits normally allow for a prolongation, mainly for reasons of complexity of the case at hand. The administration has to justify why it makes recourse to a deadline prolongation and it needs to preannounce when the final act will be issued. In case the administration issues an act after a prescribed deadline, this might trigger the Union's obligation to pay damages, but in general it does not affect the validity of the act, unless the substance of the act is affected by the delay.

As regards the legal treatment of administrative silence, EU law does not contain a general rule which transforms inaction into a positive or negative implied decision. The main tool against administrative action, which is provided in primary law, is the possibility to make a claim before the CJEU, so that it is declared that an institution, body office, or agency of the Union failed to act. In such a case, an action for damages may also

[92] On this, see Harlow and Rawlings (2014, p. 156 et seq).

be brought before the court. Secondary law contains specific rules which may transform silence into an implied act. The two main sectors which contain general provisions on the creation of an implied negative decision in case of non-compliance of the administration by the prescribed time-limits are EU civil service law and the rules on access to documents, i.e., fields which presuppose an action by the EU and are thus not suitable for the use of implied positive decisions. EU secondary law provides for implied positive decisions in cases when the applicant seeks permission in order to proceed to a desired action which does not involve a risk for human health or the environment, such as merger control and authorization of State aid.

Among the examined fields, the main areas where general rules providing for fictitious decisions are absent are the areas of risk regulation and the distribution of funds, i.e., areas where a decision has important consequences for human health or the EU budget.

The examination of the European Ombudsman's annual reports and the case-law of the CJEU has shown that administrative inaction and delays are not major issues in EU administrative governance. The main field which forms the subject matter of Ombudsman's investigations in the last two years has been risk regulation procedures. In this field, the foreseeability of the total length of a procedure should be strengthened. To conclude, the EU administration has achieved not to be a "silent" administration and this contribution may thus convey a positive "sound."

References

Athanasiadou, N. (2017). *Der Verwaltungsvertrag im EU-Recht* [Administrative Contracts in European Union Law]. Tübingen: Mohr Siebeck.

Auby, J.-B. (2014). General Report. In J.-B. Auby (Ed.), *Codification of Administrative Procedure* (pp. 1–27). Brussels: Bruylant.

Azoulai, L., & Clément-Wilz, L. (2014). *Le principe de bonne administration* [The principle of good administration]. In J.-B. Auby & J. Dutheil de la Rochère (Eds.), *Traité du Droit Administratif Européen* [Treaty of European Administrative Law] (2nd ed., pp. 651–678). Brussels: Bruylant.

Barents, R. (2016). *Remedies and Procedures before the EU Courts*. Alphen aan den Rijn: Wolters Kluwer.

Chevalier, E. (2014). *Bonne administration et Union européenne* [Good administration and European Union]. Brussels: Bruylant.

Craig, P. (2018). *EU Administrative Law* (3rd ed.). Oxford: Oxford University Press.

Cremer, W. (2015). *Art. 265 AEUV*. In C. Calliess & M. Ruffert (Eds.), *EUV/AEUV Kommentar* (5th ed.). Munich: CH Beck.

Eliantonio, M. (2014). Judicial Review in an Integrated Administration: The Case of 'Composite Procedures'. *Review of European Administrative Law, 7*(2), 65–102.

European Commission, Notice on the Handling of Complaints by the Commission Under Articles 81 and 82 of the EC Treaty, 2004/C 101/05. (2004).

European Commission, Notice on Best Practices in Proceedings Concerning Articles 101 and 102 TFEU. (2011). https://eur-lex.europa.eu/legal-content/GA/TXT/?uri=CELEX:52011XC1020(02).

European Commission, Rules of Procedure [C(2000) 3614], as Last Amended by Commission Decision of 9 November 2011 amending Its Rules of Procedure. (2011). https://eur-lex.europa.eu/legal-content/GA/TXT/?uri=celex:32011D0737.

European Commission, Code of Best Practice for the Conduct of State aid Control Procedures. (2018). https://eur-lex.europa.eu/legal-content/EN/TXT/PDF/?uri=CELEX:52018XC0719(01)&rid=1.

European Ombudsman, European Code of Good Administrative Behaviour. (2002). https://www.ombudsman.europa.eu/en/publication/en/3510.

European Ombudsman, Annual Report 2013. (2013). https://data.europa.eu/euodp/en/data/dataset/ombudsman-annual-report-2013.

European Ombudsman, Annual Report 2014. (2014). https://data.europa.eu/euodp/en/data/dataset/ombudsman-annual-report-2014.

European Ombudsman, Annual Report 2015. (2015). https://data.europa.eu/euodp/en/data/dataset/ombudsman-annual-report-2015.

European Ombudsman, Annual Report 2016. (2016). https://data.europa.eu/euodp/en/data/dataset/ombudsman-annual-report-2016.

European Ombudsman, Annual Report 2017. (2017). https://www.ombudsman.europa.eu/en/annual/en/94827.

European Parliament, Resolution on the European Ombudsman's Special Report to the European Parliament Following the Own-Initiative Inquiry into the Existence and the Public Accessibility, in the Different Community Institutions and Bodies, of a Code of Good Administrative Behaviour. (2001). http://www.europarl.europa.eu/sides/getDoc.do?pubRef=-//EP//TEXT+TA+P5-TA-2001-0455+0+DOC+XML+V0//EN&language=EN.

European Parliament, Resolution of 15 January 2013 with Recommendations to the Commission on a Law of Administrative Procedure of the European Union. (2013). http://www.europarl.europa.eu/sides/getDoc.do?type=TA&reference=P7-TA-2013-0004&language=EN.

European Parliament, Resolution of 9 June 2016 for an Open, Efficient and Independent European Union Administration. (2016). http://www.europarl.europa.eu/sides/getDoc.do?pubRef=-//EP//TEXT+TA+P8-TA-2016-0279+0+DOC+XML+V0//EN.

Galetta, D.-U., et al. (2015). *The General Principles of EU Administrative Procedural Law*. Brussels: European Parliament.

Gogos, K. (2005). *Η δικαστική προσβολή παραλείψεων της διοίκησης* [The Judicial Challenge of Administrative Silence]. Athens-Thessaloniki: Sakkoulas.

Harlow, C., & Rawlings, R. (2014). *Process and Procedure in EU Administration*. Oxford: Hart Publishing.

Hofmann, H. C. H. (2009). Decision-making in EU Administrative Law—The Problem of Composite Procedures. *Administrative Law Review, 61,* 199–221.

Hofmann, H. C. H., et al. (2011). *Administrative Law and Policy of the European Union*. Oxford: Oxford University Press.

Hofmann, H. C. H., et al. (2014). *The Model Rules*. ReNEUAL.

Jansen, O. (2016). Silence of the Administration: General Comments and Dutch Law. In J.-B. Auby (Ed.), *Droit comparé de la procédure administrative* [Comparative Law of Administrative Procedure] (pp. 623–646). Brussels: Bruylant.

Laule, G. (1999). Action for Failure to Act in State Aid Cases: Case T-95/96, Gestevision Telecinco SA v Commission of the European Communities, Judgment of 15 September 1998. *Comparative and International Law Journal of Southern Africa, 32,* 376–385.

Lenaerts, K., et al. (2014). *EU Procedural Law*. Oxford: Oxford University Press.

Sant'Anna, J. (2016). *Le silence ou l'inertie de l'Administration en droit de l'Union européenne* [The silence or the inaction of the Administration in European Union law]. In J.-B. Auby (Ed.), *Droit comparé de la procédure administrative* [Comparative Law of Administrative Procedure] (pp. 735–738). Brussels: Bruylant.

Spiliotopoulos, E. (2015). *ΕγχειρίδιοΔιοικητικούΔικαίουII* [Administrative Law II]. Athens: Nomiki Vivliothiki.

Temple Lang, J., & Raftery, C. (2011). Remedies for the Commission's Failure to Act in "Comitology" Cases. *European Law Review, 36*(2), 264–275.

von Danwitz, T. (2008). *Europäisches Verwaltungsrecht* [European Administrative Law]. Berlin: Springer.

Ziller, J. (2014). *Les concepts d'administration directe, d'administration indirecte et de coadministration et les fondements du droit administratif européen* [The Concepts of Direct Administration, Indirect Administration and Shared Administration and the Foundations of European Administrative Law]. In J.-B. Auby & J. Dutheil de la Rochère (Eds.), *Traité du Droit Administratif Européen* [Treaty of European Administrative Law] (2nd ed., pp. 327–334). Brussels: Bruylant.

PART III

National Perspectives – Western and Southern Europe

CHAPTER 3

Administrative Silence in Germany

Bettina Engewald

3.1 The Legal and Administrative Background for Analyzing the Administrative Silence

In order to understand the different approaches of the German administrative authorities with regard to the reduction of administrative silence, the legal and structural background needs to be pointed out. The following section gives a brief introduction to the historical development of German administrative law and the accompanying efforts to optimize administrative processes (Sect. 3.1.1) as well as a description of the administrative sovereignty and responsibility prevailing in German administrative law (Sect. 3.1.2).

B. Engewald (✉)
Institute for Regulatory Impact Assessment and Evaluation (InGFA),
German Research Institute for Public Administration (FOEV),
Speyer, Germany
e-mail: engewald@foev-speyer.de

D. C. Dragos et al. (eds.),
The Sound of Silence in European Administrative Law,
https://doi.org/10.1007/978-3-030-45227-8_3

3.1.1 History of German Administrative Law, Making Administration More Efficient

Research about administrative silence mentions three major impacts on the evolution of the German administrative law: (1) its origins in the French administrative law, (2) the rule of law, and (3) the reduction of bureaucracy. In the nineteenth century, German administration, German administrative law, and its doctrine were significantly influenced by the French administrative system.[1] In particular, this French impact on the evolution of German administration may be found in the work of the *Übervater* of the German administrative law, *Otto Mayer*.[2] These impacts are particularly related to the interrelationship between the authorities and the courts.[3] Existing attempts to deal with administrative silence were abolished due to the strict separation of powers.[4] The courts were prohibited from interfering with the administration and had to halt trials until the authority came to a decision.[5] Comparatively, literature concerning administrative jurisdiction kept silent about administrative silence.[6] This trend continued even in the new Federal Republic of Germany after World War II.[7]

This changed partially with the codifications of the administrative procedure and the administrative court procedure. The Administrative Court Acts of Baden-Wuerttemberg, Bavaria, and Hesse included the possibility of legal actions against administrative silence in Section 35 (2).[8] For the first time, these regulations defined administrative silence as a circumstance whereby an authority is not deciding about an application in due time. Baden-Wuerttemberg and Hesse added that silence meant for the application to be rejected. "Due time" was not defined at all and could be influenced by how busy the authorities were, by the authority's

[1] Leisner (2000, p. 231) and Stelkens (2016, p. 197).

[2] Stelkens (2016, p. 297).

[3] Leisner (2000, p. 231).

[4] Leisner (2000, p. 231).

[5] Leisner (2000, p. 231).

[6] Leisner (2000, p. 230).

[7] Leisner (2000, p. 230).

[8] The German text of Section 35 of the Administrative Court Acts of all three can be found in Eyermann and Fröhler (1950, p. 10).

desire to find a correct decision or even life experience at which time one could expect a decision.[9]

In contrast to the most parts of German administrative law, the two major federal codifications, the Federal Administrative Procedure Act (VwVfG) and the Code of Administrative Court Procedure (VwGO), were not influenced by French law or comparative law at all.[10] While the VwVfG does not mention silence, it mentions by which means the authority can issue a decision: written, electronic, oral, or in another way, Section 37 (2) sentence 1 VwVfG. Section 75 VwGO implements the action for failure to act. Its existence excludes any possibility to understand administrative silence as a negative decision as long as a *lex specialis* does not order something else.[11] The implementation of Section 75 VwGO did not trigger a discussion about administrative silence.

For some time past, Germany aimed at reducing its bureaucracy. German bureaucracy has already been criticized over 200 years ago.[12] This continued during the Republic of Weimar[13] and during the new Federal Republic.[14] Starting in Bavaria in 1978, the *Länder* aimed to make their administration more citizen-friendly.[15]

During the 1990s, the debate around safeguarding of the economic competitiveness of Germany made room for administrative reforms.[16] An independent commission audited the administration to be meticulous and objective but took a long time for decisions.[17] They admitted to not finding sufficient empirical data to support this but international investors believed this.[18] It followed a reform of the VwVfG in 1996 which tried to accelerate the approval procedures[19] and in 2006, followed another

[9] Leisner (2000, p. 231).

[10] Stelkens (2016, p. 198).

[11] Kopp and Schenke (2018, p. 923).

[12] Cf. Cancik (2017, p. 3 f.).

[13] Cancik (2017, p. 9 f.).

[14] Cancik (2017, pp. 12 f.).

[15] Cancik (2017, p. 24).

[16] Jacquement-Gauché and Stelkens (2016a, pp. 365, 367).

[17] Bundesministerium für Wirtschaft (1994, p. 49).

[18] Bundesministerium für Wirtschaft (1994, p. 49).

[19] Jacquement-Gauché and Stelkens (2016a, p. 368) and Mehde (2011, p. 316).

reform with the same aim which modified the plan approval procedure by mainly reducing the cases of citizen participation.[20]

At the same time, two other evolutions took place. First, the doctrine of "New Public Management" was introduced to Germany[21] but its principles were never codified in the VwVfG.[22] Second, serious budget deficits forced local communities, the *Länder*, and the Federation to consolidate their budgets and to reform their administrative apparatus for the sake of cost reduction.[23] In 2018, the parties forming the new cabinet of the German Government highlighted the importance of a modern, streamlined administration aiming to reduce bureaucracy and accelerate procedures in the coalition agreement.[24]

Conventional, German administrative science and administrative procedural law stem from the rule of law.[25] Therefore, the classical authors do not concern themselves with administrative silence.[26] In the nineteenth century, the idea of liberalism advocated a smaller state with limited scope of action rather than an activation of the authorities.[27] *Otto Mayer* mentions in his main opus the idea that the citizen files an application[28] and that the civil servant does not have a right "*in dubio abstine*."[29] But he then only speaks about an authority that does something the citizen does not like it to do.[30] This line of thought ended up with an administrative law and science only concerned with tying and controlling the administration and not with fighting its inactivity.[31] However, even

[20] Cf. Jacquement-Gauché and Stelkens (2016a, p. 370).

[21] Mehde (2011, p. 318).

[22] Mehde (2011, p. 320).

[23] Mehde (2011, p. 314).

[24] CDU et al. (2018, p. 63).

[25] Leisner (2000, p. 231).

[26] Leisner (2000, p. 231).

[27] Leisner (2000, p. 232).

[28] Mayer (1914, p. 155).

[29] Mayer (1914, p. 195).

[30] Cf. Mayer (1914, pp. 159 f.).

[31] Leisner (2000, p. 232).

modern approaches regarding the rule of law do not cover administrative silence either.[32]

3.1.2 Distribution of Administrative Sovereignty Due to Legal-Administrative Tradition

The organization of German administrative law follows two main ideas. On the one hand, general principles are separated from sector-specific material law. On the other hand, there exists a clear demarcation between the responsibilities of federal laws and laws of the Länder.

To begin with, the general administrative law is the administrative procedural law which is found in the VwVfG. The VwVfG regulates only the procedure and does not state any material law. It encompasses regulations about the hearing of the citizens during an administrative procedure, the definition, the criteria, and the formalities of an administrative act, as well as the binding effect of administrative acts, only to name a few. The special administrative law is material law and consists of various laws. These regulate the individual rights and obligations, their origin, their change, and their ending. Each special act may have provisions which alter the general procedure.

The distinction among federal law and the laws of the *Länder* exists separately from the division between general and special law. The VwVfG is the Federal Administrative Procedure Act and is the administrative procedure law for the authorities of the Federation, Section 1 VwVfG. Each *Land* has its own administrative procedure law which regulates the procedures for the authorities of the *Land* and the local communities of this *Land*. Additionally, Articles 73 and 74 of the Basic Law for the Federal Republic of Germany (GG) give the Federation the legislative power over some but not all special administrative fields. Accordingly, special administrative law may also be the law of a *Land*.

However, the VwGO stands apart from this distinction and states a federal law that is applicable for all administrative courts in Germany. For historical reasons, tax law and social welfare law have their very own procedure and court procedure acts. All of them are federal laws.

Generally, the *Länder* execute all laws in their own right, Article 83 GG. They provide for the establishment of the requisite authorities and

[32] Leisner (2000, p. 233).

regulate their administrative procedures, Article 84 (1) sentence 1 GG. In most cases, the *Länder* allow for the local communities to execute the laws. When assigning administrative tasks in this way, however, the federal authorities and the administrative authorities of the Länder often overlook the fact that local communities have to execute both federal laws and the laws of the *Länder*.

3.2 The Legal Framework of Administrative Timeliness

The Basic Law for the Federal Republic of Germany (GG) does not mention the administrative procedure and the rights of the citizens against the administration. In German law, there exists only one mention of silence as a legal term. This instance can be found in Section 362 (1) sentence 1 of the Commercial Code: a merchant who gets an offer from another merchant with whom they regularly do business has to answer without undue delay. By remaining silent, they accept the offer.

In all other cases in German civil law, silence is not defined as a legal concept.[33] This became an overall unwritten principle of German civil and administrative law.[34] However, public liability handles activity and inactivity in the same way.[35] It considers the imperfect fulfillment of the official duty as a violation of said duty.[36]

Deadlines for administrative action cannot be found in the VwVfG itself. For a long time, the VwVfG did not know a written principle of timeliness. Instead, one was derived from the principle of administrative efficiency and—if a citizen had requested a decision—from the rule of law and the fundamental rights of said citizen.[37] In 1996, a written expression of timeliness was added to Section 10 sentence 2 VwVfG.[38]

[33] Instead of all: Busche (2018, p. 1663 f.).

[34] Cf. Jacquement-Gauché and Stelkens (2016b, p. 647).

[35] Leisner (2000, p. 232).

[36] Leisner (2000, p. 232).

[37] Kopp and Ramsauer (2018, p. 317). Cf. also Schmitz (2018, pp. 528 f.). The idea that there is one single principle of administrative efficiency which encompasses all administrative procedures has been criticized (Cf. Ziekow 1998) who refers back to the fundamental rights of the citizens (pp. 56 ff.).

[38] Kopp and Ramsauer (2018, p. 317) and Schmitz (2018, pp. 528 f.).

The procedure has to be performed easily, conveniently and expeditiously. Meanwhile, the *Länder* all have identical rules.[39] However, this addition served only to emphasize its significance.[40] Nevertheless, the rule of rapidity constitutes an obligation for the administration.[41] The authority must refrain from taking any unnecessary measures and particularly time-consuming investigations.[42] But the decision has to be just, lawful and rightful.[43]

Schmitz doubts that the addition in Section 10 sentence 2 VwVfG leads to any practical consequences.[44] *Leisner* criticizes that the distinction between long and too long is not clear-cut and, likewise, that it remains unclear how to determine a deadline if the authority adheres to Section 10 sentence 2 VwVfG. Attempts to find case groups or form categories for cases of administrative procedures which take too long could barely be found.[45] *Leisner* misses any dogmatic handling of administrative silence but does not offer a dogmatic approach either.[46] She speculates that the scholars hesitate to do so because administration is already largely bound by the courts' rulings.[47] Furthermore, *Leisner* states that administrative questions are so diverse that general rules cannot do justice to all possible cases.[48]

[39] Section 10 sentence 2 LVwVfG BW; Article 10 sentence 2 BayVwVfG; Section 1 (1) VwVfG BE and Section 10 sentence 2 VwVfG; Section 1 (1) sentence 1 VwVfGBbg and Section 10 sentence 2 VwVfG; Section 10 sentence 2 BremVwVfG; Section 10 sentence 2 HmbVwVfG; Section 10 sentence 2 HVwVfG; Section 1 (1) NVwVfG and Section 10 sentence 2 VwVfG; Section 10 sentence 2 VwVfG M-V; Section 10 sentence 2 VwVfG NRW; Section 1 (1) LVwVfG RLP and Section 10 sentence 2 VwVfG; Section 10 sentence 2 SVwVfG; Section 1 (1) SächsVwVfG and Section 10 sentence 2 VwVfG; Section 1 (1) VwVfG LSA and Section 10 sentence 2 VwVfG; Section 10 sentence 2 LVwG; Section 10 sentence 2 ThürVwVfG.

[40] Kopp and Ramsauer (2018, p. 317) and Schmitz (2018, pp. 528 f.).

[41] Ziekow (1998, pp. 62 f.).

[42] Leisner (2000, p. 235).

[43] Leisner (2000, p. 235).

[44] Schmitz (2018, pp. 528 f.).

[45] Leisner (2000, p. 240). She actually does not cite any.

[46] Leisner (2000, p. 240).

[47] Leisner (2000, p. 240).

[48] Leisner (2000, p. 240).

3.3 The Length of Administrative Deadlines

While there are no general deadlines for administrative procedures, jurisdiction and interpretation of the law give rise to various indications of the length of the proceedings and the timing of administrative action (Sect. 3.3.1). On the basis of this information, it is possible to determine the prescribed procedure duration as well as a legal deadline from the legal requirements (Sect. 3.3.2).

3.3.1 The Length of Deadlines in General Law and in Special Laws

The duration for administrative action as well as the determination of a precise deadline depends on the individual case.[49] A rule of thumb states that the deadline is shorter when the individual case is important (for the citizen or the community) and longer when it is not.[50] Complex matters and matters which require extensive investigations are allowed to take longer.[51] However, work overload, huge workloads, as well as absenteeism due to illnesses or vacations do not justify delays since the authority has to resolve these issues.[52] Nevertheless, it is possible to halt a procedure if all involved parties agree.[53]

Indications about the length of a normal procedure can be found in Section 75 VwGO, the action for failure to act.[54] If the authority has not decided about an objection or an application to carry out an administrative act within a suitable period without sufficient reason, the applicant may call the administrative court for intervention. The action may not be lodged prior to the expiry of three months, unless a shorter period is required because of special circumstances of the case. Thus, Section 75 VwGO states the benchmark for the length of an administrative procedure.[55]

[49] Kopp and Ramsauer (2018, p. 319) and Schmitz (2018, pp. 527 f.).

[50] Kopp and Ramsauer (2018, p. 319).

[51] Kopp and Ramsauer (2018, p. 319).

[52] Kopp and Ramsauer (2018, p. 319) and Schmitz (2018, pp. 528 f.).

[53] Kopp and Ramsauer (2018, p. 319) and Schmitz (2018, p. 530).

[54] Kopp and Ramsauer (2018, p. 319).

[55] Kopp and Schenke (2018, p. 924).

Nevertheless, a generally valid period for administrative action is difficult to define because the authority needs an adequate time slot for reflection and processing which has to take into account the legal complexity and the need of (extensive) investigations.[56] A "reasonable" deadline accounts for the urgency of the decision for the applicant/claimant and the duration of the decision of the authority.[57] The latter takes the associated workload, the difficulty of finding the facts, and the legal complexity into consideration.[58] These aspects need to be balanced.[59] Due to the deadline of three months determined by Section 75 sentence 2 VwGO, the interpretation of the term "suitable period" has thus little practical importance.[60] Section 46 of the Code for Fiscal Courts (FGO) and Section 88 of the Code for Social Welfare Courts (SGG) have similar rules whose deadline is six months long.

The deadline of three months only means that the administrative court cannot dismiss the action for failure to act because it was filed too early.[61] *Leisner* understands the deadline as the regular processing deadline.[62] She argues that interpreting the deadline only as a vesting period would be detrimental to the authority.[63] The authority has to pay the court fees if the filed action for failure to act is later dropped in court.[64] *Leisner* considers the fact that the authority has to pay the court fees even though the legislator did not assume the authority being able to finish a procedure in the regular time slot of three months to be unjust.[65]

56 Brenner (2018, p. 1669).

57 Brenner (2018, p. 1669).

58 Brenner (2018, p. 1669).

59 Brenner (2018, p. 1669).

60 Brenner (2018, p. 1669).

61 Kopp and Schenke (2018, p. 926).

62 Leisner (2000, p. 241).

63 Leisner (2000, pp. 241 f.).

64 Leisner (2000, p. 242).

65 Leisner (2000, p. 242).

3.3.2 *Calculating Deadlines*

Sections 187 till 193 of the Civil Code (BGB) are applicable for calculating deadlines, Section 31 (1) VwVfG. If the last day is on a weekend or a public holiday, the deadline expires to the following weekday, Section 31 (3) sentence 1 VwVfG. If a period starts with the occurrence of an event, the day of the event is not part of the period, Section 187 (1) BGB. A period of time specified by days ends on the expiry of the last day of the period, Section 188 (1) BGB. A period of time specified by weeks, by months, or by a duration of time comprising more than one month—year, half-year, quarter—ends on the expiry of the day of the last week or of the last month which, in its designation or its number, corresponds to the day on which the event or the point of time occurs, Section 188 (2) BGB. If a period of time is extended, the new period is calculated from the expiry of the previous period, Section 190 BGB.

3.3.3 *Overview: Some Deadlines in Federal Law*

Technically, two kinds of deadlines are possible: processing and decision deadlines. During the first one, the authority has to gather the facts and to decide. The latter one only starts after all the facts are gathered. The probably best-known deadline can be found in Section 48 (4) VwVfG. The authority can revoke an unlawful administrative act within one year after learning about the unlawfulness. The deadline is a decision deadline and starts only after the authority has gathered all the facts.[66] Nothing is said about how long the authority is allowed to gather facts and investigate.[67] This is still criticized in science and seen as a processing deadline.[68]

Various deadlines can be found scattered among the field-specific laws and their details vary greatly but they are all decision deadlines.

Various deadlines can be found in various laws. Complicated procedures are allowed to take longer and cases in which an individual has a special interest should be faster. Otherwise, a general rule cannot be found. Some deadlines are examined in detail below.

[66] BVerwGE 70, 356 (362 ff.).

[67] Cf. Leisner (2000, 235).

[68] Kopp and Ramsauer (2018, pp. 1234 f.).

Table 3.1 Deadlines shorter than a month

Act	*Length*	*Prolongation possible?*
Section 13 (3a) sentence 1 of Volume V of the Social Security Statute Book	3–5 weeks	Yes
Section 6 sentences 4 and 5 of the Pressurised Air Decree	4 weeks	Yes
Section 12 (1) of the Pressurised Air Decree	4 weeks	Yes

Source The table includes lists found in Kopp and Ramsauer (2018, p. 1043), Stelkens (2018, pp. 1590 f.), Ziekow (2010, pp. 74 ff.), and own findings

A very short one is the deadline in Section 13 (3a) sentence 1 of Volume V of the Social Security Statute Book, which gives health insurance funds a deadline of three weeks to decide whether to finance medical performances or not. If the health insurance funds need to obtain the statement of an expert, the deadline is extended to five weeks. Furthermore, two comparatively short deadlines can be found in the Pressurised Air Decree. Neither regulation foresees any discretionary power in these cases (Table 3.1).

More common are deadlines which are a bit longer ranging from one month to two months with some odd lengths in between. Deadlines of a month can be found in laws as various as the Energy Industry Law, the Federal Immission Control Act, the Federal Building Code, the Genetic Engineering Law, the Medicinal Products Act, and the Property Commerce Law. A rather odd deadline of five weeks can be found in Section 171 (2) of the Competition Act. Section 7f (2) of the General Railway Act and Section 7 (6) of the Environmental Impact Assessment Act both introduce a deadline of six weeks (Table 3.2).

Most common are deadlines with a duration of three months. As part of the already mentioned Medicinal Products Act, Volume V of the Social Security Statute Book, Federal Immission Control Act, and Energy Industry Law, they can also be found in the Industrial Code, the Public Transport Act, the Infection Protection Law, the Crafts Code, the Closed Substance Cycle and Waste Management Act, and the Chemicals Act (Table 3.3).

Deadlines longer than three months are less common, although the legislator is free to set a regular processing time longer than three

Table 3.2 Deadlines of a month but shorter than three months

Act	*Length*	*Prolongation possible?*
Section 42 (2) sentence 4 of the Medicinal Products Act	30 days	No
Section 16 (3) sentence 2 and 3 of the Genetic Engineering Law	30–60 days	No
Section 15 (2) of the Federal Immission Control Act	1 month	No
Section 17 (2) sentences 1 and 2 of the Medicinal Products Act	1 month	+2 months
Section 20c (5) sentence 2 of the Medicinal Products Act	1 month	+2 months
Section 22 (5) of the Federal Building Code	1 month	+3 months
Section 145 (1) and Section 22 (5) sentence 4 Federal of the Building Code	1 month	+3 months
Section 6 (1) of the Property Commerce Law	1–3 months	No
Section 7f (2) of the General Railway Act	6 weeks	No
Section 7 (6) of the Environmental Impact Assessment Act	6 weeks	+3–6 weeks
Section 13 (3a) sentence 4 of Volume V of the Social Security Statute Book	6 weeks	Yes
Section 10 (6) sentence 1 of the Genetic Engineering Law	45 days	No
Section 10 (6) sentence 2 of the Genetic Engineering Law	45 days	No
Section 12 (5) of the Genetic Engineering Law	45 days	No
Section 10 (5) sentences 2 and 3 of the Genetic Engineering Law	45–90 days	No
Section 42 (2) sentence 8 of the Medicinal Products Act	60 days	No
Section 4a (6) sentence 1 of the Energy Industry Law	2 months	No
Section 4b (5) sentence 1 of the Energy Industry Law	2 months	No
Section 31 (3) of the Energy Industry Law	2 months	+2 months +a second prolongation if the applicant agreed

Source The table includes lists found in Kopp and Ramsauer (2018, p. 1043), Stelkens (2018, pp. 1590 f.), Ziekow (2010, pp. 74 ff.), and own findings

Table 3.3 Deadlines of three months

Act	*Length*	*Prolongation possible?*
Section 52a (3) sentence 2 of the Medicinal Products Act	3 months	No
Section 29 (2a) of the Medicinal Products Act	3 months	No
Section 17 (1) of the Medicinal Products Act	3 months	No
Section 6a (1) of the Industrial Code	3 months	No
Section 11 (2) and (3) of the General Railway Act	3 months	No
Section 34d (4) sentence 2 of the Industrial Code	3 months	No
Section 27 (1) sentence 2 of the Medicinal Products Act	3 months	No
Section 27 (1) sentence 3 of the Medicinal Products Act	3 months	No
Section 137g (1) sentence 4 of Volume V of the Social Security Statute Book	3 months	No
Section 36a (4) sentences 2 and 3 of the Industrial Code	3 months	+1 month
Section 20c (5) sentence 1 of the Medicinal Products Act	3 months	+2 months
Section 15 (1) Sentences 2 and 3 of the Public Transport Act	3 months	+3 months
Section 13b (5) sentences 6 and 7 of the Energy Industry Law	3 months	If the applicant agreed
Section 53a (2) of the Infection Protection Law	3 months	Yes
Section 10 (1) sentence 2 of the Crafts Code	3 months	Yes
Section 54 (6) sentence 2 of the Closed Substance Cycle and Waste Management Act	3 months	Yes
Section 19b (1) sentence 5 of the Chemicals Act	3 months	Yes
Section 16 (3) of the Federal Immission Control Act	3–6 months	Yes

Source The table includes lists found in Kopp and Ramsauer (2018, p. 1043), Stelkens (2018, pp. 1590 f.), Ziekow (2010, pp. 74 ff.), and own findings

months.[69] A deadline of four months can be found in Section 11 (5) sentences 2 and 3 of the Animal Protection Law. A long deadline of seven

[69] Leisner (2000, p. 243).

months for deciding upon an application to build and operate a hazard-related power plant can be found in Section 23b (4) sentence 1 of the Federal Emission Control Act (Table 3.4).

Similarly, the possibilities to prolong a deadline may vary. Both the shortest and the longest deadline stated in Tables 3.1, 3.2, 3.3, and 3.4 can be prolonged. While Section 13 (3) sentence 1 of Volume V of the Social Security Statute Book does not state how much longer the health insurance funds are allowed to take, Section 23b (4) sentence 1 of the Federal Immission Control Act states that 3 months maximum can be added to the deadline. In both cases, the authority notifies the applicant of the prolongation and must justify the reasons for prolonging the deadline.

Likewise, it is possible to prolong a long deadline just as a short one and often a maximum duration for the prolongation or the procedure itself is included in the calculation. Due to their shortness, prolongations of short deadlines easily double the length of the procedure while prolongations of longer deadlines only add about half of the original deadline.

Table 3.4 Deadlines longer than three months

Act	*Length*	*Prolongation possible?*
Section 7a (6) sentence 1 of the General Railway Act	4 months	No
Section 42 (4) of the Competition Act	4 months	+2 months
Section 11 (5) sentences 2 and 3 of the Animal Protection Law	4 months	+2 months
Section 10 (6a) of the Federal Immission Control Act	3–7 months	+3 months
Section 21a (4) sentence 1 of the Medicinal Products Act	5 months	No
Section 23a (4) sentences 2 and 3 of the Energy Industry Law	6 months	If the applicant agreed
Section 23b (4) sentence 2 of the Federal Immission Control Act	6 months	+3 months
Section 27 (1) sentence 1 of the Medicinal Products Act	7 months	No
Section 23b (4) sentence 1 of the Federal Immission Control Act	7 months	+3 months

Source The table includes lists found in Kopp and Ramsauer (2018, p. 1043), Stelkens (2018, pp. 1590 f.), Ziekow (2010, pp. 74 ff.), and own findings

Two prolongations take the requests of the applicant into account. Both Section 13b (5) sentences 6 and 7 of the Energy Industry Law and Section 23a (4) sentences 2 and 3 of the Energy Industry Law foresee a prolongation only if the applicant agreed to it. The prolongation itself does not have a time constraint.

Similarly special is Section 31 (3) of the Energy Industry Law which allows two prolongations. The deadline expires within two months and it can be extended by another two months if the authority needs more information. Afterward, it might be extended again and for an indefinite time if the applicant agrees to it. If the application concerns a bigger new generation plant which shall be connected to a network or a reservoir, the authority can prolong the original deadline as well as the first prolongation.

In almost all cases, the applicant needs to be informed about the intended prolongation. Only Section 7 (6) of the Environmental Impact Assessment Act and Section 42 (4) of the Competition Act do not foresee a notification obligation.

However, in all these cases, the authority almost always needs to justify the prolongation. Only in Section 15 (1) sentences 2 and 3 of the Public Transport Act does not specify a justification obligation. In Section 6 sentences 4 and 5 of the Pressurised Air Decree, Section 12 (1) of the Pressurised Air Decree, and Section 36a (4) sentences 2 and 3 of the Industrial Code, it is only mentioned that the prolongation is possible in "justified" cases. Section 54 (6) sentence 2 of the Closed Substance Cycle and Waste Management Act states that both the notification and the justification are only necessary if the applicant is situated within the European Union or the European Economic Area.

Even when there is no obligation for notification, it is safe to assume that the authority will notify the applicant. Otherwise, the applicant might sue in accordance with Section 75 VwGO and thus might condemn the authority to pay the costs and fees of the court procedure even though the court finds that the deadline was prolonged and the prolongation was justified by the court because they failed to notify the applicant about the prolongation. If the authority fails to give a notification or to provide sufficient reasons for the prolongation, neither the longer deadline nor the administrative act are unlawful. Both are violations of procedural and formal requirements. Section 45 VwVfG stipulates that violations of procedural and formal requirements can be supplemented even during the court procedure (Table 3.5).

Table 3.5 Prolongation possibilities and notifications necessities

Act	*Length*	*Prolongation?*	*Notification necessary?*
Section 13 (3a) sentence 1 of Volume V of the Social Security Statute Book	3–5 weeks	Yes	Yes, with reasons why
Section 6 sentences 4 and 5 of the Pressurised Air Decree	4 weeks	Yes	None mentioned, but prolongation only in "justified" cases
Section 12 (1) of the Pressurised Air Decree	4 weeks	Yes	None mentioned, but prolongation only in "justified" cases
Section 17 (2) sentences 1 and 2 of the Medicinal Products Act	1 month	+2 months	Yes, with reasons why and before the original deadline ends
Section 20c (5) sentence 2 of the Medicinal Products Act	1 month	+2 months	Yes, with reasons why and before the original deadline ends
Section 22 (5) of the Federal Building Code	1 month	+3 months	Yes, with reasons why and before the original deadline ends
Section 145 (1) and Section 22 (5) sentence 4 Federal of the Building Code	1 month	+2 months	Yes, with reasons why and before the original deadline ends
Section 7 (6) of the Environmental Impact Assessment Act	6 weeks	+3–6 weeks	No
Section 13 (3a) sentence 4 of Volume V of the Social Security Statute Book	6 weeks	Yes	Yes, with reasons why
Section 31 (3) of the Energy Industry Law	2 months	+2 months +a second prolongation if the applicant agreed	First prolongation only if the authorities needs additional information

(continued)

Table 3.5 (continued)

Act	*Length*	*Prolongation?*	*Notification necessary?*
Section 36a (4) sentences 2 and 3 of the Industrial Code	3 months	+1 month	None mentioned, but prolongation only in "justified" cases
Section 20c (5) sentence 1 of the Medicinal Products Act	3 months	+2 months	Yes, with reasons why and before the original deadline ends
Section 15 (1) Sentences 2 and 3 of the Public Transport Act	3 months	+3 months	Yes
Section 13b (5) sentences 6 and 7 of the Energy Industry Law	3 months	If the applicant agreed	No
Section 53a (2) of the Infection Protection Law	3 months	Yes	Yes and has to be communicated in due time
Section 10 (1) sentence 2 of the Crafts Code	3 months	Yes	Yes and has to be communicated in due time
Section 54 (6) sentence 2 of the Closed Substance Cycle and Waste Management Act	3 months	Yes	Yes and has to be communicated in due time
Section 19b (1) sentence 5 of the Chemicals Act	3 months	Yes	Yes and has to be communicated in due time
Section 16 (3) of the Federal Immission Control Act	3–6 months	Yes	Yes and reasons must be given
Section 42 (4) of the Competition Act	4 months	+2 months	No
Section 11 (5) sentences 2 and 3 of the Animal Protection Law	4 months	+2 months	Yes and reasons must be given

(continued)

Table 3.5 (continued)

Act	*Length*	*Prolongation?*	*Notification necessary?*
Section 10 (6a) of the Federal Immission Control Act	3–7 months	+3 months	Yes and reasons must be given
Section 23a (4) sentences 2 and 3 of the Energy Industry Law	6 months	If the applicant agreed	No
Section 23b (4) sentence 2 of the Federal Immission Control Act	6 months	+3 months	Yes and reasons must be given
Section 23b (4) sentence 1 of the Federal Immission Control Act	7 months	+3 months	Yes and reasons must be given

Source The table includes lists found in Kopp and Ramsauer (2018, p. 1043), Stelkens (2018, pp. 1590 f.), Ziekow (2010, pp. 74 ff.), and own findings

Empirical data about the actual length of procedures is hard to obtain and is not collected officially. While all the above-mentioned laws are federal laws, only some of them are executed by the Federation. The remaining laws are executed by the *Länder* while their mode of execution varies greatly across the several *Länder*. While one *Land* creates a single authority to deal with all cases under a specific law, another *Land* delegates the execution to the local communities. Neither the *Länder* themselves nor the local communities (Germany has about 11,000 local communities) seem to be interested in an (official) statistic.

3.4 Responses to Administrative Silence

German administrative law does not know a general response to administrative silence because as mentioned before silence is not defined as a legal term. This means, originally Germany had neither a positive nor a negative construct of administrative silence. Instead, a legal remedy, the action for failure to act, was installed (presented later on in Section 6). An administrative act resulting from a non-expeditious procedure is not necessarily unlawful.[70] Following the implementation of the Services in the Internal Market Directive 2006 (DLRL), a positive construct was installed (cf. Sect. 3.5).

3.5 The Positive Silence: Genehmigungsfiktionen

In 2009, the DLRL was implemented, which lead to the implementation of *Genehmigungsfiktionen*. The term roughly translates as "fiction of an authorisation." The *lex generalis* can be found in Section 42a VwVfG. When a specified deadline expires, an approval is granted if this is stipulated by law. The regulations concerning the validity of administrative acts and the proceedings for legal remedy apply mutatis mutandis. The deadline takes three months unless otherwise stipulated by law. It can be prolonged and the prolongation has to be justified and communicated. The fictitious administrative act has to be confirmed upon request. In accordance, the *Länder* all have identical rules.[71]

The implementation led to an extensive discussion among scholars[72] on questions such as: Is Section 42a VwVfG constitutional? Is a fictitious administrative act an administrative act? When does a fictitious administrative act enter into force, particularly if a third party is involved? What if the fictitious administrative act is unlawful? What if the applicant believes that their request is complete while it is not and the deadline expires? What if the deadline expires and an administrative act (mostly the rejection of the request) reaches the applicant shortly thereafter?

However, the implementation did not trigger a debate about administrative silence itself. Some scholars speculated that an expiring deadline

[70] Kopp and Schenke (2018, p. 924), Kopp and Ramsauer (2018, p. 319), and Schmitz (2018, pp. 526 f.).

[71] Section 42a LVwVfG BW; Article 42a BayVwVfG; Section 1 (1) VwVfG BE and Section 42a VwVfG; Section 1 (1) sentence 1 VwVfGBbg and Section 42a VwVfG; Section 42a BremVwVfG; Section 42a HmbVwVfG; Section 42a HVwVfG; Section 1 (1) NVwVfG and Section 42a VwVfG; Section 42a VwVfG M-V; Section 42a VwVfG NRW; Section 1 (1) LVwVfG RLP and Section 42a VwVfG; Section 42a SVwVfG; Section 1 (1) SächsVwVfG and Section 42a VwVfG; Section 1 (1) VwVfG LSA and Section 42a VwVfG; Section 42a LVwG; Section 42a ThürVwVfG.

[72] Cf. only: Bernhardt (2009), Broscheit (2016), Eisele (2014), Guckelberger (2010), Heiß and Jedlitschka (2009), Hullmann and Zorn (2009), Jäde (2009), Jarass (2009), Kluth (2011), Lenders (2009), Scheidler (2012), Schmitz and Prell (2009), Stelkens (2018), Vigaranan (2015), and Ziekow (2007).

would lead the authority to reject the request without following the normal procedure[73] but they all failed to produce statistical evidence for their claims. Section 42a VwVfG implements Article 13 (4) DLRL[74] which demands the silent authorization to be the norm and not the exception[75]. As long as a norm like Section 42a VwVfG is installed within the scope of the DLRL, this is no breach of EU law.[76]

The DLRL only provides a general and consistent procedure but does not stipulate the application of *Genehmigungsfiktionen* to all administrative procedures.[77] It only indicates that an authorization was granted but not that this authorization is lawful.[78]

The deadline is modeled following the deadline in Section 75 VwGO[79] and is an average deadline which allows for the legislator to set longer or shorter deadlines.[80] The deadline being a processing period,[81] the starting point is the point of time when objectively all necessary documents deciding the application are submitted.[82]

While Section 42a VwVfG did not lead to the implementation of *Genehmigungsfiktionen* in every administrative procedure,[83] they can be found in various laws. They exist independently of the length of the original deadline and a possible prolongation. Given the importance of an objectively complete application, I was surprised that I did not find a single law which foresees a notification to the applicant for a completed application.

Section 42 (4) of the Competition Act foresees special regulations. It regulates the fusion of two or more companies which the Federal Cartel Office opposed. The Federal Economics Minister can nevertheless allow

[73] Biermann (2009, p. 382), Stelkens (2018, p. 1583), and Ziekow (2010, p. 103).

[74] Kopp and Ramsauer (2018, p. 1040).

[75] Cf. Mirschberger (2012, p. 259 f.).

[76] Mirschberger (2012, p. 260).

[77] Mirschberger (2012, p. 259).

[78] Mirschberger (2012, p. 260).

[79] Kopp and Ramsauer (2018, p. 1048).

[80] Kopp and Ramsauer (2018, p. 1048).

[81] Cf. Kopp and Ramsauer (2018, p. 1048).

[82] Mirschberger (2012, p. 258).

[83] Seckelmann (2012, pp. 553 f.).

the fusion. If he does not decide within the (prolonged) deadline, the request to fuse is rejected (Table 3.6).

3.6 Legal Remedies

When looking at legal remedies, one must differentiate between legal remedies against the silence itself and legal remedies against the fictitious administrative act. Since according to Section 42a (1) sentence 2 VwVfG the proceedings for legal remedy shall apply mutatis mutandis, a fictitious administrative act can be challenged in court like a normal administrative act. The citizen can file an action for failure to act against a silent authority (Sect. 3.1.1). They may claim damages too (Sect. 3.3.2). Additionally, the officer may face internal disciplinary consequences.[84]

3.6.1 Action for Failure to Act

The action for failure to act is regulated in Section 75 VwGO, 88 SGG, and 46 FGO. It should be noted that the action for failure to act is a special case of the enforcement action. It only lets the claimant skip the administrative appeal in cases of silence.[85] Section 75 VwGO only changes the criteria for admissibility of the claim and not the possibilities of the court to decide.

If there is a sufficient reason for silence, the court sets the authority a deadline during which the authority has to decide upon the matter, Section 75 sentence 3 VwGO. This deadline can be prolonged once. If the authority comes to a decision during this deadline, the court declares the main case settled, Section 75 sentence 4 VwGO.

If the authority does not decide during the deadline or during the prolonged deadline, the court procedure goes on and the court may decide upon the matter.[86] The same happens if there is no sufficient reason for the delay. If the case is ripe for adjudication, the court announces the obligation on the administrative authority to effect the

[84] Kopp and Ramsauer (2018, p. 319).

[85] Kopp and Schenke (2018, pp. 922 f.).

[86] BVerwGE 42, 108-115 (111).

Table 3.6 Genehmigungsfiktionen in various laws on the Federal level

Act	*Length*	*Prolongation possible?*	*Nature*
Section 13 (3a) sentences 1 and 6 of Volume V of the Social Security Statute Book	3–5 weeks	Yes	Positive
Section 6 sentences 4–6 of the Pressurised Air Decree	4 weeks	Yes	Positive
Section 12 (1) of the Pressurised Air Decree	4 weeks	Yes	Positive
Section 42 (2) sentence 4 of the Medicinal Products Act	30 days	No	Positive
Section 22 (5) Federal of the Building Code	1 month	+3 months	Positive
Section 145 (1) and Section 22 (5) sentence 4 of the Federal Building Code	1 month	+3 months	Positive
Section 15 (2) of the Federal Immission Control Act	1 month	No	Positive
Section 6 (1) and (2) of the Property Commerce Law	1–3 months	No	Positive
Section 7f (2) of the General Railway Act	6 weeks	No	Positive
Section 13 (3a) sentences 4 and 6 of Volume V of the Social Security Statute Book	6 weeks	Yes	Positive
Section 12 (5) of the Genetic Engineering Law	45 days	No	Positive
Section 29 (2a) of the Medicinal Products Act	3 months	No	Positive
Section 6a (1) of the Industrial Code	3 months	No	Positive
Section 11 (2) and (3) of the General Railway Act	3 months	No	Positive
Section 15 (1) sentences 2–4 of the Public Transport Act	3 months	+3 months	Positive
Section 19b (1) sentence 5 of the Chemicals Act	3 months	Yes	Positive
Section 13b (5) sentences 6 and 7 of the Energy Industry Law	3 months	Yes if the applicant agreed	Positive
Section 53a (2) of the Infection Protection Law	3 months	Yes	Positive

(continued)

Table 3.6 (continued)

Act	*Length*	*Prolongation possible?*	*Nature*
Section 10 (1) of the Crafts Code	3 months	Yes	Positive
Section 54 (6) sentence 2 of the Closed Substance Cycle and Waste Management Act	3 months	Yes	Positive
Section 42 (4) of the Competition Act	4 months	+2 months	Negative
Section 23a (4) sentences 2 and 3 of the Energy Industry Law	6 months	Yes if the applicant agreed	Positive

Source The table includes lists found in Kopp and Ramsauer (2018, p. 1043), Stelkens (2018, pp. 1590 f.), Ziekow (2010, pp. 74 ff.), and own findings

requested official act, Section 113 (5) VwGO. If this is not the case, the court hands down the obligation to notify the plaintiff, taking the legal view of the court into consideration. The case is ripe for adjudication if the authority has no discretionary power or the discretionary power is limited to zero, Section 114 sentence 1 VwGO. A limitation to zero means that only one decision is found to be lawful and rightful which means it will not overstep the statutory limits of discretion or uses discretion in a manner not corresponding with the purpose of the empowerment.

Empirical data about the use of the action for failure to act is very difficult to gather. While empirical data about the new cases filed with the courts and the finished cases is collected, it can only be found sorted by fields. 230,801[87] new proceedings were opened in Germany in 2016 alone, and the data only differentiates between normal and summary proceedings.

Since 2016, empirical data about Section 88 SGG is collected by the Federal Statistical Office for each *Land* and the Federation. All 68 social courts of the Federal Republic of Germany were surveyed for their number of actions for failure to act and the number of all actions including actions for failure to act for 2016 and 2017. 51 courts replied and provided data. Some courts referred to other authorities such as the

[87] Statistisches Bundesamt (2017b, p. 11).

higher social court, their respective state statistical office, or their respective Ministry of Justice. I was able to gather data from all courts in eight *Länder*, including Saarland, which possess only one court, and the cities Hamburg and Bremen. The authorities in Bavaria and Mecklenburg-Western Pomerania only reported number of cases per *Land* and year. To increase the number of answering courts, I followed up by phone all those who did not answer the first call after some months. Data collection was closed on July 15, 2018 (Table 3.7).

In some *Länder*, the aggregation of the acquired data differs from official data (Table 3.8).

Table 3.7 Actions for failure to act and other actions by Land in 2016 and 2017

	2016			*2017*		
	Actions for failure to act	*Other actions*	*All actions*	*Actions for failure to act*	*Other actions*	*All actions*
Federation	17,454	339,108	356,562	20,715	322,052	342,767
Baden-Württemberg	864	30,634	31,498	1364	29,196	30,560
Bavaria	1459	37,139	38,598	1741	34,286	36,051
Berlin	3885	23,611	27,496	4121	21,778	25,899
Brandenburg	1666	15,162	16,828	1362	14,898	16,260
Bremen	394	3303	3697	540	3306	3846
Hamburg	415	9015	9430	747	8239	8986
Hesse	391	20,323	20,709	393	19,694	20,086
Lower-Saxony	1505	32,298	33,803	1554	30,057	31,658
Mecklenburg-Western Pomerania	449	9382	9831	443	8735	9193
North Rhine-Westphalia	2601	77,407	80,008	3898	73,680	77,474
Rhineland-Palatinate	468	13,986	14,454	480	12,959	13,447
Saarland	105	4054	4159	91	4049	4142
Saxony	154	25,285	25,439	653	26,007	26,660
Saxony-Anhalt	1292	15,703	16,995	1702	14,545	16,245
Schleswig-Holstein	387	11,026	11,804	830	10,481	11,311
Thuringia	1028	10,780	11,808	796	10,157	10,949

Source The data from 2016 stem from Statistisches Bundesamt (2017c, pp. 14–17). The data from 2017 are own findings

Table 3.8 Differences between the official and my own data

	Total of claims		*Actions for failure to act*		*%*	
	Official data	*Own data*	*Official data*	*Own data*	*Official data*	*Own data*
2016						
Bavaria	38,598	38,592	1459	1459	3.7800	3.7806
Hesse	20,714	20,709	391	391	1.8876	1.8881
Lower-Saxony	33,803	33,803	1505	1504	4.4523	4.4493
Mecklenburg-Western Pomerania	9193	9178	443	443	4.8189	4.8268
North-Rhine Westphalia	80,008	80,052	2601	2601	3.2509	3.2491
Rhineland-Palatinate	14,454	14,446	468	468	3.2379	3.2397
Thuringia	11,808	11,817	1028	1028	8.7060	8.6993
2017						
Bavaria	36,051	36,027	1741	1741	4.8293	4.8325
Hesse	20,086	20,087	393	393	1.9566	1.9565
Lower-Saxony	31,658	31,611	1554	1554	4.9087	4.9160
North-Rhine Westphalia	77,474	77,580	3898	3900	5.0314	5.0271
Rhineland-Palatinate	13,447	13,439	480	480	3.5696	3.5717
Thuringia	10,949	10,953	796	796	7.2701	7.2674[a]

[a]I could not completely clarify why the data differs. However, those inconsistencies are small (third and fourth decimal place). Such inconsistencies can always happen when transferring data due to typos or conversion problems. Considering the high number of cases (up to around 80,000), the margin of error is small (up to about 100)

Only the official data will be used as long as only data from the *Land* is discussed. If data from the individual courts is discussed, then my own data will be used

Source Own presentation

In 2016, the number of actions for failure to act ranges from about 100 to almost 4000 with the lowest number (105) in Saarland and the highest (3885) in Berlin (Fig. 3.1).

However, the case numbers only made up a small percentage of the total number of claims which ranges from about 3700 to about 80,000. While the Saarland has the lowest number of actions for failure to act, Bremen has the lowest number of overall claims (3697). The *Land* with the lowest percentage of actions for failure to act is Saxony with only 0.61%. It is followed by Hesse with 1.89%. The *Land* with the highest number of actions for failure to act is Berlin which has the fifth highest

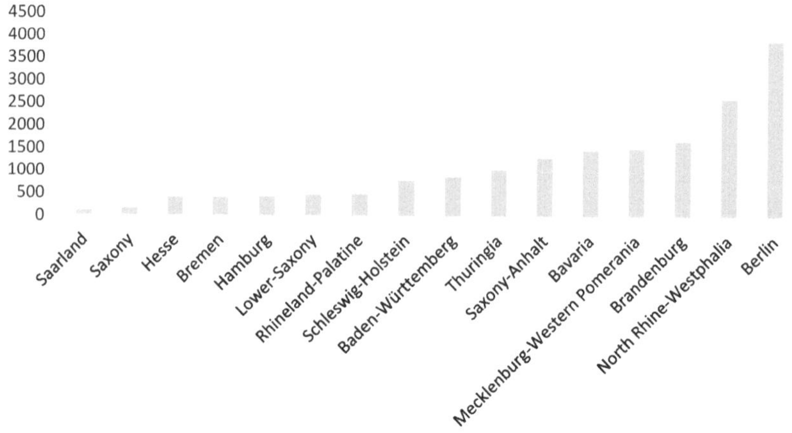

Fig. 3.1 Actions for failure to act by Land in 2016 (*Source* Statistisches Bundesamt 2017a, pp. 14–17)

number of claims (27,496). But Berlin is also the *Land* with the highest percentage of actions for failure to act (14.13%) followed by Bremen with 10.66%. Overall, 4.895% of all claims are actions for failure to act (Fig. 3.2).

On the courts' level, the picture becomes much more diverse. In Hesse, the number of actions for failure to act ranges from 1 at the SG Fulda and the SG Kassel to 164 at the SG Gießen. The number of all claims ranges from 1341 at the SG Fulda to 4078 at the SG Frankfurt/Main. At the SG Kassel, only 0.03% of claims are actions for failure to act, while 5.56% of all claims are actions for failure to act at the SG Gießen.

In Lower-Saxony, the number of actions for failure to act ranges from 48 at the SG Hannover to 659 at the SG Hildesheim. The overall number of claims ranges from 1980 at the SG Aurich to 9934 at the SG Hannover. The percentage ranges from 0.48% at the SG Hannover to 16% at the SG Hildesheim.

In North Rhine-Westphalia, the number of actions for failure to act ranges from 8 at the SG Münster to 1027 at the SG Düsseldorf. The number of all claims ranges from 4094 at the SG Aachen to 16,817 at the SG Düsseldorf. At the SG Köln, only 0.07% of all claims are actions

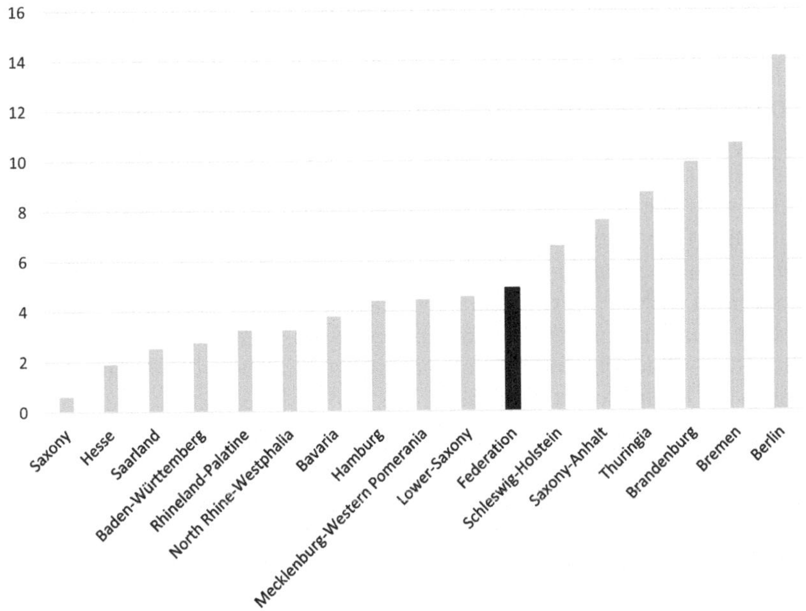

Fig. 3.2 Percentage of actions for failure to act by Land in 2016 (*Source* Statistisches Bundesamt 2017a, pp. 14–17)

for failure to act while 8.77% of all claims are actions for failure to act at the SG Düsseldorf.

In Rhineland-Palatinate, the SG Trier shows the lowest and the SG Speyer the highest numbers of claims. At the SG Trier, only 32 of 1501 claims are actions for failure to act (2.13%). 180 of the 4955 claims (3.64%) are actions for failure to act at the SG Speyer.

In Saxony-Anhalt, the SG Magdeburg has the highest number of claims (7075) and the SG Dessau-Roßlau has the lowest (3411). But the SG Dessau-Roßlau has both the highest number of actions for failure to act (597) and the highest percentage (11.5%). The SG Halle has the lowest number of actions for failure to act (290) and the lowest percentage (4.46%).

In Thuringia, the SG Nordhausen and the SG Gotha have the lowest and highest numbers of claims. At the SG Nordhausen, 109 of 2256 claims are actions for failure to act (4.83%). At the SG Gotha, 531 of the 4153 claims are actions for failure to act (12.79%) (Table 3.9).

In 2017, the number of actions for failure to act ranges from under 100 to almost 4000. Again, Saarland has the lowest (91) and Berlin has the highest (4121) number of actions for failure to act (Fig. 3.3).

Again, these numbers only make up a small percentage of the claims with the total number of claims ranging from 3846 to 77,580. Once again, Saarland accounts for the second lowest number of claims (4049) behind Bremen (3846). The *Land* with the lowest percentage is Hesse with 1.96%. North Rhine-Westphalia is again the *Land* with the highest number of claims (77,580). Berlin has with 15.91% the highest percentage of actions for failure to act. Overall, 6.04% of all claims were actions for failure to act (Fig. 3.4).

Like in 2016, the numbers are more diverse on the courts' level. In Hesse, the SG Marburg has had not a single action for failure to act while it had 1917 other claims. The SG Gießen has with 192 the highest number of actions for failure to act. The SG Fulda has with 1192 the lowest number of claims while the SG Frankfurt/Main has with 4492 the highest number. The SG Wiesbaden has with 0.03% the smallest percentage of actions for failure to act after the SG Marburg. The SG Gießen has the highest percentage with 6.84%.

In Lower-Saxony, while the SG Aurich has 81 actions for failure to act, the SG Hildesheim has 439. The SG Aurich has with 1873 the lowest number of claims while the SG Hannover has the highest with 8843 claims. The SG Osnabrück has the lowest percentage with 0.86% and the SG Hildesheim has the highest percentage with 11.29%.

In North Rhine-Westphalia, the SG Münster shows the lowest number of actions for failure to act (3) while the SG Düsseldorf shows the highest number (1315). The SG Aachen has the lowest number of claims (3985) and the SG Köln the highest (11,944). The SG Münster has the lowest percentage (0.05%) while the SG Düsseldorf has the highest (11.51%).

In Rhineland-Palatinate, the SG Trier and the SG Speyer have the lowest and highest numbers of claims. At the SG Trier, only 36 of 1411 claims are actions for failure to act (2.55%). At the SG Speyer, 194 of 4893 claims are actions for failure to act (3.96%).

In Saxony-Anhalt, the SG Magdeburg has again the highest number of claims (6551) but it has the lowest number of actions for failure to act (382) and the lowest percentage (5.83%). The SG Dessau-Roßlau has again the lowest number of claims (3283) and the highest percentage

Table 3.9 Actions for failure to act and other actions in Hesse, Lower-Saxony, North Rhine-Westphalia, Rhineland-Palatinate, Saxony-Anhalt, and Thuringia by court in 2016

	All actions	*Actions for failure to act*	%
Hesse			
SG Darmstadt	3962	128	3.23
SG Frankfurt/Main	4078	66	1.62
SG Fulda	1341	1	0.07
SG Gießen	2951	164	5.56
SG Kassel	3075	1	0.03
SG Marburg	2315	4	0.17
SG Wiesbaden	2987	27	0.90
Lower-Saxony			
SG Aurich	1980	73	3.69
SG Braunschweig	4792	299	6.24
SG Hannover	9934	48	0.48
SG Hildesheim	4118	659	16.00
SG Lüneburg	3293	183	5.56
SG Oldenburg	3960	136	3.43
SG Osnabrück	3438	50	1.45
SG Stade	2266	56	2.47
North Rhine-Westphalia			
SG Aachen	4094	23	0.56
SG Detmold	6975	162	2.32
SG Dortmund	16,817	331	1.97
SG Duisburg	13,505	701	5.19
SG Düsseldorf	11,711	1027	8.77
SG Gelsenkirchen	8943	295	3.30
SG Köln	12,686	9	0.07
SG Münster	5321	8	0.15
Rhineland-Palatinate			
SG Koblenz	4530	137	3.02
SG Mainz	3460	119	3.44
SG Speyer	4955	180	3.63
SG Trier	1501	32	2.13
Saxony-Anhalt			
SG Dessau-Roßlau	3411	597	17.50
SG Halle	6509	290	4.46
SG Magdeburg	7075	405	5.72
Thuringia			
SG Altenburg	3063	219	7.15

(continued)

Table 3.9 (continued)

	All actions	*Actions for failure to act*	%
SG Gotha	4153	531	12.79
SG Meiningen	2345	169	7.21
SG Nordhausen	2256	109	4.83

Source Own presentation

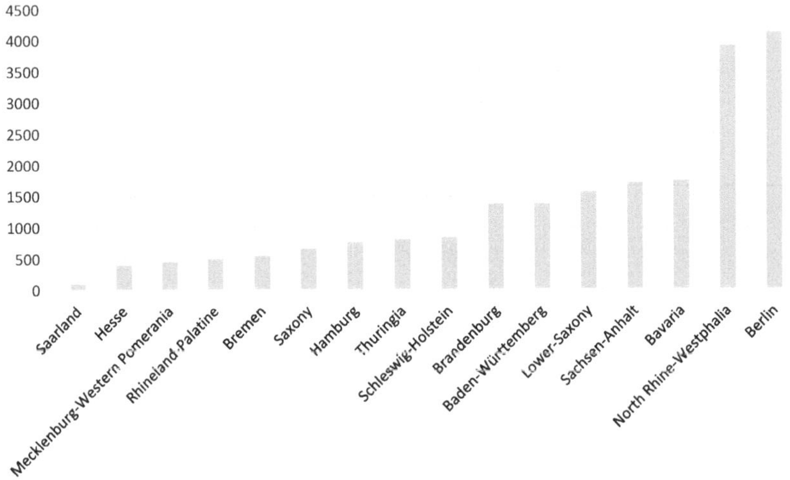

Fig. 3.3 Actions for failure to act by Land in 2017 (*Source* Statistisches Bundesamt 2018a, p. 16 f.)

(19.49%). The SG Halle has the highest number of actions for failure to act (678).

In Thuringia, the SG Nordhausen and the SG Gotha have the lowest and highest numbers of claims. At the SG Nordhausen, only 69 of 2096 claims are actions for failure to act (3.29%). At the SG Gotha, 408 of 3850 claims are actions for failure to act (10.6%) (Table 3.10).

Overall, the number of actions for failure to act rose nationwide by 3261 or 18.68% in 2017. At the same time, the number of claims dropped by 13,795 or 3.87% although this trend could not be observed in all of the *Länder*. In Brandenburg, Saarland, and Thuringia, the number of

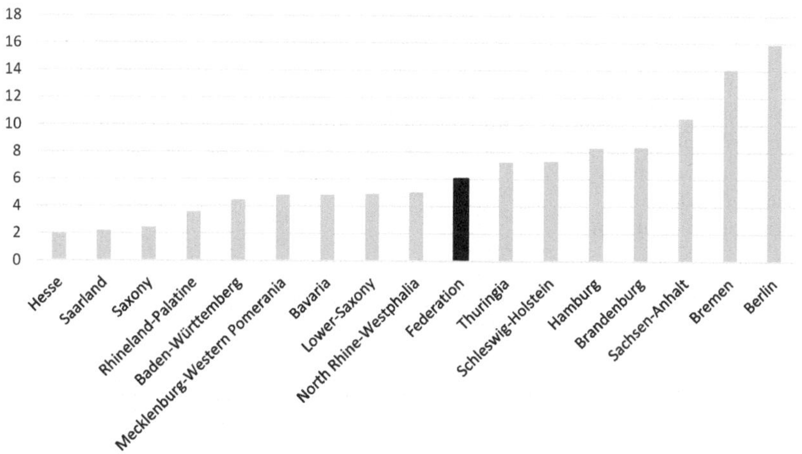

Fig. 3.4 Percentage of actions for failure to act by Land in 2017 (*Source* Statistisches Bundesamt 2018a, p. 16 f.)

actions for failure to act dropped alongside the total number of claims. In Bremen, the Saarland, and Saxony, the number of claims even rose.

The highest drop in actions for failure to act can be observed in Brandenburg with 304 actions less for failure to act. The lowest drop may be observed for Mecklenburg-Western Pomerania with 6 actions less for failure to act. The lowest rose occurred in Hesse with 2 actions more for failure to act. The highest rose was reported for North Rhine-Westphalia with an increase of 1297 actions for failure to act (Fig. 3.5).

This data shows that at least for 2016 and 2017 administrative silence existed in social security law and was an issue the courts had to deal with. Administrative silence could be found almost all over Germany but it does not seem to state a serious problem. One out of 20 claims (2016) or 1/6th of all claims (2017) was an action for failure to act. It should be noted that the social security law knows summary proceedings, and in 2016 and 2017, 43,038[88] and 39,317[89] new summary proceedings were filed, respectively. While the percentage was lower in most of the *Länder*, it was considerably higher in some other, particularly the City

[88] Statistisches Bundesamt (2017a, p. 15).

[89] Statistisches Bundesamt (2018a, p. 15).

Table 3.10 Actions for failure to act and other actions in Hesse, Lower-Saxony, North Rhine-Westphalia, Rhineland-Palatinate, Saxony-Anhalt, and Thuringia by court in 2017

	All actions	*Actions for failure to act*	%
Hesse			
SG Darmstadt	3711	135	3.64
SG Frankfurt/Main	4492	51	1.14
SG Fulda	1192	10	0.84
SG Gießen	2805	192	6.85
SG Kassel	2865	4	0.14
SG Marburg	1917	0	0
SG Wiesbaden	3105	1	0.03
Lower-Saxony			
SG Aurich	1873	81	4.32
SG Braunschweig	4736	323	6.82
SG Hannover	8843	255	2.88
SG Hildesheim	3887	439	11.29
SG Lüneburg	2964	127	4.28
SG Oldenburg	4044	195	4.82
SG Osnabrück	3137	27	0.86
SG Stade	2127	107	5.03
North Rhine-Westphalia			
SG Aachen	3985	12	0.30
SG Detmold	7120	241	3.38
SG Dortmund	16,997	641	3.77
SG Duisburg	11,819	1183	10.00
SG Düsseldorf	11,427	1315	11.51
SG Gelsenkirchen	8392	428	5.10
SG Köln	11,944	77	0.64
SG Münster	5896	3	0.05
Rhineland-Palatinate			
SG Koblenz	3902	130	3.33
SG Mainz	3233	120	3.71
SG Speyer	4893	194	3.96
SG Trier	1411	36	2.55
Saxony-Anhalt			
SG Dessau-Roßlau	3283	640	19.49
SG Halle	6411	678	10.58
SG Magdeburg	6551	382	5.83
Thuringia			
SG Altenburg	2875	175	6.09

(continued)

Table 3.10 (continued)

	All actions	*Actions for failure to act*	%
SG Gotha	3850	408	10.6
SG Meiningen	2132	144	6.75
SG Nordhausen	2096	69	3.29

Source Own presentation

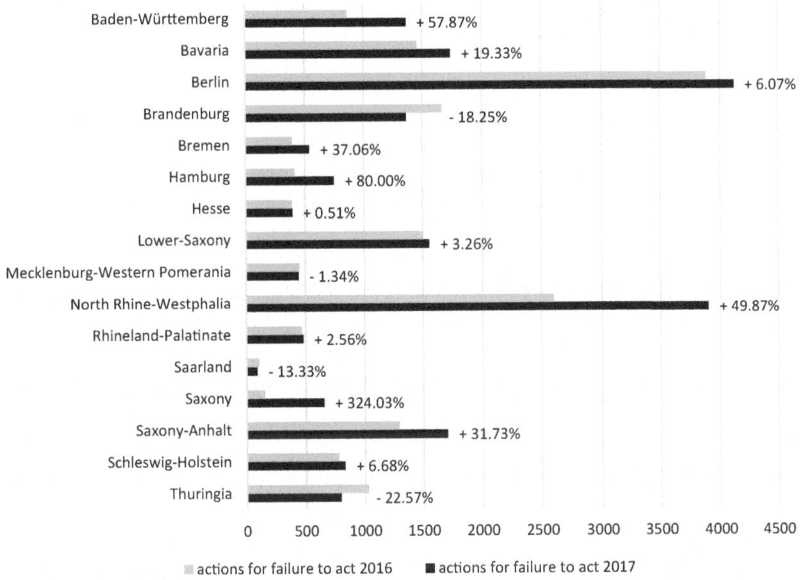

Fig. 3.5 Drop and rose of actions for failure to act between 2016 and 2017 (*Source* Own presentation)

States Berlin, Bremen, and Hamburg, and the eastern *Länder* Brandenburg, Saxony-Anhalt, and Thuringia. One can only speculate about the reasons. One possible explanation could be that the City States have a poorer population which needs more assistance from social systems. Another possible explanation could be that these *Länder* themselves are less wealthy than the others and thus have fewer employees to deal with requests. A third possible explanation is a combination of the first and the second explanation. A possible explanation for the generally low numbers is that the applicants can get legal protection with summary proceedings and did not have to resort to actions for failure to act. Broader and deeper research is needed to (dis)prove these hypotheses.

The number of actions for failure to act increased in 2017 in some *Länder* but it is impossible to predict future trends. More and broader research is needed to find out how the numbers evolved before 2016 and to find out why they increased in 2017.

Additionally, the data from social courts does not give any indication about the number of actions for failure to act before the administrative courts. One might formulate the hypothesis that the numbers are equally low. To determine if this is correct, further research regarding this topic is needed.

3.6.2 *Right for Compensation*

The citizen may have a claim for damages.[90] The right for compensation is found in Article 34 GG and Section 839 BGB. If an officer violates his official duty, liability rests principally with the state or the public body that employs him. The officers themselves are only liable if they intentionally did wrong or grossly neglected their duty.

If the property of the citizen was damaged, they might also have a claim for damages. This entitlement is not found in any law but the judges derived it from the concept behind Section 74 and Section 75 of the introduction of the General Prussian Land Law which dates back to 1794. Personal rights have to step back behind the common good but the state has to compensate those who are forced to sacrifice their rights.

Both claims only apply if the citizen has done everything to repel the wrongdoing that is the administrative silence, Section 839 (3) BGB. This includes filing an action for failure to act.[91]

Data about the finished claims for compensation is collected by Higher Regional Court, *Land*, and Federation.[92] No difference is made between claims for compensation because of administrative silence and for other reasons. Property damage is included.

[90] Kopp and Ramsauer (2018, p. 319).

[91] Kopp and Schenke (2018, p. 924).

[92] Statistisches Bundesamt (2014, 2015, 2016, 2017c).

In 2013, 348,651 proceedings were finished at the German District Courts and 4553 of them were claims for damages.[93] In 2014, 334,499 proceedings were finished at the German District Courts and 4464 of them were claims for damages.[94] In 2015, 332,085 proceedings were finished at the German District Courts and 4078 of them were claims for damages.[95] In 2016, 322,371 proceedings were finished at the German District Courts and 4158 of them were claims for damages.[96] In 2017, 308,026 proceedings were finished at the German District Courts and 3757 of them were claims for damages.[97] Between 2013 and 2016, claims for damages made 1.3% of all claims[98] and they made 1.2% of claims in 2017.[99] One could conclude that the overall numbers of claims for damages are stable on a very low level. Given the low percentages of actions for failure to act at the social courts one may formulate the hypothesis that claims for damages in this case are comparably low because administrative silence only makes a small part of all claims for damages. To verify this argument, more research is needed.

3.7 Overall Assessment of the Legal Regime and the Practice of Administrative Silence

The German way of dealing with administrative silence is a non-treatment and (administrative) silence is only scarcely mentioned in the codes. While we know the principle of timeliness—since 25 years even codified by the law—we do not know a general deadline. At the same time, various different deadlines are scattered among various laws, but failing to meet these deadlines does not necessarily have consequences whatsoever. Silence itself has not defined as a legal construct and therefore, originally, neither a positive nor a negative silence existed. The positive silence known as *Genehmigungsfiktionen* is a new product established by EU law.

[93] Statistisches Bundesamt (2014, p. 42).

[94] Statistisches Bundesamt (2015, p. 48).

[95] Statistisches Bundesamt (2016, p. 48).

[96] Statistisches Bundesamt (2017c, p. 48).

[97] Statistisches Bundesamt (2018b, p. 48).

[98] Statistisches Bundesamt (2014, p. 46; 2015; 2016, p. 52; 2017c, p. 52).

[99] Statistisches Bundesamt (2018b, p. 52).

There is little to no interest in the law in action. Scholars do not discuss administrative silence. Empirical data is close to non-existent and not officially collected. The discussion of efficiency ignores silence while it declares procedures to be too long without sufficient empirical data.

The data about the actions for failure to act is only a small glimpse and does not allow for any more than the formulation of hypotheses. The approach of non-treatment expects that the system works in a more or less effective manner. This mentality proves to be a better solution than the model of a positive silence. While the applicant can seek legal protection, the decision itself is always up to the authority. The authority can still balance the rights of all parties involved, especially third parties. A fiction does not replace this kind of balancing the interests and rights of the involved parties.

Nevertheless, silence exists and administrative science should try to assess to which extent this issue impedes swift and effective administrative action, and under which circumstances it might occur. This research should focus not only on the courts' level but first and foremost on the authorities' level.

List of German Abbreviations

BayVwVfG	Bayerisches Verwaltungsverfahrensgesetz (Bavarian Administrative Procedure Act)
BGB	BürgerlichesGesetzbuch (Civil Code)
BremVwVfG	Bremisches Verwaltungsverfahrensgesetz (Bremen Administrative Procedure Act)
BVerfGE	Entscheidungen des Bundesverfassungsgerichts (Journal)
BVerwGE	Entscheidungen des Bundesverwaltungsgerichts (Journal)
DLRL	Dienstleistungsrichtlinie (Services in the Internal Market Directive 2006)
EU	Europeen Union
FGO	Finanzgerichtsordnung (Code for Fiscal Courts)
GG	Grundgesetz für die Bundesrepublik Deutschland (Basic Law for the Federal Republic of Germany)
HmbVwVfG	Hamburgisches Verwaltungsverfahrensgesetz (Hamburg Administrative Procedure Act)
HVwVfG	Hessisches Verwaltungsverfahrensgesetz (Hesse Administrative Procedure Act)
LVwG	Allgemeines Verwaltungsgesetz für das Land Schleswig-Holstein (General Administrative Procedure Act for the State Schleswig-Holstein)
LVwVfG BW	Verwaltungsverfahrensgesetz für Baden-Württemberg (Administrative Procedure Act for Baden-Württemberg)

(continued)

(continued)

LVwVfG RLP	Landesverwaltungsverfahrensgesetz (State Administrative Procedure Act (Rhineland-Palatinate))
NordÖR	Zeitschrift für das Öffentliche Recht in Norddeutschland (journal)
NVwVfG	Niedersächsisches Verwaltungsverfahrensgesetz (Lower-Saxony Administrative Procedure Act)
SächsVwVfG	Verwaltungsverfahrensgesetzes für den Freistaat Sachsen (Administrative Procedure Act for Saxony)
SG	Sozialgericht (social court)
SGG	Sozialgerichtsgesetz (Code for Social Welfare Courts)
SVwVfG	Saarländisches Verwaltungsverfahrensgesetz (Saarland Administrative Procedure Act)
ThürVwVfG	Thüringer Verwaltungsverfahrensgesetz (Thuringian Administrative Procedure Act)
VwGO	Verwaltungsgerichtsordnung (Code of Administrative Court Procedure)
VwVfG	Verwaltungsverfahrensgesetz (Federal Administrative Procedure Act)
VwVfG BE	Gesetz über das Verfahren der Berliner Verwaltung (Act on the Procedure of the Berlin Administration)
VwVfG LSA	Verwaltungsverfahrensgesetz Sachsen-Anhalt (Administrative Procedure Act Saxony-Anhalt)
VwVfG M-V	Verwaltungsverfahrens-, Zustellungs- und Vollstreckungsgesetz des Landes Mecklenburg-Vorpommern (Administrative Procedure, Delivery, and Enforcement Act of the State Mecklenburg-Western Pomerania)
VwVfG NRW	Verwaltungsverfahrensgesetz für das Land Nordrhein-Westfalen (Administrative Procedure Act for the State North Rhine-Westphalia)
VwVfGBbg	Verwaltungsverfahrensgesetz für das Land Brandenburg (Administrative Procedure Act for the State Brandenburg)

References

Bernhardt, D. (2009). Fingierte Genehmigungen nach der Dienstleistungsrichtlinie - Möglichkeiten der Regelung und Einschränkung. *Gewerbearchiv*, 100–106.

Biermann, H. (2009). Verfahrens- und Entscheidungsfristen. Sinnvolle Instrumente zur Beschleunigung von Verwaltungsverfahren oder „Irrweg der Fiktionen“? *NordÖR* 377–384.

Brenner, M. (2018). § 75 [Klage bei Untätigkeit der Behörden]. In H. Sodan, & J. Ziekow (Eds.), *Verwaltungsgerichtsordnung*. Großkommentar. Baden-Baden: Nomos.

Broscheit, J. (2016). *Rechtswirkungen von Genehmigungsfiktionen im Öffentlichen Recht* (1st ed.). Berlin: Duncker & Humblot.

Bundesministerium für Wirtschaft (Ed.). (1994). *Investitionsförderung durch flexible Genehmigungsverfahren. Bericht der Unabhängigen Expertenkommission zur Vereinfachung und Beschleunigung von Planungs- und Genehmigungsverfahren* (1st ed.). Baden-Baden: Nomos-Verl.-Ges.

Busche, J. (2018). BGB § 147 Annahmefrist. In F. J. Säcker, R. Rixecker, H. Oetker, & B. Limperg (Eds.), *Münchener Kommentar zum Bürgerlichen Gesetzbuch. Band 1. Allgemeiner Teil* (§§ 1–240). ProstG. AGG. München: C.H. Beck.

Cancik, P. (2017). Zuviel Staat? – Die Institutionalisierung der „Bürokratie"-Kritik im 20. Jahrhundert. *Der Staat, 56*(1), 1–38.

CDU, CSU, & SPD (2018). Ein neuer Aufbruch für Europa. Eine neue Dynamik für Deutschland. Ein neuer Zusammenhalt für unser Land. Koalitionsvertrag zwischen CDU, CSU und SPD. https://www.cdu.de/system/tdf/media/dokumente/koalitionsvertrag_2018.pdf?file=1.

Eisele, J. (2014). Die verwaltungsrechtliche Genehmigungsfiktion im Straf- und Ordnungswidrigkeitenrecht. *Neue Juristische Wochenschrift*, 1417 1420.

Eyermann, E., & Fröhler, L. (1950). *Verwaltungsgerichtsgesetz für Bayern, Bremen, Hessen und Württemberg-Baden. mit einem Anhang ergänzender Vorschriften*. München und Berlin: C. H. Beck'sche Verlagsbuchhandlung.

Guckelberger, A. (2010). Die Rechtsfigur der Genehmigungsfiktion. *Die öffentliche Verwaltung*, 109–118.

Heiß, G. and Jedlitschka, N. (2009). Einheitliche Stelle - elektronisches Verfahren - Genehmigungsfiktion: Neuerungen im Verwaltungsverfahren aufgrund der EU-Dienstleistungsrichtlinie. *Thüringer Verwaltungsblätter*, 265–273.

Hullmann, C., & Zorn, M. (2009). Probleme der Genehmigungsfiktion im Baugenehmigungsverfahren. *Neue Zeitschrift für Verwaltungsrecht*, 756–760.

Jacquement-Gauché, A., & Stelkens, U. (2016a). La simplification administrative en Alemagne. In J.-B. Auby (Ed.), *Droit comparé de la procédure administrative. Comparative law of administrative procedure*. Bruxelles: Bruylant.

Jacquement-Gauché, A., & Stelkens, U. (2016b). Le traitement du silence de l'Administration et de l'inertie administrative en droit allemand. In J.-B. Auby (Ed.), *Droit comparé de la procédure administrative* [Comparative Law of Administrative Procedure]. Bruxelles: Bruylant.

Jäde, H. (2009). Die verwaltungsrechtliche Genehmigungsfiktion. *Umwelt- und Planungsrecht*, 169–173.

Jarass, H. D. (2009). Probleme um die Entscheidungsfrist der immissionsschutzrechtlichen Genehmigung. *Das Deutsche Verwaltungsblatt*, 205–212.

Kluth, W. (2011). Die Genehmigungsfiktion des § 42a VwVfG - Verfahrensrechtliche und prozessuale Probleme. *Juristische Schulung*, 1078–1082.

Kopp, F. O., & Ramsauer, U. (Eds.). (2018). *Verwaltungverfahrensgesetz*. Kommentar (19th ed.). München: C.H. Beck.

Kopp, F. O., & Schenke, W.-R. (Eds.). (2018). *Verwaltungsgerichtsordnung*. Kommentar (24rd ed.). München: C.H. Beck.

Leisner, A. (2000). Die untätige Behörde. - Zum „zureichenden Grund" der Entscheidungsverzögerung bei der Untätigkeitsklage. *Verwaltungsarchiv, 91. Band*, 227–260.

Lenders, B. P. (2009). Aktuelles zum Verwaltungsverfahrensrecht - Teil I.*Nordrhein-Westfälische Verwaltungsblätter*, 457–463.

Mayer, O. (1914). Deutsches Verwaltungsrecht (2nd ed.). München und Leipzig: Verlag von Duncker & Humblot.

Mehde, V. (2011). Haushaltskonsolidierung und betriebswirtschaftliche Steuerung. In H. Hill, K.-P. Sommermann, U. Stelkens, & J. Ziekow (Eds.), *35 Jahre Verwaltungsverfahrensgesetz – Bilanz und Perspektiven*. Vorträge der 74. Staatswissenschaftlichen Fortbildungstagung vom 9. bis 11. Februar 2011 an der Deutschen Hochschule für Verwaltungswissenschaften Speyer. Berlin: Duncker & Humblot.

Mirschberger, M. (2012). The Implementation of the Services Directive in Germany. In U. Stelkens, W. Weiß, & M. Mirschberger (Eds.), *The Implementation of the EU Services Directive. Transposition, Problems and Strategies*. The Hague: T.M.C. Asser Press.

Scheidler, A. (2012). Die Genehmigungsfiktion im Personenbeförderungsrecht. Kritische Anmerkung zu OVG Hamburg, GewArch 2011, 120. *Nordrhein-Westfälische* Verwaltungsblätter, 340–343.

Schmitz, H. (2018). § 10 Nichtförmlichkeit des Verwaltungsverfahrens. In P. Stelkens, H. J. Bonk, & M. Sachs (Eds.), *Verwaltungsverfahrensgesetz*. Kommentar. München: C.H. Beck.

Schmitz, H., & Prell, L. (2009). Verfahren über eine einheitliche Stelle - Das Vierte Gesetz zur Änderung verwaltungsverfahrensrechtlicher Vorschriften. *Neue Zeitschrift für Verwaltungsrecht*, 1–12.

Seckelmann, M. (2012). § 42a Genehmigungsfiktion. In R. Bauer, D. Heckmann, K. Ruge, M. Schallbruch, & S. E. Schulz (Eds.), *Verwaltungsverfahrensgesetz und E-Government*. Wiesbaden: Kommunal- und Schul-Verlag.

Statistisches Bundesamt. (2014). *Rechtspflege*. Zivilgerichte. https://www.destatis.de/DE/Publikationen/Thematisch/Rechtspflege/GerichtePersonal/Zivilgerichte2100210137004.pdf?__blob=publicationFile.

Statistisches Bundesamt. (2015). *Rechtspflege*. Zivilgerichte. https://www.destatis.de/DE/Publikationen/Thematisch/Rechtspflege/GerichtePersonal/Zivilgerichte2100210147004.pdf?__blob=publicationFile.

Statistisches Bundesamt. (2016). *Rechtspflege*. Zivilgerichte. https://www.destatis.de/DE/Publikationen/Thematisch/Rechtspflege/GerichtePersonal/Zivilgerichte2100210157004.pdf?__blob=publicationFile.

Statistisches Bundesamt. (2017a). *Rechtspflege*. Sozialgerichte. https://www.destatis.de/DE/Publikationen/Thematisch/Rechtspflege/GerichtePersonal/Sozialgerichte2100270167004.pdf?__blob=publicationFile.

Statistisches Bundesamt. (2017b). *Rechtspflege*. Verwaltungsgerichte. https://www.destatis.de/DE/Publikationen/Thematisch/Rechtspflege/GerichtePersonal/Verwaltungsgerichte2100240167004.pdf?__blob=publicationFile.

Statistisches Bundesamt. (2017c). *Rechtspflege*. Zivilgerichte. https://www.destatis.de/DE/Publikationen/Thematisch/Rechtspflege/GerichtePersonal/Zivilgerichte.html.

Statistisches Bundesamt. (2018a). *Rechtspflege*. Sozialgerichte. https://www.destatis.de/DE/Publikationen/Thematisch/Rechtspflege/GerichtePersonal/Sozialgerichte2100270177004.pdf;jsessionid=AEDA740E9FE6EFA59A11463B22427644.InternetLive1?__blob=publicationFile.

Statistisches Bundesamt. (2018b). *Rechtspflege*. Zivilgerichte. https://www.destatis.de/DE/Publikationen/Thematisch/Rechtspflege/GerichtePersonal/Zivilgerichte2100210177004.pdf?__blob=publicationFile.

Stelkens, U. (2016). L'influence actuelle du droit administratif français sur le droit administratif allemand. In P. Cossalter & C. Witz (Eds.), *Soixante ans d'influences juridiques réciproques franco-allemandes*. Jubilé des 60 ans du Centre juridique franco-allemand, Université de la Sarre. Paris: Société de Législation Comparée.

Stelkens, U. (2018). § 42a Genehmigungsfiktion. In P. Stelkens, H. J. Bonk, & M. Sachs (Eds.), *Verwaltungsverfahrensgesetz*. Kommentar. München: C.H. Beck.

Vigaranan, V. (2015). *Die Genehmigungsfiktion im allgemeinen Verwaltungsrecht. Fortbestehender Umsetzungsbedarf im Hinblick auf die europäische Dienstleistungsrichtlinie*. München: Utz.

Ziekow, J. (1998). Zügige Verwaltungsverfahren. In J. Ziekow (Ed.), *Beschleunigung von Planungs- und Genehmigungsverfahren*. Vorträge und Diskussionsbeiträge auf dem gleichnamigen Forum von 25. bis 27. März 1998 an der Deutschen Hochschule für Verwaltungswissenschaften Speyer. Berlin: Duncker & Humblot.

Ziekow, J. (2007). Die Auswirkungen der Dienstleistungsrichtlinie auf das deutsche Genehmigungsverfahrensrecht. *Gewerbearchiv*, 217–225.

Ziekow, J. (2010). *Möglichkeiten zur Verbesserung der Standortbedingungen für kleinere und mittlere Unternehmen durch Einführung von Genehmigungsfiktionen*. Berlin: Duncker & Humblot.

CHAPTER 4

Silence in the French Administrative System: A Failed Revolution?

Emilie Chevalier

4.1 Introduction

The question of the regulation of silence of the administration, and the broader question of time limits in France, is a manifestation of the specificity of the French administrative system and the conception of administrative law.

4.1.1 General Overview of French Administrative Law and System

French administrative law started developing in the nineteenth century, following the French Revolution. In this context, its development was an answer to ensure that the separation of powers would be effective, in

E. Chevalier (✉)
University of Limoges, Limoges, France
e-mail: emilie.chevalier@unilim.fr

D. C. Dragos et al. (eds.),
The Sound of Silence in European Administrative Law,
https://doi.org/10.1007/978-3-030-45227-8_4

order to prevent judiciary power to adjudicate on administrative matters.[1] Promotion of administrative law was a way to give a specialized set of rules to deal with administrative matters. Consequently, the promotion of administrative law was developed in order to ensure that administrative matters would be excluded from the scope of jurisdiction of judiciary (*juge judiciaire*). To this extent, it was not really regarded as a way to promote limitation to administrative powers, but rather as a way to take into account the peculiarities of administrative function.[2] The basic idea was to say that administrative matters should be adjudicated and reviewed by administrative authorities themselves. The Council of State, which was set up under Napoleon Bonaparte regime in 1799, was not at that time an independent court, but rather a "council" to the State. It is only from 1872 that the Council of State became a proper court granted with jurisdiction to rule on the cases involving administrative authorities.[3] This led to the development of a specific corpus of rules applicable to administrative authorities and activities, under the authority of the Council of State.[4] The French system is then dualistic, meaning that there are two different judicial orders, judiciary courts and administrative courts (which are now composed, a part of the Council of State, of administrative tribunals and administrative courts of appeal). The jurisdiction of judiciary courts is related to application of private law and private activities, whereas the jurisdiction of administrative courts encompasses administrative activities which imply the enforcement of prerogatives of public power (*prérogatives de puissance publique*).[5] For long, administrative law had been mainly

[1] Loi du 16 et 24 et août 1790 sur l'organisation judiciaire—Article 13: "Judicial functions are separate and shall always remain separate from administrative functions. Courts shall not, on pain of forfeiture, disrupt in any way the operation of administrative bodies, or summon administrators to appear before them by reason of their duties."

[2] See Sordi (2017).

[3] Loi du 24 mai 1872 portant réorganisation du Conseil d'État—Article 9: "The Council of State (Conseil d'État) adjudicates … on actions for the annulment (annulation pour excès de pouvoirs) of the acts of the various administrative authorities"; see McCleave Cake (1972).

[4] Tribunal des conflits, 8 February 1873, *Blanco*.

[5] Conseil constitutionnel, Décision n° 80-119 DC, 22 July 1908, Loi de validation législative; Conseil constitutionnel, Décision n° 86-224 DC, 23 January 1987, Loi relative au Conseil de la concurrence.

developed through case law. Thus, French administrative law is qualified as judge-made law. Case by case, the Council of State developed the fundamental principles and rules underlying administrative action.[6]

For a long time, due to the little promotion and weakness of constitutional law, the legality principle was understood as compliance with legislative rules. From the second part of twentieth century, the promotion of individual rights started being included in administrative law, through the development of general principles of law (*principes généraux du droit*). From the 1978, written administrative law has been developed through the adoption of specific statues related to the principles applicable to the administrative decision-making process and to the accountability of administrative power, such as access to documents. In addition, codification process has been enforced, but still focused on specific issues.[7]

Concerning its internal organization, France is a unitary State. Administrative system is strongly centralized, organized around the State administration (*administration centrale*), which gathers all the services of ministers, having a national competence, under the responsibility of prime minister and the government.[8] The ministers are represented at local level, through decentralized services (services déconcentrés), which ensure the enforcement of national decisions at local level, within a part of French territory. In addition, the decentralized administration (administration décentralisée) is made of the local and sub-state authorities (cities, departments, and regions). They are in charge of the interest of people on certain parts of territory. They are granted with a certain degree of autonomy, noticeably financial, and political power. However, their prerogatives are limited to regulatory power and do not include legislative competences. Indeed, the autonomy granted should not lead to the infringement of equality principle among citizens, which is deeply anchored in the French system.[9] The administrative power shall be then enforced under the same conditions on the whole French territory.

Aside this strongly hierarchical system, there are independent administrative authorities, that are state institutions responsible, on its behalf,

[6] See Chevallier (2007).

[7] *Code général de la propriété des personnes publiques* (General Code on the Property of Public Entities), *Code des marchés publics* (Public Procurement Code), *Code général des collectivités territoriales* (Local Authorities Code), *Code de justice administrative* (Code on administrative justice).

[8] Articles 20 and 21 of the French Constitution (Constitution of 4th October 1958).

[9] Article 1 of the Declaration of human and citizen's rights.

for regulating sectors considered essential and for which the government wishes to avoid direct intervention (fundamental rights, economic regulation…). They are outside the traditional administrative structures and are not subject to the authority of a minister. Their activity is under the review of the Parliament.

4.1.2 Silence in French Administrative Law

The central role of the administrative judge, and especially of the Council of State, is immediately apparent in the approach adopted by French administrative law dealing with the issue of silence kept by the administrative authorities. Basically, it is dealt with in relation to litigation. Giving a meaning to silence aimed at avoiding to leave the individual in a position of endless waiting and uncertainty, but especially not to prevent him/her from having access to the administrative judge. Indeed, this is closely linked to an important rule of French administrative litigation, according to which judicial review can only be exercised against a preliminary decision (décision préalable).[10] Consequently, the absence of the adoption of a decision by the administrative authority hinders access to judge for individuals. Thus, this rule responds to a desire to fight against the inertia of the administration, which must not hinder the intervention of the judge, and at the same time to encourage the interventionism of the judge in the control of the acts of the administration.[11] And, that's why, the basic rule was to opt for negative silence, the silence kept by administrative authorities creating a refusal decision, which grants interest to the individual to challenge it before the judge.[12]

However, since a reform in 2013, the system has evolved significantly, establishing in principle the rule that silence kept by the administration is equivalent to acceptance (positive silence). This evolution is the

[10] Art. 1er al. 1 of the decree of 11 January 1965 relatif aux délais de recours en matière administrative: « La juridiction administrative ne peut être saisie que par la voie d'un recours formé contre une décision ».

[11] See Deguergue (2015).

[12] See CE, 30 July 1920, *Servan*, n° 65585, Rec. p. 780: the provisions of article 3 of the law of 17 July 1900 were adopted "in order to facilitate the exercise of judicial remedies before the Council of State for the defence of their rights by preventing administrations from making it impossible for claimants to bring legal proceedings by virtue of their silence on the claims they are hearing."

result of various influences on French administrative system. Since the 1990s, a discourse on the efficiency of the administration is being developed. In order to promote this efficiency, in addition to the important need for structural reforms, one of the points of attention is the acceleration of administrative proceedings. Thus, the question of the time limit for administrative action is closely linked to its effectiveness. In addition, the increasing promotion of administrative simplification (the so-called simplification shock)[13] was another element taken into consideration while leading the reform of silence. The evolution of the meaning given to administrative silence is also the result of a greater consideration for individual rights in administrative relationship. In its report dedicated to this issue,[14] the Council of State explained this evolution. The basic rule of negative silent "embodied the initial conception of public power. It guaranteed respect for the mission entrusted to the administration, i.e. to always act in the general interest." The silence meaning refusal, the inertia of administrative authority could not lead to something prejudicial to general interest. The starting of an action depended on the individual, and then, the inertia of administration could be reviewed by the administrative judge, as the ultimate protector of general interest. Thus, "the mechanism of silence meaning refusal thus ensured a perfect safeguard a priori of the general interest since it was protected in principle."[15] The reversing of the rule by the Law of 12 November 2013[16] is then a change of balance between general interest and individual rights. So, the rule of positive silence aims at making prevailing the latter, "possibly to the detriment of the general interest that the acceptance of its request may threaten."[17] Such a conception aims at reactivating the administration, because the silence of the administration, which could mean that

[13] Circulaire n° PRMX1318686C, 17 July 2013 related to the administrative simplification and to the protocol of relations with the deventralized services *relative à la simplification administrative et au protocole des relations avec les services déconcentrés* (JORF n° 0165 du 18 juillet 2013, page 11993), https://www.legifrance.gouv.fr/affichTexte.do?cidTexte=JORFTEXT000027721598&categorieLien=id.

[14] Report of the Council of State, L'application du nouveau principe "silence de l'administration vaut acceptation," 2014 (La Documentation française).

[15] Council of State (2014).

[16] Loi n° 2013-1005 du 12 novembre 2013 habilitant le Gouvernement à simplifier les relations entre l'administration et les citoyens (JORF n° 0263 du 13 novembre 2013, page 18407).

[17] Council of State (2014).

the administration has not dealt with the request, can affect the general interest. The general interest "can only prevail eventually if the administration takes the initiative to make it prevail. It will then have to either oppose an explicit decision to reject the application before the expiry of the time limit for the appearance of an implicit decision of acceptance or, if such a decision has been adopted, to withdraw it."[18]

4.1.3 The Regulation of Timeliness, Mainly Grounded on Legal Certainty

French administrative law includes a set of general principles of law that intend to provide a framework for administrative action. These principles have a higher value than administrative acts, but lower than the legislation. Some of them also have constitutional value and are therefore also binding on the legislator. The general principles of law have played an important role in the development of administrative law, given that until the 1990s there were only a few written texts applicable. From a substantial point of view are part of this category classical principles known in the other member states. Among them, the equality principle is fundamental and has constitutional value.[19] However, it is not really relevant while dealing with timeliness of administrative activities. Other principles may be more expected to play a role here, such as the principles of proportionality, of legal certainty, and of legitimate expectations. First, in the French system, there is no legal rule that enshrines proportionality as a general principle of administrative law. The principle of proportionality was implicitly introduced as a means of control of the administrative discretion in specific situations. Thus, up until today, proportionality is not understood as an overriding principle of public law, but only applied in certain fields of law, particularly related to human rights. Second, it is worth recalling that the principles of legal certainty and of legitimate expectations have not been recognized for a long time in the French system. Especially, the principle of legitimate expectations is not recognized as such, since it is regarded as contravening the objective conception of administrative law, which serves the promotion of the general interests. In French law, individual expectations can, as a matter of principle, not limit the freedom

[18] Council of State (2014).

[19] Article 1 of the Declaration of human and citizen's rights.

of the administration in its pursuit of the public interest. However, as general principle of EU law, it shall be applied by national courts, while enforcing EU law.[20] The principle of legal certainty is now a general principle of administrative law.[21] It is obviously taken into consideration in the whole system, even if it has no constitutional value. This limited scope may be justified by the objective conception of French administrative system and the weight of general interest, which is opposite to a subjective individual-centered conception of administrative law. Consequently, legal certainty and the protection of individual acquired rights must sometimes be limited in the name of general interest.

The definition of time limits or the statement of the requirement to respect "a reasonable deadline" is first and foremost a matter of legal certainty. The judge bases the respect of the defined time limit or a reasonable deadline on this requirement. However, the control of administrative action on this ground remains limited. According to the prevailing view, the determination of time limits applicable to the administrative procedure is primarily based on the desire to ensure the efficient functioning of the procedures. It is only in case of excessive delay to adopt decisions that the administrative judge would sanction the administrative authority. For example, the administrative judge may limit the possibilities of initiating disciplinary proceedings, especially in a case where there was no limitation period for such actions. In a case of 29 January 2013, the Administrative Court of Appeal of Marseille ruled that a disciplinary proceedings against a civil servant could not be initiated "beyond a reasonable time after the day on which the authority becomes aware of the facts for which it intends to impose a sanction."[22] In this case, a civil servant had been dismissed and expelled from the hospital public service by his administration more than 15 years after the wrongdoing. Therefore, the requirements of legal certainty are included in the reasoning of the administrative judge, without, however, except in extreme cases, serving as a basis for sanctioning the administrative authority having ignored the requirement of a reasonable time limit.

[20] CE, 9 May 2001, *Entreprise personnelle de transports Freymuth*, n° 210944; CE, 10 April 2009, *Association pour le maintien de l'élevage en Bretagne*, n° 310184.

[21] CE, 24 March 2006, *KPMG*, n° 288460.

[22] CAA Marseille, 29 January 2013, n° 11MA02224.

4.2 The Legal Framework of Administrative Timeliness

Generally speaking, the French Constitution does not provide for provisions related to administrative procedures and requirements. So, expectedly, there is no general administrative timeline referred to in the Constitution, nor the requirement to act within a reasonable time. However, the Constitutional Council, through its case law, referred to the principle of negative silence. It provided for explicitly, in a decision of 26 June 1969, Protection des sites (n° 69-55 L), that "negative silence is a general principle of law of our system."[23] Consequently, only legislative acts could provide for exceptions to the principle. It is then applicable if there is no text regulating time line.[24] That's why also legislation needed to be adopted to reverse the principle.

4.2.1 *Time Limit and Silence in Administrative Procedure Act*

French administrative law has been widely developed through case law. The adoption of general act related to administrative procedure is recent. On this occasion, the rules applicable to the administrative silence were amended.

Eventually, the Code on relations between the public and administration was adopted in 2015. A first legislation was adopted in 2000,[25] but the idea of a Code really came out in 2013. Interest for codification of administrative proceedings was renewed from 2012. Article 3 of Law of 12 November 2013 empowered the government to simplify the relations between administration and citizens through an ordinance. It gave the government the power and the mission to adopt a Code that should gather "*the general rules related to administrative proceedings applicable to the relations between the public and administrative bodies of the State and local entities, public establishment and bodies performing a public service*

[23] Constitutional Council, 26 June 1969, *Protection des sites*, n° 69-55 L; Constitutional Council, 18 January 1995, *Vidéosurveillance*, n° 94-352 DC.

[24] See also for the Council of State case law: CE, 14 February 2001, *Ministre de l'emploi et de la solidarité c/M. Bouraïb*, n° 202830.

[25] Loi n° 2000-321 du 12 avril 2000 relative aux droits des citoyens dans leurs relations avec les administrations (JORF 13 avril 2000, p. 5646).

task. (...) It gathers the general rules related to the regime of administrative acts. The codified rules are those which are in force at the date of the publication of the ordinance and, if needed, the already published rules, but not yet in force at this date." Two years later, the ordinance n° 2015-1341 of 23 October 2015 related to legislative provisions of the Code on relations between the public and administration and the decree n° 2015-1342 related to regulatory provisions of the Code on relations between the public and administration were adopted.[26]

The Code does not provide for a new principle with regard to deadlines. Indeed, the requirement to adopt decision or to act within a reasonable time is not even mentioned in the Code. However, it brings new developments with regard to the meaning of silence. Indeed, according to Article L231-1 of the Code, "Silence kept by an administrative authority upon an individual request is equivalent to a decision of acceptance." However, this new statement did not fully set aside the application of the rule of negative silence. First, when an administrative act or action does not fall within the scope of the Code, the previous rule of negative silence remains applicable, noticeably in the context of relationship between civil servants and administrative authority.[27] Second, activities of the courts are obviously outside the scope of the rule. Third, specific regimes, providing either positive or negative silent, or specific deadlines to be complied with when a decision is adopted are still applicable.[28]

4.2.2 Sector-Specific Legislation (Special Laws)

As stated before, despite the recognition of the general rule of positive silence, specific legislation and regulations remain in force, providing for specific meaning given to silence kept by administrative authorities, or for specific deadlines to be complied by administrative authorities when

[26] JORF 25 octobre 2015, p. 19872 et p. 19895.

[27] See Article L100-1 and Article L100-3 of the Code on relations between the Public and the Administration: « *For the purposes of this Code and unless otherwise provided in this Code, the following definitions shall apply: 1° Administration: State administrations, local authorities, their public administrative establishments and bodies and persons governed by public and private law entrusted with a public administrative service mission, including social security bodies. (...)* »

[28] Article L231-4 of the Code on relations between the Public and Administration, see below.

adopting a decision. It is then a case-by-case approach. Such an approach, as derogating to the general principle, may be justified by legal certainty (the need to have an explicit decision in order to comply with individual rights, or not to infringe them) or by the need to leave more time to the competent administrative authority to adopt a decision. It is the case, for example, in technical area, as in planning legislation, related to building permit. The planning code provides for specific deadlines applicable to the instruction of building permit request.[29] The deadline is then for two months.[30] Furthermore, it is worth noticing that the planning code provides for exception to those deadlines extending them to six months, for example, where the future building will be in a protected area. The extension of deadline may be justified by the need of consultation. The huge current tendency is to ensure the acceleration of proceedings to deliver building permit. Legislation and ordinances were adopted in order to reduce the time of instruction for huge development projects.[31] The objectives of those legislative developments were to reduce the length of proceedings to deliver building permit, having a huge economic impact. So, the way to proceed is not to exclude the positive silence principle, but to reduce the deadline to get an implicit decision, and to constrain the competent administrative authorities to act faster. Indeed, in case there is no decision adopted within the time of instruction, the building permit is considered as delivered. However, it is possible for the competent administrative authority to withdraw an implicit decision of authorization of a building permit, by adopting a decision of refusal, after the expiry of the deadline to get an implicit decision. Requirements need to be met, since there is an impact on the rights of the petitioner. Consequently, according to Article L424-5 of the planning code, the withdrawal of the building permit is only possible if the implicit decision is illegal and within the deadline of three months, after the date of constitution of the positive implicit decision.[32] The objective of such reform was to reduce the length

[29] Article R423-23 of the planning Code.

[30] There are specific deadline for déclaration préalable (1 month) and three months for other projects.

[31] See, for example, Decree n° 2015-836 of 9 July 2015 on the reduction of time limits for the examination of urban planning authorizations (JORF n° 0158 du 10 juillet 2015, page 11770).

[32] Article L424-5 of the planning Code: "The building, development or demolition permit, tacit or explicit, may be withdrawn only if it is illegal and within three months

of delivery of a building permit to five months, instead of an average of nine months, knowing that such a deadline depends on the need of the administrative authority to ask and to get complementary files.[33] It is always possible for the competent administrative authority within the time limit of instruction to adopt an explicit decision authorizing the building. It happens most often when the favorable decision is adopted but conditioned by the compliance with additional requirements prescribed by the administrative authority.

The approach concerning the definition of deadline strongly depends on the type of proceedings and the type of interests which are at stake. For example, in migrant cases, the deadline to register an asylum seeker is limited to three days, and can be, for exceptional reasons, extended to ten days.[34]

Concerning the grant of social benefit, the approach is slightly different. Indeed, since the decision has a financial impact,[35] the principle of negative silent is still applicable, and most often within a deadline of two months.

As far as we know, there is no procedure where there is no deadline for answering petitions. Moreover, when it is provided for the adoption of an explicit decision, the silence kept by the administrative authority within the deadline set up by regulatory decisions or legislation, does not lead to an implicit decision.[36] The petitioner needs then to wait for an explicit decision of the administrative authority. In case of the absence of decision, the only solution is to introduce an action in liability.[37]

of the date of this decision. After this period, the permit may only be withdrawn at the explicit request of the beneficiary."

[33] See below.

[34] Article L741-1 of alien's code: Registration shall take place no later than three working days after the request is submitted to the competent administrative authority, without any preconditions of domiciliation. However, this period may be extended to ten working days where a large number of foreign nationals apply for asylum simultaneously.

[35] See below for the exceptions to the rule of positive silence.

[36] CE, 9 May 1995, Époux Tchijakoff, n° 127763; CE, 2 May 2007, Min. de l'Écologie c/ Coopérative agricole Le Dunnois, n° 295024; CAA Marseille, 2 May 2011, Commune de La Roque-d'Anthéron, n° 08MA04208.

[37] See below.

4.3 The Length of Administrative Deadlines

4.3.1 Counting Deadlines

As stated before, the Code on relations between public and administration does not provide for general deadline, nor for a general requirement to act within a reasonable time. When sectorial legislation set up deadlines, the solutions provided for are various. Those deadlines are provided for the decision-making stage. The applicable deadlines are different in case of administrative appeal and to introduce an action before the judge.

The time limit for adopting an administrative decision is counted in calendar days. The time limit for the examination of the request expires two months after the request is made by the person concerned to the day. As it is not a judicial deadline, the time limit may end on Sunday, especially in the event of an implicit decision.[38] Furthermore, the countdown of the time limit is different depending on whether it is the time limit for administrative action, or the time limit for appeal, before the administrative authority or before the judge. In addition, where the calendar of the month used as the starting point for calculating the two-month period for contentious appeals does not have a corresponding calendar in the month in which the period expires (30 days or 28/29 days for February), the end of the period for appeals must be brought forward to the last day of that month. When the request is introduced, the administrative authority is first under an obligation to issue a receipt for the application, containing a registration number and the date on which the file is received. This date is the starting point of the time limit. However, the starting point of the time limit remains dependent on the completeness of the file. Therefore, if the administrative authority requests additional documents for the individual, the period will only start on the date of submission of these additional documents.

A preliminary administrative appeal shall be introduced within two months. This period starts the day on which the decision is notified to the person concerned or made public. In the case of implicit decisions, the time limit for appeal starts at the end of the time limit for the constitution of the decision. It is counted in calendar days. However, if the deadline is a Sunday or a public holiday, the deadline is postponed to the following Monday. The introduction of a prior administrative appeal has the effect

[38] CE, 28 February 1986, n° 38325 39132.

of suspending the time limit for an appeal in court, which will restart once the decision upon the appeal has been adopted. In French administrative law, there are cases where the introduction of a prior administrative appeal is mandatory, which conditions the admissibility of the appeal in court. Otherwise, the possibility for the individual to lodge an administrative appeal is an option left open.

An action in administrative court to challenge an administrative act is admissible if it is introduced within two months from the notification of the decision, or, in the case of the implementation of a prior administrative appeal, from the date of notification of the decision adopted in the context of that appeal, or from the date on which an implicit decision to reject is taken. This period is counted in the same way as in the case of prior administrative appeal. Sometimes, the time limit is different, because of special statutory provisions: For example, a permission for polluting installations can be challenged within one year by residents of the area and associations.[39]

4.3.2 The Concept of "Reasonable" Deadline

The concept of "reasonable deadline" is not really developed in administrative proceedings. It is widely developed, under the influence of Article 6 ECHR, in relation to courts. It is widely taken into account in assessing the speed of administrative courts in the exercise of the function of judging. It led in particular to the establishment of a regime of State liability in case of failure to comply with the obligation to judge within a reasonable time.[40] However, this concept of a reasonable deadline has not been taken into consideration the field of administrative procedure. Administrative courts consider that Article 6 ECHR is not applicable to administrative procedures, including tax matters or procedures leading to the adoption of sanctions. This does not mean, however, that other requirements set out in Article 6 ECHR are not taken into account, in particular with regard to respect for the principle of impartiality.[41]

[39] Article R514-3-1 of the Environment Code.

[40] CE, 28 June 2002, *Magiera*, n° 239575.

[41] CE, 3 December 1999, *Didier*, n° 207434.

Perhaps the most significant jurisprudential development, dealing with review of the reasonable deadline, is related to the adoption by the regulatory power of regulatory acts implementing legislation. The Council of State thus considers that "the exercise of regulatory power includes not only the right, but also the obligation to take, within a reasonable time, the measures necessarily required for the application of the law."[42] However, the administrative judge points out that the authority vested with implementing competence is, in principle, not bound by the time limits provided by legislation, while enforcing its implementing competence,[43] and a delay can be justified by the complexity of the matter in question or the need to fulfill formalities.[44]

4.4 Responses to Administrative Silence

4.4.1 The Prevailing Model: Positive or Negative

In the French administrative system, it may be rather difficult to decide what the prevailing model is.

For a long time, the principle was that silence kept by the administrative authority meant rejection. Following the reform of 2013, the general principle has then been changed; the common principle is then positive silent. However, it is still difficult to consider that it is the prevailing model. Indeed, there are so many exceptions, that they impact the scope of the general principle. But, even before the rule changed, the rule of positive silence applied already in three main fields: regulations related to the exercise of occupational activities and freedom of trade and industry, employment law, and regulations related to property rights.[45] Now, the question is regulated by Article L231-1 of the Code on relations between the public and administration. It rules that silence kept for two months by the administrative authority upon the request of the individual means a decision of acceptance. Article D231-2 of the Code states that the lists

[42] CE, 7 mars 2008, *Féd. nat. des mines et de l'énergie CGT*, n° 298138.

[43] CE, 3 févr. 1999, *Nodière*, n° 178785.

[44] See Deffigier (2003).

[45] Article 22 of Loi du 12 avril 2000 relative aux droits des citoyens dans leurs relations avec les administrations: « *Silence kept for two months by the administrative authority upon a request implies a positive decision when provided for by decree adopted following an opinion of the Council of State* ».

of proceedings where the principle is applicable are published on the prime minister website. However, Article L231-4 of the Code provides for a series of exceptions, cases where silence kept means rejection of the request. There are five categories of exception. First, in case the request is not about the adoption of an individual decision, but rather of a regulatory decision. Second, when the request is not based on proceedings provided for legislation, or is dealing with a preliminary internal appeal (recours administratif préalable). Third, if the request has a budgetary impact (except in the field of social security). Fourth, in case positive silent would not be compatible with international agreement, fundamental freedoms and rights, and protection of public order. Fifth, if the request deals with the relationships between the administrative authority and the civil servants.

Thus, the possibilities for derogations are still very important. The legislative and regulatory authorities have a wide margin of discretion in determining exceptions. Vigilance seems important on the part of the doctrine and legislative and regulatory authorities to preserve the rule of negative silence, particularly when the exercise of rights and freedoms is at stake.[46] Nowadays, there are about 2400 exceptions to the rule of positive silence, provided by more than 50 decrees and legislation.[47] Consequently, it is hard to talk about a prevailing model, but rather we can assume that the French system is of a hybrid nature, with regard to the question of the meaning of silence.

4.4.2 National Doctrine on the Administrative Silence: Advantages and Side Effects Envisaged by the Literature of the Preeminent Model

The question of silence of administrative authority was not part of the subjects of huge interests of academic doctrine for a long time. However, the 2013 reform made it a central and has raised new concern from the academic doctrine, at least for some time.

[46] In 1995, in a Decision *Loi relative à l'installation de systèmes de vidéosurveillance*, the Constitutional Council stated that the positive silence regime provided for by the legislation was in breach with the Constitution "taking into account the risks that the installation of video surveillance systems may entail for individual freedom".

[47] See Froger (2016).

The reform process is quite recent. It has been extensively presented and discussed by the academic doctrine. Indeed, scholars widely questioned its merit and its interest for the French administrative system.

The reform process aimed at tackling three kinds of issues, according to the government which impulsed this reform.[48] First, it is part of the promotion of improvement of the relationship between administration and individuals, enhancing the consideration for their rights. Second, it aimed at accelerating the proceedings, in order to facilitate the economic growth. Third, it should contribute to the simplification of the legal process, of the decision-making process. So, the reform is also part of a wider modernization process, enhancing the efficiency of administrative functioning.

However, the reform has been widely criticized in academic doctrine. Three types of criticisms were made. First of all, the reform has not led to a simplification and has been even considered as a source of intense complexification. The government has published about 31 decrees providing for exceptions to the new rule. The situation looked so complicated that those proceedings are listed on the website of the prime minister. Furthermore, early from 2014, a report from the Council of State was dedicated to the enforcement of the new rule,[49] explaining the reasons for change and the potential benefits of the new rule.

Second, the irrelevance of the reform was pointed out. Some counted precisely the number of exceptions,[50] showing that the scope of the old rule has not been really questioned. The number of derogations is now more important than the 1200 proceedings where positive silence is applicable. So, even if the basic principle is now a positive silent, in the majority of the cases, the rule of negative silent still applies.[51] The academic works stressed that the stated political objectives of the reform have taken precedence over legal rationality.

Finally, some also pointed out that there was no need to question the principle that silence is rejection. Arguments related to the French conception of the administrative system are developed, showing a certain fear toward the risks of positive silence, particularly for the satisfaction

[48] See Ribes (2014).

[49] Council of State (2014).

[50] Derosier (2014).

[51] Cassia (2015).

of the general interest. Positive silent has much more important legal consequences than negative silent. On the opposite, negative silent has no impact on the state of law, no change in the legal order, whereas positive silence creates new legal situations, and rights for the benefit of the person who introduces the request, and has impact on third parties.[52] However, it was shown that setting the new general principle impacts the logic grounding the use of silence in the legal system. Indeed, positive silence implies the creation of rights to individuals, to be enforced, and implies then, maybe paradoxically, action from the public authorities, in order to fight against its own inertia.[53]

The implementation of the rules relating to silence kept by the administration is limited to proceedings initiated upon request. The management of the administration's silence is closely linked to guaranteeing the rights of individuals and balancing them with the general interest.

So, the change of paradigm did not appear to be justified either by the quest for legitimacy, or for improving efficiency of administration.

4.4.3 The EU Influence Over National Rules and Practices—Especially the Impact of the EU Service Directive

As in other member states, European law has influenced administrative law and administrative functioning.

The design of the reform first of all appeared, for some, to be the result of the influence of the right to good administration, enshrined in Article 41 of the Charter of Fundamental Rights.[54] But, obviously, this influence seems limited, or, in any case, if the principle of good administration is taken into account, it is rather in its dimension of promoting the efficiency of the administration, which can precisely counterbalance the rights of individuals.[55] Indeed, good administration is one of the grounds for derogation from the rule that silence is a decision to accept.

The most significant impact is probably due to the adoption and implementation of the Services Directive. Indeed, member states have

[52] Denoix de Saint Marc (1998).

[53] Lafaix (2012).

[54] Sirinelli (2011).

[55] Chevalier (2014).

been encouraged to simplify their administrative authorization regimes, noticeably by promoting implicit decision-making after a certain period of time, in order to facilitate the freedom of establishment of economic operators.[56] The implementation of internal market requirements has promoted the liberalization of the regulation of authorizations with an economic scope. The mechanism of implicit authorization is a way to soften the regulation, promoting freedom and individual autonomy. The generalization of the implicit authorization mechanism in the economic field "would thus reflect the new balance between the protection of individual freedom and the protection of the general interest."[57]

4.5 The Negative Silence

4.5.1 The Legal Character of Prescribed Deadlines (Instructive/Preclusions)

The principle of negative silence still persists, despite the 2013 reform. Indeed, the hypotheses of silence as rejection are now provided for by a series of decrees. According to Article L231-4 of the Code on relations between public and administration, such derogations are based on five types of grounds.[58] The first set of exceptions concerns requests for regulatory decisions, including requests to the author to repeal illegal regulations. The second set of exceptions concerns requests that do not fall within the scope of a procedure provided for by a legislative or regulatory text, or that have the character of a complaint or administrative appeal. The third exception concerns requests of a financial nature. The fourth exception concerns the obligation to comply with international commitments (this is the case, for example, with regard to the implementation of the Services Directive). The fifth exception concerns the relationship between administrative authorities and their agents, a situation that was already excluded from the scope of implicit decisions of acceptance under previous law. The Council of State justified this exclusion by pointing out that "the nature of the relations that a civil servant maintains, in his capacity as a person employed by a public person, with

[56] Deguergue (2015).

[57] Sirinelli (2011).

[58] Article L231-4 of the Code on the relations between the Public and the Administration.

the public person who employs him, is different from that which he is likely to maintain in his capacity as a citizen or as a user with that public person as an administrative authority." In addition, Article L231-5 of the Code on relations between public and administration provides for that a decree adopted following the opinion of the Council of State may state derogation on the ground of good administration.

In cases of negative silence, the deadline for silence to mean a decision may be distinct according to the subject matter. The principle is for two months. But, it can go from 15 days to 18 months,[59] and even 3 years (in matters related to installation of nuclear plants).

The deadline then defined is binding. There can be no derogation from this. However, the duration can be adjusted due to some reasons. In particular, if the administrative authority requests documents from the individual in order to complete the file, the starting point of the time limit is postponed to the date of the complete preparation of the file. The time limit may always be shortened if the administrative authority adopts an explicit decision, whether positive or negative.

4.5.2 The Possibility to Issue a Valid Act After the Deadline Expired

Once the time limit has expired, and therefore a negative implicit decision has been adopted, it is possible for the administrative authority to adopt a decision upon an individual request. The intervention of an implicit decision to reject an administrative appeal does not in principle preclude the subsequent taking of an express negative decision and its notification. But, in order to define the extent of the prerogatives of the administrative authority, several cases shall be distinguished, depending on whether the deadline has expired or not. Indeed, once the deadline has expired, the implicit decision exists, and then, the issuance of an explicit decision would be assimilated as the withdrawal of the implicit decision. Then, the administrative authority has to comply with specific rules.

First, an explicit negative decision was adopted before the expiry of the period within which the negative existed, but was notified after the expiry of that period. The fact that the express rejection decision was notified

[59] Article R. 543-162 of the Environment Code: Initial approval of the operator of an installation for the storage, depollution, dismantling, cutting or shredding of end-of-life vehicles; see also a deadline of 345 days in case of marketing authorization of GMOs (Articles L. 533-5 et R. 533-25 à R. 533-51 of the Environment Code).

after the silence period is without influence on its legality, the explicit negative decision remains valid and in force.[60]

Second, an implicit negative decision exists because of the expiration of the deadline, and it is illegal. Pursuant to Article L243-3 of the Code on relations between public and administration, the implicit decision can be withdrawn either within four months from its birth, either within six months from the introduction of the individual request.

Third, an implicit negative decision exists and it is legal. The administrative authority cannot withdraw it. However, the authority can adopt a positive explicit decision, and this will be considered as abrogating the implicit decision (abrogation having "only" for effect to remove the future effects of the act, and not the past ones). It can do that at any time.

4.5.3 Legal Consequences/Fictions: Finality and Enforceability

The effect of a negative implicit decision is the same as that of an explicit decision. Silence creates a fiction of an administrative decision that was taken despite the inertia of the administration. It has legal effects, which can be considered as adversarial, and is binding. Above all, and this is the main purpose of the mechanism, it constitutes a preliminary decision (*décision préalable*), which can be challenged before the administrative judge.

The implicit nature of the decision implies adjustments of application of procedural requirements, such as the duty to give reasons. As a refusal decision, it must be stating the grounds on which the decision is adopted. According to Article L232-4 of the Code on relations between the public and the administration, the lack of motivation does not make the decision illegal, whereas such motivation would have been mandatory in the case of an explicit decision. So, there is a dispense of motivation for any implicit decision. Within the period open to challenge it before the judge, i.e., two months, the individual who initiated the implicit decision may request the administrative authority to provide him/her with the grounds of the decision. The administrative authority must inform him/her of the reasons within one month of the request. In such a case, the time limit to seize the court to challenge the decision shall be extended until the end of a two-month period, having started the day on which the reasons

[60] Conseil d'Etat, 15 juillet 1964, *Dunand*.

were communicated to it. If the public authority does not communicate the grounds within one month, the implicit decision is then illegal.[61]

The individual who wants to challenge the implicit refusal shall introduce a claim before the court within two months. The central issue is then the question of the starting point of the deadline for appeal. According to Article R421-2 of the Code on relations between the public and the administration, the individual has two months from the date on which an implicit decision to reject was taken. The date of submission of the application to the administrative authority, proved by any means, shall be established in support of the appeal. In particular, the individual may request from the administrative authority a certificate proving the constitution of the implicit decision and its meaning.[62] However, the starting point of the appeal period may be extended if, within the time limit for appeal, an explicit decision is adopted. In this case, the two-month appeal period starts again from the date of adoption of the explicit decision.[63]

Another element which may affect the starting point of the deadline for an appeal in court is the general principle according to which the deadline to make an appeal starts only if the individual became aware of time limits and available appeal proceedings.[64] The implementation of this requirement may be more difficult to satisfy in the case of an implicit decision. According to Article R421-5 of the Code on relations between the public and the administration, the remedies must be indicated while notifying the decision. This mention is very important because its failure means that the time limits for appealing do not start to run, and the decision can therefore be challenged at any time.[65] However, the case law of the Council of State restricted recently the possibility to introduce an

[61] In the field of public health, the legislator has established a rule according to which the absence of communication of the reasons for an implicit decision rejecting the request for the creation of medical beds leads to the birth of an implicit decision of acceptance, see Article L6122-10 of the Code on public health; see also CAA Marseille, 15 May 2008, n° 06MA01050.

[62] Article L232-3 du Code on relations between the Public and the Administration; see Koubi (2018).

[63] Article R421-2 of the Code on relations between the Public and the Administration.

[64] General principle stated by Article R421-5 of the Code on relations between the Public and the Administration.

[65] For a negative implicit decision in tax matter: CE, 8 February 2019, n° 406555, *SARL Nick Danese Applied Research*.

action before court in such a case. In the Czabaj case,[66] where the remedies and time limits for appeal have not been indicated to the addressee of the decision, the Council of State stated that "*the addressee of the decision may not exercise judicial review beyond a reasonable period*," which has been set at one year, from "*the date on which he was notified of an express decision or from the date on which it is established that he was aware of it.*" By a decision of 18 March 2019, the Conseil d'Etat transposed this deadline to the case of negative implicit decisions. It considered that a "reasonable" period of one year is also applicable to appeals against negative implicit individual decisions, if the addressee was aware of the decision. The Council of State then specified that "Proof of such knowledge cannot result solely from time spending from the submission of the application. It may, however, result from the fact that it is established either that the person concerned was clearly informed of the conditions of birth of an implicit decision when submitting his request, or that the implicit decision was subsequently expressly mentioned during exchanges between the individual and administration, in particular in case of an internal appeal against that decision." The starting point of the "reasonable time" is either the date of birth of the implicit decision or the date of the event establishing that the individual became aware of the decision.[67]

If an action for annulment against the negative implicit decision is introduced before court, the judge will review it as any explicit administrative decision. The individual must, when bringing the matter before the Court, provide proof of the existence of the implicit decision of rejection, either by the notification that the application has been lodged (the individual will be able to use the certificate issued by administration, upon his/her request[68]) or by the notification, if it exists, of the decision of rejection. If the judge considers that the negative implicit decision is illegal, it will be annulled, and its effects will disappear ex tunc. If the individual wants to have a positive decision, he/she will have to re-start all the proceedings, from the administrative stage, and submit a request before the administrative authority. Indeed, the administrative judge has no power to adopt a decision to replace the administrative decision.

[66] CE, 13 juillet 2016, *Epoux Czabaj*, n° 387763.

[67] CE, 18 March 2019, n° 417270.

[68] See Article L232-3 of the Code on relations between the Public and the Administration: "The implicit decision of acceptance shall be the subject, upon the request of the individual concerned, of a certificate issued by the administrative authority."

Through case law, the administrative courts have developed the potential to "rescue" an unlawful decision from annulment. In the *El Bahi* case, the decision was illegal since it was based on a wrong legal or factual ground. However, the public authority would adopt the same decision, once it was grounded on the correct legal or factual basis. In order to avoid what is then considered as a "useless" annulment, the court can change the legal or factual ground,[69] by referring to the lawful ones, while dismissing the claim. According to the *El Bahi* case, the requirements to substitute the legal grounds are the following: The provision which will be substituted must have an "equivalent scope" to the legal basis wrongfully used; the administrative authority must hold the same margin of discretion; and the applicant must have benefitted from the guarantees (formal and procedural) he would have had if the correct legal basis had been applied. The parties must also have the opportunity to comment on the substitution before the court carries it out. But, there is one important limit to the power of substitution: The court cannot substitute its own decision for the illegal decision. Indeed, the possibility to substitute the legal or factual grounds of a decision is conditioned by the fact that this substitution has no consequences on the substance of the final decision.

Generally, an annulment ruling does not indicate precisely which measures are to be adopted to enforce it, leaving the administration free to decide how to use its margin of discretion. However, the court may provide for guidance addressed to the public authorities when reconsidering the case of the claimant. In some cases, as the *Société Toulouse Football Club*[70] case, the administrative courts may also state clearly what the administrative authority should do to comply with the ruling.

Moreover, when an action for annulment is lodged against a decision, the court may, at the same time as pronouncing the annulment of the challenged decision, issue an injunction. In France, there has traditionally been a reluctance to provide the courts with injunctive powers, as this was seen as an encroachment upon the powers of the administration. According to the old position of case law, the administrative courts could not depart from the fundamental principle according to which "it is not for the administrative court to address injunctions to the

[69] CE, 6 February 2004, *Hallal*, n° 240560.

[70] CE, 25 June 2001, Société Toulouse Football Club v National Football League, n° 234363.

administration."[71] However, the absence of explicit powers of injunction was criticized in the doctrine.[72] The adoption of the Law of 8 February 1995[73] provided the administrative courts with powers to grant injunctive relief grounded on three new provisions of the Code on administrative justice, namely Article L911-1 to Article L911-3. Two conditions are to be met for an applicant to be able to seek an injunction. First, an applicant must request the injunction. Second, the case must fall within the scope of application of Articles L911-1 and L911-2. These provisions require that either the administrative authority has to adopt a specific decision in order to implement the ruling (Article L911-1) or the authority has to take a new decision, after having reconsidered the case (Article L911-2). However, the judge has the power to order the adoption of a specific measure only in case where the administration has no remaining discretion to adopt the act and determine its content, either within Article L911-1 or Article L911-2. Whenever an administrative authority is given a margin of discretion, an injunction could only require the reconsideration of the case, but should not determine the content of the decision to be taken by the authority. For example, in the case *Haras d'Achères*,[74] the Council of State did not order to the public authority to grant a building permit, but only to reconsider the request of the applicant within a time period of two months. The administrative judge also made use of the power of injunction in case where the government failed to adopt the regulatory acts to implement legislation within a reasonable deadline, taking into account the specificity and the complexity of each case.[75]

Moreover, the court can order a recurring penalty pursuant to Article L911-3 of the Code on administrative justice, the amount of which has to be paid until the judgment is complied with, according to a deadline defined by the order. The determination of the amount of penalty is at

[71] This formula is frequently used by the administrative judge himself, see CE, 22 November 1968, *Miss Y.*, n° 67843.

[72] See Rivero (1962) and Moderne (1990).

[73] Law n° 95-125 of 8 February 1995 on the organization of courts and civil, criminal and proceedings (*Loi relative à l'organisation des juridictions et à la procédure civile, pénale et administrative*, JORF n° 34 du 9 février 1995, p. 2175). See also Sauvé (2014).

[74] CE, 7 February 2003, *Haras d'Achères*, n° 220215.

[75] CE, 26 July 1996, *Association lyonnaise de protection des locataires*, n° 160515; CE, 28 July 2000, *Association France Nature Environnement*, n° 204024. See Deffigier (2003).

the discretion of the administrative court. The penalty must be paid partly to the applicant and partly transferred to the State budget.

4.6 The Positive Silence

4.6.1 The Legal Character of Prescribed Deadlines

Positive silence is the new principle stated by Article L231-1 of the Code on relations between public and administration. It reverses the old principle of negative silent. However, as stated before, the rule is not so new. Even before the adoption of the law, there were numerous exceptions (about 500) meaning that the "new" rule concerning the meaning of silence has already been known in the French legal system. Then, once the amendment has been adopted, it was still possible to provide for exceptions to the new rule. Thus, this new rule would not increase the number of cases of positive silence. Proof of the uncertainty and complexity brought by the reform, the legislator immediately provides for the need for editing a website, listing all the cases of positive silence, which seems at the same time questions the scope of the principle and the interest to set up such a principle.

The existence of a positive implicit decision depends on the expiration of the deadline of two months, as a principle. In case of emergency, the deadline may be shorter.[76] On the contrary, it may be longer in case of a need of deeper investigation. It shows that to this extent positive silent implies to go deeper in the examination of the request, since the implicit decision will create rights.

The starting point of the time limit is the day when the request has been lodged before the administrative authority. It ends two months later, whatever the day is. The deadline is counting according to calendar days. Article L114-3 of the Code on relations between the Public and Administration provides for a case of prorogation of the deadline, only applicable to the request for a positive implicit decision. If the request has been lodged before the incompetent authority, the latter is under an obligation to transmit the decision to the competent authority,[77] and, it is only then

[76] Article D. 1332-5 of the Code on Public Health: a one-month silence kept by the administrative authority is an authorization of derogation to the applicable norms of swimming waters.

[77] Article L114-2 of the Code on relations between the Public and the Administration.

that the time limit to have an implicit decision will start. It shows that in case of positive silence, there is a special attention paid to the fact that the competent administrative authority would have enough time to decide on the case. Also in case of positive implicit decision, the time limit can be prorogated and suspended if the administrative authority asks the individual for new documents, necessary to decide upon the request, until the individual delivers the requested documents.[78] Consequently, the positive implicit decision can exist much after the deadline of two months. Indeed, the legislation did not provide for specific deadline applicable to the administrative authority or to the individual while exchanging those documents.[79]

4.6.2 The Possibility to Issue a Valid Act After the Deadline Expired

Unlike the negative implicit decision, a positive implicit decision creates rights for individuals. Consequently, in compliance with legal certainty requirements, the possibilities to challenge such a decision, noticeably by issuing an act after the deadline expired, are restricted. They are limited in case where the positive implicit decision is illegal. A legal decision creating individual rights can only be challenged before the judge by third parties, and never by administrative authorities themselves. However, according to Article L242-4 of the Code on relations between the public and the administration, "Upon the request of the beneficiary of the decision, the administration may, without time limit, repeal or withdraw a decision creating rights, even a legal one, if its withdrawal or repeal is not likely to affect the rights of third parties and if it is to replace it with a decision more favourable to the beneficiary." Such a request will be relevant only if there is a chance for the individual to get a more favorable decision.[80]

In the event that the implicit decision of acceptance is illegal, the administrative authority, on its own initiative or upon the request of a third party, may repeal or withdraw it within four months following the birth of the implicit decision.[81] If the addressee of the decision requests

[78] Article L114-3 of the Code on relations between the Public and the Administration.

[79] Deguergue (2015).

[80] Eveillard (2015) and Seiller (2016).

[81] Article L242-1 of the Code on relations between the Public and the Administration.

it, then the administrative authority is under an obligation to do so.[82] It is worth mentioning that the 2013 reform also amended the rules applicable to the withdrawal of administrative decisions, unifying the applicable regime for explicit and implicit decisions, and making them simple.

So, the administrative authority may, pursuant to those conditions, adopt an opposite decision to the initial implicit decision or a more favorable one. However, if an appeal is lodged against the decision, the administrative authority loses the possibility to withdraw the decision.

4.6.3 Legal Consequences/Fictions: Finality and Enforceability

After the expiry of the deadline, silence kept means the adoption of an individual administrative decision, with the same consequences as for an explicit decision. It may therefore confer rights on the applicant or third parties. Therefore, where appropriate, the authorized activity may be carried out. The positive implicit decision does not need to be proven. However, at the end of the deadline, the individual may request from the competent administrative authority a certificate of the implicit decision of acceptance. It should be noted here that a priori the individual does not need such a certificate for litigation purposes, since the individual will not lodge an appeal challenging a favorable decision. As the Council of State points out in its report, there is no time limit for issuing the reception notice, and its absence does not prevent the implicit decision of acceptance from existing from a legal point of view, and so, being enforceable. However, if the administrative authority challenges the implicit decision, and the possibility to perform activities on its ground, the individual will have to proof that he/she initiated a request and the date of the request, by any means. Consequently, being in possession of the reception notice or of the certification might be helpful!

Administrative authority shall complete specific formalities to ensure that the positive implicit decision is made public to third parties. Thus, Article L232-2 of the Code on relations between the public and the administration provides that the competent administrative authority must publish the initial request, if necessary by electronic means, indicating the date on which it will be deemed accepted if no express decision has been taken. However, this requirement does not seem fully favorable to third

[82] Article L242-3 of the Code on relations between the Public and the Administration.

parties, who may spend long hours on Internet to find any print of an implicit decision, and then, risk to overtake the deadline of two months to go to court.[83]

The scope of positive silence is rather limited. Decisions that may affect the rights of third parties, or the exercise of fundamental rights, are generally excluded from the scope of the principle of positive silence, such as decisions that have a financial impact. Traditionally, there was a fear and a reluctance toward positive silence, seeing as granting rights because of the inertia of the administration. One important criticism is that it makes individual interests to prevail over general interests since the administrative authority is not anymore in a position to balance them.[84] Indeed, under the previous rule, the administrative authority was guaranteed that an absence of action would not commit itself to anything and would not grant any right. If the applicant wanted a positive decision, he then had to lodge an intra administrative objection or an action before the judge. Therefore, the applicable regime to positive silent is stricter, noticeably concerning the starting point of the implicit decision.[85]

4.7 Supervision of the Administrative Timeliness

As explained before, access to judge in case of infringement of the requirement to act within a reasonable time is if a limited interest. In the case of action for annulment, the annulment of administrative decisions on this ground is pretty rare. Action in damages seems more adequate.[86]

The promotion of respect of administrative timeliness and action in due time, upstream, seems more relevant. In terms of internal administrative policy, this requirement has been more and more taken into consideration, and implied different types of measures to improve administrative functioning toward this objective. Noticeably, while amending the rules on administrative silence, one of the objectives of the 2013 reform was

[83] See Deguergue (2015): It seems that "the legislator wanted to reduce the litigation generated by implicit decisions and therefore favoured an administrative logic, which should encourage the Administration to respond expressly to the request."

[84] Cassia (2015).

[85] Chapus (2008).

[86] See below.

to speed decision-making process, and the production of administrative decisions.[87]

Concerning individual decisions, the requirement to act and to reply to individual petition within a reasonable time is part of the code on conduct applicable to public services.[88]

From a wider perspective, the need for speed is constantly reaffirmed, grounding structural and functioning administrative reforms. It is part of the quest for always greater efficiency of public action.[89] The compliance with deadlines is one of the indicators to assess performance of public action. The question of compliance with deadlines is a central aspect of the managerial culture of performing public action,[90] and introduced by the Loi organique related to Finance Act in 2001,[91] which introduced a performance approach in the French public sector.[92] It is now part of the bigger issue of legitimacy of public institutions, which has implied reform and modification of the internal organization.[93]

From the personal perspective of the civil servant, as any other legal obligations, the timeliness requirement shall be complied with by any civil servants. To a certain extent, in case of a repetitive behavior, a disciplinary fault cannot in principle be characterized because of the lack of intention, but it would be rather a professional deficiency. It can be sanctioned by the dismissal of the civil servant.[94] But, we should stress that it seems hardly possible to reach such scenario. Indeed, the delays in administrative action are not originated only in individual behavior but are rather the combination of various factors (lack of human resources, in adaptation of competencies, misunderstanding of the meaning of reforms...). It seems more likely that a persistent behavior would be, in a certain

[87] Backes et al. (2010).

[88] See Articles 7 and 8 of the Marianne Charter (Charte Marianne), available at https://www.modernisation.gouv.fr/etudes-et-referentiels/referentiels/le-referentiel-marianne-nouvelle-version.

[89] Chevallier (2000).

[90] Baudot (2015).

[91] Loi organique n° 2001-692 du 1 août 2001 relative aux lois de finances.

[92] Calmette (2006) and Demeestere and Orange (2008).

[93] For a study of the management of deadline in a public service of allowance of social benefits: see Baudot (2015).

[94] Article 70 of Loi n° 84-16 du 11 janvier 1984, portant dispositions statutaires relatives à la fonction publique de l'Etat.

way, sanctioned, through the reduction of premiums, knowing that those premiums are granted with regard to the results of an administrative department and not of one civil servant.

4.8 Legal Remedies

4.8.1 Administrative Appeal

Individuals are always entitled, unless special legislation has created special procedures, to first bring their complaints against an administrative act before the author of the act (*recours grâcieux*) or before his/her direct supervisor (*recours hiérarchique*) the minister, who is superior, and to appeal through litigation only when the complaint has been rejected. The nature of this objection procedure is, however, predominantly facultative; yet regarding certain administrative decisions, an administrative appeal procedure is of obligatory character before bringing a claim to court. If the individual is the addressee of the contested decision, he or she will be entitled to bring an objection procedure. If this is not the case, he or she will have to prove to have a sufficient interest in the procedure. According to Article L411-2 of the Code on relations between the public and the administration, any administrative decision may be appealed against within two months. In that case, the deadline to lodge an appeal before court is extended. It shall not start running again until the administrative appeal has been rejected. On the opposite, if following the administrative appeal, the request of the individual is successful; the action in court is pointless. There is no specified time for the administrative authority to reply to the appeal; however, generally after 2 months, silence on the part of the administration creates a decision that can be appealed. The decision of the authorities is fully reconsidered at the objection procedure stage, including its merits. Article L411-4 of the Code on Relations between the public and the administration states that “The administrative authority shall decide on the appeal lodged against a decision creating rights on the basis of the factual and legal situation prevailing at the date of that decision. In the event of an appeal against a decision that does not create rights, it shall be based on the factual and legal situation prevailing on the date on which it decides on the appeal.” The decision on the objection procedure may result in a worse decision for the applicant.

So, administrative appeal is a way open to individuals to challenge administrative decision. Since the decision is fully reviewed at this stage, the applicant can raise points related to the infringement of deadlines or reasonable deadlines requirements. However, at this stage, it seems rather unlikely that it would lead to the repeal of the decision, if the content of the decision would not have been different.[95]

4.8.2 *Judicial Review*

As mentioned before, although the requirement related to the compliance of deadline, or the obligation to decide within a reasonable time are binding on the administrative authorities, and thus, are reviewed by the administrative judge in judicial review (recours en excès de pouvoir), it leads very rarely to the annulment of the administrative decision. On the one hand, the judge is quite reluctant to limit the margin of discretion of the competent administrative authorities, especially in this area which is widely a matter of internal management and organization. On the other hand, an infringement of procedural rule only leads to the annulment of the decision if this infringement has consequences on the content of the decision or has deprived individuals from procedural safeguards.[96] Hence, infringement of deadline requirements will ground the annulment of an administrative decision, only in case of excessive delay in administrative action.

Silence kept by administrative authority shall not be regarded automatically as an obstacle to judicial review. It is precisely the *raison d'être* of the implicit decisions mechanism. Indeed, silence kept constitutes an implicit decision, which may be regarded as an administrative decision (decision préalable) then challengeable before the judge. However, in the case where the deadline to adopt a decision is expressly stated, if the administrative authority does not adopt a decision within the time limit, judicial review is not accessible. Indeed, in this case, no implicit decision could be constituted. Furthermore, there is no judicial action in case of inaction from the administrative authorities.[97] But, in this case, individual might find a way to get access to the judge. He/she needs to introduce an

[95] See below.

[96] CE, 23 December 2011, *Danthony*, n° 335033.

[97] Cassia (2015).

internal appeal before the competent administrative authority, asking it to act. In case of silence kept by the administrative authority for two months, a refusal implicit decision exists, and then can be challenged before the judge, who will review the legality of refusal of action. Nevertheless, if applicable, annulment of the refusal decision may have limited effects for the situation of individual.

4.8.3 Court Remedies for Silent Rejection and Silent Approval

Court remedies to challenge implicit decisions are limited to judicial review and action in liability, which will be detailed below.

From a general perspective, according to Article 11 of the Code on administrative justice, "Judgments are enforceable," meaning that the administrative authority has to adopt all the measures to comply with the ruling. An excessive delay in the execution of a court decision renders the State liable.[98] However, the question of enforcement is most often about the understanding of the ruling and what it implies, than the persis tent unwillingness of the administrative authority. That's why, sometimes, the administrative judge decides to provide for guidance in its ruling, in order to "help" the administrative authority while enforcing the judgment. Obviously, when a ruling is about the annulment of an implicit decision, it may seem less easy to define what its enforcement implies.

Once the administrative judge rules that a negative implicit decision is illegal and annuls it, the ruling is binding on administrative authority. As a negative decision is concerned, the ruling does not affect legal order or impacts directly the addressee of the implicit decision. Indeed, the ruling has no effect to replace the decision. The individual, if she/he still wants to get a positive decision, will have to reintroduce a request before the administrative authority, and so, to restart the proceedings ab initio. The administrative authority will have to reconsider the request. While challenging the implicit refusal decision, the individual may ask the judge for adopting injunction to order the administrative authority to reconsider the request, but not indicating what the content of the decision would

[98] CE, 23 June 2014, *M. Wespelaere*, n° 369946.

be.[99] The administrative judge can also impose fines, if the administrative authority persists by not adopting the expected measures.[100]

As a positive decision is concerned, and is annulled, it has for effect to withdraw if from the legal order ex tunc, meaning that all the effects already performed should be erased. This means for example that the activity authorized implicitly shall be stopped, since it is then illegal. In case of annulment of positive decision, there is no point to ask for injunction (especially because here the addressee will not be one of the applicants), since it does not imply specific reaction from the administrative authority.

4.8.4 Right to Compensation—Damages

Right to compensation is accessible for individuals, before administrative judge, in case they can claim for a damage caused by administrative acts or actions. The French public liability system is based on fault (*faute simple*), which is understood broadly. Furthermore, the claimant needs to prove the existence of damage and a causal link between the administrative act or action and the damage. When damage results from an administrative decision, any violation of the law is considered in and by itself as a fault.[101] No further evidence of fault is needed. However, illegality will not lead to liability, where it appears that a decision, which is only illegal because of procedural flaws, is justified in fact and in substance.[102] Consequently, the violation of the requirement to act in due time may be regarded as a fault, only if the delay is excessive.

Indeed, delays are not systematically considered as fault because the administrative authority does not have a general obligation to act in due time. The judge will only sanction delays if they are excessive or abusive. But there is no prefixed time limit, everything will depend on the circumstances, and on what it is considered by the judge as a "normal" deadline for action. In the case law, examples of liability found because of excessive delays are mostly about delays in acting, not in decision-making. They are

[99] See above.

[100] See above.

[101] CE, Sect., 26 January 1973, *Ville de Paris c/Driancourt*, n° 84768.

[102] CE, 15 July 1964, *Prat-Flottes*, n° 59536.

numerous noticeably in medical matters,[103] or related to delay of public authority to provide individuals for the assistance of police forces in order to enforce a decision (i.e., eviction from housing).[104] Concerning delay in decision-making, the main hypothesis is about the adoption of regulatory decisions implementing laws. The administrative judge considers that one-year delay to adopt such measures is a fault, which may ground the liability of the State.[105]

With regard to third parties who would be affected by an implicit authorization decision, there are no specific requirements for liability, in case the implicit decision is illegal. If a third party wants to ask for compensation because of a legal implicit decision, special regime is applying. Lawful action of the administrative authority can also cause state liability. But damages are granted exceptionally, in case a lawful decision would cause special and abnormal damages. The liability regime is then grounded on equality principle. Due to the very strict conditions to be fulfilled, it is very hard to get compensation on this ground.

4.8.5 The Role of the Ombudsman

In the French system, the Defender of Rights performs the function of Ombudsman.[106] Its task aims at ensuring that administrative authorities comply with the rights and freedoms. The Defender of Rights may amicably resolve the disputes that are brought to his attention via mediation. Any individual can send a complaint to the Defender of Rights, whose decisions are not legally binding upon the public authorities.

Basically, the Defender of Rights is competent to investigate complaints related to delays. In its annual reports, the Defender of Rights pointed out several failures in the functioning of administrative department, and public services.

The cases are mainly related to the question of access to social rights and social benefits. In the 2018 Activity report, the Defender of rights

[103] See, for example, Cour administrative d'appel de Paris, 2 May 2017, *M. A.*, n° 15PA00325; Cour administrative d'appel de Marseille, 30 March 2017, *Centre hospitalier d'Avignon*, n° 16MA02034.

[104] CE, 27 January 2010, n° 320642; CE, 21 January 2011, n° 339647.

[105] CE, 27 November 1964, *Veuve Renard*, n° 59068; CE, 27 July 2005, n° 261694.

[106] Article 71-1 of the French Constitution; Organic Law no. 2011-333 of 29 March 2011 on the Defender of Rights.

stressed the silence kept by the administrative authorities in case of request related to those topics is an element which finally discourages the individuals to claim for those benefits (about 12% of their recipients finally do not claim for allowance they are supposed to be granted for). Half of the complaints processed by the services of the Defender of Rights, more than half were related to the lack of listening and attention paid to the points raised by the individuals, the deadline to get answers and even the absence of answer. Then, violation of education right was pointed out concerning especially Roma children,[107] or unaccompanied minors who are facing with very long deadline to get appointment with the competent authorities to get assistance.[108] So, the Defender of rights considers that the "no reply" phenomenon expands in the public services, so that users are "tossed around from a calling centre platform inaccessible to a website that is difficult to access too. To such an extent that it is now possible to wonder whether the reply, if necessary within a time frame that allows it to be relevant, is still part of the relationship with users."[109] On the basis of this statement, the Defender of Rights stresses that its institution is an alternative way which may look quite relevant for individuals to get the respect of their rights.

The role of the Defender of Rights is here central to point out the failure of public services, with regard to the management of delays, which has direct consequences on the effectiveness of rights. However, its authority is limited to the proposal of structural reforms.

[107] See, for example, decision 2018-005 of 25 January 2018 concerning a refusal to send Roma children to school by a major; decision 2018-011 of 30 March 2018 concerning a refusal of schooling by a mayor for a family hosted by an association; decision 2018-221 of 12 October 2018 concerning the refusal by the mayor to allow a child to attend a nursery school on the grounds that a procedure to expel him from the squat in which he was domiciled with his family was in progress.

[108] Decision 2018-137 of 29 April 2018 relating to the refusal by the department of a contract for the reception of a young adult in favor of an unaccompanied minor who has reached the age of majority.

[109] Defender of Rights, Annual Report for 2018, p. 28, available at https://www.defenseurdesdroits.fr/sites/default/files/atoms/files/raa-2018-num-19.02.19.pdf.

4.9 Overall Assessment of the Legal Regime and the Practice of Administrative Silence

The rule of negative silence, which was the principle in French administrative system for decades, was stated in order to grant rights to individuals, and to safeguard the right to access to judge. Classically, giving a meaning to silence is regarded as promoting the Rule of law. This rule looked necessary under French system in order to safeguard an effective access to administrative judge. Indeed, the individual is then granted with a decision, being not affected by the inertia of the public authority. Furthermore, it is a way for the individual to get within a reasonable time limit a decision and then to challenge it if necessary. However, the rule was mainly justified to protect general interest, under the review of administrative judge, rather than taking into consideration individual rights at stake. The legislative reform initiated in 2013 has for consequence to modify the meaning of silence kept by administrative authorities. From now on, "the silence kept for two months by the administrative authority upon a request means a decision of acceptance." This amendment has been widely criticized, considering the law was drafted in a context of emergency, while generating more complexities than simplification.[110] Indeed, the amendment was drafted in the context of the codification process of administrative proceedings.

After a few years of enforcement, it is possible to take a look at the situation.

First, the reversing of the rule dealing with the meaning of silence appeared quite brutal from the administrative authorities point of view.[111] It has really changed the way of managing proceedings, implying adaptation from the public department. However, clearly, in a context of constant downsizing of civil servants, it seems that the human resources are lacking to enforce a new role of investigator, especially in particularly complex decision-making process.

[110] Braconnier et al. (2013).

[111] Pauliat (2013): If certain provisions contained therein were expected, in light of the main principles laid down by the inter-ministerial committees for the modernization of public action, such as, for example, the adoption of the legislative part of a Code on relations between administrations and the public, others have emerged as a result of a government amendment; this is the case with the principle that silence for two months by the administrative authority on an application is equivalent to a decision to accept it; see Pastor (2016).

Second, the risk is then to have counter-effects. Indeed, one idea if the rule of positive silence is to favor legal certainty, while protecting individual rights. It should be in principle a guarantee that the administrative authority would, concretely and seriously, investigate to decide upon the individual request. However, there is a huge risk that, facing difficulties to cope with the situation, especially when dealing with matters involving potentially a lot of individuals (migrants, students, pupils...), that the administrative authority would prefer adopting an explicit decision of refusal. It would be a way to preserve general interest, by adopting a decision having no effect on legal order.[112] Such a situation would completely impair the aim of the reform, by increasing the number of disputes, rather accelerating decision-making process.

Third, this huge change of philosophy might be a change for a deeply reform of the French administrative system. On the one hand, it may be an opportunity to stress the responsibility of the administration in the correct enforcement process of regulation of individual situations. Indeed, the intervention of the judge shall be the last option left to the individual to make heard his arguments. But, an efficient administration shall be able to avoid most often the litigation step. On the other hand, it is also about restoring the relationship between administrative authorities and individuals. Indeed, the compliance with deadlines and the proper investigation of individual petitions express the degree of consideration for individuals. Such an evolution would not be incompatible with the French conception of general interest, which must ensure compliance with fundamental rights and democracy and transparency requirements.

Giving a meaning to silence seems absolutely necessary for flexibility reasons of the administrative system, but shall be handled with care: the intrinsic characteristics of an administrative system may blur the sounds of silence.

References

Backes, C., Chevalier, E., Eliantonio, M., Jansen, A. M. L., Portinga, M. A., & Seerden, R. J. G. H. (2010). Versnelling besluitvorming over complexe projecten – niet alleen in Nederland een hot issue Nerderlands! *Tijdschrift voor Bestuursrecht*, 58–66.

[112] Seiller (2014).

Baudot, P.-Y. (2015). L'invention des délais - Pourquoi l'administration doit-elle répondre dans les temps? *Revue des politiques sociales et familiales*, 5–18.

Braconnier, S., Cassia, P., Gonod, P., Petit, J., Plessix, B., & Seiller, B. (2013). Le silence de l'administration vaudra acceptation. Big Bang ou trou noir juridique? *JCP*, 2309–2310.

Calmette, J.-F. (2006). La loi organique relative aux lois de finances (LOLF): un texte, un esprit, une pratique. *Revue française d'Administration Publique, 117*, 43–55.

Cassia, P. (2015). Silence de l'administration: le "choc de complexification". *Dalloz*, 201.

Chapus, R. (2008). *Droit du contentieux administratif*. Paris: LGDJ.

Chevalier, E. (2014). *Bonne administration et Union européenne – Contribution à l'étude de l'espace administratif européen*. Bruxelles: Bruylant.

Chevallier, J. (2000). L'accélération de l'action administrative. In P. Gerard, F. Ost, & M. Van de Kerchove (Eds.), *L'accélération du temps juridique* (pp. 489–508). Bruxelles: Presses universitaires de Saint Louis.

Chevallier, J. (2007). Le Conseil d'Etat, au coeur de l'Etat. *Pouvoirs, 123*, 5–17.

Council of State. (2014). *L'application du nouveau principe "silence de l'administration vaut acceptation"* (Annual Report). Paris: La Documentation française.

Deffigier, C. (2003). L'obligation pour le gouvernement de prendre les règlements d'application de la loi littoral (à propos de l'arrêt du Conseil d'Etat du 28 juillet 2000, Association France Nature Environnement). *Revue Française de Droit Administratif*, 116–125.

Deguergue, M. (2015). Le silence de l'administration. *Les Cahiers de droit, 3/4*, 389–410. Available at https://id.erudit.org/iderudit/1034456ar.

Demeestere, R., & Orange, G. (2008). Gestion publique: qu'est-ce qui a changé depuis 25 ans? *Politiques et Management Public, 27*, 127–147.

Denoix de Saint Marc, R. (1998). Le silence de l'administration. In IFSA, *Droits et attentes des citoyens* (p. 123). Paris: La Documentation française.

Derosier, J.-P. (2014). La nouvelle règle "le silence vaut acceptation" si rarement applicable. *JCPA*, 14–16.

Eveillard, G. (2015). La codification des règles de retrait et d'abrogation des actes administratifs unilatéraux. *Actualité Juridique du Droit Administratif*, 2474–2484.

Froger, C. (2016). Le cantonnement des dérogations au principe du « silence vaut acceptation ». *Actualité Juridique du Droit Administratif*, 1986–1991.

Koubi, G. (2018). Le « silence attesté ». In G. Koubi, L. Cluzel-Métayer, & W. Tamzini (Eds.), *Lectures critiques du Code des relations entre le public et l'administration* (pp. 211–224). Paris: LGDJ.

Lafaix, J.-F. (2012). Le sens du silence. *Revue du Droit Public*, 1032–1054.

McCleave Cake, H. (1972). The French Conseil d'État—An Essay on Administrative Jurisprudence. *Administrative Law Review, 24*(3), 315–334.

Moderne, F. (1990). Etrangère au pouvoir du juge, l'injonction, pourquoi le serait-elle? *Revue Française de Droit Administratif*, 798–821.

Pastor, J.-M. (2016). Le silence vaut accord: une revolution administrative à la peine. *Actualité Juridique du Droit Administratif*, 1892.

Pauliat, H. (2013). Le silence gardé par l'administration vaut acceptation: un principe en trompe-l'oeil? *JCPA, 38*, 737.

Ribes, D. (2014). Le nouveau principe « silence de l'administration vaut acceptation ». *Actualité Juridique du Droit Administratif*, 389–394.

Rivero, J. (1962). Le Huron au Palais-Royal ou réflexions naïves sur le recours pour excès de pouvoir. *Dalloz*, 37–40.

Sauvé, J.-M. (2014). *L'injonction – la loi du 8 février 1995 après vingt ans de pratique*. Available at http://www.conseil-etat.fr/Actualites/Discours-Interventions/L-injonction-la-loi-du-8-fevrier-1995-apres-vingt-ans-de-pratique.

Seiller, B. (2014). Quand les exceptions infirment [heureusement] la règle: le sens du silence de l'administration. *Revue Française de Droit Administratif*, 35–42.

Seiller, B. (2016). La sortie de vigueur des actes administratifs. *Revue Française de Droit Administratif*, 58–68.

Sirinelli, J. (2011). La transposition de la directive Services, l'expression d'une nouvelle approche de l'intervention publique en matière économique. *Revue Du Droit Public, 4*, 883–919.

Sordi, B. (2017). Révolution, Rechtsstaat and the Rule of Law: Historical Reflections on the Emergence and Development of Administrative Law. In P. Lindseth & S. Rose-Ackerman (Eds.), *Comparative Administrative Law* (2nd ed., pp. 23–37). Cheltenham: Edward Elgar.

CHAPTER 5

Legal Instruments to Confront Administrative Inaction in Belgium: A Gift for the Citizen but a Curse for the Government?

Bengt Verbeeck, Ivo Carlens, Jurgen Neuts, and Ludo M. Veny

5.1 The Legal and Administrative Background for Analyzing the Administrative Silence

5.1.1 The Distribution of Administrative Competence Within the Legal-Administrative Tradition in Belgium

When the Kingdom of Belgium gained its independence from the UK of the Netherlands in 1831, it was a decentralized unitary state: There

Ludo M. Veny: Deceased

B. Verbeeck (✉)
University College Ghent, Ghent, Belgium
e-mail: bengt.verbeeck@hogent.be

I. Carlens · J. Neuts · L. M. Veny
Ghent University, Ghent, Belgium
e-mail: ivo.carlens@ugent.be

D. C. Dragos et al. (eds.),
The Sound of Silence in European Administrative Law,
https://doi.org/10.1007/978-3-030-45227-8_5

was a central government, there were 9 provinces and there were 2739 municipalities. From the 1970s on, the state reform has started, and it has proved to be an ongoing process of devolution that yet has not come to its end. From 1993 on, Belgium is officially a federal state.

This Belgian federal state consists of communities and regions. These, in turn, are at the root of law within the powers allocated to them under the Constitution and by certain special laws, i.e., the special law act of 1980. The communities and regions are competent to draw up acts, called decrees (ordinances in the Brussels-Capital Region). The regional and community governments must enforce all enacted decrees and ordinances.

Actually, Belgium is also divided into 10 provinces[1] and 581 municipalities. At the corresponding levels, provincial and municipal councils also enact regulations and ordinances in the fields for which they are responsible. The provincial executive (Deputation)[2] and municipal executive (College of Burgomaster and Aldermen)[3] implement these regulations (as well as higher norms such as acts, decrees, ordinances, and orders, within the limits of their powers). Judicial power is not divided in this way. Organization of the courts is solely a federal responsibility.

So, in Belgium, there are 6 parliaments and 6 governments. Laws and decrees can be reviewed by the Constitutional Court. All other decisions issued by governmental bodies and by provincial and local government can be reviewed by the Council of State, the highest administrative court, created by the law act of December 23, 1946. Although this Council of State was traditionally described as part of the executive power, this was not experienced that way: The Council of State was in no way dependent on the executive power to fulfill its task and it displayed great impartiality and independence, and almost immediately grew into the highest independent court in the administration.

J. Neuts
e-mail: jurgen.neuts@ugent.be

[1] The former province Brabant was split up into Flemish Brabant and Walloon Brabant in 1995.

[2] "Provincial College" in the Walloon part of Belgium, "Deputation" in the Flemish part of Belgium.

[3] "Municipal College" in the Walloon part of Belgium, "CBA" in the Flemish part of Belgium and in the Brussel Capital Region.

From 1993 on, the new article 160 of the Belgian constitution stipulates that there is a Council of State for all of Belgium, whose composition, authority, and functioning are determined by law, with the understanding that the law can grant the King the power to organize jurisdiction in accordance with its given principles.

Following its incorporation into the Constitution, it was emphasized that the Council does not belong to the "Judiciary," as is the case for the ordinary courts and tribunals, but neither can it simply be considered a part of the executive power, as had been positioned in the preceding decades. To the contrary, the Council of State has a *sui generis* status.[4]

5.1.2 The Broader Social/Cultural Context of Understanding Timeliness of Administrative Procedure

In 1831, the Constituent Assembly opted for a compromise system to ensure the legal protection of the citizen against the administration. Initially, they started from a monistic system of legal protection. They did not, however, wish to exclude definitively the possibility of establishing administrative courts in Belgium, which would handle administrative disputes.

The rule of law was one of the main features in the first Belgian constitution, and one aspect of administrative silence appeared in Belgian legislation yet in 1860: Article 150 of the Municipal Law Act gave citizens of a municipality the right to take legal action on behalf of the municipality in cases where the municipal council failed to act. This "substitution" provision was in fact one of the earliest legal instruments allowing citizens to act against administrative silence or more specifically in this case against the inaction of local governments.

The shift from a nineteenth-century "night-watchman state" into a twentieth-century "welfare state" made its activities grow tremendously; the number of potential conflicts between the citizen and the state increased making the state increasingly vulnerable and its actions to be considered less self-evident.

Of course, in present time, the abovementioned substitution provision, recently abolished by the Flemish legislator, is no longer the only example in Belgian law of a legal instrument that can be used by a citizen

[4] Van Damme (2001, p. 74).

to react against administrative inaction. Belgian administrative procedural law, e.g., makes it possible for a citizen to lodge an appeal with the Council of State against the continuing "silence of an administration" (cf. infra nr. 2.2).

By the time the constitution was coordinated in 1994, the Belgian system of legal protection in administrative disputes has developed into a rather French like, dualistic model. The thus developed mixed system of legal protection has led to the fact that at present, certain disputes in Belgium involving the administration can only be heard by ordinary courts, that other disputes can be submitted only to a specific administrative court and that in certain cases, albeit infrequent, both the judicial and the administrative courts are involved in the jurisdictional procedure.

As more administrative procedures were gradually established, and the principles of administrative law emerged, the notion of timeliness became more and more important.

5.1.3 The Main Principles of Administrative Law Regarding Timeliness of Administrative Procedures

Timeliness has always played an important role in Belgian administrative procedural law, and principles of good administration are, for some decades yet, intrinsic to the system. The traditional principles of good administration, as emerging in legal doctrine since the 1970s and based on decisions issued by the Council of State, are: the right to be heard, due care, legitimate expectations, and proportionality.[5] These principles function as a guarantee when unilateral decisions by administrative authorities are issued and as a correction of the predominant position of the administration in relationship with the citizen.

According to the Council of State, *the right to be heard* must be applied from the moment that an administration considers taking a serious measure against a person that is based on his personal behavior, which is considered to be a shortcoming, and when the measure is of that nature that it affects severely his interests.[6] Only in a very limited number of situations, this principle is not to be applied, e.g., when it concerns very

[5] See Mast et al. (2017, pp. 56–73).

[6] CoS 27 May 2004, nr. 131.827.

simple facts.[7] The involved person should neither be heard when he had the chance to anticipate to the reasons of the new decision in a prior stage of the procedure.[8]

The due care principle implies that the administration must prepare its decision carefully. Decisions must be based on correct fact finding. The administration must inform itself sufficiently; technical decisions may force the administration to be informed by external specialists. A policy guideline cannot automatically be applied in every individual case without any additional enquiry.[9] Also, when executing its duty to inform, an administration must act carefully.[10]

The legitimate expectations principle is considered to be the counterweight for the earlier low predictability of administrative acting as a consequence of the administration's policy freedom. It is up to the administration to omit that the citizen gets frustrated due to legitimate expectations that he expects from the administration's acting. The Council of State has ruled that, when this principle is applied, the citizen must be able to rely on a fixed course of action by the authority or on commitments of promises that were done by the authority in the concrete case.[11] Three conditions were traditionally linked to this principle: a mistake by the authority, the granting of an advantage to a citizen as a consequence of this mistake, and the absence of weighty reasons to take away this advantage.[12] Other aspects of this principle are the nature/quality of the administrative body that has caused the expectations, the way this has been done, the legitimate character of the expectations, the citizen's acting as a consequence of the expectations and possible factors that resist against these expectations.[13]

The proportionality principle is frequently applied in disciplinary matters. Violation of it is usually invoked when the choice made by the authority is esteemed to be a mismatch between the general interest and the particular interest. The Council of State usually qualifies sanctions being a complete mismatch with regard to the proved facts as illegal which

[7] CoS 30 January 2015, nr. 230.037.

[8] CoS 8 August 1997, nr. 67.691.

[9] Cos 17 March 1981, nr. 21.037; 7 April 1981, nr. 21.094; 8 June 2015, nr. 231.462.

[10] CoS 21 April 2008, nr. 182.185.

[11] CoS 26 May 2015, nr. 231.330; 6 October 2015, nr. 232.435.

[12] CoS 15 June 2004, nr. 132.404; 22 January 2015, nr. 229.956.

[13] CoS 6 October 2015, nr. 232.440.

means that the administration cannot impose a sanction which would be opposed for similar facts by another administration.[14]

5.2 The Legal Framework of Administrative Timeliness

5.2.1 *Constitutional Basis?*

As the Belgian constitution does not contain many provisions on administration, it does not provide any general administrative deadline. Nor does it mention any effect of administrative silence. It often does refer to the law (in broader sense, thus also referring to decrees issued by regional and community parliaments) as the basis of rights, duties, and decisions by any authority or administration.

As to the administration, the Belgian constitution, i.e., article 162, guarantees some principles on direct election of local councils, publicity, and transparency on accounts and budgets. Finally, article 28 of the Belgian constitution must be mentioned here: It says that "everyone has the right to address petitions signed by one or more persons to the public authorities."

5.2.2 *Administrative Procedure Act or Other General Laws*

Until 1971 there was no general law act that could serve for the citizen as a legal basis to lodge his appeal against an authority that fails to decide within due deadline. Belgian public law doctrine, however, accepted that it was the Council of State's duty to examine whether the silence of the administrative authority could be interpreted as an implicit rejection.[15]

The law act of June 3, 1971, intended to guarantee a better protection against the silence by an administrative authority, as well when it concerns individual decisions as executive acts, i.e., when executing a law act. It introduced a new article that stipulates that when an administrative authority is obliged to decide and there has been no decision issued by the end of a deadline of 4 months, the silence of by the administrative authority is considered to be a dismissive decision.

[14] CoS 20 February 1990, nr. 34.108.

[15] See Mast et al. (2017, p. 1270).

Apart from this general rule, other deadlines can and must be found in different legal acts, as well issued by the federal level as by the regional, community, or local level. Most of them are in the nature of being sector-specific legislation. In these acts, the effect of administrative silence and the right to judicial review are incorporated.

On the other hand, the legal tradition rules that the lack of acting by an administrative authority when it is not obliged to do so cannot be contested.

5.2.3 Sector-Specific Legislation (Special Laws)

Timeliness is applied in several fields of administrative law, i.e., the environmental permits area, the building permits, but also in other fields such as permits to start up a commercial enterprise, the real heritage area, and social benefits.

In many cases, the legislator determines that when an administration is competent it is also obliged to take administrative legal actions in certain matters. As such, the legislator often stipulates the time period during which a decision must be taken by the administration. However, holding an administration to a particular deadline is only meaningful when there are explicitly legal consequences connected to exceeding the deadline.

Just like real decisions, fictitious decisions can either be positive (a tacit *permit* which allows the citizen to proceed with a certain action) or negative (a tacit *rejection* which often means that the citizen won't receive a certain benefit).

Examples of tacit refusal can be found in the federal Law on Transparency of April 11, 1994, which says the request to have access to an administrative document should be considered to be rejected without decision, and in past Flemish legislation on urban development.

As to social benefits, the Social Security Charter comprises strict rules about information to the requesters and contact between the social services and the requesters: When no decision has been taken within 4 months, the requested benefits should be paid, or damage interests must be added. When a request for support or right to social integration is introduced at a Public Centre for Social Welfare (PCSW), which is a local authority, and no decision has been taken after 30 days, the requested support is considered not to be granted and the citizen can lodge an appeal before the labor tribunal against this fictitious rejection within 3 months.

5.3 The Length of Administrative Deadlines

5.3.1 What Is the Length of Deadlines in General Law and in Special Laws?

It is important to note from the outset that there is no general legislation on the federal (Belgian) level which stipulates a certain fixed deadline that all administrations must adhere to when taking administrative actions. Special laws and decrees determine specific deadlines; exceeding these deadlines can have consequences concerning the legitimacy or the legality of the final decision. For a deadline to have legal consequences, these consequences must be explicitly mentioned in the same regulation which stipulates the deadlines. If there are no consequences stipulated, then the administration can in theory still act even when it exceeds the time limit and this until the moment a higher administrative authority, an appeal body or an administrative court acts with regard to the same subject matter.

To determine whether a "reasonable deadline" is exceeded or not, the Council of State will take into account the possibility for an administration to gather all necessary facts, information and advisory opinions to come to an informed, carefully considered administrative decision.[16] As such the complexity of a specific case often determines what is "reasonable."[17] However, practical or organizational problems which an administration may experience cannot be used as justification for unduly delaying an administrative decision.[18]

5.3.2 Possibilities of Prolongation (How Many Times, Communication to Petitioners)

There is no general rule on prolongation of deadlines; if the sector-specific regulation does not mention it explicitly, it is not possible to prolong the deadline.

[16] CoS 3 June 1997, nr. 66.519.

[17] CoS 19 January 1995, nr. 51.211: the Council of State found that an administration which decided on the inadmissibility of an appeal after 15 months exceeded a "reasonable deadline"; in another case, the "reasonable deadline" was deemed to be exceeded after 2 months, see CoS 8 February 2001, nr. 93.156.

[18] CoS 19 June 2014, nr. 227.766.

Some sector-specific laws do mention this possibility: In environmental permits law, e.g., a prolongation of the deadline is only possible when a new public enquiry is necessary. The administration can organize a new public enquiry or gain different advices a second time. Doing so prevents the decision to be annulled. The due deadline within which the decision has to be taken is in this case prolonged by 60 days.[19] This prolongation must be communicated to the applicant.

The same happens when a PCSW is not able to decide within 30 days on a request for any kind of support due to necessary information that is not supplied in due time. The decision can be delayed, must be motivated and the requester must be informed about it.

5.3.3 Counting Deadlines

There is a variety of rules stipulating the start of the deadlines. We only can mention few examples here. Generally, deadlines are calculated in *calendar days* but there are some exceptions: Article 291 Local Government Decree states that if the expiry date is on a Saturday, Sunday, or a legal holiday then the expiry date is moved to the first working day. If there is no decision or event to trigger a deadline, then the deadline is calculated backward starting with the event that ends the deadline. The day of this event is not included in the deadline. In Flemish education law with regard to elementary and secondary education, deadlines are sometimes calculated using *schooldays* as a basis instead of working days, thus excluding Saturdays, Sundays, legal holidays, and all school holidays. This is especially the case when it's a deadline the parents of a pupil must comply with.[20] There are different kinds of deadlines: Two important deadlines in this perspective are the so-called term of order and the "expiration period."

The first one is a deadline stipulated by the law within which an administrative authority must exercise a competence (e.g., deciding on a permit), but if this deadline is exceeded, there is no expiration of competence.[21] This exceeding is not sanctioned either by an annulment of the

[19] Article 32, §2 Flemish Decree of 24 April 2014 on environmental permits, further referred to as the 2014 Environment Decree

[20] Article 110/24, §1 Codex Secondary Education.

[21] SeeOpdebeek (1992, p. 79) and Van Hoorick (2011, p. 57).

issued decision[22] and the competent authority remains competent to act, however, not unlimitedly for it has the duty to act within a reasonable deadline.[23] Exceeding this reasonable deadline can lead to liability claims.[24]

The second one, the expiration period, is a deadline stipulated by the law within which an administrative authority must exercise a competence (e.g., granting a permit) under penalty of expiration of this competence.[25] When exceeding this deadline, the authority loses its competence to take a decision.[26] Some of these deadlines occur in urban planning regulations as well in first instance as on administrative appeal level[27]: "…If no decision has been taken within the term of expiration, mentioned in §1, the request is considered to be rejected."

Article 21 of the 2014 Environmental Decree[28] stipulates that the result of the inquiry (completeness and receivability) must be communicated within a deadline of 30 calendar days starting the day after the day of submission of the permit request. No decision within this deadline means the request is valid. Then, a new deadline of 105 (or 120) days starts on the day after the request is declared valid or silently on the 30th day after introduction of the request.

On the Flemish level, too, there are some major general decrees, e.g., Local Government Decree, Flemish Government Decree, and some codifications, e.g. Codex Higher Education, Codex Spatial Planning, in which the use and calculation of deadlines are—to a certain degree—streamlined within the context of said legislation, but even then, there is no "standardised" deadline. Again, the specific subject matter determines which deadline must be followed, even within the same general decree or codification.

[22] CoS 17 December 2014, nr. 209.855; CoS 24 October 2011, nr. 215.967.

[23] Opdebeek (2015, p. 159).

[24] Lust (2003, p. 859).

[25] Opdebeek (1992, p. 79).

[26] CoS 12 November 2008, nr. 187.846; CoS 7 February 2013, nr. 222.423.

[27] Maes (2015, p. 134).

[28] Flemish Decree of 24 April 2014 on environmental permits, further referred to as the 2014 Environment Decree.

5.3.4 *The Concept of "Reasonable" Deadline*

The concept of "reasonable deadline" has been developed and influenced by European Law. The provision of the ECHR on reasonable deadline (article 6 §1), drafted in 1950, was the first to introduce the "time" factor in connection with justice on a statutory level. Being much more than a simple recommendation, this article stipulates that every judge is bound to treat a case within a reasonable deadline. The Court of Justice prefers evaluating the duration of the single separate phases. It is important to stress that as to the ECHR's case law, every case is a story to itself, and the Court examines each case in order to decide whether in the actual situation there has been a breach of the reasonable time clause. Step by step, this principle was applied in other legal branches, such as administrative law.[29] Today it is taken for granted that this principle is part of the general principles of good administration.[30] However, the provision of article 6§1 ECHR must be distinguished from the reasonable deadline as a principle of good administration.[31]

The violation of treaties (ratified by the federal parliament) can be invoked before any tribunal, court, or judicial body. In 2012, the Council of State ruled that a deadline of 10 or 11 months, taken into account the complexity of the case, was not unreasonable. Recent judgments of the Council of State show that this concept is still valuable and applied in different procedures. In 2016, the Council of State ruled that the exceeding of the reasonable deadline does not lead to a loss of competence by the Council of Permit litigations as this body *must* decide.[32] So, this body must take a decision.

5.4 Responses to Administrative Silence

5.4.1 *The Prevailing Model: Positive or Negative*

Although the *Lex silencio positivo* technique exists in Belgium in some very specific domains, is not applied very often (cf. infra nr. 6). Generally spoken, Belgian doctrine and jurisprudence are very dismissive toward this

[29] Marneffe et al. (2011, p. 10).

[30] De Taeye (2002, p. 172).

[31] Opdebeek (1992, pp. 110–111).

[32] CoS 29 March 2016, nr. 234.284.

technique as the Council of State has ruled that it is hardly compatible with the principle of legal certainty. A set of classic arguments has been developed to argue against it: First, there is the duty for an administration being competent to decide on a permit, to do this within due time. This decision, then, must be founded on a careful enquiry during which the administration takes all interests into consideration. It was argued that the *Lex silencio positivo* allows the interests of the applicant to take precedence over the general interest. And this is completely against one of the basic principles of administrative law, notably the fact that the general interest always has to take precedence over the private interest. Furthermore, it is likely to happen that at insufficient research will precede the positive decision. In this respect, it is important to look at the initial objective of gaining advise when deciding on a permit request, notably a careful preparation of the final decision. So, when a fictitious decision is taken, there can be no question of careful enquiry preceding this decision. Thirdly, this method can make the possibilities of appeal by third persons more difficult: When a decision is taken ex officio, one can wonder how and within which deadline a mean of appeal can be applied. Finally, it must be taken for granted that a permit that has been granted by applying *Lex silencio positivo*, is not motivated at all; this implies that lodging an appeal against this permit will probably be little effective as the arguments used to grant the permit cannot be contested.

In building permit legislation, tacit rejection rules.[33] This happens too, when, by applying article 66, §3, 2 of the 2014 Decree on environmental permits. In the past, both the Council of State and the Council of permit litigations have ruled that there is no question of a tacit refusing decision if an authority does not take any decision within due time.

In later jurisprudence, both councils rule in the opposite direction[34]: Both the Council of State and the Council of permit litigations have decided that the deadline within which an order must be obeyed, is indeed a term that makes that the authority when failing to decide is considered to have taken a silent or tacit decision.[35] The Council of State has ruled several times that this kind of tacit decision is a fully contestable administrative decision.

[33] Art. 4.7.18 §2 Flemish Code of environment planning; art. 32 §4 2014 Environment Decree.

[34] See Denys (2015, pp. 280–283); CoS 17 March 2015, nr. 230.559, nv Imbos.

[35] CPL 13 December 2016, nr. RvVb/A/1617/0402; CPL 30 August 2016, nr. RvVb/A/1516/1491.

5.4.2 *National Doctrine on the Administrative Silence: Advantages and Side Effects Envisaged by the Literature of the Preeminent Model*

In Belgium, there is not such a thing as a national doctrine on the administrative silence, but case law by the Council of State and (later) also by the Council of Permits Litigations indicates that the tacit decision— even: Tacit refusal—is the preeminent model.

It seems only natural that when discussing legal protection in administrative law the emphasis is first and foremost on protecting citizens against potentially harmful actions of governmental administrations. This was also the rationale which led to the creation of the Belgian Council of State in 1948. As is stipulated in the Coordinated Laws of the Council of State (article 14, §1), the Council of State can decide on the legality of administrative decisions or administrative regulations that affect the legal position of an individual citizen. These administrative legal actions must be definitive and ready to be executed. It therefore stands to reason to assume that within the framework of legal protection this left a major loophole for administrations: By refusing to take a decision, e.g., about a citizen's request for a permit or about an administrative appeal, an administration could in effect escape judicial supervision. At first, this indeed seemed to be the case and there was—and in some circumstances there still is—a real risk that an administration may, with or without obvious intent, hold a citizen "hostage" by keeping strategically silent.

However, solutions to this kind of problems were quickly found in administrative law, either by creative reasoning of legal scholars and administrative judges or by adapting legislation and strengthening administrative appeal procedures.

In some cases, the legislator decided to stipulate what the legal consequences are of administrative silence. But for those cases where there is no such explicit stipulation, a solution was found by expanding the judicial review of the Council of State. As mentioned before, under certain conditions a citizen can start an "annulment procedure" against an administration that won't decide on a certain issue (article 14, §3 Coordinated Laws on the Council of State).

Talking about advantages of tacit decisions, the main advantage of a fictitious or tacit decision, either positive or negative, is that it creates legal consequences or prevents them. As such, it can be viewed as an administrative legal action which can be—if taken in final instance—subjected to judicial review by the Council of State.[36] However, there also some major disadvantages which must be mentioned, especially if the lack of a timely decision by the administration brings about a tacit positive decision.

5.4.3 *The EU Influence Over National Rules and Practices*

In literature on administrative silence, there is often referred to the EU Service Directive. This directive had to be transformed into Belgian legislation by December 28, 2009. Legal modifications had to be issued at all levels: federal, regional, community, and local: Law acts, decrees, federal and regional government decisions, provincial regulations, and local regulations were involved. Two law acts were needed: The federal level the law act of December 22, 2009, modified with its article 18 the conditions to be taken into account when granting a permit to a commercial enterprise. Another law act, the so-called Service Law Act, was issued on March 26, 2010,[37] about 4 months after the ultimate date of implementation. This law act contains one very important article, i.e., article 11, 4th paragraph, being the implementation of article 13, 4 of the Service Directive. The importance lies in the fact that by lack of decision within a determined deadline, the permit is considered to be granted. As mentioned before, this *Lex silencio positivo* technique occurs in Belgium in some specific areas but is not often applied, mainly because of the Council of State's point of view that decisions can only be issued after careful assessment and after taking into consideration the points of general interest.[38]

5.4.4 *Is Administrative Silence Restricted to Procedures Based on Application or also for Ex Officio?*

When no deadline is mentioned is any law, the requester can rely on the concept of exceeding the reasonable deadline. However, case law on this subject proves not to be in favor of the requester but rather in favor of the administration.[39] There are only a few cases in which the requester successfully appeals in a case without deadline determined by law.

[36] CoS 18 March 2004, nr. 129.417, Salaets e.a.

[37] See Pieters (2010, p. 746).

[38] See Opdebeek (1992, p. 222).

[39] CoS 27 May 2003, nr. 120.004; 27 June 2002, nr. 108.523.

When the legislation doesn't stipulate which consequences are connected to a certain type of administrative inaction, then, in particular circumstances and with respect of certain conditions, article 14, §3 Coordinated Laws of the Council of State can be applied.[40] This back-up stipulation can only be applied if and when there is no specific regulation dealing with a certain type of administrative inaction.

An administration can however have an obligation to decide when for instance there is an organized administrative appeal procedure or when there is a precise request from a citizen to gain a benefit within a certain regulated framework (e.g., permission to hold a protest march).

Of the utmost importance is the fact that article 14, §3 requires the citizen formally reminding the administration to act.[41] The citizen must make it clearly understood that he is invoking the abovementioned article of the Coordinated Laws of the Council of State and that further administrative silence will—after the prescribed period of four months—will result in an appeal procedure with the Council of State against the tacit decision to reject the request of the citizen.[42]

As a result of a formal reminder by the citizen, the administration is confronted with a definitive time period during which the administration must decide on the matter. Either there is a regular administrative decision against which an administrative and/or a judicial appeal is possible, either there is no decision which must be seen as tacit rejection and the regular appeal period of 60 days (with the Council of State) starts from the day after the period of four months ends. If after four months an explicit decision is taken, then the tacit rejection becomes non-existent and is replaced by the explicit decision.[43] The citizen will of course still be able to appeal against the explicit decision.

[40] Referred to before as the Law act of 3 June 1971, actually incorporated as article 14, §3 in the CoS coordinated laws.

[41] Opdebeek (2006, p. 13).

[42] See, e.g., CoS 25 November 2003, nr. 125.670.

[43] CoS 16 January 2014, nr. 226.105; *TBP* 2014, 475; *T.Gem.* 2014, 145.

5.5 The Negative Silence

5.5.1 The Legal Character of Prescribed Deadlines (Instructive/Preclusions)

In general, deadlines are to be respected. However, some reasons are accepted in order to prolong the deadline. Administrations often prolong the deadlines because of inability to decide within due time. If it concerns a "term of order," this does not produce any consequences. They remain competent to decide when exceeding the deadlines. When it concerns an expiration deadline, the lack of decision is considered to be a negative decision. Only few exceptions can lead to the prolongation of the deadline.[44]

5.5.2 The Possibility to Issue a Valid Act After the Deadline Expired

As mentioned before,[45] it is perfectly possible to issue a valid act after the deadline has expired if this deadline is a term of order. However, more and more, penalties are provided in case an administration fails to act in due time.[46] This occurs in the federal social benefits law where a requested amount has to be paid within a deadline of 4 months.[47]

5.5.3 Legal Consequences/Fictions: Finality and Enforceability

The former environmental decree and the decision of the Flemish government of February 6, 1991, made it possible to prolong or to refuse tacitly an environmental decision. If the competent authority in first instance does not take a decision on the permit request, then the permit is considered to be refused. But if the appeal decision has not been taken in due time, the permit is considered to be granted. On June 14, 2001, Belgium

[44] Cf. supra, nr. 3.2.

[45] Cf. supra, nr. 3.3.

[46] E.g.: MHCC/M/1617/0015, 31 January 2017: In which the administrative court found that although the regional administrative entity could act outside the given deadline the fact that the administration had acted so unreasonably late (23 months after the deadline) was reason for significantly reducing the administrative fine the administration had issued. See also: MHCC/M/1718/0021, 17 October 2017.

[47] Cf. supra, nr. 2.3.

was condemned by the Court of Justice for this. According to the court, the tacit permit was not compatible with several European directives: A permit can only be prolonged by means of an explicit administrative decision. So, Belgian legislation was adapted afterward.[48]

As discussed before (cf. supra, nrs. 4.1 and 4.2), tacit refusal is the preeminent model in Belgian public law. When a request is rejected, it gives right to judicial review. Both the Council of Permit Litigations[49] and the Council of State concluded that a silent decision must be considered to be a real decision that can be contested.[50]

5.5.4 *Case Law*

In a case, the regional urban planning officer requested for the annulment of a silent decision by the provincial executive body—the Deputation—on its administrative appeal against a permit granted in first instance. The provincial executive body disputed the receivability of the request and argued that not the silent decision but the in first instance issued decision by the municipality had to be the object of the request. Furthermore, the Deputation thought that due to the absence of any decision taken by itself, the municipality's decision was the last instance decision. The Council of Permits Litigation from its side ruled that the Deputation had issued a "silent decision" which could be fully contested.[51]

In a case concerning a building permit where both the local executive body and the provincial executive body—as the requester was appealing against the first silent decision—failed to take a decision within due time, the requester finally appealed to the competent minister who, finally, granted the permit. Due to the absence of financial revenues during the period, the competent authorities remain silent, the requester lodges a damage claim before the tribunal. After rejection by the tribunal of first instance and the court of appeal, the case is dealt with by the Court of Cassation. This court rules that these administrative bodies have to decide

[48] Decree Flemish Parliament of 6 February 2004 (Official Gazette 20 February 2004, 2nd edition).

[49] CPL 14 February 2012, nr. A/2012/0052, 8.

[50] Larmuseau et al. (2012, p. 276).

[51] CPL 8 August 2017, nr. RvVb/A/1617/1110; CPL 28 April 2015, nr. A/2015/0270.

in due time but if they don't, the exceeding of a "term of order" might be the reason for a liability damage claim if some conditions are met, but is not sufficient to annul the decisions.[52]

5.5.5 *Empirical Evidence*

Earlier statistics showed that Belgian and Flemish administrations were not able to respect the narrow deadlines. As to Building permits, more than 50% of the requesters said that their request as treated with a deadline from only a couple to 456 days.[53] As to environmental permits, more than 50% was not treated within due time and causing a silent decision of refusal.[54]

This situation has improved over the years: A report issued by the Flemish Environment Agency in 2017, mentioned that in the period 2010–2016, there was an average of only 0.2% of silent refusals "issued" by the provincial executive bodies acting as appellate bodies concerning building permits.[55]

In general, in 2012 there were still 212 tacit refusals, in 2013 this number decreased to 180, in 2014 to 117, and in 2015 there were only 88 tacit refusals.[51] Actual data show that in the year 2017–2018, 916 annulment requests have been introduced (888 in 2016–2017) about 20% (21% in 2016–2017) of it against a silent refusal.

This implies that the number of decisions that have been issued within due time, has been drastically increased in recent years, and that the number of silent refusals has decreased. A large majority of the contested decisions concerns building permit decisions (76%).[56]

As to requests for allocation by persons with a handicap, the legal deadline is 6 months, but it was well known that this deadline was exceeded in many cases. Recent data show there is still vary according to the province the requester lives in: In 6 from the 10 provinces the deadline is respected,

[52] Cass. 10 April 2014, C.11.0796.N.; see also Haentjens (2016).

[53] Test Aankoop (2010).

[54] UNIZO-studiedienst (2011).

[55] https://www.ruimtelijkeordening.be/Portals/108/201709_SV_beroepen_rapport.pdf.

[56] See DBRC, Annual Report 2017–2018, Brussels, 2018, pp. 28–35.

but in the other provinces it can mount up to 12 months.[57] Reasons seem to be technical problems and a shortage of staff.

PCSW's seem to be the only administrations that decide in due deadline about request for social help or the right to social integration, as there are no reports on exceeding times.[58]

5.6 The Positive Silence

5.6.1 *The Legal Character of Prescribed Deadlines (Instructive/Preclusions)*

As mentioned before yet, deadlines must be respected but exceeding them generally does not always produce consequences. In some very specific cases, e.g., minor regulations *Lex silencio positivo* technique is applied. These deadlines cannot be prolonged as they produce consequences just by exceeding the deadline. Apart from the regulation mentioned before (see nr. 3.2.), this is possible in Flemish environment legislation where the expiration deadline of an environmental permit can be prolonged in case of odds. In case the appellate authority does not decide ultimately on the day of the initial date of expiration, the prolongation is considered to be approved. A similar regulation is provided in case a permit is suspended of abolished. When appealing against this decision, the Flemish government must respect a deadline of 120 days. Exceeding this deadline implies the approval of the appeal.[59]

For certain works and activities on protected real heritage, like monuments and historical town or village views, the involved agency (Space and Heritage, Real Heritage) grants own allowances and permits, away from the building permit procedure. The deadline for these allowances and permits is 30 days, to be counted from the reception of the complete file. Failing to decide within this deadline leads to a tacit allowance.

[57] See www.handicap.belgium.be.

[58] Earlier case law reports (2002 and 2012) revealed 0 or 1 case a year for exceeding the deadline; actual data—a fact check carried out in March 2019 by Exello, the union of General directors of Flemish municipalities—show that more than 90% of the decisions is taken within 30 days after applying for support.

[59] Art. 93, 2014 Environment Decree.

Another application of it could be found in the law act on the permits of commercial enterprises where from April 9, 2012, on, a permit of a commercial enterprise could be granted silently by lack of decision.[60]

5.6.2 *The Possibility to Issue a Valid Act After the Deadline Expired*

There is a principle difference between a silent approval and an explicit administrative act issued afterward, but both kinds of administrative decisions are in fact kinds of *unfair* decisions.

As to the technique of silent approval, this mechanism is not conducive for attaining legal certainty. There is no written decision which can lead to evidentiary problems and there is in principle no communication or promulgation of a tacit decision as is the case with regular decisions. This means there can also be problems about the knowability and questionability of tacit decisions. As such with the mechanism of the tacit decision there could be a greater risk the interests of third parties might be harmed, albeit implicitly but nonetheless substantially. In some cases, a tacit permit can be against public interest. Tacit decisions come about without careful preparation and without consideration of all the involved interests. The question arises whether the use of tacit decisions doesn't increase the risk that the consequences of exceeding deadlines will be seen solely in function of the legal position of the citizen requesting a permit and that the administration will simply bypass the weighing of other interests—those of third parties or the public interest.

An appeal procedure which makes use of tacit decisions should for the same reasons not be considered preferable.

As to issuing administrative acts after the deadline has been expired, and even if the Council of Permit Litigations and the Council of State rule that valid decisions can be taken that way, it must be stressed that this kind of decisions are breaching the rights of the requester/citizen. The Council of State has ruled that the competent authority does not remain competent unlimitedly because is it bound to issue a decision within a reasonable deadline. Furthermore, case law by the Council of State recognizes that delayed decisions can be harmful and lead to legitimate liability claims.

[60] Art. 11, §7, Law on Commercial Enterprises 2004.

5.6.3 Legal Consequences/Fictions: Finality and Enforceability

As discussed before, it may be difficult to use rights granted by a fictitious decision, and many questions can raise on the implementation of these rights. However, tacit (positive) decisions are valid decisions that can be appealed against, which usually won't happen because of it grant benefits to the citizen/requester. It might be difficult for the latter one to enforce the tacit decision as there has been no formal communication.

5.6.4 Case Law

As there is nearly no application of *Lex silencio positivo* in important Belgian or Flemish law, there is almost no case law available.

However, some examples can be given. The 2014 Environment Decree stipulates that, when an environmental permit is suspended or annulled by an administrative authority and the citizen appeals against this decision, the latter one expires if the Flemish government does not decide within the deadline.[61] This is a kind of positive tacit decision. Criticism against this kind of regulations in general refers to the violation of article 10 §6 of the Service directive which forbids the principle of tacit decision and which stipulates that every refusal of a permit must be motivated explicitly.[62]

According to article 11 of the law act of August 13, 2004, the inter-ministerial committee is as an administrative appeal body competent to handle appeals against some decisions of the municipal executive body concerning socio-economic requests. When deciding, this body must communicate its decision within a deadline of 40 days after postage date of the written appeal.[63] When this body does not decide in due time, the initial decision of the College of Burgomaster and Aldermen is considered to be confirmed.[64] This implicit decision is a consequence of the mere exceeding the deadline and is usually not communicated the appellant. As to the general principles of good government, problems rise when in these kind of decisions there is no mentioning of appeal possibilities. Article 19, 2, of the coordinated laws on the Council of State, the appeal

[61] See art. 93, 2014 Environment Decree.

[62] Parl. Doc., Flemish Parliament, 767 (2015–2016), nr. 6.

[63] Article 11 §5 Law act of 13 August 2004.

[64] Article 11 §7 Law act of 13 August 2004.

deadline is to start as soon as the deadline of 40 days is expired. The Council of State has ruled that also an implicit decision can be the object of an annulment request.[65]

The Constitutional Court from its side concludes that the legislator has not had the purpose to make article 19, 2 of the Council of State coordinated laws applicable on implicit decisions.[66] The legislator's choice aims a legal goal and tries to combine the principles of legal certainty and of the right to access to the judge. The Court rules that, doing so, the legislator does not harm in an unreasonable way the rights of the involved persons by not providing communication of the consequences when communicating the first instance decision. So, when an appeal is lodged based on article 11 of the law act of August 13, 2004, the citizen cannot, according to the Constitutional Court, ignore the consequences linked by the law to a possible lack of decision issued by the interministerial committee, notably that the appeal deadline begins when the decision's deadline is expired.

5.6.5 *Empirical Evidence*

Exact data were hardly available: A minister answering a question put by a MP mentioned 10% as the number of lacking decisions causing a tacit approval.[67] A study by UNIZO, the Union of Independent Enterprises mentioned 20% of tacit approvals due to the lack of decision by local authorities.[68] This problem was reported to be continued until last year by the Flemish Agency of Entrepreneurship; reasons for these tacit approvals could be the lack of knowledge of the legislation by local civil servants.[69]

The whole system of tacit permit was abolished on January 1, 2018, and integrated in the 2014 Environmental Decree. In this decree, exceeding the deadline usually means an implicit refusal.

[65] See CoS 15 January 2016, nr. 233.486; CoS 30 June 2016, nr. 235.278.

[66] Const. Court, 25 June 2015, nr. 93/2015.

[67] Senate, Session 2006–2007, Question nr. 3-6505 by Mr. Steverlynck dd. 28 December 2006 (N).

[68] UNIZO-Studiedienst (2007).

[69] https://www.detailhandelvlaanderen.be/wetgeving/tijdige-betekening-van-beslissingen-inzake-socio-economische-vergunning.

5.7 Supervision of the Administrative Timeliness

5.7.1 *Supervision of the Timeliness: Administrative Control, Judicial Review, Etc*

Belgian or Flemish legislation does not contain an automatic control on administrative timeliness. It is up to the citizen to react when he wants to activate any instance to judge about timeliness. So, the Council of State has ruled that the citizen/requester must take himself the necessary steps in order to force the administration to act within reasonable time.[70]

As to the environmental permits' legislation, no decision is usually considered to be a negative decision: So, when a citizen applies for an environment permit, and the local executive body fails to take a decision within the prescribed deadline, the decision is considered to be a silent refusal.[71] It is up to the requester to appeal against this negative (fictitious) decision. This occurs, too, in other legislations, e.g., when a PCSW fails to take a decision within 30 days after the request for social support, the requester can lodge an appeal before the labor tribunal against the absence of decision.[72]

5.7.2 *Governmental Strategies, Studies, Actions, and Their Effects on Tackling Excessive Length of Procedures*

In Flemish parliament, several discussions were held on tackling excessive length of procedures. The involved minister on environmental affairs was hopeful that a new decree on environmental permits—the 2014 Environment Decree, applied from January 1, 2018—would limit the procedural delays.

Other departments (e.g., social affairs), too, have recently taken measures in order to limit the delays: In February 2017 a roadmap with

[70] CoS 18 April 2005, nr. 143.267; 29 May 1998, nr. 73.931.

[71] See art. 32, §4, 2014 Environment Decree.

[72] Art. 66, §3, 2, of the 2014 Environment Decree; PCSW Law, Social Benefits Law, etc.

time schedule was announced[73]; one year later, the involved minister again announced a reduction of all delays.[74]

5.8 Legal Remedies

5.8.1 Administrative Appeal

As mentioned before, according to article 28 of the Belgian constitution, everyone has the right to address petitions signed by one or more persons to the public authorities. Constituted bodies are alone entitled to address petitions under a collective name. Interpreted in a broader sense, administrative appeals can be lodged before public authorities. The administrative appeal is directed to an organ of active administration, to an administrative authority that in this frame does not exercise any jurisdictional competence.[75] An administrative appeal allows the citizen to question an authority's decision before the same or before another of higher authority. This kind of appeal is an important instrument of legal protection against the authority.[76] It must be stressed that under Belgian public law, a specific administrative appeal excludes other possibilities.[77] When no solution can be found by means of an administrative appeal, judicial review remains possible.[78]

When provided by the law—included deadlines, competent instances, and executable decisions—the administrative appeal is called organized administrative appeal.[79] The main character of such an appeal is that the administration is obliged to answer to the appeal.[80] The appellate body that will judge about the organized administrative appeal is usually

[73] https://www.presscenter.org/nl/pressrelease/20170221/reactie-van-de-fod-sociale-zekerheid-naar-aanleiding-van-de-stakingsactie-van-.

[74] https://www.lachambre.be/kvvcr; answer to question by MP V. Yüksel, nr. 0667—Session: 54.

[75] See Mast et al. (2014, p. 948).

[76] See Wouters (2008, p. 251).

[77] CoS 10 May 1995, nr. 53.223; Veny and De Munck (2011, p. 278).

[78] See Mast et al. (2009, p. 948).

[79] See De Roy (2003, p. 8).

[80] CoS 13 November 1995, nr. 56.211; *T.Gem.* 1996, p. 101.

a higher administrative body. This body is competent to reform the initial decision and to decide itself about the case.[81]

There is no general deadline for organized administrative appeal procedures. As is the case for initial decisions, special laws and decrees determine the deadline for each specific administrative appeal (supra 3.1.). These are the same laws and decrees providing for the initial decision. For example, administrative appeal against an administrative refusal to release a copy of an administrative document must be lodged within a deadline of 30 calendar days, starting the day after receiving the refusal decision.[82] The appeal body has in turn 30 calendar days—which can be prolonged to 45 calendar days—to decide on the administrative appeal.[83] In the context of environmental permits, the administrative appeal body in question must adhere to a deadline of 120 days if the initial decision was taken following the regular procedure while there is also a deadline of 60 days if the initial decision was taken following the simplified procedure.[84]

As mentioned before, the Belgian system adheres to judicial dualism. So, judicial review as such belongs to the ordinary courts, but administrative redress is possible before an administrative court, where the highest administrative court is the Council of State. After the Council of Permits Litigations has issued a decision, it is possible to lodge a so-called cassation appeal before the Council of State. As to liability matters—even when authorities are involved—the ordinary tribunals and courts until the Court of Cassation are competent to judge.

The scope of judicial review seems not always to be obliging the authority to answer or to issue the act: In the social benefits area, the interests (cf. supra nrs. 2.3 and 5.2) and measures[85] are clearly meant to force the authority to act, but in other areas the scope (e.g., certain procedures) rather seems to be to protect *both* parties' rights.[86]

[81] See Goris (2007, pp. 189–194).

[82] Article II.48, §1 Flemish Government Decree.

[83] Article II.50, §1 Flemish Government Decree.

[84] Article 66 Flemish Decree on environmental permits.

[85] E.g., the deadline of 30 days after request to decide on social support, see article 10 Social Security Charter, article 62bis, §1, PCSW Law Act of 8 July 1976, and article 21, §3 Social Integration Law Act of 26 May 2002.

[86] CPL 17 October 2017, nr. RvVb/A/1718/0145; CPL 8 May 2018, nr. RvVb/A/1718/0814.

5.8.2 *Court Remedies for Silent Rejection and Silent Approval*

Administrative inaction can take on many forms, like an administration neglecting to protect a collective interest forcing citizens take legal action instead of the administration or indecisive of procrastinating behavior of an administration in individual cases which forces a citizen to take legal action against a non-existent, fictitious, decision—as described before.

But administrative inaction can also manifest itself in other ways and this in turn can bring about some other—unintended—legal consequences: In 2010 the Court of Appeal of Brussels held the municipality of Grimbergen liable for not acting with proper care regarding the actualization of the population register.[87] After a police enquiry in February 1998, it was ascertained that a certain resident of the municipality no longer lived at the registered domicile within the municipality. As a result, the municipal administration should have within an appropriate timeframe stricken the resident from its records. However, even though in July 1998 another family came to live at this address, the former resident was still officially domiciled at the same address. As a result, when because of a substantial financial debt of the former resident a bailiff confiscated the goods found at this address in September 1998 (while the residents were temporarily absent) and consequently sold the seized goods the following day… it was deemed that confiscating the wrong goods was a result of negligent inaction of the municipal administration which had had plenty of time to act on information gathered by the aforementioned police enquiry.

In 2017, a judge ruled that when an administration decides to start in 2006 an urgent expropriation procedure as foreseen in the law on expropriation but then fails to take any further steps during the following eight years this can only lead to the conclusion that there has been no real urgency. As such the judge stated that the current expropriation claim has become invalid and must be rejected because it is founded on an illegitimate decision of 2006 (invoking urgency where there is none).[88]

Another issue regarding administrative silence is whether continued inaction of a government can lead to legitimate expectations on the part of a citizen that the government will remain silent forever. The Council of State has, on occasion, stated clearly that a citizen cannot derive any

[87] Court of Appeal Brussels, 10 June 2010 http://jure.juridat.just.fgov.be.

[88] Justice of Peace, Aalst, 27 February 2017, AR 16/1153.

rights from the continuing existence of an illegal situation.[89] It must be clear that silent decisions can be annulled.[90]

There are only few cases in which a judge can replace an administrative decision by his own decision: This occurs for instance when a citizen lodges an appeal against a decision of the lack of any decision by the PCSW. The judge can confirm, adapt, or replace the authority's decision.[91]

5.8.3 *Right to Compensation—Damages*

Very exceptionally, compensation is provided. This is the case in the new environmental legislation: If the competent authority—usually the local executive body—does not decide in due time, a penalty is to be applied.

Damage claims can always be demanded in case of exceeding the deadlines. A claimant always has the right to prove—according to the civil liability procedure—that there is a direct damage as a consequence of the silence.

With the Flandria judgment of November 5, 1920,[92] the Court of Cassation stated that when it comes to civil liability there is no distinction to be made between the government as a private law actor and as public law actor. Even when a government administration acts in the public interest, it doesn't mean that these actions cannot harm an individual citizen. If it can be proven that the administration didn't act with due care and due diligence, then that administration can be sued for compensation of the damages its actions caused.

The Flandria judgment is also interesting with regard to government's inaction: The City of Bruges was held liable because it was considered to have been negligent by not having chopped down a tree that had fallen on to the greenhouse of the Flandria Company.

[89] CoS 12 December 2002, nr. 113.571.

[90] CPL 17 October 2017, nr. RvVb/A/1718/0145, case nr. 1516/RvVb/0386/A.

[91] See: Art. 71, PCSW-Law 8 July 1976.

[92] Cass. 5 November 1920, *Pas.*, 1920, I, 193–240.

Further jurisprudence refined all sorts of issues regarding government liability.[93] But it is clear that failure to take a decision or failure to properly execute a decision may lead to liability issues.

5.8.4 *The Role of the Ombudsman*

As well the federal Ombudsman as the regional ombudsman can accept complaints with regard to administrative silence. They report about it annually. However, their recommendations and investigations do often not produce many effects, unless in the case of environmental permits.

The Flemish Ombuds service reports that there are hardly any complaints about the functioning of the Council of permit litigation. When receiving complaints about the wrong functioning of administrations, it first examines the receivability of the complaint: It checks whether it is competent to handle it and whether it concerns a real complaint. Is so, it asks for explanations by the involved agency. The answer by the agency explaining the delay, is reported. Local authorities are mainly competent to deal with building and environmental permits. So, these numbers are not found back in the Ombudsmen's reports; it is not a federal nor a regional competence.

In 2017 there were 19 complaints about the social benefit "help to elder people"; 12 of them were about the unreasonable delay to treat the request for a benefit.[94]

The federal Ombudsman reports the violation of the reasonable deadline as the most formulated complaint. Of course, it does not always deal about decisions but also about treatment of other files, requests for information, etc.[95]

5.8.5 *Empirical Evidences*

Officials and heads might be held accountable for delays, they are in no way personally accountable in a way that they are to pay indemnities. Several initiatives have been taken to improve this kind of service

[93] Cass. 7 March 1963, *Pas.* 1963, I, 744; Cass. 26 April 1963, *Pas.* 1963, I, 905; Cass. 16 December 1965, *Pas.* 1966, I, 513.

[94] Annual Report 2017 Flemish Ombudsman, p. 20.

[95] Federal Ombudsman, Annual Report 2017, p. 140.

to the public. In the environmental permits law area, the exceeding of the deadline can lead to pay indemnities. Then the Flemish Union of towns and municipalities (VVSG) has lobbied to not impose this legislation as this would weigh up the local budgets. The competent Flemish minister defended the introduction of indemnities but stressed that a monitoring report showed that the number of silent refusals was in a few years diminished from 2.7 per 1000 to 1.5 per 1000. This implies that the overwhelming majority of decisions on permits is granted in due time.[96]

The deadlines of the new Environment Decree are strict but most authorities seem to succeed in respecting them. After 105 days counting from the day after applying for the permit, the decision should be taken by the competent authority when no additional advice is needed.[97] This deadline can be prolonged once by 60 days for some specific reasons.[98]

Requesters can lodge an appeal against this decision within a deadline of 30 days before the Council of Permits Litigations. This administrative judicial body is competent to deal with not only explicit decisions but also with silent decisions.[99] As mentioned before, in 2017–2018, there were 916 annulment appeals lodged before this body. 76% of the appeals lodged in 2017–2018 concerned building permits. This body issued 1276 judgments in 2017–2018, of which 1040 were final decisions. The number of pending files diminishes year by year but has not yet disappeared. The Council's objective now is a deadline of 6 months.[100] Also the Flemish ombudsman reports an enormous progress in the backlog and considers it no longer as a problem.[101]

[96] Flemish Parliament, Commission meeting, Commission for environment, urban planning, nature, energy and animals' welfare, Tuesday 12 April 2016, question by MP Lydia Peeters to minister Joke Schauvliege, nr. 1677 (2015–2016).

[97] Art. 32, §1, 2014 Environment Decree.

[98] Art. 32, §2, 2014 Environment Decree.

[99] Art. 66, §3, 2, of the 2014 Environment Decree stipulates that the silence of the Deputation (or the Flemish government), not treating in due time administrative appeal can lead to a silent rejection of this appeal.

[100] DBRC Annual Report 2017–2018, pp. 30–36.

[101] Annual Report 2017 Flemish Ombudsman, p. 21.

5.9 Overall Assessment of the Legal Regime and the Practice of Administrative Silence

As there are many ways in which "administrative silence" can manifest itself, there are many ways within the Belgian legal framework in which a citizen or a group of citizens can take legal action against government inaction that may harm individual or collective interests.

In this paper, certain manifestations of administrative silence were explored and some legal instruments to combat administrative inaction were discussed, mainly in theoretical terms. This leads us at this point to two—tentative—conclusions.

First of all, there is no definitive solution—no "one size fits all" kind of instrument—against the failure or the unwillingness of an administration to take a decision or execute a decision. Sometimes the cure—e.g., "lex silencio positivo"—may be deemed worse than the disease because there is no longer any form of careful examination before the effects of an "implicit or tacit" decision are felt. Or the solution, for instance the substitution of an inactive administration, is viewed by some as contradicting democratic principles. To offer citizens more adequate protection against administrative silence a diversified array of legal instruments must be developed. This means not only fine-tuning existing instruments but also find new creative ways to balance between legal certainty and respecting the interests of all involved actors. Secondly, while legal protection against government action has been a field of study in Belgium for a long time, the same cannot be said about legal protection against *government inaction*. Notwithstanding several interesting academic explorations and analyses of the phenomenon of "administrative silence" in the past,[102] it continues to be seen mainly as something "extraordinary" or "exceptional," as a side-effect of inefficient or ineffective governing, not as a potential problematic phenomenon worth studying in its own right. A more comprehensive, interdisciplinary approach certainly seems recommended. Finally, it must be clear that some recent innovations (e.g., in environmental law) impose some strict deadlines that seem to improve decision-making on permits.[103]

[102] Opdebeek (1988), Bolt (1988), and Opdebeek (1992); see also more recently: De Coninck (2016).

[103] Cf. supra nr. 7.2.

References

Bolt, H. (1988). *Het inactieve bestuur, administratiefrechtelijke bescherming tegen stilzitten van de overheid*. RW 1988–1989, 1137–1139.

De Coninck, L. (2016). *Le silence de l'administration: décision implicite d'accord ou de rejet?*. Louvain: Université catholique de Louvain.

Denys, S. (2015). Rechtskarakter van de beslissingstermijnen bevolen door de Raad voor Vergunningsbetwistingen. *T.Gem.*, afl. 4, 280–283.

De Roy, C. (2003). *Het georganiseerd administratief beroep*. Mechelen: Kluwer.

De Taeye, S. (2002). Het rechtszekerheidsbeginsel en het vertrouwensbeginsel. In B. Hubeau & P. Popelier (Eds.), *Behoorlijk ruimtelijk ordenen*. Brugge: die Keure.

Goris, J. (2007). Het georganiseerd bestuurlijk beroep en het algemeen bestuurlijk toezicht: de soms vage scheidingslijn wordt steeds vager. *T.Gem.*, afl. 3, 189–194.

Haentjens, F. (2016). Aansprakelijkheid bij overschrijding ordetermijn. *TOO*, nr. 3, 433–434.

Larmuseau, I., et al. (2012). Stilzwijgend geweigerd, onwettigheid verzekerd. *TOO*, nr. 4, 276.

Lust, S. (2003). *De aansprakelijkheid van de Overheid voor het niet in acht nemen van een beslissingstermijn* (noot onder Cass. 8 November 2002). RABG, afl. 15, 859.

Maes, A. (2015). Dwingende beslissingstermijnen in de VCRO. Of toch niet (altijd)? *TOO*, afl. 1, 134.

Marneffe, W., Ooms, A., & Vereeck, L. (2011). Rechtseconomische analyse van het beginsel van de redelijke termijn bij vergunningen. *TVW*, 10.

Mast, A., Dujardin, J., et al. (2009). *Overzicht van het Belgisch administratief recht*. Mechelen: Kluwer.

Mast, A., Dujardin, J., et al. (2014). *Overzicht van het Belgisch administratief recht*. Mechelen: Kluwer.

Mast, A., Dujardin, J., et al. (2017). *Overzicht van het Belgisch administratief recht*. Mechelen: Wolters Kluwer.

Opdebeek, I. (1988). *Het inactieve bestuur. Administratiefrechtelijke rechtsbescherming tegen stilzitten van de overheid in België*. Zwolle: Tjeenk Willink.

Opdebeek, I. (1992). *Rechtsbescherming tegen het stilzitten van het bestuur*. Brugge: die Keure.

Opdebeek, I. (2006). Artikel 14, §3, RvS-Wet. In *Publiek Procesrecht, Artikelsgewijze commentaar met overzicht van rechtspraak en rechtsleer* (p. 13). Mechelen: Kluwer.

Opdebeek, I. (2015). *De sanctie voor schending van de redelijke termijn bij het opleggen van bestuurlijke boetes in het milieurecht: geen zwart-witverhaal, maar wel een verhaal van 50 tinten grijs...* (noot onder Milieuhandhavingscollege 13 June 2014, MHHC-14/38-K2). MER, 159.

Pieters, E. (2010). La loi du 28 mars 2010 sur les services. *TBH*, nr. 8, 746.
Test Aankoop. (2010). *Stedenbouwkundige vergunning: de overheid neemt een loopje met de termijnen.*
UNIZO-Studiedienst. (2007). *Handelsvestigingenbeleid ontspoort*. Unizo-analyse van enkele belangrijke distributie-indicatoren, Brussel.
UNIZO-Studiedienst. (2011). *Investeringsprojecten van ondernemers, snel en efficiënt vergunnen*. Brussel.
Van Damme, M. (2001). The Council of State: Institution on the Junction of the Three Traditional Powers of State. In J. Vande Lanotte (Red.), *The Principle of Equality: A South African and Belgian Perspective* (p. 74). Antwerpen and Apeldoorn: Maklu.
Van Hoorick, G. (2011). *Handboek Ruimtelijk bestuursrecht*. Intersentia: Antwerpen.
Veny, L., & De Munck, E. (2011). Effectiveness of Administrative Appeals Within the Framework of Administrative Justice in Belgium. *TRAS*, 278.
Wouters, K. (2008). *Het administratief beroep*. Antwerpen: Maklu.

CHAPTER 6

Remedies Against Administrative Silence in the Netherlands

Kars J. de Graaf, Nicole G. Hoogstra, and Albert T. Marseille

6.1 The Legal and Administrative Background for Analyzing Administrative Silence

The Netherlands is a decentralized unitary state. That means that within the public domain the state is composed of primarily general-purpose governmental bodies. Although exceptions to that general rule exist, for instance for water management, the Dutch state in addition to the central government is made up out of decentralized public bodies, such as "municipalities" that are situated within "provinces," that fulfill legislative and administrative tasks. The Netherlands became a kingdom in 1815, of

K. J. de Graaf (✉) · N. G. Hoogstra · A. T. Marseille
Department of Constitutional Law, Administrative Law and Public Administration, University of Groningen, Groningen, The Netherlands
e-mail: k.j.de.graaf@rug.nl

N. G. Hoogstra
e-mail: n.g.hoogstra@rug.nl

A. T. Marseille
e-mail: a.t.marseille@rug.nl

D. C. Dragos et al. (eds.),
The Sound of Silence in European Administrative Law,
https://doi.org/10.1007/978-3-030-45227-8_6

which Belgium and Luxembourg also belonged until 1830. The Netherlands is a parliamentary constitutional monarchy, in which the king is the ceremonial head of state and governs under the responsibility of the ministers without having any legal influence. The Netherlands is one of the founders of European cooperation, and in 1952 joined the European Coal and Steel Community, the predecessor of the European Union.

Om general there are two kinds of legal rules concerning administrative law in the Netherlands. First, administrative authorities are granted the power to act for the purpose of performing a public service in many statutory provisions; those provisions usually regulate such action in detail. This includes substantive rules in numerous areas of public law, such as social security law, immigration law, or environmental law. Second, in 1994 the Netherlands introduced the General Administrative Law Act (GALA), or in Dutch the *Algemene wet bestuursrecht* (Awb), which contains rules for orders made by administrative authorities and creates the right of appeal to an administrative court against single-case decisions or orders. The GALA provides provisions on the process of administrative decision-making in a general sense and also a general framework for legal protection against the orders issued.

In the past two decades, administrative silence has been given high priority on the political agenda. In many cases, timely decision-making by administrative authorities has been a problem. Research shows that administrative authorities have a hard time responding to a variety of license applications within the set time limit. Not only does this mean that an applicant was left in the dark for too long with regard to the authorization of starting an activity or project, but in the past, it was also problematic to force the administrative authority to make a decision. There has therefore been much attention devoted to both administrative practice and the introduction of legal remedies against administrative silence. This attention was necessary in spite of the general rule that an administrative authority is obliged to take a decision on a license application within a prescribed limit of time.

Timely decision-making by the administration ensures predictability and legal certainty in the relationship between government and its citizens. For any government to function properly within a democratic society that is based on the rule of law, it is also important that public authorities take decisions within a reasonable time and certainly within the time period prescribed by law. In the past few years, the Dutch national legislator has invested in various legal instruments to stimulate timely decision-making. The objective of these instruments is to sanction the administrative authority in case decisions are not made within the prescribed time limit. Non-legislative causes of failures in timely decision-making, such as insufficient employee competence, the workload being too high for government officials, or the complexity of applications, are generally not considered potentially successful arguments to justify administrative silence. However, the legislator does acknowledge the fact that finding a solution for the problem cannot be guaranteed with (only) legislation and regulation. In this contribution, we will discuss the rules and provisions that the Netherlands has introduced to guarantee that government takes decisions on time.

6.2 Legal Framework for Timely Decision-Making

6.2.1 Constitution, the General Administrative Law Act and Sector-Specific Acts

The Dutch Constitution (*Grondwet*) does not refer to timely decision-making by public authorities specifically and does not provide specific provisions on judicial protection against untimely decision-making by government.[1] The Netherlands is however familiar with regulation stimulating timely decision-making and sanctioning administrative silence. In the past, there have been relevant provisions in sector-specific legislation concerned with this issue, but since its introduction the GALA provides general provisions on timely decision-making and on several different sanctions. However, as it is a general act on administrative law, there is always the possibility of prevailing provisions of sector-specific legislation.

The GALA provides one of the key provisions on timely decision-making in Article 4:13(1) GALA. For single-case decisions that are requested by an interested party, this provision provides as follows:

> An administrative decision shall be made within the time limit prescribed by statutory regulation, or, in the absence of such time limit, within a reasonable period after receiving the application.

[1] Article 6 ECHR implies a right to a fair and public hearing within a reasonable time by an independent and impartial tribunal. Case law concerned with this right does not apply directly to administrative silence.

Article 4:13 GALA stipulates that the statute in which the particular public competence to make the single-case decision is provided (e.g., a permit or a license) can provide how much time an administrative authority has to decide on an application. Nowadays, many of the sector-specific regulations provide not only specific competences but also prescribe a time limit for making a decision when a request has been made. An example can be found in the General Act on Environmental Licensing (*Wet algemene bepalingen omgevingsrecht*, GAEL). Article 3.9 GELA provides that an application for a building permit should be decided on within 8 weeks. Another example is Article 5.1 of the Dutch Nature Conservation Act (*Wet natuurbescherming*); it provides for a term of 13 weeks to decide on an application.

When a specific legislative act awards an administrative authority the competence to decide on a permit application but does not provide a specific time period to decide on an application, Article 4:13 GALA stipulates that the decision shall be taken within a reasonable period after receiving the application. Then also Article 4:13(2) GALA is relevant. It stipulates the following:

> The reasonable period (…) shall in any event be deemed to have expired if the administrative authority has not made an administrative decision or given communication as referred to in article 4:14, subsection 3, within eight weeks of receiving the application.

This means that unless specified otherwise, the general time period to take a decision is eight weeks. The provision does however also refer to Article 4:14(3) GALA in order to ascertain what is in fact a reasonable period to decide on an application. It reads:

> If, in the absence of a time limit prescribed by statutory regulation, an administrative decision cannot be made within eight weeks, the administrative authority shall inform the applicant within this time limit, stating a reasonable time limit for the administrative decision to be made.

From these two relevant provisions, read in conjunction with each other, the following can be deduced.[2] Starting point is that a reasonable period is eight weeks after the application is received but it can be longer. This

[2] *Parliamentary Papers II* 1988/89, 21 221, 3, pp. 105–107.

is the case when there is not a reasonable possibility for the administrative authority to take a decision within eight weeks after receiving the application. Extending the reasonable period should not just be notified by the administrative authority to the applicant but this should be done in writing before the eight-week period is over. On the other hand, the reasonable period can also be shorter than eight weeks; if a permit is requested for a demonstration to be held in a week's time, then—if reasonable—a decision should be taken before the date the demonstration is planned.[3]

6.2.2 *Assessing the Length of the Decision Period*

For both the situation that a period is stipulated in a sector-specific legislative act and for the situation that, in the absence of a statutory time period, the "reasonable" period applies, the GALA provides a number of provisions on assessing the beginning and the end of the decision period. Article 4:13 GALA provides that the decision period starts after the public authority has received the application and ends after the time period provided in a specific statute or after a reasonable time period, which is in principle eight weeks.

Article 4:15 GALA mentions a number of reasons for suspending the decision period. Perhaps the most important reason for suspension occurs when the applicant has not complied with all the requirements stipulated in either the GALA, a sector-specific act or a regulation for sending in a complete application. A proper assessment of the received application is only possible if the application provides all relevant information. If the applicant has not supplied the administrative authority with the required information, the time limit for making an administrative decision will be suspended from the day the administrative authority requests of the applicant to complete his application until the day the application has been completed or the day the time limit set for this purpose expires. This way of calculating the time period seems—where applicable—at odds with Article 13(3) Services Directive as this provision states that the period "shall run only from the time when all documentation has been submitted." Suspension of the decision period is also possible when the applicant has agreed to an extension, when there is a delay for which the

[3] Van Wijk et al. (2014, p. 306).

applicant is to blame or when the administrative authority is unable to make a timely decision due to *force majeure*.

The GALA provides in cases where the public authority comes to the conclusion that the time limit for making a decision will not be met, that the public authority is obliged to notify the applicant and inform him of the timeframe for expecting a decision, which should be as short as possible (Article 14(1) GALA). This notification was originally not intended to extend the time limit for taking a decision and was simply meant to make sure the applicant was notified. Many of the sector-specific regulations explicitly provide a possibility to extend the deadline (e.g., Article 3.9(2) GAEL). However, there has been some discussion whether the GALA implies the opportunity for extending the time period. In the explanatory memorandum for the implementation of the Services Directive (2006/123/EC)[4] in the Dutch Services Act (*Dienstenwet*) the government argued that Article 4:14(1) GALA does offer the possibility to extend the time period.[5] In that perspective it is also noteworthy that Article 31 of the Dutch Services Act explicitly states that—for any decision that falls within the scope of the Services Directive—Article 4:14(1) may only be used once, for a limited time and only if extending the time period can be justified by the complexity of the issue. Furthermore, it states that the notification provided for in Article 4:14(3) GALA shall take place before the end of the original time period and shall be accompanied by reasons for the extension.

6.2.3 *Timely Decision-Making in Practice?*

In the Netherlands, as far as our knowledge is concerned, there has recently been no systematic research into the extent to which administrative bodies make a decision before the deadline. However, there are countless indications that administrative bodies do not decide on time in a substantial number of cases. An illustration is provided by an analysis concerned with the handling of appeals by the administrative courts, which is currently being conducted by one of the authors of this contribution. In the context of that research, we looked at how quickly

[4] Directive 2006/123/EC of the European Parliament and of the Council of 12 December 2006 on services in the internal market (*PbEU* 2006, L 376/36).

[5] See *Parliamentary Papers II* 2007/08, 31 579, no. 3, pp. 108–109.

administrative bodies decide on objections to their decisions. In most cases, the period for deciding on an objection is 12 weeks after the period to lodge an objection of 6 weeks. The research shows that in less than half of the cases (45%) a decision on the objection is made within these 18 weeks. In particular in cases in the field of environmental law and in disputes about compensation, decision periods are frequently exceeded.

6.3 Responses to Administrative Silence in the Netherlands

6.3.1 Different Legal Consequences of Administrative Silence

Dutch administrative law provides several possible legal consequences in cases where a public authority does not make a decision within the given time limit. Before the introduction of the General Administrative Law Act in 1994, one could point to the Administrative Law Act on Administrative Decisions of 1976 (*Wet administratieve rechtspraak overheidsbeschikkingen*, ALAAD) that provided in Article 3 that administrative silence should be interpreted as a refusal of the administrative decision requested. The ALAAD was revoked and the GALA now regulates the main legal consequences of administrative silence. What is the prevailing model in Dutch administrative law? From the moment the GALA was introduced, Article 6:2(b) provides that administrative silence as a response to an application by an interested party will be considered as an order that is subject to judicial review. Only the provisions of the GALA that are concerned with judicial review are applicable to administrative silence (Chapters 6, 7 and 8 GALA). Besides the opportunity of judicial review (see Sects. 6.4 and 6.6), Article 4:17 GALA stipulates that the public authority could be subject to a penalty for its silence if certain specific conditions are met (see Sect. 6.6.2).

Although these sanctions could be considered sufficient, the legislator has in 2009 also introduced a system of fictitious positive decision-making in section 4.1.3.3 GALA which is considered an alternative to the sanctions mentioned above. The reason for the introduction has been to strengthen the applicant's position vis-à-vis the public authority and to stimulate that authority to decide within the given time limit, but also to implement the EU Services Directive. The provisions in this section 4.1.3.3 GALA provide for an immediate legal consequence when the time period has been exceeded: A fictitious positive response to the application is created automatically (*ex lege*). The decision-making period therefore has a fatal character and for the public authority it is no longer possible to allow the time period for taking the decision to expire unused with impunity. However, we should keep in mind that this particular section of the GALA is only applicable when its applicability is explicitly stipulated in a specific legislative act, regulation, or ordonnance. An important example of this can be found in the General Act on Environmental Licensing (*Wet algemene bepalingen omgevingsrecht*, GAEL) which prescribes that section 4.1.3.3 GALA applies to applications for licenses that will be decided upon after using the so-called standard decision-making procedure, with the exception of Article 4:20b(3) and Article 4:20f GALA.[6] For these specific provisions, the GAEL provides its own regulatory scheme which will be discussed below. Another example is provided by the Dutch Services Act that implements the European Services Directive in the Netherlands.[7] Although normally sector-specific legislative acts will designate a specific permitting system to which section 4.1.3.3 GALA is applicable, the Dutch Services Act simply stipulates that this section is applicable to all licensing systems that fall within the scope of the European Services Directive, except when the applicability is specifically ruled out by a legislative act.

6.3.2 *The EU Influence on National Rules and Practices*

When the EU Services Directive was implemented in the Netherlands in December 2009, there were changes to the GALA and a dedicated legislative act was introduced, the Dutch Services Act. In Sect. 6.2.2, we discussed some provisions of the Services Act that changed the Articles 4:14 and 4:15 GALA in case of an application for a decision that falls within the scope of the Services Directive. The implementation also led to the introduction of section 4.1.3.3 GALA that provides general provisions on fictitious authorizations. The provisions in this section are only applicable when another legislative act has stipulated that they are and can

[6] It is hardly surprising that a strict deadline for taking an administrative decision is incorporated in the GAEL, since this instrument did already apply to several licensing systems—for example the building permit based on the former Housing act—that now are included in the ELA.

[7] In Dutch: *Dienstenwet*. Also see on this subject K. J. de Graaf and N. G. Hoogstra (2013) and Sect. 6.3.2.

therefore potentially be relevant for all applications by an interested party to use a competence awarded by the legislator to a public authority.[8] Article 13(4) of the Services Directive was one of the main reasons to introduce section 4.1.3.3. GALA. Member states are obliged to introduce a system of fictitious positive decisions when the nature of a specific decision falls within the scope of the Services Directive, although exceptions can be justified. It reads as follows.

> Failing a response within the time period set or extended in accordance with paragraph 3, authorisation shall be deemed to have been granted. Different arrangements may nevertheless be put in place, where justified by overriding reasons relating to the public interest, including a legitimate interest of third parties.

The Services Directive therefore demands the implementation of a system of fictitious positive decisions in case where the time period set is exceeded, but allows the member states some leeway. The Dutch Services Act therefore stipulates in Article 28 that all licensing systems that fall within the scope of the European Services Directive are subject to a system of fictitious positive decisions, except when the applicability is specifically ruled out by a legislative act.

Despite the fact that section 4.1.3.3 GALA has only been in force since 2009,[9] tacit authorizations were not a new phenomenon in the Netherlands. For some licensing systems, legislation already stipulated that failure on the part of the administrative authority to take a decision within the given time limit would result in fictitious approval. An important example of this system of tacit authorization is the permitting system for building permits. For a long time these could be granted tacitly under the Housing Act if no decision has been taken within the statutory time

[8] In other words, this section can be applicable to application for decisions within and outside the scope of the Services Directive. Before introducing the new section, the Government launched a project to assess whether existing permitting systems could be deleted or converted into a system of general binding rules and many were. Remaining licensing systems now usually include a strict deadline to take a decision. See *Parliamentary Papers II* 2007/08, 29 515, no. 224.

[9] In the Netherlands, this part of the implementation of the European Services Directive has been discussed most. Stelkens et al. (2012, p. 37).

limit.[10] Section 4.1.3.3 GALA has introduced important general provisions to replace and enhance different regimes of fictitious approvals in specific legislative acts.[11] Legal scholars in the Netherlands quite often refer to the rules on fictitious authorizations as the *Lex silencio positivo* (LSP), which seems to be a strange mix between Latin and Spanish.

6.4 From a Negative Interpretation to a Procedural Instrument

In the first years after the introduction of the GALA in 1994, the appeal against the failure to process an application within the set time limit on the basis of Article 6:2(b) GALA was treated by administrative courts as a fictitious refusal. The omission of a decision was interpreted as a substantive reaction and the judicial review therefore also covered the substance of the matter as if the application was refused. Judicial review against administrative silence did not only concern the question whether the administrative authority had exceeded the decision period, but also whether the administrative authority could lawfully refuse the application. This situation was explained as being a continuation of the case law under the ALAAD, that provided explicitly in Article 3 that administrative silence shall be considered a refusal of the application.

However, a judgment of the highest administrative court (the Administrative Jurisdiction Division of the Council of State) in December 1998 changed this role of the courts in judicial review against administrative silence quite drastically.[12] The Administrative Jurisdiction Division decided that from now on an appeal against the failure to deliver an administrative decision within the set period would not be considered an appeal against a refusal but will simply be seen as the appeal lodged against the omission of a decision.

[10] Other former examples are the Monuments and Historic Buildings Act and the Mining Decree.

[11] This division only applies when stated in a specific Act. For legislation within the scope of the Services Directive this is the standard based on Article 28(1) of the Services Act. For legislation outside the scope of the Services Directive an explicit provision that division 4.1.3.3 of the GALA is applicable is required.

[12] Administrative Jurisdiction Division of the Council of State 3 December 1998, ECLI:NL:RVS:1998:ZF3644.

> Using Article 6:2(b) of the GALA by making an objection or lodging an appeal against the absence of a decision can primarily be seen as a procedural means to get an administrative body to take a decision. In general, the administrative body is still obliged to take a real decision – which can also be done pending the procedure for not taking a decision in time – against which judicial review is possible. The GALA does not stipulate that non-timely decision-making shall be considered a substantive decision of any kind. [...] In the absence of such a provision, the Council of State considers that there is no reason in general nor in this specific case to equate the absence of a decision with a real substantive decision based on what the administrative body has put forward in the course of the procedure.[13]

In short, an appeal against failure to take a timely decision should no longer be interpreted as being a substantive decision, but is merely a procedural instrument for an interested party to allow the administrative court to force the public authority to take a real decision. It was rather remarkable that the Administrative Jurisdiction Division of the Council of State choose a different route than the legislator had envisaged according to the explanatory memorandum of the GALA, which states the following.

> Because an untimely decision on an application is equated with a real decision for the purpose of the provisions concerned with the objection and appeal scheme, the content of the decision to be taken can also be discussed in the objection and appeal procedure. If, for example, it becomes apparent during the proceedings before a court which decision should have been taken, then it is not sufficient to state that the administrative body did not make a timely decision, but the court can also provide judicial review against the content of the decision.[14]

In general, this approach of the Administrative Jurisdiction Division is explained by legal scholars in literature as being justified, specifically because a substantive interpretation of untimely decision-making can put administrative courts in a difficult position as many believe that the judge shall not take over the task of the administration to take decisions.[15]

[13] Translated from the judgment.

[14] *Parliamentary Papers II* 1988/89, 21 221, no. 3, p. 120 (translated).

[15] Ten Veen and Collignon (2010, pp. 319–341).

The main and mostly only question within such an appeal is whether the administrative authority did indeed fail to process the application within the set time period. This is often a simple calculation: Whether the set time period to decide has expired without the administrative authority having taken a decision or whether the decision period did not expire (yet). Consequence of this procedural change in judicial review is that, from a substantive point of view, the applicant's substantive legal position is not made clear by the outcome of the appeal procedure since the court's ruling will only be about the question whether there was a case of untimely decision-making. If that is the case, the administrative court shall order the administrative body to take the decision within a time period under penalty of paying a penalty if this period is exceeded, which obligation has been laid down in Article 8:55d GALA since October 2009. An appeal procedure against untimely decision-making does of course not relieve the administrative body of the obligation to take a real decision. If this decision is taken during the procedure against the untimely decision-making, the judicial review will also include the real decision. In principle, however, the appeal procedure is regarded as simply a procedural means for encouraging the public authority to make a real decision.

6.5 Fictitious Positive Authorizations: Positive Silence

6.5.1 Introduction

The introduction of a broad system of fictitious approvals has been severely criticized.[16] In fact the idea of the system of tacit authorization is that it stimulates administrative authorities to decide within the prescribed time limit. So, in an ideal scenario the instrument will be never applied, because the administrative authority always decides before the end of the strict deadline. Looking at the case law based on the GAEL this is not the case in practice. In particular, the Council of State, in its advisory role, was

[16] Jacobs (2010) and see also Schiebroek and De Waard (2011).

not in favor of the introduction of tacit authorizations and even recommended to withdraw this legal instrument from national administrative law in the Netherlands.[17]

The main point of criticism directed at this instrument is that it is very likely that the public interest and the interests of third parties are not (sufficiently) taken into consideration. In addition, a tacit authorization places the applicant's interest above the public interest and the interests of third parties. In other words, public interests, as well as private interests of third parties, can be set aside in favor of the licensee. The exercise of activities requiring prior authorization must now be allowed without, as is customary, being tested for compatibility with the public interest. In a system of tacit authorization, activities contravening the public interest are all of a sudden allowed, which means that, as with the legal certainty of third parties, protection of this interest is no longer safeguarded without further regulation.

A fictitious approval will cause legal uncertainties, considering the fact that this type of permit does not comply with the procedural and substantive demands which normally apply to formal administrative decisions. Moreover, the Council of State, in its advisory role, notes that a tacit authorization is not based on an adequate balancing of interests.[18] The interests of third parties are not properly weighed up against other interests, either because a substantive assessment of the license application has not taken place at all or because this assessment has not resulted in an actual administrative decision.[19] In addition, the decision will not be properly motivated, especially because of the fact that there is not even a written decision. Normally, the administrative authority has to fulfill the

[17] The Council of State has been reserved with regard to the introduction of a system of tacit authorization. See *Parliamentary Papers II* 2007/08, 29 515, no. 224, *Parliamentary Papers II* 2007/08, 31 579, no. 4, *Parliamentary Papers II* 2007/08, 32 844, no. 4 and *Parliamentary Papers II* 2009/10, 32 454, no. 4.

[18] The Council of State believes that a fictitious approval can have harmful effects for third parties or society as a whole. This is especially the case when the tacit authorization occurs with licensing systems regulated in the ELA, because these licensing systems do almost always affect the physical living environment, the interests of third parties and the public interest. See *Parliamentary Papers II* 2007/08, 32 844, no. 4, pp. 9–10.

[19] See Article 1:3(2) of the GALA: "Administrative decision" means an order which is not of a general nature, including rejection of an application for such an order.

obligation to provide reasons for the administrative decision that explain why the decision was taken.[20]

The legislator took notice of the criticism and acknowledged that a tacit authorization might have harmful effects on the public interest and the interests of third parties. In order to protect these interests several provisions were introduced in the GALA.[21] These provisions will be discussed in this section. In addition, there will be attention to supplementary provisions in the GAEL that are also designed to safeguard the public interests and the interests of third parties.

We will focus here on three questions. The first question is when a fictitious approval enters into force and how interested parties are given notice that authorization has been granted. A second question is which legal powers an administrative authority has to protect the public interests and the interest of third parties, after an authorization is granted tacitly. A third question is how legal protection against tacit authorizations is regulated.

6.5.2 Notification and the Entering into Force of Tacit Authorizations

When section 4.1.3.3 of the GALA has been declared applicable to a certain licensing system, then tacit authorization can be granted if the statutory time limit has expired and the administrative authority has not responded to the application.[22] In case a statutory time limit is missing in a specific Act, the "reasonable time limit" of eight weeks will apply.[23] Since exceeding the strict deadline results in a fictitious approval, it is important that both the applicant and third parties stay informed of the strict deadline. For that reason, it is strongly recommended that the competent administrative authority send an acknowledgment of receipt of the application as soon as possible, stating both the time limit for

[20] Article 3:46 of the GALA.

[21] The expectation of the legislator is that these instruments will only be used in exceptional cases. *Parliamentary Papers II* 2006/07, 30 844, no. 3, p. 36.

[22] For example, there is a prescribed time limit of eight weeks for applications covered by the standard preparatory procedure as set out in Article 3.9(1) of the ELA. This time limit can only be extended once by the administrative authority for 6 weeks at most. So the time limit is fourteen weeks at most.

[23] See also Article 31 of the Services Act and Article 4:14 of the GALA.

the response and the fact that tacit authorization will be granted if no response is sent within the given time limit.[24] In case a tacit authorization is deemed to have been granted, this approval takes effect on the third day after the time limit has expired.[25] The legislator has chosen the third day after expiry of the time limit to ensure that a formal decision sent by the administrative authority on the last day of the time limit could be delivered by mail.

A notice that the authorization has been granted tacitly based on the GALA is not required for the entry into force of the fictitious permit. Normally, an administrative decision shall not take effect until it has been notified.[26] Positive consequence of the rule that a tacit authorization enters into force automatically is that the administrative authority has no influence on the moment the license takes effect.[27]

Article 4:20b(3) GALA is however not applied mutatis mutandis in the GAEL.[28] According to the GAEL, a fictitious permit needs to be notified before it can become effective. In addition, the licensee that holds such a fictitious permit can only benefit from this license once the time limit for formally lodging an objection against it has expired or in case a notice of objection has been filed, after a decision has been made in the following objection procedure.[29] And in Dutch law the time limit to formally lodge an objection will start after official notification of the permit that was tacitly granted. In other words, the entering into force of a tacit permit on the basis of GAEL will be automatically suspended for a number of weeks after the official notification of the permit.[30]

[24] This is mandatory by applications for an environmental license. See Articles 3.8 and 3.9(1) of the ELA.

[25] Article 4:20b(3) of the GALA.

[26] Article 3:40 of the GALA: "An order shall not take effect until it has been notified." Article 3:41 of the GALA: "Orders which are addressed to one or more interested parties shall be notified by being sent or issued to these, including the applicant."

[27] *Parliamentary Papers II* 2007/08, 31 579, no. 3, pp. 129–130.

[28] This means that a tacit authorization based on the GAEL does not enter into force after three days after the time limit has expired.

[29] Article 6.1(4) of the ELA.

[30] Moreover, it is possible for the licensee of the fictitious permit to ask for a preliminary injunction in order to reverse the suspensive effect. See also C. M. Saris, "Tijdig beslissen. Het doel dichterbij met de Wet dwangsom en beroep bij niet tijdig beslissen en de verruiming van de lex silencio positivo?", *De Gemeentestem* 2008, nr. 30.

Nevertheless, for both the regime in the GALA and the GAEL the administrative authority is obliged to give notice of the fictitious authorization within two weeks of its entry into force (GALA) or its emergence (GAEL). In addition, the administrative authority is required to give public notice that an approval has been awarded fictitiously instead of a formal (real) license. With this public notification, third parties are informed of the fictitious approval. However, it is questionable whether public notification of tacit authorization always takes place. It has been discussed whether an administrative authority, unable of making a decision within the prescribed time limit, would announce an issued fictitious license in time.[31] In other words, it would be highly likely that the administrative authority fails to give a notification within two weeks after the strict deadline, the expiration of which has led to a tacit authorization.

If the administrative authority fails on the duty of notification, there is a risk that the administrative authority has to pay a penalty.[32] This is the case when the applicant has asked for notification by a written notice of default and the administrative authority has not answered this request within two weeks.[33] The penalty is the same as when there is an untimely decision.[34] The exact amount of the penalty payment depends on the amount of time it takes before the administrative authority notifies the tacit authorization. With this instrument, the administrative authority is once again sanctioned for the fact that a decision has not been made before a strict deadline. Next to the sanction of a penalty, it is also possible to force the administrative authority to officially send notice of the granted permit by filing an appeal with the administrative court, again after a written notice of default has been issued and two weeks have passed.[35] The court will be able to order the administrative authority to officially notify or publish the permit that was granted tacitly.

[31] Robbe (2011) and see also Robbe (2012).

[32] Article 4:20d of the GALA.

[33] Article 6:12 of the GALA.

[34] See the rapport "Monitor Wet dwangsom" attachment by *Parliamentary Papers II* 2012/13, 29 934, no. 29.

[35] Article 8:55f of the GALA.

6.5.3 Competence to Amend or Revoke Tacit Authorizations

One of the key consequences of the fact that a permit has been granted tacitly is that the administrative authority is no longer competent to issue a valid act or order. The legal basis for such a substantive decision on the matter is non-existent because a decision was already "taken." Judicial review must lead be to annulment of the decision.

In order to safeguard interests after a license has been granted tacitly, so-called standard conditions are automatically considered conditions of the fictitious approval. If a statutory provision or a policy guideline stipulates the standard conditions that are normally to be included in the permit, they apply by operation of law to tacit authorizations.[36] This particular regulation aims to equalize license conditions for substantive administrative decisions and fictitious decisions.[37]

Besides standard conditions the administrative authority has the power to either add conditions to the fictitious approval or to revoke the license if this is needed to avoid *serious consequences for the public interest*.[38] Both can be done within a time limit of six weeks after sending a notification of the tacit authorization.[39] The licensee is entitled to compensation if the administrative authority decides to amend or revoke a tacit authorization. Only the damage resulting from the amendment or revocation of the license is considered for compensation, not the damage which may arise after a license issued by right is granted.[40]

The GAEL contains specific other provisions about the competence of public authorities to either attach conditions to the environmental license that was tacitly granted or to revoke it in case of serious consequences

[36] By way of example, in the explanatory memorandum attached to this instrument, the case of a license that gives permission to set up a terrace is mentioned. Attached to this type of license, most municipalities in the Netherlands have a standard condition with regard to closing times. The same closing time applies in case of a fictitious terrace permit, irrespective of whether or not this is included in the license application (*Parliamentary Papers II* 2007/08, 31 579, no. 3, p. 133).

[37] A standard condition is a rule which is included in a legal provision or a policy rule. However, which exact rules can be seen as standard conditions is unclear. This has led to some debate in Dutch literature. See De Kam (2010) and see also Kocken (2011).

[38] Article 4:20f of the GALA.

[39] Notification in the sense of Article 4:20c of the GALA.

[40] Article 4:20f(3) of the GALA.

for the physical living environment.[41] As a consequence of the provisions regulating when such a license will enter into force, no detrimental effects for the environment will occur within at least six weeks after the license is notified. This gives the administrative authority the opportunity to examine if the fictitious license has detrimental consequences for the environment and which measures might offer an adequate solution. Consequently, together with the notification of the tacit license to the applicant, the conditions attached to the tacit decision or the (partial) revocation of the license can also be notified. The wording used in the GAEL is different from the terminology used in the GALA. The scope of this regulation in the GAEL appears to be more restrictive, since "*serious consequences for the environment*" is a more restricted concept than "*serious consequences for the public interest*," which is used in the GALA. Furthermore, the GAEL provides for quite a rigorous obligation for the administrative authority to amend or to revoke the fictitious approval, whereas the GALA only stipulates the competence to do so. Also, in the GAEL, the administrative authority is not subject to a strict period of time in which conditions need to be attached to the license or in which the license has to be revoked. Naturally it would be best if the administrative authority takes measures within a short period of time in light of the serious detrimental consequences that the tacit authorization might have.

6.5.4 Empirical Evidence

How often are administrative bodies allowing positive fictitious decisions to come into existence? Research that was conducted in 2013 shows that quite a number of administrative bodies are occasionally confronted with the fact that they did, but very few administrative bodies experience this frequently (Fig. 6.1).[42]

38% of the administrative bodies indicates that, in the 5 years following the introduction of this instrument, they were never confronted with the fact that a positive fictitious decision was granted, 53% occasionally (1–10 times), 9% regularly (10 or more times).

[41] Article 2.31 and 2.33 of the ELA.

[42] https://www.wodc.nl/onderzoeksdatabase/evaluatie-van-de-werking-van-de-lex-silencio-positivo.aspx.

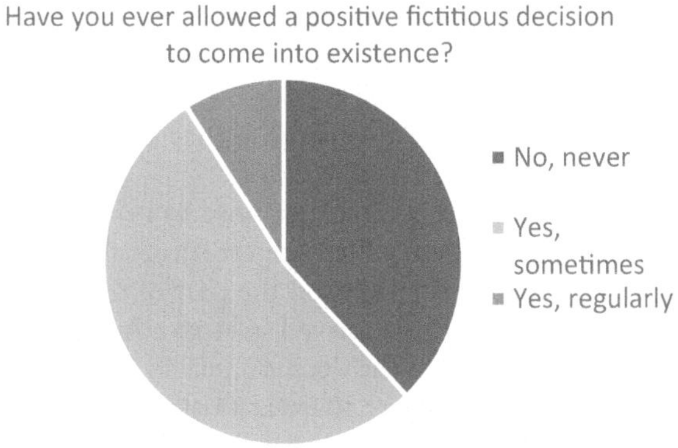

Fig. 6.1 Positive fictitious decisions

Looking at the nature of the applications that were tacitly granted, we see that most decisions relate to permits in the field of environmental and planning law.

What is the impact of the introduction of the *lex silencio positivo*? Does the decision-making process proceed more quickly now than before the introduction of this law? 38% of the administrative bodies believes this is the case, whereas 62% believes this is not the case. A number of administrative bodies believe that the law has a positive effect on the punctuality of decision-making. They believe that the most important reason for this is an increased alertness to respecting the decision period. This alertness seems to be greater compared to situations where the *lex silencio positivo* is not applicable and where there is, at most, a risk that a party concerned will put the administrative body into default on the grounds of failure to make a timely decision. To forfeit a penalty is annoying, but if it happens, the damage is manageable. Administrative bodies are, however, much more reluctant to allow a positive fictitious decision to come into existence. They want to avoid a permit from being granted *ex lege*. The reason for this is that such a permit has unwanted social consequences, especially if the permit is contrary to the law. If, for example, an entrepreneur obtains a fictitious positive decision (permit) that should have been denied by the administrative body, his competitors will be damaged and are likely to lodge an objections or an appeal.

In practice, the following occurs in situations where the *lex silencio positivo* applies and where there is a risk of not meeting the deadline for rendering a decision. The administrative body contacts the applicant and asks him to withdraw his application and to submit a new one, so as to allow the administrative body to render a timely decision. Applicants often comply with this request, also because they have an interest in the administrative body rendering a real decision.

More side effects are mentioned in response to one of the open questions of the survey. One of these is that the creation of a positive fictitious permit will generate false expectations on the part of the permit holder, as the positive fictitious permit is not carved in stone. Another negative side effect is that, in situations where the decision period for the administrative body has almost expired and where there is a risk that a positive fictitious decision will be rendered, the application is denied for safety reasons. The ball is then in the applicant's court: If they still want to obtain a permit, they must file an objection against the denial. Another negative side effect mentioned is that the positive fictitious permit weakens the position of third parties. In the event that a positive fictitious permit is granted while the rules do not allow the granting of such a permit, the third party must take action to avoid the unlawful permit from applying.

6.6 Legal Remedies

6.6.1 Appeal Against the Failure to Take a Timely Decision

The standard in the GALA is that an appeal to the administrative court is only allowed against written decisions of public authorities. No appeal can be made to the administrative court against other acts or omissions of public authorities. That would mean that if an administrative authority did not make a (timely) decision (yet), no legal remedy would be available with the administrative court against that act or omission. In the case of administrative silence or untimely decision-making, there is no decision. The legislator has deemed such a situation undesirable. That is why a number of provisions have been introduced in the GALA that make it possible to litigate before the administrative court against the absence of a decision.

To this end, Article 6:2(b) GALA stipulates the following: "For the purposes of statutory regulations governing objections and appeals, the following shall be equated with an order: failure to make an order in due time."

This provision allows interested parties to lodge an appeal against untimely decision-making with the administrative courts in the Netherlands.

Article 6:12 GALA stipulates special provisions about the appeal against administrative silence or late decisions in cases an interested party has applied for a single-case decision, like a permit. In the past, that provision meant not only that it was possible to appeal against the absence of a decision to the administrative court, but also that the appeal with the administrative court could only be lodged after the interested party had first lodged a formal objection with the administrative authority about the decision that was not taken. In 2009 Article 6:12 GALA was amended and now reads:

1. If the notice of appeal is brought against failure to make an order in due time or against failure to notify that an authorization is deemed to have been granted, it shall not be subject to any time limit.
2. A notice of objection or appeal may be submitted at such time as
   a. the administrative authority has failed to make an order in due time or has failed to notify that an authorization is deemed to have been granted and
   b. two weeks have passed since the day the interested party sent the administrative authority a written notice of default.
3. If it is not reasonably possible to require the interested party to declare the administrative authority to be in default, the notice of appeal may be submitted as soon as the administrative authority fails to make an order in due time;
4. The objection or appeal shall be ruled inadmissible if the notice of objection or appeal is submitted unreasonably late.

The provision provides that as soon as an administrative authority has allowed the decision period to expire, an interested party (Article 1:2 GALA) can send the administrative authority a notice of default. Two weeks later, he is allowed to lodge an appeal with the administrative court against the absence of the decision. There is, however, a limit to the possible appeal against the absence of a decision. Such an appeal shall not be lodged "unreasonably late." When an appeal is made "unreasonably late" depends on the circumstances of the case. The case law of the highest administrative courts shows that those who wait more than half a year before appealing against the absence of a decision run the risk that their appeal will be declared inadmissible because it was submitted unreasonably late.[43]

The way in which that appeal is handled is provided in Articles 8:55b up to and including 8:55f GALA. The arrangement entails the following. In the first place, the appeal is handled by the court in a simplified manner. This means that the appeal is not handled at a hearing (Article 8: 55b(1) GALA). The judge will rule on the appeal within eight weeks (Article 8:55b(1) GALA). If the appeal is well founded and the administrative authority has still not taken a decision at that time, the court will determine that the administrative body shall take a decision within two weeks (Article 8:55d (1) GALA). The administrative court shall attach a penalty to this decision for each day that the administrative body fails to comply with the decision (usually a penalty of 100 euro until a maximum of 15.000 euro).

The only available remedy against the ruling of the court in a procedure against administrative silence is the possibility to object against the judgment of the court with (another chamber of) the court. The administrative court will then decide within six weeks on the objections brought forward. If the objection is well founded, the administrative law court will then again decide as quickly as possible on the appeal (Article 8:55e GALA).

The administrative court can refrain from the simplified handling of the appeal against administrative silence. The appeal will then be dealt with at a hearing (Articles 8:55b(2 and 3) GALA). In that case, the court decides if possible, within thirteen weeks (Article 8:55b(3) GALA). Appeal against the court's decision is possible.

The Articles 8:55b to 8:55f GALA show that the legislator does not consider the absence of a decision as a fictitious negative decision. The assessment of the appeal against the absence of the decision therefore only concerns the question whether the administrative body has exceeded the decision period that applies to him. However, this was not always the case.

[43] Trade and Industry Appeals Tribunal (*College voor Beroep van het bedrijfsleven*) 16 April 1998, ECLI:NL:CBB:1998:AN5693, Administrative Jurisdiction Division of the Council of State (*Afdeling bestuursrechtspraak van de Raad van State*) 15 January 2003, ECLI:NL:RVS:2003:AF2904, Central Appeals Tribunal (*Centrale Raad van Beroep*) 4 October 2005, ECLI:NL:CRVB:2005:AU4243.

6.6.2 *Penalty for the Failure to Take a Timely Decision*

Due to the entry into force of the Act on Penalty Payment and Appeals in the event of administrative silence in October 2009, the GALA was amended in the sense that an interested party that is waiting for a decision of an administrative body has been given an alternative instrument (in addition to the appeal against the failure to take a timely decision) to persuade an administrative body that is in default to decide within the set time limit. The administrative authority can forfeit a penalty for each day that it is in default to take a decision, with a maximum of 42 days. The regulation, included in section 4.1.3.2 GALA, applies to both decisions on demand and decisions on objections, but only when the decision is considered a single-case administrative decision (in Dutch a *beschikking*). With this penalty payment scheme, the legislator has intended to include a financial incentive in the GALA to stimulate timely decision-making.

The penalty payment is due from two weeks after the administrative authority has received a written notice of default. The way to give notice to an administrative body of late decision-making is not subject to any other legal requirements than that it must be done in writing (Article 6:12(2)(b) GALA). A notice of default is therefore free of form. However, the baseline is based on consistent case law that it must be sufficiently clear to which application for a decision the notice of default relates.

Similar to a notice of default in the context of an appeal procedure for late decision, the administrative authority is also warned by the notice of default that the decision period has been exceeded. Equally similar is that the administrative body in this way obtains an additional time period, as it were, to still take a decision. If the administrative authority is able to take a decision on the application within two weeks' time, it will not owe a penalty payment to the applicant.

This penalty payment is €23 per day for the first 14 days, €35 per day for the second 14 days, and then €45 per day. The total amount could rise to a maximum of €1442. A penalty payment by an administrative authority is not required under all circumstances. Article 4:17(6) GALA stipulates three exceptions. The first exception is the situation in which a notice of default is received by the administrative authority unreasonably late. Secondly, no penalty payment is due if the applicant of the penalty is not an interested party. It is unclear whether the legislator has thought this to mean that the person applying for the penalty payment could be a different person than the applicant for the decision. After all, the alternative is that the applicant is not considered an interested party for his own request. A third exception is that no penalty payment is due if the application is non-admissible or manifestly unfounded. This legislative text is somewhat remarkable since the term inadmissible or manifestly unfounded is normally used in legal procedures as the objection procedure and the procedure of judicial review. In the words of the GALA an application can be put out of consideration (see Article 4:5 GALA).

Within two weeks after the last day a penalty payment was owed, the administrative authority must, by decision, determine the total amount of the penalty payment. This last day may mean that maximum penalty payment of €1442 has been reached or that the administrative body has taken a decision and published it. Payment of the penalty must be made within 6 weeks of the announcement of the decision determining the total amount of the penalties.

The penalty payment scheme aims to stimulate the administrative authority to decide on an application in time. It is clear to the attentive reader that although the administrative authority can be sanctioned in the event of a time limit, it is not necessarily guaranteed that the administrative authority ultimately takes a decision either granting or refusing the application. After all, the payment of a penalty is not equivalent to obtaining a decision on the original application. In order to force the administrative authority to take a decision, the applicant has no choice but to (also) lodge an appeal procedure for failure to take a decision timely.

6.6.3 *Legal Protection in Case of Tacit Authorizations*

A fictitious authorization can be legally challenged the same way a formal (real) decision on an application is challenged.[44] This generally means that first an objection shall be made by submitting a notice of objection to the administrative authority which "made" the fictitious approval.[45] Next, the fictitious approval can be challenged at the district court and the decision can be appealed the Administrative Jurisdiction Division of the Council of State.[46] The six-week period during which an appeal can

[44] Although theoretically a tacit authorization is not an "order" (defined in Article 1:3(1) of the GALA as a written decision of an administrative authority constituting a public law act), Article 4:20b(2) simply states that it is regarded as an order.

[45] Article 6:4 of the GALA.

[46] Articles 8:1 and 8:104 of the GALA.

be lodged against a tacit authorization begins when notice is given of the authorization.[47] As explained earlier there can be a substantial difference between the moment the tacit authorization takes effect and the moment an administrative authority gives notice of this license.[48] This means that third parties have to wait until notice is given before they can officially object against the tacit authorization.

Judicial review of a decision that was tacitly granted starts with the obligatory objection procedure by lodging an objection with the competent authority. The time period to lodge an objection commences at the moment the decision is officially notified in accordance with Article 3:41 or 3:42 GALA, as follows from Article 6:8 GALA. The notification of the fictitious decision is therefore essential for both the applicant and third parties with an interest as it marks the start of the time period set to officially lodge an objection and also determines the moment when the fictitious authorization becomes irrevocable as lodging an objection is no longer possible.

Although Article 4:20c GALA contains an explicit obligation for the administrative body to notify that a fictitious authorization was granted, it is conceivable that—certainly now that it is clear that the administrative body has not taken a decision within the time period set—timely notification is also not to be expected. The GALA therefore provides interested parties access to the administrative courts in case a fictitious authorization is not notified correctly (see Article 8:55f and 6:12 GALA).

Another issue—which automatically occurs in case of a fictitious license—is that there is no written document in which the reasons for the decision are stated. It is assumed that it is not really possible to check for compliance with procedural requirements, such as the requirement that sound reasons are given; that would mean that any legal action would lead to a successful appeal which could hardly have been, the intention of the legislature.[49] If the administrative court completely or partially annuls the tacit authorization, the authority must make a new decision. Failure

[47] Article 6:8 of the GALA: 'The time limit shall start on the day after that on which the order is notified in the prescribed manner'.

[48] See in detail Sect. 6.3.2.

[49] See also Buteijn (2009).

to comply with the administrative court's order to make a new decision cannot lead to another tacit authorization.[50]

6.6.4 *The Role of the Ombudsman*

An analysis of the National Ombudsman's annual reports of the past years reveals that a large number of complaints per year relate to the lack of timely decision-making. The lack of will of the power to expeditiously grant or refuse applications is a persistent problem. Timeliness is included in the most recent version of the National Ombudsman's Guide to Good Administration and is described as follows.

> The government is acting as quickly and decisively as possible. The legal deadlines are final deadlines. The government strives for shorter periods whenever possible. If decision-making takes longer, the government will inform the citizen in good time. If no period is specified, the government acts within a reasonable - short - period.[51]

In the annual report of 2000, the National Ombudsman states that a fictitious granting of a permit can offer a solution in a number of cases and suggests the legislator to investigate in which licensing systems this can be introduced.[52] It is striking that the National Ombudsman is relatively positive about a system of fictitious licensing.

The moment a citizen turns to the National Ombudsman to lodge a complaint about untimely decision-making, he has often waited a considerable time for a response from an administrative authority. The National Ombudsman finds it unacceptable that the patience of the citizens is put to the test by the government that does not comply with the stipulated terms of the GALA for timely decision-making. According to the National Ombudsman, failing to take timely decisions leads to a deterioration of confidence in the government.

[50] *Parliamentary Papers II* 2009/10, 32 454, no. 3, p. 4.

[51] www.nationaleombudsman.nl.

[52] Jaarverslag 2000, *Kamerstukken II* 2000/01, 27 645, 1–2.

6.6.5 Empirical Evidence

Introduction

How often these legal remedies are used? In 2013, the use and impact of the penalty for and the appeal against the failure to make a timely decision were extensively analyzed on behalf of the Research and Documentation Centre (WODC) of the Ministry of Justice of the Netherlands.[53] To this end, a written survey was conducted among 253 administrative bodies as well as 16 face-to-face interviews within administrative bodies.

Penalty for Failure to Make a Timely Decision

The survey shows, in the first place, that a vast majority of the administrative bodies has been put into default one or more times for failure to make a timely decision.

Figure 6.2 shows that, since the introduction of this instrument, 15% of the administrative bodies has never been put into default, 70% occasionally, and 15% frequently.

Administrative bodies that are put into default do not necessarily also forfeit a penalty. This clearly happens less often (Fig. 6.3).

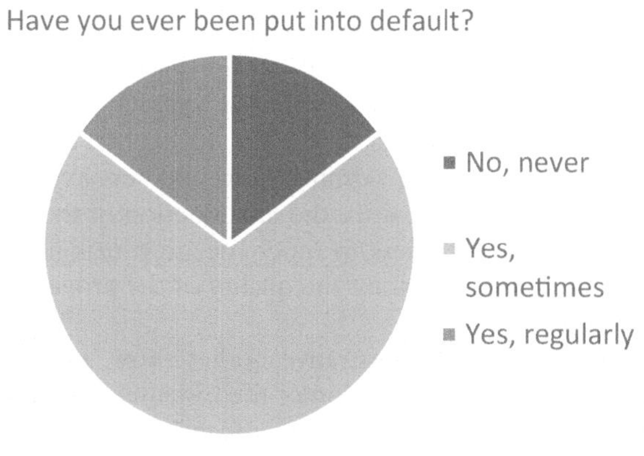

Fig. 6.2 Put into default?

[53] https://www.wodc.nl/onderzoeksdatabase/evaluatie-van-de-werking-van-de-lex-silencio-positivo.aspx.

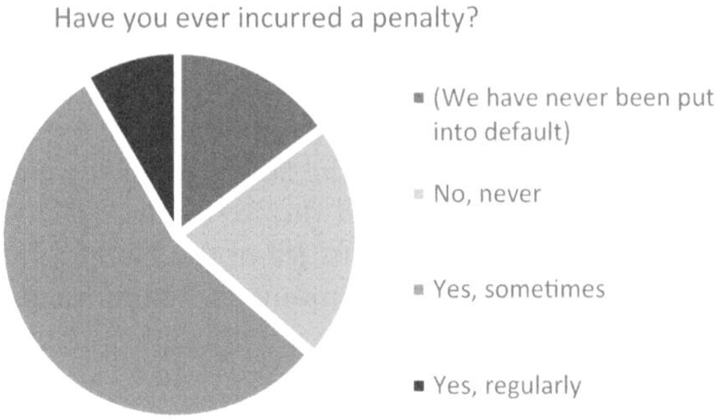

Fig. 6.3 Incurred a penalty?

25% of the administrative bodies that have been put into default has never incurred a penalty, 65% occasionally (1–10 times), and 10% (relatively) frequently (10 or more times).

What is the effect of the possibility to put an administrative body failing to make a timely decision into default and to ensure that it incurs a penalty? A minority of the civil servants to whom this question was submitted (33%) indicated that the effect of that possibility is that decision-making procedures proceed more quickly. A clear majority (67%), however, saw no effect. Of the group that saw no effect, a clear majority considered that the positive effect is limited.

The group that saw an effect was asked to explain that effect. Two explanations prevailed. Firstly, administrative bodies are more alert to respecting the decision period since the introduction of the arrangement. Secondly, the increased alertness to timely decision-making is consistent with the general efforts to increase the quality of the provision of services by public authorities.

The interviews within administrative bodies show, more clearly than the survey does, that the introduction of the instrument of a penalty does have an impact. Civil servants who were subjected to a face-to-face interview indicated that this is an important incentive to respect the decision period.

The arrangement not only has a direct impact, but also some side effects. One of the negative side effects mentioned is that the risk of forfeiting a penalty for failure to make a timely decision results in less careful decision-making. There is more pressure to make a timely decision, which may negatively affect a careful preparation of the decision. There are, however, also positive side effects. Since it has become possible to put an administrative body into default for failure to make a timely decision and to have it forfeit a penalty, it has been easier for administrative bodies to highlight the importance of timely decision-making. In addition, administrative bodies have become more alert to meeting deadlines. The citizens involved are contacted earlier if there is a risk of not meeting a deadline. The introduction of the arrangement has made administrative bodies more aware of the importance of good communication. People who are not informed by the administrative body will put that body into default more quickly than those who are informed that the deadline will not be met.

Appeal Against the Failure to Make a Timely Decision

One of the questions of the survey held among administrative bodies was how often, in the past 5 years, the arrangement was invoked. It appeared that the arrangement was invoked only occasionally (Fig. 6.4).

70% of the administrative bodies indicated that the arrangement was never invoked, 25% occasionally (1–10 times), 5% frequently (10 or more times). Appeal on the grounds of failure to make a timely decision mainly pertains to decisions pursuant to the Government Information (Public

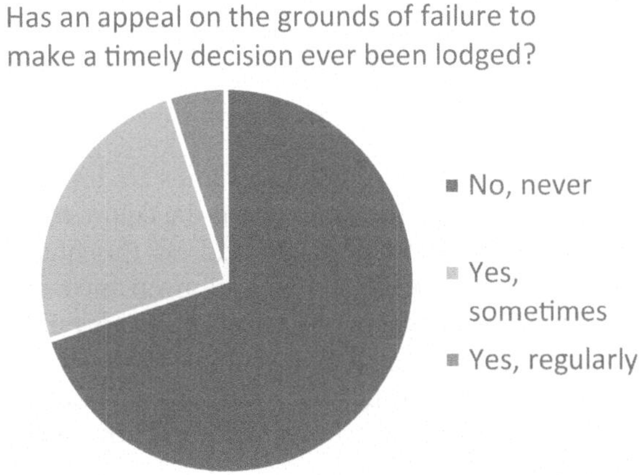

Fig. 6.4 Appeal against the failure to make a timely decision

Access) Act, enforcement decisions, environmental permits, and decision on objections.

Administrative bodies believe that the arrangement has limited impact because it is not invoked very often. What they find positive about the arrangement, is the obligation to put the administrative body into default before lodging an appeal before the court. This allows the administrative body to take action. In many cases, the notice of default is not followed by an appeal on the grounds of failure to make a timely decision.

One of the reasons why the arrangement is so little used is that citizens want to maintain constructive contacts with the administrative body. If an applicant hopes for a positive decision by the administrative body, he often finds it too risky to put the administrative body into default if it has not yet rendered a decision on the expiry of the decision period. Applicants fear that a notice of default reduces the chance of a positive decision.

Citizens who want to take action, if an administrative body has exceeded the decision period, may invoke the penalty arrangement for failure to make a timely decision, or lodge an appeal on the grounds of failure to make a timely decision, or do both. A significant factor in making this choice is the importance attached to the decision. If, for example, the decision relates to a large infrastructure project, the administrative body may decide to postpone its decision, even if this means that it will incur the full penalty of €1442. In this case, it may be more efficient for the person who is waiting for the decision to lodge an appeal on the grounds of failure to make a timely decision. After all, incurring the penalties is, in this case, no incentive for the administrative body to render an early decision. However, an order from the administrative court to render a decision is a real incentive.

It is not easy to find out how often proceedings are brought before the administrative courts in the Netherlands about the failure to make a timely decision. The study from 2013 does not address this question. Courts do not provide information about this question on their own initiative. Moreover, not all judgments of administrative courts are published. Those court judgments that are published almost always concern cases that have been discussed during a formal hearing, while cases about the failure to make a timely decision are almost never dealt with in a procedure with such a formal hearing.

Nevertheless, we can make an estimate of the frequency with which disputes about the failure to make a timely decision are brought before the court. From information that we have obtained from three of the eleven districts courts in the Netherlands, it can be deduced that in one court almost 3% of the total number of administrative cases concern an appeal about the failure to make a timely decision, in the second court almost 4% of the cases, in the third court in more than 5% of the cases. It should be noted that for some of these cases, incidentally, the administrative body still makes a decision during the court-procedure against the absence of a decision. In that case, the nature of the dispute will change from the relatively simple question about untimely decision-making to a substantive argument on the merits of the decision during the court proceedings. In such a case the central question at the time the appeal is lodged is whether the administrative body has exceeded the decision period, but in the judgment the court gives a judgment on the legality of the decision that has since been taken.

6.7 Overall Assessment of the Legal Regime and the Practice of Administrative Silence

Legislation in the Netherlands usually provides competent administrative authorities with a specific decision period that it shall not exceed. Is no specific time period for making the decision prescribed, then Article 4:13 GALA provides that a decision shall be made within a reasonable time, which it stipulates as being 8 weeks. The period to decide on an application starts when the application is received but will be considered suspended for a number of reasons. The most important is when an application is considered incomplete, for instance, when the applicant does not provide all relevant and required information in his application. This applicant has to be warned and offered the opportunity to make his application complete. During the time between the warning and the moment when the application is complete, the decision period will be suspended. Also, other reasons for the suspension of the decision period are mentioned in the Dutch General Administrative Law Act (GALA). What will happen if the decision period is exceeded by the competent administrative authority?

The remedies that the Dutch legislator over time introduced against untimely decision-making by administrative authorities are stipulated in the GALA. Dutch administrative law basically provides for three different remedies when the period to make a decision has expired. The first is the possibility for an interested party to ask for judicial review of the administrative silence. This legal procedure allows the administrative courts to review questions such as whether the competent administrative authority has indeed not taken a decision and whether the decision period to take the decision has indeed expired like the interested party has claimed. Although there are some formalities that the interested party has to overcome, this procedure seems an accessible legal instrument that can potentially lead to a court order to make a decision subject to a penalty payment (Sect. 6.6.1).

The second and third remedy against administrative silence in the Netherlands have a scope that is slightly less broad since these remedies only apply in cases where a single-case decision has been applied for by an interested party. The second remedy is applicable for all single-case decisions that were applied for by an interested party and comes down to a penalty payment by the administrative authority for each day that has passed while is has been put in default and two weeks have passed since then (Sect. 6.6.2). The third remedy was discussed in Sect. 6.5, the so-called *Lex silencio positivo* (LSP). While the Netherlands had some experience with tacitly granted authorizations since 1993, a specific section in the GALA was introduced in 2009 with general provisions about the fictitious approval in order to properly implement the EU Services Directive. This remedy is only applicable when a specific legislative act provides a provision that activates the applicability of this section of the GALA. The legislator introduced in section 4.1.3.3 GALA some special provisions in order to safeguard the public interest and the interests of third parties in cases where an authorization is tacitly granted.

After describing the three legal remedies against administrative silence, we looked at the practical use and the impact of those three instruments. The effectiveness of the various instruments to persuade the government to make timely decisions seems rather limited. With the remedy that provides for the penalty payment the administrative body can forfeit penalty payments if it is late in making its decision. However, invoking the regulation cannot effectively force the administrative authority to actually take a decision. On the other hand, civil servants (experiential experts) have the impression that since the introduction of the possibility of the penalty payment for administrative silence the government has been more alert to taking decisions within the prescribed decision period. Also, administrative authorities seem more aware of the importance of good communication with the applicant, certainly if there is a risk that the decision period is not long enough to take the decision. The provisions that stipulate that any interested party can lodge an appeal against the administrative silence of any administrative authority have a limited scope (the court order is no more than a relevant new incentive for the administrative authority to decide) and there are very few cases that have been brought to court. Striking about the effects and the use of the tacit authorization scheme (in the Netherlands named *Lex silence positivo*) in many cases is that the cure is worse than the disease itself. The occurrence of a fictitious positive decision results in so many complications that administrative authorities do everything they can to prevent them from having to issue and notify a fictitious positive decision. The effect of the *Lex silencio positivo* is often not that decisions are taken more often within the prescribed decision period, but that procedural techniques are applied to avoid the negative effects, without the potential positive effects (timely decision-making) being realized.

References

Buteijn, M. I. P. (2009). Lex silencio positivo: spreken is zilver, zwijgen is goud…of niet. *Journaal Bestuursrecht, 15,* 238.

De Graaf, K. J., & Hoogstra, N. G. (2013). Silence is Golden? Tacit Authorizations in the Netherlands, Germany and France. *Review of European Administrative Law, 6*(2), 7–34.

De Kam, B. (2010). De vergunning van rechtswege en standaardvoorschriften. *De Gemeentestem,* 107.

Jacobs, M. J. (2010). Lsp in de Awb. De totstandkoming en regeling van de positieve fictieve beschikking bij niet tijdig beslissen. In T. Barkhuysen, W. den Ouden, & J. E. M. Polak (Eds.), *Bestuursrecht harmoniseren: 15 jaar Awb* (pp. 627–653). The Hague: Boom Juridische uitgevers.

Kocken, B. M. (2011). Lex silencio positivo. *Stand van zaken. Vastgoedrecht, 1,* 5–11.

Robbe, J. (2011). De omgevingsvergunning van rechtswege. In A. A. J. de Gier e.a. (Eds.), *Goed verdedigbaar, Vernieuwing van bestuursrecht en omgevingsrecht* (pp. 477–490). Deventer: Kluwer.

Robbe, J. (2012). De Awb en de omgevingsvergunning van rechtswege. *TO, 3,* 55–63.

Schiebroek, M. J., & De Waard, B. W. M. (2011). In alle talen zwijgen: de Lex silencio positivo. *JBplus,* 94–112.

Stelkens, U., Weiß, W., & Mirschberger, M. (2012). *The Implementation of the EU Services Directive: Transposition, Problems and Strategies.* The Hague: T.M.C. Asser Press.

Ten Veen, A., & Collignon, A. (2010). De redelijke termijn voor bestuursorgaan en rechter. In T. Barkhuysen, W. den Ouden, & J. E. M. Polak (Eds.), *Bestuursrecht harmoniseren: 15 jaar Awb* (pp. 319–341). The Hague: Boom Juridische uitgevers.

Van Wijk, H. D, Konijnenbelt, W., & Van Male, R. (2014). *Hoofdstukken van Bestuursrecht*. Wolters Kluwer.

CHAPTER 7

Administrative Silence in Italy, Between (Desired) Simplification and (Practical) Complication

Anna Simonati

7.1 Introduction: The Legal and Administrative Background

In Italy, the Constitution indicates the basic purposes to be pursued by the authorities, and ordinary legislation imposes more specific rules. Administrative action is primarily up to the municipalities (in accordance with the principle of subsidiarity), but of course all the institutional levels are involved

The exercise of administrative power (which is separate from the legislative and the judicial) is normally subject to different kinds of appeals. A general tool (whose use is always allowed) is the appeal to the authority which is hierarchically superior than the one that issued the measure; the rules in force in specific fields may provide for different kinds of appeals (to either the authority author of the act or third public

A. Simonati (✉)
Faculty of Law, Trento University, Trento, Italy
e-mail: anna.simonati@unitn.it

D. C. Dragos et al. (eds.),
The Sound of Silence in European Administrative Law,
https://doi.org/10.1007/978-3-030-45227-8_7

subjects). At the Regional level, the Ombudspersons work to contrast maladministration, but they have not specific powers to promote the respect by the authorities for the principle of timeliness. Finally, the administrative courts may always be asked to verify compliance with the rules in force.

From the point of view of the distribution of competence between different kinds of courts, the Italian legal system is rather complicated. Beside the ordinary courts (before whom the actions concerning individual rights may be brought) there are the administrative courts, working on a double level (the Regional Administrative Courts—Tribunali Amministrativi Regionali, T.A.R.—as first-degree courts, and the Consiglio di Stato as second-degree court). Their relationship with the ordinary courts is based on the distinction between individual right and "legitimate interest" (interesse legittimo). The former is traditionally considered as the strongest legal position and its protection is normally granted by the ordinary courts; the latter is traditionally described as the position held by the private subjects in their relationship with administration. Such idea still corresponds to a guide criterion. However, in some fields, where the exercise of an administrative power is surely involved[1] and the distinction between individual rights and "legitimate interests" is objectively complicated, the national legislator may give all the judicial competence on specific issues to the administrative courts. These are the cases of exclusive jurisdiction, where "legitimate interests" and individual rights jointly may be known and protected by the administrative courts. So happens, for instance, for the judicial review on non-significant silence, where there is not an administrative measure (not even a tacit one) and the object of the appeal is a material behavior (an inaction) by the competent authority.

Discretionary administrative power cannot be the object in its substantive content of a judicial review; its exercise can be checked by the administrative courts, not on its merits, but only from the point of view of whether it is in accordance with the aims indicated in the statutes. In other words, judicial review is permitted to check whether or not the discretionary power was correctly used: in the negative, the measures are vitiated with excess of power. A fundamental parameter for checking whether an administrative measure is voidable because of excess of power,

[1] This was made clear by Constitutional Court, 6.7.2004, No. 204.

is the principle of proportionality. This ensures that the desired result in the public interest is obtained with the least sacrifice of private interests.[2] Another important parameter is the prohibition of unequal treatment.[3]

7.2 The Legal Framework of Administrative Timeliness and the Length of Deadlines

7.2.1 The Constitutional Basis

In Italy, the timeliness of administrative action is considered as a corollary of the principle of good administration, codified in art. 97.2 of the Constitution. Of course, this issue is strictly connected with the legal value of administrative inaction. Sometimes, in fact, a rule of law states that the administrative silence kept in specific cases has a legal meaning: it corresponds either to the emission of a measure (positive silence), or to the denial of the measure desired by the applicant (negative silence). Sometimes, instead, the inaction by the authority has no legal meaning: this is the case of non-significant silence. Since administrative silence is not mentioned in the Constitution, a preliminary point concerns the allocation of the normative competence on it.

In Italy, the legislative power is shared by the national and the Regional level. Art. 117 of the Constitution contains two lists of tasks: on the first, only the State may issue statutes; on the second, the ordinary Regions may issue statutes about the details, respecting the principles laid down by the central legislator. In the non-listed tasks, the Regional legislators own the legislative competence. Exceptions to such mechanism are indicated in favor of some Regions, which, depending on historical and geographical reasons, have a status of special autonomy.

Sometimes, the Regional legislators issued statutes on administrative silence, which were partially incoherent with the rules in force at the national level. In particular, whenever a national statute compelled administration to produce expressed measures in specific fields, in the older case law, the Constitutional Court excluded any derogation by the Regional

[2] Cons. St., V, 6.9.2012, No. 4733; Idem, VI, 10.12.2015, No. 5615; Idem, VI, 28.1.2016, No. 287.

[3] However, the prohibition of unequal treatment cannot be used to obtain a favorable unlawful measure, even if it has been already applied to someone else. Cons. St., VI, 5.3.2013, No. 1298; Idem, VI, 23.5.2011, No. 3044.

legislators, where primary public interests (for instance, to the protection of environment or health) were directly involved.[4] Moreover, the Court held that, according to a general principle, neither the central[5] nor the Regional legislators[6] may provide for a case of tacit consent whenever there is strong administrative discretionary power.

More recently, on issues covered by a concurrent legislative competence, the Court recognized the power of the Regional legislators to rule the significance of an administrative silence differently than the central legislator did.[7] When the competence is solely reserved to the national legislator, instead, according to the Constitutional case law the Regions cannot introduce "new" cases of significant silence. Besides, in order to ensure equal treatment all over the Country, the Regional legislators cannot reduce, in comparison with the one provided for in the national statutes, the deadline for the production of positive silence,[8] except when the Regional rules have a narrow space of implementation and an administrative power of *ex post* control survives.[9]

The administrative courts sometimes held that the legal qualification of the administrative inaction as positive, negative, or non-significant silence in a national statute, in fields of joint (central and Regional) competence, is not necessarily binding.[10] Consequently, a Regional statute may consider as non-significant a case of inaction, which is instead classified in a national rule as a case of positive silence.[11] However, in fields of particular importance for the satisfaction of fundamental rights of citizens (such as the production of energy), the "central" rule containing the deadline for the emission of the measure was considered immediately binding for the Regional legislators.[12]

[4] Constitutional Court, 18.6.1992, No. 306.

[5] Constitutional Court, 7.10.1992, No. 393.

[6] Constitutional Court, 2.8.1993, No. 408; Constitutional Court, 21.2.1996, No. 26.

[7] Constitutional Court, 7.7.2004, No. 196.

[8] Constitutional Court, 21.7.2014, No. 209, and 9.12.2009, No. 313.

[9] Constitutional Court, 11.7.2012, No. 171.

[10] Cons. St., VI, 15.12.2014, No. 6155.

[11] Cons. St., VI, 17.12.2013, No. 6042.

[12] Cons. St., V, 27.12.2013, No. 6279; Cons. St., V, 14.10.2013, No. 5000.

7.2.2 *Timeliness in the Administrative Procedure Act (and Beyond)*

In the national general statute on administrative procedure (Law 7.8.1990, No. 241), art. 2 regards the deadline of conclusion of procedures. The legislator clearly pursues a balance between the public interest to respect for the principles of sound administration[13] and the interest by the involved private parties to timeliness, clearness, and compliance with the rule of law.[14]

According to art. 2 (which was deeply amended many times since 2005, especially by Law 18.6.2009, No. 69, and later on again in 2010 and in 2012), each authority has a legal duty to conclude with a final measure all the procedures, both when they have begun with a request by a private party and *ex officio*. In the *ex officio* procedures, the starting point is commonly indicated in the date of the first official document. The terms, provided for in specific fields, are indicated by various statutes or national regulations. When they fix just the minimum and maximum, the length of the single procedures is decided (always within the general term of 90 days), by the competent administration. These rules show a strong effort in finding out a compromise between the need for completeness of the inquiry step and the economy of public action, especially in the interest of the private parties who aim at obtaining permissions.

The time-limit is indicated in 180 days for national-level procedures that are particularly complicated.[15]

In special fields (basically, when citizenship and immigration are considered), where individual fundamental rights are concerned and in the inquiry step deep attention must be paid, no binding deadline is provided for.

Finally, when no term is indicated in specific rules and there is no need for special dilation, the general deadline for administration to issue the final measure is fixed in 30 days from the beginning of the procedure.

[13] Clarich (1995, p. 37), Colavecchio (2013, p. 94), Posteraro (2015, p. 2676), and Vese (2017, p. 779).

[14] Ramajoli (2014, p. 710f).

[15] See art. 2.4, Law No. 241/1990.

When the procedure starts, the responsible officer must send to the interested parties a formal communication, containing various information, among which the indication of the deadline for the emission of the final decision and of the remedies in case of delay.[16]

In other articles of Law No. 241/1990, special deadlines are indicated for the emission of "internal" acts during the inquiry step, such as advices (normally, 20 days, plus other 15 days if necessary),[17] technical evaluations (normally, 90 days, plus other 15 days if necessary),[18] and preliminary denial of favorable measures, in order to allow the applicant to add further papers or reasons (normally, 10 days).[19]In case of delay, the production of this kind of acts may be by-passed, with some exceptions where the defense of primary public interests is involved. The deadline may be postposed only once (normally, within 15 days), whenever the consulted authority asks for a few days more to express itself.

The emission of "self-defence" measures (especially annulment and revocation of acts) is ruled in art. 21 *quinquies* and art. 21 *nonies* of Law No. 241/1990, introduced in 2005 and amended in 2015. In the original version, in compliance with the traditional idea of inexhaustibility of administrative power, such rules fixed no deadlines, but contained just a broad reference to the reasonable term, within which the "secondary-degree" acts should have been produced. Of course, such legislative choice gave administration a very strong discretionary power. The courts constantly stated that, when the facts were particularly complicated, the power could be exercised also after a long time since the emission of the first-degree measure.[20] Law 7.8.2015, No. 124 amended the text and fixed the duration of the reasonable time, within which the "self-defence" measure may be produced, in 18 months. Such recent change is a proof of the increasing importance of the principle of protection of legitimate expectations; therefore, the interest of the private parties to the timeliness of administrative action nowadays in tendency may prevail on the public interest to lawfulness.

[16]See art. 8.2.c bis, Law No. 241/1990.

[17]See art. 16, Law No. 241/1990.

[18]See art. 17, Law No. 241/1990.

[19]See art. 10 bis, Law No. 241/1990.

[20]Cons. Stato, V, 30.6.2013, No. 3037.

Besides, according to the 2015 reform,[21] a regulation had to be issued by the Government, in order to make some administrative procedures faster and more efficient.[22] The decree of the President of the Republic 12.9.2016, No. 194 contains some rules about the so-called fast track method.[23] It requires the indication each year of the group of administrative procedures whose particularly strong public interest needs their quick conclusion. In those cases, the deadline for the emission of the final measure is reduced (normally to the half) and the substitution of the non-acting authority with another, indicated by the Government, is provided for as well. The concerned procedures have basically to do with relevant public works or productive units or with starting of commercial activities. Such "acceleration" rules apply also to the procedures about environment, public health, and cultural heritage are comprised. Therefore, the legislator, who in the past had considered these fields too strictly connected with fundamental public interests to allow the prevalence of quickness on completeness of the inquiry step,[24] seems to have changed its mind.

7.3 Sector-Specific Legislation

7.3.1 Some Examples of Significant Silence

In Law No. 241/1990, art. 20 broadly rules the case of tacit consent, but various cases of significant silence are contained in numerous special legal sources. Describing or even summarizing all of them is impossible. Anyway, some provisions are particularly interesting, because in the perception of the practitioners who responded to the questionnaire related to this research, their implementation is rather frequent.

The first example concerns the requests for access to administrative documents and data. According to art. 25.4 of Law No. 241/1990, in front of a request for access to administrative documents, when the 30 days term expires without any answer by the competent administration, a negative decision is tacitly produced. Notwithstanding normally the authority answers with an expressed decision, negative silence is often

[21] Torchia (2016, p. 23).

[22] Napolitano (2014, p. 709).

[23] Basilica and Barazzoni (2014, p. 146).

[24] Cons. St., VI, 13.5.2016, No. 1935; Cons. St., ad. plen., 27.7.2016, No. 17.

practiced, especially when no counter-interested parties are involved. With reference to the more recent right of access to administrative data which are not compulsorily to be published in the institutional Web sites, the inaction by administration is instead considered a case of non-significant silence. This is interesting, as it shows that the legal relevance of transparency and of the right of information of citizens is increasing in the perception of the Italian legislator. Moreover, it shows that negative silence is currently considered as a potentially excessive tool for simplification, when the matter is the satisfaction of individual rights, which are deeply rooted in Constitutional values (as the right of information is).

A different example has to do with the emission of building permissions, asked for by a private party to the municipal authority. The relevant rule is art. 20.8 of Legislative Decree 6.6.2001, No. 380, according to which, after 60 days since the reception of the private party's request, if the responsible officer of the procedure has not expressed a contrary opinion, there is a case of positive silence. Therefore, this rule is a sectorial coverage of the general provision contained in art. 20 of Law No. 241/1990. An explicit exception is ruled when the land is covered by a landscaping or cultural constraint. According to the recent case law, the tacit positive silence cannot work not only whenever an administrative constraint has been issued by the competent authority, but also when the area lays within a site where a public landscaping or cultural interest is presumptively present (such as in the historical town-center).[25] Such tendency demonstrates that a restrictive interpretation is applied by the courts in order to reduce the practical effects of positive silence, when they are considered potentially dangerous for the protection of important public interests.

7.3.2 *Some Remarks on Significant Silence*

It is clear that "negative" silence normally does not produce any change in the legal reality. On the contrary, "positive" silence has the substantial effect of replacing an administrative decision with the private one.[26]

In Italy, by progressive steps of legislative reform, positive silence has become the rule—excluding some cases (listed in art. 20.4, Law No.

[25] Cons. Stato, 27.9.2017, No. 4516.

[26] D'Orsogna and Lombardi (2017, p. 965).

241/1990) where strong public interests are involved—when the procedure starts with a request by a private subject, who aims at obtaining a favorable administrative measure.[27] Such choice gives priority to the protection of the interest of the private applicant, but it produces an evident sacrifice of the public interest to obtain an informed and sound decision by the competent authority.

In general, the effect of significant silence is quite paradoxical. A decision is supposed to be taken but the inquiry step is strongly reduced (or it does not concretely exist at all) and the reasons are not expressed. Notwithstanding this, secondary-level powers may be used by administration[28] and a power of annulment may be used by the administrative courts,[29] despite there is not a first-degree decision upon which they are exercised.

The lack of an effective procedural inquiry step, during which all the relevant elements of the case are properly taken into account by the competent authority, is probably the reason of an orientation held in the recent case law. According to this line, even though positive silence can be considered as the source of a tacit permit requested by the private interested subject, if further action by administration is needed in order to allow him/her to concretely implement the tacit permit and such action is not already done, relating to this part of power there is just a non-significant silence. Consequently, before starting his/her activity, the private party must obtain an expressed decision by administration.[30]

7.4 Non-significant Silence and the Possibility to Issue a Valid Act After the Deadline Expired

According to a strict interpretation of art. 2, Law No. 241/1990, when the deadline has expired and the final measure has not been issued yet, the competent authority should lose its power. The officer who breaches the legal deadline or does not issue the due administrative measure may be punished on the ground of the individual professional performance; together with the senior officer, he/she is liable to disciplinary and

[27] Parisio (2006) and Torchia (2017, p. 15).

[28] See art. 20.3, Law No. 241/1990.

[29] Torchia (2017, p. 15).

[30] Cons. St., IV, 13.12.2017, No. 5869.

administrative-accounting action.[31] Anyway, each administration indicates, with a general act, the subject who must intervene with substitutive powers in case of inaction by the competent authority. In such case, the deadline to conclude the procedure corresponds to the half of the "original" one.

Therefore, generally speaking, the expression of administrative discretionary power is allowed, in accordance with the organizational needs, only within the legislative boundaries.[32] However, in the Italian legal system a traditional presumption is commonly accepted, according to which public power—as it is based on the necessity to pursue a general interest and as it derives from a rule of law—is inexhaustible.[33] Such view was confirmed by the rule previously contained in art. 21 *bis* of Law 6.12.1971, No. 1034 (as amended by Law 21.7.2000, No. 205), whose object was the judicial review on non-significant silence. Quite similarly with the rule at present in force, art. 21 *bis* described a peculiar and simplified kind of appeal, possibly ending with the emission of an order to exercise the administrative power and the appointment by the court, when necessary, of a commissioner with substitutive powers. According to that rule, one of the duties of the commissioner was to check whether meanwhile the competent authority had produced the administrative measure. This was the proof that a late administrative act, even though not compatible with the legal deadline, was considered lawful. Anyway, this provision was later on erased by the Administrative Judicial Review Code (Legislative Decree 2.7.2010, No. 104); consequently, a legislative argument in favor of the inexhaustible nature of administrative power disappeared.

To make the rules at present in force compatible with such view, art. 2 of Law No. 241/1990 should be read as if it contained just a presumptive but not binding indication of the average duration of the procedure. This interpretation is probably not totally in line with the Constitutional values of impartiality and efficiency of administrative action. Consistently, according to the case law, the duty to conclude the procedure with an expressed final measure, even in absence of a specific

[31] See art. 2.9 bis-9 quater, Law No. 241/1990.

[32] Sica (2017, p. 985).

[33] Francario (2017).

rule of law, derives from the general principles of good administration.[34] According to the principle of justice, then, the recipient of an administrative unfavorable measure has always the right to challenge it before a court[35] and non-significant silence is not prevented by the emission of just elusive or interlocutory non-necessary acts.[36] Moreover, the provisions concerning the administration's duty to conclude procedures within the pre-established time frame and those relating to the maximum duration of procedures pertain to the essential levels of benefits, referred to in article 117.2.m of the Constitution, which must be uniformly granted in the whole Country.[37] So, one could probably infer that—differently than in the past—nowadays, after the consumption of the deadline, the competent authority should lose its original power to issue the final measure.[38]

Both the theories of consumption and of survival of administrative power, after the deadline indicated in the rules, have strong and weak points. Perhaps, none of them may absolutely prevail, because the context is nowadays very complex.

In the *ex officio* procedures (which often start in order to produce unfavorable measures for the recipient), when the deadline has passed, the private party has a strong interest to maintain his/her original position. Whenever for the private subject the final measure may still be useful, the power may be exercised, as so corresponds to the fulfillment of a duty in the public interest and—at the same time—in the interest of the private single interlocutor. Hence, a late measure may be issued when it satisfies a private's request and when, even though it is the result of an *ex officio* procedure, it is satisfactory for the private party. Differently, when the measure is unfavorable for the recipient, time should be considered as a constitutive element of public power. Consequently, its late

[34] Cons. St., IV, 20.5.2014, No. 2545; Cons. St., IV, 29.5.2015, No. 2688, Cons. St., 12.2.2015, No. 741 and No. 742; Cons. St., VI, 8.2.2016, No. 508; Cons. St., IV, 15.9.2014, No. 4696; Cons. St., IV, 4.12.2012, No. 6183.

[35] Cons. St., V, 9.3.2015, No. 1182; Cons. St., III, 14.11.2014, No. 5601.

[36] Cons. St., III, 10.12.2013, No. 5924; Cons. St., VI, 17.12.2013, No. 6037; Cons. St., V, 28.4.2014, No. 2184.

[37] See art. 29.2 *bis* of Law No. 241/1990.

[38] Partially *contra*, for instance, Pinelli (2015, p. 2216) and the case law, among which recently, for instance, Cons. St., VI, 1.9.2017, No. 4160 and Cons. St., IV, 6.8.2013, No. 4150.

exercise could make it unlawful. Notwithstanding one could object that even receiving an (expressed) unfavorable measure may be useful for the recipients (who have the opportunity to ask for the annulment of it), the above-mentioned opinion is shared especially among the scholars.[39] Speaking of the cases where the late exercise of power is not allowed, two different views are expressed. According to one of them, the violation of the deadline produces the extinction of the power itself, since the legislator gave it to the competent authority at certain conditions, whose breach produces a total inexistence of such power. According to the other, instead, the violation of the deadline is a mere breach of law and the measure would be voidable and not void. The difference matters especially on the ground of judicial review, as the defense tools in the two cases are different.[40]

However, in the recent case law, it was held that an action against non-significant silence cannot be brought whenever the competent authority issued a measure, notwithstanding it was late and different than the expected one according to the rules. In such case, an action for annulment is the proper defense tool.[41] Moreover, if the action against non-significant silence has already been brought when the competent authority issues the measure, the appeal must stop.[42] On the contrary, the emission of an infra-procedural act is not able to interrupt the deadline for the creation of non-significant silence.[43]

7.5 Cases of Administrative Inaction Other Than Silence in Strict Sense

The distinction between significant and non-significant silence is of course fundamental, but in Italy things are even more complicated.[44] In some cases, the emission of an expressed permission has been replaced with the maintenance for the authority of just a power of supervision (after

[39] Vese (2017).

[40] Vese (2017, p. 779).

[41] Cons. St., V, 27.11.2017, No. 5556; Cons. St., III, 21.11.2017, No. 5417; Cons. S., VI, 8.10.2013, No. 4949.

[42] Cons. St., III, 4.5.2018, No. 2660; Cons. St., 13.10.2015, No. 4710.

[43] Cons. St., IV, 15.9.2010, No. 6892.

[44] Lipari (2015) and Torchia (2017, p. 17).

the beginning of the action by the private parties) and later on of a power of self-protection in the public interest. Both the powers have to be implemented within specific terms.

In fact, sometimes a private party, in quite simple and clear circumstances, may just communicate his/her will to do something (for instance, to make very small works on a building)[45] and this is enough to enable him/her to immediately start the works, with a duty to add some relevant documents when requested.[46] This is an effect of the influence played by the European Directive 2006/123/EC on the internal market, according to which the cases of positive silence may survive only if they are rooted in strong reasons of public interest. There is a clear reference to the need for strengthening the legal tools which are able to allow a private subject to start an activity without previously obtaining a permit, by replacing the traditional *ex ante* administrative power with an *ex post* power of control.

In such cases—which are admitted only when there is not discretionary power—administration can act after the beginning of the private initiative, controlling if all the legal conditions are respected. In other words, the private act is substitutive of a permit and administration has only a power of check and prohibit (within a specific deadline) the going on of the concrete action, if it is unlawful. As an alternative, when the breach of law is mild, a chance must be given to the interested private party to make the situation compatible with the legal system, within another deadline (after which a sort of tacit denial is created).[47]

Sometimes, in the short deadline for the exercise of the power of lawfulness-check, the competent authority does not take any initiative and just after the consumption of the legal term it realizes that the private party's initiative should have been forbidden. If the private party lied about the substantial conditions, his/her behavior is normally relevant as a type of crime and it cannot be regularized. Moreover, after the consumption of the legal deadline, the competent authority may also use its ordinary power of "annulment"... which of course does not work on a first-degree decision (that does not exist), but on the legal effects

[45] See arts 6 *bis* and 22 of Legislative Decree No. 380/2001, in their current formulation.

[46] See, in a general perspective, art. 19, Law No. 241/1990, in the text in force.

[47] Donato (2015) and Scotti (2016, p. 620).

connected with the concrete action held by the private party.[48] Such peculiar secondary-degree power has anyway to be enrooted in the pursue of the public interest and its exercise is submitted to the general deadline of 18 months. Later on, the secondary-degree measure cannot be issued any more, but the action is still unlawful, and the author may be punished, for instance, with economic penalties.[49] According to the case law, the private party is anyway responsible for the truth of his/her statements.[50] Consequently, from the point of view of the citizens, this mechanism does not create real simplification, since many actions previously up to the competent authority now must be performed by the private subject.[51]

This scheme produces many systemic problems, al least because the difference between the deadline for the exercise of the power of checking the lawfulness of the private action and the deadline for the exercise of the power of "annulment" is not clear. Hence, notwithstanding at the beginning of its history this mechanism was the general one (with numerous exceptions), nowadays it may be implemented in a number of hypothesis which are listed in specific rules (such as, primarily, Legislative Decree 25.11.2016, No. 222).[52] The cases frequently regard situations where an administrative discretionary power (that requires a comparison between different interests) is excluded, but technical discretionary power may be involved.

Besides, third parties may be interested in stopping the activity, which is for them harmful. Therefore, after the deadline for the exercise of the power of control of lawfulness by the competent authority has expired, the subjects, who suffered a damage as a consequence of the activity carried out, may bring before an administrative court an action against the non-significant silence. As a result of the previous debate among the scholars, this solution is laid down in art. 31 of the Administrative Judicial Review Code. The source of the non-significant silence is in this case not a request by a private party for the emission of a favorable measure, but the legal duty to exercise the power of control.[53] According to the

[48] Gualdani (2017), Macchia (2015, p. 621), and Sinisi (2015).

[49] See art. 21, Law No. 241/1990.

[50] Cons. St., ad. plen., 29.7.2011, No. 15; also Cons. St., advice 15.3.2016, No. 839.

[51] Torchia (2017).

[52] Carbone (2017) and Contessa (2018).

[53] Cons. St., VI, 3.11.2016, No. 4610.

courts, then, after the consumption of the deadline for the exercise of the checking power (but perhaps also before the consumption of that deadline, according to a minority orientation),[54] the third parties who have suffered a damage may bring an action before an administrative court, to obtain an order to the competent authority to use the power of "annulment," to which art. 19 of Law No. 241/1990 refers.[55]

7.6 Administrative Non-significant Silence: A Special Case of Judicial Review

7.6.1 Preliminary Remarks

Traditionally, non-significant silence was not ruled in any statute. Therefore, the first effort was made in the administrative case law, in order to allow the private party, who had asked for a favorable measure, to use the action of annulment also in front of an inaction by the competent authority. This "creative" orientation was based on the implementation by analogy of art. 25 of the consolidated text of rules on public employees (Decree of the President of the Republic 10.1.1957, No. 3). When the competent authority did not issue an act that was expected to be produced, the interested subject had to make an expressed request. After 60 days with no answer by administration, the applicant had to send a formal notice and after the following 30 days a significant negative silence was considered to be legally existing; therefore, the tacit denial could be challenged.

Only in Law No. 205/2005 a legal regime of the judicial remedy against non-significant silence was provided for. Similar rules are now contained in the Administrative Judicial Review Code in force.[56] At present, notwithstanding non-significant silence is still in principle considered as a pathological phenomenon, a specific action may be brought, in order to obtain at the end an explicit decision.

[54] T.A.R. Veneto, 5.3.2012, No. 298.

[55] Cons. St., VI, 3.11.2016, No. 4610.

[56] See arts 31, 34, 117 and 133.

7.6.2 *The Judicial Action: Conditions and Possible Results*

The judicial review on significant silence does not pose particular problems, because the applicant may ask for annulment of the tacit administrative measure, and the process follows the ordinary rules on appeal against expressed acts.[57] In the Administrative Judicial Review Code, some rules specifically regard, instead, the judicial action which may be brought before an administrative court, in front of a non-significant administrative silence.[58]

When the legal deadline for the conclusion of the procedure has expired, the interested subject may bring an action before an administrative court, in order to obtain the declaration of the duty of the competent authority to take an expressed decision.[59] The action can be brought until the inaction lasts and anyway within one year after the consumption of the deadline for the conclusion of the administrative procedure.[60] The court may decide on the merits of the substantial interest of the applicant, only when the administrative power involved is not (or not any more) discretionary and no further inquiry step is required.[61] In such case, the court can order the production of a specific measure.[62] When either a discretionary power is involved or additional inquiry is required, instead, the court cannot replace administration, depending on the principle of separation between public powers; therefore, just a general judicial order is issued and, in case of further inaction by the competent authority, the court appoints a special commissioner who exercises the administrative power.[63] Anyway, it is clear in the case law that the judicial decision must take into account the factual changes that have meanwhile occurred.[64]

[57] Cons. St., VI, 11.6.2018, No. 3556; Cons. St., VI, 6.6.2018, No. 3417; Cons. St., IV, 26.3.2012, No. 1757.

[58] Cerbo (2017, p. 1), Occhiena (2012, p. 583), Meale (2016, p. 1719), Scognamiglio (2017, p. 450), Vese (2017, p. 779), and Posteraro (2017, p. 793).

[59] Cerbo (2017, p. 2ff.) and Guacci (2012, p. 195ff.). In the Administrative Judicial Review Code, see art. 31 and art. 34.1.c.

[60] Cons. St., V, 20.4.2012, No. 2337; Cons. St., III, 3.3.2015, No. 1050; Cons. St., V, 29.8.2016, No. 3710; Cons. St., III, 25.1.2016, No. 255.

[61] Scognamiglio (2017, p. 450).

[62] See art. 31.3 of the Administrative Judicial Procedure Act.

[63] Cons. St., VI, 9.2.2016, No. 557; Cons. St., VI, 23.22016, No. 736.

[64] Cons. Stato, ad. plen., 9.6.2016, No. 11.

In the judicial procedure against non-significant silence, almost all the deadlines are reduced to the half and the court deliberates in closed session.[65]

The action may be brought directly, with no need of a previous formal notice to the competent authority,[66] differently than it used to be in the past.[67] This means, of course, that art. 2 of Law No. 241/1990 is considered as a direct source of duties for the competent authority. This is also a consequence of the overcoming of the orientation, according to which, when a discretionary power was given to administration on the *an* and the *quomodo* of its intervention, one could suppose that the discretionary power automatically covered the choice on *quando*. After the introduction of the new formulation of art. 2 of Law No. 241/1990, this interpretation is not possible anymore, because, also in absence of a sectorial rule about the deadline, the 30 days general one works.

The court issues a simplified decision, which means that the reasons are just briefly indicated. When the appeal is totally or partially successful, the court orders administration to act, normally within 30 days.[68] When necessary, the court appoints a commissioner in the final judicial decision (or even after the conclusion of the appeal, when the interested party asks for that). The judicial decision may cover the matters related with the emission of the final administrative measure, here comprised the issues about the intervention by the commissioner. If during the appeal against non-significant silence an expressed measure is produced by the competent authority, the trial may go on being converted into an appeal for annulment of such act.

Finally, the appeals against non-significant silence correspond to a case of exclusive jurisdiction of the administrative courts.[69] According to the case law, however, there is not always exclusive jurisdiction whenever an authority, which is requested to act, does not take any initiative. The special "appeal" against non-significant silence, instead, may work only if

[65] Cons. St., VI, 11.2.2011, No. 919; Cons. St., V, 24.3.2016, No. 1208. In the Administrative Judicial Review Code, see art. 87.

[66] See art. 117 of the Administrative Judicial Procedure Code and art. 2.4 *bis* of Law No. 241/1990.

[67] Cons. St., V, 22.11.2005, No. 6500; Cons. St., III, 20.4.2015, No. 1989; Cons. St., V, 31.3.2016, No. 1272; among the scholars, Police (2017, p. 285).

[68] See art. 117.2 of the Administrative Judicial Procedure Code.

[69] See art. 133 of the Administrative Judicial Procedure Code.

the substantial field of the case corresponds to an administrative power.[70] Consequently, the special action against non-significant silence cannot be brought, for example, when an authority has entered into a contract with a private subject and the dispute regards the implementation of such obligations.[71]

7.6.3 *Critical Remarks in the Case Law on Non-significant Silence*

The parties who can bring their case to the administrative court are primarily, of course, those who requested a favorable measure. But also the possible recipient of an unfavorable measure could hold an interest to obtain an expressed act (containing reasons), in order to challenge it and get its annulment by a court.[72] In fact, the breach of the principle of timeliness of the exercise of administrative power can be brought before a court by the private parties who own a concrete interest in getting the power exercised, even though they are not surely the recipients of an expected favorable measure.[73]

The court should declare the action non-admissible, not only if it is brought too late,[74] but also if it is brought before the deadline for the emission of the final administrative measure has expired.[75] Nonetheless, according to the recent case law, a less rigid orientation starts to be accepted, especially when the deadline is not perfectly clear in light of the concrete development of the administrative action.[76] Moreover, some scholars point out that, as numerous rules provide for "intermediate" deadlines for the issuing of internal acts, it is possible that the action is brought before the expiration of the very final deadline for the conclusion of the procedure. In light of the breach of some "internal" terms, in fact, even before the final deadline has formally expired it may be evident that

[70] Cons. St., VI, 7.9.2012, No. 4758; Cons. St., III, 1.2.2012, No. 501.

[71] Cons. St., IV, 7.6.2018, No. 3429; Cons. St., V, 24.2.2011, No. 1194.

[72] Cons. St., IV, 15.9.2014, No. 4696.

[73] Cons. St., IV, 6.4.2016, No. 1358.

[74] Cons. St., IV, 26.3.2014, No. 1460.

[75] Cons. St., VI, 12.10.2010, No. 7432; Cons. St., VI, 2.9.2011, No. 4922; Cons. St., IV, 20.5.2014, No. 2538.

[76] Cons. St., ad. plen., 29.7.2011, No. 15 and Cons. St., V, 8.2.2012, No. 523.

respecting it has meanwhile concretely become impossible.[77] However, in the administrative case law it was held that the breach of the "internal" deadlines for the conclusion of single procedural steps, if no rule clearly defines such silence as a significant one, does not produce for the competent authority the loss of power.[78]

The action against non-significative silence may be brought whenever there is a duty to conclude the administrative procedure. Therefore, notwithstanding there is discretionary power on the *an* of the beginning of the procedure, if it has begun it has to end with an expressed measure and such case is not deeply different than the procedures started with a request by a private party. This is the result of a long evolution, which was carried out primarily by the doctrine[79] and later on also by the courts.[80] According to the recent case law, besides, the action against non-significant silence may start when administration has a legal duty to start a procedure, but it has taken no procedural steps at all.[81] On the contrary, when the discretionary power regards the *an* of the administrative action and a procedure has not formally begun, there is not a duty to issue a final measure and the judicial review for non-significant silence may not be activated.[82]

An open problem has to do with the borders of the technical notion of "procedure on private request." According to a shared opinion, it is necessary to distinguish the requests by private subjects, holders of a differentiated interest to obtain the final measures (from which a legal duty of administration to answer arises),[83] and other kinds of initiatives (such as simple reports or alerts, made by the holders of general interests). The latter are not able to start an administrative procedure in formal sense, although recently the doctrine has held the opposite whenever the alert by the private party corresponds to a duty whose implementation

[77] Sica (2017, p. 985).

[78] Cons. St., VI, 13.5.2016, No. 1935; Cons. St., V, 28.4.2014, No. 2184.

[79] Greco (1980).

[80] Cons. St., ad. plen., 30.5.1960, No. 8; Cons. St., 10.31978, No. 10; Cons. St., 24.11.1989, No. 16; Cons. St., 4.12.1989, No. 17; Cons. St., 14.12.2001, No. 9; Cons. St., 9.1.2002, No. 1; Cons. St., 15.9.2005, No. 7.

[81] Cons. Stato, V, 27.11.2012, No. 6002.

[82] Cons. St., IV, 27.12.2017, No. 6096.

[83] Cons. St., IV, 13.11.2015, No. 5015; Cons. St., IV, 19.3.2015, No. 1503.

ex officio is required by a rule (for instance, with reference to the reports about breaches of law in re-development zones).[84] The action cannot be brought, then, when the competent authority has chosen not to issue a regulation, that is a legal source; in such case, there are not differentiated interests by specific private parties, whose existence is a necessary condition.[85]

Sometimes, the request by the private subject may be considered inadmissible. It has been held that the duty to start the procedure does not arise when the request is posed to an authority which is totally deprived of competence,[86] or when the request is not complete of all its elements,[87] or when it has a too general content,[88] or else when it is just the renewal of a previous request which was expressly rejected by the competent authority.[89]

The case law often adds that a duty to exercise the administrative power can arise from a general principle of good administration,[90] and sometimes also from a previous act of the competent authority (even not a legal source) stating its intention to issue an administrative measure.[91]

Besides, according to the case law, the recipient of an unlawful measure, who did not timely challenge it, may not bring the action on non-significant silence to obtain a judicial order to the competent authority to exercise the power of self-annulment.[92]

[84] Cerbo (2017, p. 6).

[85] Cons. St., V, 9.3.2015, No. 1182; Cons. St., V, 6.9.2012, No. 4718.

[86] Cons. St., V, 28.9.2015, No. 4499; Cons. Stato, ad. plen., 27.4.2015, No. 5.

[87] Cons. St., IV, 18.12.2013, No. 6105.

[88] Posteraro (2015, p. 2685).

[89] Cons. St., IV, 7.6.2017, No. 2751.

[90] Cons. St., IV, 18.2.2016, No. 653; Cons. St., III, 2.5.2016, No. 1660; Cons. St., V, 13.10.2016, No. 4235; Cons. St., 28.12.2016, No. 5529; Cons. St., V, 2.8.2017, No. 3871.

[91] Cons. St., V, 1.7.2014, No. 3293; Cons. St., IV, 21.9.2015, No. 4378; Cons. St., VI, 20.7.2018, No. 4406.

[92] Cons. St., IV, 14.3.2016, No. 1012; Cons. St., V, 4.5.2015, No. 2237; Cons. St., IV, 29.11.2012, No. 6095; Cons. St., V, 30.12.2011, No. 6995; Cons. St., IV, 12.9.2018, No. 5344, and Cons. St., III, 11.6.2018, No. 3507.

7.6.4 *The Right to Compensation as a Consequence of the Delay*

Some scholars observe that the judicial review on non-significant silence seems to grant an immediate defense but not necessarily a full satisfaction of the private party's interest.[93]

Actually, one of the main results of the current formulation of art. 2, Law No. 241/1990 is the possibility to ask for an economic compensation, whenever administration does not comply with the rules on the deadline for the conclusion of procedures.[94] According to art. 2 *bis*, the private party who has a legal interest to the timely emission of an administrative measure may obtain an economic compensation, not only when the delay has caused a specific damage, but also as a mere consequence of the delay itself. In this case, anyway, the emission of detailed rules in other (legislative or regulatory) sources is expected.

This shows that both the general interest to timeliness of administrative action and the correspondent individual right are seriously considered in the rules in force.[95]

From the point of view of liability of administration, two different duties of the competent authority should be distinguished. The first is the duty to respect the legislative deadline of the procedure; the second is the duty to issue the requested administrative measure, if compatible with the legal landscape and with the discretionary evaluation when necessary. So, non-significant silence always may be considered as a breach of the (autonomous) interest of the private party to obtain an expressed measure. Such interest is independent from the favorable or negative outcome of the procedure.[96] The applicant has to prove all the objective and subjective elements of liability, in order to obtain a condemnation of administration.[97] However, occasionally, in the recent case law, it was held that a very general assert about the big number of procedures to be

[93] Ramajoli (2014, p. 735).

[94] Before the 2009 reform, the negative orientation prevailed in the case law: Cons. St., IV, 27.12.2001, No. 6415; Cons. St., V, 18.11.2002, No. 6389; Cons. St., VI, 31.3.2006, No. 1637; Cons. St., V, 30.11.2007, No. 6138; Cons. St., IV, 29.1.2008, No. 248; Cons. St., V, 2.3.2009, No. 1162; Cons. St., ad. plen., 5.9.2005, No. 5; Cons. St., ad. plen., 15.9.2005, No. 7.

[95] Ramajoli (2014, p. 711) and Criscuolo.

[96] Cons. St., VI, 26.7.2017, No. 3696.

[97] Cons. St., VI, 24.7.2017, No. 3662; Cons. St., V, 21.4.2016, No. 1584.

closed within a short term and about the complication of the inquiry step of the single procedure is in itself sufficient to exclude the obligation of the competent authority to give the applicant an economic compensation for the damage suffered because of the breach of the legal deadline.[98]

Finally, in the case law it is clear that the special procedural rules working for judicial review on administrative silence do not work also for the connected judgments about economic compensation, which consequently normally follow their own rules.[99]

7.7 Final Remarks: Administrative Inaction… in Action

In Italy, the timeliness nowadays is one of the criteria, according to which administration should act. The respect for legal terms is considered as an instrument of lawfulness; it works in the perspective of the issuing of the final measure and of the conclusion of the internal steps of the procedure. At the same time, the respect for the legal deadlines corresponds to a right of citizens. In such perspective, non-significant silence is especially relevant on a systemic ground. In fact, according to the latest evolution, the principle of timeliness of administrative action works differently in light of the nature of the decision to be issued and of the interests to be taken into account. A delay may produce different effects on the survival of administrative power, depending especially on the favorable or unfavorable content of the expected final measure.

From the point of view of the strength of the protection of the interest of private parties, when administrative silence is non-significant, the power of the courts to order the issuing of a final decision within a short term—or even to satisfy the applicant's interest, when there is no discretionary power—surely is an important instrument. According to art. 2.8 of Law No. 241/1990, each definitive judicial decision, condemning administration in case of unlawful inaction, must be sent to the Corte dei Conti, that is the court competent to judge on financial liability of public subjects. Therefore, the delay matters as a form of administrative inefficiency.[100]

[98] Cons. St., III, 5.6.2018, No. 3411.

[99] Cons. St., III, 10.11.2017, No. 5188; Cons. St., VI, 26.7.2017, No. 3696; Cons. St., V, 2.7.2012, No. 3844; Cons. St., IV, 4.12.2012.

[100] Immordino (2010, p. 74) and Ursi (2016, p. 21).

Notwithstanding this, art. 117.2 of the Administrative Judicial Review Code does not fix a maximum length of the term indicated by the court to the competent authority, in order to take the final decision; consequently, the court has a broad discretionary power in doing so.

The right to obtain an economic compensation for the delay may be considered as an adjunctive defense tool, but the existence of a right of private parties to timeliness of administrative decision as an independent legal interest is sometimes denied (even recently) in the case law.[101] Besides, its concrete implementation seems to be rather weak, because of the lack for effective instruments for enforcement. From this point of view, a useful proposal could be the extension to this case of the *astreinte* mechanism, that allows the court to condemn administration to pay a sum of money for each day of delay in complying with a judicial decision. This tool is provided for in art. 114.4.e of the Administrative Judicial Review Code only for the "judgement on compliance" (giudizio di ottemperanza), but, according to an extensive interpretation, it could be activated whenever an administrative judgment is not complied with by the competent authority. This may be perhaps a good idea,[102] even though till now the case law does not agree.[103]

The provision for cases of significant silence in practice has not had the effect of incentivizing administration to take expressed decisions, in order to avoid dangerous presumptions of (tacit) exercise of power without a procedure and without giving reasons. On the contrary, tacit decisions are perceived as an instrument of partial simplification; third parties are allowed to ask for their annulment and the competent authority may erase them through the implementation of its secondary-degree power.[104] Unfortunately, there is not empirical data on the concrete implementation of the rules about significant and non-significant silence in Italy. Therefore, information about practice may be inferred by the case law, that offers—as it has been shown in the paper—food for thought in many different ways. Such solicitations go hand-in-hand with the doctrine's ones.

[101] Cons. St., IV, 6.4.2016, No. 1371.

[102] Sica (2017, p. 985).

[103] T.A.R. Abruzzo, l'Aquila, 26.5.2016, No. 339; T.A.R. Campania, Salerno, I, 2.1.2017, No. 13; T.A.R. Campania-Naples, III, 28.11.2016, No. 5524; T.A.R. Sicily, Catania, III, 30.8.2016, No. 2186.

[104] Torchia (2017, p. 19).

From the point of view of the analysis of case-law, an interesting source of empirical data may be indicated in the annual reports that the regional administrative courts publish every year describing their previous activity.[105] There is not a general rule about the content of such reports, but quite often they offer a quantitative overview on the kind of cases decided.[106] Anyway, from the reports one can infer that the judicial review on administrative non-significant silence is in the recent times slowly decreasing, as it is shown by the statistics calculated by some regional courts.[107] Besides, a relevant information concerns a sort of geographical fragmentation. In the administrative courts working

[105] They are available on line in https://www.giustizia-amministrativa.it/web/guest/inaugurazione-degli-anni-giudiziari, retrieved April 2019.

[106] Some reports indicate also the average length of the duration of the judicial appeals. For instance, in the report on 2017 by the Regional administrative court of Friuli Venezia Giulia, it is stated that the average duration of special appeals—among whom are the ones on non-significant silence—is of 109 days.

[107] In Abruzzo, in 2017 546 appeals were totally issued, 30 of which against non-significant administrative silence. In Molise, in 2017 the received appeals were 527, 10 of which on administrative silence. In Apulia (section of Bari), in 2017 59 appeals on non-significant silence were issued, corresponding to a decrease of 18% than the data on 2016; according to the 2018 report by the special section of Lecce, in 2016 70 appeals on administrative silence were issued and 64 in 2017 (with a decrease of 8%). In Liguria as well the appeals on non-significant silence are progressively decreasing (they were 25 in 2016, 19 in 2017 and 13 in 2018). In Sicily, in 2018, 88 of the 2634 new appeals concerned non-significant silence. In the 2019 report by the Regional administrative court of Piemonte, it is shown that the appeals on non-significant silence were 16 in 2016 (of comprehensively 1325), 23 in 2017 (of comprehensively 1208) and 10 in 2018 (of comprehensively 1129). In Calabria, the special section of the regional administrative court working in Reggio Calabria calculated in 2018 19 new appeals on non-significant silence (of comprehensive 653). According to the 2018 report, in 2017 the appeals on non-significant silence before the Regional administrative court in Lazio were 799 (corresponding to 5.96% of the total amount) and in the same field the court issued in 2017 114 decisions accepting the appeal; in 2018, the appeals on non-significant silence were instead 1115, with an increase of 39.5%, representing 7, 18% of the total amount; in 2018, then, 679 judicial decisions were published on administrative silence (192 of whom accepting the appeal). According to the 2018 report by the Regional administrative court of Sardinia, in 2017 the appeals on non-significant silence were 19 (1.80% of the total amount of appeals in the same year) and the decisions on the same subject were 20; in 2016 the appeals were 33, in 2015 they were 27, and in 2014 they were 24. In 2017, the Regional administrative court of Umbria received comprehensively 510 appeals, 16 of which on non-significant silence; in 2018, the total amount was of 651 appeals, 8 of whom on non-significant silence. In Veneto, in 2017, the Regional administrative court received 26 appeals on non-significant silence; they were 22 in 2018.

in the north of the Country, in fact, the number of appeals against non-significant silence is often particularly low,[108] which shows that in such Regions the administration normally answers to the requests by the private parties.

It is also clear in some reports that the most complicated side of the judicial action in the case of non-significant silence concerns the appointment of the special commissioner with substitutive powers: the main problem regards the choice of the commissioner him/herself. In practice, the administrative court asks for help by administration (usually, an authority that is different than the one originally competent for issuing the measure) in choosing the person with the required skills.[109]

Finally, one may infer that the case law on significant silence is seldom put in evidence in the reports as a relevant part of the annual activity, because it rarely involves complicated problems.[110]

In order to learn something more about the practitioners' opinion, some interviews have been conducted.[111] The respondent people were asked to explain how often, in their practice, positive, negative, and non-significant silence are used in administrative action; moreover, information was asked about the fields were the various kinds of silence are concretely used. From the point of view of justiciability, the questionnaire

[108] For an example, see the 2018 report of the administrative court in South Tyrol, where in 2017 just three appeals against non-significant silence were made (5.9%). In the report by the Regional administrative court of Friuli Venezia Giulia, it is pointed out that the appeals on non-significant silence in the year were just six (seven in 2016, four in 2015).

[109] See especially the 2018 report by the administrative court of Abruzzo.

[110] Some examples may be found in the 2018 report of the administrative court in Calabria: see T.A.R. Calabria, Catanzaro, II, 15.3.2017, No. 865, Idem, 20.2.2017, No. 284; Idem, 20.1.2017, No. 1584. Similarly, see the 2019 report by the special section of Reggio Calabria: T.A.R. Calabria, Reggio Calabria, 2.7.2018, No. 402, and Idem, 17.12.2018, No. 758. In Liguria, in the 2018 report, among the most relevant cases some appeals against silence are indicated, in the field of planning law and protection of environment (T.A.R. Liguria, I, 20.3.2017, No. 225, and Idem, 29.6.2017, No. 579) and in the field of access to documents, were a case of negative silence is provided for (T.A.R. Liguria, II, 23.1.2018, No. 51). Litigation on access to administrative documents seems to be relevant also in Campania, with 253 appeals (of comprehensively 5275) in 2017 and 223 appeals (of comprehensively 5256) in 2018. Planning law is indicated as a relevant field for litigation on non-significant silence in the report on 2017 by the Regional administrative court of Piemonte.

[111] The respondent people were a few dozen: public servants, ombudspersons, and administrative judges, working in different Italian regions.

asked how often tacit decisions (both positive and negative ones) and non-significant silence are concretely challenged before a court and how often an economic compensation is the consequence for administrative non-action or delay.

It is a clear result of the questionnaire that significant silence is concretely often used by administration; in such case, tacit denials are sometimes challenged by the applicants, while tacit permits are almost never challenged by third parties. In the perception of the practitioners (that seems to be partially confirmed by the case law), the majority of controversies on non-significant silence before the administrative courts concern access to data. Also the actions for compensation of the damage, suffered because of the delay, are not frequent[112]; according to the respondent practitioners, the main reason for that lays in the difficulty of proving that the prejudice was a direct consequence of the delay itself and of quantifying its amount. Finally, an interesting element rising from the questionnaires is the idea, expressed by some practitioners, according to which often a simple inaction is the reaction of officers in front of requests of clarification by the citizens. In a technical perspective, this of course has nothing to do with administrative silence in strict sense, since this kind of requests are not able to produce a duty to start a procedure; nonetheless, this may be a sign of an attitude of scarce transparency, using inaction as a sort of weapon "against" the citizens and as a tool of illegal simplification in the implementation by the public officers of their institutional duties.

Bibliography

Basilica, F., & Barazzoni, F. (2014). *Diritto amministrativo e politiche di semplificazione*. Sant'Arcangelo di Romagna: Maggioli.

Carbone L. (2017). *La riforma dell'autotutela come nuovo paradigma dei rapporti tra cittadino e amministrazione pubblica*. https://www.giustizia-amministrativa.it/documents/20142/147937/nsiga_4375342.doc/c99dda0a-2b2a-265b-0b96-9857567c3d29?version=. Retrieved December 2018.

[112] A recent example is indicated among the particularly relevant case law in the report on 2017 by the Regional administrative court of Lombardia (autonomous section of Brescia): see T.A.R. Lombardia, Brescia, II, 4.5.2017, No. 599. See also T.A.R. Calabria, Catanzaro, I, 12.6.2018, No. 1177, mentioned as relevant case law in the report on 2018 by the administrative court of Calabria. Finally, in the field of planning law, see T.A.R. Campania, Naples, 3.5.2017, No. 2365, Idem, 24.5.2017, No. 2764, and Idem, 11.7.2017, No. 3734.

Cerbo, P. (2017). L'azione di adempimento nel processo amministrativo ed i suoi confini. *Diritto processuale amministrativo*, 1–43.

Clarich, M. (1995). *Termine del procedimento e potere amministrativo*. Turin: Giappichelli.

Colavecchio, A. (2013). *L'obbligo di provvedere tempestivamente*. Turin: Giappichelli.

Contessa, C. (2018). *L'autotutela amministrativa all'indomani della "legge Madia"*. https://www.giustizia-amministrativa.it/documents/20142/147937/nsiga_4626619.docx/98e4df94-b075-f366-b25c-a22eaf5456b0?version=. Retrieved December 2018.

Criscuolo R. *Il risarcimento del danno derivante da ritardo della PA nell'emanazione di un provvedimento favorevole al privato e l'indennizzo da mero ritardo nella conclusione del procedimento amministrativo*. http://www.neldiritto.it/appdottrina.asp?id=13119#.W92CKWepWUk. Retrieved December 2018.

Donato, L. (2015). *Le autocertificazioni tra "verità" e "certezza"*. Naples: Editoriale Scientifica.

D'Orsogna, M., & Lombardi, R. (2017). Il silenzio assenso. In M. A. Sandulli (Ed.), *Codice dell'azione amministrativa* (pp. 965–981). Milan: Giuffré.

Francario, F. (2017). *Riesercizio del potere amministrativo e stabilità degli effetti giuridici*. Fedralismi. https://www.federalismi.it/ApplOpenFilePDF.cfm?artid=33885&dpath=document&dfile=13042017123943.pdf&content=Riesercizio%2Bdel%2Bpotere%2Bamministrativo%2Be%2Bstabilit%C3%A0%2Bdegli%2Beffetti%2Bgiuridici%2B-%2Bstato%2B-%2Bdottrina%2B-%2B. Retrieved December 2018.

Greco, G. (1980). *L'accertamento autonomo del rapporto nel giudizio amministrativo*. Milan: Giuffré.

Guacci, C. (2012). *La tutela avverso l'inerzia della pubblica amministrazione secondo il codicedel processo amministrativo*. Turin: Giappichelli.

Gualdani, A. (2017). *Il tempo nell'autotutela*. Federalismi. http://www.sipotra.it/wp-content/uploads/2017/06/Il-tempo-nell%E2%80%99autotutela.pdf. Retrieved December 2018.

Immordino, M. (2010). Tempo ed efficienza nella decisione amministrativa. In A. Contieri, F. Francario, M. Immordino, and A. Zito (Eds.), *L'interesse pubblico tra politica e amministrazione* (pp. 57–94). Naples: Editoriale Scientifica.

Lipari, M. (2015). *La SCIA e l'autotutela nella legge n. 124/2915: primi dubbi interpretativi*. Federalismi. https://www.federalismi.it/ApplOpenFilePDF.cfm?artid=30592&dpath=document&dfile=20102015123142.pdf&content=La%2BSCIA%2Be%2Bl%27autotutela%2Bnella%2Blegge%2Bn%2E%2B124%2F2015%3A%2Bprimi%2Bdubbi%2Binterpretativi%2B%2D%2Bstato%2B%2D%2Bdottrina%2B%2D%2B. Retrieved December 2018.

Macchia, M. (2015). Sui poteri di autotutela: una riforma in senso giustiziale. *Giornale di diritto amministrativo*, 634–639.

Meale, A. (2016). Il rito del silenzio, come azione di carattere generale e il rapporto con la giurisdizione del Giudice amministrativo. *Giurisprudenzaitaliana*, 1719–1722.

Napolitano, G. (2014). Diritto amministrativo e processo economico *Dirittoamministrativo*, 695–724.

Occhiena, M. (2012). Art. 31. Azione avverso il silenzio e declaratoria di nullità. In R. Garofoli and G. Ferrari (Eds.), *Codice del processo amministrativo* (pp. 579–600). Rome: NelDiritto.

Parisio, V. (Ed.). (2006). *Silenzio e procedimento amministrativo in Europa*. Milan: Giuffré.

Pinelli, C. (2015). Il silenzio non può per Costituzione concludere il procedimento amministrativo, malgrado una "giurisprudenza tradizionalmente rispettosa della scelta del legislatore". *Giurisprudenzacostituzionale*, 2216 2218.

Police, A. (2017). Il dovere di concludere il procedimento e il silenzio inadempimento. In M.A. Sandulli (Ed.), *Codice dell'azione amministrativa* (pp. 226–290). Milan: Giuffré.

Posteraro, N. (2015). Considerazioni critiche sul generalizzato potere di provvedere della p.a. *Foro amministrativo*, 2676–2701.

Posteraro, N. (2017). Riflessioni a proposito del rito avverso il silenzio inadempimento. *Foro amministrativo*, 793–809.

Ramajoli, M. (2014). Forme e limiti della tutela giurisdizionale contro il silenzio inadempimento. *Diritto processuale amministrativo*, 709–745.

Scognamiglio, A. (2017). Rito speciale per l'accertamento del silenzio e possibili contenuti della sentenza di condanna. *Diritto processuale amministrativo*, 450–497.

Scotti, E. (2016). La segnalazione di inizio attività. In A. Romano (Ed.), *L'azione amministrativa* (pp. 582–652). Turin: Giappichelli.

Sica, M. (2017). Il rito del silenzio inadempimento: limiti e proposte. *Giurisprudenza italiana*, 990–995.

Sinisi, M. (2015). *La nuova azione amministrativa: il "tempo" dell'annullamento d'ufficio e l'esercizio dei poteri inibitori in caso di s.c.i.a. Certezza del diritto e falsi miti*. Federalismi: http://www.ptpl.altervista.org/dottrina_contributi/2015/sinisi_martina_23122015_la_nuova_azione_amministrativa.pdf. Retrieved December 2018.

Torchia, L. (2016). *I nodi della pubblica amministrazione*. Naples: Editoriale scientifica.

Torchia, L. (2017). Teoria e prassi delle decisioni amministrative. *Diritto amministrativo*, 1–41.

Ursi, R. (2016). *Le stagioni dell'efficienza. I paradigmi giuridici della buona amministrazione*. Maggioli: Sant'Arcangelo di Romagna.

Vese, D. (2017). Termine del procedimento amministrativo e analisi economica. *Rivista trimestraledi diritto pubblico*, 779–830.

CHAPTER 8

The Sound of Silence in Spain

Patricia Valcárcel Fernández, Rafael Fernández Acevedo, and Sara Sistero Ródenas

8.1 Introduction

The kingdom of Spain is a decentralized State consisting of 17 regions, known as autonomous communities, and two autonomous cities (Ceuta and Melilla). Art. 2 and 137 of the 1978 Spanish Constitution state that there are three levels of government and public administration (national, regional, and local). The distribution of competences is set out in Art. 148 and 149 of the Spanish Constitution. Most importantly for this paper, Art. 149.1.18 grants the State exclusive powers over "general administrative procedure, without limiting the ability of the autonomous communities to organise themselves."

P. Valcárcel Fernández (✉) · R. Fernández Acevedo
Faculty of Legal and Labour Sciences, University of Vigo, Vigo, Spain
e-mail: pvalcarcel@uvigo.es

R. Fernández Acevedo
e-mail: racevedo@uvigo.es

S. Sistero Ródenas
Faculty of Law, University Jaume I of Castellón, Castellón de la Plana, Spain
e-mail: sistero@uji.es

D. C. Dragos et al. (eds.),
The Sound of Silence in European Administrative Law,
https://doi.org/10.1007/978-3-030-45227-8_8

In the context of European traditions, Spain is usually identified with the German notion of Rechtsstaat. Nevertheless, the principal feature of Spain's constitutional history has been its extreme instability. The nature of administrative silence runs parallel to this particular development of the rule of Law.[1]

Authoritarianism was the dominant reality in the nineteenth and twentieth centuries. With limited parliamentary control and ministerial responsibility, which were never enforced, despotism and the mercantilization of the public administration increased.[2] In fact, administrative silence began, not as a protective mechanism but rather as a tool in the service of the public administration itself. It occurred for various reasons, notably to improve the public image[3] of the authorities and to emphasize the final character of administrative action.

The history of administrative silence in Spain is the history of the administrative disputes courts, particularly their traditional task of reviewing decisions. Administrative silence was not generally regulated in Spain until well into the twentieth century.[4] In the meantime, case Law was declared to be without effect in the absence of any previous decisions capable of being monitored (*décision préalable*).[5] Throughout the

[1] Aguado i Cudolà (1997, pp. 29–75).

[2] Varela Ortega (1977) and Sánchez Morón (1991, p. 50).

[3] Awareness begins of the damage caused to the image of the State by delays in administrative procedures. In the explanation of the reasons for the Regulations for processing business at the Finance Ministry (Royal Decree 18/02/1871), it is considered that simplicity and speed in the office will not only end the delays but also that "most importantly, they will make the public administration appear in the eyes of the country and the judgment of public opinion in such a way that many of the criticisms hanging over it will disappear. These are the result of the sluggishness, confusion and obscurity that sometimes predominate."

[4] The expression "administrative silence" appears for the first time in local administration in the approval of the Municipal Statute of 8 March 1924. However, the scope of silence there was limited to the prior administrative route without any effect on the use of the courts. See García Pérez (2001, p. 176).

[5] From the origins of the administrative dispute courts, the requirement for a prior executive administrative act to allow access to the judicial route constantly hampered their work. The courts declared themselves incompetent to proceed and sent the case back to the administration to complete the process. This led to situations of legal defenselessness so flagrant some of them took 30 years to process. Spanish case Law failed to make a decisive impact on the new control mechanisms or the speeding up of administrative action. See Aguado i Cudolà (1998).

last century, administrative practices remained immutable. Administrative silence became a way of completing the administrative procedure.[6] Such a perversion of legal technique allowed the authorities to benefit from neglecting their duties.

More extensive protection was provided under pre-constitutional regulations enacted in 1956 and 1958.[7] However, the coming into force of the 1978 Constitution provided the most favorable interpretation of the fundamental right to effective judicial protection.[8]

The principle of procedural economy took the constitutional requirement for effectiveness into administrative procedure (103 CE; Judgment of the Supreme Court, 6 February 1998). Furthermore, Art. 20 of the Law on General Administrative Procedure (Law 39/2015, of October 1, hereafter LPAC) established the principle of responsibility for processing, so that the public administration must take all measures necessary to ensure a final decision. Finally, Art. 71 completes the measures with the principles of urgency, transparency, and electronic processing.

[6] The acceptance of silence as a kind of fictitious (tacit or presumed) "administrative act," translating the doctrine of express resolutions, became a way for administrative bodies to evade obligations, moving away from the initial aim, which was to allow citizens to benefit from delays caused by the administration. See García Pérez (2001).

[7] The first circumstances of administrative silence arise in the financial administration in the first half of the nineteenth century.

In 1956, the Administrative Procedures Law was published, regulating negative administrative silence as a general rule when faced by formal inactivity of the administration (Art. 38). Art. 94 of the Administrative Procedures Law makes similar provisions. Positive silence was somewhat secondary in this legislation, requiring special regulation. See Morillo-Velarde Pérez (2002, p. 92).

[8] STC 86/1986, 21 January, ECLI:ES:TC:1986:6. This judgment marks the adaptation of administrative silence to the requirements of the Rule of Law promulgated in the Constitution of 1978 (Art. 1). Full subjection to the Law and to the Law (Art. 103.1); court supervision of all administrative action (Art. 106.1); and the principle of effectiveness (Art. 103.2). The repeal of the pre-constitutional regulations for administrative disputes (1956) and administrative procedure (1958) did not arrive until 1998 and 1992 respectively. The judgment is crucial in considering that it would not be reasonable to consider an appeal against administrative silence out of place. This would mean putting the administration "in a better position than if it had given notice with all legal requirements."

8.2 Legal Context of the Obligation to Resolve Administrative Procedures

Part IV of the Spanish Constitution refers specifically to issues relating to "Government and Administration" (Art. 97 to 107). More specifically, Art. 103 to 107 refer to the "Administration." Inferred from these precepts is the obligation that the Law regulates an administrative procedure, and that all acts of a public administration must necessarily be issued while observing the procedure provided in Law. The obligation to ensure a hearing for the interested party, when applicable, is also established.

That said, the Constitution makes no mention of any other formalities that must exist in the procedure; nor does it expressly establish a maximum period within which each administrative procedure must be decided on. However, Art. 103 of the Constitution does refer to a series of principles that must guide the actions of public administrations. The most notable of these is "effectiveness," which is understood to include the obligation to resolve all administrative procedures within a reasonable time. The rules governing each procedure must determine this reasonable period within which the procedure must be resolved and notification given of the decision.[9]

The Spanish Constitution does not, therefore, refer expressly and directly to administrative silence.

With regard to judicial review of administrative acts, Art. 103 of the Constitution establishes the principle of full respect for the rule of Law and for administrative Law. This determines that no actions by the Administration are exempt from judicial control, as can also be inferred from Art. 24.1, which recognizes the "right to effective judicial protection." More specifically, Art. 106.1 establishes that the courts control the lawfulness of administrative action, as well as its submission to the ends that justify it.

As has already been explained, Art. 149.1.18 of the Spanish Constitution gives the State exclusive jurisdiction to regulate the common administrative procedure. This jurisdiction has been fulfilled by the State legislators though LPAC. Consequently, this Law regulates the general

[9] Art. 21 LPAC provides that the maximum period within which notification must be given of the express resolution will be that established by the regulation for the corresponding procedure. If the regulation does not establish a maximum period, it will be three months.

formalities comprising the common administrative procedure. Thus, it is possible to establish other formalities or adapt those set out in the LPAC to a particular sector. This should always relate to the provisions of Art. 1.2 of the LPAC, which requires that these formalities or adaptations be made through the Law (State or autonomic, depending on which has jurisdiction over the matter requiring the introduction of procedural exception) and only "*when it is effective, proportionate and necessary for the achievement of the proper purposes of the procedure, and with justification (...)*." However, by means of a regulation (approved by the State, autonomous community, or local government), procedural exceptions referring to the following issues may be established: competent bodies, periods of time inherent in the specific procedure because of the matter being dealt with, forms of beginning or ending the procedure, publication and reports to be obtained.

Accordingly, by virtue of subject matter, the duration of each special administrative procedure may be established in these sectorial regulations. If this regulation is not issued, or no mention is made of the maximum period of time for this area of administrative procedures, Art. 21.3 LPAC stipulates that the time allowed for resolving an administrative procedure is three months. In addition, Art. 21.2.2 of the LPAC places a limit on the sectorial regulation of a regulatory scope by setting the time limitv for the procedures it regulates: This period cannot exceed 6 months. Therefore, whenever a longer period needs to be established, a State or autonomous community Law must be enacted.

In any case, from Art. 21.1 of the LPAC, it can be inferred that administrations must always issue an express decision and notify the interested parties of it within the period of time established by the regulations governing the applicable administrative procedure.

Finally, where appropriate for reasons of public interest, the application of urgent processing to the procedure may be agreed, *ex officio* or at the request of the interested party. Should this occur, the periods of time set for the ordinary procedure are halved, except for those relating to the submission of applications and appeals (Art. 33.1 LPAC).

8.3 Concerning the Maximum Duration of Administrative Proceedings

8.3.1 General and Special Deadlines

The general maximum period of time established "in the first or initial instance" by Spanish legislation for deciding and providing notification of administrative acts that expressly resolve procedures is three months, as already indicated, unless there is a special rule making any other specification, with a maximum of six months if the rule has regulatory status.

In administrative appeal procedures, the period of time allowed depends on the type of appeal lodged. The LPAC only regulates ordinary appeals (to higher courts and optional administrative reconsideration appeals) and extraordinary appeals for review and leaves special appeals in the hands of special legislation (e.g., special appeals in the field of procurement, appeals in the area of sports, and economic-administrative appeals).

The maximum period of time allowed for deciding and reporting on the resolution of these appeals, which is always counted from the date they are lodged, is 3 months for appeals to higher courts (Art. 122.2 LPAC) and for extraordinary review (Art. 126.3 LPAC), and 1 month for appeals for reconsideration (Art. 124.2 LPAC).

With regard to the special appeals referred to above:

a. In the case of a special appeal concerning procurement, the maximum period of time allowed for resolution is two months.[10]
b. In the case of appeals in the area of sport, as no specific period of time for resolution is established in the sectorial regulations. The general three-month period set out in Art. 21.3 of the LPAC applies.
c. Finally, in the economic-administrative context, the period of time allowed for resolving the ordinary procedure, in any of its instances (the Law establishes several), is one year from the filing of the complaint[11] (Art. 240 of Law 58/2003, of 17 December). If the

[10] Art. 57.5 of the Public Sector Contracts Act, 9/2017, transposing the Directives of the European Parliament and the Council 2014/23/EU and 2014/24/EU, of 26 February 2014, into the Spanish legal system (LCSP).

[11] Art. 240 of the General Taxation Law 58/2003, 17 December (LGT).

fast-track procedure has been applied, the period of time allowed for resolution will be six months[12] (Art. 247.2 of Law 58/2003, of 17 December). Additionally, various extraordinary remedies are regulated with different time limits for resolution (three or six months, depending on the case), always counted from the date on which the appeal is lodged[13] (Art. 242, 243, 244 of Law 58/2003, of 17 December).

Regarding the character or nature of these deadlines, from Art. 95.1 and 25.1.b) LPAC it clearly follows that both the general deadline and any special deadlines determined by the sectorial legislation have the nature of peremptory deadlines (expiry deadlines). This is the general rule in administrative proceedings. Among other consequences, this means that, even if an administrative procedure has expired a new one with the same purpose could be begun, as long as the actions of the individual or of the administration have not lapsed (Art. 95.3 LPAC).

The nature of the deadline is completely independent of whether the lack of resolution and notification within the procedure's time limit constitutes a case of negative or positive silence.

Overall statistical data in relation to compliance or non-compliance with the deadlines for resolution of administrative procedures are scant. In summary, it can be indicated, for example, that failure to meet the deadline for resolving and notifying urban planning applications is estimated to be very high. This is due to the fact that the periods established in regional planning legislation are short[14] in relation to the material and personal resourced available to most local councils, which are insufficient in order to comply with them.

Finally, it is usual to state that administrative procedures may be resolved by express act or by silence, but this is a mistaken conception. Administrative silence is clearly not, and cannot be envisaged as, a way of resolving administrative procedures. Administrative silence is always a failure by the authorities to comply with their duties.

[12] Art. 247.2 LGT.

[13] Art. 242 to 244 LGT.

[14] Normally three months. See Art. 143.2 of the Galician Land Law 2/2016, of 10 February, or Art. 172.5 of the Andalusian Town Planning Law 7/2002, of 17 December.

8.3.2 Extension and Suspension of Deadlines

The LPAC regulates three different cases relating to the extension of the maximum periods of time allowed for deciding and giving notice of an administrative procedure. The objective is to provide solutions to three different types of problem:

(A) When the number of requests made or people affected could lead to non-compliance with the time limit for resolution. In this case, firstly, the Law requires the body competent for processing the request to provide sufficient human and material resources to comply with the proper and timely completion of the procedure (Art. 21.5 LPAC).

Exceptionally, when these personal and material resources are depleted, the body competent to decide, at the suggestion of the examining body or hierarchically superior body, where applicable, may, by giving reasons, agree to extend the time limit for resolution and notification, although this cannot be greater than that established for dealing with the procedure (Art. 23.1 LPAC).

As underlined by the case Law, a literal understanding of this precept shows that "the possibility of extending the processing period is governed by the following notes: (1) it is an exceptional power and must therefore be applied in a limited way; (2) express reasons must be given for using it; (3) the reasons given must not be based on general considerations but on specific reference to the circumstances of the case; and (4) it may not be adopted *a priori*, but will only be appropriate after all relevant means for resolving it within the established period have been exhausted."

Precisely for this reason, the STS in the case quoted cancels the decision to extend the period in the case judged because "it was not adopted in view of the vicissitudes of the case and the incidents occurring in processing it, but was agreed in the agreement to start the proceedings, without any reasons given concerning the particular features of the case. On the contrary, only purely general references to the relevant sector of activity were given." The TS understands that this way of proceeding "involves making a procedural power legal established as exceptional into a general one. Indeed, to accept it would mean leaving without effect and de facto repealing the period established in the regulations for processing the case, making the extended period the normal one." Ultimately, the TS considers that if the general characteristics of the sector considered along justify the extension of the period from six to 12 months, a similar decision could, on principle, be extended to any proceedings of this kind.

This is a clearly unacceptable conclusion because if the regulations establish a particular period for processing and resolution it is on the basis that the proceedings can reasonably be concluded within this period. For this very reason, if in a specific case the period is considered to be insufficient, this must be recorded, giving reasons based on these circumstances.

(B) Principally for the benefit of the interested parties, and unless otherwise established, Art. 32 of the LPAC also stipulates that, if the circumstances make it advisable and no third-party rights are prejudiced, the administration must, *ex officio* or at the request of the interested parties, grant an extension of the periods of time set for dealing with the procedure. This extension may not exceed half of the period envisaged in each case. All parties interested in the procedure affected must be notified of the extension agreement. This extension is mandatory for the maximum time allowed for procedures processed by diplomatic missions and consular offices, as well as those, which, although occurring within Spain, require the completion of any procedure abroad, or involving interested parties resident outside Spain.

When a technical incident has rendered the ordinary operation of the corresponding system or application impossible, and until the problem has been resolved, the administration may decide to extend the unexpired period of time. To this end, it must publish, in its online office, details of both the technical incident that has occurred and the specific extension of the unexpired time limit.

Under no circumstances can any agreement be made to extend the period of time for this second case if the extended time limit has already expired. In other words, the decision on the extension must be taken before the deadline in question.

(C) During the course of the administrative procedure, certain circumstances may arise in which the Law allows the countdown to the deadline for the decision to be stopped. This will ultimately result in an increase in the actual time taken to resolve the procedure. These circumstances and the maximum period allowed applying in each case may be optional or mandatory, in accordance with the following scheme (Art. 22 LPAC):

(a) The Law allows the counting of the maximum legal period established for resolving a procedure and giving notice of the decision to be suspended in the following cases[15]:

a. When any interested party is required to correct defects or provide documents and other supporting evidence that may be necessary. The suspension covers the time between notification of the request and effective compliance with it by the recipient. Failing this, the period granted is 10 days, "reasonably" extendable by up to five additional days, except in cases of selective procedures or competitive tendering.
b. When a prior, mandatory judgment from a European Union body must be obtained. The suspension covers the time between the request, notification of which must be sent to the interested parties, and notification of the judgment to the examining administration, which must also be notified to the parties.
c. When there is an uncompleted procedure within the scope of the European Union, which has a direct bearing on the content of the resolution in question. The suspension covers the time from when its existence becomes known (the interested parties must be notified) until its resolution (notification of this will also have to be given).
d. When mandatory reports are requested from a body responsible to the same administration or a different one. The suspension covers the time between the request (the interested parties must be notified of this) and receipt of the report, which must also be notified to them. Under no circumstances may this suspension period exceed three months.
e. When technical tests or contradictory analyses or settlements need to be performed at the behest of the interested parties. The suspension covers the time required to incorporate the results into the file.
f. When undertaking negotiations aimed at reaching an agreement or a settlement to finalize the procedure. The suspension covers the period between the formal declaration in this regard and the conclusion of any negotiations without effect.

[15] Art. 22.1 LPAC.

g. When a preliminary court judgment needs to be secured to resolve the procedure. The suspension covers the period from the request for the judgment, which must be notified to the interested parties, until the administration has proof of the judgment. Notification must be given of this.

(b) The Law determines the suspension of the maximum legal period allowed for resolving a procedure and reporting the decision in the following cases[16]:

a. When one public authority requires another to annul or review an act that it deems to be illegal and which constitutes the basis for the act that the first authority must order within the scope of its powers. The suspension covers the period from the time when the request is made until it is dealt with; or, where appropriate, the time when the appeal lodged before the administrative disputes courts is resolved. The interested parties must be notified of both the making of the request and compliance with it; or, where appropriate, the resolution of the corresponding administrative disputes appeal.
b. When the body competent to decide resolves to perform some additional action. The suspension covers the period from the moment when the interested parties are notified of the agreement for the start of the complementary actions, with reasons, until their completion.
c. When the interested parties move to request recusal at any time during a procedure. The suspension covers the period from the moment the matter is raised until its resolution by the hierarchical superior of the recused party.

8.3.3 How Are the Periods Calculated?

The period of time set for deciding and notifying on the express act that concludes the administrative procedure is calculated differently, depending on how the procedure was begun (Art. 21.3 LPAC)[17]:

[16] Art. 22.2 LPAC.
[17] Art. 21.3 LPAC.

a. In proceedings initiated *ex officio*, counting commences with the resolution by the body that is competent to begin the procedure.
b. In procedures initiated at the request of the interested party, the calculation begins on the date when the application was received by the electronic registry of the administration or body competent to process it.

The last point is because Art. 16.4 LPAC allows interested parties to submit their requests, pleadings, appeals, and all manner of documents to the computerized registry of any public sector body, as well as at post offices, diplomatic representations, or consular offices of Spain abroad, registry help desks, or any similar registry established under current regulations. In such cases, counting will, logically, not begin until the application is received in the computerized registry of the body competent for processing it.

With regard to the rules on the expiry of time limits, the LPAC distinguishes between procedures initiated *ex officio* which could have unfavorable effects on the interested parties and all other procedures. In the former case, the consequence of the expiry of the maximum period of time allowed for deciding and giving notice is the expiry of the procedure (a typical example being sanctioning procedures). However, in all others (i.e., procedures initiated *ex officio* liable to give rise to favorable effects and procedures initiated at the request of the interested party), the consequence is administrative silence.

Regarding the nature of the periods of time, in the vast majority of cases, periods of this kind are established in months or years, in which case they are counted from date to date. This formula has not been without controversy.

Firstly, the date-to-date rule for calculation is not spelled out in Art. 30.2 LPAC, unlike Art. 5.1 of the Civil Code, which provides that "if the periods are fixed in months or years they will be calculated from date to date." This expression, which was contained in the LPA/58[18] and in Law 30/92,[19] was removed by the reform of the latter in 1999, and the elimination was maintained in the current LPAC.

[18] Administrative Proceedings Law 17 July 1958.

[19] Public Administrations Legal System and Common Administrative Procedure Law 30/1992, 29 November (Law 30/92).

The question remains as to why this expression has disappeared from the current wording of Art. 30.2 LPAC and why, despite this, we still continue to state that the calculation is from date to date.

The explanation lies in relating this rule with another stating that *dies a quo no computatur in termino*. This means the period begins "from the day after notification or publication" (or, as appropriate approval or rejection through administrative silence).[20] Note that if *dies a quo* is the day after notification and the calculation begins from date to date, the final result would determine a period of the number of months indicated by the period plus one day. This result appears to go against the legal provision of periods in calendar months or years. It was therefore necessary to specify which had to be the *dies a quo*: the day of notification or the day afterward, as expressly established by Law and still applicable today.

Case Law had to mediate in this controversy. STS 8133/1994, referring to Art.5.1 del of the Civil Code, states that the interpretation of this precept has given rise to a fertile doctrine in case Law which "is highlighting the fact that in periods counted by months, the period ends the following month on the day of the month with the same number as the day of notification or publication."[21] And, at the same time, STS 7301/1997[22] states: "In accordance with the date-to-date rule included in Art.5.1 of the Civil Code, the initial wording of Art. 48.4 of Law 30/92, following the observation drawn up by the Council of State, does not maintain the day following the date of notification or publication as a criterion for fixing the initial date of all periods. Instead, it is maintained only when the periods are expressed in days (Art. 48.4). In the periods indicated in months or years, the latter precept establishes the general rule that the dies *a quo* will be the same day as the notification or publication of the act. Ultimately, both the current tendency in case Law and the regulations arising from Law 30/92 try to prioritise the specific rule for periods established in months or years of calculating date to date. In this way *dies ad quem* is the equivalent to the day of notification or publication in the month concerned. The ultimate significance of this tendency in case Law is very significant for all of them. The STS dated 9-3-88 states that the doctrine of case Law is now categorical and conclusive in

[20] Art. 30.3 LPAC.

[21] STS 8133/1994, 13 December, ECLI:ES:TS:1994:8133, legal basis 2.

[22] STS 7301/1997, 2 December, ECLI:ES:TS:1997:7301, legal basis 3.

establishing that in periods indicated by months, although date to date calculation begins the day after notification or publication, the final day of such a period will always be that corresponding to the ordinal number of the day of notification or publication".

Finally, the applicable LPAC, correctly taking up this doctrine from case Law, clarifies that "if the period is fixed in months or years, these will be calculated from the day after the day of notification or publication of the act concerned or the day after the one when approval or rejection by administrative silence is assumed."[23]

Note that, with everything, in the circumstances we are referring to, for the calculation of the period for resolving and giving notice of the proceedings, the *dies a quo* clearly does not begin with the notification or publication of an administrative act but rather, as has been said, from the request by the individual or the agreement to begin proceedings, as appropriate.

However, the LPAC envisages and regulates the possibility that periods of time could be established by days and even hours.

a. If the period of time is set in hours, all hours of the day are understood to be working hours and they are computed from hour to hour and from minute to minute from the hour and minute. The duration may not be more than 24 hours, or the period must be expressed in days.
b. If the period is established in days, and if it is not expressly stated that these are calendar days, they are understood to be working days, and Saturdays, Sundays, and public holidays are excluded from the calculation, unless otherwise established in Law or by an EU regulation. Thus, in terms of public procurement, LCSP Additional Provision 12 stipulates that periods of time established in days will be understood to be in calendar days unless otherwise specified.

Taking into account that the State, the autonomous communities, and the municipalities have different non-working days, the labor calendar approved every year by the general State Administration and the administrations of the autonomous communities, specifying precisely which days are working days and which are not, must be taken into account in

[23] Art. 30.4 LPAC.

computing the number of working days. The calendars approved by the autonomous communities will also include the non-working days of the local authorities included in their territorial scope.

These calendars must be published in the corresponding official journal before the beginning of each year, as well as in other media ensuring that they are widely circulated.

Any day that is a non-working day in the place of residence of the interested party or in the locality where the body dealing with the procedure has its headquarters is considered a non-working day (Art. 30.6 LPAC).[24]

However, this rule does not apply to the administration's online office, where applications, documents, etc., are submitted via computerized registries[25] (Art. 31.3 LPAC). This is the case, for example, when interested parties are obliged to interact electronically with public administrations[26] (Art. 14 LPAC). It should also be borne in mind that, within the framework of electronic administration, the online office of the registry of each administration determines the days considered to be working days in line with its territorial scope and the official calendar.

It is important to stress that, for the purpose of calculating deadlines, the electronic registry of each administration or body is governed by the official date and time of electronic access to the site, which must have the security measures necessary to ensure its integrity and must be accessible and visible.

The operation of the computerized registry is governed by the following rules:

a. It must allow the submission of documents 24 h a day, 365 days a year.
b. For the purposes of computing the period of time established in working days, and concerning compliance with deadlines by the interested parties, submission on a non-working day will be understood to be made in the first hour of the next working day, unless a rule expressly allows receipt on a non-working day.

   Documents will be considered to have been submitted in the actual order in which they are submitted on the non-working

[24] Art. 30.6 LPAC.

[25] Art. 31.3 LPAC.

[26] Art. 14 LPAC.

day. Documents submitted on a non-working day will be deemed to precede, in consecutive order, those submitted on the first subsequent working day.

c. The starting point for the time limits that must be met by public administrations is determined by the date and time of submission in the electronic registry of each administration or organization. In any case, the person submitting the document must be notified of the actual date and time of the starting point for these periods.

Whatever the nature of the time limit (in hours, days, months or years), it must always end on a working day. Otherwise, if the final day set for the period is not a working day (Saturday, Sunday, or public holiday), the Law determines that it will be extended to the next working day. This rule can be understood as being for the benefit of individuals.

Finally, the non-working status of Saturdays was established for the first time in the Spanish administrative area by the LPAC in 2015. It can be considered that this decision has been influenced by European administrative Law, which has always considered Saturdays as non-working days (Art. 2 of Regulation 1182/71, of the Council, of June 3, 1971).

8.4 Effects of Administrative Silence

8.4.1 General Rules

The LPAC distinguishes[27] between procedures initiated at the request of the interested party and those initiated *ex officio* which are likely to have unfavorable effects on the interested parties. While in the latter the rule is of negative silence, with no exceptions, in those initiated at the request of the interested party, the general rule is that silence approves requests, in other words positive silence.

There are, however, several exceptions to this general rule, which are listed in the Law itself.[28] Thus, in procedures initiated at the request of the interested party, silence will be negative in the following cases:

1. When a legal instrument with the status of a Law, or an EU Law, or an international Law applicable in Spain, establishes otherwise.

[27] Art. 54, 24 and 25 LPAC.

[28] First subparagraph of Art. 24.1 LPAC.

When the purpose of the procedure is to access or carry out activities, the Law that provides for negative silence must be based on the concurrence of compelling grounds of public interest.

2. In procedures relating to the exercise of the right to petition, recognized in Art. 29 of the Spanish Constitution.
3. In procedures whose approval would result in the transfer of powers relating to the public domain or to the public service to the applicant or to third parties.
4. In procedures which entail the exercise of activities that may be harmful to the environment.
5. In procedures relating to the recognition of capital liability of the public administrations.
6. In procedures which challenge administrative acts and *ex officio* review procedures initiated at the request of the interested parties. As the doctrine has it,[29] the negative meaning of silence, considered as rejection in this type of proceedings of challenge, is an exception to the general rule of positive silence justified with the principle of the presumption that administrative acts are legal. However, in 1992[30] Spanish legislators introduced an exception to this exception which the current LPAC, from 2015, maintains with some nuances: It established a specific circumstance of positive silence granting approval as a response to inactivity by the administration in proceedings of challenge.

These circumstances, known in the doctrine as "double silence exception," require various requirements to be fulfilled: (a) The initial proceedings must have been begun at the request of the interested party; (b) the request must be unresolved, with no decision notified within the period established, producing negative silence (an exception to the general rule of positive silence); (c) the appropriate appeal against this negative silence should be to a higher court (hierarchical appeal), not an appeal for reconsideration; (d) that, if such an appeal has been lodged, it has not been resolved or notification given of a decision within three months. If all these requirements are fulfilled, silence is considered positive, upholding the appeal (Art. 24.1 of the LPAC). In this way, the legislators "punish"

[29] Morillo-Velarde Pérez (2002, p. 118).

[30] Art. 43.3.b) Law 30/92.

repeated failure by the administration to comply with the legal obligation to resolve and give notice of all procedures within the established period (Art. 21 of the LPAC).

Overall, the original formulation of the double silence exception generated doubts in the interpretation of its specific scope.[31] A large number of authors[32] have upheld a broad interpretation of the scope of this exception. The literal interpretation of Art. 43.3.b) Law 30/92 would lead us to understand that the positive effect of double silence would apply if the silence was considered to refuse a request. This would be regardless of the matter concerned or the rule establishing the negative silence (general administrative proceedings Law, special Law, European Community regulation). In all these cases, because of the effect of double silence, what for Spanish or European Community legislators is negative becomes positive.

By contrast, another interpretation[33] considered that the double exception could not be applied when the general administrative procedural Law determined that silence should be negative. So, the positive effect of double silence would not come into play when the exceptions included in the general Law were operative, making silence automatically negative, without any exception, in proceedings to exercise the right of petition in Art. 29 of the Constitution and those whose approval would result in transferring powers relating to public property or public services to the requester or to third parties.

This last solution was the one taken up in the case Law. STS 2/2013[34] states, without giving reasons, that the double silence exception "**should not apply in cases of the right to petition or powers related to public property**, but it does undoubtedly apply in cases exempted from positive silence" by European Community legislation or rules. And it concludes

[31] On this problem, see Casado (2015, pp. 271–316).

[32] Among others, Santamaría Pastor (1993, p. 173), Ballesteros Moffa (1999, p. 12), Morillo-Velarde Pérez (2002, pp. 119–120), and Fernández Acevedo (2005, pp. 269–270), and, by the same author (2004, pp. 847 and 923). In this last work, after setting out the possibility that concessions will be obtained from the public domain through positive silence, the author critically warns that "besides other considerations such as those concerning the legal insecurity generated by positive silence, this result is barely coherent with the basic legal system established in the Constitution for the public sphere (Art. 132)" (p. 923).

[33] Among others, Parejo Alfonso (1993, pp. 578–579) and Gallardo Castillo (2010, p. 194).

[34] STS 2/2013, of 8 January, ECLI:ES:TS:2013:2, legal basis 4.

by stating that "in cases of presumed rejection of an appeal to a higher court lodged against a presumed rejection, Law 30/92 wants silence to be positive even though, **under another Law**, negative silence might apply for the petition route." In this decision, the higher public interest present here (public property, public service) is a factor in this decision.

Finally, the applicable LPAC has taken up this doctrine from the case Law, extending the list of circumstances for not applying the positive effect of double silence in the new case of negative silence that it introduces in the first paragraph of Art.24 (proceedings "involving the exercise of activities that could damage the environment"), as well as in procedures concerning the property-related liability of public authorities (claims for losses and damages).

However, when an administrative appeal to a superior court has been filed against the dismissal of a request due to administrative silence owing to the expiry of the maximum period, the silence is positive if, when the deadline is reached, the competent administrative body does not issue and give notice of an express decision, provided it does not concern the matters listed in cases (2), (3), (4), and (5).

As can be deduced from the above exceptions, there are numerous procedures in which the lack of an express decision determines that the applications or resources of the interested parties can be understood to have been dismissed owing to negative administrative silence. In the opinion of Prof. Muñoz Machado,[35] this means that—despite the emphasis legislators have placed on restructuring the system so that positive silence prevails as fair compensation for the anomaly produced by the administration not responding to the inducements of the administered parties—there is still some doubt as to whether the rule actually does prevail in the current legislation. The transposition of the Services Directive,[36] through Law 17/2009,[37] which amended the Law that previously regulated this matter, required a review of the procedures exempted in the positive administrative silence rule, which the current LPAC has not fully conducted.

[35] Muñoz Machado (2017, p. 151).

[36] Directive 2006/123/EC of the European Parliament and the Council of 12 December 2006, relating to services in the internal market.

[37] Law 17/2009, of 23 November, on free access to and exercise of service activities.

In any case, positive administrative silence is not always the most favorable option for citizens. This is the case when the administrative act is required to enable the individual to proceed in legal transactions. The lack of a document accrediting that the administration has granted the power or right requested may cause more harm than good. In particular, when dealing with regulated acts, the rule of negative administrative silence allows the interested party to make a challenge before the administrative appeals courts and to request the court to issue the regulated act omitted by the administration. The court may also determine the content of the annulled act in its judgment (Art. 71.2 LJCA[38]-, *a contrario sensu*). Precisely for this reason, in the matter of planning permission for construction, the Spanish legislators have deemed it necessary to reverse the positive sense of administrative silence to negative silence, as will be later.

As explained, the concept of administrative silence also applies to procedures initiated *ex officio*. In this case, they are distinguished depending on whether the procedure has favorable or unfavorable effects for the interested parties: In the former case, the rule of negative administrative silence applies; in the latter, expiry, rather than administrative silence, is applicable.

In any event, we need to distinguish between applications that initiate a procedure and those that can be incorporated once a procedure has already been initiated. In this regard, the jurisprudence has stated that the positive silence currently contemplated in a general way in the LPAC is not applicable to all requests made by interested parties, only to procedures initiated at their request (Judgment of the Supreme Court 1358/2007)[39]. For this reason, STS 7070/2008[40] negated the claim that the lack of response to a request meant approval, understanding the contractual modification procedure as having been initiated *ex officio*, even if there had been a prior request from the interested party.[41]

It is not surprising, however, that the administration should attempt to pass off instances falling under the umbrella of the former case as if they belonged to the latter. As determined by the aforementioned STS

[38] Law 29/1998, of 13 July, governing the Administrative Disputes Courts (LJCA).

[39] STS 1358/2007, of 28 February 2007, ECLI:ES:TS:2007:1358.

[40] STS 7070/2008, of 17 December 2008, ECLI:ES:TS:2008:7070, legal basis 2.

[41] See García de Enterría and Fernández (2017, p. 652).

1358/2007, in cases where the interested party's request is completely independent of the initial *ex officio*-initiated procedure, it must be understood as a procedure initiated at the request of the interested party and, therefore, of positive administrative silence. This was the case, in the example of the aforementioned judgment, with the claim for interest generated *ex lege* on an acknowledged and paid principal debt which arose as part of the execution of a public works contract.

8.4.2 The Influence of EU Law

Law 17/2009, of November 23 and Law 25/2009 transposed the Services Directive into Spanish legislation.[42] In accordance with these Laws, a large part of Spanish legislation (State, autonomic, and local) was amended to eliminate the requirement of prior administrative authorization as a prerequisite for access to activities or for exercising them. These authorizations were transformed into "responsible statements" or "prior communications" from the interested parties. These instruments ("responsible statements" or "prior communications") are currently regulated in Art. 69 LPAC.

In all other cases in which this transformation has not taken place (i.e., the requirement for prior administrative authorization has been maintained), the general rule that administrative silence in proceedings initiated at the request of the interested party is positive is applied. In order to establish exceptions to this general rule, as has already been mentioned, a Law is required. However, this Law is not entirely free to establish negative silence. It can only do so based on the concurrence of compelling grounds of public interest. The only such reasons are those which have been defined or interpreted by the jurisprudence of the CJEU. They are limited to the following: public order, public safety, civil protection, public health, preservation of the financial equilibrium of the social security system, protection of the rights, safety and health of consumers, recipients of services and workers, requirements of good faith in commercial transactions, the fight against fraud, protection of the environment and the urban environment, animal health, intellectual and industrial property, the conservation of national historical and artistic heritage, and the objectives of social and cultural policy (Art.

[42] Law 25/2009, of 22 December, amending various Laws to adapt them to the Law concerning free access to and exercise of service activities.

3.11 Law 17/2009). In this respect, the impact that European Law and jurisprudence have on the Spanish regulation of administrative silence is clear.[43]

8.5 The Legal Nature of Negative Silence

The sole purpose of dismissal owing to administrative silence is to allow the interested parties to file the appropriate administrative or and administrative dispute appeal (Art. 24.2 LPAC). That is to say, as the doctrine states,[44] it is a mere legal fiction with purely procedural effects. This is neither an administrative act nor a way of resolving the procedure; it is the Law's response to a breach by the administration of its obligation to decide in a timely manner. Therefore, in these circumstances, there are two options open to individuals:

1. to continue awaiting the administration's compliance with its obligation to decide, even though it is late, because, as clearly follows from the LPAC, the obligation to resolve the matter can only be met in one way: by deciding (without prejudice to cases when the procedure is terminated by agreement or arrangement, as well as the procedures relating to the exercising of rights subject only to the duty of "responsible declaration" or "prior communication" to the administration).
2. to lodge the appeal they deem appropriate.

Consistent with this twofold option, as well as with the fact that incorrectly notified resolutions will have no effect unless the interested party acknowledges notification, the LPAC has eliminated all time limits on challenging negative silence, both through appeal to a superior court and through an appeal for reversal. The time limit for lodging an administrative appeal is also eliminated, in addition to that already made for the administrative disputes procedure through the jurisprudence of the Constitutional Court.[45] Indeed, the Constitutional Court has interpreted

[43] A critique of how the transposition of the Service Directive has been carried out in relation to administrative silence is made by García Pérez (2013, pp. 77–80).

[44] See García de Enterría and Fernández (2017, pp. 652–654).

[45] STC 52/2014, of April 10, 2014, ECLI:ES:TC:2014:52.

that, as Art. 46 LJCA only sets a time limit for contesting assumed acts, and, as negative silence is not an act, the provision sets no time limit whatsoever on contesting negative silence.

No requirement of proof is required in the case of administrative silence.

As we have already said in point 4.2, in the case of regulated acts, the judicial authority is fully competent to replace the administration. If, on the other hand, it is a discretionary act, it cannot do so and must limit itself to annulling the administrative silence that has arisen, demanding that the administration dictates the express act in accordance with the Law.

In relation to the execution of judicial sentences, the process must commence by stating that competence is vested exclusively in the courts and tribunals of justice (Art. 117 CE). On the other hand, the enforcement of judgments is regulated in Art. 103 to 113 LJCA. Based on those precepts, it is important to stress that parties are obliged to comply with judgments, in the form stated in them and in line with their content, and that acts and provisions of the administration contrary to the dictums of the judgments and issued with the aim of circumventing compliance with them are null and void.

Regarding the periods allowed for complying with judgments, Art. 104 LJCA establishes that once these are final, the Court Clerk will notify the body that has conducted the activity which is the subject of the appeal within ten days. Having received the communication, the latter must duly put it into effect and implement what is required by compliance with the declarations appearing in the judgment, and, within the same period of time, indicate this to the body responsible for fulfillment. As a general rule, two months after this notification, or when the period of time set out in the judgment itself for compliance with its ruling has elapsed, any of the parties and persons affected by it may request enforcement.

Finally, in accordance with Art. 112 LJCA, once the periods allowed for full compliance with the ruling have expired without their content having been implemented, the court, after hearing the parties, will adopt the measures necessary to enforce the mandate.

Exceptionally, having confirmed an authority or official's responsibility for failure to execute, and after giving them a warning, the judicial authority will be able to:

a. Impose penalty payments of between €150,000 and €500,000 and, where appropriate,
b. Take action concerning corresponding criminal liability.

In Spain, one of the most serious problems to be addressed is the high level of non-compliance with administrative dispute court judgments, which can be regarded as a systemic problem that the latest legal regulations have attempted to resolve, so far with differing degrees of success.[46]

Despite the clear reluctance of jurisdictional bodies to impose fines of this type and to take action over criminal liability, it can be seen that, in recent years, they have begun to impose them more frequently.

As an example of a Law that establishes a special case of negative silence in proceedings initiated at the request of the interested party on compelling grounds of public interest, we could refer to Additional Provision 19 of Law 21/2003, of July 7, on Air Safety, amended by Royal Decree-Law 8/2014, of July 4, approving urgent measures for growth, competitiveness, and efficiency. The second paragraph of this Provision stipulates that, due compelling grounds of public interest in security, and if the time limit for giving notice of the authorization procedures for operations and activities performed by remote-controlled aircraft elapses without there having been an express resolution, the authorizations requested shall be deemed to have been rejected by administrative silence.

Another interesting example arises in relation to planning permission. In Spanish Law, it has been traditional, even when the general rule was of negative silence, to attribute approval (positive silence) to the lack of a decision on municipal license applications in general and particularly for permission for land use and building work.

In time, this rule has been nuanced with the idea that rights or powers going against planning regulations cannot be acquired through administrative silence. This rule generated great legal insecurity among individuals who could not be entirely sure that their applications were entirely in line with particularly complex regulations like those governing planning.

Finally, in 2011 legislators decided to change the sense of silence from positive to negative in relation to the most important procedures relating to the transformation and use of land and the subsoil, as well as building

[46] See Gómez-Ferrer Rincón (2008).

and construction. This was done for reasons of legal security, and the change has been maintained in current town planning legislation.[47]

It can therefore be seen that in certain spheres positive silence can generate disadvantages which negative silence, by contrast, does not produce.[48]

Overall, reality is showing, as the doctrine has highlighted,[49] that the change in the direction of the silence we have mentioned can also cause practical disadvantages. In fact, it requires individuals to undertake long processes through the courts which unnecessarily delays them in obtaining and legitimately exercising their rights. This is particularly serious in circumstances where it is clear that the permission applied for is legally permitted.

The problem referred to in this question is known in Spanish Law as "late decisions." The treatment of these "late decisions" is different

[47] See Art. 11.4 of Royal Legislative Decree 7/2015 of 30 October approving the new draft of the Law concerning land and urban renewal.

[48] A similar situation has arisen with the promulgation of transparency Laws. While the State regulations applying to the General State Administration (and, subsidiarily, in the territories) have established the criterion of negative silence when faced with failure to resolve requests for access to information within a month, some Autonomous Communities have established the criterion of positive silence in their own Laws. With this, the Autonomous Community parliaments of Catalonia, Valencia, and Aragon wanted to provide better guarantees of access to public information. However, an average of five years after these rules began to be applied, it has been made clear that:

1. Administrative silence will be positive provided it is not "*contra legem*"; in other words, provided it does not go beyond the limits of the Law. This is possibly difficult for the person making the request to discover, increasing legal insecurity.

2. If there is negative silence, there is an immediate administrative or judicial appeal. However, the guarantee mechanisms against positive silence take a long time (both in the case of administrative and judicial appeals). This is because, despite the presumed approval, the administration must once again demand information in the case of any objection. This is an additional bureaucratic burden and another deadline period ensuring that defense is possible.

3. Aware of this, the guaranteeing authorities or commissions responsible for transparency at these Autonomous Communities have encouraged the inclusion of an interpretation of positive silence more favourable to citizens in their transparency Laws. This allows a generally clear and rapid way of obtaining guarantees without the need to specify the requested direction of the silence and without the administration benefiting from its own poor practice. (*Criterios Interpretativos sobre reclamación a la GAIP en caso de silencio administrative*, 7 January 2016).

See Ballesteros Moffa (2014).

[49] See González Botija (2015).

depending on the different effects associated with administrative silence (Art. 24.3 LPAC). Thus, if governed by rule of negative administrative silence, the subsequent express decision (late decision) will be adopted with no connection whatsoever with regard to the meaning of silence, which here is a mere legal fiction with effects that are purely and exclusively procedural, i.e., to allow interested parties to appeal if they consider it appropriate. Therefore, the late express act can be either affirmative or dismissive.

The second question posed by "late decisions," and which is totally independent of the direction of the silence—and therefore common to positive and negative silence—has to do with whether they can be contested. Even though it may be late, the express act determines when the clock starts on the period allowed for appeals, which will now be those periods established for contesting the express acts (1 month in the case of appeals to a superior court and optional appeals for administrative reconsideration).

8.6 The Legal Nature of Positive Silence

Positive silence determines that everything requested by interested parties in their application is upheld and (by contrast with the situation for negative silence) the Law grants the same, so that such silence is considered to have the same effect as an express resolution. It is binding on both the administration that is resumed to have issued it and on third parties, who, if they do not agree, will need to challenge it if they are entitled to do so.

The activity covered by an assumed act may legally be put into practice. Administrative acts produced by administrative silence give rise to effects as of the expiry of the maximum period during which the express decision must be issued and notified without it having been issued. They can be accredited by any element of proof admitted in Law. Despite this, the LPAC has provided an *ad hoc* element of proof, referred to as the silence accreditation certificate. This certificate is issued *ex officio* by the body with competences to decide within 15 days from the date of the expiry of the period allowed for resolving the procedure. Additionally, the interested party may request it at any time, with the period indicated being counted from the day following that of the request's entry in the computerized registry of the administration or body competent for resolving the matter.[50]

The form of executing assumed acts (i.e., affirmative or positive silence) is exactly the same as that for express acts. If the assumed act imposes an obligation on the administration to do something and it fails to comply, the individual can exercise the action envisaged in Art. 29.2 LJCA. In accordance with this, interested parties may request their execution by the administration, and, if this does not occur within one month from the request, they can file an appeal under an administrative dispute procedure within two months.

In relation to the question regarding the possibility of using the assumed act (positive silence) for fiscal purposes, obtaining other rights or conducting additional procedures, the response is clearly positive. This is true in as far as these assumed acts are fully equated with positive or favorable express acts.

Concerning "late decisions," as explained in point 5 regarding negative silence, they are treated differently depending on the different effects associated with administrative silence.[51] In cases where the rule of positive administrative silence must apply, a subsequent express decision (late decision) must always confirm this; that is., it must consist of an express affirmative act. A late express act must therefore be in the same sense as the prior alleged act, otherwise it would effectively be a reversal of a prior favorable act without following the procedure legally established for the review of favorable acts[52] and would, therefore, be null and void.[53]

8.7 Supervision of Administrative Timeliness

8.7.1 Supervision of Timeliness: Administrative Control, Judicial Review, Etc

According to Art. 21 LPAC, infringement of the obligation to resolve administrative procedures will entail disciplinary responsibility. However, the specific figure and fines are intentionally omitted. In the absence of

[50] Art. 24.4 LPAC.

[51] Art. 24.3 LPAC.

[52] Art. 106 LPAC.

[53] Art. 47.1.e) LPAC.

sectorial legislation, the Statute for Civil Servants includes the infringement of essential functions as a very serious infringement. In addition, it should be noted that the lack of performance is considered as a serious infringement,[54] but, otherwise, the negligence infringement could be also considered a minor infringement.

Traditionally, the demand for accountability in Spain involves practical difficulties in effectively implementing the regulation. The reasons vary from the very complexity of these organizations to a certain tendency to protect themselves rather than looking after the public. As various legal writings have stated, it is still important to improve the status and broaden the role of the public prosecutor in this field.

It is recalled that in terms of civil liability, damages are the direct responsibility of the public authority.

Under the 2013 Spanish Freedom of Information Act, persistent non-compliance with the obligation to make a resolution constitutes a breach (although the unjustified failure to provide information does not). In spite of all efforts, the system of responsibility relating to the duty of transparency shows some significant legal shortcomings. There is no express mention of sanctions, and officials filling political positions or political advisory positions, or indeed private bodies, are not held responsible.

8.7.2 *Governmental Strategies, Studies, Actions, and Their Effects on Tackling Excessive Length of Procedures*

The duration of proceedings remains the aspect with the lowest ratings when it comes to citizens' perception of public services. Therefore, the first report presented by the Commission for Public Administration Reform (CORA)[55] in 2011 proposed to extend these systems already up and running in certain State general administration units across the board to allow for the measurement of administrative unit workloads, calculate average processing times for procedures, assess the productivity of each unit, and compare it with its counterparts.

[54] STJCLM 103/2002, 21 January, ECLI:ES:TSJCL:2002:103.

[55] Available at the Transparency Portal: http://transparencia.gob.es/transparencia/dam/jcr:16c7ed96-bab3-4adb-943e-6c1730dd5785/reforma-AAPP-ingles.pdf.

This will allow for the reallocation of resources and adjustment of remuneration. With this, it will be possible to correct the delays in processing procedures in the processing units.

Processing times and variations in them can be posted on the websites of these bodies for matters most affecting citizens.

As a first step in the implementation of the CORA report, the ten most common procedures for the general State Administration have been selected to reveal their average processing times every month. The selected procedures are:

1. Request for initial retirement benefits;
2. Request for initial maternity benefits;
3. Traffic sanctioning procedures;
4. Complaints and claims by the users of telecommunication services;
5. Tax certificates;
6. Deferrals and payment in installments of arrears in tax administration;
7. Holidays for senior citizens;
8. Request for unemployment benefits;
9. Residence and work permits.

In the peripheral State Administration, efforts to reduce the backlog of compulsory expropriation procedures by 89.26% should be mentioned. Average processing times for these procedures has moved from 12 months in 2012, to 2–3 months in 2017.[56]

8.8 Legal Remedies

8.8.1 Administrative Appeals

There are two ordinary appeals on Spanish administrative system. On the one hand, there is a hierarchical appeal (known as an "alzada"), which is essential so that administrative review procedures can be exhausted. In addition, within the framework of appeals against administrative inactivity,

[56] Ministerio de Política Territorial y Función Pública. *Informe sobre el funcionamiento de los Servicios de la Administración Periférica del Estado en 2017*, p. 85. Available at: http://www.mptfp.gob.es/dam/es/portal/delegaciones_gobierno/informe-evaluacion/Informe_Ejecutivo-2017/Informe_Ejecutivo_2017.pdf.pdf.

the hierarchical appeal could be used by citizens to lodge complaints with a superior official. On the other hand, there is an informal appeal (known as a "reposición"), which puts forward a facultative request for reinstatement.

Over the years, the existence of time limits for applying for such remedies has been criticized. The major problems were concentrated in negative silence and hierarchical appeals. In accordance with case Law from the Supreme Court, while the public authority gains from a breach, the time limits put citizens in an even worse position. Citizens are responsible for knowing about and calculating the deadline. At that time, the main argument was that there was no notification when no express decision was made. Not only, therefore, was there no express decision, there was also no starting date for counting the period for appeal.[57]

Today, since the adoption of LPAC (39/2015) there are no time limits, irrespective of whether the silence is positive or negative. In this respect, the Law makes no distinction between a hierarchical appeal and an informal one. The person concerned may lodge an appeal at any time after silence comes into effect.

To conclude whether no response is obtained from the administrative authorities, the criteria differ according to the type of administrative appeal. In the case of an informal appeal, the general rule applies, after a month without a decision. That means negative silence comes into effect, because, as stated earlier, although this is a procedure at the request of one of the parties, there is a specific provision under Art. 24 LPAC. By contrast, in the case of hierarchical appeal, after three months have elapsed without a decision it is assumed that the response is positive. This rule is also known as "double silence" in relation to Art. 21.1 and 122.2 LPAC.

8.8.2 Judicial Review

Under Art. 46, LJCA provides a six-month time limit for lodging a judicial appeal against non-express decisions. This provision has been interpreted by extensive case Law; otherwise, it would have had to be repealed in accordance with the fundamental right to effective judicial

[57] STS 1952/1984, 7 November, ECLI: ES:TS:1984:1952; STS 9860/1986, 10 January, ECLI: ES:TS:1986:9860; STS 5317/1999, 21 July, ECLI: ES:TS:1999:5317.

protection. The Constitutional Court[58] argues the proportionality rule takes precedence over excessive formalism. The Supreme Court, in its Judgment of 23 January 2004, concludes that it is no longer right to speak of "rejecting implied acts," but only of a legal fiction allowing the use of administrative and judicial remedies, always for the benefit of the person concerned. Legal uncertainty is caused by the legal infringement and not by the absence of preclusive periods.

As a result, it is possible for there to be late decisions: in other words, decisions enacted after the use of judicial remedies. In such a case, the person concerned could withdraw or extend the complaint (Art. 36.4 LJCA). If the late decision was a confirmation of a previous positive silence, it is understood that there could be no appeal against the second decision under Art. 28 LJCA. Nevertheless, some case Law has suggested a nuanced approach.[59]

8.8.3 Court Remedies for Silent Rejection and Silent Approval

As shown in Sect. 8.4.2, the scope of judicial review depends on whether the administrative act is discretionary or regulated. In the latter case, a full judicial review is possible. Below is a summary of latest case Law on the field of administrative silence:

- Claiming default interest: The Supreme Court does not recognize an assumption of administrative silence in this field, because there is no procedural autonomy. The judgment understands that this application is in the context of a contractual procedure.[60]
- Positive silence on regional transparency Laws: The Constitutional Court finds this discrepancy from State Law unconstitutional, which maintains negative silence as a rule, unconstitutional.[61]
- Lack of prescriptive report: The Supreme Court considers positive silence fully functional, even in the absence of a prescriptive report. Once the positive silence produces legal effects, checks for intrinsic

[58] STC 188/2003, 27 October, ECLI:ES:TC:2003:188; STC 14/2006, 16 January, ECLI:ES:TC:2006:14; STC 39/2006, 13 February, ECLI:ES:TC:2006:39.

[59] STS 15825/1992, 22 September, ECLI:ES:TS:1992:15825.

[60] STS 1358/2007, 28 February, ECLI: ES:TS:2007:1358.

[61] STC 104/2018, 4 October, ECLI:ES:TC:2018:104.

legality must not be used as an excuse. For these purposes, there are specific review procedures.[62]

- In spite of the application to the public authority, selective and recruitment procedures are considered *ex officio* procedures, so positive silence does not apply.[63]
- Positive silence will not take effect if it harms third parties, whose right to be heard in administrative procedures was not properly guaranteed.[64]

8.8.4 The Right to Compensation—Damages

Administrative silence could mitigate the effects of a breach of the Law, but it does not evade other responsibilities. In the Spanish system, State liability is mainly objective. Nevertheless, if a legal duty exists, public inactivity will be always a sign of "abnormal" behavior.

It is interesting that compensation does not depend on complying with the legal deadline, but rather on the specific circumstances. The person concerned has right to achieve a decision within a "reasonable period." Case Law associates the State's liability with the "undue delay".[65] Exhausting the time limit could therefore not be justified because of the specific circumstances of an individual case. Conversely, a delay may be justified; therefore, the breach of the deadline is just one indication of the undue delay.[66]

8.8.5 The Role of the Ombudsman

It is very common for the national and regional Ombudsmen to have to deal with citizens' dissatisfaction or frustration. Administrative inactivity is a standard type of "maladministration." The Ombudsmen's control is focused on effectiveness and practices rather being another legal control.

[62] STS 908/2018, 19 March, ECLI:ES:TS:2018:908.

[63] STS 3785/2018, 6 November, ECLI:ES:TS:2018:3785.

[64] STS 4405/2014, 28 October, ECLI:ES:TS:2014:4405.

[65] STC 5/1985, 23 January, ECLI:ES:TC:1985:104. In the same sense: Council of State 15 December 1988.

[66] Sabela Oubiña Barbolla, Dilaciones indebidas. Undue delay. *Eunomía. Revista en Cultura de la Legalidad*, N°. 10, abril–septiembre 2016, pp. 250–264.

Cases of inactivity presented to the Ombudsman are widespread, but many more remain concealed by a degree of resignation among citizens.

Complaints are notably frequent at regional and local levels. A substantial proportion of these are confined to urban design (namely, restoration of legal standards and planning sanctions) and selective and recruitment procedure. In recent years, however, as a result of the 2006 Dependency Law and the lack of funds, these complaints have increased. The role of the Ombudsmen in such emergency scenarios reduced the time frames by 50% and even achieved financial compensation for the heirs of those who died before they could receive the benefit.

8.8.6 Empirical Evidence

The administrative courts are the most congested. According to General Council of the Spanish Judicial Authority,[67] in 2011 the system of administrative justice was congested in 214%. However, the rate was reduced each year since then. As stated in the latest report (2018), this rate has fallen to 168%.[68] It is clear that the Law 10/2012 on Fees Regimes for Justice System has a role to play here. Nonetheless, the appeals against administrative silence are exempt from the payment of any fees or taxes.[69]

Studies provided by the Barcelona Bar Association[70] stress that legal remedies against an administrative silence stand for 42.9%—a very high percentage, whose further analysis and careful consideration is needed. For instance, the number of appeals against silence increases in the second instance (61.9%). An explanation might be the acceptance deficit[71] as

[67] 2012 Report on Activity of Judicial Bodies. Available at: http://www.poderjudicial.es/stfls/CGPJ/ESTADÍSTICA/RESÚMENES%20ESTADÍSTICOS/FICHERO/NA-2012-Nacional-T1T4_1.0.0.pdf.

[68] 2018 Report on Activity of Judicial Bodies. Available at: http://www.poderjudicial.es/stfls/CGPJ/ESTADÍSTICA/RESÚMENES%20ESTADÍSTICOS/FICHERO/NA-2018-NACIONAL-T1T4_1.0.0.pdf.

[69] Similarly when the appeal concerns fundamental rights o a public agent in defending their status.

[70] 2015–2018 Reports on Justice by ICAB (Barcelona Bar Association). Available at: http://www.icab.es/?go=eaf9d1a0ec5f1dc58757ad6cffdacedb1a58854a600312cceb548f19444db1eaf474775f0204467c4d6653e813159c9da993b6be01c348c510b76d60556439961cc12e9a9c6329b47f5d27d4f2e7c7e1dafa2e16bbd0cab30dd1320eb50775c2.

[71] Langenbach, Pascal. *Der Anhörungseffekt: Verfahrensfairness und Rechtsbefolgung im allgemeinen Verwaltungsverfahren*. Vol. 3. Mohr Siebeck, 2017.

a result of the lack of motivation, namely on complex cases. On the contrary, the aim of cassation is concerned mainly with appeals against explicit administrative acts.

Another interesting issue emerges in the field of State liability.[72] At the local level, remedies against administrative silence pose the 8% of remedies, while at the regional level the percentage drops to 6.2%. Finally, these kinds of remedies continue to decline to 1.5% at the national level. This trend is explained by the distribution of competences, and because of the local administration is responsible for building permits and activities licenses.[73]

Within the framework of Special Appeal for Human Rights Protection, the percentage of remedies against administrative silence in 2018 is relatively low, only 10.1%. Insofar as the former percentage was 0%, this trend is largely driven by new Art. 121 LPAC. On the basis of this provision, there is no time limit for contesting the silence.[74]

8.9 Conclusions

In Spain, the technique of administrative silence has developed considerably since it was first regulated in 1924. The concept has gradually matured, and this has been shown in the way the regulations have been perfected. The development we are talking about can clearly be seen, for example, in the change in the general rule of silence from negative to positive that began in 1992. This change must be considered to progress in that it does not see administrative silence as a normal way of ending administrative proceedings but rather as a technique for guaranteeing individuals their rights when if an administration fails to comply with one of its principal duties: to answer and attend to citizens, as required by "the right to good administration." Good administration responds to the

[72] 2015 Report on Administrative Justice by Centro de Investigación sobre Justicia Administrativa de la Universidad Autónoma de Madrid(CIJAUAM). Available at: https://www.google.com/url?sa=t&rct=j&q=&esrc=s&source=web&cd=1&cad=rja&uact=8&ved=2ahUKEwjRw6OGo-XhAhXLxIUKHRtXCoQQFjAAegQIARAC&url=http%3A%2F%2Fcija-uam.org%2Fwp-content%2Fuploads%2F2015%2F03%2FInforme-sobre-la-Justicia-Administrativa-2015.pdf&usg=AOvVaw3N_MppXC-JADGRttygXEKA.

[73] Dalays on these procedures undermine not only the rights of citizens, but also create an economic damage.

[74] According to Constitutional Court (explained above).

citizens who are administered and who have held rights and interests for decades, including the right to obtain an express, well-founded response to their requests.

In this sense, it must not be forgotten that the Charter of Fundamental Rights of the European Union expressly recognizes this "right to good administration" (Art. 41). This states generally that "every person has the right to have his or her affairs handled impartially, fairly and within a reasonable time." Extending this declaration to Spanish Law, it is easy to see within the right of citizens to have their affairs handled within a reasonable time, a more specific right to have them expressly resolved. Could failure to resolve matters raised by citizens be considered as anything other than "poor administration"? Art. 41 of the Charter, referring in greater detail to the specific rights involved in good administration, specifically lists "the obligation of the administration to give reasons for its decisions," which cannot be understood without the logical premise that there must, in all cases, be an express administrative decision giving reasons, and not a fictitious or a presumed one.

There is similar logic in the context of the influence of EU Law in Spain, particularly through the Services Directive. This directive, firstly, has eliminated the need for many prior administrative interventions requiring individuals to request the administration to carry out many activities which were in their interests and permitted by the legal system. Secondly, it determined the change in direction of silence, establishing more circumstances for positive silence, and, in turn, determined that the exceptions to the general rule of positive silence can only be established by a Law based on overweening reasons of general interest in accordance with the case Law of the TJUE.

Some sectorial legislations, as in the case of planning Law, or more recently transparency Law, have shown the limits and difficulties that positive administrative silence raises compared to negative silence. So, the effects of this silence are being debated and corrected, which in principle should be more favorable to citizens but, in practice, could generate greater legal insecurity (as positive silence "*contra legem*" is prohibited), and even greater difficulties in access to administrative and legal remedies. Moreover, as in the case of the right of access to information, the existence of positive silence depends on real commitment by the administration.

In any case, if there is a real desire to ensure that the administration complies with its obligation to resolve and give notice of all proceedings within the established period, it is essential to provide it with sufficient material and human resources and to finally and decidedly implement computerized administration. As studied in Sect. 8.7, with regard to the CORA report on the reform of the public authorities, in the last few years central government has launched various strategies to reduce average resolution times, resulting in satisfactory statistical data. Overall, the regional and local authorities essentially concern Ombudsmen, who act and become involved in the most flagrant cases while citizens remain resigned and accustomed to too many delays.

Bibliography

Aguado i Cudolà, V. (1997). La evolución histórica del silencio administrativo: de los estatutos de Calvo-Sotelo hasta la Ley 30/1992. *Revista de estudios de la administración local y autonómica*, no. 273.

Aguado i Cudolà, V. (1998). Los orígenes del silencio administrativo en la formación del Estado constitucional. *Revista de Administración Pública*, no. 145.

Aradas García, F. (2016). La configuración del silencio administrativo. De la Ley 30/1992 a la Ley 39/2015. *El consultor de los Ayuntamientos y de los Juzgados*, no. 19.

Arzoz Santiesteban, X. (2015). Apogeo y crisis del silencio administrativo positivo. *Revista Española de Derecho Administrativo*, no. 170.

Ballesteros Moffa, L. Á. (1999). El nuevo régimen jurídico del silencio administrativo. *Sentencias de Tribunales Superiores de Justicia y Audiencias Provinciales y otros Tribunales*, vol. V, Aranzadi.

Ballesteros Moffa, L. Á. (2014, May). Administration's inaction against citizens' "right to know". *Revista Jurídica de Castilla y León*, no. 33, pp. 1–29.

Casado, L. (2015). El silencio en los recursos administrativos: el alcance del efecto positive del doble silencio en el recurso de alzada. *Revista Española de Derecho Administrativo*, no. 172.

Fernández Acevedo, R. (2004). *Utilización de los bienes y derechos públicos: studio de su regimen jurídico.* Madrid: El Régimen Jurídico General del Patrimonio de las Administraciones Públicas.

Fernández Acevedo, R. (2005). Sobre la figura juridica del precario administrativo (con especial referencia a su aplicación al dominio publico). *Revista Española de Derecho Administrativo*, no. 126.

Fernández Ramos, S. (2017). El silencio administrativo en el ejercicio del derecho de acceso a la información pública: entre el abuso de la Administración y el voluntarismo del legislador. *Revista Española de la Transparencia*, no. 4.

Gallardo Castillo, M. J. (2010).*Régimen Jurídico de las Administraciones Públicas y Procedimiento Administrativo Común. Comentario sistemático a la Ley 30/1992, de 26 de noviembre*, Madrid.
García de Enterría, E., and Fernández, T. R. (2017). *Curso de Derecho Administrativo I*, Cizur Menor (Navarre).
García Pérez, M. (2001). El silencio administrativo negativo. *Cuadernos de derecho público,* no. 12, pp. 171–214.
García Pérez, M. (2013). El silencio administrativo en España. *Misión Jurídica: Revista de Derecho y Ciencias Sociales,* 6(6), 85–94.
Gómez-Ferrer Rincón, R. (2008). *La imposibilidad de ejecución de sentencias en el proceso contencioso-administrativo*, Cizur Menor (Navarre).
Gómez Puente, M. (2002). *La inactividad de la Administración,* Aranzadi, Cizur Menor (Navarre).
González Botija, F. (2015). Seguridad jurídica y crisis económica no justifican el silencio negativo: a propósito de la STC 29/2015, de 19 de febrero. *Revista de urbanismo y edificación*, no. 35, pp. 113–130.
Martín Valdivia, S. (1999). El silencio administrativo como garantía de los derechos de los particulares (Análisis comparativo de la nueva regulación legal de la institución). *Revista de Administración Pública*, no. 149.
Morillo-Velarde Pérez, J. I. (2002). El silencio administrativo tras la reforma de 1999: Un cambio inadvertido y unas posibilidades inéditas. *Revista de administración pública*, no. 159, pp. 87–135.
Muñoz Machado, S. (2017). *Tratado de Derecho administrativo y Derecho público general*, Volume XII, administrative acts and administrative sanctions, Madrid.
Nieto Garrido, E. M. (2006). Silencio administrativo y acceso a la jurisdicción en la reciente jurisprudencia del Tribunal Constitucional: a propósito de las SSTC 14/2006, de 16 de enero, y 39/2006, de 13 de febrero. *Revista de administración pública*, no. 170.
Oubiña Barbolla, S. (2016). Dilaciones indebidas. Undue delay. *Eunomía. Revista en Cultura de la Legalidad*, no. 10, abril – septiembre, pp. 250–264.
Parejo Alfonso, L. (1993). El silencio administrativo en la Ley de Régimen Jurídico de las Administraciones Públicas y del Procedimiento Administrativo Común. In *La protección jurídica del ciudadano (procedimiento y garantía jurisdiccional). Estudios en Homenaje al Profesor Jesús González Pérez*, Madrid.
Pérez Andrés, E. (2004). Una sentencia trascendental sobre la inexistencia de plazo para interponer el recurso contencioso-administrativo frente al silencio administrativo negativo. *Revista de administración pública*, no. 164.
Santamaría Pastor, J. A. (1993). La actividad de la Administración. In *Comentario sistemático a la Ley de régimen jurídico de las administraciones públicas y del procedimiento administrativo común (Ley 30/1992 de 26 de noviembre)*, Madrid.

Tornos Mas, J. (2007). La Sentencia del Tribunal Supremo de 28 de febrero de 2007 relativa a la reclamación de intereses de demora.¿ una drástica reducción del silencio administrativo?. *Revista de administración pública*, no. 173.

Sánchez Morón, M. (1991). *El control de las Administraciones Públicas y sus problemas*. Ed. Instituto de España, Espasa-Calpe, Madrid.

Soriano, J. E. (2000). Silencio administrativo e impugnación jurisdiccional: la resurrección de un Lázaro administrativo. *Revista de Administración Pública*, no. 151.

Varela Ortega, J. (1977). *Los amigos políticos. Partidos, elecciones y caciquismo en la Restauración (1875–1900)*. Madrid: Alianza Universidad.

CHAPTER 9

Administrative Silence in Portugal

Miguel Assis Raimundo, João Tiago Silveira, Tiago Fidalgo de Freitas, and Gonçalo De Andrade Fabião

9.1 The Legal and Administrative Background for Analyzing Administrative Silence

9.1.1 Administrative Law in Portugal: General Remarks

The Portuguese system of administrative law can be described as a system of the French *droit administratif* tradition, whose roots date back to the European expansion of liberal ideas inspired by the French in the

M. A. Raimundo (✉) · J. T. Silveira · T. F. de Freitas · G. De Andrade Fabião
School of Law, University of Lisbon, Lisbon, Portugal
e-mail: miguelraimundo@fd.ulisboa.pt

Centre for Research in Public Law (CIDP), University of Lisbon, Lisbon, Portugal

J. T. Silveira
e-mail: joaotiagosilveira@fd.ulisboa.pt

T. F. de Freitas
e-mail: tfreitas@fd.ulisboa.pt

G. De Andrade Fabião
e-mail: goncalofabiao@fd.ulisboa.pt

D. C. Dragos et al. (eds.),
The Sound of Silence in European Administrative Law,
https://doi.org/10.1007/978-3-030-45227-8_9

nineteenth century, being deeply influenced, in the twentieth century, by other traditions (mainly, German administrative law), and later on, by the convergence of two main forces: the principles of the democratic constitution of 1976 and the influence of European Union law, following Portugal's joining the European Union in 1986.[1]

After several periods of evolution along with the current Portuguese Constitution,[2] the system stabilized in a model of dual jurisdiction, with separate judicial and administrative courts—Articles 209 and 212 of the Portuguese Constitution.[3]

9.1.2 *The Main Principles of Administrative Law and Their Connection with the Timeliness of Administrative Procedure*

Portuguese Public Administration, following its tradition, aims to pursue the public interest, in the respect of the legal rights and interests of citizens (Article 266, nr. 1 of the Portuguese Constitution) and is subject to the principles of conformity with the Constitution and statute law [Article 266(2)]. Article 266(2) adds that Public Administration is bound to the principles of equality, proportionality, justice, impartiality, and good faith. Article 267 calls for an effective and non-bureaucratic public administration, and Article 268 mentions several manifestations of the principles of transparency and general due procedure. The Constitution also states that all public entities are bound by the provisions granting fundamental rights [Article 18(1)]. The system is completed by a provision (Article 22) establishing the liability of the State (here, in the broad sense of public authorities) for damages caused by its activity. This provision explicitly covers liability originating from both action *or omission*.

The Portuguese Constitution does *not* provide explicitly for a *general* duty to act in a timely fashion in administrative procedures, and, as a

[1] For the historical roots, and general characteristics, of the Portuguese administrative law and administrative courts system, see, *ex multis*, Caetano (2001), Freitas do Amaral (2016a), Garcia (1994), and Sérvulo Correia (2005a).

[2] The Portuguese Constitution is available, in English and French translations, at https://www.parlamento.pt/Legislacao/Paginas/ConstituicaoRepublicaPortuguesa.aspx.

[3] For reference regarding the current configuration of the Portuguese system of administrative justice, see Amado Gomes et al. (2016), Pereira da Silva (2009), Sérvulo Correia (2005a), and Vieira de Andrade (2017); and, in English, still relevant despite some legislative changes that occurred in 2015, Sérvulo Correia (2006).

consequence, does not provide for any time limit to do so. There are two important exceptions to this statement.

The first exception is the so-called right of petition, under which citizens can direct any requests or complaints to any public bodies, on any matters of their own personal interest, or on matters of collective interest [Article 52(1) of the Constitution]. In this case, the Constitution does state that the petitioner has the right to an answer in a reasonable amount of time. However, the right in question is not construed as applying, at least directly, to administrative procedures, or at least, to all of them: Citizens can exercise the right of petition before the Parliament, for example.[4]

The second exception regards the right of access to administrative information. The Constitution states that the law will provide for a maximum deadline for public authorities to respond to requests of access to administrative information [Article 268(6)].

The lack of a specific constitutional provision regarding a duty to decide administrative procedures at a given deadline, however, is mitigated by: (i) an understanding, among some scholars, that these provisions give grounds for a broad constitutional duty of timely decision,[5] and (ii) the application of Article 6(1) of the European Convention on Human Rights and/or Article 41(1) of the Charter of Fundamental Rights of the European Union, which scholars[6] and courts[7] use to state a fundamental right to a timely decision.

9.2 The Legal Framework of Administrative Timeliness

9.2.1 The Treatment of Administrative Silence in the Constitution

In addition to the principles set out in the Portuguese Constitution (and international law) mentioned in the previous section which refer to the matter of timeliness, the Constitution contains several options which are also relevant to the general topic of administrative silence.

[4] Framing the right in question in these restrictive terms, Miranda and Machete (2010, pp. 1025–1026).

[5] This is the case of Otero (2013, pp. 389–390; 2015, p. 111).

[6] Amado Gomes (2013a), (b), and Neves (2012).

[7] Decision of the Supreme Administrative Court of 02-03-2004, proc. 1531/03; and decision of the Central Administrative Court (South), 11-04-2013, proc. 7084/11. These decisions are available (in Portuguese) at www.dgsi.pt.

The most relevant reference for the topic of administrative silence [not considering the specific cases of Articles 52 and 268(6), already mentioned above] is a provision which refers to *judicial protection* of the rights and interests of citizens before Public Administration. Article 268(4) of the Constitution reads as follows (authors' translation):

> Citizens are entitled effective judicial protection of their legal rights and interests, which includes, namely, the recognition of said rights and interests, the setting aside of any harmful administrative acts, regardless of their form, *the injunction to issue any administrative acts that are legally due*, and adequate means of interim relief.

The section of this provision referring to the injunction to issue legally due administrative acts is a constitutional guarantee of judicial protection against administrative inaction. This is very meaningful, since it is common knowledge that in French inspired administrative justice systems, forms of injunction in matters related to administrative acts were traditionally not in place, or were difficult to obtain, because of the understanding of the principle of the separation of powers.[8] The evolution of the Portuguese system is an example of this. A new type of lawsuit (inspired by the German model of the "*Verpflichtungsklage*") directed at obtaining an injunction to issue a legally due administrative act (Articles 66 to 71 of the Code of Procedure before Administrative Courts or CPAC) was only created in 2004.[9]

9.2.2 Administrative Procedure Code (APC) of 2015

Statute law rules on administrative timeliness and reaction to omission in considerable detail. The first general Administrative Procedure Code in Portugal was created in 1991, and it set out a general time limit of 90 days to decide procedures upon request.

Currently, the general act on administrative procedure is the 2015 Administrative Procedure Code (henceforth, the "APC"). It treats the matter of administrative timeliness both at the level of principles and specific, detailed rules.

[8] Aroso de Almeida (2016, p. 87).

[9] See, on this matter, Calçada Pires (2004), Pereira da Silva (2002), and Sousa da Fábrica (2010).

Article 13 of the APC states the duty to decide on any application made by a citizen to an administrative authority. This duty is accompanied by the relevant exception of cases in which a prior decision has been taken, by the same authority, on an identical application, by the same person, less than two years ago. In this last case, the application does *not* create a duty to decide.[10] This exception is meant to avoid cases in which applicants would overload administrative authorities with the same, repeated requests, in an attempt to obtain new answers which would open up judicial litigation yet again.[11]

Articles 5(1) and 59 of the APC both refer to the duty to conduct the procedure and act in a timely fashion. While the former refers to timeliness in general, the latter is more specific, in the sense that it refers to the duty to carry out the procedure in a timely fashion. Based on this principle, the public authority may, e.g., reject any procedural act that it deems unnecessary.

In addition to these principles, the APC provides for general rules stating the maximum delays for decision in administrative procedures. The contents of these rules will be analyzed below.

9.2.3 *The Interplay Between the APC and Special Laws*

Administrative timeliness is not treated in the same way throughout the whole administrative law sector. There are specific laws in which the deadlines for decision and the consequences of administrative silence are deemed to have different legal effects than those foreseen in the APC.

However, the rules of the APC are applicable to any administrative procedure ruled by law, which does not set out its own specific time limits [this flows from the general provision of Article 2(5) of the Code].

9.3 The Length of Administrative Deadlines

9.3.1 *The Length of Deadlines in General Law and in Special Laws*

For procedures which begin by an application made to a public authority, the general time limit for a decision is 90 days [Article128(1) APC].

[10] Otero (2015, p. 417). On the requirements for the rule to apply, see Freitas do Amaral (2016b, p. 284); see also Raimundo (2016).

[11] Otero (2015, p. 113).

These are 90 *business days* (see below, Sect. 9.3.3). The law safeguards special rules, and these do exist, with very different deadlines, some longer, some shorter than the one set out in the APC.[12]

A special case of a deadline for responding to an application is that of a request of access to administrative information. In cases where the application is made in an ongoing procedure, the answer must be given in 10 days [Article 82 (3) of the APC], or 3 days, in the case of simpler requests [Article 84(3)]. In cases of a request of access to information relating to a procedure which is already finished (or, in general, information held by public authorities but not linked to an administrative procedure), the deadline is 10 days in all cases [Article 15(1) of Law nr. 26/2016, of 22 August].[13]

In addition to these deadlines applying to the issuing of a *final decision*, specific provisions rule on the general deadline for *intermediate* actions to be carried out by administrative authorities, in the context of an administrative procedure, for which there is no specific deadline set in the law. This general deadline for carrying out any action is 10 days (Article 86 of the APC).[14]

Finally, a distinction must be drawn between the general deadline for a decision (90 days), the intermediate deadlines for specific actions (10 days) which we just mentioned, and the regime of what the law designates as the "defection" (*deserção*) of the procedure. A procedure (initiated by application) ends (with no decision) if it is halted for a period of more than six months by reasons related to the applicant [Article 132(1), of the APC]. This is, of course, a negative consequence, not due to administrative silence, but to silence (or inaction) *of the applicant*.

[12] As a matter of example, for Environmental Impact Assessment procedures, the deadline is 100 days; in building permits, deadlines of 30 or 45 days apply, according to the type of work to be carried out by the applicant.

[13] For an overview of the provisions regarding transparency and right of access to public information in Portuguese law, see Fidalgo de Freitas (2016).

[14] As a matter of example, the law states that upon receiving an application, the authority must invite the applicant to correct any insufficiencies in the application (Article 108 of the APC); but it does not state *when* this should be done. Article 86 of the APC should be applied.

In a relevant provision, Article 128(5), of the APC, obliges the officer responsible for the procedure to *justify*, after the deadline, if no final decision has been taken, why the deadline could not be met. This justification *may be*[15] relevant for *disciplinary* purposes.

Ex officio procedures—that is, procedures which are initiated at the initiative of a public authority—which might lead to a disadvantageous decision to interested parties—are subject to a different, also general, rule: 180 days, or else the procedure *expires*[Article 128(6) of the APC]. An example of *ex officio* procedure which might lead to a disadvantageous decision is the procedure to apply a disciplinary sanction to a worker of a public body.

The existence of this general deadline in these types of procedures is a recent novelty in Portuguese law, as it was introduced by the 2015 APC. The general rationale for this deadline is the idea that the person possibly affected by the negative outcome of the procedure should not be kept indefinitely in a situation of uncertainty.[16] This novelty has prompted some questions regarding its functioning.[17] A pertinent point is how to apply the concept of a procedure leading to a disadvantageous decision in contexts (common, for example, in Environmental or Urban Planning law) where legal relations tend to be, not bilateral (administration "vs" a single private party), but *multilateral* (administration "vs" several persons with different rights and interests).[18]

Ex officio procedures which do *not* lead to a disadvantageous decision (i.e., those that can lead to an advantageous decision, for example, a procedure to attribute an honor or award to someone) do not have a specific deadline for decision or expiry, which prompts the question of whether the public authority can choose to terminate these procedures with no decision.[19]

The deadlines mentioned above apply to general administrative procedures, *at first level*. In administrative review procedures (second instance

[15] In fact, there is consensus among authors that the mere breach of the deadline for decision is not enough to give rise to disciplinary action—see Aroso de Almeida (2015, p. 121) and Quadros et al. (2016, p. 259).

[16] Amado Gomes (2013a, p. 145) and Quadros et al. (2016, p. 260).

[17] Otero (2015).

[18] Raising the issue, Amado Gomes (2013a, p. 145).

[19] See, on the point, Cortez (2001, p. 371).

procedures), the deadline for a decision is 30 days counting from the moment the reviewing authority receives the complaint [Articles 192(2), and 198(1) APC]. In the case where the reviewing authority is the same which issued the decision, this deadline of 30 days to decide cannot be extended. If the authority hearing the complaint is different (typically, the highest-ranking officer of the hierarchy, e.g., a minister), the deadline can be extended up to an aggregate total of 90 days, but only in case the review procedure requires additional gathering of evidence [Article 198(2)].

9.3.2 Possibilities of Extension

Deadlines for a decision of procedures upon application can be extended, in "*exceptional circumstances, (…) for one or more times, not exceeding the maximum limit of 90 days*" of extension [Article 128(1)]. The total aggregate duration of deadline for decision can, therefore, reach 180 days, which is probably excessive. The decision (which must be explicit) to extend the deadline is notified to the applicant and also any other participants in the procedure [Article 128(2)].

In cases where the law does not attribute any special effect (e.g., positive silence) to silence, the breach of the duty to decide within the time limit has several consequences (see below), but the possibility of deciding on the application remains intact. This means that the lapsing of the deadline for a decision does *not* affect the lawfulness of the decision which is taken later on.[20]

9.3.3 Counting Deadlines

Despite proposals to change this state of affairs,[21] administrative procedures still have special rules regarding calculating deadlines; that is, the general rules applicable to the setting of any deadline (i.e., payment due in a sale of goods contract) are not the same rules applying to administrative deadlines.

[20] See, e.g., decisions of the Supreme Administrative Court of 31-03-2011, proc. 57/11; decision of the Supreme Administrative Court of 09-05-2012, proc. 1118/11.

[21] Silveira (2013).

The deadline for deciding a procedure begins, as a rule, when the competent body receives the application [Article 128(3), of the APC). It is important to stress that it begins when the *competent* body receives the application, because there is an important provision (Article 41 of the APC) stating that when the applicant files the application with the wrong administrative body, the latter must forward it to the competent body.

Special provision is made, regarding this matter, for administrative procedures carried out through an electronic single point of access (such as the one implemented by transposition of the Services Directive): In this case, the deadline begins when the system acknowledges receipt of the application.[22]

For *ex officio* procedures (possibly leading to a disadvantageous decision), since there is no application, the relevant moment to begin counting the 180-day expiry of the deadline of Article 128(6) should be the moment when the interested party (or parties) receives notice of the beginning of the procedure.

The rules for calculating deadlines, as mentioned, are specific and are set in Article 87 of the APC. As a rule, administrative deadlines are counted in business days.[23] Business days exclude Saturdays, Sundays, and holidays [Article 87(c), of the APC].

The rationale behind the use of business days is that the deadline should be aligned with the working days of the employees and opening hours of public services.[24]

In addition to these rules, there is one specific case of suspension of the deadline, which must be mentioned, since it gives rise, in most administrative procedures, to an increase in the global deadline for decision. In the majority of administrative procedures, there is a specific phase in which participants have the right to be heard (fair hearing) on the intended

[22] Only in cases where there is a "fair impediment," with no fault of the competent authority (such as a proven technical malfunction not due to the authority's conduct), will the risk of the "electronic delay" run on the part of the applicant. See, on this matter, França Jardim and Raimundo (2016).

[23] A relevant exception to the rule of deadlines in business days are deadlines which are by law superior to six months: These are counted in calendar days [Article 87(d) of the APC].

[24] This type of justification, however, seems to counter, e.g., the rule according to which citizens can carry out any action in administrative procedures by electronic means any day of the week [Article 104(2) of the APC].

decision, before it is taken (Articles 121–125 of the APC).[25] The deadline granted for a person to give his or her view on the intended decision is, as a rule, 10 days, and during this period, all deadlines in the administrative procedure are suspended [Article 121(3)]. This is subject to criticism: The 90-day period is already a generous time limit, and it should contain every normal phase of administrative procedures, such as the fair hearing phase.

An administrative deadline to which an administrative authority is bound is considered to have been complied with if the decision is taken before the end of the deadline (this results, although not too clearly, from Article 155 of the APC). However, as a rule, administrative decisions which are negative to the persons involved only become *effective* in relation to those persons, after they are notified (Article 160 of the APC). Since administrative decisions must, as a rule, be notified within eight days after the approval of the decision [Article 114(5), of the APC], this means, for example, a decision subject to a 90-day deadline will be considered to have been taken in a timely fashion, if it was *approved* on day 90, but was only *notified* five days later. The result is different in the case of positive silence (see below).

9.3.4 The Very Limited Relevance of the Open Concept of a "Reasonable" Deadline in Portuguese Law Regarding Administrative Decisions

In many jurisdictions, the concept of a *reasonable deadline* for administrative action is very relevant in the everyday application of the duty to act in a timely fashion. This is not the case in Portuguese administrative law, due to the existence of a general rule providing for a time limit. Reference to an open concept of a "reasonable deadline" would only be necessary if there was not a strict deadline in place. Since there are discussions in case law and among scholars do not go in this direction.

This does not mean, of course, that reference to such an open standard cannot carry out a relevant function in the legal system. However,

[25] These cases are provided for by Article 124 of the APC and include, for example, urgency in the decision, or risk of harm to the public interest if the participant is warned beforehand of the intended decision.

it is essentially limited to acting as a standard for control (of compatibility with the Constitution and EU law) of the specific rules (legal and administrative rules) defining the length of procedures.[26]

9.4 Responses to Administrative Silence

9.4.1 The Prevailing Model: The Absence of Decision as a Simple Breach of the Duty to Decide, and the Existence of Special Rules Providing for Positive (and, Marginally, Negative) Silence

Historically, tacit administrative acts first appeared in Portuguese administrative law to dismiss an application and so providing applicants a possibility for a judicial review.[27] This was the 1991 Administrative Procedure Code's framework: a negative response to administrative silence.[28] The figure of tacit decisions—which were, mainly, negative decisions—was the object of criticism, with arguments ranging from the negative effects for the effectiveness of judicial review, to arguments which underlined how the regime promoted administrative inertia.[29]

The Administrative Courts Procedure reform, in 2002/2004, and the CPAC which then came into force, changed the traditional model for responses to administrative silence.

Indeed, since the CPAC brought about a judicial injunction against an administrative authority ordering it to act in the wake of Article 268(4), of the Constitution, as explained above, the rule of a tacit administrative act of dismissal as legal consequence for silence lost its reason to be and was consensually considered, among scholars, to have been revoked.[30] Nowadays, Article 129 of the APC clearly states that administrative silence within procedures initiated by application means, simply,

[26] It is not impossible to think of a decision by a court (namely the Constitutional Court), stating that the deadline established by a given law is too long for the decision in question. Significantly enough, though, such a decision has never been taken by Portuguese courts.

[27] Otero (2003, p. 1006).

[28] Sérvulo Correia (2005b, pp. 12–15) and Silveira (2004).

[29] Freitas do Amaral (2011, pp. 366–367) and Rebelo de Sousa (1999, p. 134).

[30] Rebelo de Sousa and Salgado de Matos (2009, p. 390).

the default or breach of the duty to decide, thus enabling the applicant to use administrative and judicial remedies. Administrative silence is therefore acknowledged as being a procedural requisite.[31]

This doesn't mean the end of tacit administrative acts. Although tacit administrative acts of dismissal lost their major significance, there's still room for tacit administrative acts of approval/authorization.[32]

Article 130(1) of the APC requires a specific provision in a special law or regulation to create a situation of tacit administrative act of approval/authorization. The APC only mentions tacit administrative acts of approval/authorization, not tacit administrative acts of dismissal. This means two things: (i) There are no longer, *as a rule*,[33] negative tacit administrative acts, and (ii) there are only positive tacit administrative acts when a specific legal regime or regulation prescribes it.[34]

From this last fact some authors offer the view that, despite the appearances, administrative silence, as a rule, pertains to a dismissal.[35]

Article 130(1) APC provides that a positive tacit administrative act is created in the absence of ***notification*** of a decision, meaning that if a decision was taken within the prescribed deadline, but not notified, the positive tacit act is still created.[36]

Portuguese authors, in general, are not great supporters of the model of silent decisions (negative or positive), viewed as a situation in which there is a breach of the duties of Public Administration, namely the duty to decide all requests submitted.[37]

[31] Otero (2015, p. 419).

[32] Rebelo de Sousa and Salgado de Matos (2009, p. 390) and Otero (2003, p. 1004).

[33] In fact, some laws, not so aware of the change in paradigm, continue, occasionally, to provide for situations of negative tacit acts. See, e.g., on the law of access to insurance and reinsurance activities—see Articles 56(2) and 219(2) of Law n. 147/2015, of 9 September; measures of reinforcement of the dynamism of the Portuguese capital market—see Article 7(5) of Decree-Law n. 77/2017, of 3o June; also, in Public Procurement law—see articles 102(2), 274(1) of the Public Contracts Code; and Article 106 of the Code of Tax Procedure and Process.

[34] T. Antunes (2016, p. 784) and Freitas do Amaral (2016b, pp. 300 303).

[35] Otero (2015, pp. 417–418).

[36] Antunes (2016, p. 784).

[37] In this line, for example, Otero (2003, p. 1007). See also Pereira da Silva and Macieirinha (2015, p. 605).

9.4.2 The EU Influence Over National Rules and Practices

Directive 2006/123/EC of the European Parliament and of the Council of 12 December 2006 on services in the internal market defines "authorisation scheme" as any procedure under which a provider or recipient is in effect required to take steps in order to obtain from a competent authority a formal decision, or an implied [tacit] decision, concerning access to a service activity or the exercise thereof, thus enabling implied decision within administrative procedures. Portugal's Decreto-Lei n.° 92/2010, of 26 July and Decreto-Lei n.° 48/2011, of 1 April, transposed Directive 2006/123/EC.

The first Portuguese legislative act simplifies the access and exercise of services activities. Its Article 9(2)(b) mentions the possibility of tacit positive administrative acts as a consequence of administrative silence beyond the legal deadline. This rule has an exception whenever an imperious reason of public interest dictates otherwise. An imperious reason of public interest is an exceptional circumstance based, inter alia, on grounds of public policy, public security, civil protection, personal safety, public health, preservation of the financial balance of the social security system, consumer protection, recipients of services and workers, loyalty of transactions trade, fraud prevention, protection of the environment and the urban environment, animal health, intellectual and industrial property, conservation of national historical and artistic heritage, social or cultural policy objectives.

The second Portuguese legislative act, regarding the use of public space (e.g., streets, town squares), prescribes that authorization for the use of public space will be implied whenever the municipality does nothing within the deadline of 20 days (Article 15).

9.5 The Negative Silence

9.5.1 The Legal Character of Prescribed Deadlines (Instructive/Preclusions)

The legal character of the deadlines to decide procedures initiated by an application is instructive, in the sense that their breach does not preclude the power to decide, as seen above. The possibilities for extension have also been analyzed.

However, the legal character of the deadline to decide *ex officio* procedures which might lead to a disadvantageous decision can be understood to be preclusive, given that the procedure expires. This deadline cannot be extended.

9.5.2 The Possibility to Issue a Valid Act After the Deadline Expired

In procedures initiated by an application, there is no unlawfulness regarding an administrative act issued after the deadline has expired. In addition to the indications in this sense given above, this is noticeable in Article 70 of the CPAC: The judicial injunction against an administrative authority ordering it to act may experience changes if the administrative authority finally issues the decision (which means that the latter *can* be issued).

Differently, within *ex officio* procedures which might lead to a disadvantageous decision, any decision made after the deadline expired is unlawful, as recently stated by the Portuguese Supreme Court of Justice.[38] According to recent case law, when the act is issued after the deadline of 180 days, it is void.

9.5.3 Legal Consequences/Fictions: Finality and Enforceability

As stated above, administrative silence, in general, doesn't have the effect of rejecting a request or application. In accordance with the dichotomy presented, it may be considered as a non-act and grounds for a judicial review in the form of an injunction against an administrative authority, compelling it to act. In these injunction lawsuits, the general limits derived from the principle of separation of powers apply (Article 71 of the CPAC).

The proof requirements are set in Article 67 of the Code of Procedure in Administrative Courts. There must have been an application, followed by an absence of decision, i.e., administrative silence.

Regarding the scope of the court's decision, see below, Sect. 9.8.

[38] Decision of the Supreme Court of Justice of 16-05-2018, proc. 76/17.1YFLSB.

9.6 The Positive Silence

9.6.1 Legal Definition of Positive Silent Decisions: Conditions of Existence and Lawfulness

Positive silence is a legal fiction by which a positive administrative decision is considered to have been issued to a private interested party when the deadline to decide was not met.[39] It is usually recognized as a legal instrument to streamline administrative procedures thus avoiding a natural person or a private entity to be harmed by the absence of an administrative decision issued in due time.

Positive silence should be distinguished from other legal instruments such as (a) "previous communications," (b) "previous communications with an associated term" for the Public Administration to issue a decision and (c) positive silence regarding requests presented by public entities/private entities with administrative powers before other public entities/entities with administrative powers.

"Previous communications" and "previous communications with an associated term" are also used to streamline administrative procedures. In the first case, a natural person or a private entity is required to send a communication to an administrative entity prior to an action, but there is no decision to be issued by the administrative powers after such communication nor term to issue said decision.[40] In the second case, a natural person or a private entity is required to send a communication to an administrative entity prior to an action but there is a term for such entity to issue a decision. However, the absence of a decision within the term is not considered as an illegal omission (as in the positive silence) but rather a legal option that the administrative entity may wish to take. Therefore, the possibility of a private party to take an action after the term of a previous communication with an associated term is not the result of a legal fiction with the same effects of an administrative decision, but simply the result of the expiry of the term.[41] Thus, an administrative decision after such term is not to be considered as an administrative act aiming to revoke a legal fiction with the same effects of an administrative decision but simply an illegal act.

[39] Silveira (2004, p. 101).

[40] See Article 134(1) of APC.

[41] See Article 134(2) and (3) APC.

Previous communication and previous communications with associated terms are being increasingly used in administrative law as legal tools to streamline administrative procedures. In relevant cases, they are replacing the positive silence as effective tools to protect private parties against the absence of administrative decisions.[42]

Finally, positive silence regarding requests presented by public entities/private entities with administrative powers before other public entities/entities with administrative powers [provided for by Article 130(4) APC] aims to ease decisions and procedures between administrative entities when an approval is required to undertake a certain action. This is different from the positive silence because it refers to relations between administrative entities.

As mentioned above, positive silence is not the rule, and depends on a specific provision set by law. However, it is clear that in recent years, it is used by the Portuguese legislator. Examples of tacit approval can be found in multiple regimes: (a) waste management[43]; (b) environmental permit[44]; (c) environmental impact assessment[45]; (d) building permits[46]; and (e) "zero licensing" regime.[47] The Portuguese law does not establish any legal matters where positive silent approvals are not accepted and even in traditional sovereignty areas, such as tax law, positive silence is used as a legal instrument.[48]

Combining all the relevant provisions regarding positive silence (especially, Article 130 APC), we can state that Portuguese law explicitly refers to four requirements or conditions of a positive silent decision: (a) an application or request, that is, a claim presented by someone; (b) the *competence* of the administrative body to which the request was directed;

[42] The "zero licensing" regime sets several cases of previous communications (Article 12) as well as several laws and decree-laws aimed to transpose the EU Services Directive (Article 4).

[43] See Articles 29(4) and 37(3) of Decree-Law n. 178/2006, of 5 September, as amended.

[44] See Article 23 of Decree-Law n. 127/2013, of 30 August, as amended.

[45] See Article 19(2) and (4) of Decree-Law n. 151-B/2013, of 31 October, as amended.

[46] See Articles 111(c) and 113 of Decree-Law n. 555/99, of 16 December, as amended.

[47] See Article 15(2) of Decree-Law n. 48/2011, of 1 April, as amended.

[48] For instance, Article 183-A of the Code for Tax Procedures before Tax Administration and Courts sets forth a case of positive silence for claims concerning the recognition of the expiry of guarantees.

(c) the *timeliness* of the presentation of the request by the applicant; and (d) the necessary lapsing of the term which is set, by law for the decision to be issued.[49]

If we distinguish between requirements of *existence* and requirements of *lawfulness* (or *validity*) of an administrative decision, then requirements (a) and (d) are, clearly, requirements regarding *existence*: If no application was submitted, or until the term for the decision has lapsed, legally, there is no possibility of claiming that there is a silent decision.

However, the same clarity is not present in what regards requirements (b) and (c). If a request is made to an authority which is not competent on the matter, but this authority retains the request without sending it to the competent authority (which, as we saw earlier, it should do: Article 41 of the APC), it is arguable if this means that the silent decision is not produced, or if it means that *an invalid silent decision* is produced, or even if it means that a valid silent decision is produced. The question, which is the object of debate among Portuguese authors,[50] has serious consequences: a decision taken by an incompetent authority is unlawful, but within a short period of time, that unlawfulness may become irrelevant (*maxime,* in what concerns statute of limitation for judicial review).[51] However, if competence is understood as a requirement for the very *existence* of a silent act, then obviously the simple passing of time will never be sufficient to create a positive decision. It can easily be understood that the first possibility of interpretation *maximizes* the scope of positive silent

[49] In a somewhat different structure, Freitas do Amaral (2016b, p. 303) and Silveira (2004, pp. 167–188).

[50] The few authors taking position on the matter treat competence of the public body as a requirement for existence of the silent decision—Esteves de Oliveira et al. (1999 p. 484); or accept that a request presented before an entity not entitled to decide does not prevent a positive tacit decision to be formed if such entity has the duty to send the claim to the competent entity Silveira (2004), pp. 168–169.

[51] This happens because the time limit for reacting to an unlawful administrative decision before the administrative courts, as a rule (for situations of *anulabilidade*) is of only three months, in some cases less. Portuguese Administrative Law distinguishes these situations from the more severe situations of unlawfulness (*nulidade*), which, as of 2015, need to be provided for by a specific rule. For cases of *nulidade*, the law states that judicial review can be initiated at any time (i.e., it is under no statute of limitation).

decisions, while the latter obviously limits that same scope. There are relevant arguments to sustain this last position after the publication of the new APC,[52] and this is also present in other systems.[53]

Similar considerations can be made about requirement (c). On face value, the rule provides that the request which justifies the positive silent decision must be made in a timely fashion. This, of course, supposes that the request is under law subject to some kind of term.[54] Arguably, in this case, we stand before a requirement concerning the very existence of a positive silent decision.[55]

9.6.2 Formal and Substantial Lawfulness as Conditions? The Principle of Equivalence Between Silent and Explicit Decisions and Some of Its Consequences

Another comment to be made about the Portuguese general rules regards formal completeness, simply to notice the *absence* of any specific reference to such a requirement as a condition for the issuance of positive silent decisions.

Also, without any explicit reference, in Portuguese law, is the topic of *substantial* lawfulness of the applicant's claim. By substantial lawfulness, we understand the conformity or compatibility of the claim with the legal parameters against which it is to be evaluated: For example, a building permit must comply with the parameters set in urban planning instruments and regulations.

It is, of course, a possibility that the application does not comply with some of these legal parameters. The traditional position is based on the idea that the unlawfulness of the request does *not* prevent the production of a silent decision, but it may cause the unlawfulness of that decision, in much the same way as would happen if an explicit act were issued.[56]

[52] Not only Article 130(1), but another rule [Article 128(3) of the APC], regarding the moment when the time limit for decision begins.

[53] Deguergue (2015, p. 400).

[54] For example, if the law states that a request to obtain a certain permit to undertake seasonal economic activities should be presented up to 30 days prior to the beginning of the relevant season.

[55] It has been treated as such by authors: see Esteves de Oliveira et al. (1999, p. 485).

[56] Esteves de Oliveira et al. (1999, p. 485), Silveira (2004, pp. 188–194), Vasques (2013), and Folque (2016). This is a statement backed by the courts; see, inter alia,

This last conclusion is merely a consequence of the general theoretical assumption that treats silent decisions under the same principles and according to the same rules as explicit decisions, unless the nature of silent decisions excludes those rules.[57]

This is also the reason why if a silent decision has emerged, there can be no explicit administrative act of a different sense, except in strict conditions which allow (in general) for favorable acts (*atosconstitutivos de direitos*) to be annulled or revoked (Articles 167 and 168 of the APC). And it is the same reason why silent positive acts are, generally, enforceable in the same way as explicit decisions.

It should be mentioned, however, that although it is the prevailing position, it is not unanimous among Portuguese authors that positive silent decisions deserve the same treatment, in general, as explicit decisions.[58]

Finally, although the above-mentioned principles apply, in some cases (namely some environmental procedures), formal completeness, as well as material completeness, is legally required as conditions for the positive silence.[59]

9.6.3 *Proof Requirements, Enforcement and Effectiveness*

In general, there is no special requirement to demonstrate a positive silent act and the law does not require the issuance of an administrative document to confirm that no expressly adopted decision was issued. Moreover, there is no general requirement to present a claim before an administrative court in order to recognize the positive silent act.

the Supreme Administrative Court decision of 10 September 2008, proc. 171/08-30; and the Central Administrative Court (South) decision of 26 September 2012, proc. 1538/06.1BEPRT. Some authors suggested that there would be a *distinguo*: For the most serious cases of unlawfulness (*nulidade*), there would be no production of the silent positive act; that would only happen with the less severe situations of unlawfulness (*anulabilidade*), which, as mentioned above, are the rule in Portuguese law; see, defending this position, Alves Correia (1993). However, this suggestion did not receive support.

[57] For a statement of this general principle, Silveira (2004, pp. 94, 101) and *passim*.

[58] Strongly disagreeing with this position, see, recently, Pereira da Silva and Macieirinha (2015).

[59] Article 23(1) of Decree-Law n. 127/2013, of 30 August, as amended, sets forth that the positive silence is formed if there is no ground to reject the claim.

Usually, the document used for the presentation of the claim, duly stamped with the date of its presentation, is accepted as providing evidence of the positive silent act.

The silent positive decision is often criticized as an inadequate legal tool to protect private entities before the absence of a due administrative decision because it does not provide a robust credential that such entity was granted a right.[60] On the one hand, it is more difficult to enforce rights before public and private entities due to the absence of a document. On the other hand, it is common practice for public entities to issue explicit decisions after the term is elapsed, and the positive silent act is formed. These decisions are accepted by Portuguese courts as valid, if the claim presented did not comply with the law, and therefore private parties may face expressly adopted decisions which in practice prevent the enforcement of the silent positive act.[61]

Because of these factors, private parties often prefer to keep waiting for an explicit administrative decision, even when the law sets forth positive silence. This is also the reason why Portuguese law is increasingly using legal instruments as previous communications and previous communications with associated terms, rather than positive silence.[62]

When e-government tools are used, the law frequently provides for automatically generated documents to demonstrate that rights were granted in the absence of decisions in due time, which seems to be an effective means of proof.[63]

9.7 Supervision of the Administrative Timeliness

The law does not foresee any specific type of control over administrative timeliness other than those that derive from the different legal remedies analyzed in paragraphs 8.1–8.3, *infra*. The officials (or the departments) not meeting the deadlines may be liable in general terms, as described in paragraph 8.4, *infra*.

[60] Silveira (2004, pp. 281–296).

[61] In the more severe cases of unlawfulness (*nulidade*), there is no deadline to adopt such decision but in the other cases of unlawfulness of *anulabilidade* there is a term to issue the decision.

[62] Article 9 of Decree-Law n. 92/2010 of 26 July sets forth that previous communication should be preferred instead of legal instruments where a decision from an administrative body is required.

[63] E.g., Article 62(4) of APC, article 23(3) of Decree-Law n. 127/2013, of 30 August, as amended.

9.8 Legal Remedies

9.8.1 Administrative Appeal

The APC establishes review procedures which are applicable also in the case of administrative silence. The reviewing body is the same body if a complaint (*reclamação*) is filed, or a higher office if an administrative appeal (*recursohierárquico*) is filed. The deadline to file these requests is, respectively, of 15 days and of 30 days—Articles 191(3) and 193(2) of the APC. The law also foresees other types of administrative appeals to bodies that exercise supervision (*supervisão*) competencies within the same entity, to entities that exercise administrative oversight (*superintendência*) or monitoring (*tutela*) competencies over other entities, or to the plenary of the collegial body whose members have taken decisions, but those are conditional upon provision in special bills—Article 199 of the APC. These procedures are the same that are applicable in general administrative law; they are therefore not particularly aimed at addressing administrative silence. The deadlines for decision of these administrative complaints have been indicated *supra*. It is hard to state whether they are efficient or effective in general: it depends more on how each specific administrative authority uses them, and information is not collected about that matter.

The lack of an answer to an administrative appeal has no specific consequence, except in the case of necessary appeals—i.e., those for which the law requires the petitioner to file an administrative appeal before being able to seek judicial review. In those cases, the absence of reply allows the petitioner to file an action before an administrative court.

9.8.2 Judicial Review

Judicial review for administrative silence can be sought, as mentioned several times above, through administrative actions, filed before administrative courts. The typical remedy available is an injunction for the authority to provide the applicant with a reply to his request. There is not a general pre-established deadline for the administration to act in accordance with the court's judgment, but in order to ensure the effectiveness of this remedy, the court may both set a deadline for such purpose, even *ex officio*, and/or establish a penalty payment to be paid for by the public official in charge for further undue delay when justified—cf. Articles 3(2),

95(4) and 119 of the CPAC. In the (rare) cases in which only one solution may be legally adopted by the administrative authority, the court can order the latter to issue an administrative act with that specific content or at least specify the legal constraints the latter must take into account when issuing one such act—cf. Articles 3(4) and 95(5) of the CPAC.

If the administrative authority does not comply with the court's judgment, the applicant can request the court to enforce it by means of an executive procedure. In doing so, the administrative court can either resort to a penalty payment to compel the administrative authority to issue the due administrative act, or, when its content is legally bound, to directly issue the decision—Articles 3(4), 164(4)(c) and (d), 167(6), 169, 172(6)(b), 176(4), and 179(3) and (5) of the CPAC.

9.8.3 Right to Compensation—Damages

As mentioned in Sect. 9.1.2, the right to compensation for damages related to action *or inaction* of administrative bodies is set out in the Constitution. Damages caused by administrative silence fall under this general right to compensation, and Article 9(1), of the specific act ruling civil liability of public administration (Law nr. 67/2007, of 31 December) refers to*o missions* as facts that can give rise to liability.[64] This point has been acknowledged unequivocally in case law.[65]

The right to compensation for damages under Portuguese law depends on the verification of a set of conditions, provided for by law. The verification of silence alone—in the sense of a situation of inaction—is not, in itself, enough to provide a right to compensation. There must be a situation of *unlawfulness* in the said inaction (as seen above, silence is not always considered unlawful), for which the authority bears *fault*. In addition, there must be *damages*, and they must be linked to the inaction by a causal process; i.e., there must be a link of adequate *causation* between them, for liability to be asserted. The general conditions of civil liability are applicable in these types of cases.[66]

[64] See, on this matter, Antunes (2018, pp. 540–543) and Cadilha (2011, p. 178).

[65] See decisions of the Supreme Administrative Court of 1 October 2008, proc. 842/07; 31 March 2011, proc. 57/11; and 9 May 2012, proc. 1118/11.

[66] For a general overview of the rules on civil liability of the State and other public bodies, see, inter alia, Amado Gomes et al. (2018a).

There is discussion as to whether it is possible for authorities to *justify* for not complying with a deadline. The authorities often assert, for example, the understaffing, or lack of means, in public services. In the general system of civil liability of public bodies, as it was understood traditionally, this type of argument can be accepted, according to the circumstances of the case.[67] However, at least since Law 67/2007, it seems that, unless a serious *force majeure* event occurs, arguments such as the lack of resources, or funds, or even an abnormal increase or difficulty in managing applications, are not enough to exclude liability. In fact, Law 67/2007 sets out a parameter of *faute du service*. According to this parameter, if the performance of the administrative body in a given situation is inferior to a general standard of due quality, liability is still asserted, even if there is no *individual* fault [Article 7(3) and (4) of Law 67/2007]. This may be the case, e.g., when everyone in the public authority has done their job managing applications, but delays were still not avoided, because staff was insufficient. This reason is not enough to exclude liability.

Finally, it should be mentioned that, according to the Constitution (Article 22) and the law (Article 7 of Law 67/2007) both the public authority *and* the public officers may be held liable.

The law states that when civil liability is established, the full extent of damages should be compensated (Article 3 of Law 67/2007). Damages include both pecuniary damages and moral damages, as well as damages already occurred in the past, or those that will take place in the future [Article 3(3)]. Under Portuguese law of civil liability (in general and in the liability of public bodies), moral damages are only subject to compensation if they are sufficiently serious (Article 496 of the Civil Code, *ex vi* Article 3 of Law 67/2007). This is relevant for omissions in general,[68] and therefore, also for administrative silence. There have been cases in which, due to the gross breach of the deadline, moral damages were awarded.[69]

[67] In general, concerning causes for exclusion of civil liability of public bodies, see Otero (2010).

[68] See, e.g., decision of the Central Administrative Court (South) of 21-04-2016, proc. 8639/12.

[69] In the decision of the Central Administrative Court (South) of 20-06-2013, proc. 6542/10, moral damages were awarded in a situation where a retirement pension, which

Silence can also give rise to damages to persons who are considered third parties to the procedure—this is clear in cases of *positive* silence. In these cases, the absence of the exercise of *powers of refusal or control* by the public authorities may be harmful to those affected by the activity which is deemed to be allowed by positive silence. If this occurs, there is an unlawful omission, which may give rise to civil liability.

9.8.4 The Role of the Ombudsperson

Petitioners can also lodge a complaint before an Ombudsperson about administrative silence, as its mandate encompasses not only actions, but also omissions from public authorities—see Article 23(1) of the Constitution. However, the Ombudsperson's competencies are limited to issuing recommendations—see also Articles 20–22 of Law n. 9/91, of 9 April. There are no publicly available statistics or published data regarding how often the Ombudsman deals with administrative silence and the effectiveness of its recommendations and investigations.

9.9 Overall Assessment of the Legal Regime and the Practice of Administrative Silence

Despite the significant legal regime covering timeliness and reaction to administrative silence, the general perception is still that there are long delays in deciding administrative procedures in Portugal,[70] which has been confirmed yet again by a recent Government survey,[71] as well as the last Annual Report of the Portuguese Ombudsperson, which reports, for example, that procedures such as the award of retirement pensions in

was due by law, was requested in 2003, but only decided (favourably) by the competent authority in 2007.

[70] In this sense, e.g., Freitas do Amaral (2016b, p. 277), one of the most authoritative scholars in Portuguese administrative law claims that decisions being taken within the time prescribed by law is "a thing quite rare in Portugal!"

[71] See Portuguese Government (2016, p. 21), indicating that in a survey among citizens regarding the biggest problems identified with the functioning of public services, the problems most referred were "long waiting times" (with 61% of respondents) and "long times for reply from public services" (59% of respondents).

many cases take over a year to decide,[72] even though the general deadline of 90 days applies.

This is undoubtedly related to cultural issues, which are difficult to change in a short period of time. However, legal provisions can also play a role, and on this matter, it is probably safe to say that a general deadline of 90 (business) days to decide administrative procedures does *not* help administrative timeliness. It is doubtful that returning to a situation of a general clause of a "reasonable deadline" for decision would be a good solution.

Another point that should be noted is the apparent contrast between the legal regime—which provides several instruments to react to administrative silence, from the possibility to award injunctions to civil liability and disciplinary sanctions—and the abovementioned perception regarding the existence of too long delays. There is still no solution in sight for this problem of the *ineffectiveness* of the rules regarding timeliness, a situation which seems to find some tolerance on the part of courts.

Finally, it must also be mentioned that, as with other systems, cases of positive silence are growing in Portuguese law, and this under several forms (positive decisions, but also previous communication mechanisms), despite the continuing criticism by authors, who continue to hold that silence is not the best way to pursue the public interest and citizens' rights. On this note, and even though no general numbers exist on the effectiveness of positive silence systems in reducing decision deadlines, the truth is that, at least in limited cases where information on average response times is available, there seems to be a positive effect.[73] Further empirical research is necessary in order to ascertain if this is a coincidence, or an actual correlation.

[72] See Portuguese Ombudsperson (*Provedor de Justiça*) (2018), p. 79. The Government has also recently acknowledged that applications for retirement pensions take, on average, 5 months to decide—even though the legal deadline is 90 days: see https://www.publico.pt/2018/09/18/economia/noticia/vieira-da-silva-admite-problema-no-pagamento-das-novas-pensoes-1844389, last accessed 5 April 2019.

[73] The authority responsible for giving public and private works permits (i.e., permits for acting as a contractor in public and private construction) and real estate broker permits (IMPIC, I.P.) advertises its average response times, which range from 9 to 20 days, according to the type of request—see http://www.impic.pt/impic/relatorios-e-dados-estatisticos/prazos-medios-de-licenciamento_3, last accessed 5 April 2019. This information is relevant, since Law nr 41/2015, of 3 June, puts in force a system of positive silence for these types of permits.

Bibliography

Alves Correia, F. (1993). *As grandes linhas da recente reforma do direito do urbanismo português*. Coimbra: Almedina.

Amado Gomes, C. (2013a). A «boa administração» na revisão do CPA: depressa e bem… *Direito & Política* (4), 142–145.

Amado Gomes, C. (2013b). A decisão do procedimento em prazo razoável: uma nova responsabilidade administrativa. Anotação ao Acórdão do TCA-Sul de 11 de Abril de 2013 (proc. 07084/11). In C. Amado Gomes & T. Serrão (Eds.), *Responsabilidade Civil Extracontratual das Entidades Públicas: Anotações de Jurisprudência* (pp. 25–32). Lisboa: Instituto de Ciências Jurídico-Políticas (e-book).

Amado Gomes, C., Neves, A. F., & Serrão, T. (Coords.). (2016). *Comentários à revisão do CPTA e do ETAF*. Lisboa: AAFDL.

Amado Gomes, C., Neves, A. F., & Serrão, T. (Coords.). (2018a). *Organização Administrativa: Novos Actores, Novos Modelos* (2 vols.). Lisboa: AAFDL.

Amado Gomes, C., Pedro, R., & Serrão, T. (Coords.). (2018b). *O Regime de Responsabilidade Civil Extracontratual do Estado e demais Entidades Públicas: Comentários à luz da Jurisprudência*. Lisboa: AAFDL.

Antunes, T. (2016). A decisão no novo Código do Procedimento Administrativo. In C. Amado Gomes, A. F. Neves, & T. Serrão (Coords.) (Eds.), *Comentários ao Novo Código do Procedimento Administrativo*. Lisboa: AAFDL.

Antunes, T. (2018). Comentário ao artigo 9.º (ilicitude). In C. Amado Gomes, R. Pedro, & T. Serrão (Coords.) (Eds.), *O Regime de Responsabilidade Civil Extracontratual do Estado e demais Entidades Públicas: Comentários à luz da Jurisprudência* (2ª ed., pp. 537–567). Lisboa: AAFDL.

Aroso de Almeida, M. (2015). *Teoria Geral do Direito Administrativo. O Novo Regime do Código do Procedimento Administrativo* (2ª ed.). Coimbra: Almedina.

Aroso de Almeida, M. (2016). *Manual de Processo Administrativo* (2ª ed.). Coimbra: Almedina.

Cadilha, C. A. F. (2011). *Regime da responsabilidade civil extracontratual do Estado e demais entidades públicas anotado* (2ª ed.). Coimbra: Coimbra Editora.

Caetano, M. (2001, 7th reprint of 10ª ed.). *Manual de Direito Administrativo* (Vol. I). Coimbra: Almedina.

Calçada Pires, R. (2004). *O pedido de condenação à prática de acto administrativo legalmente devido. Desafiar a modernização administrativa?* Coimbra: Almedina.

Caupers, J., & Eiró, V. (2016). *Introdução ao Direito Administrativo* (12ª ed.). Lisboa: Âncora.

Cortez, M. (2001). A inactividade formal da Administração como causa extintiva do procedimento e as suas consequências. In AA/VV (Ed.), *Estudos em*

Homenagem ao Prof. Doutor Rogério Soares (STUDIA IURIDICA 61, Ad Honorem 1) (pp. 723–796). Coimbra: Coimbra Editora.
Deguergue, M. (2015). Le Silence de l'Administration en Droit Administratif Français. *Les Cahiers de Droit, 56*(3–4), 389–410.
Esteves de Oliveira, M., Pacheco de Amorim, J., & Gonçalves, P. (1999, reprint). *Código do Procedimento Administrativo Comentado.* Coimbra: Almedina.
Fidalgo de Freitas, T. (2016). Administrative Transparency in Portugal. *European Public Law, 22*(4), 667–688.
Folque, A. (2016). *Notas sobre a Revisão do Ato Administrativo no Novo Código.* Coimbra: Almedina.
França Jardim, A., & Raimundo, M. A. (2016). Balcão único electrónico. In C. Amado Gomes, A. F. Neves, & T. Serrão (Coords.) (Eds.), *Comentários ao novo Código do Procedimento Administrativo* (3ª ed., Vol. I, pp. 515 ss.). Lisboa: AAFDL.
Freitas do Amaral, D. (2011). *Curso de Direito Administrativo* (2ª ed., with P. Machete & L. Torgal, Vol. II). Coimbra: Almedina.
Freitas do Amaral, D. (2016a). *Curso de Direito Administrativo* (4ª ed., with L. Fábrica, J. Pereira da Silva, & T. Macieirinha, Vol. I). Coimbra: Almedina.
Freitas do Amaral, D. (2016b). *Curso de Direito Administrativo* (3ª ed., with P. Machete & L. Torgal, Vol. II). Coimbra: Almedina.
Garcia, M. d. G. F. P. D. (1994). *Da justiça administrativa em Portugal: sua origem e evolução.* Lisboa: Universidade Católica Portuguesa.
Miranda, J., & Machete, P. (2010). Anotação ao art. 52.°. In J. Miranda & R. Medeiros (Eds.), *Constituição Portuguesa Anotada* (2ª ed., Tomo I, pp. 1022 ss.). Coimbra: Coimbra Editora.
Neves, A. F. (2012). O direito a uma decisão administrativa em prazo razoável. In L. Pinto e Netto & E. Bittencourt Neto (Coords.) (Eds.), *Direito Administrativo e Direitos Fundamentais - Diálogos necessários* (pp. 51 ss.). Belo Horizonte: Fórum.
Otero, P. (2003). *Legalidade e Administração Pública. O sentido da Vinculação Administrativa à Juridicidade.* Coimbra: Almedina.
Otero, P. (2010). Causas de exclusão da responsabilidade civil extracontratual da Administração Pública por facto ilícito. In AA/VV (Ed.), *Estudos em Homenagem ao Prof. Doutor Sérvulo Correia* (Vol. II, pp. 965 ss.). Lisboa: Faculdade de Direito da Universidade de Lisboa.
Otero, P. (2013). *Manual de Direito Administrativo* (Vol. I). Coimbra: Almedina.
Otero, P. (2015). *Direito do Procedimento Administrativo* (Vol. I). Coimbra: Almedina.
Otero, P. (2016). Problemas constitucionais do novo Código do Procedimento Administrativo - uma introdução. In C. Amado Gomes, A. F. Neves, &

T. Serrão (Coords.) (Eds.), *Comentários ao novo Código do Procedimento Administrativo* (3ª ed., Vol. I, pp. 21–40). Lisboa: AAFDL.

Pereira da Silva, V. (2002). Todo o contencioso administrativo se tornou de plena jurisdição. *Cadernos de Justiça Administrativa* (34), 24 ss.

Pereira da Silva, V. (2009). *O Contencioso Administrativo no Divã da Psicanálise. Ensaio sobre as acções no novo processo administrativo* (2ª ed.). Coimbra: Almedina.

Pereira da Silva, V., & Macieirinha, T. (2015). Agir não agindo. Da insustentabilidade do ato tácito. In AA/VV (Ed.), *Estudos dedicados ao Professor Doutor Bernardo da Gama Lobo Xavier* (Vol. 3, pp. 597–621). Lisboa: UCP.

Portuguese Government. (2016). *Relatório da Volta Simplex+ - Ainda mais simples*. Available online at https://www.simplex.gov.pt/app/files/33d9ef89f2328ba7f54385c3927153b9.pdf. Last accessed 5 April 2019.

Portuguese Ombusdsperson (*Provedor de Justiça*). (2018). *Relatório à Assembleia da República 2017*. Available online at http://www.provedor-jus.pt/site/public/archive/doc/RELATORIO__2017_web.pdf. Last accessed 5 April 2019.

Quadros, F. d., Sérvulo Correia, J. M., Machete, R. C. d., Vieira de Andrade, J. C., Garcia, M. d. G. F. P. D., Aroso de Almeida, M. et al. (2016). *Comentários à revisão do Código do Procedimento Administrativo*. Coimbra: Almedina.

Raimundo, M. A. (2016). O acto confirmativo - elementos para uma reapreciação, a propósito do Anteprojecto de revisão do CPTA. In M. Rebelo de Sousa & E. Vera-Cruz Pinto (Coords.) (Eds.), *Liber Amicorum Fausto de Quadros* (Vol. II, pp. 429 ss.). Coimbra: Almedina.

Rebelo de Sousa, M. (1999). *Lições de Direito Administrativo* (Vol. I). Lisboa: Lex.

Rebelo de Sousa, M., & Salgado de Matos, A. (2009). *Direito Administrativo Geral* (2ª ed., Tomo III - *Actividade administrativa*). Lisboa: D. Quixote.

Sérvulo Correia, J. M. (2005a). *Direito do Contencioso Administrativo* (Vol. I). Lisboa: Lex.

Sérvulo Correia, J. M. (2005b). O incumprimento do dever de decidir. *Cadernos de Justiça Administrativa* (54), 6–32.

Sérvulo Correia, J. M. (2006). Judicial Resolution of Administrative Disputes (Administrative procedure in Portugal). In D. Moura Vicente (Ed.), *Comparative Law Portuguese-American Perspectives* (Vol. I, pp. 323–336). Coimbra: Almedina.

Silveira, J. T. (2004). *O deferimento tácito (esboço do regime jurídico do acto tácito positivo na sequência de pedido do particular à luz da recente reforma do Contencioso Administrativo*. Coimbra: Coimbra Editora.

Silveira, J. T. (2013). A decisão administrativa no anteprojecto de revisão do CPA. *Cadernos de Justiça Administrativa* (100), 109 ss.

Sousa da Fábrica, L. (2010). A contraposição entre acção comum e acção especial no Código de Processo nos Tribunais Administrativos. In AA/VV (Ed.),

Estudos em Homenagem ao Professor Doutor Sérvulo Correia (Vol. II, pp. 631 ss.). Lisboa: Faculdade de Direito da Universidade de Lisboa/Coimbra Editora.

Vasques, S. A. (2013). *As Intimações no Regime Jurídico da Urbanização e Edificação.* Coimbra: Almedina.

Vieira de Andrade, J. C. (2017). *A Justiça Administrativa (Lições)* (16ª ed.). Coimbra: Almedina.

PART IV

National Perspectives – Central and Eastern Europe

CHAPTER 10

Legal and Administrative Challenges of Administrative Silence in Slovenia

Tina Sever, Polonca Kovač, and Mirko Pečarič

10.1 The International and Constitutional Context for Analyzing Administrative Silence

Slovenia is a parliamentary democratic republic independent since 1991 and was previously a part of the former Yugoslavia. It has been a member of the Council of Europe since 1994, of EU since 2004, and of the OECD since 2010. The Slovenian culture and its political and legal systems are closely related to the Austrian continental framework that Slovenia made part of before 1930. Slovenia can thus be considered

T. Sever (✉) · P. Kovač · M. Pečarič
Faculty of Public Administration, University of Ljubljana, Ljubljana, Slovenia
e-mail: tina.sever@fu.uni-lj.si

P. Kovač
e-mail: polonca.kovac@fu.uni-lj.si

M. Pečarič
e-mail: mirko.pecaric@fu.uni-lj.si

D. C. Dragos et al. (eds.),
The Sound of Silence in European Administrative Law,
https://doi.org/10.1007/978-3-030-45227-8_10

a part of the legislature-centered *Rechtsstaat* circle. Moreover, Slovenia's culture regarding common problems places it among bureaucratic countries focused on collectivism and high uncertainty avoidance.[1]

Slovenian Constitution from 1991[2] corresponds to the requirements of Art. 6 of ECHR on due process. Firstly, Art. 23 defines the right to judicial protection. Also relevant are the procedural guarantees of equal protection of rights (Art. 22) and public nature of court proceedings (Art. 24). In accordance with Art. 22, everyone is entitled to equal protection of rights irrelevant to the nature of procedure. Constitution sets in Art. 25 the right to a legal remedy against the decisions of state bodies, municipal bodies, and bearers of public authority. However, in terms of the importance of speedy decision-making and the legal consequences of delays for individual rights, the umbrella legislation must establish mechanisms to ensure legal certainty. Based on the Austrian tradition, the principle of negative fiction has been established in Slovenia. Thus, the prevalence of the public benefit over private interests is emphasized.

Administrative silence has become recently politically and legally more relevant in Slovenia mainly in connection with Art. 6 of ECHR that requires that decisions are made within a reasonable time, although some provisions on time limits had been included in GAPA already before that. Crucial in such regard—in addition to Art. 23 of Constitution[3]—is also Art. 1 of the 2006 Protection of Right to Trial without Undue Delay Act.[4] This Act was drafted and adopted based on the ECtHR judgment in the case Lukenda v. Slovenia[5] and the decision of the Constitutional Court,[6] since the entire protection system in Slovenia was found timely inefficient. Art. 23 of Constitution indeed provides a guarantee, but its

[1] Hofstede et al. (2010).

[2] Official Gazette of the Republic of Slovenia (OGRS), No 33/91-I and revisions.

[3] Art. 23 of Constitution reads: "*Everyone has the right to have any decision regarding his rights, duties, and any charges brought against him made without undue delay by an independent, impartial court constituted by law.*"

[4] OGRS, No 49/06 and amendments. See Jerovšek et al. (2004, pp. 617–621) and cf. Šturm et al. (2011).

[5] 23032/02, 6 October 2005.

[6] U-I-65/05, 22 September 2005.

range is grammatically limited to judicial procedures.[7] Although Constitution does not provide a general administrative time limit, it nevertheless demands decision-making within a reasonable time not just in civil and criminal matters, but also in administrative matters. This inference derives from the connection between Art. 22 and 23, aligned with the ECtHR's case law on Art. 6 on the notion of "tribunal."[8] Additionally, the ECtHR considers it crucial that the dispute covers the entire period from the beginning of the administrative procedure[9] or at least from lodging an administrative appeal[10] up to the adoption of a ruling and administrative enforcement.

10.2 The Length of Administrative Time Limits

10.2.1 General and Sector-Specific Legislation

In Slovenia, the umbrella regulation on administrative silence is General Administrative Procedure Act and Administrative Dispute Act (GAPA[11] and ADA[12]). GAPA lays down the principle of economy, which demands procedures to be conducted fast, with low costs and minimum delay for the parties. In case of administrative silence, it envisages the possibility of appeal and action by the party. That is the case either in procedures initiated upon request of the party or explicitly in procedures commenced *ex officio*, at both levels of administrative decision-making (Art. 222, 255, and 256 of GAPA and Art. 28 of ADA). Additionally, GAPA allows in Art. 18 for *ex officio* devolution of competence if, due to the delay, consequences detrimental to the public interest might arise. GAPA envisages the principle of subsidiarity, which enables that particular procedural institutions are regulated by a special law differently than under Art. 3 of GAPA. However, there must be a specific need for such exception based on Art. 22 of Constitution. Sector-specific regulations in Slovenia will often set different time limits than GAPA, mainly longer due to special

[7] Up-1202/05-4, 22 September 2006.

[8] E.g. Sramek v. Austria, 8790/79, 22 October 1984; Sacilor Lormires v. France, 65411/01, 9 November 2006. More regarding Slovenian cases in Sever (2016).

[9] See Stibilj v. Slovenia, 1446/07, 5667/07, 6 October 2015.

[10] Božić v. Croatia, 22457/02, 29 June 2006.

[11] OGRS, No 80/99 and amendments.

[12] OGRS, No 105/06 and amendments.

inquisitory acts required or shorter in order to enhance enforceability of entrepreneurs' permits. For the latter purpose, sometimes laws opt for a positive silence model instead of a negative one.

According to Art. 222 and 256 of GAPA, the time limit for decision in special fact-finding and appellate procedures is—as soon as possible, but allowed up to—two months from the receipt of a complete request by the party or from the receipt of an appeal, while the time limit for decision in a summary procedure is up to one month.[13] Highly relevant is also the provision of paragraph three of Art. 28 of ADA, whereby since 2007 the party may bring action in an administrative dispute if the procedure before the two administrative instances is not finally resolved *within three years* of the beginning of the procedure.[14]

10.2.2 Possibilities of Prolongation

The time limits defined by GAPA to issue a decision are only instructive. Therefore, the obligation of issuing a decision continues to apply despite the expiration of the time limit. In case an administrative decision is not issued within the legally prescribed time limits, a party can require an explanation of the reasons for delay. The competent body needs to inform the party about the reasons for delay in three working days after receiving a request at the latest. Finally, in accordance with GAPA, after the expiry of the time limit the party is entitled to file an appeal at any time until the issuing of the decision. Some sector-specific laws like Public Information Access Act (OGRS, No 51/06 and amendments) also allow a prolongation of time limits, usually based on the justified reasons for longer proceedings.

[13] GAPA defines also five extraordinary legal remedies, such as reopening of procedure no later than in three years, annulment and abrogation of decision through supervisory right in five or one year depending on the type of violation. In terms of enforcement proceedings, the administrative body must issue a procedural decision allowing the enforcement of a decision without delay within thirty days from when the decision became enforceable at the latest.

[14] In a two-instance administrative procedure, the substantive appraisal of the appeal against the first instance act challenged by action is a precondition for bringing action against the first instance act (decision of the Supreme Court, I Up 21/2014; an exception applies in relation to action in accordance with Art. 28 of ADA).

10.2.3 Counting Time Limits

The relevant period to issue a decision as an instructive deadline starts when a party submits a complete application or, in case of procedures *ex officio*, when the administrative body performs the first official action. In case proceedings are stayed, the time limits are suspended. If the party submits an incomplete application, the body requires that it be supplemented within a certain time limit, defined by the official in charge but allowed only once. The time limit to issue a decision starts when the application is supplemented.

On the other hand, procedural time limits referring to the actions of the parties or other participants in the procedure are preclusive. The time limits can be defined in days, months, or years. The counting of the time limit defined in days starts usually the next day, after the service of an administrative act. It is not limited by weekends or work-free days. However, if the last day of the time limit falls on a weekend or work-free day, its expiry is shifted on the next working day. When the time limits are defined in months or years, they expire on the same day of the relevant month/year. Moreover, the officials in charge can define the time limits for certain actions in procedures on their own (e.g., supplementation of the application under Art. 67 of GAPA), while the time limits can also be prolonged on the party's justified request, before the expiry of the time limit. Finally, if the party has justified grounds for the miss of a time limit, restitution is possible (Art. 103–108). Unjustified conduct by the official or the other second private party that leads to a delay in the procedure could be regarded as an aggravating circumstance when demanding compensation for damages due to delay.

10.3 Responses to Administrative Silence in Slovenia

10.3.1 National Doctrine on Administrative Silence and the Prevailing Negative Model

National doctrine in Slovenia understands administrative silence as a breach of EU principles.[15] Operationally in nearly all cases, the Slovenian system follows the German model of negative fiction, providing to the party the right to appeal. In addition, the devolution of competence applies *ex officio* in some cases. If the time limit prescribed by the separate act or GAPA is violated and the general model of negative fiction applies in case of administrative silence, the umbrella acts GAPA and ADA envisage the following three possibilities.

First, in case of risk to the life and health of people, the natural and living environment or property, the delay leads to obligatory devolution of competence from the first to the second instance; the latter must take on the case and decide as soon as possible (Art. 18 of GAPA).

Second, the devolution of competence to a higher instance is established, since in silence, the consequences of a negative decision are considered irrefutable legal fiction (*praesumptio iuris et de iure*). An appellate administrative procedure or a procedure before the court also applies for cases where a party files an appeal or brings action, although both GAPA and ADA contain some restrictions, e.g., possibility for the second instance authority to prescribe an additional time limit to the first instance authority, or the necessary written call to decide on the appeal before bringing action in an administrative dispute.[16] Third, in case of

[15] Cf. Galetta et al. (2015, p. 21): "*Timeliness, which pertains to the principles of fairness, means that decisions have to be taken within a reasonable time since slow administration is a bad administration and might be in violation of the concept of legal certainty.*" There is also a direct link to the right to be heard. The same stressed by Slovenian scholars, e.g., Šturm, Jerovšek, Kovač, Kerševan, etc. More recent analysis in Sever and Kovač (2016).

[16] In an administrative dispute, a party may bring action due to the administrative silence of the second instance authority, as well as of a first instance authority when an appeal against the first instance decision is not allowed. According to case law, administrative silence applies for decisions and procedural decisions also in enforcement procedures (judgment of the Supreme Court, U 1578/93-4, 12 October 1995). In terms on estimating the legality of administrative silence under ADA, it is relevant, which body is competent to issue an administrative decision and not which body is competent to receive a request by the party (see Administrative Court, I U 2474/2017-9, 24 September 2018).

delay in relation to which the party does not claim special protection on grounds of administrative silence and there are no evident detrimental consequences for specifically protected goods, an optional devolution to the appellate authority is possible despite the otherwise strict prohibition of appropriation of competence.

In order to establish the above presumptions, however, certain conditions need to be fulfilled, cumulatively at least: (i) The case must concern a specific administrative matter; (ii) the prescribed time limit for decision must be set; and (iii) some degree of legal protection must be prescribed in case of administrative silence. In addition, theory and also case law in Slovenia distinguish between prescribed and reasonable time limit for decision because of the different legal nature of the one or the other.[17]

10.3.2 *The EU Influence Over National Rules and Practices*

The most significant respective EU influence in Slovenia is based on Directive 2006/123/EC. Slovenia adopted the Services in the Internal Market Act (SIMA[18]), which sets time limit for a positive fiction is three months from the initiation of the procedure. It allows the extension of the time limit and, in particular, derogations from such arrangement, if dictated by the public interest or the legitimate interest of accessory participants. In order to clarify the relations and estimate the arising of a right or enforceability, the authority must issue to the applicant an acknowledgment of receipt of the application stating the time limit for the issue of the authorization and the available legal remedies. Moreover, the instruction that after the expiry of the time limit the fiction of positive decision will arise is recommendable. Nonetheless, SIMA is based on

The case deals with the right of temporary stay and a right to privacy in accordance with Art. 8 of ECHR. Since there still needs to be decided on the right of Art. 8 for the first time, the administrative unit is competent to decide on the merits, the court cannot intervene in executive branch and decide instead of it.

[17] Kovač et al. (2012, pp. 42ff).

[18] OGRS, No 21/10. Cf. Pirnat (2009), and Remic and Kovač (2010). The aim of the Directive is to increase the competitiveness of the European market by enabling particularly small and medium-sized enterprises to expand their activities, specifically based on individual procedural provisions. In Art. 13, the Directive provides the fiction of positive decision that occurs if the national authority does not decide on the party's application for authorization to provide services within the time limit prescribed under national law.

an "unusual" legal technique since positive decision in case of administrative silence will not apply with the coming into effect of the SIMA, but only when or if sector-specific regulations refer to the specific provisions of this Act. SIMA is thus contrary to the principle of subsidiary application of regulations, since its addressees do not even know when they are subject to this Act and the Directive, or to GAPA or separate acts.

Additionally, from the point of view of the applicable regulation under GAPA, setting time limits under SIMA nullifies the seriousness of the "threat" of fiction of positive decision in case of administrative silence. Namely, the legally prescribed time limit at the first instance can be six months, while exactly the same could occur in case of deciding on legal remedies due to administrative silence under GAPA and ADA. Likewise, questionable is regulating positive fiction at the first instance without specifying what happens in case of administrative silence at the second instance. Here, GAPA and ADA are more consistent. Since SIMA fails to comply with the requirements of the Directive, the ECtHR case law suggests that the provisions of the Directive should be applied directly since they are clear, unconditional.[19]

10.4 The Negative Silence

10.4.1 The Possibility to Issue a Valid Act After the Expiry of the Time Limit

The mere delay does not make the decision unlawful.[20] Of course, this does not apply if competence has already been delegated due to administrative silence. In this case, second instance authority decides on appeal due to administrative silence. In the event of doubt as to the appropriation of competence by second instance, it is important that the first instance authority immediately delivers the issued decision also to the second instance authority if it believes that the party has or will file an appeal due to administrative silence. An analogy can be made when the delivery of the first instance decision and the appeal due to administrative

[19] See Kerševan and Androjna (2017, p. 69).

[20] According to the Administrative Court, case U 1171/2000, 12 September 2002, exceeding the 10-day time limit (for subsequent calculation of customs debt under Art. 154 of Customs Act) did not affect the legality of the decision since the said time limit cannot be considered a preclusive time limit.

silence coincide, since the meaning of such institution is achieved as soon as the decision is taken. Otherwise, under its supervisory right, the second instance authority should annul the decision of the first instance for violation of subject matter jurisdiction, and then take the (same) decision itself.

When it comes to appeal in the above case, GAPA does not regulate the proceeding of the second instance authority. Yet, halting the not yet initiated fact-finding procedure at the second instance does not make any sense. In such case, an official note by the second instance authority stating that the "dispute" in such part is dismissed suffices. However, if the procedure at the second instance has already started (e.g., the first instance body has already been called on to explain the reasons for the delay) such is not possible, as it would involve a violation of subject matter jurisdiction, which is an absolute procedural error.[21]

In addition to the delay being unlawful per se, the violation of prescribed time limits is a sign of malpractice or maladministration. By doing so, the party is left in uncertainty and the recognition of their right is delayed since they can only exercise such right after the decision has been issued and has become enforceable.[22] It is worth pointing out that the time limit includes not only the issuance of a decision, but also its delivery, since only then does the act have external effect—in relation to the party or other addressees of the decision.[23] The prescribed time limit does not run when a formally incomplete application is being supplemented or during the suspension (e.g., when solving the preliminary question, assessing the general legal act underlying the procedure, before the Constitutional Court). These are important correctional measures to avoid delays beyond the influence of the deciding authority.

The appeal may be filed directly with the second instance authority (Art. 255 of GAPA). The appellate authority must within its supervisory powers ensure that action is taken. Thus, it first examines the reasons for delay. Depending on the answer, it either imposes an additional time limit up to 1 month for issuing the decision at the first instance, or (finally) decides on its own, especially in the event of subjective delay and other

[21] Cf. Art. 237 of GAPA; Kovač et al. (2010, p. 41).

[22] If the body enforces a recognized right, it means that it has already decided (Kovač et al. 2015, p. 151).

[23] Theory is unanimous in such regard (e.g. Kerševan and Androjna 2017, p. 183).

circumstances and depending on the necessity of immediate decision. It is not exempted from liability even if, for example, the first instance authority does not present the case file or such cannot be found. The party may withdraw an already filed appeal on administrative silence, yet it is deemed due to devolution and incompleteness of the case that the second instance authority is still obliged to decide in the main case. Although the decision must be based on correctly established true facts of the case, fact-finding procedures may not last indefinitely, and the authority must do everything in its power to establish the decisive facts within a legally prescribed time limit and as soon as possible. Since the parties may not force the authority to issue a decision that affects their interest, the provision of Art. 255 of GAPA—envisaging the right to appeal on grounds of administrative silence or the fiction of negative decision—may be considered disputable. This procedural institution is only allowed in procedures initiated by the party when their request is being decided. However, a second instance authority that would be aware of the exceeding duration of the procedure could take over the case as well.[24]

Further, it is important to consider the regulations and facts that apply at the time of decision-making, especially if the sector-specific act does not bind the recognition of a right to the filing of the application but rather to the issuing of a decision. For example, GAPA provides that since the administrative body is bound by legality, it will decide on the basis of substantive law applying at the time of decision-making and the then existing relevant facts.[25] According to the case law of the Administrative Court, an application must be dealt with in line with applicable law and the actual circumstances existing in the course of or at the time of expiry of the time limit for decision, not after its expiration, but case law is not consistent in such regard. Some judgments favor deciding after the issuing of the first instance decision, albeit in delay.[26] In order to

[24] Art. 18 of GAPA; Kovač et al. (2015, p. 97).

[25] Paragraph one of Art. 251 and paragraph two of Art. 238.

[26] Cf. judgments of the Supreme Court, I Up 289/2005, X Ips 1642/2006, 10 March 2010. Yet, theory (e.g. Jerovšek et al. 2004, p. 59) argues that the doctrine of deciding after the issuing of a first instance decision has no constitutional or legal basis, as it relies on the surpassed principle of uniform decision-making at the first and second instance. For example, if the party's request is partially successful, the party would file the appeal only in relation to the non-successful part of the decision—however, partial finality is not possible because of the relatedness and interdependence of the two parts. It is therefore necessary to consistently observe the prohibition *reformatio in peius*.

ensure equality before the law, equal protection of the rights of the parties and trust in law or legitimate expectations under Art. 14, 22 and 2 of Constitution, the Constitutional Court in case Up-304/01-27, 20 May 2004, stressed that in cases of a substantial exceeding of the time limit for decision (e.g., four years at the first instance), the regulation that is consistent with Constitution is the one applicable at the expiry of the prescribed time limit for decision. In this way, the parties are not affected by possibly stricter conditions introduced by an amendment of the regulation during the procedure,[27] but this only applies in case of unreasonably long procedures, not at every exceeding of the prescribed time limit.

What is relevant—the state of facts and the regulations in place at the time of the expiry of the time limit for decision, or the time when the appeal due to administrative silence is filed, or does the general rule concerning the issuing of the (non-fictitious) decision apply? The argument in favor of the date of filing the appeal is based on the logical conclusion that the party has appealed precisely with the intent to enforce the then valid regulations and relevant facts—otherwise the party would not appeal at all.[28]

10.4.2 Legal Consequences and Fictions, Finality, and Enforceability

Given the fictitious nature of the negative decision, a recurrent dilemma is whether fictitious acts have the same characteristics as the actually issued acts. It is essential to define whether the act has the quality of (substantive) finality, as only a substantively final act allows for the emergence of legal consequences.[29] These legal consequences, if defined by a final decision of a state authority, should be unchangeable. However, in the event of the fiction of rejected request, the fictitious act cannot achieve substantive finality. Such an act can only become (only conditionally) administratively or formally final (a party can file an appeal *after* time limits were breached—if there were a full formal finality the appeal would not be possible), since the function of the institution of administrative

[27] If the amendment brings milder conditions for the party, the latter can withdraw the original request and initiate a new procedure under the new legislation.

[28] Kerševan and Androjna (2017, p. 419).

[29] The legal status of the party whose request is rejected is thus the same as the status of the party to whom no decision has been issued (Kerševan and Androjna 2017, pp. 104ff).

silence is to establish legal protection for the party, not to give rise to effects under substantive law.

The subject matter of an appeal on grounds of administrative silence is not to challenge the content of the decision; there is no such thing by definition. By applying a legal remedy upon administrative silence, the party claims that the authority has not decided. Indirectly, the party indeed challenges the decision that does not recognize the legal interest they claimed, but essentially the party only files an appeal or an action to claim a right, not the violation thereof.

Some experts[30] believe that the fiction of decision in case of administrative silence can only be claimed by the main active party (and its legal successor), and not by an accessory participant or public interest representative or a passive party against whom the procedure is usually carried out *ex officio*. Such narrow definition contradicts the purpose of this institution, since the point of prescribing a time limit or efficient decision-making in administrative matters is also the protection of public interest. That means that it is necessary to decide contrary to the party's request, if so required by the need to protect the public benefit. Moreover, also accessory participants if their *locus standi* is recognized should be protected.[31]

The prescribed time limit, unless the law explicitly defines administrative silence only in procedures initiated upon the request of the party, thus applies both in procedures initiated upon request and in procedures initiated *ex officio*. Even in the latter case, we can talk about the interest of the (passive) party in a prompt decision because the party is uncertain until the end of a proceeding how their obligation will be decided. Or even claims a certain parallel right within the scope of their obligation (e.g., deciding on the payment of tax by installments or on tax write-off).

[30] Arguing that a passive party cannot be interested in the decision since if the act is not issued, the party's legal status does not change either (e.g. Cvetko 1995, p. 986).

[31] Kovač et al. (2015, pp. 59ff). Unless if they cannot be affected by a decision that does not change the legal relation compared to the situation before the initiation of the procedure. In practice, the opposite is often found in inspection cases where the applicants wish to force the authorities to act so that they will be able to claim, for example, for damages insofar as they are affected by the violation (Kovač et al. 2015). However, according to the Supreme Court, cases X Ips 209/2015, 6 October 2016, X Ips 40/2016, 23 November 2016, an application is merely a motion to initiate the procedure ex officio, which means that the authority is not obliged to initiate the procedure and, consequently, administrative silence might not occur at all.

Therefore, because of the principle of legal certainty, in such a case the party has the right to appeal against administrative silence as if an unfavorable decision has been made in their respect.[32] In practice, of course, not many appeals in such regard are expected. However, a procedure can involve several parties with conflicting interests; therefore, any (fiction of) decision can thus be positive for one party and negative for the other, but both need to be ensured the relevant legal protection.

10.4.3 Case Law

Several judgments were issued in Slovenia in relation to different aspects of administrative silence. For example, the Constitutional Court judgment in case UI-147/08, 11 November 2009, when the plaintiff in connection with Directive 2006/123/EC claimed protection in the administrative dispute under Art. 28 of ADA, but in the meantime the administrative body adopted the decision and the court terminated the procedure with a procedural decision. Similar is provided by the decision of the Supreme Court I Up 235/2009, whereby the defendant carried out all the actions, which the plaintiff initially claimed when bringing action on grounds of administrative silence, therefore, silence "never actually occurred." Further on, see also case II Ips 645/2009, 17 May 2012, of the Supreme Court. Here, in relation to the preliminary question and the length of procedure, the court found the administrative authority's misunderstanding of what the preliminary question was when it came to interpreting sector-specific regulations (municipal decrees or municipal plans as the basis for a concrete building permit) and its absolute passivity since the suspension of the procedure to be unlawful.[33] In case I Up 626/2002 of 26 February 2003, the Supreme Court also emphasized that the party must exhaust legal protection upon administrative silence and thus speed up the procedure. In order to be able to appeal against unlawful conduct, the party must first exhaust the available legal remedies.[34] Failing to do so, the party will not be able to ground the

[32] Kerševan and Androjna (2017, p. 104).

[33] See more cited cases in other sections of this chapter. For empirical data, see the section on legal remedies.

[34] See Supreme Court's case II Ips 976/2007, 14 October 2010; Kovač et al. (2015, p. 188).

inadmissible conduct of the body on inadmissibly long-lasting procedures in a civil proceeding for damages.[35]

There are more cases, mainly addressing sector-specific peculiarities that are only partially regulated or formally implemented and then deviate from a generally complaint system of legally protected interests. Searching the case law of the Supreme Court and typing in "administrative silence," over 200 hits are given. However, we focused on the case law of the Supreme Court's administrative department regarding the ADA of 2006, which has been in force since January 2007. In the period from 2007 to 2018, the administrative department of Supreme Court issued 70 decisions and 10 judgments in relation to "silence." The Supreme Court's administrative department otherwise issued during the period from 2007 to 2018 altogether 7844 cases (counting together old and new ADA cases).

10.5 The Positive Silence

10.5.1 The Possibility to Issue a Valid Act After the Expiry of the Time Limit

In addition to the prevailing negative model in case of administrative silence, the Slovenian legislation also regulates the fiction of positive decision, partly under GAPA and partly under sector-specific laws (e.g., above mentioned SIMA). In both cases, administrative silence is interpreted as sustaining the party's request, particularly if a specific decision—for example, consent—is a condition for obtaining another right. Consent as an accessory act is thus in "a positive silence camp," while a final decision is still in the negative one.

This is the case of joint decisions under Art. 208 and 209 of GAPA, since it is deemed that consent—as an accessory act—has been given if the co-author of the decision does not deliver its consent/opinion/refusal to the other authority within 15 days. Administrative silence is interpreted to the advantage of the party, since otherwise, it would not be possible to issue a decision on the merits and the party could not use legal remedies because of the accessory nature of the opinion. At most, the party could file an appeal due to administrative silence of the authority that asked for the opinion, but this would not be efficient as the reasons for not

[35] With high compensation under Supreme Court's decision II Ips 645/2009, 17 May 2012.

issuing a decision within the prescribed time limit are not on the side of this authority. Should the consent-giver miss the time limit of 15 days to deliver its consent under Art. 209 of GAPA, it would be presumed that consent was given. However, if the consent-giver refuses consent before the decision is issued, even if after the expiry of the 15-day time limit, such decision cannot be sustained since the opinion of the consent-giver should be considered in accordance with the principle of legality.[36] If the decision has already been issued but consent has not been given within the prescribed time limit, then the decision is lawful. In such case, the authority competent to give consent may—by itself or through the State Attorney's Office—propose extraordinary legal remedies, provided that the conditions for the use of such are fulfilled.[37] However, it is essential that consent is required, otherwise the fiction of given consent does not occur.[38]

Exceptionally, the fiction of sustaining decision is prescribed by a special act, as is the case with the Public Assembly Act of 2002, whereby the declared gathering or event is considered to be allowed if a ban is not issued at least three or sometimes five days before the event. Consent, however, is more a type of control rather than a "classic" permit. Nevertheless, considering EU principles and Constitution, it would be acceptable if certain specific administrative procedures were regulated differently.

[36] See Administrative Court, I U 1352/2009, 21 April 2010: "*One of the legal consequences of paragraph five of Art. 50a of the Construction Act is that the negative decision concerning consent, issued by the competent authority after the legally prescribed time limit has expired, rebuts the statutory presumption that because of administrative silence, consent was given.*" See also case II U 424/2011, 21 November 2012: "... *refusing consent, even if the decision has been issued after the expiry of the legally prescribed time limit, rebuts the statutory presumption that because of administrative silence, consent was given.*"

[37] E.g. an evident infringement of a substantive regulation under paragraph two of Art. 274 of GAPA; Kovač et al. (2015, p. 217).

[38] Jerovšek et al. (2004, p. 578) and Kovač et al. (2010, p. 164). Similar applies for consent on radiation and nuclear safety—the competent authority needs to acquire this in a procedure to obtain from the Ministry of the Environment the permit to carry out activities affecting the environment, or consent to carry out activities affecting the road buffer zone in the procedure for issuing a construction permit, under the act regulating public roads (case U 677/2002). Similar provisions are found in the act regulating construction or the energy act for consents that are separate administrative acts (a separate procedure is carried out for such), but their issuing is only one step in the procedure to obtain all the permits necessary to the party.

10.5.2 *Legal Consequences and Fictions, Finality and Enforceability*

In the fiction of recognizing a right or legal interest, the assessment of the merits is by definition absent, therefore the purpose of the norm is not achieved. In such case, the administrative procedure does not make sense—without an assessment of the merits through legal principles and rules, the administrative procedure (although only in cases of fiction of sustaining decision) would be an unnecessary administrative barrier. The parties would file a request, wait for the administration's inaction, and, without weighing between the public benefit and the rights of the parties, obtain the rights. The parties would thus be bound by the law to be active, but in the formal sense without any benefit "from the other side." If so, it would be more reasonable to deregulate the area.[39] In other words, as long as there is a necessity to examine the risk to the public interest by defining a matter as an administrative one, a substantive weighing between the interests must be carried out in the procedure. In this context, it is pointless to question who is (to be) affected by administrative silence—the party or the authority.[40] Silence undoubtedly harms primarily the public interest, i.e., the value categories defined and protected with the regulations in force. In order to protect the rights of the parties against abuse of authority, in case of administrative inactivity, the party acquires procedural, not substantive law entitlements. If this was the case, it would had been easier to accept the granted appeal than the granted request, since an assessment of the party's eligibility for authorization or the weighing between private and public interests would already had been carried out at first instance.[41]

[39] More in Kovač (2012).

[40] See Pirnat (2009, p. 3).

[41] Such considerations emerged in Slovenia when adopting the new act on tax procedure in 2006, stating that the fiction of granting the appeal against a tax-related first instance decision would be established. The reason for this was a very large backlog in solving appeals in this area. Instead of two months, it took two or three years to decide, and in most cases decisions were just annulled and returned for reconsideration, which—due to non-suspensiveness of the appeal—in tax matters—led to many cases of bankruptcy among the taxpayers. Despite an extremely pressing practice, this possibility was rejected under the influence of public law theorists, as it would be a form of constitutionally inadmissible settlement, also at the expense of inequality of the parties. Ultimately, mass appeals challenging the entire tax assessment due to the limitation period could lead to the bankruptcy of the state budget.

With the fiction of positive decision, a fictitious act could gain substantive finality. This would give rise to the protection of acquired rights, even without an *ex-ante* fact-finding procedure or a (potential) procedure for the assessment of legality of the decision based on legal remedies. The classic purpose of substantive finality and, consequently, stability of legal relations is to protect the holders of rights and obligations in such relations, as a final decision binds all the involved (*res iudicata ius facit inter partes*) and is regarded as correct and true (*res iudicata pro veritate accipitur*). This also prevents double jeopardy (*ne bis in idem*). Logically, such effects only occur when the decision is issued in writing and served on the party; i.e., it must actually exist. In case of the fiction of positive decision, the problem of finality or enforceability (i.e., the arising of a right or obligation that, under Art. 224 of GAPA, is as a rule based on administrative finality) is evident because there is no actual (material) document and thus no explicit date (fiction) of legal effect.[42] If such fiction applies, it is imperative to provide some additional evidence, for example, by issuing a certificate of the receipt of the application, or a subsequent letter or note on the beginning of enforceability or the date when the right has arisen.[43]

10.6 Supervision of Administrative Timeliness

According to Art. 320 of GAPA, the head of the competent body must ensure that procedures are conducted within the prescribed time limits. Furthermore, GAPA requires that bodies have a register of the number of applications, the number of solved administrative matters, the time and means of conducting procedures, etc. In case of delays in administrative procedure, there is a possibility to inform the administrative inspection about the violation of time limitsv. According to administrative inspection reports for the last three years, for instance, the number of established violations of instructive time limits is among the highest in comparison with other violations of GAPA rules.

On the basis of GAPA amendments of 2008 (Art. 300 to 307g), in order to ensure greater efficiency, an inspector may—when, for example, an official person or head of the body has violated the prescribed time limits—decide that such official person undergoes additional training.

[42] Kovač (2011, p. 181).

[43] For empirical data and case law on positive model, see other sections.

Moreover, an inspector may propose a disciplinary procedure be initiated under the acts governing public employees or labor relations. Here, the inspection distinguishes between objective reasons for delay and subjective liability, as opposed to the ECtHR's assessment of unreasonable time for a decision where the lack of staff in the administration or in the national court does not exempt from liability.

10.7 Legal Remedies

10.7.1 Administrative Appeal, Judicial Review and Remedies for Silent Rejection and Approval

In the event of administrative silence, the party may file the appeal immediately after the expiration of the time limits (if earlier, the appeal is rejected as premature) and at any time pending the issuing of the decision. If the time limit expired after the expiry of the time limit for appeal, counted from the start of the delay, the institution of administrative silence would have no purpose. The party's statement that they will not file an appeal before the decision is issued or the prescribed time limit for decision expires, has no effect and the party is not precluded. Although the party knows that the decision has been issued but the time limit for issuing such has already expired, they have the right to file an appeal due to administrative silence, because the decision has not yet been served and the legal effects thereof only arise upon service. In such case, what is known as partial administrative silence occurs, but partial silence is usually considered equal to complete silence since legal effects only arise upon service.[44] If the second instance administrative body does not decide on the appeal due to administrative silence within two months, the party will have to lodge a repeated request to the second instance administrative body before bringing an action to the court. In case of a repeated request, the decision must be issued within seven days following the request. If the decision is not issued within this time limit, the party can bring an action due to administrative silence to the Administrative Court.

Only when administrative silence is unjustified and the lawsuit itself justifiable, the court can decide on the merits, providing that the

[44] According to Supreme Court case I Up 42/2002, 12 September 2002, a decision is deemed issued after it has been served, while in establishing administrative silence it is necessary to assess whether the reasons preventing the serving were justified or not.

following conditions are fulfilled: The plaintiff has filed a request to decide on the merits; substantive decision-making is in accordance with the nature of the matter; and the court has the necessary data or establishes the relevant facts by itself at the oral hearing. If deciding on the merits is not possible, the court instructs the administrative authority to issue the administrative decision. However, the latter can again fail to issue a decision, thus placing the burden of appeal back on the party. However, one needs to be aware of the pros and cons of merit system, since it indeed speeds up effective protection of the parties (no "yo-yo" effect as in the cassation system), but there is the risk of the judiciary taking over the tasks of the executive (the principle of separation of powers), as well as the problem of sufficient number and (specific) competences and/or organization of administrative judges and courts.[45]

In the period from 2007 to 2018, the administrative department of Supreme Court altogether issued 70 decisions and 10 judgments in relation to "silence." Out of 70 decisions, appeal was granted only 10 times and partly granted four times. In 47 cases, appeal was refused and in three cases rejected. Further on, the court rejected the submitted revision[46] five times and granted it once and partly granted one time. In the rest of the cases, revision was refused.[47] In terms of content of administrative matters, the most common issues during 2007–2018 were taxes, environment and spatial-related matters, agriculture, denationalization, state legal aid, children with special needs, and asylum.

[45] Sever et al. (2016, p. 160). According to Art. 65 of ADA, the court may decide on the matter if this is permitted by the nature of the matter and if the data on the procedure provide reliable foundation/facts established at hearing, particularly if: (1) Removal of contested administrative act and the new procedure would cause damage for the plaintiff which would be difficult to redress; (2) After the administrative act removed, the administrative body issues a new act, which is contrary to the legal opinion of the court; (3) Administrative silence; on second instance or in 30 days after removal; and (4) Necessary for protection of constitutional rights.

[46] A possible extraordinary legal remedy in administrative dispute.

[47] Looking at decisions, we identified some typical cases, e.g. the parties file appeals due to administrative silence although silence actually could not happen, since the matter was not administrative but, for example, civil (e.g., contract on scholarship); or the issued decision is not an administrative act as defined by Art. 2 of ADA (only procedural decisions); or the body was not obliged to issue a decision so administrative silence could not occur, etc. On the other hand, the appeal was granted when there was no final decision issued in 3 years as the final time limit defined by ADA (Art. 28, see also case I Up 105/2011, 18 April 2012).

10.7.2 Right to Compensation for Damages

The violation of the prescribed time limit for decision with the fiction of negative decision is not (yet) an unlawful act; more so, an appeal or action due to administrative silence even "legalises" the violation. This does not apply when the delay results in detrimental consequences and it can be demonstrated that the delay by the administrative authority has caused damage to the party.[48] The damage caused by the delay would, on the other hand, lead to the (objective) tort liability of the State under Art. 26 of Constitution, if the party would prove in a civil procedure all elements of the tort. Several judgments were issued in Slovenia in such regard. Particularly relevant is the Supreme Court's case II Ips 186/2015, 1 October 2015, concerning health inspection (the presence of THC in beer production), where the Court found that errors in the assessment of evidence and misapplication of substantive law did not constitute unlawfulness,[49] less so the operative part of the decision which merely repeated the legal norm. As regards considering the operative part and the reasoning as well all the relevant circumstances within the framework of proportionality, the Higher Court in the case II Cp 177/2018, 4 April 2018—in line with the previous decision of the Constitutional Court, Up 998/2015-19, 30 November 2017, noted: "*The state must organise the work of its services in such a way that the legal remedies by which the regularity of a decision is tested are decided on quickly. In the specific case, the administrative procedure, which started with the taking of the sample for analysis on 3 November 1998 and ended with the decision to stop the procedure on 1 June 2004, lasted unacceptably long and exceeded the allowed reasonable time in a relatively simple matter.*"

[48] Some authors make no distinction among such and claim unlawfulness at any delay of the prescribed time limit. About the fact that violation of the prescribed time limit is unlawful (Tratar 2000, pp. 213–215).

[49] See Šturm et al. (2011). Cf. judgment VSK Cp 826/99, 15 February 2000, where the court finds that due to the instructional character and without any consequences determined for the body under GAPA, the exceeding of this time limit does not automatically mean liability of the State. In the specific case, deciding at second instance took nine months in total, but the court considered that this time limit—in light of the generally known fact about administrative burden and the usual time limits in which these authorities decide—does not constitute unnecessary delay, which would be the basis for compensation, contrary to the mere administrative silence. The same can be found in decisions U-I-147/08 and Up-1547/08, 11 November 2009.

10.7.3 The Role of the Ombudsman

In Slovenia, the Ombudsman protects human rights in relation to state, local self-government bodies and bearers of public authority. The parties need firstly to exhaust all available legal remedies and the Ombudsman cannot interfere with ongoing procedures, except when these are unjustifiably delayed or authority is obviously abused.[50] The Ombudsman's yearly reports show that administrative silence is a problem in certain administrative fields, e.g., water rights and social affairs. In the reports for 2016 and 2017, one of the more problematic bodies was the Ministry of Labour, Family, and Social Affairs due to constant delays when deciding as a second instance on administrative appeals. This is a particularly sensitive area since the Ministry decides on the rights that are crucial for survival, e.g., financial social assistance, state scholarship, etc. The Ministry should decide within 2 months, but sometimes it takes even 2 years or longer.[51] The Ombudsman issued recommendations and several warnings, but the procedures have not yet improved significantly.

10.7.4 Empirical Evidence of Administrative and Court Procedures

Administrative statistics is kept on a yearly basis for all administrative authorities according to the Rules on the Keeping of Records of Administrative Procedures.[52] For our research, the summary reports concerning decisions in administrative matters in 2013 and 2016,[53] and court statistics on administrative matters[54] were considered.

In 2016, Slovenian administrative authorities reportedly dealt with a total of 8.005.576 cases, of which 250.020 (3%) in the municipalities. Most cases concerned finances (40%), social affairs (25%), and various matters at the local units (11%), although these shares do not necessarily reflect the complexity of the procedures. In 2016, a total of 57,395 appeals were filed (e.g., 0.8% of all administrative matters at first instance) and a further 18,049 were left from 2015. At the end of 2016, the number of unresolved appeals was 10,778, mostly in social affairs (47%),

[50] See Art. 24 of Human Rights Ombudsman Act, OGRS, No 71/93 and amendments.

[51] See Ombudsman (2018), reports for 2016 and 2017.

[52] OGRS, Nos 18/03, 7/06; adopted based on Art. 322 of GAPA.

[53] MPA (2018).

[54] See Supreme Court (2018) and EC (2018).

public fees (24%), and health care (17%). Moreover, 132,309 extraordinary legal remedies were filed. In addition to the 8 million cases, over half a million administrative enforcement procedures were carried out; 83% thereof were carried out within the legally provided time limit. According to summary data of administrative statistics, it is especially outstanding for Slovenia that the various indicators to monitor the activities of administrative authorities do not show any deviations—except in terms of solution time in individual sectors. Thus, it appears from the data in Figs. 10.1 and 10.2 and Table 10.1, taking into account the aforementioned GAPA rules, that in general there are almost no delays, since an average of 92% of the cases is settled on time. According to Fig. 10.1, the most responsive authorities are local administrative units and financial offices, while more problems are identified in individual, unfortunately the most sensitive areas such as social affairs.

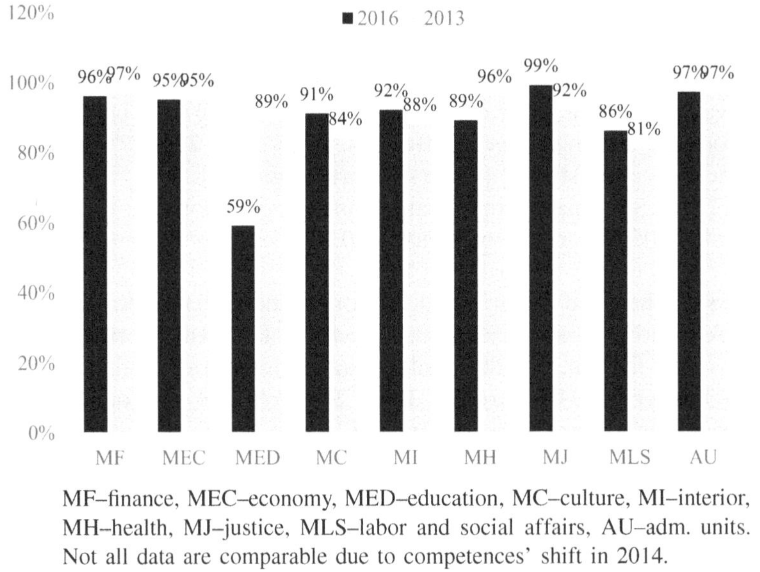

Fig. 10.1 Share of cases resolved within prescribed time limits, 2013 and 2016 (MPA [2018])

In order to overcome this problem—identified already in 2013—and for the government to adopt corrective measures, the MPA carried out the analysis also in September 2017 for 2016. The analysis led to administrative inspection controls, additional employment in problematic areas, and simplification of procedures under sector-specific acts (e.g., automatic calculation of social rights), but the results are yet to be seen and a new analysis should follow in about 2–3 years.

According to the analysis for 2016 and Fig. 10.2, most delays are recorded in social affairs and health care. The situation is improving in social affairs and in general, but deteriorating in particular in health care, which raises concern because of the sensitive position of the parties in such matters. Of the total 54,902 officially recorded backlogs in 2016 (129,739 in 2013), around 40% (and 69% in 2013) were recorded by the Ministry of Social Affairs, and 22% (from 6% in 2013) by the Ministry of Health, while other exposed sectors with exceeding timings are also construction licenses and taxation.

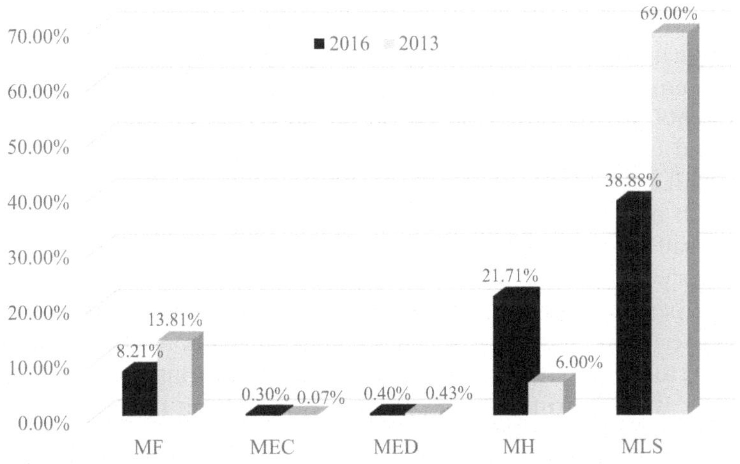

MF–finance, MEC–economy, MED–education, MH–health, MLS–labor and social affairs.

Fig. 10.2 Share of backlogs by ministries in total backlogs in 2013 and 2016 (MPA [2018])

Looking at the data by ministries for 2016 only, we note that the time limits are mostly exceeded in matters pertaining to the Ministry of Labour, Family, and Social Affairs (177,419 backlogs of the approx. 2 million cases in total). The backlogs are most evident in the social work centers, which are first instance authorities. In addition, there are even more backlogs at the same ministry when dealing with appeals, among these over 3000 appeals from 2015 not yet resolved in 2017! Most of these cases concern social rights, where the thresholds are already low and fast decision-making is of the utmost importance. Second is the Ministry of Finance with nearly 75,000 backlogs out of the approx. 3 million cases at the first instance and evident delays at the appellate instance. These data suggest that the ministries for social affairs and finance do not handle the quantity of cases attributed to them nor the appeals, since the number of backlogs in 2016 was higher than in the previous years. Third is the field of environment or construction (approx. 265,000 cases in total), closely followed by health care (almost 500,000 cases in total), recording over 20,000 backlogs at the first instance. Finances and the environment have been a problem for quite some time now, but things are getting better. Unfortunately, the opposite is true for socially deprived parties (Table 10.1).

Moreover, there are some other problematic sectors, such as access to information, since almost 40% of all appeals filed with the Information Commissioner were due to administrative silence (nearly 200 out of approx. 500 in 2016). Legislation on this subject has been in force since 2003 and one would expect administrative authorities to comply therewith (with a time limit of 20 working days to respond) more strictly over time with 67% of appeals in 2008 or 2009. Yet the unresponsiveness in almost half of the cases 14 years since the adoption of the law is not satisfactory.

A further issue opens up in relation to Art. 251 of GAPA in appellate procedures: If the appeal is justified, the appellate authority has the discretion to return the case for reconsideration to the first instance, given that the latter is closer to the parties and the case and can thus establish the facts more economically.[55] This can prolong the procedures or postpone

[55] However, the appellate decision is not a decision on the merits and the party needs to exhaust all legal remedies against the new administrative decision, if they wish to access to the court and succeed in claiming any violation, also of constitutional rights (case Up-114/97).

Table 10.1 Administrative statistics of delayed cases in 2016 by sector (MPA [2018])

Ministries and executive agencies within such	*First instance cases after prescribed time limit*	*Appeal cases unsolved in December 2016**
Environment	24,458	338
Interior	126	29
Foreign affairs	0	0
Justice	30	15
Education	5,414	80
Finance	74,796	4,301
Infrastructure	1,203	7
Health	20,830	121
Agriculture	2,214	265
Labour, family, social affairs	177,419	5,522
Economy	14,727	30
MPA	301	/
Culture	354	23
Outside ministries: AU	3,257	/
Outside ministries: Municipalities	21,588	41
All	**346,717**	**10,778**

*Not necessarily backlogs yet but likely to become such in the same percentage

administrative finality and, as a rule, the enforcement of the challenged initial decision. The same applies in an administrative dispute where the action does not stay the enforcement and the court may decide in cassation.[56] Therefore, in its report for 2017, the Slovenian Ombudsman suggested to the Ministry of Public Administration to amend GAPA so that the line ministries would be obliged to solve the appeals in administrative procedure on their own. A topic that also comes up in expert debates in this regard is the option of full jurisdiction as a rule instead

[56] More in Kerševan and Androjna (2017, pp. 588ff).

of cassation in the administrative dispute.[57] Yet data do not justify the proposed changes,[58] particularly considering the systemic function of the supervisory authority or the legal remedies. The role of the latter is in fact to supervise the legality of lower instance authorities and not to decide on the merits. If such decisions were delegated to a higher instance, the parties would be deprived of several levels of legal protection and the constitutional guarantees would be interfered with.[59]

In an administrative dispute, the time limit set by the Court Rules is six months. Data for the Administrative Court for 2018 show that it takes on average seven to eight months, more precisely, the solution is to be expected in 7.6 months from bringing action. A year before that, the expected time was only 5.3 months, but increased due to asylum-related cases. The time limit at the appellate Supreme Court raises more concern. For administrative matters, the average time limit in 2017 and 2018 was 13 months (although significantly less for other areas), which was nevertheless an improvement compared to 2016 when the time limit was 22 months. According to the EU Justice Scoreboard,[60] Slovenia is in the EU average as regards Administrative Court cases ranking 13th in the EU-25. Data for 2010–2016 indicate that on average, about 280 days are needed to solve administrative cases at the Administrative Court, and about 300 days at all instances. Here, Slovenia ranks 9th in the EU-25.

In such context, it is interesting that the parties usually—except in case of access to public information—rarely file appeals for administrative silence. Thus, the ministries record 0 to 10 appeals per year on such grounds, even if cases concern, e.g., investment in construction, where greater activity of the parties would be expected (e.g., only 9 appeals for administrative silence, and only 1 action before the court, out of the total 884 appeals in 2010). Between 150 and 250 requests for damages due to delays are filed, and in about one-third of the cases settlement is reached,

[57] Sever et al. (2016, p. 151).

[58] The report for 2016 (MPA 2018) reveals that the appeal was sustained and the case returned to the first instance in 2469 cases, the second instance authority decided on its own in 4205 cases, while in the remaining 24,059 cases the appeal was rejected or dismissed or the procedure was suspended. This means that a new procedure at the first instance occurs in only 8% of all appeals or 37% of sustained appeals.

[59] Cf. Šturm et al. (2011); comments to Art. 22, 23, 25, and 157.

[60] EC (2018, pp. 12ff); see particularly Figs. 10 and 11.

amounting to EUR 215–365,000 per year. Moreover, 30–40 constitutional complaints are filed every year to the Constitutional Court; as well as up to 10 for unreasonable time for decision and about 20 for inefficient legal remedies to the ECtHR. Typing the words "administrative silence" and similar into the search engine of the Constitutional Court, only 30 decisions are found between 1997 and 2018, of which one-third relates to constitutional review and two-thirds relate to individual constitutional complaints, with areas tackled such as construction permits, inspections, denationalization, citizenship, asylum, social affairs, etc.

10.8 Overall Assessment of the Legal Regime and Practice of Administrative Silence

It can be concluded that in some administrative areas in Slovenia, a systematic problem of exceeding the prescribed time limits is identified, and in some cases even unreasonably long decision-making. The questions are whether (i) the violation of the prescribed time limit is due to abuse of authority, or (ii) whether an actually unrealistic time limit has been set where sector-specific regulations do not regulate the specifics of their field, e.g., in case of a more demanding fact-finding and evidence-taking procedure which would require a generally longer period than two months set by GAPA. Based on the empirical data, we conclude, that it definitely depends on the administrative area as such, what is the reason and what would be the best solution for delays. For example in social affairs, as being evidently problematic in terms of deciding in reasonable time, we think option under (i) is relevant, i.e., a higher awareness of the line Ministry of the importance of decision-making on time and efficient, mostly organizational, measures taken to improve it.

The parties *rarely* take advantage of the possibility of appeal or court action, due to relatively small backlogs and probably because they are aware of their *subordinate* position in relation to the administration and hope that if they patiently wait for the decision, the latter will be more favorable. In addition to the said subjective reasons, there are increasing delays at higher instances, which reduce the effectiveness of this timeliness institution in practice.

In the case of Slovenia, there is a need to revisit the regulation of sector-specific acts and examine whether a certain relation needs to be regulated by administrative law at all (e.g., issuing permits for the implementation of activities, if ex-post control suffices), or it should be deregulated by legislator. Furthermore, if the matter is defined as administrative, the sector-specific act should take into account the specifics of the field first in prescribing a realistic time limit for decision at both instances, with due account of the complexity of the case, the necessary procedural actions, the obtainment of consents, etc. If a sudden liberalization seems too radical, or if empirical analyses show that the administration is evading its duties (e.g., as regards transparency), only then a separate act should provide for the legal fiction of positive silence. Additionally, the authorities should introduce various forms of system mediation, so that a dispute over inaction of the administration could be overcome by an agreement between the parties involved. Experience shows that such an approach eventually leads to greater direct efficiency of the administration, i.e., shorter procedures, fewer appeals, higher customer and employee satisfaction.

The institution of administrative silence is, at least in Slovenia, a corrective measure under GAPA that plays a role if and when the current government or line ministry strengthens its efforts to reduce backlogs, but does not have major consequences in the share of legal remedies used by the parties of the procedure. This means that the issue of delays can be much more efficiently resolved from top to bottom rather than from bottom to top, by prescribing realistic time limits and introducing organizational improvements. This is confirmed also in practice since the parties only seldom have recourse to appeal or court action, either because they are unaware thereof or they prefer to call on the first instance authority directly. Hence, empirical data in Slovenia do not provide a basis for the introduction of positive silence as a main legal fiction in GAPA. On the other hand, it seems reasonable to introduce legal fiction of positive silence to a limited extent in individual acts governing special rights, such as access to public information.

In order to ensure efficiency in administrative matters, it is imperative to ensure the accountability of the authorities. If one authority is inefficient, the whole vertical system becomes inefficient. Therefore, a lawful and timely proceeding is first expected by every official person authorized to conduct the procedure or carry out individual procedural actions. Next, the head of the competent authority must supervise the efficient organization and work of the official persons, which is why the head has *ex lege* a certain decision-making competence (Art. 28 and 320 of GAPA). In general, the line minister is accountable for efficiency in an individual field. Of course, the whole corpus of administrative authorities must work in concert since quite often the rights of individuals are linked to different authorities—if one authority proceeds as it should, but the other does not, the party is not granted their lawful rights. [61] In this sense, the results of the analysis serve as a call, primarily for the competent public administration coordinators to improve, *inter alia*, the system of administrative statistics. This should be done by introducing more relevant and comparable composite indicators and monitoring the entire public administration or at least the authorities that carry out most of their activities through measurable units. Administrative efficiency should stand for politically legitimate, professional and lawful, transparent and responsive action that focuses on areas that are essential for the public interest, always proportionately within the entire administrative and societal system.

References

Constitutional Court of the RS. (2018). http://www.us-rs.si/.

Cvetko, A. (1995). Še enkrat o molku organa [Once More on Administrative Silence]. *Podjetje in delo*, *21*(7), 985–995.

European Commission. (2018).*The 2018 EU Justice Scoreboard*. Luxembourg: Publications Office of the EU. https://ec.europa.eu/info/sites/info/files/justice_scoreboard_2018_en.pdf.

Galetta, D.-U., et al. (2015). *The General Principles of EU Administrative Procedural Law*. Brussels: European Parliament.

Hofstede, G., Hofstede, G. J., & Minkov, M. (2010). *Cultures and Organizations: Software of the Mind*. New York [etc.]: McGraw-Hill.

Jerovšek, T., & Trpin, G., et al. (2004). *Zakon o splošnem upravnem postopku s komentarjem* [GAPA with a Commentary]. Ljubljana: Institute for Public Administration & Nebra.

Kerševan, E., & Androjna, V. (2017).*Upravno procesno pravo* [Administrative Procedural Law]. Ljubljana: GV.

Kovač, P. (2011). Šutnja uprave između teorije i prakse u Sloveniji [Administrative Silence between Theory and Practice in Slovenia]. *ZbornikPravnogfakultetaSveučilišta u Rijeci*, *32*(2), 869–900.

[61] It needs to be noted that case law recognizes the correlation of cases, but assesses the effects for each case individually. For example, according to Supreme Court judgment I Up 1433/2002, 23 June 2005: "*Although the procedures are correlated, under the Slovenian GAPA with the fiction of negative decision, it cannot be considered that a preliminary request was granted – despite the fact that the same authority is competent for both cases.*"

Kovač, P. (2012). Fighting Administrative Silence in European and Slovene Law and praCtice. In D. C. Dragos, F. Lafarge, & P. Willemsen (Eds.), *PSG Law & PA: Proceedings*(pp. 79–106). Bucharest: Economică.
Kovač, P., et al. (2010). *Upravno-procesne dileme pri rabi ZUP* [Administrative-procedural Dilemmas in the Use of GAPA]. Ljubljana: Official Gazette of Republic of Slovenia.
Kovač, P., et al. (2012). *Upravno-procesne dileme pri rabi ZUP* [Administrative-procedural Dilemmas in the Use of GAPA]. Ljubljana: Official Gazette of Republic of Slovenia.
Kovač, P., et al. (2015). *Upravno-procesne dileme pri rabi ZUP* [Administrative-procedural Dilemmas in the Use of GAPA]. Ljubljana: Official Gazette of Republic of Slovenia.
Ministry of Public Administration (MPA). (2018). http://www.mju.
Ombudsman. (2018). *Varuh človekovih pravic*. http://www.varuh-rs.si/.
Pirnat, R. (2009). Molkorgana mora škodovatiorganu in ne stranki [Administrative Silence Must Harm the Authority not the Party]. *Pravna praksa, 28*(14), 3.
Remic, M., & Kovač, P. (2010). Storitvenanotranjemtrgu – fikcijapozitivneodločitvealikonkurenčnostposlovensko [Services in the Internal Market—Fiction of Positive Decision or Competitiveness in Slovenia]. *Pravna praksa, 29*(3–4), 6–8.
Sever, T. (2016). Conducting Procedures in Administrative Matters in Reasonable Time—Analysis of Selected Case Law by the European Court of Human Rights Versus Slovenia. *International Journal of Public Policy, 12*(3–6), 149–167.
Sever, T., Đanić, A., & Kovač, P. (2016). Effective Legal Protection Against the Excessive Length of Administrative Decision-Making: The Cases of Slovenia and Croatia. *The NISPAcee Journal, 9*(1), 135–166.
Sever, T., & Kovač, P. (2016). EU Principles as a Guide for Modelling Timely Administrative Procedures in Slovenia. *Netherlands Administrative Law Library*, http://www.nall.nl/tijdschrift/nall/2016/03/NALL-D-15-00007.pdf.
Šturm, L., et al. (2011). *Komentar Ustave RS* [Commentary on Constitution of the RS]. Brdo: Faculty of Government and EU Studies.
Supreme Court of the RS. (2018). https://www.sodnapraksa.si/.
Tratar, B. (2000). Varstvo pravic v upravnem postopku v primeru molka uprave [Protection of Rights in Administrative Procedure in Case of Silence]. *Dignitas, 5–6*, 213–227.

CHAPTER 11

Administrative Silence in Croatia: Between Fiction and Reality

Marko Šikić, Anamarija Musa, and Bosiljka Britvić Vetma

11.1 Introduction: The Background of Administrative Silence in Croatia

The timeliness of administrative procedure is a key prerequisite for the exercise of citizens' rights and for the fulfillment of their legal obligations. The inactivity of administration within a prescribed deadline is contrary to all principles of administrative procedure, because all these principles imply the activity and fulfillment of official duties of public authorities and their jurisdiction. It is clearly contrary to the principles of effectiveness

M. Šikić · A. Musa (✉)
Faculty of Law, University of Zagreb, Zagreb, Croatia
e-mail: amusa@pravo.hr

M. Šikić
e-mail: marko.sikic@pravo.hr

B. B. Vetma
Faculty of Law, University of Split, Split, Croatia
e-mail: bbritvic@pravst.hr

D. C. Dragos et al. (eds.),
The Sound of Silence in European Administrative Law,
https://doi.org/10.1007/978-3-030-45227-8_11

and efficiency which demand that public authorities conduct administrative procedures as simply as possible, without delays and at a low cost, but at the same time in a manner that enables all relevant facts and circumstances to be determined. This principle is clearly stated in Article 10 of the Croatian Law on General Administrative Procedure (hereinafter: LGAP).[1] Moreover, silence of administration violates the rule of law as the main principle of legal systems, which is also stated as a main value of the constitutional order in Croatia.[2] This is why modern administrative procedure legislation allows the parties to protect their rights not only against administrative decisions but also in cases of non-decisions—silence of administration. This is also the case with the Croatian LGAP which guarantees the right to legal remedy.[3]

In this paper, first we examine the issue of deadlines in administrative procedures, next we present the approach to silence of administration in the Croatian legal system, and then we provide an analysis of legal protection against silence of administration in second instance administrative procedures and before the court. In the final part, the issue of silence of administration in administrative procedures related to administrative justice cases and access to information cases is discussed, followed by an overall assessment.

The system of public administration and administrative law in Croatia—an EU member since 2013 and a post-socialist, transitional, and newly independent state (since 1991)—falls under the group of the German *Rechtsstaat* model. The regulation of administrative procedures and administrative disputes by general laws has been present since the 1920s, with the current regulation having been adopted in 2009 (Law on General Administrative Procedure, hereinafter: LGAP) and 2010 (Law on Administrative disputes, hereinafter: LAD)[4] within the reform of the public administration process which had been incentivized by the prospect of EU membership.

The Croatian administrative system consists of three main parts: state administration, territorial self-government (local and regional), and public

[1] Official Gazette 47/2009 (hereinafter the Official Gazette will be referred to as OG).

[2] Article 3 of the Constitution of the Republic of Croatia, OG 85/2010 (consolidated), 5/2014.

[3] Article 12 LGAP.

[4] OG 20/2010, 143/2012, 152/2014, 94/2016, 29/2017.

services. Currently, there are approximately 6000 public bodies at all levels in Croatia,[5] including approximately 130 bodies at the central level (35 state administrative organizations, 75 public agencies, 20 state bodies), 575 local and regional governments, approximately 4000 public institutions, 25 professional chambers, etc. Public tasks can be delegated to local government units and legal persons (agencies, public establishments, statutory or other associations, public companies, etc.)

The possibility to control any administrative act before the administrative judiciary is granted by Article 19§1 of the Constitution. The decisions of the public bodies (second instance and first instance, if the appeal is not allowed) as well as their general acts can be challenged in terms of legality before the four regional administrative courts and the High Administrative Court as the second administrative instance court. The two-tiered system of administrative judiciary has been in function since 2012, replacing the former one-tiered system inherited in 1991 from the previous system.

11.2 The Legal Framework of Administrative Timeliness

11.2.1 The Framework for Administrative Timeliness and Silence of Administration

In Croatia, legal protection against administrative silence has been developing for a long time—ever since the laws governing general administrative procedures in the Kingdom of Yugoslavia and Croatian Banovina were adopted in 1920 and 1930. However, since the regulation on legal protection against administrative silence in these laws suffered significant shortcomings, a better protection system only emerged in Socialist Yugoslavia with the adoption of the LAD of 1952 and the LGAP of 1956. These laws provided for legal protection against the silence of first instance and second instance bodies by applying a negative fiction system, which is legal protection based on the construction that a party may file an appeal in the administrative procedure "as if its application were rejected" or in other words, to initiate an administrative dispute "as if the appeal were rejected."

[5] For the types of public bodies, see Musa (2018, pp. 345–348).

After its independence in 1991, Croatia assumed the former federal LGAP and the LAD. In spite of some minor changes, there were no significant changes in the administrative silence protection system. Thus, it can be said that in Croatia a negative fiction system was applied and gradually developed from the mid-twentieth century up until 2009 when the current LGAP was brought, by which Croatia regulated the general administrative procedure as an independent state for the first time.[6] The 2009 LGAP was followed by the new LAD in 2010 (LAD), and the two new laws, together with a decrease in the number of special procedures, constitute the core of the administrative reform implemented in Croatia in the process of EU accession and democratic institutions building. In addition, the amendments of the Constitution in 2000 introduced the concept of the reasonable deadline in accordance with the European convention of human rights (*infra* 3.3.). This is the only mention of the timeliness of procedure (albeit not specifically administrative) in the Constitution. Moreover, in its Article 18 the Constitution specifically states that the right to appeal is granted against individual administrative acts, not mentioning situations where a decision is absent.

However, despite the introduction of some new important legal institutes, such as administrative contracts, legal protection against public administration bodies' conduct, objections, and one-stop shop, the new LGAP largely retained the structure of the former law, almost all of its principles, and a majority of the most important institutions. Along with the introduction of new institutions, the most significant difference between the earlier and the new LGAP is in the latter's length; it is almost half its length. The shortening of certain institutions contributed to the visibility and clarity of legal norms. Unfortunately, in some cases, it also led to ambiguity and legal gaps in the legal text.

The LGAP states, among its principles, in Article 10 a principle of efficiency and economy, demanding that the procedure is conducted "without delays," which is an addition compared to the former LGAP. The very institution of legal protection against administrative silence was retained in the new LGAP. In respect to its earlier organization, the institution has undergone certain changes, the most important of which is the abandonment of the earlier system of negative fiction and the introduction of a "neutral" approach that does not attach any meaning to

[6] See Koprić et al. (2017).

silence. Also, a provision on the application of a positive fiction system was introduced in the law's text.

11.2.2 Special Administrative Procedures

Before the adoption of the 2009 LGAP, the special administrative procedures dominated the administrative landscape. The reason was that the former LGAP was only subsidiary applicable, if otherwise not prescribed by a special law for the reasons of the necessity of the procedure. The incentive for a special regulation of certain administrative procedures gave rise to special administrative procedures. In the sole comprehensive analysis of special administrative procedures conducted in 2006 within a public administration reform project,[7] 65 special administrative procedures were identified. An additional analysis in 2010 claims that number of administrative procedures which deviate from the LGAP even increased to more than 100 by the time the new LGAP was adopted.[8]

The 2006 analysis has shown that a dozen laws significantly depart from the LGAP, such as the Customs Law, the General Tax Law, the Maritime Law, the Family Law, the Law on Constructions, the Law on Expropriation, the Law on Pension Insurance, and the Law on Health Insurance Other laws adjust the procedure to specific circumstances to a lesser degree (e.g., the Law on Environmental Protection, the Law on Railways, the Law on Electronic Media). One of the main departing elements in the special procedures is a special regulation of the deadlines for the issuing of decision.

In the attempt to ensure the consistent implementation of the general administrative law, the new LGAP has abandoned the de facto principle of subsidiary application and prescribed in Article 3 its implementation in all administrative matters. While the specific elements of the administrative procedure may be regulated differently by law, it is necessary for adjudicating in individual administrative fields, provided that it is not contrary to the basic provisions and the purpose of the LGAP. However, despite the new principle, the special regulation of particular issues of administrative procedure is fairly widespread.

[7] For detailed list see Ljubanović (2006).

[8] Cf. Ljubanović (2010) and Koprić et al. (2016).

11.3 The Length of Administrative Procedures

11.3.1 The Length of Deadlines in General Law and in Special Laws

The general deadlines for issuing an administrative decision in the *first instance* are prescribed by Article 101 of the LGAP. Depending on the type of the procedure, the public authority has to decide in the matter "without delay," within maximum time limit of 30, in case of direct adjudication,[9] or 60 days, when conducting an investigatory procedure.[10] Moreover, the time limit incorporates the obligation to issue and deliver a decision to parties, which, in combination with relatively short deadlines counted in calendar days, creates a pressure for the public authority to act efficiently and speedily.

In *the appeal procedure*, the general deadline for issuing a second instance decision is 60 days, but the appellate authority is required to issue a decision "as soon as possible."[11]The LGAP allows for a shorter deadline to be set by a special law. However, given the fact that the appeal is submitted through the first instance authority (which examines the formalities of appeal and reconsiders the substantive part, and then forwards it along with the case to the appellate body), and that the decision upon appeal has to be sent by the second to the first instance body which then has to deliver the decision to the parties, it leaves not much time for the second instance body to complete the procedure and deliver the decision within the deadline.[12] Thus, relatively short deadlines in both instances of general administrative procedure may be a cause for significant delays in administrative decision making.

[9] In situations when facts are determined or known or when the reasons of urgency require such a procedure, see Articles 48–50 LGAP.

[10] It has to be conducted whenever it is necessary to determine the facts and circumstances relevant for the clarification of the legal situation, or when two or more parties with opposing interests participate in the procedure, see Articles 51–57 LGAP.

[11] Article 121 LGAP.

[12] For example, the State Public Procurement Appeal Commission states in its annual reports that the average time for the appeal decision in 2016 was 34 days, and 38 days in 2015, slightly beyond the statutory deadline (30 days). However, it also states that the average time for a decision, after the file has been completed (data from the first instance body received) was 11 days.

Compared to the general deadlines regime determined by the LGAP, for some special administrative procedures *shorter or longer deadlines*[13] are prescribed, usually counted in months.[14] Included the group of laws that prescribe shorter deadlines are, for example, the Law on Civil Servants, the Law on the Right of Access to Information (*infra* 6.1) other Law on Agriculture, etc. On the other hand, longer deadlines are prescribed in more complex cases: six months for issuing a decision on international protection on the request[15]; four months for the evaluation of the environmental impact and six months for the environmental permit[16]; six months for the decision on work ability or disability[17]; four months for the decision on the dispute between operators[18]; three months for the decision on the recognition of a foreign professional qualification[19]; etc.

The *prolongation of deadlines* for issuing a decision in the administrative procedure is not envisaged in the LGAP, but some special laws enable public bodies to prolong(an already prolonged) deadline in exceptional circumstances[20] or if there are justified reasons, but for 1 month at the most.[21]

11.3.2 Counting Deadlines

In comparison with the former LGAP which prescribed the deadlines in months, the deadlines in first instance procedures are counted in calendar days. This change in the approach may be considered as fairer and contributing to the procedural equality of the parties, especially given the fact that months have an unequal number of days, which led to different positions depending on which month the request is submitted in.[22] On

[13] The previous LGAP allowed only the prescription of shorter deadlines.

[14] Cf. Šikić et al. (2011) and Ljubanović (2010).

[15] The express procedure requires 2 months. See Articles 40§1 and 41§1 of the Law on International and Temporary protection (Law on Asylum).

[16] Articles 88 and 99§3 of the Law on the Environmental Protection.

[17] Article 59 of the Law on Pension Insurance.

[18] Article 20 of the Law on Electronic Communication.

[19] Article 19§1 of the Law on Regulated Professions.

[20] Article 20§4 of the Law on Electronic Communications.

[21] Article 19§1 of the Law on Regulated Professions.

[22] Cf. Šikić (2013).

the other hand, the deadlines are not interrupted by non-working days (holidays, Sundays), but if the final day falls on a non-working day, the deadline expires the following working day.[23] Moreover, in cases when the deadlines are determined in months, such as in the cases of some special procedures or appeal procedures, the deadlines are counted in months.

The deadlines for issuing (and delivering) a decision begin from the day the public authority has received an orderly application from the party.[24] Thus, the LGAP prescribes the deadline for issuing a decision only for procedures initiated by the party, departing from the former LGAP which required that the deadlines for issuing a decision are applied also to the ex officio procedure, if such a procedure is in the interest of the party. This change of approach might be considered as a step back in legal certainty and legal protection.[25]

11.3.3 The Concept of Reasonable Deadline

The general and special procedural provisions related to the timeliness of administrative decisions do not refer to reasonable deadlines. Instead, expressions such as "without delay" (for the first instance decision and delivery)[26] or "as soon as possible" (for the decision on an appeal)[27] are used for the purpose of speeding up the procedure, but only within a prescribed maximum deadline.

However, the concept of reasonable time became embedded in the Croatian legal doctrine by means of the legal institute of the right to trial within a reasonable time. This institute found its application in Croatia from the moment the European Convention of Human Rights and its Article 6, the right to fair trial, had started to bound Croatia in 1997. From that moment on, intense legislative activity began which sought to protect Croatian citizens from unreasonably long deadlines in the resolution of judicial proceedings.[28] Through amendments to the Constitution

[23] Article 81 LGAP.

[24] Article 40§2 LGAP.

[25] Cf. Šikić et al. (2011).

[26] Articles 101§1 and 97§3 LGAP.

[27] Article 101 LGAP.

[28] Cf. Šikić (2013, p. 458) and Šikić (2010, pp. 96–99).

from 2000, the right to trial within a reasonable time was introduced as a constitutional right[29] in the Croatian legal system. Furthermore, Article 63§1 of the Constitutional Law on the Constitutional Court[30] stipulates that the Constitutional Court will initiate proceedings with a constitutional complaint, among others, before the legal remedy is exhausted in the event of the court not bringing a decision within a reasonable time on a party's rights or obligations or on their suspicion and/or accusation of a criminal offense. Article 27 of the Law on Judiciary[31] prescribes a party's right to trial within a reasonable time. Within the context of the presented assertions, it is important to note that the 2010 LAD is imbued through the principle of efficiency stated in Article 8 requiring the Administrative Court to conduct the administrative dispute quickly and without delay thus avoiding unnecessary costs, to prevent the abuse of rights of parties and other participants in the dispute, and to bring the decision within a reasonable time.

The aforementioned rules for the right to a fair trial include the standards of realization of one's rights before an independent and impartial tribunal, with the obligation to conduct a fair trial that will end within a reasonable time. The standards (criteria) set by the European Court to determine the term "reasonable time" were accepted by the Constitutional Court, by regular and specialized courts, and by the Supreme Court of the Republic of Croatia when they became competent to provide protection in this type of proceedings. The court judges all these criteria at the same time and considers their effect on the duration of the procedure. The European Court's first judgment finding a violation of the European Convention for the Protection of Human Rights by the Republic of Croatia was passed in 2001,[32] and it had to do with a violation of the right to trial within a reasonable time.

[29] Everyone has the right to an independent and impartial court established by law which fairly and within a reasonable time brings a decision on their rights or obligations, or on their suspicion and/or accusation of a criminal offense (Article 29§1 of the Constitution).

[30] OG 99/1999, 29/2002, 49/2002.

[31] OG 28/2013, 33/2015, 82/2015, 82/2016, 67/2018.

[32] The cases Rajak v. Croatia, ECHR no. 49,706/99 [2001]; Horvat v. Croatia ECHR 51585/99 [2001] have had significant effect on the development of the legal framework on the reasonable time.

From the onset of its decision making in this type of proceedings, in general the Supreme Court tied the beginning of the consideration period for the violation of a party's right to a trial within a reasonable time to when a suit was filed with to the administrative court. However, in the last decade the Constitutional Court, by harmonizing the interpretation of the application of the right to trial within a reasonable time in proceedings conducted in administrative matters with the practice of the European Court of Human Rights,[33] took a stand on the terms for protection relating to the legally relevant period for the assessment of the right to trial within a reasonable time; as such, in this period of time it covers not only the length of the administrative dispute proceedings, but also the administrative procedure before the competent administrative body.[34] This position affected the Supreme Court's reasoning in the subsequent cases.

As pointed out by legal scholars,[35] determining the general meaning of the term "reasonable time" in resolving all administrative matters because of their specificity and diversity does not yield results; timely resolution is most often ensured by setting specific deadlines for resolving these issues in certain administrative matters, which are then tailored to the specifics in these areas.

However, resolving administrative and judicial matters within deadlines and within a reasonable time remains a challenging task for Croatian public administration and administrative judiciary. According to the EU Justice Scoreboard 2018,[36] Croatia has the 6th largest caseload among EU countries (despite being the champion in number of judges), and when it comes to the length of administrative proceedings, Croatia is 6th among EU countries, although a decrease has been recorded from the period of 2010, when Croatia came 4th.

[33] There were several ECHR judgments related the issue of reasonable time: Počuča v. Croatia ECHR no. 38550/02 [2006]; Božić v. Croatia ECHR no. 22457/02 [2006]; Vajagić v. Croatia ECHR no. 30431/03 [2006].

[34] Cf. Constitutional Court, Decision and Judgment U-IIIA-4885/2005 of 20 June 2007.

[35] Cf. Đerđa (2013, p. 4).

[36] European Commission (2018, pp. 11–12).

11.4 Responses to Administrative Silence

11.4.1 From Negative Fiction to Neutral Position

The protection against administrative silence system, which is based on the *principle of negative fiction* and had been implemented in Croatian law for over half a century, on the whole was deemed to be quite high quality.[37] However, despite such a long period of validity based on the same protection system, in legal practice (of both public administration bodies and administrative courts) legal provisions have often been misunderstood, whereby the starting point for such erroneous interpretations was most often due to an insufficient understanding of the negative fiction system.[38] At the same time, particular laws envisaged the application of positive fiction.

The new 2009 LGAP departs from the negative fiction system, no longer attributing meaning to a failure to act. Rather, silence is simply considered a procedural prerequisite for filing an appeal, or for initiating an administrative dispute.[39] Such a *"neutral" approach* to administrative silence enables parties legal protection: following the silence (inaction) of a first instance body, a party may file an appeal with the second instance body, and in cases of silence on the behalf of bodies against whose administrative acts an appeal cannot be filed or in cases of silence on the behalf of second instance bodies, it is possible to seek legal protection through an administrative dispute.[40] This way, incorrect interpretations of legal provisions which result from a misunderstanding of the system of negative fiction are avoided. Also, in the new 2010 LAD, this new direction in the organization of administrative silence was recognized (*infra* 6).

Application (Request) of a Party as a Condition for Silence

Administrative silence is explicitly restricted to procedures based on application of the party and, in contrast to the former LGAP, may not be

[37] Šikić (2006, 2008).

[38] Cf. Šikić (2008, 2010, 2013); Šikić et al. (2011).

[39] Such a protection system was introduced by the world's first codification of the administrative procedure, the Austrian General Administrative Procedure Act of 1925. According to it, the protection of citizens was provided only against the silence of first-degree bodies, because after the expiry of the six-month application deadline parties could request a transfer to a hierarchically more competent authority.

[40] Article 101§3 LGAP.

applied in cases where the procedure is instituted ex officio.[41] This position is even more visible in the case of the silence of second instance bodies, since the prerequisite for the failure to act of the appeal body is the submission of an appeal by a party.[42]

Legal Character of Prescribed Deadlines

Compared to the preclusive deadline for lodging an appeal against the decision of a first instance body (in general 15 days from the day of the reception of the decision, if the special law does not prescribe a longer deadline),[43] deadlines for issuing a decision in first instance or second instance procedures are instructive—they do not automatically result in consequences, and the public body may issue a decision well beyond the deadline. However, an omission to issue a decision gives the party the possibility to lodge an appeal against silence of administration or initiate an administrative dispute, which the party may or may not use. In comparison with the procedural deadlines which are official deadlines, the deadlines to issue a decision are statutory deadlines.

11.4.2 A Tale of Positive Fiction

As a strict exception to the fundamentally neutral concept of legal protection against administrative silence, the new LGAP introduces a concept of ***positive fiction***: When so prescribed by a special law, the party's request is considered to have been adopted if the body in the proceedings initiated by formal request on the behalf of the party in which it is directly authorized to resolve the administrative matter does not issue a resolution within the prescribed deadline.[44] It follows that the application of positive fiction is limited in relation to several elements. Namely, the legislator provides the possibility of applying positive fiction only in cases where it is prescribed by some (more than one hundred) special laws regulating administrative proceedings. Given that the application of positive fiction was enabled by special laws before the LGAP's entry into force (and is further expected to be applied), the legislator has actually only recognized

[41] Articles 101 and 102 LGAP.

[42] Article 119§1 LGAP.

[43] Article 109 LGAP.

[44] Article 102§1 LGAP.

this fact and has decided to set the guidelines and limits of this standardization through the LGAP as a general law. Secondly, the possibility of occurrence through a positive act only applies to orderly requests on the behalf of a party. Thirdly, the application of positive fiction is limited by the fact that it is tied only to direct adjudication (applicable in simpler cases) and therefore positive fiction is not possible if investigatory procedures are carried out. Given the fact that positive fiction is envisaged in only few cases its application is extremely limited,[45] which is highlighted by the facts that administrative proceedings are long-lasting and that the widespread use of positive fiction in practice could cause adverse effects.

Additionally, the party has the right to request the body to issue a decision establishing that the party's request has been adopted and it is obliged to issue such a decision within eight days.[46] Legal theory states that this is a declarative act by which the authority establishes that the legal deadlines for the decision have expired, and that due to this, by force of law, the party's request was adopted.[47] In this way, it tries to eliminate the legally insecure situation in which the party finds itself. However, imposing the obligation (and deadline) on the public authority to issue such a decision brings up the problem of the disruption of public interest and objective legal certainty, especially if any (even a completely unfounded and unlawful) request on the behalf of the party, solely because of the fact that the legal deadlines have expired, in addition to the legal fiction itself, would be additionally confirmed by the public authority by issuing an administrative act.[48] The LGAP also applies a similar technique in situations where more than one body is involved in administrative matters and then prescribes that in cases when one of the public authorities involved, within the prescribed period of 30 days, does not decide on a request for consent, confirmation, approval or opinion, it shall be considered that such an act was issued in favor of the party.[49]

[45] In Article 25§8 of the Law on the civil society associations regarding the registration of the association (OG 74/2014, 70/2017); Articles 10§9 and 19§3 of the Law on regulated professions in relation to the recognition of professional qualifications (OG 82/2015), Article 8§3 of the Law on establishments in relation to the eligibility of the founding act (OG 76/1993, 29/1997, 47/1999, 35/2008), and few others.

[46] Article 102§2 LGAP.

[47] See Šikić (2010) and Šikić et al. (2011).

[48] Cf. Šikić (2010).

[49] Article 21 LGAP.

It follows that though the positive fiction system, the LGAP intends to resolve the situations involving a delay in the decision making, which is expected to have a positive effect on administrative action itself.

11.5 Supervision of Administrative Timeliness: Legal Remedies

11.5.1 Appeal Against the Silence of Administration

Appeal against the silence of first instance administrative bodies has its own specifics that are quite different from appeals against administrative acts. An appeal filed due to administrative silence may also be directly submitted to the second instance body[50] thus departing from the rule that an appeal must be submitted to the first instance body which in appeal proceedings has extensive competence in regards to appeals. This option has been standardized so that parties, justifiably doubting the ability of first instance bodies to decide within a reasonable time, could "skip" the first instance bodies and directly seek protection from the supervising body.

The processing of appeals filed against administrative silence is regulated in Article 119 of the LGAP, and may be assessed as relatively purely regulated institute.[51] The second instance body, upon receiving the appeal against the silence of a first instance body, demands to know the reasons why the decision was not issued within the deadline. These reasons, of course, can be very different, and the appellate body's task is to evaluate them and decide whether they warrant neglecting the deadline for bringing a decision (justified reasons include the exceptional complexity of the subject itself which requires the submission of a large amount of evidence, the hearing of witnesses that are absent at the time, the fault of the party, etc.)[52] or whether they unjustifiably neglected the deadline (ex. officials taking vacation leave). Depending on whether the appellate body determines that the reasons for silence are justified or not, the consequences can be different: in the first case, it can award the first instance body a new deadline of 30 days, and in the second case, the second instance body can resolve the administrative matter itself or order

[50] Article 110 § 1 LGAP.

[51] Cf. Šikić (2009a).

[52] Cf. Šikić (2013) and Šikić and Staničić (2009).

the first instance body to bring the requested decision within 15 days. However, when administrative silence—which is an unlawful silence—is unjustified, instead of two equal alternatives it would be more efficient and logical to prescribe (based on the earlier LGAP) the second instance body's obligation to simply bring a decision—with the exceptional possibility, if it is deemed to be quicker and more economical, to order the first instance body to carry out all or some of the proceedings. Namely, if the second instance body decides to order the first instance body to resolve the matter (it has the right to file an appeal against the decision) the party can rightfully have concerns about deadlines and the outcome of the proceedings.

The second instance body is limited by the deadline—it is obliged to bring a decision on the appeal and to deliver it to the party through the first instance body as soon as possible and no later than 60 days from the date of the filing of an orderly appeal, with the possibility that a deadline of less than 60 days may be prescribed for a decision on an appeal through a special law. If the appellate body does not issue (and deliver) a decision on the appeal within a deadline, the party may initiate an administrative dispute.

11.5.2 Legal Remedies: Judicial Protection

The system of administrative justice has undergone a thorough reform through the adoption of the 2010 LAD (in force since 1 January 2012)—the subject of the administrative dispute has been expanded (to general normative acts among other things); the previous one-tiered court model has been replaced by a two-tiered model; mandatory public hearings have been introduced; administrative courts have become courts of full jurisdiction; etc. Legal protection against administrative silence has also been altered and aligned with the reform that affected administrative procedures, i.e., with the fact that protection against administrative silence is no longer based on negative fiction.[53]

Among other things, also encompassed in administrative disputes, is the assessment of the legality of the failure of administrative bodies to,

[53] See Đerđa and Šikić (2012), Musa (2014), and Koprić et al. (2017).

within the legally prescribed deadline, decide on the party's right, obligation or legal interest or its regular legal remedy.[54] The matter at hand is the failure to bring a decision within the statutory deadlines i.e., administrative silence. Even protection by the LAD is no longer based on a feigned negative act (as was the earlier LAD); rather, it simply bases protection against silence as a prerequisite for initiating an administrative dispute.[55] The LAD enables legal protection against silence in the procedure initiated by a request of the party if the appeal is not allowed (first instance) and by an appeal (second instance). Furthermore, the LAD also enables legal protection due to the widespread inactivity of public authorities. Namely, protection is also made possible for the purpose of evaluating the legality of the failure of public sector bodies in the field of administrative law to act in accordance with the regulation within the statutory deadline, that is, in cases where no administrative procedure is conducted that could result in individual administrative act (e.g., failure to issue a decision on objection against other administrative action).[56]

An administrative silence lawsuit is to be filed to the court eight days after the expiry of the prescribed time limit at the earliest, which means that the lawsuit can be filed up until the moment the individual decision is brought or the public authority has proceeded.[57] In contrast to the former LAD which prescribed the obligation for the party to send a rush note to the administrative body, the new LAD determines an additional deadline which further prolongates the decision-making process. Among other reasons, the court will have to dismiss the lawsuit if it is filed prematurely, as well as in cases where the party did not use regular legal remedies in the administrative procedure.[58]

In addition, the defendant—public body that failed to decide or act—must be given the opportunity to respond to the lawsuit within a period of no less than 30 days or no more than 60 days. This long timeframe adds to the already prolonged administrative procedure but also allows the administrative body to decide on the matter, meaning that the dispute has the role of a reminder to action. If the defendant fully proceeds in

[54] Article 3§1/3 LAD.

[55] Staničić et al. (2017, p. 42) and Šikić (2009b).

[56] Cf. Đerđa and Šikić (2012, pp. 90–91, 94); Articles 122, 155 and 156 LGAP.

[57] Staničić et al. (2017, pp. 89–92), Article 24§2 LAD.

[58] Article 30 LAD.

accordance with the claim over the course of the dispute by bringing a decision or acting in accordance with the regulation, the court suspends the administrative dispute and the plaintiff (a party in the administrative procedure) will have the opportunity to initiate the dispute against the now available decision.

If the court decides that the reasons for the administrative silence are justified (i.e., that the claim is unfounded), the court would have to reject the claim.[59] The legal theory claims that, given the particularities of administrative silence, it would be more appropriate to dismiss the lawsuit because rejecting a claim leads to a situation in which parties, should public authorities continue to use delay tactics (now perhaps unjustifiably), would no longer be able to initiate an administrative dispute because of the concept of *res judicata*.[60] If the court finds that the reasons for administrative silence are unjustified, it will adopt the claim and resolve the matter itself, i.e., decide with full jurisdiction,[61] unless this is impossible due to the nature of the matter or the defendant has settled at his own discretion. It would then order the defendant to bring a decision and set an appropriate deadline.

Failure to comply with court judgments represents an even more serious form of disobedience on the behalf of public authorities and an even greater problem for the functioning of the rule of law.[62] In Article 81, the LAD prescribes that the execution of the judgment must be ensured by the defendant i.e., the authority competent for the execution who are required to comply with the judgment at the latest within 60 days of the date of the final judgment whereby he is bound to legal considerations and court observations. If the judgment is not executed in time (or contrary to its contents), the plaintiff is allowed to request the execution of a judgment. The LAD also makes it possible to impose fines on the head of the public authority that did not ensure the execution of the verdict. Also, due to damage caused by failure to execute or an improper execution of the verdict in an administrative dispute, the plaintiff has the right to a remedy that is pursued before the competent court.

[59] Article 57 LAD.

[60] Staničić et al. (2017, p. 96).

[61] Article 58§3 LAD.

[62] In its decision Hornby vs Greece (1997), the ECHR connected the execution of the court decisions with the right to fair trial.

11.5.3 Other Forms of Legal Protection Against Administrative Silence

Other forms of legal protection against administrative silence include legal protection in the process of *issuing certificates*—if the public authority, at the request of the party, does not issue a certificate on the facts on which the official records are kept, or fails to bring and deliver a decision rejecting the request, or does not issue an amended certificate, an appeal can be filed.[63] The same mechanism is also applied to for the issue of factual evidence on which no official records are kept, in which case the deadline is 30 days.[64]

As a special form, the LGAP also regulates the possibility of legal protection against the inactivity of public administration in the institute of *information on the conditions for the protection and fulfillment of rights*.[65] This is not an administrative procedure, rather a situation where an interested person, before the administrative procedure, is considering whether to initiate it. In the case of a written notice, within 15 days a complaint may be filed as a remonstrative remedy, by which the head of the body brings a decision within 15 days. This situation is an expression of legitimate expectations, which although not explicitly mentioned as one of LGAP's principles, is established as a principle of the Croatian legal order in the decision of the Constitutional Court.[66]

The possibility of ombudsman protection is recognized widely—anyone can complain to an ombudsman on the grounds of infringements of one's rights,[67] but in substance it is limited due to the ombudsman's non-binding decisions. The ombudsman acts by seeking an explanation and recommending the remedying of the maladministration. According

[63] Article 159 LGAP.

[64] Article 160 LGAP.

[65] Article 155 LGAP.

[66] Decision No. U-IIIB /4366/2005, 5 April 2006. The Constitutional Court accentuated the principles of legal certainty and the related principle of protecting the legitimate expectations of the parties in the proceedings in which they decide on their rights and obligations as the core constituents of the rule of law and the respect of human rights, which are the highest values of the constitutional order of the Republic of Croatia.

[67] Article 93 of the Constitution and the Law on Ombudsman, OG 76/2012.

to the annual reports of the Ombudsman,[68] the long duration of administrative procedures, especially in relation to tax matters, civil service status and social care, is one of the key challenges for the effective exercise of citizens' rights. However, the ombudsman underlines that citizens are not aware of their right to initiate an administrative dispute, which points to the more general problem of citizens' awareness and civic education, as well as the service orientation of administration.

11.6 The Practice of Silence–Some Empirical Evidence

The absence of official statistical or analytical data on administrative proceedings in Croatia in general, and timeliness and administrative silence in particular, is striking. Quite some time has passed since the Ministry of Administration ceased to collect information on "administrative" and "non administrative" proceedings in public administration. Official data can only be found in the reports of some public authorities, with the data not being presented in a unified manner (even from the same body in different years). For example, data on the decisions of certain state offices (first instance administrative bodies in regions) shows that in the State administration office in the Sisacko-Moslavacka County 12.15—15.53% of cases in 2017 were solved beyond the deadline, with most cases being in the area of free legal aid, agriculture, tourism and proprietary rights. Similarly, in the Medjimurska County in 2015, 255 out of 4781 cases (5.33%) were closed after the deadline with an additional 590 cases still opened after the expiration of the deadline out of total of 5787 cases (10.2%).[69]

In sum, the administrative policy is not based on the extensive data on administrative proceedings which would reveal the key issues, allow the policy makers and the theory to draw conclusions on the justifications of certain legal solutions, and indicate the need for improvements in the law or practice.[70] However, in order to assess at least some aspects of

[68] Annual reports of the Ombudsman are accessible here: http://ombudsman.hr/hr/izvjesca-hr.

[69] http://www.udu-mz.hr/?gid=52&aid=341.

[70] However, the attempts of the central administration to introduce the unique IT system for documenting the administrative procedures might become a platform for data collection in the near future.

the incidence of administrative silence in Croatia, the data on the specific administrative procedure of access to information and the data obtained from the administrative courts are presented.

11.6.1 Access to Information and Silent Administration

The right of access to information is exercised in a special administrative procedure which is regulated by the Law on the right of access to information (LRTI).[71] Compared to the general procedure regime, which applies insofar other regulated by the LRTI, it is expected that citizens' requests for access to information are dealt with in a speedy and less formalized manner, with an effective, efficient and independent protection mechanism. In comparison with the general regime, among other specificities of the procedure,[72] there are several key differences in relation to timeliness of the procedure. First, the deadlines are significantly shorter in both instances—15 days for deciding on the request in first instance procedures (compared to 30 and 60 days in general procedures), with the possibility of prolongation (not envisaged in the general regime) by additional 15 days in strictly prescribed cases[73]; in second instance procedures, the Information Commissioner has 30 days to decide on the appeal (compared to 60 days in general procedures), with two special deadlines of 60 days (if the public interest test has to be performed) and 90 days (if the opinion of the Office of the National Security Council has to be obtained).[74] The second difference, which is expected to shorten the procedure overall, is that administrative disputes are solved before the High Administrative Court, the second instance administrative judicial authority. Thirdly, in comparison with the LAD which does not prescribe the deadlines for judicial decisions, the LRTI obliges the Court to decide within a 90-day deadline.

As shown in Table 11.1, more than 90% (92–96%) of all requests for information are decided by public bodies within the deadline, with

[71] OG 25/2013, 85/2015; See Musa (2018).

[72] E.g., formal decision is not required if the right is granted, etc. See Ofak (2016).

[73] Article 20§1 and Article 22§2 LRTI; Prolongation is possible if the information has to be sought outside the seat of the authority; in case of voluminous requests; if it is necessary to ensure the completeness and correctness of information; if public interest test has to be performed.

[74] Article 25§3,5,6 LRTI.

Table 11.1 Silence of administration in first instance procedures on access to information

	1st instance cases					*Appeals*			
Year	*Requests (No.)*	*Adopted requests—information disclosed*[a]	*Requests not adopted (eligible for appeal)*[b]	*Requests decided within deadline (%)*	*Cases pending after the deadlines have expired*	*Total number of appeals*	*Appeals against silence of administration (SoA)*	*Share of SoA appeals in the total number of appeals (%)*	*Share of SoA in relation to cases closed after expiration of deadlines (%)*
2013	24.330	23.852 (82.57%)	5.035	96.64	815	515	331	64.27	40.61
2014	21.078	19.299 (88.27%)	1.789	92.80	1314	658	400	60.79	30.44
2015	18.007	15.428 (84.46%)	2.401	93.55	1123	624	402	64.42	35.80
2016	17.059	15.797 (91.10%)	3.274	95.25	795	635	384	60.47	48.30
2017	22.226	17.444 (82.94%)	3.785	94.95	1063	1172	498	42.49	46.85

Source Information Commissioner's Annual Reports for 2018, 2017, 2016, 2015, 2014, 2013 (www.pristupinfo.hr)
[a]includes requests from previous year
[b]Total number includes partially adopted requests, refused requests, dismissed requests, pending cases, suspended cases, and cases in which the public authority issued a notice (information not available)

approximately 1000 requests reported annually(800–1500 cases per year) as being delayed and qualifying as silence of administration. Slightly less than half of these cases do actually get before the Commissioner through an appeal against silence of administration (46–48%). However, silence of administration appeals still composes a significant share of all appeals before the Commissioner, indicating the importance of this problem among first instance bodies—64.27% of all appeals in 2013 to 42.49% of all appeals in 2017 were filed due to silence, with approximately 330–500 cases of silence being appealed to per year.

With regard to second instance procedures, an indicator of the timeliness may be found in data on the appeals received by the Information Commissioner (IC) in 2017.[75] Out of 1178 appeals before the Commissioner in 2017, 624 were lodged against decisions on refusal or dismissal by first instance bodies (52.3%). Out of 575 appeals on decisions on refusal of the request by the first instance bodies, the IC found in 379 cases that the appellant was right and annulled the decision and the case was returned to the first instance body (240 cases) or the IC decided on the case *in meritum* (139). In sum, when the suspectable data is removed, there were 363 cases where the citizens were right when seeking the protection of their rights. Out of 363 cases, 147 were supposed to be decided upon within 30 days (40.46%), and 216 within 60 days (59.50%).

The average duration was 101 days in the first group, and 9447 days in the second group, ranging from 1 day to 422 and 433 days.[76] Only 40 cases in the 30-day group and 105 cases in the 60-day group were solved within the time limit, making only 39.94% of all cases resolved within the statutory deadline. Out of the rest of the 60% of the late cases, 93 were solved within 30 days after the expiration of the deadline (25.62% of all cases), and 81 were not solved within 100 days of the expiration of the deadline (22.32% of all cases). This data indicates that the IC manages to decide on appeals within the statutory deadline in only 2/5 of the cases, and that every fourth to fifth user (whose appeal is grounded) will have to wait for the decision 100 days or more upon the expiration of the deadline for the decision.

[75] The data retrieved from the Office of the Information Commissioner.

[76] The beginning date is the date of the receipt of the appeal in the Office of the Commissioner, the end date is the date of the decision (delivery, which also has to be included in the deadline, is not included because data is not available).

The reasons for the striking delays in the appellate procedure are the well-known low capacity of the Commissioner to deal with the constantly increasing number of appeals, but also in the procedural shortcomings in practice: public authorities' delays in sending the files and information that is sought by the requestor, and in responding to the Commissioner's letters. Some cases also contain a large piece of information, which has to be thoroughly examined. Moreover, if the appeal is sent to the Commissioner, it has to be redirected to the first instance body which has to follow the procedural steps prescribed by the LGAP. Moreover, the majority of the appeals are being submitted directly to the Commissioner, which significantly slows down the procedure.

Although the Commissioner frequently remains silent, the appellants do not always use the possibility to institute an administrative dispute. Roughly, if the conditions for a dispute emerged in 117 cases with 30 days deadline and 109 cases with 60 days deadline, meaning that the users may have lodged a complaint against the Commissioner's silence in at least 226 cases (not counting the cases when the first instance decision was upheld), the number of 40 silence disputes (out of 175 total disputes) shows that the appellants will use this instrument in approximately 17.7% of cases.

The access to information data points to the various reasons for the delays in administrative procedure, ranging from the incapacity of administrative authorities (at both levels), to overburdening with requests/appeals in the specific period (e.g., beginning of summer holidays), to technical reasons (poor records management). Sometimes, the bodies delay the procedure on purpose, in order to avoid disclosing information that can lead to reputational damage. The duration of the procedure may work as a deterrent to the use of the LRTI by users, especially journalists. However, it remains that 15-day deadlines (counting calendar days) for the first instance decision and 30-day deadlines for the second instance decision are not always sufficient to decide on the right of the user in the current circumstances, at least not in 3–8% of cases at the first instance or 60% of cases in the second instance. The delays and silence, as a result, lower the trust in both public administration and the protection authorities.

11.6.2 When the Silence Is Brought to Court

Administrative disputes against the failure of administrative bodies to issue a decision within a prescribed time are solved by the four first instance regional administrative courts (in Zagreb, Split, Rijeka and Osijek), while in some specific cases (such as in cases of access to information, some competition or electronic communications cases) administrative disputes in the first instance are solved by the second instance High Administrative Court.

In order to assess the prevalence of the administrative silence that ends up before administrative courts, the data on the administrative courts' cases in the period from 2015 to 2017 was collected (the number of all opened and closed cases, the number of administrative silence cases, the types of decisions adopted in the silence of administration cases) and the presidents of the courts were asked to assess the most frequent cases of silence of information by area. The data in Table 11.2 shows that the five courts opened 34,361 administrative dispute cases in the three-year period from 2015 to 2017 with an average closing rate of 111%.

Silence of administration disputes constitutes 5.10% of all opened cases (1753 cases), with the share being the largest in the Osijek court where 13.05% of all administrative disputes emerge from the administrative silence. The number of administrative silence disputes in the five courts has experienced an increase of 23.25% in the three-year period, from 529 in 2015 to 652 in 2017 as well as an increase in the relative share of the administrative disputes' cases, from 4.10 in 2015 to 620 in 2017. In other words, while the number of all administrative cases has experienced a significant decrease of 17.4%, the number of administrative silence cases has continued to rise. The increase is recorded in all courts except in the Rijeka court, with fourfold increase in the High administrative court (access to information appeal cases, see supra 6.1). This might be attributed to the greater awareness of the parties on their right to initiate a dispute on the grounds of administrative silence, but also to the greater acceptance of administrative cases which have been decided upon within the prescribed time. In other words, one may conclude that the parties are increasingly satisfied with the administrative decision (and thus initiate less administrative disputes in total), or give up challenging the decision before court (to avoid the loss of time and resources), and that the parties, when faced with the failure of the administrative body to issue a decision, more often react by initiating a dispute.

The Administrative Court in Zagreb has the greatest share of all disputes (42.14%), but administrative silence complaints are most frequent in the court in Osijek where 38.85% of all administrative silence disputes have been initiated, followed by the Zagreb court (28.35%). This might mean that in some parts of the country administrative bodies tend

Table 11.2 Administrative disputes 2015–2017

Administrative disputes 2015-2017		*Administrative court in Zagreb*			*Administrative court in Split*			*Administrative court in Rijeka*			*Administrative Court in Osijek*			*High Administrative court*			*Total*		
Administrative disputes - all cases	Year	Cases opened (N)	Cases closed (N)	Cases closed (%)	Cases opened (N)	Cases closed (N)	Cases closed (%)	Cases opened (N)	Cases closed (N)	Cases closed (%)	Cases opened (N)	Cases closed (N)	Cases closed (%)	Cases opened (N)	Cases closed (N)	Cases closed (%)	Cases opened (N)	Cases closed (N)	Cases closed (%)
	2015	5335	4425	82.94	2769	3256	117.59	2015	1797	89.18	1825	1600	87.67	395	610	154.43	12339	11688	106.36
	2016	4680	4129	88.23	2719	4200	154.47	1827	2185	119.59	1933	1757	90.89	354	331	93.50	11513	12602	109.34
	2017	4465	5670	126.99	2359	3453	146.38	1727	2421	140.19	1462	1589	108.69	496	452	91.13	10509	13585	122.67
	∑/av	14480	14224	98.23	7847	10909	139.02	5569	6403	114.98	5220	4946	94.75	1245	1393	111.89	34361	37875	111.77
Silence of administration cases	Year	Cases opened (N)*	Share in total AD (%)	Index	Cases opened (N)	Share in total AD (%)	Index	Cases opened (N)*	Share in total AD (%)	Index	Cases opened (N)*	Share in total AD (%)	Index	Cases opened (N)*	Share in total AD (%)	Index	Cases opened (N)*	Share in total AD (%)	Index
	2015	174	3.26		51	1.84		100	4.96		191	10.47		13	3.29		529	4.29	
	2016	143	3.06	82.18	80	2.94	156.86	92	5.04	92.00	245	12.67	128.27	12	3.39	92.31	572	4.97	108.13
	2017	180	4.03	125.87	77	3.26	96.25	97	5.62	105.43	245	16.76	100.00	53	10.69	441.67	652	6.20	113.99
	∑/av	497	3.43	104.03	208	2.65	126.56	289	5.19	98.72	681	13.05	114.14	78	6.27	266.99	1753	5.10	111.06
Silence of administration cases closed	Year	Cases closed (N)	Cases closed (%)	Index	Cases closed (N)	Cases closed (%)	Index	Cases closed (N)	Cases closed (%)	Index	Cases closed (N)	Cases closed (%)	Index	Cases closed (N)	Cases closed (%)	Index	Cases closed (N)	Cases closed (%)	Index
	2015	159	91.38		84	164.71		100	100.00		121	63.35		10	76.92		474	89.60	
	2016	149	104.20	93.71	116	145.00	138.10	88	95.65	88.00	243	99.18	200.83	16	133.33	160.00	612	106.99	129.11
	2017	157	87.22	105.37	85	110.39	73.28	94	96.91	106.82	153	62.45	62.96	41	77.36	256.25	530	81.29	86.60
	∑/av	465	93.56	99.54	285	137.02	105.69	282	97.58	97.41	517	75.92	131.89	67	85.90	208.13	1616	92.18	107.86

to remain silent more often than in others (e.g., Split with 11.87%) or that the parties are much more aware of their rights.

Regarding the outcomes of the administrative disputes initiated on the grounds of administrative silence, the data presented in Table 11.3 indicates that in a significant number of cases (705 out of 1616 or 43.63%) the dispute was suspended because in the meanwhile the administrative body issued a decision and the reasons for the dispute (silence) ceded to exist. This suggests that the initiation of administrative disputes on the grounds of administrative silence serves as an incentive for the administrative body to speed up the procedure. It can also indicate, especially in relation to the fact that the highest share of the suspended cases has been reported by the High Administrative Court, mainly in relation to the access to information appeals before the Information Commissioner (61.19% cases), that the time limits for administrative decisions might be insufficient, given the large number of cases before the Commissioner and the fact that first instance bodies tend to cooperate reluctantly in appeal procedures (e.g., delayed responses, failure to send the file or information sought). On the other side, one-third of all silence of administration disputes (534 cases out of 1616, all before the four first instance courts) prove to be justified—the courts adopt the claim and confirm that the failure of the administration to decide in the matter is not legally grounded and justified. In addition, almost each tenth decision (10.95% of all cases) is likely to be dismissed because there are no conditions for conducting a dispute (e.g., the deadline has not expired).

The responses from the courts regarding the types of cases indicate that the most common administrative silence disputes, although differently emphasized by different courts, include cases related to the civil servants' status and rights (Civil Service Commission), pensions (Croatian Pensions Insurance Fund), expropriation and indemnification of deprived property (Ministry of Justice), taxes (Tax Administration—Ministry of Finance), and social rights and benefits (Ministry of Demography, Family, Youth and Social Policy). The High Administrative Court, given its role as the first (and only) instance administrative court in only a restricted number of issues, receives administrative silence complaints regarding the failure of the Information Commissioner to decide upon the appeals in cases of access to information.

For example, the Civil Service Commission is an extreme case of long-standing administrative silence mostly due to the fact that within 3-year period from 2013 to 2015 more than 25,000 appeals were lodged (out of

Table 11.3 The silence of administration disputes 2015–2017 by outcomes

Outcomes of the dispute	*Administrative court in Zagreb*		*Administrative court in Split*		*Administrative court in Rijeka*		*Administrative court in Osijek*		*High Administrative court*		*Total all courts*	
Claim adopted	102	21.94	45	15.79	118	41.84	269	52.03	0	0.00	534	33.04
Claim rejected	25	5.38	12	4.21	10	3.55	23	4.45	9	13.43	79	4.89
Claim dismissed	74	15.91	40	14.04	18	6.38	41	7.93	4	5.97	177	10.95
Dispute suspended	201	43.23	154	54.04	128	45.39	181	35.01	41	61.19	705	43.63
Claim ceded	59	12.69	27	9.47			2	0.39	13	19.40	101	6.25
Discontinuation			2	0.70			1	0.19		0.00	3	0.19
Other (merging, etc.)	4	0.86	5	1.75	8	2.84				0.00	17	1.05
	465	100.00	285	100.00	282	100.00	517	100.00	67	100.00	1616	100.00

44,126 total in a 10-year period), mostly due to the 2014 law by which the rights of civil and public servants to a salary increase were suspended as an austerity measure. In 2017 the capacities of the Commission were strengthened but also the grounds for appeals were limited, while the protection of the rights from the collective agreement (e.g., annual leave, travel expenses, etc.) was deemed to be a matter of labor law and delegated to the general courts. This extreme case of administrative silence shows that administrative silence may easily be provoked by an inadequate organizational setting, as a consequence of a regulation that affects a large group of people and their rights, and too broad grounds for setting in motion an administrative procedure, which generate negative effects on all concerned appellants.

11.7 Concluding Remarks

The problem of silence of administration in Croatia is one of the key challenges for the rule of law and administrative action. In fact, the failure to decide on citizens' rights within a prescribed time limit is not only public administration's problem, but also the judicial system's. These circumstances not only violate the rights of citizens, but also have a negative impact on the functioning of the economy and society in general. The negative effects on public administration are numerous: from the burdens of files, to low quality decisions, and, more far-reaching, to a lower trust in institutions.

The legal framework for the timeliness of administrative decision making and for dealing with administrative silence has changed in the last decade. The most significant change relates to the general approach to administrative procedures, with a greater emphasis on the protection of citizens' rights and greater effectiveness. The treatment of silence, after decades of negative fiction, has taken a neutral stance, with positive fiction being recognized in some specific but not numerous procedures (e.g., recognition of qualifications). The available statistical data shows that in first instance central administration 10–15% of cases are solved after the deadline, as well as that approximately 3–8% of access to information cases are decided upon after the deadline. It shows that only 5% of administrative disputes are initiated on the grounds of administrative silence, and it also shows that some second instance administrative bodies (Information Commissioner, Civil Service Commission) face a significant problem in dealing with appeals within statutory deadlines. Sometimes the reasons can be found in a broad legal basis for complaints or the material law which creates a high number of cases that could be appealed against.

The reasons for the delays and silence in Croatia, however, are not primarily to be found in the legal framework, but rather in the general problems of public administration—the low capacities of public administration, low-quality human resources management and records management, ineffective leadership and lack of responsibility, sometimes passive citizens who do not use legal instruments out of the fear that using legal remedies can only worsen their legal situation.

The fact that the ministry responsible for administration and administrative procedures does not collect data on administrative proceedings and their timeliness indicates that the "silence problem" however is not perceived as central issue in administrative action and citizens' rights, although the decisions of Constitutional Court and the ECHR would indicate so. In addition, the current Strategy of development of public administration 2015–2020 does not accentuate this problem specifically, but only underlines the necessity of fast and efficient public administration, and plans to establish a system for the collection of data on administrative procedures.

References

Đerđa, D. (2013). Učinak europskih pravnih pravila na pravno normiranje upravnog postupka u Hrvatskoj. *Zbornik Radova Pravnog Fakulteta U Splitu, 50*(2), 393–427.

Đerđa, D., & Šikić, M. (2012). *Komentar Zakona o upravnim sporovima*. Zagreb: Novi informator.

European Commission. (2018). *The EU Justice Scoreboard 2018*. Luxembourg: Publications Office of the European Union. https://ec.europa.eu/info/sites/info/files/justice_scoreboard_2018_en.pdf.

Koprić, I. et al. (2016). *Legal Remedies in Administrative Procedures in Western Balkans*. Danilovgrad: ReSPA. https://www.respaweb.eu/11/library#respa-publications-2016-7.

Koprić, I., Kovač, P., & Britvić Vetma, B. (2017). Zaštita prava građana u odnosu s javnom upravom: povijesni razvoj, sadašnje stanje i perspektive razvoja u Hrvatskoj i Sloveniji. In I. Koprić, A. Musa & T. Giljević (Eds.), *Građani, javna uprava i lokalna samouprava: povjerenje, suradnja i potpora* (pp. 295–340). Zagreb: Institut za javnu upravu.

Ljubanović, B. (2006). Posebni upravni postupci u Republici Hrvatskoj. *Hrvatska javna uprava, 6*(3), 5–22.

Ljubanović, B. (2010). Novi Zakon o općem upravnom postupku i posebni upravni postupci. *Hrvatska javna uprava, 10*(2), 319–328.

Musa, A. (2014). Administrative Law and Public Administration. In T. Josipović (Ed.), *Introduction to the Law of Croatia* (pp. 55–93). Alphen aan den Rijn: Wolters Kluwer Law & Business.

Musa, A. (2018). Croatia: The Transparency Landscape. In D. Dragos, P. Kovač, & B. Marseille (Eds.), *The Laws of Transparency in Action: A European Perspective* (pp. 339–387). London: Palgrave Macmillan.

Ofak, L. (2016). The Right of Access to Information as a Right Protected by The European Convention and Other International Human Rights Treaties. *Zbornik Pravnog Fakulteta Sveučilišta U Rijeci, 37*(2), 921–951.

Šikić, M. (2006). Temelji zaštite građana od šutnje uprave u Republici Hrvatskoj. *Hrvatska javna uprava, 6*(2), 121–148.

Šikić, M. (2008). Primjena pravnih fikcija u institutu zaštite građana od šutnje uprave. *Zbornik Radova Pravnog Fakulteta U Splitu, 45*(1), 149–175.

Šikić, M. (2009a). Pravo na suđenje u razumnom roku u postupcima pred Upravnim sudom Republike Hrvatske. *Zbornik Pravnog fakulteta Sveučilišta u Rijeci, 30*(1), 333–372.

Šikić, M. (2009b). Pravna zaštita od šutnje uprave prema novom Zakonu o općem upravnom postupku. In I. Koprić & V. Đulabić (Eds.), *Modernizacija općeg upravnog postupka i javne uprave u Hrvatskoj* (pp. 191–213). Zagreb: Društveno veleučilište & Institut za javnu upravu.

Šikić, M. (2010). Vremenski okviri odlučivanja u Hrvatskom upravnom sporu. *Zbornik radova Pravnog fakulteta u Splitu, 47*(1), 93–112.

Šikić, M. (2013). Utjecaj prakse (presuda) Europskog suda za zaštitu ljudskih prava na upravno sudovanje u Republici Hrvatskoj. *Zbornik Radova Pravnog Fakulteta U Splitu, 50*(2), 357–471.

Šikić, M., & Staničić, F. (2009). Uređenje žalbe u posebnim upravnim postupcima. *Hrvatska pravna revija, 9*(4), 43–52.

Šikić, M., Staničić, F., &Turudić, M. (2011). Pravna zaštita od šutnje uprave u posebnim upravnim postupcima. *Hrvatska pravna revija, 11*(3), 80–92.

Staničić, F., Britvić Vetma, B., & Horvat, B. (2017). *Komentar Zakona o upravnim sporovima*. Zagreb: Narodne novine.

CHAPTER 12

The Privilege of Silence in Serbian Administrative Law

Vuk Cucić

12.1 Introduction

Serbia has a long administrative law tradition. The principle of legality and the right to administrative appeal were introduced by the Constitution of 1835.[1] The judicial control of administration was introduced by the Constitution of 1869.[2] The rules of administrative judicial procedure were codified in 1922 and the rules of administrative procedure in 1930. Two pillars of administrative procedural law are the General Administrative Procedure Act of 2016[3] (hereinafter: **GAPA**) and Administrative Disputes Act[4] (hereinafter: **ADA**). Serbia has a two-tier administrative

[1] https://sr.wikisource.org/sr/Устав_Кнежевине_Србије_(1835). The first Serbian constitution, however, was suspended only a month after its promulgation, Batakovic (2007, p. 134).

[2] https://sr.wikisource.org/sr/Устав_Кнежевине_Србије_(1869).

[3] Official Gazette of the Republic of Serbia (hereinafter: OGRS), no. 18/2016.

[4] OGRS, no. 111/2009.

V. Cucić (✉)
University of Belgrade, Belgrade, Serbia
e-mail: vukcucic@ius.bg.ac.rs

D. C. Dragos et al. (eds.),
The Sound of Silence in European Administrative Law,
https://doi.org/10.1007/978-3-030-45227-8_12

procedure and one single Administrative Court (hereinafter: "**AC**"), which is the only court conducting judicial control of administrative acts.[5]

The legal protection against administrative silence was prescribed in several phases. Firstly, only against non-appealable [*konacno*] administrative silence, against which judicial review is open. This type of administrative silence was introduced by the Council of State and Administrative Courts Act of 1922. The protection against the failure of administrative authorities to enforce judgments rendered in administrative court proceeding was prescribed by the Administrative Disputes Act of 1952.[6] The next step was introduction of the administrative appeal against the silence of the first-instance administrative authority, done by the General Administrative Procedure Act of 1956.[7] Lastly, protection against the failure of administrative authorities to undertake factual acts [*upravne radnje*] was prescribed by GAPA.[8]

All other components of substantial and procedural legality of the work of the administration preceded administrative silence. Hence, in Serbia, the administrative silence was the final building block of legal protection against arbitrary action of the administration.

12.2 Normative Regulation

12.2.1 General Legal Principles

The principles of procedural efficiency and economy are among the basic principles of administrative law. They represent the foundation for the provisions regulating deadlines for undertaking of administrative activities and legal protection against administrative silence.

The principles of efficiency and economy are prescribed by two general, systemic laws in this field—Article 9 GAPA and Article 9 of the State Administration Act.[9] However, they are not contained in the Constitution,[10] which regulates only the right to trial within reasonable time (Art.

[5] Cucic (2011, pp. 53–54).

[6] Dimitrijevic (1996a, pp. 126–127).

[7] Ibid.

[8] Davinic and Cucic (2017, pp. 235–236) and Tomic et al. (2017, pp. 161–163).

[9] OGRS, no. 79/2005, 101/2007, 95/2010 and 99/2014.

[10] OGRS, no. 98/2006.

32). This includes trials before AC, but has no impact on the duration of administrative proceedings.

12.2.2 Obligation to Decide

The administration is not always obliged to decide a case within a certain period of time. Pursuant to Article 145 GAPA such duty exists only in two instances, when the procedure was initiated by a party's request and when it was initiated *ex officio*, but in a favor of a party (e.g., when a minor has to be provided with a legal guardian). The rationale behind this legal norm is said to be the fact that in these proceedings the party has an interest to have its case decided.

While this statement is true, it is incomplete when it assumes that parties would never have the interest to have the procedure that was initiated *ex officio* and with the aim to determine obligations for the parties, ended within a certain period of time. This is not always the case. Namely, let us assume that a procedure was instigated *ex officio* in order to determine whether a party has to pay certain taxes. Then let us assume that the party is a company that is being sold to another company. For that purpose, the other company asks for a due diligence report on its liabilities. A law firm preparing the due diligence report would have to state that there is an administrative proceeding initiated and that it is possible that the company would have to pay certain taxes, even if there is no ground for determining such legal obligation. This would lower the value of the company and aggravate the bargaining position of the seller. Therefore, the company/seller would have the interest to have the administrative proceeding decided and the legal situation clarified.[11]

There is a single example of special policy domain in which this interest was recognized. Pursuant to Article 38 of the Inspection Supervision Act,[12] a party, who is supervised has the right to request that the inspector ends the inspection supervision proceeding (initiated *ex officio*) within a deadline prescribed by the law. If it fails to do so, the proceeding is going to be permanently suspended [*obustavljen*] *ipso lege*. This way the supervised party can have legal certainty with respect to its legal position. Otherwise, this "Sword of Damocles," i.e., the possibility of having

[11] This yields constant uncertainty, Kostic (1998, p. 145, fn. 12).

[12] OGRS, no. 36/2015.

the party sanctioned for improper conduct, would constantly be over the party's head.

12.2.3 Types and Deadlines for Administrative Silence

Serbian administrative law prescribes deadlines for deciding or acting for various acts of administration and all procedural levels.

The deadlines concerning administrative silence are generally counted in days (certain special domain laws prescribe hours instead, e.g., election laws[13]). The deadlines set in days commence on the day following the day when the event from which the deadline is counted occurred (Art. 80, para 2 GAPA). As a rule, in the case of administrative silence, this is the day of initiation of the proceeding, i.e., when the party submitted its request to the authority (or sent it via post) or, in the case of a proceeding initiated *ex officio* in the party's favor, the day when the authority undertook the first procedural action with the aim of commencing the proceeding (Art. 91 GAPA). The deadlines can commence in non-working days (Saturdays, Sundays, holidays) (Art. 80, para. 4 GAPA). However, if the last day of the deadline is a non-working day, then the deadline lapses on the first following working day (Art. 80, para. 5 GAPA).

GAPA prescribes general deadlines (can be shortened or prolonged by special laws) for performance of different types of administrative activities—rendering of the first-instance decision, deciding on administrative appeal and extraordinary legal remedies, issuance of public documents, issuance of guarantee acts, deciding in enforcement procedure. Additionally, ADA prescribes the deadline for issuance of an administrative act in the process of enforcement of judicial decisions. All of these deadlines are instructive in case of negative legal fiction of administrative silence; that is, authorities are still allowed to issue decisions or perform other activity after the deadline passes. In case of a positive legal fiction, the deadline is preclusive, since an administrative appeal filed in such a situation will be dismissed [*a limine, odbacena*]. For certain types of administrative silence, the law prescribes two or more consecutive deadlines, the first counted

[13] Members of the Parliament Election Act, OGRS, no. 35/2000, 57/2003, 72/2003, 75/2003, 18/2004, 101/2005, 85/2005, 28/2011, 36/2011 and 104/2009; Local Elections Act, OGRS, no. 129/2007, 34/2010 and 54/2011; National Councils of the National Minorities Act, OGRS, no. 72/2009, 20/2014 and 55/2014.

from the day of initiation of the proceeding, and the second from the day of submission of a subsequent request ("reminder") for deciding (e.g., for lawsuit).

Finally, Serbian law in certain instances regulates the *duration of the procedure of judicial control of administrative acts*. Article 2 ADA stipulates that trials before AC have to be conducted within a reasonable time. This is backed up by the provisions of Article 32 of the Constitution and Article 6 of the European Convention of Human Rights (both regulating the right to a fair trial) and a special law regulating this matter.[14] Additionally, there are special laws prescribing fixed deadlines for deciding on the legality of an administrative act.[15]

Deadlines for undertaking administrative activities are, as a rule, non-extendable. Nonetheless, there are special laws prescribing exceptions. Article 62 of the Competition Protection Act allows the Competition Protection Commission to extend the deadline for deciding on merger requests. Likewise, Article 16 of the Free Access to Information of Public Importance Act[16] permits a public authority to extend the deadline for providing requested information if there are justified reasons for such an extension. GAPA does not authorize the first-instance authorities to extend the deadlines for deciding on their own, but gives the appellate authorities that power, if there was a justified reason preventing the authority to decide timely.[17] The extended deadline is equal to the period covered by the justified reason, but it cannot be longer than 30 days (Art. 173, para. 1 GAPA).

12.2.4 Responses to Administrative Silence

The Negative Legal Fiction—The General Model

The negative legal fiction [*negativna pretpostavka cutanja uprave*] is the main mechanism of legal protection against administrative silence in

[14] The Protection of the Right to a Trial within a Reasonable Time Act, OGRS, no. 40/2015.

[15] Members of the Parliament Election Act, Local Elections Act, and Competition Protection Act (OGRS, no. 51/2009 and 95/2013).

[16] OGRS, no. 120/2004, 54/2007, 104/2009 and 36/2010.

[17] In Germany, the courts do this, Gelevska Trajcevski (2011, p. 225).

Serbian administrative law. The silence is considered as inactivity (non-act) giving the party right to a legal remedy. This mechanism represents the general rule, prescribed by two systemic laws—GAPA and ADA.

The Positive Legal Fiction—The Exception

The other option is a positive legal fiction of the silence of administration [*pozitivna pretpostavka cutanja uprave*], where the lapse of the deadline leads to an *ipso lege* approval of a party's request. This is the exception in Serbian administrative law, and it is *prescribed by special laws*.[18] Such examples are most often found in fields of business and other registration and entrepreneurship. For instance, there is a positive legal fiction with a very short deadline of only five days as of the day of receipt of a party's request in the Registration Procedure with the Agency for Commercial Registers Act[19] (Arts. 15 and 19). This relates to all types of business and commercial registers, registers of collaterals, register of civil associations, etc. Similar is the example of registration of political parties, where the deadline is somewhat longer—30 days as of the day of submission of a request.[20] Another example is Article 62, paragraph 2 of the Competition Protection Act. If the Commission for Protection of Competition does not decide upon parties' request for merger, the parties are free to merge. The positive legal fiction can be found in elections legislation as well. Art. 96 of the Members of the Parliament Election Act prescribes that an objection lodged with the State Elections Commission against election irregularities shall be considered accepted if the Commission fails to reject it within 48 h as of its submission.

Even *GAPA, as the general law*, stipulates a case of positive legal fiction of administrative silence. It concerns complex administrative acts, i.e., the situations in which one authority renders an act, but with prior or subsequent consent or opinion of another administrative authority. Article 138, para. 4 GAPA prescribes that in such cases, the second administrative authority is obliged to give (or deny) its consent or opinion within 30 days as of the day it was requested. If it fails to do so, it shall be

[18] These exceptions appeared before 1937 in Labor Act, Krbek (1937, p. 82). Yugoslavia, looked up to the French administrative law that introduced the positive presumption in 1852, Gelevska Trajcevski (2011, pp. 221–222).

[19] OGRS, no. 99/2011 and 83/2014.

[20] Political Parties Act, OGRS, no. 36/2009 and 61/2015.

considered that it gave consent or positive opinion and the first authority shall proceed with the issuance of the administrative act.

In the case of positive legal fiction of administrative silence, *the deadline for deciding is preclusive*; that is, authorities are no longer authorized to decide on the request. In such situations, the authority can only be obliged to execute this implicit positive administrative act (e.g., to insert the company's name in the commercial register) or to refrain from preventing the party to exercise its implicitly recognized rights (e.g., to merge with another company in the same market). Furthermore, in this case, the party is explicitly not allowed to submit an administrative appeal against administrative silence, because its request is approved the way it was submitted (Art. 151, para. 5 GAPA).

The same logic, but the opposite effect has *the legal mechanism for ending of the inspection supervision proceeding*. As it was described (see *supra* 2.2), if the inspection supervision is not completed within the legally prescribed deadline, the party can request the inspector to end it. If it fails to do so within the following eight days, it is considered that the proceeding is permanently suspended and that the party's behavior and conducts were legal and appropriate (Art. 38 of the Inspection Supervision Act). The party cannot be controlled for the same behavior or conduct again (Art. 20, para. 4 of the Inspection Supervision Act).[21]

The Negative v. the Positive Fiction

Domestic[22] legal doctrine, among others, tackled the theoretically and practically most important issue concerning regulation of administrative silence—the issue of *whether the predominant legal fiction should be negative or positive*. This issue became particularly important in 2012, when the Draft GAPA (which was later not adopted) proposed a radical shift from the negative to the positive legal fiction of the administrative silence as a rule.[23]

[21] Expect if the circumstances of the case changed in the meanwhile or if the inspection supervision is necessary for prevention of immediate threat to human life or health, environment or flora and fauna.

[22] Given the common legal heritage, domestic legal doctrine does not include only Serbian authors, but also authors from the other countries that used to be part of Yugoslavia.

[23] Same happened in Bulgaria in 2006, when the negative presumption remained in force by difference of only one vote in the Parliament, Hrusanov (2011, pp. 91–92).

The legal scholars mainly opt for the current system, where there is the negative legal fiction as a rule and the special laws could prescribe exceptions.[24] Even those that favor positive legal fiction as a general rule make it with significant reservation, i.e., under numerous conditions.[25] More important than their stances are their arguments *pro et contra* the negative or the positive legal fiction.

The main argument for the positive legal fiction is the fact that it *does not require the party to resort to legal remedies*.[26] *Ipso lege* the party gets its request accepted when the deadline for deciding passes. Additional argument is that the positive legal fiction shortens the overall duration of the proceeding, thus reinforcing the principle of procedural economy; i.e., it saves time and money. Furthermore, arguments against the negative legal fiction are those supporting the positive one. It is claimed that the negative legal fiction "legalizes" administrative silence instead of sanctioning it.[27] Consequently, there is no incentive for proper sanctioning of administrative inaction. To the contrary, certain authors consider that the positive legal fiction would provide the necessary motivation for that.[28] Those favoring the positive legal fiction add that the negative legal fiction amounts to abuse of power and that it is founded on the premise that the administration is always right or, at least, that it should not rush and that "this legal formalism and excessive concern about the legality of administrative activities undermine the administration's efficiency."[29] All in all, the negative legal fiction is found to be revolutionary for the nineteenth and the beginning of the twentieth centuries, but inapt for the twenty-first century, given that "it is outdated, detrimental and inappropriate for contemporary prospective administration" and it "feeds the untimeliness of the administration, its inertia and strengthens the feeling of irresponsibility of civil servants."[30] It could be added that the negative legal fiction does not give the parties the possibility to genuinely protect their rights, given that the presumed rejection is not justified as it would be in an

[24] Kovac (2011, p. 287) and Sikic (2007, pp. 114–116).

[25] Dimitrijevic (1996b, pp. 444–448).

[26] Sikic (2007, p. 103).

[27] Dimitrijevic (1996b, p. 107).

[28] Dimitrijevic (1996b, p. 441).

[29] Ibid., pp. 438, 440.

[30] Ibid., pp. 441–442.

explicit negative decision. Hence, it is more difficult for the parties to fight such implicit negative acts.

On the other hand, there are arguments backing-up the negative legal fiction as a general rule (of course, with exceptions in special policy domains). There are *two conceptual arguments against the general positive legal fiction* (the positive legal fiction as a rule). The first is that it should not and could not be used as a *panacea* against the poor organization and lack of competence and necessary managerial skills within the administration.[31] The second is the argument that the purpose of the negative legal fiction is not only to protect the procedural rights of parties, but also to safeguard the public interest.[32] When a party is recognized a right *ipso lege*, merely by the silence of the administration, the administration failed to counterweight such private rights and interests against the public interest. The decision has been made without going to the merits of the case.[33]

The supplementary arguments against the positive legal fiction target its *practical shortcomings*. These arguments can also be understood as an invitation for the amelioration of the legal regulation of the positive legal fiction, not only as a general rule, but also when it is prescribed as a sector-specific exception.

The argument that the positive legal fiction shortens the overall proceeding before the administration is to a certain extent offset by a counterargument that a request *ipso lege* accepted by administrative silence can be illegal.[34] In such a situation, it is *necessary to rectify the consequences of administrative inaction and the illegal result of that inaction*. This means that the law has to foresee extraordinary legal remedies and that administrative authorities must initiate additional proceedings to correct this illegality.[35] This in turn prolongs the overall proceeding before the administration. Moreover, this leads to legal uncertainty for the party.[36] A party formally got the right recognized by positive legal fiction, but is not certain whether the implicit positive decision is going

[31] Kovac (2011, pp. 282, 287).

[32] Sikic (2007, p. 114).

[33] Kovac (2011, pp. 284, 287).

[34] Sikic (2007, pp. 103–104).

[35] Ibid., p. 104.

[36] Ibid., p. 105.

to be withdrawn by the authority. The problem is amplified if the deadlines for withdrawal are longer. Parties then have to bear the legal risk and the burden of suspense linked with legal uncertainty.[37]

Additional drawback for a party is the fact that he or she somehow *has to prove that he or she had acquired a right and the content and scope of that right*.[38] Proving that to other public authorities and third parties solely with his or her request, date of submission of request and legal provisions regulating the positive legal fiction of administrative silence is difficult, if at all possible. Furthermore, the party's position is aggravated by the mentioned possibility of withdrawal of an implicit positive decision.[39] Another disadvantage of the positive legal fiction concerns *the legal certainty of third conscientious parties* in such situations.

Moreover, *there are special administrative proceedings in which the positive legal fiction cannot function even if there would be necessary capacities.* The very logic of these procedures disables the positive legal fiction. This is the case with the competitive proceedings,[40] such as the proceeding for obtaining agricultural subsidies (when there is not enough financial means for all the applicants) or civil service employment procedures. Obviously, not all of the participants in the procedure can get approval, hence, none of them can.

The final argument, the one that decisively influenced the general and professional public to dismiss the general positive legal fiction proposed in the 2012 Draft GAPA, was *the argument that this legal solution was prone to corruption*. Explicitly, it was said that a corrupted civil servant could take a bribe for and produce an illegal decision purely by not working on a certain case and letting the deadline to pass, without the need to justify its illegal decision.[41] Not only that it eases the corruption, but it makes it more difficult to prove. A civil servant could on paper have great results, for instance timely deciding 95% of all its cases, but choosing the "right" 5% of the cases, which he or she will not resolve in time. Who could prove that this civil servant is bad or corrupt? The data gathered by

[37] Ibid.

[38] Hrusanov (2011, pp. 94–95).

[39] Sikic (2007, p. 104).

[40] Ibid., p. 93.

[41] The same argument was raised Bulgaria, which has similar difficulties with corruption, Hrusanov (2011, p. 95).

potential controlling authorities would not indicate that a problem exists, thus putting this type of corruption "under the radar." Generally, this argument could not stand because any power and any authorization can be abused and the state has to put in place mechanisms to prevent such behavior (and they do exist, e.g., criminal and civil liability of corrupt civil servants). However, it feels that in a country like Serbia, struggling with corruption,[42] this argument should not be disregarded.

12.2.5 Legal Remedies

There are two types of remedies with respect to administrative silence—"*the remedies 'in case of'* and *the remedies 'against' administrative silence*."[43] The prior merely cure the consequences of administrative silence, while the latter invoke liability of the administration, on a general and individual level, offering relief to the parties facing detrimental consequences of administrative silence. The first group encompasses administrative appeal, judicial review, objection, and devolution. The second includes inspection supervision, Ombudsman's protection, disciplinary, misdemeanor, and criminal liability and damages claims.

Administrative Appeal, Judicial Review and Objection

There are three legal remedies that a party can use in case of a negative legal fiction of administrative silence—administrative appeal, lawsuit to AC (judicial review), and objection.

A party has the right to file an *administrative appeal* (Art. 151, para. 3 GAPA) or *lawsuit to AC* (Art. 15 ADA) if an administrative authority failed to decide upon its request (appeal or extraordinary legal remedy) within a legally prescribed deadline. The deadline for deciding is instructive for the authority. It has the right to decide until the appeal or the lawsuit against its silence has been decided upon. Provided that the administrative silence is illegal (the authority was obliged to decide within a deadline and did not do so), the appellate administrative authority and AC can either order the authority to issue an act within a certain period

[42] In 2017, Serbia ranked 77th in the Corruption Perception Index, https://www.transparency.org/news/feature/corruption_perceptions_index_2017.

[43] Dimitrijevic (1996b, p. 446).

of time or decide the case on the merits themselves (Art. 173 GAPA and Art. 44 ADA).

In certain situations, *the higher authority has to decide the case on the merits.*[44] This mechanism protects parties against the "Ping-Pong Effect." GAPA prescribes that in the case of *repeated silence of the first-instance authority*, the appellate authority has to decide the case itself.[45] The second example is the protection provided by AC in the case of failure of the defendant (administrative authority) to issue a new administrative act in accordance with its judgment—*silence concerning the judgment enforcement* [*cutanje u izvrsenju presude*]. In that situation, AC should *resolve the case on the merits* (Art. 71 ADA).

GAPA (adopted in 2016) brought a novelty with respect to deadlines concerning administrative silence. There are two deadlines for submitting an administrative appeal against the silence of the first-instance administrative authority (Art. 153, para. 2 GAPA). The first deadline is *dilatory* [*odlozni rok*] (30 or 60 days, or deadline prescribed by a special law—see *supra* 2.1), i.e., the party cannot submit the appeal before this deadline for deciding lapses. Otherwise, the appeal shall be dismissed as premature. The new GAPA introduced *preclusive* deadlines for the appeal as well. Specifically, the party can file an appeal when the deadline for deciding lapses (dilatory deadline), but only within the following one year as of that day (preclusive deadline). Once that second deadline expires, the party cannot file an administrative appeal against the silence of the first-instance administrative authority. The inspiration for this legal solution was found in the Dutch General Administrative Law Act.[46]

The same protective mechanism—negative legal fiction and legal remedy against the silence—is established for *the factual acts of the administration.* If an authority fails to perform a certain factual act, which it was legally bound to undertake within a certain time period, the party can submit an objection [*prigovor*] to the authority whose inaction was illegal. The authority must either perform the factual act or reject the objection

[44] This model originated from the Austrian law, Krbek (1937, pp. 90–91) and Gelevska Trajcevski (2011, p. 223).

[45] Davinic and Cucic (2017, pp. 239–240).

[46] Article 6:12, para. 3 of the Dutch GALA, https://www.acm.nl/en/publications/publication/15446/Dutch-General-Administrative-Law-Act. Same exists in French and EU law, Gelevska Trajcevski (2011, pp. 221, 228–229).

with a decision (administrative act) against which an administrative appeal and/or lawsuit are open (Art. 147-150 GAPA).

Inspection Supervision and Misdemeanor Liability

A party confronted with administrative inaction can request *the Administrative Inspection* to initiate control of the work of particular administrative authority and civil servant. The Administrative Inspection is a state authority in charge of controlling adherence to the law in the work of administrative authorities, as well as other state and non-state authorities exercising administrative powers, including services and civil servants within courts, public prosecutor offices, public attorney offices, the National Parliament, the Government, the President of the Republic, and provincial and local authorities (Art. 2 of the Administrative Inspection Act[47]). Judges, MPs, and other elected officials in these authorities are not encompassed by the control. It relates only to the work of the employees (civil servants) thereof. Among other matters, the Administrative Inspection controls whether authorities are deciding and undertaking other administrative actions within legally prescribed deadlines (Art. 18, subpara. 2 of the law). If they find that an authority does not perform its duties timely, it shall order it to rectify its behavior. If an authority fails to meet the orders of the Administrative Inspection, the person responsible for the work of the authority shall be charged for *misdemeanor* (Art. 39 of the law).

Ombudsman's Protection

Parties are also allowed to address *the Ombudsman* (*officially, the Citizens' Protector*). As a rule, a party first has to exhaust all the other available legal remedies before approaching the Ombudsman. One of the exceptions to this rule is that parties can reach out to the Ombudsman without exhausting available remedies and even in parallel with the remedial procedures if the complaint concerns administrative silence (Art. 25, paras. 4 and 5 of the Citizens' Protector Act).

[47] OGRS, no. 87/2011.

Disciplinary and Criminal Liability
The following form of accountability for administrative silence is the ***disciplinary responsibility under the Civil Servants Act***.[48] This law stipulates that untimely execution of its duties, including deciding in an administrative case represents a serious breach of its work duties and can lead to sanctions ranging from salary reduction to loss of employment. The disciplinary responsibility does not exclude the possibility of other type of legal (civil, misdemeanor, or criminal) liability (Art. 109-110 of said law). There was also an attempt in the new GAPA to introduce misdemeanor responsibility of civil servants for administrative silence. The Draft contained such provision, but it was eliminated during the public debate process.[49]

The authority that failed to enforce judgment of AC, i.e., failed to issue a new act in accordance therewith, can face ***criminal liability***. The official person failing to enforce final judicial decisions can be fined or imprisoned for up to three years (Art. 340 of the Criminal Code[50]).

Right to Compensation—Damages
It should be noted that ***damages*** can be sought only with respect to a specific type of administrative silence—when the defendant/authority failed to enforce a judgment of AC (Art. 72 ADA). This liability can be extended to civil servants, who did not perform their work timely, provided the damage was caused on purpose or due to gross negligence (Art. 121 of the Civil Servants Act).

In all other cases, parties can use just legal remedies (administrative appeal, lawsuit, objection, complaint to the Ombudsman or the Administrative Inspection) that can only result in undertaking or ordering an authority to undertake certain administrative activity. Parties cannot ask for compensation for damage they suffered in those instances. The problematic issue here is that the inaction of the administration is not illegal.[51] The deadline for deciding or acting in case of negative legal fiction is

[48] OGRS, no. 79/2005, 81/2005, 83/2005, 64/2007, 67/2007, 116/2008, 104/2009, 99/2014 and 94/2017.

[49] The Bulgarian law foresees pecuniary fine for the civil servant, who failed to decide timely, Hrusanov (2011, p. 90).

[50] OGRS, no. 85/2005, 88/2005, 107/2005, 72/2009, 111/2009, 121/2012, 104/2013, 108/2014 and 94/2016.

[51] Dimitrijevic (1996b, p. 432).

instructive. Hence, the authority is still competent to decide or act and there is no illegality. Given that illegality of the detrimental action is a necessary element for claiming damages, civil liability does not exist in these instances of administrative silence. This is a good justification for referring to administrative silence as the "privilege of silence."[52]

12.3 Empirical Research

12.3.1 Methodology

In order to obtain relevant data, the author sent requests to *nine public authorities*—AC, seven central government authorities (the Ministry of Interior, the Ministry of Public Administration and Local Government, the Ministry of Construction, Infrastructure and Traffic, the Ministry of Finance, the Customs Authority, the Tax Authority and the State Pension Fund) and one local government authority (the City of Belgrade, as the biggest local government unit in Serbia). The author sent official request for access to public information. The following data were sought: (1) Total number of administrative appeals submitted to relevant public authorities in 2015, 2016 and 2017; (2) Number of administrative appeals submitted to relevant public authorities against administrative silence of the first-instance authorities in 2015, 2016, and 2017; (3) How were administrative appeals against administrative silence decided upon (number of dismissed, rejected and accepted appeals) in 2015, 2016, and 2017. Additionally, the author used the pertinent data published online by two independent state authorities—the Data Protection Commissioner and the Ombudsman.

Unfortunately, given that the data were unavailable or incomplete, it was necessary (and useful) to conduct interviews with persons working in the administration and AC. The author *interviewed four civil servants* (one from the Ministry of Public Administration and Local Government, two from the Administrative Inspection and one from Novi Sad, the second largest local government unit Serbia), *one public official* (Deputy Ombudsman) and *one former Administrative Court judge*, to get a grasp of what is actually going on in practice. In order to obtain truthful information, the author guaranteed the interviewed persons anonymity (some of them requested this). Only the authority they work at and their line

[52] The expression used by Maurice Hauriou, cited from Gjidara (2007, p. 124).

and field of work shall be stated. The conducted interviews were semi-structured. They were, depending on the interviewee, oriented on the questions enabling the author to better understand obtained data and/or to fill in the gaps where data were not available, but they were also open to new ideas concerning causes, consequences, and potential solutions for administrative silence.

It would be logical to present first the data concerning appeals and then the data on lawsuits against administrative silence. Nevertheless, the data shall be displayed vice versa because the data concerning the lawsuits are complete, while the data on administrative appeal are unavailable and incomplete and had to be backed up by interviews with the civil servants. In the end, the author shall turn to other protection mechanisms.

12.3.2 Lawsuits Against Administrative Silence

AC sent the following answers. In 2017, there were 5212 lawsuits filed against administrative silence, 3607 in 2016 and in 3388 in 2015—12,207 in total for these three years. They were decided upon in the following manner: 1169 were dismissed (*a limine*), 1135 were rejected, in 3309 cases the proceeding before the Court was permanently suspended and 2201 were accepted (Tables 12.1 and 12.2).

The first thing to be observed is that in these three years AC received 12,207 lawsuits against administrative silence. In the same period, it resolved only 7814 cases thereof. Thus, 4393 cases less than what it received, i.e., 36% less. This is troubling, given that AC never decides the cases of administrative silence on the merits. It only checks whether an authority was obliged to decide within a certain deadline and whether

Table 12.1 Lawsuits submitted to AC[a]

Year	*No. of lawsuits against administrative silence*	*Total number of lawsuits*	*% of silence lawsuits*
2015	3388	20,315	16.68
2016	3607	21,548	16.74
2017	5212	21,741	24
Total	12,207	63,604	19.19

[a]The data was taken from AC's annual reports (http://www.up.sud.rs/cirilica/izvestaji-o-radu) and obtained by requests for access to public information

Table 12.2 Manner of deciding upon lawsuits against administrative silence[a]

Year	*Accepted*	*Rejected*	*Dismissed*	*Permanently suspended*
2015	265	154	256	216
2016	926	260	316	1296
2017	1010	721	597	1797
Total	2201	1135	1169	3309

[a]The data was taken from AC's annual reports (http://www.up.sud.rs/cirilica/izvestaji-o-radu) and obtained by requests for access to public information

it failed to do so. Hence, despite being fairly simple to decide upon, there are at least 4393 outstanding cases of administrative silence pending before AC for more than one year.

The data further show that the lawsuits against administrative silence, given a specific year, comprise roughly between one-sixth and one-fourth of all lawsuits submitted to AC (16–24%).

Presented data further show that parties were successful in 5510 cases. This includes the number of *accepted appeals* (2201) and the number of *permanently suspended proceedings* (3309). The latter cases are counted as a success due to the fact that proceedings are permanently suspended when defendants subsequently, during AC proceedings, issued belated acts and the plaintiffs declared themselves to be satisfied with the acts (Art. 29 ADA). Therefore, parties had been successful in 70.5% of the cases.

On the other hand, parties were not successful in 1169, i.e., 15% of cases, when their *lawsuits were dismissed*. The lawsuits against administrative silence are dismissed if the plaintiff did not submit proof that a subsequent request for issuance of the act had been submitted and that relevant deadlines had passed (*supra* 2.3).

The most puzzling are the cases in which the *lawsuits were rejected*. These constitute 14.5% of the cases (1135). In order to shed a light on this peculiar situation, the author of this paper interviewed a recently retired Administrative Court judge.[53] Given the fact that AC's case law is not easily accessible and is not searchable, the author had to determine the stances of AC *vis-à-vis* administrative silence through this interview.

[53]She was the head of the case law department, thus having a good overview of the Court's practice.

The judge explained what actually happened in practice. The cases in which AC rejected the lawsuits against administrative silence were those in which the authority subsequently issued requested acts, while proceedings before AC were ongoing. However, the act was not beneficial for the party and, consequently, the party challenged it, but by a separate lawsuit. Then, the party said that it requires AC to decide on both lawsuits. Since in the first case there was no more administrative silence, AC had to reject the lawsuit as ungrounded. The judge also informed us why this is occurring in practice. She believes that this is a consequence of a struggle of certain attorneys to earn more money, given that they usually do not charge their clients up-front, but agree with them to get the attorney fees from the other party if they win the case. Obviously, given the number of rejections, this is not an isolated example.

Two things can be inferred from this.

Firstly, these cases should also be counted as a win against administrative silence. The lawsuit forced the defendant to render an act and put an end to the silence. Accordingly, the number of successful lawsuits then rises to 6645, i.e., 85% of all cases.

Secondly, this is a flaw in the legal regulation of the lawsuit against administrative silence. Namely, the parties in these instances were right, but they will not necessarily be victorious in the proceeding before AC. The party caused the silence to end, but its request or appeal was rejected by the defendant's subsequently issued decision. Had they extended their lawsuit against the act, they could end up losing the case altogether. This can happen if the negative belated decision is later proven to be legal, in which case the plaintiff has to pay the costs of the entire proceedings to the defendant, even though he/she was right to challenge the administrative silence. Since the plaintiff was partially victorious, the costs should be split between the plaintiff and the defendant.

12.3.3 Appeals Against Administrative Silence

As was said, the author sent requests for access to public information concerning administrative appeals against administrative silence to *seven central government authorities* and one local government authority. Given that there is no centrally gathered information on the administrative appeals against administrative silence, these authorities were chosen because they each get hundreds or even thousands of appeals annually. In the lack of any systematic data, they were selected as the authorities that could make up a representative sample for the study.[54]

Only two (*the Customs Authority and the City of Belgrade*) sent all the requested data. From 2015 to 2017, the Customs Authority received 5797, out of which only two were against administrative silence. In the same period, City of Belgrade received 968 appeals, out of which 29 were against administrative silence. 21 appeals against administrative silence were accepted (i.e., 72.4%). Additionally, the data on appeals against administrative silence were obtained from the *Data Protection Commissioner*'s annual reports. In the field of access to information, from 2015 to 2017, 10,536 appeals were received, out of which 9355 (88,8%) were against administrative silence. In the field of personal data protection, for the same period, the Commissioner received 1014 appeals, out which 403 (39.7%) were against administrative silence.[55]

Three authorities (*the Ministry of Finance, the Ministry of Construction, Infrastructure and Traffic, and the State Pension Fund*) sent only the data concerning the total number of administrative appeals. They explained that they do not separate administrative appeals against administrative silence from other administrative appeals. The remaining three sent no data (*the Ministry of Interior, the Ministry of Public Administration and Local Government, and the Tax Authority*). Thus, this showed that only some administrative authorities keep records of the total number of administrative appeals they receive and that even fewer of them distinguish the appeal against administrative silence.

After facing this revelation, the author went on to inquire whether the authorities abide by their obligation to keep *records as to the number and manner of deciding upon administrative law cases* (Art. 211 GAPA). In order to check if these official records are kept, the author interviewed civil servants from the two authorities competent to supervise keeping of these records (Art. 209 GAPA)—the Ministry of Public Administration and Local Government (civil servant working in the department competent for administrative proceeding) and the Administrative Inspection (one currently employed and one former inspector). It appeared that almost none of the administrative authorities keep these records, including the Ministry of Public Administration and Local Government.

[54] See Cucic (2014, pp. 473–478) and Milovanovic et al. (2012, pp. 98–104).

[55] https://www.poverenik.rs/sr/извештаји-повереника.html.

They do have information on when a particular proceeding was initiated and ended, but they do not have and cannot electronically produce an overall statics on the number of cases that did not finish within legally prescribed deadlines. In order to obtain such information, one would have to check every single case separately. Evidently, since particular authorities do not keep such records, there is no central database with this statistic either. Due to the lack of information, it is impossible to understand how widespread is administrative silence in general and in different special policy domains.

Also, it is not possible to understand *the ratio between the number of cases in which the authorities failed to decide* within legally prescribed deadlines and *the number of those cases in which an appeal or a lawsuit against administrative silence had been submitted*. Without this information, it is not possible to exactly determine how many people consider these legal recourses to be an efficient protection mechanism and how often they use them and, if not, then why. The author tried to obtain the answer to the question concerning this ratio. One of the interviewed civil servants, a person working in the administration of Novi Sad (second largest city in Serbia), stated that the appeals against administrative silence are rarely filed, approximately less than 1% of all the cases in which the authority failed to render a decision in time. This can be confirmed by an older research. Namely, data show that in Slovenia, in 1987, when it was still a part of Yugoslavia, the administrative authorities failed to decide timely in 647,057 cases, but in the same period only 287 administrative appeals against administrative silence were submitted.[56] Hence, the parties decided to fight the silence with administrative appeals in 0.44% of the cases. One of the explanations for this behavior could be the lack of knowledge on the part of citizens.[57] Distrust in the efficiency of the system, as it will be displayed in the following section, could be another one.

12.3.4 Other Legal Remedies

Given that the authorities do not keep records concerning administrative silence, they obviously do not sanction civil servants, who did not

[56] Radjenovic (1988, p. 109, fn. 139).

[57] Ibid., pp. 109–110.

decide timely. Therefore, described mechanisms of ***disciplinary, misdemeanor, and criminal liability*** for administrative silence (see *supra* 2.5) were never used in practice. This has been explicitly confirmed by the interviewed civil servants from the Ministry of Public Administration and Local Government, the Administrative Inspection, and the administration of Novi Sad.

It was not possible to gather information concerning ***civil liability for non-execution of AC's judgments*** (*supra* 2.5). Records of such litigation claims are not kept. Nevertheless, it is unlikely that a plaintiff, who despite winning the case before AC did not manage to have such judgment executed by the defendant (sued administrative authority), would opt for another court procedure—civil litigation, which usually lasts for years, and be successful in it.

The alternative protection mechanism that proved to be fruitful is the ***complaint sent to the Ombudsman*** (Citizens' Protector). The Ombudsman regularly receives a few hundred complaints with regard to administrative silence (see Table 12.3).

In order to verify the fruitfulness of complaints, the author interviewed the ***Deputy Ombudsman*** (public official elected by the Parliament). In practice, as soon as authorities are informed of the fact that a complaint against their administrative silence has been lodged, they render the requested act. Only in a minority of cases, the Ombudsman actually conveys the entire procedure and issues a recommendation to the authority. The Deputy Ombudsman confirmed that it happens sometimes that the authority does not abide by the recommendation, but in her opinion this occurs in less than 3% of all the cases. Consequently, this appears to be the fastest formal legal cure against administrative silence.

Table 12.3 Complaint to the Ombudsman concerning administrative silence[a]

Year	*Complaints against silence*	*Total no. of complaints*	*% of silence complaints*
2014	355	2146	16.54
2015	385	2765	13.92
2016	352	2032	17.32
Total	1092	8943	12.21

[a] http://ombudsman.rs/index.php/izvestaji/godisnji-izvestaji

Finally, few *informal protection mechanisms* shall be mentioned. They were revealed in *the interview with the civil servant from the administration of Novi Sad*. Previously employed in the Department for Construction Permits and now is the Deputy Head of the Department for Public Property. This shift in employment helped to compare the work in these two departments, which have a completely different attitude toward administrative silence. This provided valuable insights.

The proceeding for issuance of construction permits in Serbia used to be excessively long (months, even years). The (then) Prime-Minister and the Minister for Construction, Infrastructure and Traffic made their top political priority to expedite this procedure because this was necessary for Serbia to climb the ladder on the Doing Business List.[58] They succeeded by significantly shortening deadlines (5 days as of the day of submission of the entire documentation) and eliminating administrative silence. In order to achieve this, they entered into a public–private partnership, establishing an electronic unified procedure for issuance of construction permits and trained all local and central government employees working in this field. So as to eradicate administrative silence, they established the Central Records of Unified Procedure (*Centralna Evidencija Objedinjene Procedure—CEOP*) and engaged in each local government unit one person—registrar—in charge of communicating with CEOP and resolving problems in the procedure. The electronic system automatically sends notification to CEOP if any deadline for deciding has been breached. If that happens in a sequence of cases, CEOP calls the local registrar and requests an explanation or solution for the problem. The interviewed civil servant informed us that there was a case in another local government unit, where CEOP asked why has there been a delay in 120 cases and these cases (and these are fairly complicated legal and factual matters) were then decided upon within 4 days. We were informed that sometimes administrative silence is a consequence of lack of knowledge on the part of local civil servants. In such situations, the Ministry, as the central authority, sends a unit of civil servants and privately engaged experts to help them resolve any trouble they encounter. Therefore, strong political will coupled with training and technical and legal support did the trick. In other words, good organization and management are curing the cause of

[58] www.doingbusiness.org/rankings.

the problem, unlike appeals, lawsuits, and complaints, which are healing the consequences.

The interviewed civil servant went on to compare the construction permit procedure with *the work in the Department for Public Property*, her current employment. In the latter, where the described political will and technical and legal support lack, civil servants do not care about administrative silence (as is the case in most special policy domains, the construction permits are a rare exception). There are no records of the number of cases in which the deadline was breached and in which administrative appeals were filed, nor is there any strive to resolve the silence related problems when they occur. In her words, administrative appeals against administrative silence are scarce (as was said, in her opinion, they are submitted in less than 1% of cases where the authority did not decide timely) and inefficient. What indeed enables the parties to resolve their problems are *two other alternative informal protection mechanisms*. The first one is the *Open Office of the Mayor* of Novi Sad.[59] This is an organizational unit established by the current Mayor, which helps citizens with the troubles they are having with the city administration and public service providers. She compared them to the local and provincial ombudsman (the Ombudsman of Novi Sad and the Ombudsman of the Autonomous Province of Vojvodina), which are, unlike their central level counterpart, inefficient in resolving the issue of administrative silence. In her words, the Open Office manages to resolve problems because they are "very hard, persistent" and civil servants "cannot get rid of them." On the other hand, the local and provincial ombudsman only sends a paper asking them what the problem is and, in the sources words, "one can slide just by sending them any kind of answer." The other protection mechanism, the one to which probably most of the parties resort, is *unofficial pleas or complaints to the competent civil servant themselves or better yet, their superiors*. The interviewed civil servant confirms that this gives results in practice, especially if the superior "nags" the civil servant to do his or her job. Again, disappointing as it may be, we have to quote her conclusion: "any alternative mechanism is better than the [*administrative*] appeal."

[59] http://www.novisad.rs/lat/otvorena-kancelarija.

12.4 Overall Assessment and a Possible Way Forward

A verse of the famous song used for the title of this book says "the silence like a cancer grows."[60] This goes for administrative silence as well. If the legislator, public officials, civil servants, and citizens do not fight it, it shall grow and endanger the proper functioning of the public administration. This paper deals with the ways in which this fight can be sustained and be successful.

The paper gives detailed overview of the "*remedies concerning administrative silence*" (*the administrative appeals and the lawsuits* to AC) and "*remedies against administrative silence*" (*disciplinary, misdemeanor, civil and criminal liability, supervision of the Administrative Inspection and the complaint to the Ombudsman*).

The paper presents *empirical data and results of the interviews* conducted with civil servants, a public official and a judge concerning this subject matter. They show that administrative silence represents a problem in Serbian administrative practice and unveil certain unexpected manners for resolution thereof.

The first thing to be done is strict implementation of the administration's obligation to establish and keep records regarding the number of cases that are not resolved in legally prescribed deadlines and information on administrative appeals and lawsuits submitted against administrative silence. This information should also be centrally kept and analyzed. Without them, any public policy aimed at combating administrative silence might amount to poking around in the dark. It is especially important to understand in which special policy domains the problem is encountered. This is the first step toward understanding why this happens (lack of human resources, equipment, training, political will, etc.) and what methods could be used for the amelioration of the situation.

Given all the arguments put forward above (*supra* 2.4.3), the author believes that the *existing general negative legal fiction of administrative silence is a better solution than the shift to the positive legal fiction as a rule*.

Nonetheless, the present legal regulation of the negative legal fiction can and should be improved in the following aspects. In the first place, the

[60] Simon and Garfunkel, "Sound of Silence," 1964.

deadlines for undertaking administrative activities should remain instructive, but the silence itself should be proclaimed illegal, thus enabling parties to seek damages in litigation (*supra* 2.5). Alternatively, the legislator could opt for direct payment of penalties by the authority to the aggrieved parties. If this option is chosen, it should be carried out with the utmost caution. It could be done only in specific special policy domains, where there are necessary human and material capacities for performing timely work. Otherwise, the country could go bankrupt. The legislator could also replicate the Slovene solution for the "Ping-Pong Effect" in cases of administrative silence. Namely, the Slovenian Administrative Dispute Act of 2006 prescribes that a lawsuit against administrative silence can be submitted to the court if the administration (including both first and second instance authority) did not render a non-appealable [*konacan*] administrative act within three years as of the day the proceeding was initiated.[61]

In spite of numerous arguments against the positive legal fiction as a rule, the positive legal fiction can be used as an exception in particular sectors. The compulsory prerequisites for this are sufficient staff, good training, supporting equipment, including ICT and the resolution of the legal deficiencies inherent to the positive legal fiction.

As to the latter, the legislator has to find an answer to the problems relating to the legal certainty, i.e., the manner of proving the content of the right that a party gained by an implicit positive decision and the legal certainty of third parties (*supra* 2.4.3). Parties have to get written confirmation about the fact that they acquired a legal right via the positive legal fiction. A way to do it could be establishment of a special administrative authority in charge only of issuance of such written confirmations and notification of the competent authority that its implicit decision has to be materialized. This could also be combined with a necessary preceding step, where the party would first have to ask the competent authority to provide written confirmation, along with a very short deadline for issuance thereof. The legal certainty for third parties could potentially be resolved by another legislative action. It could be set down in the law that the implicit act would produce its legal effects only once it has been materialized, i.e., confirmed in writing. The legislator must as well

[61] Sikic (2007, p. 209).

create the mechanisms for subsequent removal of illegal implicit decisions. The possibility of removal has to be set restrictively or, otherwise, it will strip this protection mechanism of any sense. On the other hand, the most important public interests (e.g., life, health, environment) have to be preserved even in this situation. Hence, a proper balance must be struck between the two. Lastly, these solutions must be backed up by good mechanisms for establishment of liability of civil servants.

In the end, all the mentioned mechanisms are fighting consequences of administrative silence. While some of them can help, the interviews with the civil servants indicate that the solution against administrative silence does not lie in the realm of law, but predominantly in the realm of good organization, good management, and political will. One final proposal, though the author has to admit that none of the suggested solutions represents a magic wand, could be establishment of a special authority that would be solely in charge of preventing and sanctioning administrative silence. This authority could be in charge of gathering all the data relevant for administrative silence, analyzing situations in all special policy domains, identifying the nature of the difficulties standing in the way of proper functioning of the administration and be centrally in charge of issuance of written confirmations in case of positive legal fiction. It would also be in charge of informing and aiding citizens in their struggle against administrative inaction. This work could be visible enough to the public to draw a much-needed political "sponsor" of the fight against administrative inaction and maybe put an end to this problem.

Bibliography

Batakovic, D. (2007). *Le chemin vers la démocratie - Le développement constitutionnel de la Serbie 1869–1903*. Belgrade: Institute for Balkan Studies.

Cani, E. (2014). Administrative Silence: Omission of Public Administration to React as an Administrative Decision-Taking. *Studime Juridike* [Juridical Studies], *4*, 151–173. Available at http://www.academia.edu/14059696/Administrative_Silence_omission_of_public_administration_to_react_as_an_administrative_decision-taking.

Cucic, V. (2011). Administrative Appeal in Serbian Law. *Transylvanian Review of Administrative Sciences*, *32*, 50–73.

Cucic, V. (2014). Serbia as a Part of the European Administrative Space: ADR Tools Applied to Administrative Law. In D. Dragos & B. Neamtu (Eds.), *Alternative Dispute Resolution in European Administrative Law* (pp. 461–485). Berlin-Heidelberg: Springer.

Cucic, V. (2016). *Upravni spor pune jurisdikcije – Modeli i vrste* [Administrative Dispute of Full Jurisdiction—Models and Types]. Belgrade: Faculty of Law of the University of Belgrade.

Davinic, M., & Cucic, V. (2017). The European Administrative Space—Instrument for Transforming the Serbian Administrative Law System. In A. Matei & C. Sandu (Eds.), *Enlargement of the European Administrative Space: Public Administration Reforms on the road to E.U. Membership* (pp. 223–246). Scholars' Press.

Dimitrijevic, P. (1996a). Odgovornost uprave za necinjenje sa posebnim osvrtom na "cutanje" uprave, doctoral dissertation defended at the Faculty of Law of the University of Belgrade, Belgrade.

Dimitrijevic, P. (1996b) Zakon o opstem upravnom postupku i "cutanje uprave" [The General Administrative Procedure Act and the "Administrative Silence"]. In S. Perovic (Ed.), *Aktuelna pitanja jugoslovenskog procesnog zakonodavstva* [Current Issues of Yugoslav Legislation] (pp. 427–448). Belgrade.

Gelevska Trajcevski, S. (2011). Компаративно-историски приказ на молчењето на администрацијата [Comparative-Historical Overview of the Administrative Silence]. In *Collection of Papers of the Faculty of Law "Justinian the First" from Skopje in the Honor of Naum Grizo* (pp. 219–230), Faculty of Law "Justinian the First" from Skopje, Skopje.

Gjidara, M. (2007). Le silence de l'administration publique et ses effets juridiques. In D. Aviani (Ed.), *Zbornik radova Hrvatsko-francuskog pravnog simpozijuma* [Collection of Papers of the Croatian-French Legal Symposium] (pp. 123–145). Split.

Hrusanov, D. (2011). Мълчанието на администрацията според административното право на Република България [Administrative Silence in the Administrative Law of the Republic of Bulgaria]. In *Collection of Papers of the Faculty of Law "Justinian the First" from Skopje in the Honor of Naum Grizo* (pp. 89–96). Faculty of Law "Justinian the First" from Skopje, Skopje.

Kostic, M. (1998). Cutanje uprave i ostvarivanje prava i interesa stranaka [The Silence of Administration and Fulfillment of Parties' Rights and Interests]. *Pravni zivot* [Legal Life], *10,* 143–150.

Kovac, P. (2011). Cutanje uprave izmedju zastite prava stranaka i javnog interesa [Silence of Administration Between Protection of Parties' Rights and the Public Interest]. *Pravni zivot* [Legal Life], *10,* 279–287.

Krbek, I. (1937). Upravnosudska zastita protiv sutnje upravne vlasti [Administrative Court Protection Against the Silence of administration]. *Mjesecnik* [Montly Review], *2–3,* 81–92.

Meca, M. (2014). The Evolution of Administrative Law in Albania and the Impact of the Decisions of the European Court of Justice in the Albanian Legal Reforms in Administrative Justice. *Tribuna Juridica* [Juridical

Tribune], *4*(2), 182–194. Available at http://oaji.net/articles/2017/5275-1513087163.pdf.

Milovanovic, D., Davinic, M., & Cucic, V. (2012). Efficiency of the Administrative Appeal (the Case of Serbia). *Transylvanian Review of Administrative Sciences, 37*, 95–111.

Parisio, V. (2013). The Italian Administrative Procedure Act and Public Authorities' Silence. *Hamline Law Review, 36*(1), 3–25.

Radjenovic, M. (1988). Cutanje uprave u jugoslovenskom pravu [Silence of Administration in Yugoslav Law], magistrate thesis defended at the Faculty of Law of the University of Belgrade, Belgrade.

Sikic, M. (2007). Primjena pravnih fikcija u institutu zastite gradjana od sutnje uprave. In D. Aviani (Ed.), *Zbornik radova Hrvatsko-francuskog pravnog simpozijuma* [Collection of Papers of the Croatian-French Legal Symposium] (pp. 95–121). Split.

Sikic, M. (2009). Pravna zastita od sutnje uprave prema novom Zakonu o opcem upravnom postupku [Legal Protection from the Silence of Administration in the new General Administrative Procedure Act]. In I. Kopric & V. Djulabic (Eds.), *Modernizacija opceg upravnog postupka i javne uprave u Hrvatskoj* [Modernization of the General Administrative Procedure and Public Administration in Croatia] (pp. 191–213). Zagreb.

Tomic, Z., Milovanovic, D., & Cucic, V. (2017). *Praktikum za primenu Zakona o opstem upravnom postupku* [Practicum for Application of the General Administrative Procedure Act]. Belgrade: Ministry of Public Administration and Local Self-Government of Serbia.

CHAPTER 13

Using Legal Fictions to Deal with Administrative Silence: The Case of Romania

Dacian C. Dragos, Bogdana Neamtu, and Bianca Radu

13.1 The Legal and Administrative Background for Analyzing Administrative Silence

13.1.1 The Distribution of Administrative Competence in the Context of the Legal-Administrative Tradition of the Country

Romania is one of the newest Member States of the European Union (entered EU in 2007, together with Bulgaria). Since the collapse of the communist regime in December 1989, the country has undergone

D. C. Dragos · B. Neamtu (✉) · B. Radu
Center for Good Governance Studies, Babes-Bolyai University, Cluj-Napoca, Romania
e-mail: neamtu@fspac.ro

D. C. Dragos
e-mail: dragos@fspac.ro

B. Radu
e-mail: bianca.radu@fspac.ro

D. C. Dragos et al. (eds.),
The Sound of Silence in European Administrative Law,
https://doi.org/10.1007/978-3-030-45227-8_13

a significant transition from a totalitarian regime (one of the most brutal in Eastern Europe) to a democratic one. This transition implied, among others, a complete restructuring of the political and administrative institutions.[1]

The Parliament, representing the legislative branch, has authority over many independent agencies whose attributions range from the regulation of specific areas (National Agency for Regulation of Energy Sector) to the monitoring and the assurance of fair competition (Competition Council) or the mediation of administrative disputes (the Ombudsman). At the top of the executive branch is the President of the Republic and the Government. Besides the central administration, Romania has a two-tier local public administration—intermediary level which is represented by counties and local basic level represented by rural communities and towns/cities. County and communal/city administration enjoy local autonomy. Central administration has a weak control over the decentralized and autonomous bodies of local administration (via the prefect institution). Judicial power is exercised by courts—courts of first instance, tribunals, courts of appeal, and the High Court of Cassation and Justice. From tribunals upward, all courts have specialized sections (units of judges) for administrative and fiscal matters.

The main legal instrument of the administrative law in Romania, in the absence of a law on administrative procedure (which is still at drafting stage),[2] is the Law on judicial review of administrative acts no. 554/2004, and a Law on petitions (Governmental Ordinance (hereafter GO) no. 27/2002), as well as numerous field-specific laws.

Although having a long tradition in our country, the judicial review of (communist) administration was practically inexistent during communist era. One of the first laws adopted by the new Romanian Parliament after the regime change in 1989, even before the adoption of a new Constitution, was the Law on judicial review of administrative acts (1990), replaced in 2004 by Law no. 554/2004. It remains the most important one in terms of a legal framework for administrative law.

[1] Hințea and Țiclău (2017).

[2] See Romanian Parliament (n.d.). Draft proposal of Administrative Code.

13.1.2 *The Context of Understanding Timeliness of Administrative Procedure*

The issue of timeliness is not explicitly addressed in the Romanian legal literature in terms of offering an analytical model/tool for understanding different options of the legislator with regard to administrative silence.

During the communist regime, citizens and their interests were completely disregarded in their relation with state institutions. The public sector, which overlapped with the communist party and the dictator, was supposed to know better which the public interest was. As mentioned previously, in this model it was practically impossible to challenge the action or inaction of public administration, as the state overlapped with the communist party.

After the fall of the communism, despite significant changes in the legal framework, the bureaucratic state apparatus retained some of the old habits. Organizational culture is more difficult to change than the legal framework. A state-centric approach has been in place for a long time, and it may prevail over the individual citizen even today.[3]

Some general idea on how timeliness works can be inferred from previous studies. Thus, in the area of free access to information several researches were conducted at the national level[4] and timeliness was one important aspect addressed by all these researches. At least several conclusions are very clear: In general, public institutions try to comply with the mandatory deadlines, but in a formal way—for example if clarifications are needed from the requester they wait until the last day to request the clarifications, thus extending the time needed for response; the rate of response to requests for information is still low, but despite low rates of response, public authorities report low numbers of court cases initiated by the citizens—this means that citizens often settle with their lack of response or decide not to take upon themselves the task of challenging the lack of response in courts.

[3] Liebert et al. (2013).

[4] Radu and Dragoş (2019).

13.1.3 The Main Principles of Administrative Law Regarding Timeliness of Administrative Procedures

The role of the principles of administrative law is rather difficult to identify in the context of Romanian administrative law. From the point of view of administrative law, the principles of this branch of law are "those fundamental ideas, guiding the organization and activity of the public administration."[5]

With respect to the main principles of administrative law concerning timeliness of administrative procedures (such as lawfulness, legitimate expectations, efficiency, proportionality, and reasonableness), they are not expressly provided by the law, so their source might be found somewhere else. Of importance to our analysis is also the fact that Romania does not have an Administrative Procedure Code and therefore the administrative proceedings lack an overall, logically organized, complete and coherent system of principles laid out. This is also the reason why there is no general base to resort to principles underpinning the EU law or any other source of international law.

However, there are the fundamental principles that derive from the fundamental provisions of the Constitution or are drawn from regulations issued under it.[6] Such principles are the principle of legality, the principle of access to justice, the principle of local autonomy, principle of equality, principle of non-discrimination, etc.

The question is thus whether the Romanian courts are willing to fill the gaps in written law by referring to "general principles." Examples of such judicial activism can be given, though they are limited.[7]

Romanian national courts are very receptive to the principles of administrative law, but only insofar as these principles are used as arguments in their interpretation of the national provisions of the law. In other words, except for isolated cases, principles are used by national courts either to fill in the gaps of existing legislation or in its interpretation, when ruling on the facts/merits.

This is also a consequence of the fact that Romania does not have an Administrative Procedure Code, and therefore courts are rather reluctant to apply in practice the principles of administrative procedure (such as

[5] Trăilescu (2010, pp. 8–9).

[6] Iovănaş (1977), p. 42.

[7] See, for details, Dragoş and Neamţu (2009).

weighting the conflicting interests of the parties, cost–benefit test, hearing the parties of the procedure, full motivation of the decision, and proportionality) just on the basis of legal writings (doctrine). Those principles would be natural limits for exercising discretion, but the legal culture in Romania is leaning traditionally toward legal grounds that are expressly laid down by the law.

13.1.4 Data and Method

This chapter is based on information derived from reviewing relevant national literature and doctrine on the topic of administrative silence, as well as national case law. In addition, it includes empirical data from a national wide research conducted by the authors in the period November 2018–February 2019. A survey was emailed to a sample of 636 public authorities from the whole Romania, pertaining both to decentralized local administration and to the deconcentrated one (agencies) located at the county level, as follows: 40 City Halls of county residences, Bucharest General City Hall and 6 City Halls of Bucharest sectors, 41 County Councils, 422 City Halls of municipalities, cities, and communes, 41 County Agencies for Environmental Protection, 41 County Agencies for Workforce Employment, 41 County Agencies for Public Pensions, National Agency for Workforce Employment, National Agency for Environmental Protection, and the State Inspectorate for Construction.

Public authorities were asked to provide us basic information on petitions and the way in which they handle them. It is worth mentioning that all public authorities are required by law (GO no. 27/2002) to publish twice a year a report on their handling of petitions; however, most of them do not comply with this legal obligation. The average response rate to the survey was 66.58%, though depending on the category of institutions there were somewhat significant differences (see Table 13.3). The survey included items such as number of petitions received per year, fields or subjects concerned, what types of requests public authorities include or exclude from the category of "petitions," compliance with deadlines in responding to petitions, extension of deadline for responding due to increased complexity, etc. All surveyed public authorities were also asked to describe if positive administrative silence was ever invoked or used in their handling of petitions. The empirical research investigated the period of 2016 and 2017 calendar years. 12 interviews with experts from various policy fields were also conducted in order to get a better understanding of the data collected from the survey or to obtain "unofficial" positions on delicate issues, which were not addressed in the official written responses.

13.2 The Legal Framework of Administrative Timeliness

13.2.1 Constitutional Basis

Article 51 of the Constitution establishes a general right for the citizens to address the public authorities by petitions, and the corollary obligation of public authorities to answer these petitions within the time limits and under the conditions established by law. Article 52 enshrines the citizens' right to judicial review in case public authorities do not answer within the deadlines, which is regulated by a subsequent organic law (Law no. 554/2004).

13.2.2 Administrative Procedure Act or Other General Laws

In the absence of an Administrative Procedure Code, the field is regulated through Governmental Ordinances (adopted by the Government but having the power of a law). There is a draft Code of Administrative Procedure, but it is pending adoption for more than 10 years. On the other hand, a new Administrative Code is in procedure of reconsideration by the Parliament after being declared unconstitutional by the Constitutional Court on extrinsic issues.

The main statute regulating administrative silence is GO no. 27/2002 which constitutes the general law for administrative deadlines; it provides for a general deadline of 30 days for answering petitions. In addition, Emergency Government Ordinance (hereafter EGO) no. 27/2003 specifically outlines the framework for silent approval.

There are special laws which provide for different deadlines or even explicitly state that an answer from the administrative body is needed before an action can be lodged with the court. In these situations, the deadline from the special law applies.

13.2.3 Sector-Specific Legislation (Special Laws)

There are two major pieces of legislation whose deadlines are important in practice due to their intensive use: the Code on fiscal procedure and the Law on building permits.

The Code on fiscal procedure (Law no. 207/2015) regulates the administrative procedure for establishing the tax duties for citizens and companies. *The general deadline* for the completion of this administrative task is 45 days, and it can be prolonged in justified instances, by request or ex officio (art. 77 of the Code on fiscal procedure). If an inspection is required for solving the request, then the deadline can be extended to 90 days. If new documents are requested, the deadline is prolonged with the period necessary for producing such documents. However, maximum deadlines are set also for these cases: 2 months when new information is requested from the petitioner, 3 months when other institutions must present the information, and 6 months when information is requested from fiscal authorities in other states.

The principle of *reasonableness* is guarding the possible abuses when setting intermediate deadlines. Art. 6 of the Law no. 207/2015 provides that whenever the fiscal authority needs to set a deadline for the taxpayer to exercise a right or to provide some documents, the deadline should be a reasonable one, and can be prolonged with the approval of the fiscal authority.

With respect to building authorization procedures, the law institutes a complex procedure, where the final decision is based on intermediary certificates, opinions, and legal notices—Law no. 50/1991 on building permits and Law no. 350/2001 on urban planning.

The general deadline for issuance of both certificates and building authorizations is 30 days from the moment when the documentation is submitted. A deadline of 5 days from submission is envisioned for cases in which the documents submitted by the applicant are incomplete. In practice however, public authorities make use of multiple subsequent requests for clarifications, which increases very much the final time period for the issuance of the certificate or the authorization. Other deadlines which can occur throughout the process are shorter than 30 days—for example, if an additional proof or certification is required from a different public authority, the deadline which intervenes in the overall procedures and increases the overall application period is 15 days.

During this lengthy process, the dynamic of the decision making leaves few possible instances where the applicants can challenge intermediate decisions by administrative appeal and then before a court. The final decision is based on all these intermediate internal decisions, so challenging the final decision means also discussing the legality of internal intermediate decisions. Third parties can challenge final decisions if they are aggrieved in their rights or interests, following the general judicial review procedure.

13.3 The Length of Administrative Deadlines

13.3.1 Length of Deadlines in General and Special Laws

GO no. 27/2002 which is the general law sets a 30 days deadline for responding to petitions, and this applies also for answering the administrative appeal. The same deadline can be found in some of the special laws—for example, building authorizations. Of course, there are administrative procedures where deadlines are longer—5 months, for example, for regaining nationality, but this is rather the exception than the rule. Interesting enough, during expert interviews with public servants in different fields, the issue of too short deadlines was raised. Public servants argued that sometimes the lack of response or delays are caused by workload which is unrealistic compared to the number of employees. They claimed that public institutions are inflexible in finding organizational solutions to higher workloads due to some particular circumstances—many employees retire or are on maternity leave at the same time or there are periods with specific assignments when workload increases a lot compared to regular activity.

13.3.2 Possibilities of Prolongation

The general deadline for answering petitions can be prolonged with 15 days in regular situations and with 30 days if the request regards the field of energy and natural gases, but only for reasons regarding the high complexity implied by answering the request. Notification of the petitioner regarding prolongation is mandatory. The law is salient regarding the number of successive prolongations.

The possibility given by law to prolong the deadline leaves room for discretion and abuse on the behalf of public administration, as there is no clear standard for assessing what a complex request looks like. Very often the public authorities simply prolong the deadline by claiming the complexity of the request, without explaining however what this complexity entails. Case law did not address this issue, by putting forth a test for determining what high complexity means as opposed to more regular requests/circumstances. In our own research for this chapter, the request from the public authorities of annual reports regarding petitions was labeled as complex in 40% of the cases. This needs to be corroborated however with the legal provision which imposes that such a report is drafted and published online ex officio. It is thus hard to understand how disseminating a report which in theory was already drafted can be assessed as involving a highly complex administrative activity.

13.3.3 Counting Deadlines

There are no clear rules in administrative practice regarding how the administrative deadlines are to be counted. The rules of the Code of Civil Procedure sometimes are invoked as applicable instead.[8] The law refers to calendar days and the calculation is in favor of the applicant—in the sense that calendar days prevail over working days.

13.3.4 The Concept of "Reasonable" Deadline

The question here is whether there is a standard to assess the reasonableness of the deadlines established in the Romanian law. The reference point is the standard imposed by the article 6 of ECHR. The Code of fiscal procedure refers to reasonableness (art. 6) but it does not set any standards, while as the general law, GO no. 27/2002 does not mention the principle at all.

The principle of "reasonable deadlines" has developed in the Romanian jurisprudence and doctrine mainly with respect to the administrative restitution of properties abusively taken by the communist regime. These procedures were one of the main causes of violation of article 6 (1) ECHR on account of the length of the proceedings by Romania, leading to a claim that the public authorities did not act in due time, in an appropriate manner and with utmost consistency. The law[9] provided for a procedure

[8] Art.75 of the Code on fiscal procedure.

[9] The most important ones are Law no. 18/1991, Law no. 169/1997, Law no. 400/2002, Law no. 247/2005, Law no. 112/1995, and Law no. 10/2001.

that had no deadlines so the petitioners did not have a fair representation of how long the procedure would be.

The Romanian Supreme Court rendered numerous rulings in which it argued that the state and its institutions should find administrative solutions for solving the situation.[10] A procedure must be finalized within a reasonable time and that all preliminary administrative procedures are part of this reasonable deadline and have to be taken into account when analyzing the case.[11] The High Court of Cassation and Justice stated in other cases that the term "reasonable duration" is a relative one and must be calculated by taking into account the contextual factors of the case.[12] In another case,[13] the court stated that administrative proceedings, in conjunction with the judicial proceedings, should have been carried out within a reasonable time and that the exceeding of a period of six years from the date of the request for reparation is a clear violation of the provisions of article 6 ECHR.

13.4 Responses to Administrative Silence. Legal Fictions

13.4.1 The Prevailing Model: Positive or Negative. The National Doctrine on the Administrative Silence

Based on the Constitution, GO no. 27/2002 and Law no. 554/2004 on judicial review, the prevailing legal fiction is that administrative silence means *refusal*, hence rejection of the petition.[14] The exception is the

[10] Decision no. 819/2012, File no. 491/54/2011 (http://legeaz.net/spete-contencios-inalta-curte-iccj-2012/decizia-19-2012).

[11] On 12 October 2010, the ECHR delivered a pilot judgment in the case of Maria Atanasiu and Others v. Romania (Case of Maria Atanasiu and others v. Romania, judgment of 3 October 2010, applications 30767/05, 33800/06), in which it held that the Romanian State was to take measures to ensure the effectiveness of the compensation and restitution mechanism and the effective protection of the rights set forth in article 6 (1) ECHR and article 1 of Protocol no. 1 to the Convention.

[12] Decision no. 1221/2012, File no. 911/46/2011 (http://legeaz.net/spete-contencios-inalta-curte-iccj-2012/decizia-1221-2012).

[13] Decision no. 118/2013, File no. 1233/54/2011 (http://legeaz.net/spete-contencios-inalta-curte-iccj-2013/decizia-118-2013).

[14] Manea (2014), p. 3. The same fiction was applied before the communist era—see Rarincescu 1936.

silent approval procedure, which is restricted to a few policy fields and was even further limited by the jurisprudence of the courts. Based on the findings from the empirical research, it can be concluded that silent approval was rendered almost impossible.

The legal consequence of the silence of the administration is the birth of the right to review the administrative inaction as unlawful. Law no. 554/2004 on judicial review of administrative acts is very clear in this regard: The court action can have as object the refusal (implicit or explicit) to issue an administrative act but also an administrative operation (a preliminary/preparatory act that binds the issuance of the final administrative act). So both the action and the omissions of the public authorities are challengeable in court. Based on this approach, administrative silence was assimilated to an administrative act. In the literature,[15] however, it was emphasized that silence cannot be anything else than a legal fact; it is in fact the law which attaches legal consequences to the fact that the deadline expires without receiving a response from the administration.

13.4.2 EU Influence over National Rules and Practices

The treatment of negative silence by applying the principle of reasonableness has its roots in the case law of the ECHR in article 6 of the Convention. Except from that, there is no trace of Europeanization of administrative practices as regards the timeliness of administrative procedure.

As to the positive silence, the momentum that led to the adoption of this legal fiction in Romania—namely the implementation of the services directive in Romania[16]—has passed rather quickly[17] and the courts have reduced the impact of the new legislation to minimum.

[15] Podaru (2003, p. 87).

[16] See, for details, Dragoş and Neamţu (2012).

[17] See, for details, Sect. 13.6 of the chapter.

13.5 The Negative Silence

13.5.1 Legal Character of Prescribed Deadlines

The negative silence (rejection/refusal) is regulated by GO no. 27/2002 and Law no. 554/2004 on judicial review. The deadline can be prolonged with 15 days in complex cases. The law states an obligation to inform the applicant regarding the prolongation.

If applicants are requested for new documents, the prolongation is actually even longer, due to the interplay between the prolongation itself and the additional time needed for the applicant to present new documents. The courts[18] have stated that if the applicant is requested new documents within a certain deadline and the applicant fails to present those documents within the new deadline, he/she cannot benefit from the provisions regarding administrative silence and go to court. In other words, the administrative procedure carries on. It is not clear though whether the extension can be longer than 15 days or several extensions are possible as well.

13.5.2 The Possibility to Issue a Valid Act After the Deadline Expired

As to the legal character of prescribed deadlines, it is instructive in the sense that the act can be adopted after the deadline has passed, but on the other hand failure to meet the deadline means (in principle) administrative silence and can lead to administrative appeal and court proceedings.

13.5.3 Legal Consequences/Fictions. Finality and Enforceability

The Law on administrative review no. 554/2004 provides in article 2(1)(h), a right to action in those instances when the public authority does not answer a request within the mandatory 30 days deadline. Furthermore, article 2(2) of Law no. 554/2004 equals the silent rejection with an express unjustified refuse to solve a request regarding a legitimate interest or right, which in its turn is considered to be an administrative act. So administrative acts, express refusals, and administrative silence are all equaled to a unilateral decision of the administration.

[18] Călărași Tribunal, Decision no. 40/2016.

Summarizing, the failure to answer to an application for an administrative act in 30 days could mean silent rejection of the application. However, silent rejection does not occur if the authority conducting the procedure has requested additional information from the petitioner.

The provisions from Law no. 554/2004 regulate the finality of this fiction as well as enforceability. According to article 18, the court may, where appropriate, annul the administrative act in whole or in part, oblige the public authority to issue an administrative act, to issue another document or to carry out a particular administrative operation. The court will also decide on material and moral damages caused, if the plaintiff has requested it.

If the public authority is obliged to conclude, replace, or amend the administrative act, issue another document, or carry out certain administrative operations, the final decision shall be enforced voluntarily within the time limit set out therein, and in the absence of such a term within no more than 30 days from the date of final judgment (article 24(1)).

If the debtor does not voluntarily execute its obligation, this will be enforced by forced execution. The executing court shall apply to the head of the public authority or, as the case may be, to the liable person a fine of 20% of the gross minimum salary per day of delay, which is paid to the state budget. If, within 3 months from the date of notification of the enforcement of the fine and the granting of penalties, the debtor fails to fulfill the obligation stipulated in the enforceable title, the enforcement authority shall, upon the creditor's request, set the final amount due to the state and the amount shall be due by way of penalties. At the same time, by the same decision, the court will establish, under the conditions of art. 891 of the Code of Civil Procedure damages the debtor owes to the creditor for non-performance in nature of the obligation (article 24 (2–4)).

13.5.4 Case Law

The case law of the Romanian courts is very clear on this respect: When the public authority requests amendments, clarifications, additional documents, etc., to the petitioners, the silent rejection does not occur.

In a case regarding the regaining of Romanian citizenship,[19] the court argued that the public body did not breach the 5 months period/deadline

[19] Bucharest Court of Appeal, Decision no. 3822/2012.

from the date of registration of the application, set out in article 16 of Law no. 21/1991 on Romanian citizenship, because new information was requested from the applicant. In this situation, a further period can be granted for the new verification.

A similar reasoning was applied in the case concerning the issuance of a building authorization (Călărași Tribunal[20]). Along the same lines, Bucharest Tribunal[21] argued that the request for additional documents to be submitted to the Commission for verification and approval of the documents prepared by the state-owned companies for the issuance of the attestation of ownership right on the land based on Government Decision no. 834/1991 is not equivalent to the failure to resolve the request.

The same conclusion arises in the case of a priest who did not receive the blessing to teach religious education in schools.[22] In this case, the failure to resolve the applicant's request, the non-granting of the written blessing, was determined by the fact that the applicant was unable to present the priest's recommendations, and in the absence of documents proving his participation in the liturgical, missionary, or social-philanthropic, as the cult imposes it, the refusal of the defendant appears to be justified.

13.5.5 Empirical Insights

The empirical research conducted for this study intended first to see how fast the public authorities are providing the data that they are supposed to keep in a specified format imposed by the law—a semestrial report on the handling of petitions (GO no. 27/2002). It was an exercise to test the administrative timeliness of the administration, not only to gather data about such timeliness. The average percentage of institutions that answered overall is 66.58%, but with major differences between centralized institutions and autonomous ones.

We got answers from the majority of Ministry extensions at county level (deconcentrated agencies) in no more than 2 weeks (from 1 to 14 days) with just two answers in 27 days—still within the official

[20] Călăraşi Tribunal, Decision no. 40/2016.

[21] Bucharest Tribunal, Decision no. 29/2016.

[22] Maramureş Tribunal, Decision no. 1558/2016.

deadline—and one in 46 days—outside the deadline). Local authorities answered in proportion of 80% within the deadline (from 1 day to 30 days, evenly distributed), with delays not going above 10 extra days, except some outliers. The 24 County councils responded in less than 7 days from the deadline, with just two of them in 16 days respectively 30 days, so all within the deadline. Finally, the 16 cities that are county seats that responded took more time in average, about two weeks, but they in majority complied with the deadline (only two late responses, in 34 days and 40 days). The overall conclusion is that the agencies subordinated to the ministries are more organized and centralization makes for better record keeping. The local authorities are so different in how they handle petitions, but they still manage to keep within the deadline, although as we will see the answers are not complete or meaningful. So at least procedurally speaking, administrative silence is not a common occurrence when public authorities are asked data that by law should be readily available or should be kept on record and reported. It may be different for data that is not available in reporting formats or is scattered within the institution thus harder to assemble.

The average number of days reported by public institutions to answer the petitions in 2016 and 2017 is around 14 days, which, in theory, could be considered very timely. There is however one caveat to these findings: public authorities report average deadlines, so it is very difficult to actually determine if there are cases when deadlines are not complied with. This is a very sensitive issue and public authorities do in general all they can to offer as little information as possible on failure to comply with the deadlines. This attitude goes back more than a decade ago when the FOIA legislation was first implemented. NGOs carried out monitoring campaigns, and the public authorities which failed to respond were often blacklisted. In response, public authorities are very secretive even today about cases when deadlines are missed. Several public authorities offered us access to their actual records, where each petition is registered with the date of entrance to and exit from the public institutions. In these rare cases, we were able to actually determine for each petition the actual time for issuing a response.

The situation is quite different in the case of petitions pertaining to special legislation. In the area of *building authorizations*, delays are the norm and happen quite frequently. We obtained data from interviews with real estate developers and architects. We were told that sometimes the issuance of a certificate can take up to 6 months. In our interviews one interesting finding occurred—there are significant differences in terms of timeliness among major cities. The real estate developers, who are involved in real estate projects in multiple cities, told us that cities comparable in size and pressure in terms of real estate market (Cluj-Napoca, Timișoara, Iași for instance) have very different average times for responding to similar requests. A website reporting data from the practice of lawyers in the field of real estate states that 255 days is the average time for obtaining a building authorization in Romania. Based on the legal provisions, even in complex cases, this should not take longer than 75–80 days.[23] Another interesting finding from the real estate developers was that it is very rare for them to challenge in court the delay or silence of the public authorities. They all argued that in the end, you are forced to work with the city hall (especially if doing multiple projects on a continuous basis) and it is better to be on cordial relationships with the staff from the city hall. The entire process was described as pure bargaining.

For the field of *taxation*, the Annual reports of the National Agency for Fiscal Administration state that the average time for responding to contestations (administrative appeal) was 60 days in 2016[24] and 97 days in 2017.[25] This is quite high when assessed against the general deadline for answering petitions of 30 days.

Additional information on petitions and how they are handled was collected as part of this research. Though this information is not directly related to timeliness, it offers a clearer context in which the activity of public organizations takes place. Some brief conclusions are shown below. In the tables included in the text, *N* is the number of institutions from each level of administration that answered the questionnaire in a coherent and reliable way. In Table 13.1, the total number of petitions received by category of public institution is analyzed for the two years considered during research. Though some variations are observable, overall the volume of petitions is relatively stable. Interesting information can be however obtained if we look at individual authorities included in the sample. There are clear outliers, where the number of petitions is sometimes even 10 times higher than in the case of similar institutions. In most

[23] Stoica and Maria (2016).

[24] National Agency for Fiscal Administration (2016), p. 34.

[25] National Agency for Fiscal Administration (2017), p. 27.

Table 13.1 The data on petitions based on institutions' reporting

		Total no. of petitions received	*Total no. of petitions solved within the legal timeframe*	*No. of petitions with extended deadline*	*Petitions redirected to other authorities—the deadline starts to run again*	*Classified petitions*
City Halls of municipalities, cities and communes *N = 93*	2016	44,799	44,737 (99.86%)	57 (0.13%)	4	1
	2017	45,844	45,735 (99.76%)	105 (0.23%)	4 (0.01%)	0
County Agencies for Environmental Protection *N = 40*	2016	3257	2786 (85.54%)	2 (0.06%)	442 (13.57%)	27 (0.83%)
	2017	2655	2257 (85.01%)	350 (13.18%)	42 (1.58%)	6 (0.23%)
County Agencies for Workforce Employment *N = 29*	2016	879	876 (99.66%)	0	0	3 (0.34%)
	2017	800	798 (99.75%)	0	0	2 (0.25%)
County Agencies for Public Pensions *N = 19*	2016	17,880	16,915 (94.60%)	965 (5.40%)	0	0
	2017	20,327	19,049 (93.71%)	1278 (6.29%)	0	0
County Councils *N = 31*	2016	4373	3966 (90.69%)	13 (0.30%)	347 (7.94%)	47 (1.07%)
	2017	4131	3814 (92.33%)	15 (0.36%)	246 (5.95%)	56 (1.36%)
Cities that are county capitals and 6 sectors of Bucharest *N = 17*	2016	41,906	37,479 (89.44%)	4071 (9.71%)	0	356 (0.85%)
	2017	57,478	52,945 (92.11%)	4006 (6.97%)	1	526 (0.92%)
National Agency for Workforce Employment	2016	1431	1241 86.72%	0	130 9.08%	60 4.19%
	2017	1302	1109 85.18%	0	152 11.67%	41 3.15%
National Agency for Environmental Protection	2016	76	28 (36.84%)	0	48 (63.16%)	0
	2017	73	40 (54.79%)	0	33 (45.21%)	0
Territorial Inspectorate for Construction	2016	8863	5141 (58.01%)	0	3191 (36.00%)	531 (5.99%)
	2017	8396	5206 (62.01%)	0	2751 (32.77%)	439 (5.23%)

of these cases, we found that in fact this high number is attributable to how public authorities define petitions (though law is clear on this, some public authorities include requests made under FOIA here). In terms of applicants/requesters, Table 13.2 offers valuable information. In most cases, requesters are moral persons who are applying in their capacity of citizens. Legal entities make far less inquiries using the legal tool of petitions, with one notable exception, namely in matters which are pertaining to employment. Table 13.3 includes the response rate we got from public institutions when requesting information on the petitions they handle. Granted, this request was made under FOIA but low rates of response in this case are indicative of how public authorities deal with requests from citizens and legal entities in the community (Table 13.4).

Table 13.2 Types of applicants (petitioners)

Institution		*Total*	*Citizens*	*Legal entities*	*Anonymous*
Cities and communes *N = 87*	2016	26,785	23,394 (87.34%)	3391 (12.66%)	
	2017	24,865	22,244 (89.16%)	2621 (10.54%)	
County Agencies for Environmental Protection *N = 37*	2016	3062	2318 (75.70%)	734 (23.97%)	10 (0.39%)
	2017	2460	1662 (67.56%)	795 (32.32%)	3 (0.12%)
County Agencies for Workforce Employment *N = 29*	2016	879	440 (50.06%)	439 (49.94%)	
	2017	800	376 (47%)	424 (53%)	
County Agencies for Public Pensions *N = 12*	2016	10,386	9622 (92.64%)	764 (7.36%)	
	2017	11,812	10,945 (92.66%)	867 (7.34%)	
County Councils *N = 16*	2016	1897	1538 (81.08%)	359 (18.92%)	
	2017	2011	1571 (78.12%)	440 (21.88%)	
Cities (county capitals) and 6 sectors of Bucharest N = 16	2016	108,127	68,764 63.60%	39,363 36.40%	
	2017	115,365	53,722 46.57%	61,643 53.43%	

Table 13.3 The response rate to our questionnaire by institution

	No. of requests sent	*No. of requests received*	*Response rate*
City Halls of municipalities, cities and communes	422	104 (93 valid—that could be used for research)	24.64% (22.04%)
County Agencies for Environmental Protection	41	40	97.56%
County Agencies for Workforce Employment	41	29	70.73%
County Agencies for Public Pensions	41	19	46.34%
County Councils	41	33	80.49%
Cities (county capitals) and 6 sectors of Bucharest	47	37 (23 useful but incomplete, 14 complete)	79.72%

Note In the case of two county councils, the answers could not be used—they refused to communicate the data, considered our request as abusive or invited us to their headquarters to study the documents. Also, from 37 county seats, only 23 contained the required figures, but then on closer look only 14 were actually complete with required information

13.6 The Positive Silence

13.6.1 The Legal Character of Prescribed Deadlines

EGO no. 27/2003,[26] subsequently amended through Law no. 486/2003 and Law no. 157/2010, is the main piece of legislation which regulates silent authorization. This regulation implies that the legislator regards administrative silence as an administrative act, in the sense that silence is interpreted as acceptance, as a positive answer to the request of the citizen.

As stated in article 1 of EGO no. 27/2003, the main aim of this regulation was to remove administrative barriers from the business environment, as well as fighting corruption by means of reducing discretionary powers in the decision-making process of public administration. The procedure of silent authorization was meant to apply to all authorizations issued by public administration authorities, with the exception of those issued in

[26] Official Journal of Romania no. 291 from 25 April 2003.

Table 13.4 The average time of answering petitions (data from their own reporting)

Institution		*0–4 days*	*5–10 days*	*11–20 days*	*21–30 days*	*Over the deadline*
Cities and communes *N = 62*	2016	6	22	28	6	0
	2017	7	21	28	6	0
County Agencies for Environmental Protection	2016 *N = 27*	3	18	6	0	0
	2017 *N = 26*	4	14	7	0	1
County Agencies for Workforce Employment *N = 25*	2016	0	17	5	3	0
	2017	0	18	5	2	0
County Agencies for Public Pensions *N = 12*	2016	0	0	8	4	0
	2017	0	0	8	4	0
County Councils	2016 *N = 12*	2	0	6	4	0
	2017 *N = 10*	1	2	4	3	0
Cities county residences and 6 sectors of Bucharest	2016 *N = 14*	0	0	4	10	0
	2017 *N = 13*	0	0	4	9	0

the field of nuclear activities, of those concerning the regime of firearms, ammunition and explosives, the regime of drugs, and of those in the field of national safety.

A momentum that led to this development was definitely the implementation of the services directive in Romania.[27] Following the services directive, the Romanian government was forced to create Points of Single

[27] See for details Dragoş and Neamţu (2012).

Contact for easing the communication with foreign investors.[28] A further objective was administrative simplification. In that context, it was argued that the establishment of the institution of silent authorization would be beneficial for the entire administrative system because it leads to a simplification of the procedure and speeds up its functioning mechanism. Silent authorization was regarded as an important tool for reducing bureaucracy because it generates an automatic response, without additional efforts being needed for the preparation and issuance of an administrative act.[29]

13.6.2 The Possibility to Issue a Valid Act After the Deadline Expired

The question here is whether authorities can still issue decisions after the deadline and get away with disregarding the provisions of the law. In principle, there is no provision prohibiting the public authority to issue an administrative act outside the time limit. Courts also take notice of such development and cease the proceedings meant to oblige the administration to act with no real repercussions. Such conduct may give rise to compensation though, if proven in court that the delay has produced damages.

13.6.3 Legal Fiction. Finality and Enforceability

The silent authorization means that the activity, service, or profession authorized silently can be exercised/performed by the applicant after the deadline has passed. However, a document is needed in order to claim that a silent authorization has occurred, which can be issued either by the competent public authority or by court. The applicant has to perform a "forum shopping" and choose among the two procedures; administrative, in front of the competent authority, or judicial, in front of the court. If

[28] Official website of the Romanian Point of Single Contact, available at https://edirect.e-guvernare.ro/SitePages/landingpage.aspx.

[29] Commission Staff Working Document, Detailed information on the implementation of Directive 2006/123/EC on services in the internal market, Accompanying the document Communication from the Commission to the European Parliament, the Council, the European Economic and Social Committee and the Committee of the Regions on the implementation of the Services Directive. A partnership for new growth in services 2012–2015, Brussels, 8.6.2012, SWD (2012)148.

the administrative procedure is preferred, the law states that the document shall be released within 5 days upon request, and it will state the fact that no response was given to the applicant within the legal deadline. The statement is equivalent to an authorization in front of every controlling authority or other persons. Evidently, the beneficiary will have to present also the application which was granted silently, in order to reveal the "content" of the authorization.

One interesting question is raised with regard to the nature and legal value of the document issued in accordance with articles 7 and 8, provided that the authorization which it replaces needs to be issued in a standardized format. In this situation, despite the fact that the public administration authority is forced to issue the document which allows the applicant to carry out an activity, provide a service, or exercise a profession, the document cannot be used by the applicant instead of the authorization. In this case, its practical value is questionable.

With regard to this situation, in the literature several authors[30] argued that, concerning authorizations which are valid only in standard format, regulated expressly by the law, the provisions of EGO no. 27/2003 do not apply.

However, unlawfulness can be established at a later stage as well. According to article 16 of the EGO 27/2003, if the public administration authority discovers that certain important conditions for the issuance of the authorization are not met, it will notify its holder about the irregularities identified, how they can be remedied, and the time frame within which this needs to be done, and if those remedies are not implemented it can annul the act. The deadline for remedies cannot be shorter than 30 days, but there is no deadline in which the public authority must discover the irregularities. However, regardless of the above situation, if certain conditions which cause a *severe violation of public interest, national safety, public order, and public health* are present and cannot be remedied, the act can be annulled at any time. The reasoning of this remedy is that the procedure must not have contrary effects than those envisaged by the law.[31]

[30] Puie (2010).

[31] Pitești Court of Appeal, Decision no. 2675/R-CONT/2012.

13.6.4 Exceptions to Positive Silence. The Case Law of the Courts

In practice, questions were raised on the applicability of silent authorization in domains such as building, environmental, or other sensitive fields. They are sensitive because of the high likeliness of abuses in a transitional administration like Romania's. Scholars as well as practitioners argue that it is very important to limit the fields to which silent authorization applies. This is because if this procedure applies to areas of great importance the damages it may cause could be hard to remedy afterward.[32]

First, the question was raised regarding whether the provisions of EGO no. 27/2003 apply to construction authorizations, urbanism certificates, and urbanism documentation. This controversy was settled by the Decision no. 13/16.09.2013 of the Higher Court of Cassation and Justice by a interpreting decision, by which the silent authorization was excluded from the field of *construction authorizations, urbanism certificates, and urbanism documentations.*[33]

Then, there were opinions according to which the field of environmental protection should have been exempted from the procedure of silent authorization, given its paramount importance, as well as due to the legal regime of the acts issued by environmental protection authorities, which are described as technical-legal acts.[34] The case law of the courts seems to support this opinion, stating that the issuance of environmental authorizations is regulated through a set of regulations which form a cohesive whole in the area of environmental protection, which represents a major objective of public interest, based on the principles and strategic elements which are conducive to sustainable development. The main regulations in this area are EGO no. 195/2005 regarding environmental protection and Order no. 1798/2007 regarding the approval of the procedure for the issuance of the environmental authorization.[35]

Finally, the concept of "administrative discretion" has been found not to accommodate very well the silent authorization. Hence, in a situation where the claimant requested the court to observe the meeting of the conditions necessary for the exercise of the mediator position, the court argued that silent authorization does not apply in this case. This is due to

[32] Ghencea (2013, p. 135).

[33] Radu and Chelaru (2018).

[34] Lazăr (2004, p. 182).

[35] Gorj Tribunal, Decision no. 884/2015.

the fact that authorization to exercise the mediator profession implies an assessment of the curriculum of the training program completed and not just the fact that certain documents were submitted.[36]

In a similar vein, the court argued that the procedure for granting university titles (associate professor in this case) does not fall under the provisions of EGO no. 27/2003. In this case, we are not in the presence of issuing an authorization as defined by article 3 of EGO no. 27/2003, given the fact that the court cannot substitute the evaluation done by a specialized committee and the freedom of appreciation of the competent bodies.[37]

In conclusion, the law did not have many chances in practice. The courts have settled that in those situations when granting an authorization implies an assessment done with the use of the discretionary power by public authorities, silent authorization is not possible.[38]

The silent approval does not occur when there are interruptions of the administrative procedure. Thus, if before the deadline new information is requested from the applicant, in other words if the application must be completed or amended, the deadline has no effect and no silent approval can be acknowledged.[39]

13.6.5 *Empirical Evidence*

One may wonder based on the previous section, if there is any room for application of EGO no. 27/2003 in Romania.

In the survey conducted for the research on administrative silence, all public institutions were asked about cases of silent approval. All reported that it has not been the case.

The findings from the survey indicate on the one hand that there are really no situations left when silent approval works. Courts pretty much removed by their decisions a lot of policy fields where it might have been relevant. Some of the public servants with whom we discussed also told us about the strategies public institutions use in order not to go over the deadlines. One interviewee told us that they always try to respond

[36] Highest Court of Cassation and Justice, Decision no. 131/2011.

[37] Constanţa Court of Appeal, Decision no. 106/CA/2009.

[38] See Sect. 13.6.4.

[39] Timiş Tribunal, Decision no. 1473/2011.

to requests, even if incomplete. Sometimes they know that the response is not exactly what the requester was after, but, as our responder put it, "some answer is better than no answer."

Even more interesting were the responses from real estate developers. Two of them argued that they do not like the idea of silent approval, even if it meant bypassing the public authorities which do not respond within the legal timeframe. The key word used was "insecurity." They argued that they wouldn't have invoked silent approval anyway, and called it a "recipe for disaster." They pointed that this might work in other countries but not in Romania, where there is a lot of instability and lack of clarity.

13.7 Supervision of Administrative Timeliness

13.7.1 Supervision of the Timeliness

The administrative control of the timeliness of the public administration is exercised according to the rules of administrative control. There are no special rules for dealing with situations of non-observance of deadlines. The Romanian law does not sanction the non-observance of time limits with unlawfulness of the act. The only sanction is the fact that those that consider themselves aggrieved by the lack of response within the deadline may challenge this silence in court.

GO no. 27/2002 on petitions states that failure to observe the general deadline of 30 days to answer petitions addressed to public authorities can *entail only administrative sanctions* and the *silent rejection effect* (if no additional documents were requested from the applicant). GO 27/2002 applies in subsidiary to the Environmental Impact Assessment (hereafter EIA) procedure as well, so a similar argument can be constructed for the EIA procedure.

The scope of judicial review, on the other hand, can be also to oblige the public authority to issue an act that has been silently refused until then. The delays in finalizing an administrative procedure are not considered to be punishable by administrative fees, but the court can impose fees for not observing the deadline imposed by the court as a result of the judicial review.

13.7.2 Governmental Strategies and Actions and Their Effects on Tackling Excessive Length of Procedures

In Romania, there are no specific strategies or action plans by the government which target specifically lengthy administrative procedures. There are two instances which could be associated with the issue of administrative silence.

Numerous action plans and measures are aimed at increasing transparency and free access to public sector information. The 2016–2020 National Anti-corruption strategy[40] mentions the law on petitions among the other sources of national law circumscribing this topic, but without providing more information. Reduction of bureaucracy means also reducing red tape—number of documents needed for an authorization, length of procedures, unpredictability, etc. Again, lengthy procedures are not mentioned separately, but together with other factors.

13.8 Legal Remedies

In administrative law, there are two major ways of contesting allegedly unlawful decisions/acts: the administrative appeal and the judicial review (court action). While the administrative appeal is an attempt to solve the dispute at administrative level, the judicial review is an adversarial proceeding by which an individual transfers the conflict with a public authority to the (administrative) courts.

13.8.1 Administrative Appeal

An administrative appeal implies the existence of an administrative act or the lack of action on the behalf of public administration. The administrative appeal represents a request addressed to a public authority through which the aggrieved person requests that administrative measures are taken with regard to the administrative decision: annulment, modification, and even the issuance of a new decision (in the case of refuse by public administration). The action in front of an administrative court implies that the aggrieved person will draft a claim, in contradictory with a public authority.[41]

[40] Available at http://mdrap.ro/sna-2016-2020.

[41] Dragoş and Neamţu (2013), p. 72.

In the Romanian law, the administrative appeal can be found in all of its forms: objection (internal appeal), hierarchical appeal, and external appeal to the control bodies. Objection and hierarchical appeal are expressly regulated by the Law no. 554/2004 on judicial review.

The administrative appeal needs to be answered, according to the Romanian law, within 30 days time limit,[42] which can be extended with 15 days in case the request is complex, but only after the claimant is informed about the extension.

When an initial petition was not answered in time, or when the administrative appeal against an administrative act was not answered in time, the aggrieved party can go to court against either the silent refusal (which is assimilated to an administrative act) or against the aggrieving administrative act (art. 7 of the Law no. 554/2004 on judicial review). So the administrative appeal is not mandatory when the initial request/petition was not answered in time by the administration. The alleged justification lies in the fact that the complainant should not be exposed to a negative decision twice.

Empirical data from a previous study conducted in Romania[43] seems to suggest the effectiveness of administrative appeals in general, but less so in specific fields such as tax litigation.[44]

13.8.2 *Judicial Review*

In jurisprudence,[45] it was stated that in the case of failure to resolve a request within the time limit laid down by the law, the situation recognized as "silence of public administration," the review before the administrative court can only concern the obligation of the public authority to respond to the request and, to remedy the damage caused by not issuing in time the requested act.

This solution is also in line with the provisions of art. 18(1) of Law no. 554/2004 and is important because, in the case of the second actions, the

[42] Art. 7 of the Law no. 554/2004.

[43] See Dragoş et al. (2014, p. 421).

[44] See the reports of the National Agency of Fiscal Administration, where only around 16% of administrative appeals are admitted, although at least 30% of the rest are annulled by the court.

[45] Highest Court of Cassation and Justice, Decision no. 4522/2014.

court cannot substitute itself to the administration for substantive examination of the merits of the claim but may require the administration only to issue a procedural document by which it will issue a favorable or unfavorable solution to the individual.

This approach has been shaped by the practice of the courts, a relevant judgment being the one in which the Alba Court of Appeal held that[46]:

> The applicant and the court of first instance are in error when they consider that by penalizing the silence of the administration, it is necessary for the competent authority to issue the decision with a certain content, namely to recognize the applicant's right to be admitted to the profession without examination. Verification by the court of the applicant's fulfillment of the conditions in this procedural framework is premature and constitutes an interference with the administration's attributions, as practically the court decision replaces the administrative decision, which is inadmissible.

Nevertheless, in the jurisprudence, the view is that for the purposes of admitting an administrative litigation against the failure to adjudicate an application within the legal deadline, the applicant must have fulfilled all his obligations under the law and made available complete documentation for the purpose of resolving the request.[47]

13.8.3 Court Remedies for Silent Approval

In principle, the same conditions regarding revocation, amendment, nullity that apply to regular administrative acts shall apply also to silent authorizations, as there is no specific provision of the law on this matter stating otherwise. In fact, this is considered the "safety net" for public authorities that have granted authorizations silently, in the sense that they use the opportunity to make life harder for those who benefit from the silent authorization. Consequently, the competent authority can revoke the authorization until it "entered the civil circuit," which means that the authorization was followed by another legal act or put into practice.

A more complex situation is when the authorization is confirmed by a court decision. In this case, the competent public authority who should have issued the authorization cannot revoke it or modify it. It can

[46] Alba Court of Appeal, Decision no. 2010/2011.

[47] Cluj Court of Appeal, Decision no. 184/2010.

only challenge it to the superior court, in order to get an annulment. In this context, the question is whether the court, when assessing the silent authorization or reviewing its legality, should analyze the application against the legal requirements for granting an authorization or should just acknowledge the fact that non-observance of the deadline has had as an effect a valid authorization. The courts do perform a test of lawfulness of the silent authorization, arguing that this procedure was not intended to be used passively by the administration in order to leave unlawful applications pass by, but to speed up the administrative proceedings for the benefit of those who follow the rules.

13.8.4 Damages

Law no. 554/2004 regulates, through art. 1 par. (1), art. 8 and art. 18, a subjective administrative review of full jurisdiction, in which the court has to examine not only the compliance of the administrative act with the law but also the existence of a damage to the applicant.[48]

An example in this respect is Decision no. 625 of 3 February 2010 of the Bucharest Court of Appeal, in which the court held that, by failing to solve the complainant's request within a reasonable time, he/she was damaged by the inevitable extension of the entire procedure for examining the application for the recovery of citizenship. This equals to a violation of the right to have the request assessed in a reasonable timeframe, given the time consumed with the entire process. The Court considered that, in the face of the favorable solution, the applicant was deprived of the possibility of exercising its rights as a Romanian citizen, which is likely to create frustrations, dissatisfactions, and other feelings of non-fulfillment.

13.8.5 The Role of the Ombudsman

The organization and functioning of the Romanian Ombudsman institution is regulated under the provisions of article 58 of the Constitution and detailed in the Law no. 35/1997.

In administrative matters, one of the most important attributions of the Ombudsman is the one that grants competence to verify the manner

[48] Highest Court of Cassation and Justice, Decision no. 3324/2007, not published.

Table 13.5 Complaints addressed to the Ombudsman (2015–2018)

Type of liberty breached (object of complaints)	*2015*	*2016*	*2017*	*2018*
Right to petitions (article 51 from the Constitution)	1682 (14%)	1850 (15%)	1727 (16%)	1637 (12%)
Right of the citizen agrieved by the action of public administration (article 51 from the Constitution)	923 (8%)	758 (6%)	793 (7%)	587 (4%)

Source Compiled by the authors, based on the annual reports (2015, 2016, 2017, 2018) of the Romanian Ombudsman (Available at http://www.avp.ro/index.php?option=com_content&view=article&id=50&Itemid=174&lang=ro-ro)

the authorities handle petitions received and to request the authorities or officials of the public administration concerned to cease the violation of the rights and freedoms of individuals, to restore the petitioner's rights and to compensate for the damage, according to article 15 (1) (f) of the Law no. 35/1997. Moreover, the Ombudsman has the competence to file a complaint before the administrative courts, under the terms of the administrative litigation law (article 15 (1) (m) of the Law no. 35/1997).

In the performance of his duties, the Ombudsman issues recommendations,[49] through which he shall notify the public administration authorities about the illegality of administrative acts or deeds. The silence of the public administration bodies and the late issuance of acts are assimilated to administrative acts, according to article 24 of the Law no. 35/1997.

Despite very lengthy annual reports of the Romanian Ombudsman, it is not very clear from the statistical data provided the role of the Ombudsman as redress mechanism in cases pertaining to administrative silence. From the data offered, it is very clear that the Ombudsman is solving a high number of complaints regarding the breach of the citizens' right to petitions. Also, the Ombudsman is dealing with a significant number of complaints regarding aggrieved citizens by the action or inaction of public administration. Table 13.5 includes a number of complaints addressed to the Ombudsman from 2015 to 2018 pertaining to these liberties/rights.

[49] Dragoș et al. (2010, p. 61).

13.9 Overall Assessment of the Rules and Practices Around Administrative Silence

When considering the law by the book and the general legal regime, in Romania the regulation of administrative silence is pretty scarce and legal challenges are arising as regards its legal regime.

Before 2003, the only option was that administrative silence meant rejection, and this was stated in Constitution and in laws. Then, stemming from a frustrating and lengthy administrative procedure, and prompted by the transposition of the services directive in Romania, the trend has been reversed by conferring a quite wide coverage to the regulation on silent approval in 2003, which was meant to revolutionize the administrative procedures altogether and to discipline the public authorities. However, faced with the practical implications of positive silence, the courts have reduced the coverage of silent approval procedures until they are now almost absent. So we are back to administrative silence meaning silent rejection, a principle that remains the most lasting one in the Romanian administrative law.

Our empirical research conducted for this study revealed that public authorities do not keep a structured account of timeliness in solving administrative petitions, that petitions are treated together with other requests (FOIA requests for instance), that deadlines for answering petitions are in principle not exceeded but other tricks are used, such as requesting new documents, which can prolong the procedure indefinitely. Reporting on timeliness of administrative procedure uses mean periods instead of describing cases where the deadlines were exceeded, and does not consider the completeness of the response given to the petitioner. When confronted with litigation on administrative silence, the courts try to be effective and look at the underlying legal issue at hand and treat administrative timeliness as a sideline issue. There are no strategies aimed at reducing the processing time for citizen's requests or a coordinated analysis of this phenomenon.

The main conclusion is that in Romania the positive silence is dangerous and it was abandoned as a system of dealing with administrative inactivity. The negative silence is safer although still ineffective, in the context of an administration that is endlessly trying to reform itself and to adopt the good governance principles.

References

Dragoş, D., & Neamţu, B. (2009). Europeanisation of Administrative Law in Romania: Current Developments in Jurisprudence and Legislation. *Review of European Administrative Law, 2*(1), 87–98.

Dragos, D., & Neamtu, B. (2012). The Implementation of the Services Directive in Romania. In U. Stelkens, W. Weiss, & M. Mirschberger (Eds.), *Implementation of the EU Service Directive* (pp. 513–544). The Hague: TMC ASSER Press andSpringer.

Dragoş, D., & Neamţu, B. (2013). Effectiveness of Administrative Appeals—Empirical Evidence from Romanian Local Administration. *Lex Localis—Journal of Local Self-Government, 11*(1), 71–85.

Dragoş, D., Neamţu, B., & Balica, D. (2010). The Romanian Ombudsman and Its Interaction with the Courts—An Exploratory Research. *Transylvanian Review of Administrative Sciences, 31E,* 58–75.

Dragoş, D., Neamţu, B., & Suciu, R. (2014). The Dynamic of Administrative Appeals and Other ADR Tools in Romania. In D. Dragoş, & B. Neamţu (Eds.), *Alternative Dispute Resolution in European Administrative Law* (421–459). Berlin: Springer.

Ghencea, F. (2013). *Autorizarea administrativă. Teorie. Practică. Jurisprudenţă* [*Administrative Authorization. Theory. Practice. Jurisprudence*]. Bucharest: Editura Universul Juridic.

Government Emergency Ordinance no. 27 from 18 April 2003 on silent administrative procedure, published in Official Gazette of Romania no. 291 from 25 April 2003.

Government Ordinance no. 27 from 30 January 2003 on regulating the settlement of petitions, published in Official Gazette of Romania no. 84 from 1 February 2002.

Hinţea, C., & Ţiclău, T. (2017). Public Administration Reform in Romania After 25 Years. In P. Kovač & M. Bileišis (Eds.), *Public Administration Reforms in Eastern European Union Member States. Post-Accession Convergence and Divergence* (pp. 389–426). Mykolas Romeris University and University of Ljubljana.

Iovănaş, I. (1977). *Drept administrativ şi elemente ale ştiinţei administraţiei (Administrative law and elements of administrative science)* (p. 1977). Bucharest: EdituraDidacticăşiPedagogică.

Law no. 554 from 2 December 2004 on administrative review, published in Official Gazette of Romania no. 1154 from 7 December 2004.

Lazăr, R. (2004). Pasivitatea administraţiei. Aspecte de ordin substanţial şi procedural. Procedura aprobării tacite (Passivity of Administration. Substantive and Procedural Aspects. The Silent Approval Procedure). *CurierulJudiciar*, no. 11–12.

Liebert, S., Condrey, S., & Goncharov, D. (2013). *Public Administration in Post-Communist Countries: Former Soviet Union, Central and Eastern Europe, and Mongolia*. Boca Raton: CRC Press.

Manea, M. (2014). Efectele juridice ale acceptării tacite în cadrul procesului legislativ, la iniţierea, avizarea, dezbaterea, votarea, adoptarea şi publicarea actelor normative [The Legal Effects of Tacit Acceptance in the Legislative Process, When Initiating, Debating, Voting, Adopting and Publishing Normative Acts]. *Buletin de Informarelegislativă al ConsiliuluiLegislativ, 1*, 3–15.

Ministry of Regional Development and Public Administration, National Anticorruption Strategy 2016–2020. Available at http://mdrap.ro/sna-2016-2020. Accessed 4 January 2019.

National Agency of Fiscal Performance. (2016). Performance Report 2016. Available at https://static.anaf.ro/static/10/Anaf/Informatii_R/Raport_performanta2016_07042017.pdf. Accessed 7 January 2019.

National Agency of Fiscal Performance. (2017). Performance Report 2017. Available at https://static.anaf.ro/static/10/Anaf/Informatii_R/Raport_performanta_2017_26032018.pdf. Accessed 7 January 2019.

Podaru, O. (2003). Paradoxurile tăcerii: De la non-voinţă la act. Studiu de dreptadministrativ [Paradoxes of Silence: From Non-Will to Act. Study of Administrative Law]. *Studia Universitatis Jurisprudentia*, nr. 1, pp. 88–115.

Puie, O. (2010). Consideraţii privitoare la procedura aprobării tacite în contextul dispoziţiilor modificatoare aduse Ordonanţei de Urgenţă nr. 27/2003 prin Legea nr. 157/2010 (Considerations regarding the silent approval procedure in the context of the amending provisions brought by Emergency Ordinance no. 27/2003 through Law no. 157/2010). *PandecteleRomâne*, nr. 10.

Radu, B., & Drago, D. (2019). Freedom of Information in Romania: Legal and Empirical Insights. In Dragos, D., Kovac, P., & Marseille, A. (Eds.), *The Laws of Transparency in Action: A European Perspective. Legal and Empirical Insights into the Practice of Freedom of Information in Selected Jurisdictions* (pp. 425–470). London: Palgrave Macmillan.

Radu, L., &Chelaru, M. (2018). Suntem pregătiţi pentru aprobarea tacită a cererilor pentru emiterea autorizaţiilor de construire? [Are We Ready for Silent Approval of Requests for the Issuing of Construction Authorizations?]. Hotnews.ro- Dosarejuridice – Aurorizarea de construire. Available at https://www.hotnews.ro/stiri-specialisti_stoica_si_asociatii-22839369-suntem-pregatiti-pentru-aprobarea-tacita-cererilor-pentru-emiterea-autorizatiilor-construire.htm. Accessed 6 January 2019.

Rarincescu, C. (1936). *Contenciosul administrativ roman (Romanian administrative appeal)* (2nd ed.). Bucharest: Editura Universală Alcalay.

Romanian Ombudsman, Annual reports. Available at http://www.avp.ro/index.php?option=com_content&view=article&id=50&Itemid=174&lang=ro-ro. Accessed 8 January 2019.

Romanian Parliament (n.d.). Draft proposal of Administrative Code. Available at http://www.curieruljudiciar.ro/wp-content/uploads/2016/12/Proiect-COD-procedura-administrativa.pdf. Accessed 5 January 2019.

Stoica, L., & Maria, M. (2016). Mecanismul şi utilitatea procedurii aprobării tacite în materia avizelor pentru autorizaţia de construire [Mechanism and Utility of Silent Approval Procedure in the Field of Preliminary Approvals for the Construction Authorization]. *Arena Constructiilor*. Available at https://www.arenaconstruct.ro/mecanismul-si-utilitatea-procedurii-aprobarii-tacite-in-materia-avizelor-pentru-autorizatia-de-construire/. Accessed 7 January 2019.

Trăilescu, A. (2010). *Drept administrativ (Administrative Law)* (4th ed.). Bucharest: C.H. Beck.

CHAPTER 14

Administrative Silence: A Polish Perspective

Agata Jurkowska-Gomułka, Kamilla Kurczewska, Katarzyna Kurzępa-Dedo, and Dawid Sześciło

14.1 The Legal and Administrative Background for Analyzing the Administrative Silence

The legal and institutional setup of the Polish administrative system reflects the model characteristic of the European administrative space, i.e., the system of principles, rules, and administrative procedures in European countries founded on the Weberian bureaucracy model and the

A. Jurkowska-Gomułka (✉) · K. Kurczewska · K. Kurzępa-Dedo
University of Information Technology and Management, Rzeszów, Poland
e-mail: ajurkowska@wsiz.rzeszow.pl

K. Kurczewska
e-mail: kkurczewska@poczta.onet.pl

K. Kurzępa-Dedo
e-mail: kkurzepa@wsiz.rzeszow.pl

D. Sześciło
University of Warsaw, Warszawa, Poland
e-mail: dawid.szescilo@uw.edu.pl

D. C. Dragos et al. (eds.),
The Sound of Silence in European Administrative Law,
https://doi.org/10.1007/978-3-030-45227-8_14

traditions of public law (with the *Rechtsstaat* as a governing idea).[1] The concepts of bureaucracy and *Rechtsstaat* are inevitably linked, as bureaucracy can be defined as an organizational system governed by law and structured around the concept of competence, i.e., a formal empowerment to act.[2] The current Polish administrative system clearly follows this legalistic paradigm, yet historically the relationship between the law and administrative actions was not that clear.

Currently, a legalistic paradigm of public administration is fully accepted as a foundation of public administration in Poland, and discussion over administrative liberty was concluded by the constitutional principle of legality (Art. 7 of the 1997 Constitution of the Republic of Poland), requiring a specific legal basis for all actions and operations of administrative bodies.

The key pillars of the legalistic paradigm of public administration in Poland, aside from this constitutional principle, are the codified general administrative procedures (Code of Administrative Procedure—CAP[3]) and the two-tier system of judicial review of administrative actions and omissions by specialized administrative courts. The foundation for the judicial review of administrative actions was established in the communist era. In 1980, the Supreme Administrative Court (SAC) was established, providing limited, single-instance judicial review over the state administration. The shift toward the two-tier system of administrative courts was envisaged by the new constitution adopted in 1997.[4] The process of establishing the first 16 regional administrative courts (RAC) was completed in 2003. In 2002, the new Law on Judicial Administrative Procedure (JAP)[5] was also adopted, providing a comprehensive legal framework for the handling of cases by both administrative courts.

The establishment of the two-tier system of administrative courts completed the model of four instances in administrative procedure. While this model provides an extensive review of administrative acts and other

[1] Olsen (2003).

[2] Ziller (2007).

[3] Consolidated text: Journal of Laws (JoL) 2018, item 2096. All consolidated texts available on: http://www.isap.sejm.gov.pl.

[4] JoL 1997, no 78, item 486.

[5] Consolidated text: JoL 2018, item 1302.

actions of administrative bodies, in the context of administrative silence it might also create some risks and challenges.

The key principles of general administrative procedure established by the CAP reflect the key components of *Rechtsstaat* and good administration. The normative value of the general principles of administrative procedure was confirmed by the SAC in 1982, when the Court stated that general principles are equally binding for administrative bodies pursuant to detailed procedural provisions of the CAP.[6]

The catalog of administrative procedure principles established in the CAP also explicitly addresses the issue of timeliness. Article 12 enshrines the principle of timeliness by requiring public administrative bodies to deal with cases thoroughly and quickly, resolving them using the simplest available methods. In judicial practice, the principle of timeliness was widely discussed. In particular, the SAC noted that there is no inherent conflict between the principle of timeliness and, for example, the principle of legality. There is no hierarchy between these principles—both should be taken into account equally, without prioritization of timeliness over compliance with the material and procedural regulations.[7] It is clear that the principle of timeliness does not undermine the principle of due care requiring the administrative body to investigate carefully all factual and legal aspects of the case. On the other hand, as one of the administrative courts underlined, the requirement of due care does not itself justify excessive length of the proceedings.[8]

The Polish legal system provides no explicit reference to the right to good administration, which is understood, in broad terms, as capturing key procedural guarantees of integrity, timeliness, proportionality, and legality of administrative actions. However, in judicial practice, numerous courts refer to this concept. Firstly, courts considered the relevance of the guarantees of the right to good administration established by Article 41 of the EU Charter of Fundamental Rights. Before the Charter of Fundamental Rights was ratified (altogether with the Treaty of Lisbon), the SAC pointed out that both the EU and the principles of good administration stemming from the Council of Europe documents "can be treated

[6] Judgment of SAC, I SA 258/82. All Judgments of SAC and RAC available on http://orzeczenia.nsa.gov.pl.

[7] Judgment of SAC, II GSK 916/15.

[8] Judgment of RAC, VI SAB/Wa 30/07.

as acts defining the desired standards of administration."[9] Despite the lack of binding force of European standards of good administration, the SAC recognized their importance for the interpretation of duties addressed to public administrative bodies under procedural administrative law.

14.2 The Legal Framework of Administrative Timeliness in the Polish Legal System

14.2.1 The Constitution of the Republic of Poland

The Constitution does not refer directly to the problem of administrative silence and its effects. However, some general rules expressed in the Constitution can be considered highly relevant for the discussion of the problem of administrative timeliness and of interpreting laws in this regard. Firstly, Article 2 declares Poland a democratic state ruled by law. The rule of law is considered a basis for efficient functioning of public administration oriented to meet citizens' needs (including administrative timeliness). Secondly, Article 7 demands that a public administration, as an "organ of public authority shall function on the basis of, and within the limits of, the law." This requirement of fulfilling standards settled by law is surely applied to ensuring that public administration's actions are time constrained. Thirdly, Article 9 claims that "[t]he Republic of Poland shall respect international law binding on it," imposing on public administration a duty to operate in compliance with, for example, Article 41 of the EU Charter of Fundamental Rights and Article 6 of the European Convention on Human Rights (ECHR).

The Polish Constitution provides some means to protect rights and freedoms guaranteed by the Constitution itself. Even if there are no specific provisions referring strictly to negative effects of administrative silence, general provisions on defending rights and freedoms can be successfully applied in cases of an administration's indifference to timeliness. Firstly, nobody can be barred by any specific laws from pursuing claims alleging infringement of freedoms or rights (Art. 77.2). If administrative silence causes any harm, anyone affected shall have the right to compensation for it (Art. 77.1). Additionally, persons influenced by administrative silence "shall have the right to apply to the Ombudsman

[9] Judgment of SAC, II OSK 1237/07.

for assistance in protection of their freedoms or rights infringed by organs of public authority."

14.2.2 The Code of Administrative Procedure

The Code of Administrative Procedure's (CAP) in Chapter 7 establishes a few general rules regarding administrative silence (including administrative timeliness) in proceedings before administrative bodies. For a long time, the only remedy was a complaint regarding inactivity (PL: *zażalenie na bezczynność*). Since the introduction of the amendments in the CAP in 2017,[10] the Code contains silent authorization, as well (Art. 122a–122f CAP).[11]

14.2.3 Sector-Specific Legislation (Special Laws)

A possibility of modifying deadlines in special laws, currently expressed in Article 35.4 of the CAP, was introduced on April 11, 2011 by Act of 3 December 2010 Amending the CAP and JAP.[12]

The CAP's regulations on deadlines are not applied in two cases. The first is a general derogation stating that a certain scope of matters or certain procedures before a particular administrative body are not subject to deadlines settled in the CAP, and simultaneously, specific deadlines are settled. An example of such a technique can be found in Law on Industrial Property, Article 255.3: "Provisions of the CAP regarding deadlines for dealing with cases are not applied to cases dealt with by the Patent Office in a contradictory procedure." The second technique for eliminating the CAP's regulations of deadlines, seemingly much more popular, is a simple introduction of specific deadlines in particular laws, without a direct derogation of the CAP.

Some laws follow a pattern established by the CAP for regulating deadlines (e.g., Act on Tax Law (Consolidated text: JoL 2019, item 900) also establishes deadlines for simple ("no more than 1 month") and complex ("no more than 2 months")) matters, whereas other laws solely amend

[10] Act of 7 April 2017 on Amendments to the Code of Administrative Procedure and Other Acts (JoL 2017, item 935), entered into force on 1 June 2017.

[11] As a result of doctrinal discussions: Suwaj and Perkowski (2010), Dobosz (2011), Miłosz (2011), and Suwaj (2014), and others.

[12] JoL 2011, no. 6, item 18.

a certain category of deadlines such as deadlines for dealing with appeals (e.g., Art. 16.1.2 of Act on Access to Public Information[13]).

In general, the derogations from the CAP's deadlines do not constitute any coherent system. They were created in different moments, based on rather ad hoc decisions on the duration of deadlines.

While discussing interplay between the CAP and special laws, it must be mentioned that an application of a silent authorization (Art. 122a CAP) requires direct legal basis in special laws. In November 2018, almost 18 months after the new regulation on the positive silence had gone into force, there were 15 laws referring to a silent authorization.

14.3 The Length of Administrative Deadlines in Polish Law

14.3.1 General and Specific Rules

The length of deadlines in administrative (non-court) procedures is established in the CAP. The length of administrative proceedings is identified separately for the first instance proceedings, the appeals proceedings, and the "simplified proceedings." The very basic time limits for dealing with administrative cases (at the first instance) are described as "without unnecessary delay" (Art. 35.1 CAP) and "promptly" (Art. 35.2 CAP). This proceeding duration is indicated for "cases that can be examined on the basis of evidence provided by a party, together with a demand that the proceedings be commenced; or on the basis of universally-accepted facts and evidence known to the body conducting the proceedings, or which can be established on the basis of the data which is at the disposal of that body" (Art. 35.2 CAP). In the Polish doctrine, a guideline on case completion without unnecessary delay is commonly considered as a rule of administrative procedure[14]: a case should be resolved—if possible—before an expiry of deadlines prescribed in the law, in the shortest possible time,[15] but not necessarily immediately.[16]

[13] Consolidated text: JoL 2018, item 1330.

[14] Wróbel (2018).

[15] Hauser (1997, p. 1).

[16] Przybysz (2018, para. 3).

In simple cases requiring evidentiary process, a standard time limit for a proceeding is one month; cases that are more complex can permit two months from the commencement of the proceedings. Even if the CAP does not require it, parties to the proceeding should be informed whether the case has been assigned to the "simple" or "complex" category, due to the important legal results of this activity.[17]

Appeal cases should be dealt with within a month of the appeal being received. Simplified proceedings should be completed without any unnecessary delay, one month from the commencement at the latest (Art. 35.3a CAP), regardless of the fact that the conditions concerning the evidentiary process (settled for the proceeding at the first instance) are met.

As mentioned above, deadlines for administrative proceedings settled in the CAP can be modified by special laws (Art. 35.4 CAP).

Apart from the deadlines for administrative proceedings, the CAP sets deadlines for issuing statements (a confirmation of established facts or laws) on a demand of a party ("no later than 7 days" [Art. 217.3]), as well as for dealing with complaints ("without undue delay and within one month at the latest" [Art. 237.1]).

The deadlines settled in special laws can be shorter or longer than the ones established in the CAP. A differentiated duration of deadlines is justified by the nature of the administrative matters under the regulation of special laws; usually, longer deadlines are provided for cases that require extremely thorough examination (e.g., in patent law [Art. 255.3] of the Act of Law on Industrial Property[18] provides six months for closing a contradictory proceeding before the Patent Office), or pharmaceutical law (Art. 18 of the Act on Pharmaceutical Products sets "no more than 210 days" as the deadline for dealing with an application for an access to the market). A unique example of a special law is contained in the Act of Construction Law,[19] establishing a special regime for obtaining administrative consent for some types of construction. Instead of applying for a construction permit, the investor can inform the administrative body of the project, which the administrative body can protest by administrative decision within 21 days from the delivery of the n.otification. If the administrative body does not protest within the prescribed period, the

[17] Dawidowicz (1983, p. 159) and Wróbel (2018, para. 9).

[18] Consolidated text: JoL 2017, item 776.

[19] Consolidated text: JoL 2018, item 1202.

silence is considered consent (Art. 30.5). There are acts that even calculate the time limit in hours: "not later than 96 hours before the planned date of the meeting" (Art. 14 of the Law on Public Assemblies[20]).

14.3.2 *Possibilities to Prolong Deadlines*

The deadlines prescribed in the CAP can be prolonged if the administrative body fails to complete the case within the standard time limit. The party must be informed about the reasons for the delay and the new deadline for dealing with the case. The party should be also informed about their right to present an urging claim (Art. 36.1 CAP). Information duties are not dependent on a "fault" of the public administrative body that caused the delay. Even if the reasons for the delay extend beyond the administrative body, it is obliged to fulfill the information duty (Art. 36.2 CAP). The Code of Administrative Procedure does not contain restrictions on the number of prolongations. Theoretically, parties may be informed about delays and new deadlines many times. An urging claim constitutes a sort of appeals procedure—a claim regarding inactivity or excessive duration is generally addressed to a public administrative institution of a higher level. If there is no higher-level institution, an urging claim is ruled by the administrative body involved in the faulty procedure. In this case, the body reviewing the urging claim is obliged to complete the proceeding "without unnecessary delay," to explain reasons for administrative inactivity or excessive duration of the proceeding and to identify the officials responsible. If necessary, remedies preventing future administrative inactivity or excessive duration should be enforced (Art. 37.8 CAP). An urging claim must be reviewed within seven days of the date it was received by the relevant institution (Art. 37.5 CAP). The response to the application takes the form of a ruling (Art. 37.6 CAP), which determines whether or not the administrative body remains inactive. The confirmation of a negative approach by the administrative body must be accompanied by the statement that the administrative inactivity constituted a serious violation of law (Art. 37.6.1 CAP). If the proceeding has not been completed, a new deadline is set (Art. 37.6.2a CAP). If this deadline is too short due to new circumstances, or because new evidence

[20] Consolidated text: JoL 2018, item 408.

Table 14.1 Judgments of Local Government Appeal Colleges (inactivity complaints and urging claims)

Period	*Total number of closed cases*	*Number of inactivity complaints/urging claims*[a]	*Number of inactivity complaints/urging claims admitted*	*Percentage of inactivity complaints/urging claims admitted (%)*
2015	147,388	2199	687	31.24
2016	152,837	2341	939	40.11
2017	142,675	2730	946	34.65

Source Compilation based on: https://www.bip.gov.pl/subjects/index/6942
[a]See Sect. 14.2.2

has appeared, the authority who issued the ruling is entitled to prolong the deadline (Art. 37.7 CAP).

The Polish legal system does not permit prolongation of deadlines due to a party's consent.[21]

Administrative courts are permitted to set deadlines if a claim of administrative inactivity or excessive duration of a proceeding is admitted (Art. 149 JAP).

The survey conducted among 227 public officers employed in Polish governmental and self-governmental administration[22] showed that 20% of them pointed too short deadlines as the most often reason for administrative silence (Table 14.1).

14.3.3 Counting Deadlines

Deadlines start running, in most cases, from the moment of a commencement of a proceeding. This moment is determined differently for proceedings commenced *ex officio* and proceedings commenced on the demand of a party. In the second case, the moment of commencement is "the date on which the demand is served on the public administrative body" (Art. 61.3 CAP) or, if the demand is submitted in electronic form, "the date

[21] Wróbel (2018, para. 8).

[22] The survey, conducted by researchers from University of IT and Management in Rzeszow in March-June 2018, covered 227 persons in 13 public administration units in the Podkarpackie region (2,129,138 inhabitants).

on which the demand is entered on the computer system of the public administrative body" (Art. 61.3a CAP).

The moment of commencement of an *ex officio* proceeding is more controversial because it is not regulated directly in the CAP. Currently, the prevailing approach presented in the case law of the Polish Supreme Administrative Court is that the date of the initiation of a proceeding is the date when the administrative body undertook the first activity in the case.[23]

The date of the initiation of an appeals procedure is not clearly set in the CAP. Case law shows that the period for dealing with an appeal runs from the date the administrative body of the second instance receives an appeal accompanied by the administrative files from the body.[24] If the first-instance body does not submit an appeal and files on time, the deadline is calculated from the date the applicant notified the second-instance body that an appeal was not examined.[25]

The calculation of the deadline does not include the date on which the triggering event occurs (e.g., the day on which the public administration gets a demand). The deadline expires on the last calculated day (Art. 57.1 CAP). Deadlines that are calculated in weeks or months expire at the end of the day of the last week or month, which is the day that bears the same name as the first day of the period. If there is no such a day in the last month, the expiration date is the last day of that month (Art. 57.2 and 57.3 CAP). "Days" in the CAP are calendar days, although "if the deadline falls on a public holiday, the deadline shall be deemed to be the next business day" (Art. 57.4 CAP).

14.4 Responses to Administrative Silence

While awareness of the problem of administrative silence and its practical consequences for the protection of citizens' rights were raised in both the legal doctrine and jurisprudence of courts, lawmakers have abstained from any reaction for many years.

One of the first attempts to address this issue was the process of implementation of the EU Services Directive. The Services Directive's

[23] Resolution of SAC, FPK 5/96.

[24] Judgment of SAC, OSK 111/11.

[25] Judgment of SAC, IV SAB 8/91.

implementation involved, in particular, the review of the 2004 Act on the Freedom of Economic Activity (FEA),[26] setting basic principles and procedures regulating the relationship between state administration and businesses.

The following formula of silent authorization in administrative matters relating to the businesses was added to the FEA: "If the administrative authority fails to process the application on time, it is deemed that it has issued a decision in accordance with the entrepreneur's application, unless the provisions of separate acts, due to an overriding public interest, state otherwise" (Art. 11.9). This provision is, essentially, a literal copy of the relevant provision of the Services Directive. As a case of first impression, it can be treated as a revolutionary change introducing the general principle of silent authorization in all proceedings involving the businesses. Although confirmed by the case law of administrative courts,[27] the provision had practically no actual impact. This provision's interpretation required the principle of silent authorization—even in cases involving entrepreneurs—to be explicitly confirmed in the special law regulating the respective procedure. The provision of the FEA was not sufficient as a stand-alone legal basis for applying the silent authorization in practice.

It should be also noted that in 2018 the FEA was repealed and replaced by the new Act on Entrepreneurship,[28] which excluded the above-mentioned provision.

In the case of non-issue of an individual interpretation within a statutory period, Article 14o.1 of the Tax Law finds that the interpretation fully follows the position of the applicant. The major difference is that the procedure established in the Tax Law is available to all taxpayers.

Prior to the introduction of the general formula into the CAP, Construction Law (Art. 30.5) also envisaged a form of silent consent.

In June 2017, silent consent was introduced to the CAP in a formula largely based on the German model. It applies solely in cases where it is explicitly stated in the provisions of special laws. The CAP provides a general procedural framework. For example, it enables a party to request notification of the consent. The introduction of these provisions to CAP,

[26] Consolidated text: JoL 2017, item 2168.

[27] See, e.g., judgment of SAC, II GSK 1918/14; Judgment of RAC, VI SA/Wa 1240/12.

[28] Consolidated text: JoL 2018, item 646.

however, did not extend the number of cases where silent consent is envisaged by special laws.

The Polish doctrine's approach toward silent consent is rather mixed. While the problem of excessive length of administrative proceedings is widely recognized, multiple concerns are raised in the literature about addressing this issue via introduction of silent consent. Some authors claim that when cautiously introduced, silent consent may become an effective instrument for increasing the efficiency of public administration and reducing the costs of its functioning.[29] It is also expected that the scope of silent consent will be gradually extended with the aim of reducing administrative burden and simplifying administrative procedure.[30]

However, there are also opinions indicating several risks and adverse effects of the potential expansion of silent consent in various administrative procedures. It is underlined that silent consent clearly prioritizes timeliness over all other principles of administrative procedure. Timeliness becomes even more important than the principle of balancing private and public interests. Silent consent plays a role when the process of balancing private and public interests, essential to administrative procedure, is absent or incomplete. When there is no realization of the key objectives of the administrative procedure, there is activation of silent consent.[31] As such, silent consent remains in conflict with the founding principle of administrative procedure. Silent consent also prioritizes the principle of timeliness over the duty of care. Lack of comprehensive case review is no longer an obstacle to finalizing it.

Silent consent may undermine the principle of equal treatment and consistency in the activities of public administration. Silent consent explicitly allows for a scenario in which identical—in terms of relevant facts—cases will result in different settlements. Time is the decisive factor. In one case, an authority will be able to fully investigate the case and issue a negative decision within the statutory period; in a second case,

[29] Gurba (2015, p. 100).

[30] Kubiak (2009, p. 46).

[31] Threats caused by the silent authorization, e.g., regulation (a) favors opportunistic and even corrupt behavior aimed at exceeding the deadline by the administrative body, (b) manipulating the delivery time of documents, (c) the problems of timely delivery of official correspondence (judgment of the Constitutional Tribunal, Kp 7/09).

despite identical circumstances, the settlement will be positive due to the expiration of the statutory deadline for issuing an administrative act.[32]

14.5 Negative Silence

The deadlines for public administrative bodies that adjudicate proceedings provided in the CAP and Tax Law are almost exclusively indicative. An authority is obliged to notify the parties when matters are not timely settled, stating the reasons for the delay, indicating a new date, and instructing about the right to appeal (Art. 36 CAP). The issuance of a decision after the deadline does not have a negative impact on the lawfulness of the final decision; the decision remains valid and has legal effects (judgment of SAC, III SA 696/85).

However, failure to act or non-performance by an authority within the deadline indicates that the authority violated the law. In the event of an authority's inactivity in issuing individual acts, the party acquires the right to file an urging claim (Art. 37 CAP and Art. 141 of the Tax Law) and subsequently, a complaint to the administrative court (Art. 3 JAP).

In cases of inactivity in forms other than individual acts (e.g., inactivity of a creditor who fails to perform activities prescribed by law), the party acquires the right to file a complaint, either to a higher-level body (e.g., Art. 6.1a Act on Enforcement Proceedings in Administration) or to the administrative court (e.g., Art. 101a Act on Municipal Self-Government[33]; Art. 88 Act on County Self-Government[34]; Art. 91 Act on Voivodship Self-Government[35]; Art. 64 Act on Voivode and Government Administration in the Voivodship[36]; and in numerous other filings).

Court action on an inactivity complaint: (a) obliges the authority to issue an act, interpretation or to perform an act within a specified period or obliges the authority to state or recognize the right or obligation under the law; (b) may also decide on the existence or nonexistence of a right

[32] Sześciło (2017, pp. 267–280).

[33] Consolidated text: JoL 2018, item 994.

[34] Consolidated text: JoL 2018, item 995.

[35] Consolidated text: JoL 2018, item 913.

[36] Consolidated text: JoL 2017, item 2234.

or obligation; (c) may also decide ex officio or at the request of a party to impose a fine or grant the authority a pecuniary sum (Art. 149 JAP).

Public complaints (Latin: actio popularis) are another form of citizen protection against public administration delays, which are practiced on the basis of Section VIII CAP in connection with Art. 63 of the Polish Constitution.

The case law assumes that not every inactivity or excessive length of proceeding is tantamount to a gross violation of the law.[37] Inactivity is the objectively existing state of non-delivery of a decision despite the lapse of a deadline, irrespective of the reason for exceeding the deadline and regardless of whether the deadline is statutory or designated by an administration[38] (Table 14.1).

14.6 Positive Silence

Silent consent applies only if explicitly stated in specific laws. The CAP contains only procedural regulations. Silent consent has two forms: passive "silent termination of the proceeding" without any negative or positive conclusion (Art. 122a.2(1) CAP), and "silent authorisation" (Art. 122a.2(2) CAP).

The purpose of "silent termination of the proceedings" is mobilization of the administrative body to settle the case in due time. The authority can avoid it only by issuing an administrative act in the time specified by the law.

"Silent authorisation" means approval by the authority to settle the case in the manner presented in the application—by a deliberate, intentional resignation by the body from raising timely objections. If the authority does not approve the application, it must file an objection in the form of an administrative decision no later than one month from the date of delivery of the application.

The deadline for a silent authorization of the case is one month. It is possible to introduce different dates in specific provisions (Art. 122a.2 CAP). The silent authorization of the case takes place on the day following the expiration date for issuing the decision or for filing of an objection (Art. 122c CAP). When the body informs the concerned party, before the deadline for settling the case, that there are no objections, a

[37] Judgments of SAC: I OSK 9/15, I OSK 2075/14, I OSK 1832/15.

[38] Judgment of SAC, I OPS 12/13.

silent authorization will take place on the day of delivery of the notification. Provisions regarding the prolongation will not apply to silent authorization cases (Art. 35 and 36 CAP). The date, followed by the silent authorization of the case, is referred to as the preclusion term.

A decision issued by the authority after the expiration of this period is considered defective and unlawful, and the party may challenge it in an ordinary mode, such as by appeal (Art. 127 CAP), or in an extraordinary circumstance, by annulment (Art. 156 CAP).

In the event of silent authorization of the case, the administrative body is bound by the decision issued in this mode from the day following the day on which the deadline for issuing it expires, or the day on which the deadline for filing of the objection expires (Art. 110 CAP). The authority publishes an annotation on the settlement of the case, indicating the content of the decision and its legal basis. If a party submits a request, the authority also issues a certificate of a silent authorization (Art. 122f CAP). The authority is obliged to deliver the certificate to all parties.

A party may file a complaint to the administrative body against the certificate issued in the form of a decision, and subsequently it may also file a complaint to the administrative court (Art. 122f.2 and Art. 3.2(2) CAP). There is also a possibility of "reactivating" a silently settled case by reconsideration and in the issuance of decisions in extraordinary proceedings initiated on request or *ex officio*, such as annulment (Art. 156 CAP) or resumption of the proceedings (Art. 145 CAP) in cases with serious legal defects (Art. 122g CAP).

Active "silent authorisation," exercised in place of filing objections within a specified period, is now definitely more widely used than the passive form. "Silent authorisation" is used, for example, in: Telecommunications Law (Art. 48.2)[39]; Postal Law (Art. 49.4)[40]; Environmental Law (Art. 152.4)[41]; Construction Law (Art. 30.5, Art. 54, and 71.4)[42]; Act on the Fuel Quality Monitoring and Control System (Art. 9.2)[43];

[39] Consolidated text: JoL 2018, item 1954.

[40] Consolidated text: JoL 2018, item 2188.

[41] Consolidated text: JoL 2018, item 799.

[42] Consolidated text: JoL 2018, item 1202.

[43] Consolidated text: JoL 2018, item 427.

Waste Act (Art. 11.4)[44]; Law on the Advocate (Art. 69a)[45]; Act on Legal Advisors (Art. 31.2)[46]; and in other corporate laws regarding regulated professions.

A conscious act of the will of the administrative body is also represented by the omission of, or resignation from, performing a factual act. Pursuant to Article 32.4 of the Act on the Protection of Historical Monuments,[47] if, within five days from the date of notifying about a discovery, made during construction work or earthworks, of an object that is believed to be a historical monument, the voivodship historical monuments conservators fail to inspect the discovered object, the interrupted works can be continued.

The passive form—"silent termination of the proceedings"—has a different function than the silent authorization. In this case, the desired form of the administrative body's operation is to issue an administrative act and not remain silent. The provision concerning the silent termination of the proceedings after a specified period only determines that there will be no state of inaction or excessive length. This does not mean, however, that failure to act is a desirable behavior for the legislator. Although the legal effect of the silence arises by law, this effect is not, or is not necessarily, a manifestation of the will of the authority. Assigning a legal effect to the silence of the authority in a given period constitutes a solution against inactivity and excessive duration of proceeding by the administrative body.[48]

To the best of our knowledge, by the end of 2018, only three judgments regarding the silent authorization had been issued according to the new regulation effective from 2017. These judgments resolved problems related to the change of legal status in the course of proceedings. Judgments issued based on the legal status prior to the amendment have become outdated.

It seems that the regulation of silent authorization in special Acts (before the new provision was introduced into CAP in 2017) was very effective in practice. The database shows that complaints to the

[44] Consolidated text: JoL 2018, item 992.

[45] Consolidated text: JoL 2018, item 1184.

[46] Consolidated text: JoL 2018, item 2115.

[47] Consolidated text: JoL 2018, item 2067.

[48] Gurba (2016).

administrative court were very rare—of 844,670 judgments issued since 1980, there was one postal law complaint, two telecommunications law complaints, 11 environmental law complaints, and 1187 construction law complaints.[49]

14.7 Supervision of Timeliness: Administrative Control, Judicial Review

The supervision of public administration timeliness is regulated mainly within CAP, by the means of an urging claim (Art. 37 CAP), a public complaint (Art. 227 CAP), and within the JAP by an inactivity complaint (Art. 3.2(8)–(9) JAP). These legal remedies tend to impose discipline on public administrative bodies.

From the public administration's point of view, the most efficient methods for imposing discipline on public officials (whose inactivity generated administrative silence) are the employee's liability due to the Labour Code (LC),[50] and the Act of Financial Liability of Public Officials (FLO),[51] (if inactivity was a gross violation of law). The first judgment based on FLO was delivered in April 2016. In 2018, a survey conducted among public officials in the Podkarpackie region (one of 16 Polish administrative units)[52] showed that they considered the financial liability for a gross violation of law as the most efficient way to prevent administrative silence (29.1%); second was the officials' liability based on the LC (27.8%); third, by penal liability (20.3%); fourth, by disciplinary liability (16.3%); and last, by civil liability (7.5%).

Presently, the most effective and the most frequently used remedies for counteracting administrative silence are urging claims (Art. 37 CAP); inactivity complaints to the administrative court (Art. 3 JAB); fine (Art. 154.1 JAP); and damage claims (Art. 417 Civil Code [CC]).

The reactions of administrative courts to inactivity complaints and excessive duration complaints are presented in the Annual Reports of

[49] http://orzeczenia.nsa.gov.pl/cbo/query.

[50] Consolidated text: JoL 2018, item 917.

[51] Consolidated text: JoL 2016, item 1169.

[52] The survey, conducted by researchers from University of IT and Management in Rzeszow, covered 227 persons in 13 public administration units in the Podkarpackie region (2,129,138 inhabitants).

Supreme Administrative Court (see paras. 5 and 6). The data is proof of the generally low effectiveness of inactivity complaints and specifically for abuse of this remedy by complainants (see Table 14.2).

Article 108 LC can confer employee liability for a public official's lack of activity. In this case, the employer can choose a caution (PL: *upomnienie*) or a reprimand (PL: *nagana*). Public officials failing to fulfill their duties or causing harm to the public or private interest are subject to imprisonment for up to three years (Art. 231 Penal Code).[53]

The disciplinary liability of public officials is regulated in various Acts, depending on the type of employing institution, e.g., officials in governmental administration,[54] or members of the civil service.[55] A typical catalog of disciplinary sanctions for public officials covers: caution; reprimand; qualified reprimand; demotion; and expulsion.[56]

In Poland, no single document is particularly considered to be the governmental strategy on combatting administrative silence. However, a "strategy" is implemented by the introduction of the new regulations resulting in limiting or eliminating the administrative silence. The best examples are the 2017 regulation on the urging claim, the 2015 amendments to the JAP, and the 2011 introduction of the FLO, which is also for inactivity.

The Supreme Audit Office (SAO) audits public administration units and examines administrative silence. For instance, in 2015, the SAO revealed the inactivity of customs chambers and tax offices.[57] In the post-audit report, the SAO recommended introducing internal procedures counteracting the inactivity.

[53] Kulig (2015).

[54] Act on Employees of Governmental Administrative Bodies (consolidated text: JoL 2018, item 1915); Regulation of Prime Minister on explanatory and disciplinary proceeding against public officers and on disciplinary commissions and disciplinary ombudsman (JoL no 145, item 1628).

[55] Act on Civil Service (consolidated text: JoL 2017, item 1889).

[56] Giętkowski (2013, p. 268ff).

[57] Supreme Audit Office, Information on Results of Audits of 2 April 2015—implementation of judgments of regional administrative courts and the Supreme Administrative Courts by tax offices and customs chambers, https://www.nik.gov.pl/kontrole/ (accessed 5 January 2019).

14.8 Administrative Appeal

A party has the right to submit an urging claim (Art. 37.1(1) CAP). A civic organization, the prosecutor, or the Ombudsman may do so, as well. The basis for the inactivity is irrelevant. The urging claim may be used in the course of administrative proceedings (Art. 37.6(2) (a)), as well as after its completion (Art. 37.6(2) (b)).

The petition is submitted to the higher-level body through the body conducting the proceedings, or directly to the body conducting the proceedings, if there is no higher-level authority. The higher-level body considers the urging claim within seven days. Then it issues a decision stating the inactivity of the lower-level body, accompanied by the simultaneous determination of whether it occurred with a gross violation of the law, or it refuses to declare the occurrence of inactivity. In the event of a finding of inactivity during the pending proceedings, the higher-level body obliges the authority examining the case to settle it in the time specified in the order (Art. 37.6(2) (a) CAP). However, if inactivity concerns proceedings already completed, then the higher-level body orders an explanation of the causes and a determination of the persons guilty of inaction, as well as a directive to take measures to prevent it in the future (Art. 37.6(2) (b) CAP).

If the authority ignores the urging claim, it gives the party the right to submit an inactivity complaint to the administrative court (Art. 8.2 JAP).

According to its current legal status, an urging claim cannot be treated as an appeal. It is a request to consider the matter of inactivity by the competent public administration authority.[58]

14.9 Judicial Review

An inactivity complaint can be submitted to the administrative court at any time after an urging claim has been brought before the competent authority (Art. 53.2b JAP in conjunction with Art. 37.1 CAP). The complainant submits a complaint through the authority charged with inactivity. Within the so-called self-inspection (PL: *autorewizja*), the body may accept the complaint in full within 30 days of its receipt. By accepting the complaint, it also concludes whether it was issued without a legal basis or with a gross violation of law (Art. 54.3 JAP).

[58] Judgment of RAC, III SAB/Kr24/18; Wróbel (2018).

By approving a complaint, the court (1) obliges the authority to issue an act or tax-interpretation, or to perform an act within the prescribed period; (2) obliges the authority to state or recognize a right or obligation under the law; and (3) states that the authority has committed inactivity (Art. 149.1(1-3) JAP). The court also determines whether the inactivity of the body occurred with a gross violation of the law.

The court may decide on the existence or nonexistence of a right or obligation if the nature of the case permits and the factual and legal circumstances do not raise doubts (Art. 149.1 JAP).

The court, when issuing the judgment, may optionally decide *ex officio*, or at the party's request, to impose a fine, which is10 times the average monthly remuneration in the national economy in the previous year as announced by the president of the Central Statistical Office. Under the same conditions, the court may also grant the party a sum of up to half this amount.

If the authority does not comply with the judgment regarding the inactivity complaint (Art. 149.1), the party has the right to lodge a complaint with a request to impose a fine on that body. A prior written request to the authority to comply with the judgment is needed. In addition, the court may optionally grant the complainant a sum of money up to half the amount referred to in Article 154.6. This sum should be considered as an additional disciplining method, applied when the circumstances of the case show that, without the imposition of this sanction, the body will refuse to act.[59]

There are certain court remedies for silent approval. A party may file a complaint (Pl: *zażalenie*) against a certificate issued in the form of a decision (Art. 122f.2 CAP) and may subsequently file a complaint to the administrative court (Art. 3.2(2)). The court controls the proceedings only in terms of compliance with the law.

There is also a possibility of "reactivating" a silently settled case by reconsideration and issuing of this decision in extraordinary proceedings initiated on request or *ex officio*: annulment of the decision (Art. 156 CAP) or resumption of the proceedings (at 145 CAP) in cases of serious legal defects (Art. 122g).

[59] Judgment of SAC, II OSK 880/17.

14.10 Right to Compensation

A party harmed by the inactivity of an administrative body may assert claims directly from the State Treasury or a local government unit, or another legal person performing public authority by virtue of law (Art. 417.1 CC, in connection with Art. 77.1 of the Constitution). The condition for the effective pursuit of compensation is the prior obtaining of a decision on non-compliance with the law (Art. 4171.3 CC). These may include a decision by the authority issued in response to an urging claim or a judgment by an administrative court in response to an inactivity complaint.

The liability is based on the principle of risk (Art. 417.1 CC), which makes the claims more effective and quick, because the State Treasury or a local government unit is always solvent and cannot be declared bankrupt (Art. 6.1 and 6.2 of the Bankruptcy Law).[60]

If the authority ignores the judgment of the administrative court, it entitles the person who suffered damage to claim compensation from the administrative body (Art. 154.4 and 5 JAP). If, within three months after submitting of the request, the complainant does not receive any compensation from the administrative body, they may file a suit with the common court (Art. 154.5 JAP).

There are different opinions expressed in the literature whether the aggrieved party is entitled to a claim if the administrative body has executed the court's judgment.[61]

The liability of the State Treasury for damage caused by inaction is not dependent on the gross violation of the law.[62]

14.11 The Role of the Ombudsman

The Ombudsman is obliged to undertake any activity as soon as it receives information on an infringement of human and citizens' freedoms and rights (Art. 8 of the Ombudsman Act).[63] The information on the Ombudsman's activity in the years 2013–2017, available from

[60] Consolidated text: JoL 2017, item 2344.

[61] Olejniczak (2014).

[62] Judgment of Supreme Court, IV CSK 406/11 All Judgments of SC and Appeal Courts available in: http://www.sn.pl/orzecznictwo and https://orzeczenia.ms.gov.pl/.

[63] Consolidated text: JoL 2017, item 958.

the institution's Web site,[64] shows a very small number of complaints on administrative silence (one per year in 2013 and 2014, three in 2015, and four in 2016). The Ombudsman also issued one application regarding administrative inactivity in 2013, one request for initiating changes to the regulations regarding administration inactivity in 2016, two applications for joining the administration proceedings in 2017, and one statement addressed to the General Assembly of the Judiciary of the Supreme Administrative Court regarding the growing number of inactivity complaints in 2015.

The number of all complaints submitted every year is close to 53,000, so it seems that the role of the Ombudsman in supporting citizens in the fight against illegal inactivity is not significant.

However, the Ombudsman calls for action to improve the law. For example, in 2016, in a speech addressed to the chairman of the Human Rights, the Rule of Law, and Petitions Committee of the Senate of the Republic of Poland, the Ombudsman signaled an inability to appeal to the administrative court in the case of *actio popularis* (Section VIII CAP). These are complaints and applications to which the public administration responds and provides settlement by a non-binding letter or factual action. The Ombudsman asked the legislators to consider a legislative initiative that would enable future complainants to effectively enforce their constitutional rights.[65]

14.12 Administrative Silence: Empirical Data

Different authorities handle urging claims and/or inactivity complaints, but not all of them keep records of their activities or systematically provide annual information about them. Almost all 49 Local Government Appeal Colleges publish such information on the Public Information Bulletin Web site. These reports form a large database that sufficiently serves as the material for the present research and our final conclusions in regard to the state of the administration's inactivity in practice. Local Government Appeal Colleges deal with cases from numerous fields, from taxes and spatial planning to social issues and protection of animals.

[64] www.rpo.gov.pl.

[65] 2016 Annual Ombudsman's Activity Report, pp. 77–78.

Table 14.2 Judgments of administrative courts (inactivity complaints)

Period	*Number of closed cases*	*Number of inactivity complaints*	*Number of inactivity complaints admitted*	*Percentage of complaints against inactivity admitted (%)*
2015	71,327	6240	1735	27.80
2016	72,502	6490	1087	32.92
2017	74,910	6443	1893	29.38

Source http://www.nsa.gov.pl/statystyki-wsa.php

According to the presented statistics, it seems that inactivity of administrative bodies is not a common occurrence: in 2015, it amounted to 1.49% of all cases; in 2016, 1.53%; and in 2017, 1.91%. However, as shown above, a relatively large number of inactivity complaints/urging claims remain ineffective (60–70%).

The same conclusion applies to inactivity complaints submitted to administrative courts.

Although Table 14.2 shows more complaints (8–9% of all cases), the percentage of non-effective inactivity complaints is similar (60–70%).

Regarding compensation awarded on the basis of Article 417 CC, the database of Polish case law contains 657 court decisions, from the years 2005–2018, out of which 357 relate to negligence in the exercise of public authority, and 18 relate directly to the inactivity of public administration. One hundred court rulings were issued based on Article 154.5 JAP, of which 96 concern inactivity. Out of 8400 judgments based on Article 154.5 JAP, issued in the years 2004–2018, fines for inaction were imposed in 8250 judgments.

33.8% of public officers surveyed in 2018 (see para 3.2 above) considered administrative silence as a lack of any activity in a certain case, whereas 28.9% of public officers defined administrative silence as a lack of any activity in a situation when an administrative body was obliged to act by legal regulations. The most common reason for administrative silence in public officers' view was a low quality of law (unclear content of regulations).

14.13 Concluding Remarks

The Polish legislator uses two normative strategies for preventing and combatting the pathology of inactivity or excessive duration of proceeding: (1) an urging claim (PL: *ponaglenie*), followed by an inactivity complaint to the administrative court, or (2) silent consent (silent authorization or silent termination of the proceeding). If the inactivity or excessive length of the administrative body's proceedings particularly jeopardizes the protection of citizen rights, the legislature chooses a stronger preventive measure (i.e., the silent consent, for example, as in the Construction Law and the Tax Law).

The Polish system of administrative law has yet to develop the mode of negative silent handling of cases. In the codifications of other countries, there are solutions based on a "silent negative decision" in which the lack of a response within a certain period means refusal. Fortunately, there is no such regulation in Polish law.[66]

The legislator paid a lot of attention to the problem of administrative inactivity in issuing individual decisions, which is reflected in the related CAP regulations. However, the legislature does not deal with the inaction of the authorities regarding general, analytical, planning, and reporting activities. Inactivity of administrative bodies in these matters can be claimed to the administrative court only if a solution is present in particular Acts, which is rare.

There is a growing tendency to simplify administrative procedure. Silent consent seems to be increasingly applicable, replacing the urging claim model. Undoubtedly, this type of solution improves administration and reduces operational costs. Administrative silence ceases to be a negative phenomenon and clearly becomes an alternative to the classical model of the obligatory completion of administrative procedure.[67]

It is worth mentioning that the relevant authorities exerted a lot of effort into improving the administrative procedures in Poland.

References

Dawidowicz, W. (1983). *Postępowanie administracyjne*. Warszawa: Zarys.
Dobosz, P. (2011). Milczenie i bezczynność w prawie administracyjnym. Kraków.

[66] Dobosz (2011) and Miłosz (2011).

[67] Gurba (2016, p. 96).

Giętkowski, R. (2013). Odpowiedzialność dyscyplinarna w prawie polskim. Gdańsk.
Gurba, W. (2015). Zwalczanie i zapobieganie bezczynności oraz przewlekłości postępowania administracyjnego. Państwo i Prawo, 11.
Gurba, W. (2016). Bezczynność i przewlekłość postępowania. Milczące załatwianie spraw (14 § 3, art. 36-38, 104a-104c k.p.a.). In *Reforma prawa postępowaniu administracyjnym Raport zespołu eksperckiego*. Warszawa.
Hauser, R. (1997). Terminy załatwiania spraw w k.p.a. w doktrynie i orzecznictwie sądowym, Ruch Prawniczy, Ekonomiczny i Socjologiczny, 1.
Kubiak, A. (2009). Fikcja pozytywnego rozstrzygnięcia w prawie administracyjnym. Państwo i Prawo, 11.
Kulig, M. (2015). Komentarz do art. 231. In M. Mozgawa (Ed.), Kodeks karny. Komentarz. Warszawa.
Miłosz, M. (2011). Bezczynność organu administracji publicznej w postępowaniu administracyjnym. Warszawa.
Olejniczak, A. (2014). Komentarz do art. 417. In A. Kidyba (Ed.), Kodeks cywilny. Komentarz. Warszawa.
Olsen, J. (2003). Towards a European Administrative Space? *Journal of European Public Policy, 10*(4), 506–531.
Przybysz, P. (2018). Kodeks postępowania administracyjnego. Komentarz aktualizowany, LEX/el.
Suwaj, R. (2014). Sądowa ochrona przed bezczynnością administracji publicznej. Warszawa.
Suwaj, R., & Perkowski, M. (2010). Koncepcja zapobiegania bezczynności w postępowaniu administracyjnym. Białystok.
Sześciło, D. (2017). Milcząca zgoda organu–instrument przeciwdziałania przewlekłości postępowania czy narzędzie deregulacji. In J. Supernat & B. Kowalczyk (Eds.), *Kodeks postępowania administracji Unii Europejskiej*. Warszawa.
Wróbel, A. (2018). Komentarz do art. 35. In M. Jaśkowska, M. Wilbrandt-Gotowicz, & A. Wróbel (Eds.), Komentarz aktualizowany Kodeksu postępowania administracyjnego, LEX/el.
Ziller, J. (2007). The Continental System of Administrative Legality. In B. G. Peters & J. Pierre (Eds.), *The Handbook of Public Administration*. London: Sage.

CHAPTER 15

Administrative Silence in Lithuania: Case Law and Data from the Administrative Oversight Institutions

Vidmantė Giedraitytė, Agnė Andrijauskaitė, and Mantas Bileišis

15.1 Introduction

From the point of view of contemporary trends in public administration reform, two potential paradoxes need to be taken into account when considering administrative silence: (i) a supply-side challenge of making

V. Giedraitytė (✉) · M. Bileišis
General Jonas Žemaitis Military Academy of Lithuania, Vilnius, Lithuania
e-mail: vidmante.giedraityte@lka.lt; vidmante.giedraityte@ktu.lt

M. Bileišis
e-mail: mantas.bileisis@lka.lt

V. Giedraitytė
Kaunas University of Technology, Kaunas, Lithuania

A. Andrijauskaitė
Vilnius University, Vilnius, Lithuania
e-mail: andrijauskaite@foev-speyer.de

German University of Administrative Sciences Speyer, Speyer, Germany

D. C. Dragos et al. (eds.),
The Sound of Silence in European Administrative Law,
https://doi.org/10.1007/978-3-030-45227-8_15

administrative processes more accessible and (ii) adjudication, which is a time-consuming process in itself.

On the demand side of administrative decision-making, technological development is rapidly increasing the possibilities for accessing administrative processes. Governments are under pressure to adopt electronic service provision decisions rapidly.[1] However, in many instances complex administrative decision regulation keeps multiple agents in the decision-making loop. This is likely to cause challenges on the supply side of administrative decisions. The automation and adoption of technological solutions need to keep in step with modernizing regulation to make the best use of such developments. Otherwise, paradoxically, simplification of access to administrative decision-making might create outcomes where decisions begin to take more time and demand more staff.

Adjudication is another potential bottleneck that could exacerbate the supply-side problem as it transfers the administrative procedure to other agents, both prejudicial and across the separation of powers barrier, creating new administrative costs and burdens which may be caused by the presence of existing burdens on administrative capacities in executive agencies.

One possible solution to these administrative failures is the adoption of positive administrative silence. However, this comes with its own set of risks, such as (i) the transformation of disputes from administrative into civil, as private persons and entities may come into conflict with actors that take unlawful action as a result of administrative silence or (ii) it may encourage actors to pursue a strategy of document submission that would increase the risk of administrative silence. From this point of view, some actors become incentivized to seek administrative silence by various methods, creating secondary risks of corruption and decreased trust in public administration.

A third legislative strategy is to create a nuanced system of administrative decision terms to better match actual capacities and/or differentiating between negative and positive administrative silence based on various criteria. This holds inherent risks of creating complex legislation that would be counterproductive through creating administrative burdens on

[1] M. S. Pang, G. Lee, and W. H. DeLone, "IT Resources, Organizational Capabilities, and Value Creation in Public-Sector Organizations: A Public-Value Management Perspective," *Journal of Information Technology*, 29/3 (2014), pp. 187–205.

the demand side and thus negating the benefits of technological solutions on the supply side by creating the need for highly specialized administrative staff.

Although some public administration theories opt for a plurality of tools and greater decentralization of administration,[2] such diversity, while helping with faster administrative decisions, may result in negative outcomes in cases of disputes. Also, it is by no means clear that the benefits gained in the first instances outweigh costs of the second.

All the outlined aspects need to be well understood from the *status quo* point of view before any recommendation for changes in legislation is recommended, as an existing prejudicial and judicial practice may create the basis for a more predictable dispute process and act as a better incentivizing mechanism *vis-à-vis* creating new legislation. This paper aims to chart the Lithuanian *status quo* of administrative disputes for cases which have the hallmarks of administrative silence as defined in the literature.

Further analysis includes statistics on complaints considered by competent authorities of Lithuania and their consideration in practice. The data of the highest institutions that examine such complaints are presented: the Chief Administrative Disputes Commission, the Seimas Ombudsmen's Office of the Republic of Lithuania, and the Supreme Administrative Court of Lithuania (hereafter—also "SACL"). Secondary data taken from the analyzed entities' annual reports for 2013–2017 are also used for the purposes of this chapter. The interview method was applied in order to reveal the problems of application of administrative silence in Lithuanian public administration, as well as to clarify the secondary data. Interview data were collected by interviewing experts at the Ministry of the Interior of the Republic of Lithuania, the Supreme Administrative Court of Lithuania and the Seimas (Parliament) Ombudsmen (in total 6 experts). The important aspects of complaints consideration practice regarding administrative silence will be sought, including cases of missed deadlines that must be followed by public administration entities. In this context, using the practice of the Seimas Ombudsmen's Office and the case law of the Supreme Administrative Court of Lithuania, the problems of compliance with the time limits and the application of the legal institute of administrative silence will be analyzed.

[2] Cf., e.g., H. Mosley, "Accountability in Decentralised Employment Service Regimes," *OECD Local Economic and Employment Development (LEED) Working Papers*, 10 (2012), OECD Publishing, Paris, accessible at https://doi.org/10.1787/5k98sbxn9wbw-en.

Our study is limited to those aspects of public administration in Lithuania that include the sphere of consideration of applications and complaints filed by persons. In this context, an attempt is made to establish the practice of applying the principles of the legal institute of administrative silence in Lithuania. Firstly, an analysis of the Lithuanian legal framework is carried out. The legal acts used for the analysis are taken from the official Register of Legal Acts of Lithuania (TAR) as valid on August 1, 2018. We describe the regulation of the process of considering applications and complaints submitted by persons to public administration entities by trying to identify the consequences of missed time limits, the protection of applicants' rights, and cases related to the legal institute of administrative silence.

15.2 Administrative Silence Within the Strategic and Legal Framework of Lithuania

15.2.1 Good Governance as a Strategic Objective

According to the Long-Term Development Strategy of the Republic of Lithuania,[3] the improvement of Lithuanian public administration should be a continuous, systematic process involving central, territorial, and municipal levels. Strengthening confidence in the government and legal system is identified as an important tool of good governance. These provisions are expanded in Lithuania's Progress Strategy "Lithuania 2030."[4] Therein it is emphasized that the progress of the state can only be encouraged by credible governance. Confidence in governance and public decisions calls for the active participation of all interested parties; therefore, they must be transparent and open. Public authorities should be open and accountable to the public, and public information should be understandable and clear. Also, the public sector should ensure the delivery of high-quality services that meet public demands. The services provided should be of good quality. The National Progress Program

[3] The Long-Term Development Strategy of the Republic of Lithuania approved by Resolution No. IX-1187 of the Seimas of the Republic of Lithuania of 12 November 2002, accessible at https://e-seimas.lrs.lt/portal/legalActPrint/lt?jfwid=q8i88md94&documentId=TAIS.219184&category=TAD.

[4] Lithuania's Progress Strategy "Lithuania 2030" approved by Resolution No. XI-2015 of the Seimas of the Republic of Lithuania of 15 May 2012, accessible at https://lrv.lt/uploads/main/documents/files/EN_version/Useful_information/lithuania2030.pdf.

for Lithuania for 2014–2020[5] provides an intention to achieve results from public governance that correspond to the needs of society and to the progress of the state. This program sets the target of improving the services of public administration institutions and increasing the availability of such services to society. Special strategic guidelines related to public governance are submitted in the Improvement Program on Public Governance for 2012–2020 (hereafter—"Improvement Program").[6] The strategic objective of the Improvement Program is to ensure the identification, formulation, and effective implementation of public policies that meet public needs: to increase the openness of public administration processes and to encourage society to participate actively in them, to provide good-quality administrative and public services, to strengthen the strategic thinking capacity in public administration institutions, and to improve the management of their activities. The implementation of the Improvement Program includes guidelines such as setting common standards for the provision of public sector information to society, establishing quality standards for public services and optimizing the scope of provided services, and the application of public and administrative service quality assessment. Furthermore, it is stated that in order to ensure the quality of public service the deadlines for processing applications and complaints in public administration institutions should be clarified. In accordance with the strategic provisions, legal acts regulating separate aspects of the administrative process are adopted and continue to be adopted.

15.2.2 The Main Principles of Administrative Procedures and Their Timeliness

It should be emphasized that the legal framework of the Republic of Lithuania is missing comprehensive codification of administrative procedure despite the general trend toward such codification in the continental

[5] The National Progress Programme for Lithuania for the period 2014–2020 approved by Resolution No. 14822 of the Lithuanian Government of 28 November 2012, accessible at https://e-seimas.lrs.lt/portal/legalAct/lt/TAD/TAIS.439028.

[6] Improvement Programme on Public Governance for 2012–2020 approved by Resolution No. 171 of the Lithuanian Government of 7 February 2012, accessible at https://e-seimas.lrs.lt/portal/legalAct/lt/TAD/TAIS.418407/VYOiBLpIpF.

legal systems and its significance to the daily functioning of administration.[7] The need for a Code of Administrative Procedure is a problem that has arisen from time to time in debates between scholars, politicians, and public figures since Lithuania's independence in 1991 but no specific solutions have yet been offered.[8] Nevertheless, separate aspects of administrative procedures are regulated by separate legal acts.

The foundations for organizing administrative procedures are regulated by the Republic of Lithuania Law on Public Administration (hereafter—"LPA," *Viešojo administravimo įstatymas*).[9] The procedural rules for adjudicating administrative cases are, for their part, stipulated in the Republic of Lithuania Law on Administrative Proceedings (hereafter—"LAP," *Administracinių bylų teisenos įstatymas*).[10]

The LPA is the main legal act that establishes the principles and spheres of public administration and the system of Lithuanian public administration entities, and that guarantees the right of persons to appeal against the acts, omissions, or administrative decisions of public administration entities, as well as the right to consideration of applications, complaints, and statements submitted by persons. According to this Law, a person's application to a Lithuanian public administration entity may be of a twofold nature. The first application method is "*not related to a violation of the*

[7] J. B. Auby (ed.), *Codification of Administrative Procedure* (Bruylant: 2014), p. 1.

[8] See for a call to adopt a "modern" Code of Administrative Procedure in J. Paužaitė-Kulvinskienė, "The Principle of Effective Legal Remedies in Administrative Law (Right to Access to Administrative Court) of Lithuania Under the Influence of the European Legal Order," in *Lithuanian Legal System Under the Influence of European Union Law* (Vilnius University: 2014), p. 425. Such a legislative gap on the national level is even more glaring considering "supranational tendencies" pointing toward the development of such a code (e.g., the ReNEUAL project in the EU), see more in I. Deviatnikovaitė, "Europos administracinės teisės samprata ir ES administracinių procedūrų rinkinio rengimo prielaidos [The Concept of European Administrative Law and the Background of the Development of the Law on Administrative Procedure of the European Union]," *Jurisprudencija*, 20 (3) (2013), pp. 1005–1022. See further V. Valančius and S. Kavalnė, *Europos Sąjungos teisės įgyvendinimas Lietuvos administracinėje teisėje* [The Implementation of EU Law in Lithuanian Administrative Law] (VĮ Registrų centras: 2009), pp. 101–113.

[9] Law on Public Administration of the Republic of Lithuania of 17 June 1999 No. VIII-1234 (new edition No. X-736, 27 June 2006), *Valstybės žinios* [Official Gazette], No. 60-1945, 1999.

[10] Law on Administrative Proceedings of the Republic of Lithuania of 14 January 1999 No. VIII-1029 (new edition No. XII-2399, 2 June 2016), *Valstybės žinios* [Official Gazette], No. 13-308, 1999.

person's rights or legitimate interests," it is a "*request to adopt an administrative decision or perform other actions stipulated in legal acts*" (Art. 2 (14 p.) LPA). The second application method, called a complaint, means "*a person's written application…where it is indicated that his rights or legitimate interests have been violated and it is requested to defend them*" (Art. 2 (15 p.) LPA). Complaints about a violation allegedly committed through the acts, omissions, or administrative decisions of a public administration entity against the rights and legitimate interests of the person referred to in the complaint should be considered within specified time limits and in accordance with administrative procedure (Chapter 3 of LPA).

The process of considering applications and complaints is regulated by the LPA and the Rules for Examination of Requests of Persons and for their Servicing at Public Administration Authorities, Institutions and Other Entities of Public Administration (hereafter—"Rules 2007").[11] Summarized information on consideration actions relating to applications and complaints is provided in Fig. 15.1. It is obvious from this figure that in Lithuanian legal provisions the separate administrative procedures and their execution deadlines are quite finely defined. On the one side, the meticulous regulation brings clarity in administrative procedures, but on the other side, it raises debates about the overly bureaucratic existence of such procedures.

Under the legal acts of Lithuania applications or complaints to a public administration entity should be submitted directly, through a "one-stop-shop" or sent by post or electronic means. At the request of the person, a certificate relating to the received documents should be presented on site or sent within 3 working days (Rules 2007, at par. 5, 23, 24). The consideration should be completed and a decision on the application or complaint should be adopted within 20 working days from the day of application or complaint submission (Art. 31 LPA). If it is deemed that a complaint should be dealt with by a commission set up for this purpose or for other reasons, the term of consideration may be extended for a period no longer than 20 working days (Rules 2007, at par. 26). If, due to objective reasons, the administrative procedure cannot be completed

[11] Rules for Examination of Requests of Persons and for their Servicing at Public Administration Authorities, Institutions and Other Entities of Public Administration of 22 August 2007 approved by Resolution No. 875 of the Lithuanian Government (new edition No. 933, 15 November 2017), *Valstybės žinios* [Official Gazette], No. 94-37791, 2007.

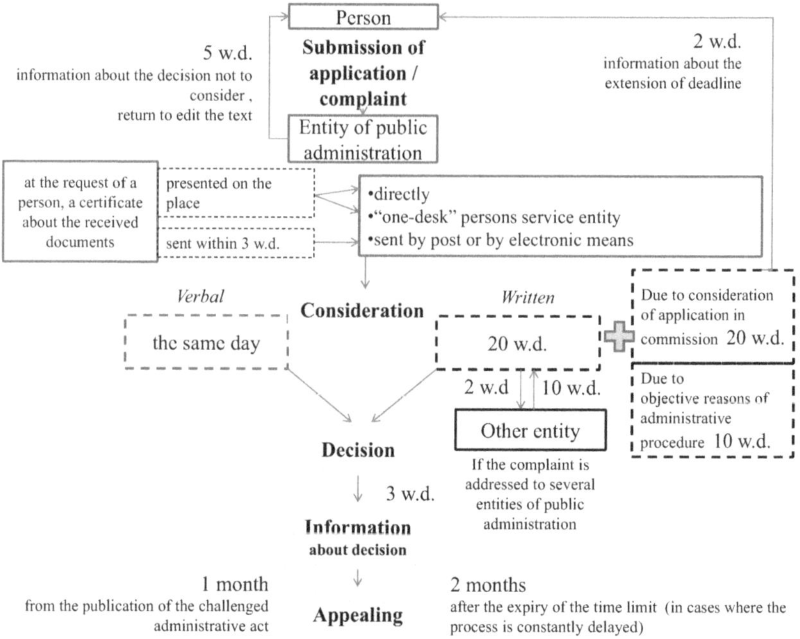

Fig. 15.1 The process of considering applications and complaints in Lithuanian public administration entities

within the set time limit, the consideration may be extended for a period no longer than 10 working days. A person should be notified about the extension of the time limit for the consideration and the reasons for the extension within 2 working days (Art. 31 LPA). Verbal requests of persons should be dealt with, if possible, on the very same day that they are received (Rules 2007, at par. 7). Within 3 working days, a person whose application or complaint has been submitted should be notified about the adopted decision (Art. 34 LPA). A person, within 1 month from the publication of the impugned administrative act (or 2 months after the expiry of the time limit—in cases where the process is constantly delayed), has the right to appeal against a decision on an application or complaint adopted by a public administration entity (Art. 28 LAP).

The answers to applications are based on their content (Rules 2007, at par. 35):

- an application for the provision of administrative services—to issue a document, a copy of document, or a statement confirming a certain legal fact—should be answered by providing the requested administrative service or indicating the reasons for refusing to consider the application
- an application for the submission of available information should be answered by providing the requested information or indicating the reasons for refusing to consider the application
- an application for an administrative decision should be answered by presenting a copy of a relevant document or indicating the reasons for refusing to consider the application
- to other applications an answer should be given in a free form or the reasons for refusing to consider an application have to be indicated.

Answers to complaints should be given by adopting a decision on the administrative procedure. A person should be notified within 3 working days about the adopted decision on the administrative procedure, the factual circumstances determined during the consideration of the complaint, and the legal acts on the basis of which the decision on the administrative procedure has been adopted, as well as the procedure for appealing against the decision (Art. 34 (3) LPA).

15.3 Different Models and a (Fuzzy) Conception of Administrative Silence

15.3.1 Positive Administrative Silence

As was mentioned in the previous part, the forms of answers to applications and complaints in Lithuania are specifically regulated by law. However, the legislation of positive and negative administrative silence is foreseen just in a separate few cases.

The EU Directive 2006/123/EC on Services in the Internal Market norms provide that in the process of granting of a licence "*authorisation procedures and formalities shall provide applicants with a guarantee that their application will be processed as quickly as possible and, in any event, within a reasonable period which is fixed and made public in advance...-Failing a response within the time period set or extended..., authorisation shall be deemed to have been granted*" (Art. 13). In implementing these provisions of special laws The Republic of Lithuania Law on Electricity,[12] The Republic of Lithuania Law on Natural Gas,[13] The Republic of Lithuania Law on the Control of Arms and Ammunition,[14] and other laws regulating the issuance of authorizations and licenses provide cases of positive administrative silence. The said legislation states that if an application for a license or authorization is not replied to within a specified time limit it is to be considered that a positive decision has been made regarding the issuance of a license or authorization (Art. 17 (2) of the Law on Electricity; Art. 21 (2) of the Law on Natural Gas; Art. 12 (4) and 12 (7) of the Law on the Control of Arms and Ammunition). The case law shows that Lithuanian administrative courts tend to give effect to positive administrative silence as stipulated in various laws, although not without some reservations (see *infra* Part 4.2).

15.3.2 Negative Administrative Silence

In other cases, silence on the part of public administration entities is perceived as an omission. In cases of silence or ignorance on the part of public administration entities (acting with intent or through negligence), one can initiate an administrative dispute. Administrative disputes may be settled by applying to the Administrative Disputes Commission or to the administrative court. In cases clearly prescribed by law, pre-trial investigation of administrative complaints is obligatory. Otherwise a person is free to choose whether to make use of a pre-trial investigation or to apply to an administrative court directly. The pre-trial investigation procedure is regulated by the Republic of Lithuania Law on Procedure of Pre-trial Administrative Disputes (hereafter—"LPPAD")[15] and other *lex specialis*,

[12] Law on Electricity of the Republic of Lithuania of 20 July 2000 No. VIII-1881 (new edition No. XI-1919, 17 January 2012), *Valstybės žinios* [Official Gazette], No. 66-1984, 2000.

[13] Law on Natural Gas of the Republic of Lithuania of 10 October 2000, No. VIII-1973 (new edition No. XI-1564, 30 June 2011), *Valstybės žinios* [Official Gazette], No. 89-2743, 2000.

[14] Law on the Control of Arms and Ammunition of the Republic of Lithuania of 15 January 2002, No. IX-705, 15 January 2002 (new edition No. XI-1146, 18 November 2010), *Valstybės žinios* [Official Gazette], No. 13-467, 2002.

[15] Law on Procedure of Pre-trial Administrative Disputes of 14 January 1999, No. VIII-1031 (new edition No. XII-2400, 2 June 2016), *Valstybės žinios* [Official Gazette], No. 13-310, 1999.

such as the Law on Tax Administration. Under the LPPAD pre-trial consideration of disputes may be effected by the Lithuanian Administrative Disputes Commission (previously (until January 1, 2018) entitled The Chief Administrative Disputes Commission) and its territorial entities (hereafter—"Disputes Commissions").

The Lithuanian Administrative Disputes Commission considers complaints (applications) contesting the legality of the individual administrative acts and actions of central state administration entities, alongside inactivity (delays) by these entities in fulfilling their competence and appeals against territorial entities. Territorial entities consider complaints (applications) contesting the legality of individual administrative acts and actions of state administration territorial entities and municipal administration entities, alongside inactivity (delays) by these entities in fulfilling their competence (Art. 5 LPAD). The pre-trial consideration of disputes may be extended for a period no longer than 20 working days. If necessary, by the reasoned decision of the Disputes Commission, the deadline for consideration may be extended by another 10 working days (Art. 12 LPAD). The decisions made by the commission may be appealed against to the appropriate administrative court.

Despite the said institutional framework for settling administrative disputes "outside the court," critical voices in the Lithuanian legal scholarship emphasize the lack of consistency in developing this institute on the part of the legislator. Above all this means that heterogeneous substantial as well as procedural standards of protecting individual rights applied by the commission and other pre-trial investigation bodies indicated in *lex specialis* persist.[16]

Another venue for an individual to defend rights is the Ombudsmen's Office, whose existence is enshrined in Art. 73 of the Constitution. The Ombudsmen are the "guardians" of Art. 5 of the Constitution stipulating that "State institutions serve the people"[17] and hence handle complaints about abuses of office or bureaucracy or instigate investigations thereof on

[16] L. Paškevičienė, "Išankstinio administracinių ginčų nagrinėjimo ne teisme institutas Lietuvoje: bendrosios normatyvinės charakteristikos [Pre-Trial Settlement of Administrative Disputes in Lithuania: General Legal Characteristics]," *Teisė* (2018), pp. 70–83.

[17] A. Normantas and M. Vasiliauskas, "Ombudsmenai kaip konstitucinio valdžios įstaigų tarnystės žmonėms imperatyvo sergėtojai [Ombudsmen as Guardians of Constitutional Principle that State Institutions should Serve the People]," in *Administraciniai teismai Lietuvoje. Nūdienos iššūkiai* [Administrative Courts in Lithuania. Current Challenges] (Lietuvos vyriausiasis administracinis teismas, Vilnius: 2010), pp. 487–509.

their own initiative. The Law on the Seimas Ombudsmen[18] (hereafter—"Law on the Seimas Ombudsmen") defines "bureaucracy" as: "*actions on the part of official when the latter, instead of dealing with the matter on the merits, observes unnecessary or invented formalities, unreasonably refuses to settle issues within the official's jurisdiction or delays decision-making or carrying out of official duties or performs other malfeasance or misfeasance in office (refuses to inform a person of his rights, gives a deliberately misleading or improper advice, etc.)*..." (Art. 2 (1)).

The Seimas (Parliament) Ombudsman is a state official appointed by the Seimas of the Republic of Lithuania. One Ombudsman is appointed to investigate the activities of officials of state institutions and agencies and one Ombudsman to investigate the activities of officials of municipal institutions and agencies.

The deadline for filing personal complaints is one year from the commission of the act (or inactivity) complained about. This "more generous" deadline as well as the "freedom of form" to file an application reflects the rationale of the Ombudsmen—to provide a "less rigid" avenue (than the judicial one) for citizens to defend their rights. A complaint must be investigated within 3 months of the day of receipt of the complaint. A proposal (recommendation) of the Ombudsman must be considered by the institution or official to whom this proposal (recommendation) is addressed, informing (no later than within 30 days from the receipt of the proposal (recommendation)) the Ombudsman about the results of the consideration (Art. 15 and 18 of the Law on the Seimas Ombudsmen).

Although the proposals (recommendations) of the Ombudsman are not legally binding and do not impose sanctions on public administration entities, they do, however, help to fix systemic problems on a regulatory level or enable authorized officials to take concrete actions (e.g., initiate investigations, apply legal liability etc.).

[18] Law on the Seimas Ombudsmen of the Republic of Lithuania of 3 December 1998, No. VIII-950 (new edition No. IX-2544, 4 November 2004), *Valstybės žinios* [Official Gazette], No. 110-3024, 1998.

15.3.3 Constitutional Roots of Administrative Silence and Its Importance as Reflected in Legislation

As already noted, the Lithuanian legal framework does not explicitly enshrine administrative silence but terms this institute as "[administrative] inaction" (*neveikimas*) or "[administrative] procrastination" (*vilkinimas*). The constitutional basis for these notions is found in the already-quoted Art. 5 of the Constitution stipulating that "State institutions shall serve the people." Hence, if they do not meet this duty their failure to act should be subject to an administrative or judicial review in order to guarantee this constitutional provision (see Art. 1 LPA). Moreover, these concepts bear a close connection with legal certainty, which is perceived as part of the rule of law in the Lithuanian legal system in line with the recurrent leitmotif in the constitutional case law that the latter principle is "especially capacious and is able to comprise a range of various interrelated imperatives."

By contrast, administrative silence (lack of reaction) may be justified when it transpires that the same issue is under judicial review in court proceedings (Art. 27 (5 p.) LPA). This requirement can be seen as a corollary of the constitutional separation of powers doctrine, namely not to interfere with the tasks entrusted to another branch of the state, and only reinforces the legal certainty of an individual.

Finally, administrative silence regarding repetitive and (or) abusive applications or other requests of an administrative character can also be partially "tolerated" and counterbalanced by the public interest in saving sparse (administrative) resources.

Both forms of such failure (administrative inaction as well as procrastination) can be challenged in front of an administrative commission or administrative court within 2 months from the date when the administrative decision in question was supposed to be adopted according to the law (Art. 8 (2) LPPAD and Art. 29 (2) LAP). Administrative courts, for their part, are (procedurally) enabled to pass judgments obliging administrative authorities to adopt a particular administrative decision or take any other action and, thus, "break" the administrative silence (Art. 92 LAP). However, according to the established praxis they cannot adopt "declaratory" judgments, i.e., state the mere fact of administrative silence. Instead applicants have to ask an administrative court to defend their "rights or interests" in a more substantial and specific way, i.e., by requiring a public body to take a certain administrative action.[19]

Safeguarding the said constitutional provision is deemed to be important by the legislator. This can be deduced from Art. 36 (1.1) LAP exempting applicants from stamp duty and, thus, facilitating access to justice in such disputes. Furthermore, this statement can be amplified by the administrative practice allowing applicants to "circumvent" statutory requirements to go through the pre-trial dispute settlement procedure. For instance, in land disputes such a pre-trial procedure is obligatory but not in cases in which the administration is procrastinating about taking action.[20] Such practice can be pragmatically explained by the fact that asking for action in such cases of "institutional inactivity" without "judicial pressure" would most likely be futile. Alternatively, it is also possible for individuals affected by "administrative silence" to submit a public liability claim, i.e., ask for damages in reliance on Art. 6.271 of the Lithuanian Civil Code *inter alia* stipulating that damage caused by unlawful action (active or passive) by public bodies must be compensated by the state. This legal option, however, places a heavier procedural burden on the applicants because they have to demonstrate not only the unlawful inaction but also the damage that was caused in a causal connection to this inaction.

15.3.4 The Lack of Definition and Blurred Lines Between Administrative "Inaction" and "Procrastination"

Lithuanian law does not define either administrative inaction or administrative procrastination in precise terms. The "black letter law" presupposes that these two categories are normatively different because (for most part) the disjunction is used in various wordings of relevant legal provisions ("inaction *or* procrastination," see, e.g., Art. 17 (1.1), 23 (1) and 92 LAP). However, this is not so in all cases: The Lithuanian legislator is far from being consistent when it comes to using these two categories and often invokes only one of them, especially while juxtaposing them with administrative action. For example, Art. 3 (2) LAP lays

[19] See, e.g., decisions of SACL, No. A7-915/2004, 21 December 2004; No. A14-261/2007, 13 March 2007, etc.

[20] See decision of SACL, No. eAS-939-756/2017, 8 November 2017.

down that "administrative courts do not assess the impugned administrative decision and [administrative] action (inaction) in terms of their economic or political reasonableness" but perform a "strict" legality review. This wording fails to include "administrative procrastination" most likely because "administrative inaction" was deemed sufficient to express the normative content of the provision. The already quoted provision exempting applicants from stamp duty, for its part, uses only the term "procrastination" and leaves out "inaction" (Art. 36 (1.1) LAP).

It can plausibly be claimed that administrative "inaction" presupposes a higher degree of passivity (such as completely ignoring an applicant's request to take administrative action) whereas "procrastination" could implicate some action which is pro forma and (or) otherwise irrelevant to actually solving an administrative matter entrusted to the particular administrative body. For example, vainly restating the content of (applicable) judicial decisions in force in administrative acts instead of actually executing what a court has ordered could be a paragon of such administrative procrastination.[21] Another illustration could be relaying the matter to another administrative authority and not following up when the latter refuses to take action. For example, in one administrative case a matter was forwarded to a self-regulatory body of the applicant's employer and thus the "vested interests" of the latter resulted in refusal to take action.[22]

However, these are only theoretical considerations not attested to by any explicit conceptualization that could be found in the case law. On the contrary, the case law blurs the lines between these two categories even further by invoking them in a mutually exclusive way and does not see the need to consider or explicate what the possible reasons for introducing these two different concepts in the legal framework may have been (if any).[23] Nonetheless it is clear from administrative case law that neither "inaction" nor "procrastination" can be equated with a negative (administrative) decision of a public body because "a court

[21] As it happened in the case of *Nekvedavičius v Lithuania* (1471/05) 17 November 2015 ECtHR, see more in A. Andrijauskaitė, "Good Governance in the Case Law of the ECtHR: A (Patch) Work in Progress," *ICON-S Conference Paper* (2018), preprint accessible at https://www.researchgate.net/publication/328354943_Good_Governance_in_the_Case_Law_of_the_ECtHR_A_PatchWork_in_Progress.

[22] See decision of Vilnius Regional Administrative Court, No. eI-3149-473/2018, 2 August 2018.

[23] See, e.g., decision of SACL, No. A173-438-2016, 18 February 2016.

can oblige an administrative body to perform a certain action only when this action has not been already taken."[24] It remains questionable how "motivated" such negative administrative decisions ought to be; however, the content of them should sufficiently express the will of administrative authorities not to take action on a matter entrusted to them.[25] The praxis shows that it remains difficult for applicants to make a distinction between negative administrative decisions and pure inaction and they often confuse the two categories. Administrative courts, for their part, tend to look "behind appearances" in such cases and focus on the "substantial nature of legal relations between individuals and public bodies" instead of "verbal formulations of the claims put together by the applicants."[26]

15.4 Administrative Silence "in Action": Relevant Data and Case Law

15.4.1 The Data on Examining Administrative Complaints in Lithuania

As can be seen from the analysis above, the procedures and terms of the actions of public administration entities are regulated meticulously, as well as the actions that individuals may take to appeal delays or other bureaucratic practices of public administration decisions. Table 15.1 shows the number of complaints to the highest Lithuanian institutions, which competences include the examination of complaints against the decisions or inactivity of public administration entities.

The data reveal that the Lithuanian Administrative Disputes Commission examines approximately seven to nine hundred complaints each year, the Seimas Ombudsman Office seventeen to eighteen hundred, and the Supreme Administrative Court of Lithuania two to three thousand. The statistics do not show the specifics of the cases in the Lithuanian Administrative Disputes Commission but it is possible to extract this information regarding the Supreme Administrative Court of Lithuania and the Seimas Ombudsman Office. The annual report of the Supreme Administrative Court of Lithuania shows that almost half (43%) of administrative cases

[24] See decision of SACL, No. A8–406/2003, 23 June 2003.

[25] See decision of SACL, No. AS11–296/2007, 11 October 2007.

[26] See, e.g., decision of SACL, No. A602-570/2014, 10 September 2014.

Table 15.1 Statistics of complaints to competent authorities of Lithuania

	2013	*2014*	*2015*	*2016*	*2017*
Chief Administrative Disputes Commission					
Complaints	966	972	945	679	n.d.
Completed cases	765	842	745	879	n.d.
Seimas Ombudsman Office					
Complaints	1805	1846	1772	1752	1784
Completed cases	1716	1953	1786	1713	1749
Supreme Administrative Court of Lithuania					
Complaints	2516	2193	3312	2840	3025
Completed cases	2135	1953	2165	2700	2593

The Annual Reports on the Activities of The Chief Administrative Disputes Commission (2013–2016); The Annual Reports on the Activities of the Seimas Ombudsmen's Office of the Republic of Lithuania (2013–2017); The Annual Reports on the Activities of Supreme Administrative Court of Lithuania (2013–2017)

in 2017 concerned administrative liability. Disputes over public service took second place (14%) in the court's docket, while tax disputes were third (7%).[27] The Ombudsmen, for their part, dealt mainly with investigations of individual applications or complaints, above all ones concerning restriction of liberty (Table 15.2).

Among the cases of investigations of individual applications/complaints are identified such problems as the activities of state and municipal institutions in the field of public administration (as well as pre-trail decision-making in disputes), taxes, consumer rights, protection of personal data, violation of deadlines for handling complaints, applications, delays in procedures, inaccurate replies, incomplete answers, failures to provide information with no reasons given, and the appeals procedure.[28]

[27] According to the interviewees representing the Supreme Administrative Court of Lithuania, a total of about 20,000 cases were investigated by the Supreme Administrative Court in the period 2014–2018, of which about 1500 were due to delay (inactivity), so the percentage varies between 5 and 7.5% depending on the year. It is not possible to say in how many decisions a clear breach of "administrative silence" was found because very often the appeal was satisfied on other grounds.

[28] On the basis of data provided by the Institution of Ombudsman, the statistics on delay (inactivity) are: 2014–40 complaints (2% of all received), 2015–71 complaints (4% of the total), 2016–62 complaints (4% of the total), 2017–84 complaints (5% of all received), and 2018–96 complaints (5% of all received).

Table 15.2 Seimas Ombudsmen completed complaint cases by area

Group by area	*Percentage per year*				
	2013	*2014*	*2015*	*2016*	*2017*
Investigation of individuals application/complaint	24	32	32	38	39
Restriction of liberty	33.5	10	27	21	26
Property	10	11	8	8	6
Environment	10	16	12	11	10
Housing	6	9	6	9	6.5
Personal and public safety and ensuring of public order	3	6	3	2	2.5
Enforcement of justice	2	2	2	2	1.5
Services	3	4	2	2	2
Social Security	4	3	2	2	2
Other	4.5	7	6	5	4.5

The Annual Reports on the Activities of the Seimas Ombudsmen's Office of the Republic of Lithuania in (2013–2017)

Table 15.3 Recommendations made by the Seimas Ombudsmen regarding the improvement of public administration procedures

	2013	*2014*	*2015*	*2016*	*2017*
Recommendations, regarding the improvement of public administration procedures	133	277	270	344	420
From them to entities of state administration	57	107	149	163	259
From them to entities of municipal administration	77	170	121	181	161

The Annual Reports on the Activities of the Seimas Ombudsmen's Office of the Republic of Lithuania (2013–2017)

Every year the Ombudsmen make proposals (recommendations) addressed to public administration entities to improve public administration procedures (see Table 15.3). They draw attention to aspects such as negligence at work, failure to comply with laws or other legal acts, violations of public servant ethics, abuse, bureaucracy or violations of human rights and freedoms. They also suggest measures that must be taken to eliminate violations (their causes and conditions) of laws or other legal acts.[29]

According to the statistics, the number of such recommendations increases every year, so it can be said that paying attention to improving public administration is becoming more significant. According to the Law on the Seimas Ombudsmen, such proposals (recommendations) must be examined by the relevant public administration entity. The results of such examinations must be communicated to the authorized Ombudsmen. It should be noted that on average 95% (data for the last 5 years) of the recommendations issued by the Seimas Ombudsmen are taken into consideration.[30] Therefore, it is considered that the Seimas Ombudsmen institution makes a significant contribution not only to the effective investigation of individual complaints but also to the promotion of the principles of the rule of law, good administration, effective democracy, and respect for human rights.

Examining complaints about failures to keep to time limits and cases related to the legal institute of administrative silence, the Seimas Ombudsman has claimed that, although laws (e.g., the Law on Electricity of The Republic of Lithuania; the Law on Natural Gas, etc.) provide that if an application for a license or authorization is not replied to within the specified time limit then it is considered that a positive decision has been made, sub-statutory legal acts often contradict legal norms. For example, the fact of a positive decision to issue a license gives an individual the right to act but at the same time the legal norms of sub-statutory legal acts in all cases require the submission of license documents. Such controversial legal regulation often misleads individuals. Therefore, the Seimas Ombudsman recommends that the responsible public administration entities change such ambiguous legal norms. Moreover, the Ombudsman notes that public administration entities should follow the general principles of law in their activities, including the principle of good administration. It is recommended that public administration entities take

[29] Information taken from The Annual Reports on the Activities of the Seimas Ombudsmen's Office of the Republic of Lithuania (2013–2017). No more detailed statistics are collected.

[30] Information taken from The Annual Reports on the Activities of the Seimas Ombudsmen's Office of the Republic of Lithuania (2013–2017).

decisions on licenses and issue supporting documents in accordance with the set time limits.[31]

15.4.2 Relevant Problems of Applying "Administrative Silence": A View of Lithuanian Public Administration Entities

According to the interview data, the term "administrative silence" is not used in Lithuanian legal regulation. Some interviewees were not aware of a definition of "administrative silence." However, according to experts at the Ministry of the Interior (hereafter—"MoI") the concept of positive administrative silence was already known and considered when the first edition of the Law on Public Administration was adopted in 1999 but neither the term nor the concept was established in the first or subsequent versions of the Law.

It further transpired from the interview data that, first of all, the definition of administrative silence is associated with the concept of "administrative inactivity" and "administrative procrastination." However, experts at the MoI perceive administrative silence "as a situation where a decision is presumed to be a positive if it has not been made within the prescribed time limit." It can be treated in several ways:

(i) A public body does not take a decision on a person's application or complaint within the prescribed time limit, and it is then presumed that a positive decision has been adopted.
(ii) A person does not respond to an inquiry of a public body within the prescribed time limit, and it is then presumed that this person has no comments or claims.
(iii) A public body does not provide comments or observations on issues that have been raised by other public bodies within the prescribed time limit, and it is then presumed that a public body has no comments or observations on this issue.[32]

[31] See Statement of Seimas Ombudsman of the Republic of Lithuania, No. 4D-2016/1-780, 10 February 2017, par. 17 and 18.

[32] For example, in Lithuania, such "internal silence" is regulated in some legal acts, as *Government work regulations (1994)*. It is presumed that, if no observations have been submitted within the prescribed time limit, there are no observations.

Interviewees believed that the time limits that are currently set in the Lithuanian legal framework are adequate, rationally justified, and take into account the fact that they are required for collecting the information necessary for a decision as well as getting horizontal and vertical alignment of the decision. According to them, the terms are already calculated considering "the longest duration possible" needed to carry out all indispensable procedural steps. Thus, they are more oriented toward the "needs" of public administration entities, i.e., making it easier for them to evaluate all possible outcomes of an administrative decision and unforeseen circumstances of the administration, e.g., the "human factor"—a subject who has to make a decision being ill, etc.

The existing time limits ensure that:

(i) the procedures are performed qualitatively
(ii) decisions are coordinated with other public administration entities or stakeholders
(iii) procedures are carried out with "minimal" burden placed on the applicants, which means that they themselves do not need to collect documents, data, etc.

Sometimes there are ideas that the time limits could be more adjustable according to the nature of the procedures but the problem is that the procedures are very difficult to group together, and the variety of terms could cause confusion.

There are also arguments that the existing time limits are no longer adequate with regard to the technology used (online data collection, process coordination, validation, etc.). New technologies, particularly information technology, help stakeholders, especially the heads of public administration entities, to be informed, to know what procedures are carried out and how, to control their execution. However, from the perspective of public administration time savings determine decisions not in terms of changes in time limits but by reducing the number of civil servants or reviewing their operational functions (identifying additional functions, etc.).

Interviewees said that there is no consensus on reviewing and reducing the number of existing procedures. Each procedure is considered to be of good quality and rationally justified. Abandoning some procedures in order to make a decision more quickly could have negative consequences, such as poor decision-making quality, lack of verification, and so on.

According to interviewees the causes of time limit violations may mostly be violated due to reasons caused by:

- undisciplined civil servants;
- malignant delay of civil servant or institution (often due to deliberate inaction or unintentional doubt by managers and heads of the entities);
- too many institutions involved in a particular administrative procedure;
- political will (in cases where political approval is required);
- the intention of a decision-maker to give full consideration to the request, to find the best solutions, to look for positive (rather than negative) arguments in order to make a decision to the favor of the applicant. Such positive reasons, according to interviewees, occur even more often than negative ones.

In the interviewees' opinion, time limits are often violated in areas such as the restoration of citizens' land ownership rights and spatial planning.

Comparing the advantages and disadvantages of positive and negative administrative silence, interviewees emphasized that positive administrative silence could help to implement the most important purpose of public administration, which is based on the principles that "all the state institutions serve the people" and "decisions benefit the citizens." The burden on the citizen in this case should be transferred to the public administration. Also, strict positive administrative silence procedures could be used to discipline civil servants. Nevertheless, wider use of positive administrative silence would require changing and tightening existing procedures. By the way, it would be difficult to identify which procedures could be implemented using positive administrative silence and which could not. Finally, according to the interviewees, positive administrative silence would have legal consequences for public administration entities that would be difficult to predict. Therefore, even greater administrative diligence would be required, which could substantially increase financial costs. Revocation of previously granted rights or other benefits as an outcome of applying "positive silence" would be especially complicated.

In such cases, the question of restitution would arise (e.g., if construction permit were abolished there would be questions about who would compensate for damage to the applicant or state, within what time limit such a permit could be revoked, etc.).

In cases of negative administrative silence if citizens do not receive a response from a public administration entity within the set time limit they have a right, but not an obligation, to appeal to the authorities responsible for complaints about non-compliance with time limits, possible abuse, delays, etc. Thus, the burden on the public administration is transferred to the person (applicant). Such a procedure currently prevails in Lithuanian public administration. It is more convenient and perhaps even cheaper for the state. For example, persons also have a right not to complain about non-compliance with time limits, in which case no additional procedures are required. This logic is attested by an observation that came from SACL representatives: Most delay (inactivity) cases are completed at first instance administrative courts and only about one-third of cases are appealed.

On the other hand, the prevailing model of negative administrative silence raises the question of implementing the principle of "serving the people." If a citizen submits a complaint, the main procedure is suspended until a decision on non-compliance with time limits has been taken. Only after the decision has been made can the main procedure be resumed. This could increase the citizens' time and even financial costs.

According to the interviewees, in order to compensate for the narrow application of positive administrative silence Lithuania has focused on providing public services using a "one-stop-shop" principle. In this way, a citizen receives full, quality service in one place. It is the fastest possible solution for a person, with no obligation placed on her to look for the needed information, to collect documents, to coordinate and get approval in separate procedures, etc.

Currently only appeal data is collected in Lithuania (although, according to the SACL representatives, in the classification of administrative cases there are no special separate categories related to delays or inaction). Collecting other data, related to compliance with set time limits, would make it possible to assess the current situation and take steps to eliminate the causes. However, it would be difficult to compile and evaluate such data, possibly the bureaucratic apparatus (number of reporting and controlling persons) would increase, and such monitoring could also lead to dissatisfaction at the institutional level (because of additional features, reluctance to be controlled, etc.). Therefore, the need to follow the time limits for all procedures is questioned. Interviewees believe that it would be an excessive requirement.

It should be noted that public authorities use "running information systems" for controlled orders. Such systems apply when dealing with issues of particular importance for which time limits are shortened by an authorized person's decision. Using this system, it is possible to control and monitor the implementation progress of such orders and compliance with the time limits and to collect data on deadline violations, omissions, or delays.

On the question of how the implementation of administrative procedures in Lithuanian public sector institutions should be improved interviewees indicated that, for the efficiency of public administration, positive administrative silence can and should be applied to certain processes or procedures. However, in order to prevent errors and abuses there should be:

- identified procedures to which positive administrative silence can be applied
- assessment of risks, i.e., possible positive and negative consequences of positive administrative silence
- the identification of completely new processes
- the setting of very clear and strictly regulated internal procedures
- tightened operational control.

According to the interviewees, the matter of when positive administrative silence could apply should be strictly individualized, e.g., positive administrative silence is possible in the examination of complaints, as well as regarding extending permissions to operate in a certain areas (if no new circumstances are established it is considered that an authorization is extended). However, in cases of the issuance of authorizations and licenses for a particular activity the state assumes responsibility for any possible consequences. Authorizations are not equivalent; thus, e.g., in cases of acquiring a permit to carry weapons special care is required.

15.4.3 "Administrative Silence" as Interpreted by Administrative Courts

The Supreme Administrative Court of Lithuania, as the supreme judicial institution in administrative cases, which forms uniform case law for administrative courts in interpreting and applying laws and other legal acts, has noted that non-observance of the time limits in public administration is not compatible with the rule of law, the protection of legitimate expectations, and the principles of legal certainty, legal security and good administration.[33] Time limits for administrative decisions are intended to ensure that the administrative procedure is not excessively extended, and that public administration entities fulfill the competence entrusted to them.[34]

According to the established practice of the Supreme Administrative Court of Lithuania, the time limit set for the subject of public administration within which an administrative decision must be taken is instructive.[35] This means that the expiration of the time limit does not invalidate an administrative decision adopted after expiration of this lime limit. The end of the statutory deadline for the adoption of an administrative decision does not invalidate the competence of the public administration entity to make an administrative decision or to take other actions. It does not directly create negative legal consequences but only extends the administrative procedure. If a public administration entity has missed the deadline for an administrative decision, it should be stated as an omission. This gives affected persons the ability to defend their rights with a complaint.

As already noted, the dividing line between administrative "inaction" and "procrastination" is far from clear in administrative case law. However, in general these notions are perceived as "full or partial inactivity of a public body by which this body fails to adopt a decision (positive or negative) regarding a question which is put before it and falls under its competence within the time limit set by law."[36] An important caveat here is "competence": Administrative authorities can only be required to act in cases where they have a legal duty to do so, and this is the

[33] See decision of SACL, No. A-525-2648/2013, 11 December 2013.

[34] See decision of SACL, No. A-602-1189/2013, 8 October 2013.

[35] See, e.g., decision of SACL, No. AS-602-285-12, 11 May 2012.

[36] See, e.g., decision of SACL, No. AS-400-502/2018, 19 June 2018.

first and foremost criterion that administrative courts will revise while solving an administrative dispute. Other criteria that need to be checked by the courts in the "administrative silence context" are whether the said competence was exercised in "due time" and according to the procedure prescribed by law. By contrast, administrative authorities not exercising a discretionary right (such as to initiate regulatory changes or, e.g., build new roads) cannot be understood as a "failure to act." The former situation would not be compatible with the separation of powers doctrine if administrative bodies were given a green light to "demand" that the legislator adopts particular laws. The latter would equal an invasion of the management of resources, which belongs to the sphere of "economic and political reasonableness" that falls outside the purview of judicial revision (Art. 3 LAP). However, such requests cannot be left "unanswered": The discretionary nature of their execution does not absolve a particular public body from the duty to consider a particular request and formulate an answer thereof according to the procedure specified in Rules 2007.[37]

Furthermore, the handling of an administrative request should not happen in a "Kafkaesque," i.e., erratic and (or) cryptic way. If this is the case, the administrative authorities in question risk being deemed as "inactive" by the administrative courts. For example, in one such case a municipal authority was eschewing its duty to restore rights to a plot of land for over a year, giving the Representative of the Government exercising supervision thereof nothing but "abstract and unsubstantiated excuses" about why it could not perform this duty "just yet" and "multiple pleas to prolong the deadline." This strategy did not sit well with the Supreme Administrative Court of Lithuania and it declared the situation to be "administrative procrastination" and attached respective consequences thereto.[38]

As already noted, in cases of omission by entity of public administration, such as failure to perform duties or delays in solving matters, an administrative court may oblige the appropriate public administration entity to take a relevant decision or to execute another court order within the prescribed time limits (Art. 92 LAP). This provision ensures that administrative procedures are not too long (fulfilling the time limit requirements) and that the public administration entity can exercise its

[37] See decision of SACL, No. A-1494-502/2018, 29 October 2018.

[38] See decision of SACL, No. A8-885-06, 13 April 2006.

assigned competence and take action if the person's request is legitimate and justified.[39]

The successful use of this provision and thus the "breaking of silence" happened in a case regarding an administrative request for exemption from paying taxes.[40] This happened in a territorial planning dispute in which a municipality was avoiding publicizing the specific conditions of the use of land, namely "sanitary zones" around pig farming complexes that were controversial due to environmental damage and caused great dissatisfaction to people living nearby,[41] in land restitution cases,[42] etc. Such cases demonstrate the negative fiction of administrative silence "in action," i.e., legal challenges caused by the passivity of administrative bodies and their eventual settlement in an attempt to repeal it.

The Supreme Administrative Court of Lithuania has also invoked the fiction of positive silence on multiple occasions, above all while examining cases on the issuance of authorizations and licenses. In a string of cases dealing with renewable solar energy and the issuance of licenses to this effect the Court emphasized that a decision on the issuance of licenses should be taken without prejudice to the set time limits by public bodies.[43] The positive fiction enshrined in the Art. 17 (2 p.) of the Law on Electricity that was applicable to a particular dispute for its part took effect if they failed to do so. Relying on this provision a person has the right to carry out licensed activities in accordance with the requirements provided by legal acts and does not have to reapply for the issuance of the license. According to the Court, under such regulation the legislator on the one hand promotes good administration by public entities while, on the other hand, establishing an additional, exclusive pathway for the protection of the rights and legitimate interests of individuals. These statements were repeated by the Court in later cases.[44]

[39] See decision of SACL, No. AS-602-82/2012, 13 January 2012.

[40] See decision of SACL, No. A-2251-756/2015, 10 December 2015.

[41] See, e.g., SACL, No. A-858-266/204, 15 May 2014.

[42] See decision of SACL, No. A-1494-502/2018, 29 October 2018.

[43] See decision of SACL, No. A-525-2648/2013, 11 December 2013.

[44] See decisions of SACL, No. A-143-2834/2013, 23 December 2013; No. A-525-1745/2014, 23 December 2014; No. A146-1273/2014, 18 August 2014; No. A143-18/2014, 14 January 2014; No. A289-525/2015, 4 February 2015; No. A91-822/2015, 4 February 2015.

However, even if legal provisions explicitly stipulate the positive fiction in the case of administrative silence this does not mean that it will be upheld under any circumstances. Whereas the "solar cases" concerned significant delays and the frustration of legitimate expectations by administration, caused by a change of policy in the dynamic field of renewable energy, slight delays in rather more "clear-cut" situations may not yield the same result. This came to the fore in a case concerning authorization to keep (carry) weapons. More precisely, even though the applicable provision in this dispute stipulated that "in case of no answer regarding the licence to keep weapons, the positive answer should be presumed" (Art. 12 (7 p.) of the Law on Control of Weapons and Ammunition) it came to no effect. This was because it transpired that, firstly, the administrative authority in charge was only 4 days late in issuing an authorization and, secondly, the applicant had a criminal record in connection with unlawful bearing of arms that (quite clearly) precluded him from getting this license in the first place.

The Court emphasized in this regard that even a positive decision on an authorization does not mean that such a decision cannot be canceled. After receiving information which could be the basis for not issuing an authorization, the decision was canceled.[45]

Therefore, the case law of the Supreme Administrative Court provides that the principles of administrative silence should help to ensure the rights of the applicant but at the same time emphasizes that usage of administrative silence should not be a pretext for public administration entities to violate persons' rights through breaches of set time limits.

15.5 Conclusions

Changes to time limits for administrative decision-making have not been on the political agenda since the adoption of the Law on Public Administration immediately before Lithuania's EU accession. The low political salience of the matter can be explained by several factors—Lithuania has adopted a long-term strategy of reform that promotes efficiency in public administration and has benchmarked its performance against a series of international indexes of governance and social welfare. To this point, the government has managed to keep up its standing in various

[45] See decision of SACL, No. A-1348-858/2016, 9 January 2017.

ratings. The executive in Lithuania is highly fragmented,[46] which means that agencies under various line ministries, as well as municipalities, have highly varying degrees of practice regarding internal management of administrative decision-making. No data are collected on how breaches of terms are prevented and managed, and only data on complaints are available. Lithuania has a well-developed system of prejudicial dispute resolution which, despite some criticism of the lack of a systematic approach,[47] seems to function well enough. However, once disputes leave the realm of a concerned agency they take up government time and resources, something which in many cases could be prevented with better internal management. However, comprehensive reform on behalf of the parliament does not appear to be likely, while disputes that reach the administrative courts are few and far between. The cases concerned are generally legally straightforward. All these arguments mean that Lithuania is best characterized as an incomplete administrative system from any one theoretical perspective but manages to muddle through with nearly no intervention on behalf of the legislative. This creates highly variable administration practice with some agencies moving ahead to automating administrative procedures so that terms will become redundant altogether (e.g., automatically issuing speeding tickets)[48] while others lag severely behind. Two recommendations stem from these observations: (i) to create an institute of positive administrative silence and (ii) to ensure data collection on administrative decision-making. The first could become a tool for agencies to consider when developing their procedures, which could reduce expenses. Under the second recommendation, evidence-based streamlining of administrative decision-making could become possible within the areas of responsibility of line ministries. The Lithuanian Law on Public Administration sets a generic term for taking administrative decisions. Once this has expired, the applicant can file a complaint with

[46] A. Stasiukynas et al., "Public Sector Reforms in Lithuania Since 1990," in M. Bileišis and P. Kovač (Eds.), *Public Administration Reforms in Eastern European Union Member States: Post-accession Convergence and Divergence* (Vilnius and Ljubljana: Mykolas Romeris University and University of Ljubljana: 2017), pp. 54–90.

[47] See footnote 16.

[48] Ministry of Interior of the Republic of Lithuania (2018) *Numatoma modernizuoti greičio matavimo prietaisais fiksuojamų nusižengimų administravimą* [Modernization of Administration of Fines for Broken Rules Registered by Speed Cameras]. Press release, Vilnius.

the Ombudsman or Administrative Disputes Commission; these institutions, if needed, can refer the case to an administrative court or, in cases where pre-trial investigation is not mandatory by law, the applicant can turn directly to administrative courts. While conceptualizing the term "*administrative silence*" in the context of Lithuania, a distinction between inaction by an administrative body and the institute that allows for treating that inaction in a particular manner needs to be made. In Lithuania, the dispute and resolution stage are well documented, although datasets from the Ombudsman or the Administrative Dispute Commission are not published, only the reports. A larger problem, though, is that in the earlier stages of the administrative process it is impossible to judge the extent of the practice of not abiding by time limitations. No data are collected centrally about the duration of administrative procedures. The relative autonomies or line ministries do not even set the definitions and classifications of the various stages of administrative processes. Administrative silence is also not a salient political issue. Cases which result in legal disputes may only constitute the tip of the iceberg. In parallel, consecutive Lithuanian governments have declared it to be their goal to settle administrative matters as soon as possible, yet this political goal has not been backed up by data from incumbents in elections. Administrative silence is therefore depoliticized to a point where the only point of reference is the standards set by administrative court practice. This is at odds with the often NPM-type rhetoric of administrative reforms in Lithuania. As a result of this study, we have come up with the hypothesis that high ministerial autonomy and low political salience result in a process of muddling through but, from the standpoint of public administration reform, this may at least partly explain the shortcomings of reforms.

Furthermore, the judiciary has not experienced a political push for new NPM-type reforms in the same way as the legislative; therefore, judicial adjudication may not be the place to create efficiency gains in cases of administrative silence. If attained, generally satisfactory outcomes of prejudicial processes might both reduce the burden on the judiciary and create a basis for improving or retaining current decision-making in administrative bodies based on the costs incurred by the outcomes of such effective prejudicial processes. An effective prejudicial dispute resolution design in such a system would need to (i) have exceedingly high levels of coincidence of resolutions with judicial decisions, (ii) be rapidly accessible and have very short durations for decisions, and (iii) include a mechanism for compensation of losses to persons and imposition of costs on administrative bodies.

In instances where the government does not comply with its own rules, a process of adjudication is available. In these instances, the final review of administrative procedures is performed by judicial actors, thus providing another avenue for individuals to fight the (possible) arbitrariness of the executive. As policymakers do not supply a definition of what good administration entails the rule of law takes precedence. Various tools can be imagined for developing effective managerial and legal protection against excessively long administrative procedures but the development of these means has costs and risks of its own. Quality data on the development of such tools in Lithuania and evidence for legislative reform are not there and can best be collected through monitoring prejudicial processes using measures of accessibility, costs, and duration.

References

Andrijauskaitė, A. (2018). *Good Governance in the Case Law of the ECtHR: A (Patch) Work in Progress* (ICON-S Conference Paper). https://www.researchgate.net/publication/328354943_Good_Governance_in_the_Case_Law_of_the_ECtHR_A_PatchWork_in_Progress.

Auby, J. B. (Ed.). (2014). *Codification of Administrative Procedure*. Brussels: Bruylant.

Deviatnikovaitė, I. (2013). Europos administracinės teisės samprata ir ES administracinių procedūrų rinkinio rengimo prielaidos [The Concept of European Administrative Law and the Background of the Development of the Law on Administrative Procedure of the European Union]. *Jurisprudencija, 20*(3), 1005–1022.

Directive 2006/123/EC of the European Parliament and of the Council of 12 December 2006 on Services in the Implementation of EU Law in Lithuanian Administrative Law (VĮ Registrų centras: 2009). Internal Market. OJ L 376, 27 December 2006, pp. 36–68.

Ministry of Interior of the Republic of Lithuania. (2018). Numatoma modernizuoti greičio matavimo prietaisais fiksuojamų nusižengimų administravimą [Modernization of Administration of Fines for Broken Rules Registered by Speed Cameras]. Press release, Vilnius.

Mosley, H. (2012). *Accountability in Decentralised Employment Service Regimes* (OECD Local Economic and Employment Development (LEED) Working Papers, 2012/10). Paris: OECD Publishing. https://doi.org/10.1787/5k98sbxn9wbw-en.

Normantas, A., & Vasiliauskas M. (2010). Ombudsmenai kaip konstitucinio valdžios įstaigų tarnystės žmonėms imperatyvo sergėtojai [Ombudsmen as Guardians of Constitutional Principle That State Institutions Should Serve the People]. In *Administraciniai teismai Lietuvoje. Nūdienos iššūkiai* [Administrative Courts in Lithuania. Current Challenges] (pp. 487–509). Vilnius: Lietuvos vyriausiasis administracinis teismas.

Pang, M. S., Lee, G., & DeLone, W. H. (2014). IT Resources, Organizational Capabilities, and Value Creation in Public-Sector Organizations: A Public-Value Management Perspective. *Journal of Information Technology, 29*(3), 187–205.

Paškevičienė, L. (2018). Išankstinio administracinių ginčų nagrinėjimo ne teisme institutas Lietuvoje: bendrosios normatyvinės charakteristikos [Pre-Trial Settlement of Administrative Disputes in Lithuania: General Legal Characteristics]. *Teisė, 108,* 70–83.

Paužaitė-Kulvinskienė, J. (2014). The Principle of Effective Legal Remedies in Administrative Law (Right to Access to Administrative Court) of Lithuania Under the Influence of the European Legal Order. In J. Bernatonis (Ed.), *Lithuanian Legal System Under the Influence of European Union Law* (pp. 397–425). Vilnius: Vilnius University.

Stasiukynas, A., et al. (2017). Public Sector Reforms in Lithuania Since 1990. In M. Bileišis & P. Kovač (Eds.), *Public Administration Reforms in Eastern European Union Member States: Post-accession Convergence and Divergence* (pp. 54–90). Vilnius and Ljubljana: Mykolas Romeris University and University of Ljubljana.

Statement No. 4D-2016/1-780 of the Seimas Ombudsman of the Republic of Lithuania of 10 February 2017 on "A", Ltd. Complaint Against the Ministry of Energy of the Republic of Lithuania. http://www.lrski.lt/seimo-kontrolieriu-pazymos/send/2-seimo-kontrolieriu-pazymos/12935-pazyma-del-skundo-pries-lietuvos-respublikos-energetikos-ministerija.html.

The Annual Reports on the Activities of Supreme Administrative Court of Lithuania (2013–2017). https://lvat.teismas.lt/veikla/teismu-praktika/teismo-metiniai-pranesimai/209.

The Annual Reports on the Activities of the Chief Administrative Disputes Commission (2013–2016). http://www.lagk.lt/veikla/veiklos-ataskaitos/.

The Annual Reports on the Activities of the Seimas Ombudsmen's Office of the Republic of Lithuania (2013–2017). http://www.lrski.lt/en/reports.html.

The Republic of Lithuania Law on Administrative Proceedings (VIII-1029, 14 January 1999; new edition XII-2399, 2 June 2016). State Gazette, 1999, No. 13-308; Register of Legal Acts, 2016, No. 2016-16849.

The Republic of Lithuania Law on Electricity of the Republic of Lithuania (VIII-1881, 20 July 2000; new edition XI-1919, 17 January 2012). State Gazette, 2000, No. 66-1984; 2012, No. 17-752.

The Republic of Lithuania Law on Natural Gas (VIII-1973, 10 October 2000; new edition XI-1564, 30 June 2011). State Gazette, 2000, No. 89-2743; 2011, No. 87-4186.
The Republic of Lithuania Law on Procedure of Pre-trial Administrative Disputes (VIII-1031, 11 January 1999; new edition XII-240, 2 June 2016). State Gazette, 1999, No. 13-310; Register of Legal Acts, 2016, No. 2016-16850.
The Republic of Lithuania Law on Public Administration (VIII-1234, 17 June 1999; new edition X-736, 27 June 2006). State Gazette, 1999, No. 60-1945; 2006, No. 77-2975.
The Republic of Lithuania Law on the Control of Arms and Ammunition (IX-705, 15 January 2002; new edition XI-1146, 11 November 2010). State Gazette, 2002, No. 13-467; 2010, No. 142-7261.
The Republic of Lithuania Law on the Seimas Ombudsmen (VIII-950, 3 December 1998; new edition IX-2544, 4 November 2004). State Gazette, 1998, No. 110-3024; 2004, No. 170-6238.
The Supreme Administrative Court of Lithuania. Case No. A-1348-858/2016, 9 January 2016.
The Supreme Administrative Court of Lithuania. Case No. A-14-261/2007, 13 March 2007.
The Supreme Administrative Court of Lithuania. Case No. A-143-18/2014, 14 January 2014.
The Supreme Administrative Court of Lithuania. Case No. A-143-2834/2013, 23 December 2013.
The Supreme Administrative Court of Lithuania. Case No. A-146-1273/2014, 18 August 2014.
The Supreme Administrative Court of Lithuania. Case No. A-1494-502/2018, 29 October 2018.
The Supreme Administrative Court of Lithuania. Case No. A-173-438-2016, 18 February 2016.
The Supreme Administrative Court of Lithuania. Case No. A-2251-756/2015, 10 December 2015.
The Supreme Administrative Court of Lithuania. Case No. A-289-525/2015, 4 February 2015.
The Supreme Administrative Court of Lithuania. Case No. A-525-1745/2014, 23 December 2014.
The Supreme Administrative Court of Lithuania. Case No. A-525-2648/2013, 11 December 2013.
The Supreme Administrative Court of Lithuania. Case No. A-602-1189/2013, 8 October 2013.
The Supreme Administrative Court of Lithuania. Case No. A-602-570/2014, 10 September 2014.

The Supreme Administrative Court of Lithuania. Case No. A7-915/2004, 21 December 2004.
The Supreme Administrative Court of Lithuania. Case No. A8-406/2003, 23 June 2003.
The Supreme Administrative Court of Lithuania. Case No. A-858-266/204, 15 May 2014.
The Supreme Administrative Court of Lithuania. Case No. A-8-885-06, 13 April 2006.
The Supreme Administrative Court of Lithuania. Case No. A-91-822/2015, 4 February 2015.
The Supreme Administrative Court of Lithuania. Case No. AS-11-296/2007, 11 October 2007.
The Supreme Administrative Court of Lithuania. Case No. AS-400-502/2018, 19 June 2018.
The Supreme Administrative Court of Lithuania. Case No. AS-602-285-12, 11 May 2012.
The Supreme Administrative Court of Lithuania. Case No. AS-602-82/2012, 13 January 2012.
The Supreme Administrative Court of Lithuania. Case No. eAS-939-756/2017, 8 November 2017.
Valančius, V., & Kavalnė, S. (2018, August 2). Europos Sąjungos teisės įgyvendinimas Lietuvos administracinėje teisėje [The Vilnius Regional Administrative Court]. Case No. eI-3149-473/2018.

Index

D. C. Dragos et al. (eds.),
The Sound of Silence in European Administrative Law,
https://doi.org/10.1007/978-3-030-45227-8

The manufacturer's authorised representative in the EU is Springer
Nature Customer Service Centre GmbH, Europaplatz 3, 69115 Heidelberg,
Germany. If you have any concerns regarding our products, please
contact ProductSafety@springernature.com

Printed and bound by CPI Group (UK) Ltd, Croydon, CR0 4YY
30/09/2026
02225644-0017